BY GRACE, I DANCE

BY GRACE, I DANCE

Surviving Suicide, Manic Depression, and Marriage

REV. MERYL ANN OLSON

LitPrime Solutions
21250 Hawthorne Blvd
Suite 500, Torrance, CA 90503
www.litprime.com
Phone: 1-800-981-9893

Published by LitPrime Solutions   08/29/2022

ISBN: 979-8-88703-040-1(sc)
ISBN: 979-8-88703-041 8(e)

Library of Congress Control Number: 2022914209

CONTENTS

By Grace, I Dance

Surviving Suicide, Manic Depression, and Marriage

By Rev. Meryl Ann Olson

You may not think that the world needs you, but it does. For, you are unique, like no one who has ever been before or will come after. No one can speak with your voice, say your piece, smile your smile, or shine your light. No one can take your place, for it's yours alone to fill.

If you are not there to shine your light, who knows how many travelers will lose their way as they try to pass by your empty place in the darkness?

Ludwig Wittgenstein

"Understand that God is everywhere, eternal and unchanging. And that you yourself are God. Know that this is the secret of an evenly balanced mind."
Jnaneshwar Maharaj 13th century Indian poet saint

DEDICATION

To my mom, Arleen Olson, who has always been here for me through every seeming obstacle to happiness. Despite her own difficulties with chronic depression on and off since her teens she still managed to care for, love, and encourage me as a child and long into adulthood. She has also been at my side to celebrate my many successes. Thank you so much, Ma. This is for you and the rest of our precious family.

My children have always been the lights of my life. Thank you for helping me to laugh at myself and to persevere through every trial in my life. If it weren't for your unconditional love, I might have lost my determination and become just another unfortunate suicide victim. I have worked hard to understand the underlying causes of this terrible disease from my perspective and to live a happy, successful life so that you would be proud of me. Now I am proud of me, too.

I also honor all the sensitive souls who've experienced the highest highs and lowest lows: the rich and famous; and unknowns like me; who have found themselves stranded in negativity, hopelessness, and terror who thought there was no way out.

DISCLAIMERS

The author is not a medical doctor. Opinions regarding medical issues are based upon her own experiences and material she has read, which reflects the experience of others and, in some – but not all – cases, material written by doctors. She is aware that individuals are physically and mentally different, and that another person may have radically different experiences. Therefore, while it is important to open discussion about medical issues, *the opinions herein are not intended as a substitute for consultation or treatment by appropriately licensed medical professionals.*

The biographical material in this book is substantially true, but names, dates and locations may be changed slightly, if necessary to protect the identity of living persons. Any resemblance to persons unknown to the author is purely accidental. Furthermore, as is so often the case, other people involved may have contrary memories of the reported events, and the author herself has sometimes written somewhat contradictory reports of events that occurred long before the reports were written. Memory is not perfect.

Editors Note

Diary excerpts and automatic writings have been minimally edited because they reflect the authors state of mind at the time they were written. - GT, July 26, 2022

PREFACE

On June 11, 1987, following a three-month period of hopelessness, self-doubt and fear, I shot myself in the head at point blank range with a 22 caliber Beretta pistol my husband brought home one afternoon for protection and target practice. It is a miracle that I am still alive to tell you this story. Even as I write these words now, years after the "accident", I am amazed and horrified by what I actually did.

Why suicide?

For some reason, I was experiencing chronic depression, hopelessness, and irrational fears that turned into acute anxiety. Maybe it was post-postpartum depression that came a year after the birth of my middle child, Kyrie. I'm not really sure what caused it, because I did not experience the same symptoms after giving birth to my son, Gabriel, at home.

Taking the drug "ecstasy", which I was told was a sacred substance, three times in a six month period prior to this entire "dark night of the soul" may have been a catalyst for this downfall. Perhaps.

The fear, anxiety, and postpartum thoughts of unworthiness finally became unbearable. Dwelling on negative thoughts became an obsession I could not control. Psychiatrists have asked me in the past if I heard voices, and I thought it was the craziest thing I'd ever heard. How could anyone "hear" voices from inside their own heads and ears?

The truth is, I never heard an actual voice, but I could swear that some type of demonic entity or disembodied soul had possessed me and was whispering the horrible ideas in my head that were not "me" or mine. My life at the time was actually pleasant, so this suicidal depression was something I did not understand at all, and it was only after reading another manic depressive's book "Bent but not Broken," by Kevin Hines, about surviving suicide, that I could understand my own dilemma a bit better. Kevin, who survived jumping off the Golden Gate Bridge at age 19, explains that he felt as if he had no choice but to kill himself because these "voices" kept telling him he and his family would be better off – that killing himself was his only option at the time. He is quite an amazing and inspiring speaker. I saw him in October, 2016, at the annual NAMI (National Alliance on Mental Illness), Mercer County, New Jersey, Harvest of Hope, celebration.

Mine was a similar experience, a spiritual, mental, and emotional trial that has taken me years to understand; and, although I'd prefer not to embarrass myself or my family, I am sharing my story in the hope that it help someone going through a similar experience. I pray no one else has to go through what I did, but if you are going through a dark night of the soul, please know there is hope. There are a lot of successful treatments for those going through chronic depressions with suicidal ideations, but only if we have the courage to share our stories and tell others how to find real help and treatment. NAMI and other mental health organizations are helping people to live productive lives amidst suicidal thoughts and ideations, have 24 hour hotlines consumers can call to get immediate help. There are also 24 hour hotlines for affirmative prayer available through the Unity churches and Centers for Spiritual Living at any time of day or night – toll free if you can not afford to pay for the call. Some additional ideas for finding help may be found in the Afterword.

After three months of entertaining irrational dark, negative, unworthy ideas about myself, I completely lost my mind, along with my faith, and I crazily forgot everything I ever knew about the power of God's love, and that I was That love itself. I did not remember God's deep love for me, I felt utterly hopeless and numb, and tried to run away from the constant depressive thoughts. I told my husband, my best friend, and my mother, but I did not believe anyone's suggestion that choosing to spend some time in a psychiatric institution would be helpful to me or that seeing a psychiatrist or psychologist would be of any help in my time of crisis and deep need.

After all, several hospitalizations and visits to a psychiatrists and psychologists did not seem to help my mother to be happy. I did not believe much in doctors or psychiatrists, so what could I do but get rid of the body/mind which I believed was the source of my problems, and return to God?

Obviously, I was irrational, and completely forgot that my mind and ego would accompany me on my journey into heaven or hell. The only way out of my problems was to go through them and surrender all limited thinking and seemingly impossible-to-solve notions to God, for if This infinitely Intelligent Being created this Universe He/She/It is intelligent enough to keep it going and to sustain me as well. The Divine Lover loves us unconditionally. If only I would not judge myself so harshly and have just a little bit of hope and faith, I would have known in my heart that all was OK; and everything would eventually turn out well. After all, God had brought me back to a place of balance and healing after previous suicide attempts.

This time, my fear and negative thinking caused me to spiral so far downward, into a pit of hellish despair, that I woke up feeling terrified of just being conscious that these terrible thoughts and ideas were still there, consuming my rational, conscious mind each morning and destroying my inherent peace of mind.

I falsely believed that Jesus, my angels, and God had abandoned me; I was convinced I was bad, and the thought that I was separate from Him and different from everyone I knew made me feel crazy, frightened, filled with sadness, deeply depressed, hopeless, and worse off than ever.

Oddly, there was no rational reason to cause this fear. It was just a lie my shadow mind told me. I had experimented with a substance called XTC on the street I was told was sacred by a trusted friend, the same man who rolfed me and introduced me to my Master, my guru, Swami Muktananda, in September of 1987. I used the ecstasy several times over a six month period, and in retrospect, I wonder if this truly might have triggered the biochemical imbalance that led to the illusions and anxiety that were normally not a part of my very positive, loving nature.

After months of suffering, I finally decided I did not deserve to live in this hellish state of mind any longer. Hopelessness and suffering were in my every thought. I could not imagine my friends, my husband, mother, or children having to live with the stigma of having a crazy mother or daughter, or my husband having to put a disloyal, dysfunctional wife into a mental institution for the rest of her life. At least that's what I began to believe in my crazy state of mind; the thought of being locked up in an insane asylum for the rest of my life was way too much for me to bear.

What to do with myself for the day gave me cause for further anxiety because absolutely nothing brought me joy or relief from these hellish thoughts. Not even being with my baby girl. I believed there was no joy or love in my heart anymore. I deserved to be punished for my lies to myself, demonic actions and negative thoughts.

I had a beautiful baby girl, my precious daughter, Kyrie, who had just turned one year old on May fifth, 1987, usually a day of celebration in many South American cultures. My husband and I had purchased a "new" historic two hundred year old brick country home several months before that, and I had a three and a half year old son named Gabriel whom I adored. But in my frightened, irrational state of mind, I could not feel the joy in my heart, and was desperate to stop my pain and crazy, unworthy thoughts.

One month earlier, I had tried to electrocute myself while in the bathtub, but the hair dryer shut itself off before the current could harm me, thank God. I told my husband how badly I was feeling, and that I tried to electrocute myself, but either he did not believe that I was serious about committing suicide, or he just didn't care. He suggested I take my nanny and Kyrie to our meditation ashram in the Catskills, but I felt so overwhelmed by hellish thoughts that the thought of just packing a bag of clothes for us seemed like a Herculean feat.

Months later he told me he was angry at me for an affair I'd had with my band leader. It was not my first affair during our brief marriage. Now I believe the guilt I stored deep within my subconscious from allowing my dad to molest me sexually, combined with much promiscuity as an aftermath, caused me to feel a lot of toxic shame. Shame led to me to disrespect my body and the sanctity of marriage, and to distrust all men in whatever committed relationships I would enter into.

My husband and I had a lot of problems with intimacy during our five and a half year marriage. I was a sensitive, sensual, and emotional 32-year-old wife and mother, but my husband lost his spark for me, or so it appeared, after I got pregnant with our first baby. He started to treat me with kid gloves and was no longer romantic. He was angry that I had chosen to keep the baby without asking him if it was OK. He even suggested that I have an abortion. I was flabbergasted, especially since he originally had so much enthusiasm when we first discussed having children.

After the failed suicide attempt with the hair dryer, I tried strangulation with a long scarf, then suffocating myself with a pillow. And after all that practice, I Still Got it All WRONG! Thank God. If it were not for Lord Jesus, Archangel Michael, Mother Mary, and my personal guardian angel, Archangel Gabriel, who all work overtime making sure I don't get myself into too much trouble anymore, I probably would be in a prison, the morgue, or a mental hospital somewhere permanently. They were around continuously guarding me and guiding me through this entire trial even though I could not consciously hear or see them in my waking state.

The spring of 1987 was not the first time I'd experienced suicidal thoughts or feelings of deep despair and hopelessness. The first time was after finishing my massage course at The Sarasota School of Natural Healing Arts in January of 1981 after my best friend and housemate, Patsy, chose to move out of our cozy garage apartment to take a job in St. Petersburg. Then Sid, a man I loved deeply, abandoned me suddenly for a younger woman the day before he was supposed to help me move my belongings into a new apartment.

I had just a few weeks to find a new place, and I was a bit anxious, so I decided to get something called an "aura balancing" in which a woman healer placed all types of crystals around my body near different points that were blocked. The crystals made me feel a bit better, but I was still anxious about finding a place to live in less than two weeks, so the healer suggested I see a gifted psychic friend she knew named Marlene. She was reasonably priced, like the aura balancing lady who only charged me $50.

Despite Marlene's predictions of an amazing, positive future, my irrational fears and skewed perceptions of reality began causing the shadow in my mind to get darker day by day. By chance, I finally ran into a man I knew at the Granary, a local health food supermarket in Sarasota that a lot of my friends from massage class shopped at in order to get bulk items like nuts, grains, cereals, tofu, and the like at a huge discount. The man I met there who was just an acquaintance told me he needed to move out of his one bedroom furnished apartment on Siesta Drive by a lovely creek at the end of the month. He said the place was fully furnished, clean, close to town, and only $350 per month. He did not give the landlord proper notice, so in essence, he was breaking his lease; and he was anxious to find another renter to take his place so he would not lose his security deposit. I did not have many belongings, and no furniture to move, so I managed to get in there with not much effort. All I owned was a few pots, pans, some dishes, my clothes, a used Schwinn three speed blue bicycle, my guitar, and my two precious kitties, Groucho and Burger.

My time there did not last very long. Thank God I did not have to sign any type of lease.

I was still in shock after Sid's, betrayal. I liked the new place, but I was terrified living on my own along with dealing with the obsessive negative thoughts after having had the safety and comfort of living with my best friend, Patsy, from New Jersey, and being able to confide in her. She not only was a great friend, a person I trusted implicitly, with whom I could share my deepest feelings and trust with my deepest secrets, but she was an assistant minister in the Psychic Science Church, of which I was also a member. Patty was and still is, years later, a very intuitive, compassionate, sweet, kind person, and a terrific psychic as well. I had no idea how much I would miss her after she moved up to St. Petersburg in order to work in our nutrition instructor, Marilyn's, holistic Clinic as a massage therapist.

So, here I was in a lovely, simple furnished apartment right near a quiet creek where I could meditate, but the ghosts that were in my mind at the moment Sid broke up with me had not left me just because I moved to a new, quieter apartment with no cockroaches and no noisy next door neighbors arguing at odd times during the night.

It was here that I really began having challenges with insomnia. I had never really had them before that. Yes, sometimes I'd be up until 1 or 2:00AM writing in my journal after taking a late night walk with Patsy, with my kitties following; and then Patty and I would share a cup of herbal tea with quiet relaxing conversation before going into our separate bedrooms to meditate and hit the sack. But that was different. I was happy and content then; and I felt as if was choosing to stay awake.

Now, in this new home, all by myself, I felt as if I was not at all in control of my thoughts. My mind just kept running amok thinking one dark, scary, negative thought after another. I was afraid I might not be able to afford such a high rent. I was afraid I had no future, or worse, that I did not know what to do in the future—even though I'd just gotten a certificate in therapeutic Swedish massage and holistic healing. I had no idea that I was going to be the first person that I would need to heal. Nobody else, just me.

The insomnia was terrible. I tried to watch the small black and white TV my old boyfriend, George, had given me one Christmas, but I could not enjoy or focus on anything for more than a few minutes. . And watching anything like love stories, situation comedies, commercials, crime dramas, live news, or any news totally depressed me. I did not care about anyone except myself—a pretty lonely, isolated place to be.

It took me hours to get to sleep, and after just two or three hours I'd wake up with suicidal thoughts. My thoughts were so frightening I could not get back to sleep for an hour or more; so if I'd not fallen asleep by 3:00 AM I would actually try to suffocate myself with my pillow; or I'd look for something in my bedroom closet with which to hang myself. I really had no idea how to tie a scarf or a rope in the right way in order to properly hang myself to death. Thank goodness. I felt no confidence even in trying to commit suicide. I was convinced I was stupid, ignorant and unworthy in everything I said or did—or did not do. Boy, did some crazy disembodied ghost have me believing a lot of crap about my precious woman self! But I just could not commit suicide successfully. After all, I did not want to hurt my mom or my grandparents. Besides, who would feed my kitties? Maybe no one else needed me, but my precious cats loved me and depended upon me for food, to clean their litter box, and for affection.

I was just numb after losing both Patty and Sid in the same month and my body, mind, and emotions were all still in shock, so I had no interest in life or anything, not even the well-being of my three precious remaining grandparents who adored me. Even petting my precious cats did not make me feel better, and I could not understand why this was happening. I'd never experienced anything like it before. I always felt comfort prior to that being with each one of my sweet, caring, and interesting grandparents. Plus, I loved cats, and had adopted strays and rescued cats from cages in pet stores from the time I was twenty-one years old and living in my own apartment. I just was too numb to feel much of anything, and that made me feel bad, guilty, ashamed, and confused since this was definitely NOT my true nature as a sensitive, empathic Cancerian.

I did not call anyone except Grammy once or twice, and the only call I ever received while living alone on Siesta Drive was from Sid asking me if I'd be interested in massaging the famous baseball star, Willie Stargell, former Captain of the Pittsburgh Pirates.

After moving two times, I ended up going to live with my grandparents. Grandpa Olson (my paternal grandfather), and Grammy and Pop Pop (my maternal grandparents) helped me carry all my belongings in their cars and trunks which I stored in Grandpa Olson's garage, I carried my kitties along in the car with me with one in my lap and the other in the back on the floor, and moved in to the safe, nurturing environment of Grammy and Pop Pop's immaculate and beautiful home in Venice Gardens, a half hour from Sarasota.

I wanted to wait for the Florida state licensing exam which was taking place in Winter Haven in a few months. I'm not sure why I wanted to do so, when I did not even want to live anymore with all the pain and fear I was experiencing, but that seemed like the next logical step. This part of my life had already been set in motion, so it just seemed like the next sensible thing to do. Except for one woman in my massage class, who had been murdered by her boyfriend, everyone was going to take the exam. I still remember Nancy's face and her long, curly auburn hair. What a tragedy!

Another one of our dear friends would die of cancer the following year. Her name was Kathy; and she was married and seemed to have a very happy life, so that was a crazy surprise too.

The practical part of the massage licensing exam was very easy for me, the written was not as easy due to my concentration being off, but I knew I had at least passed with a B or a C even in my crazy, confused state of mind. I'd find out much later when I returned to New Jersey that I'd passed both exams with flying colors, 84% on the written, and 98% on the practical.

On my way up to Winter Haven in the car with Patsy and Susan, I felt very uncomfortable because I was so terribly ashamed to share with them how crazy and suicidal I was, especially because they both knew me to be a very positive and spiritual person. However, being with two friends who talked about many "normal" things as opposed to me thinking of myself was a distraction from all the dark stuff occupying my mind at that point. I felt a slight bit of relief since I was not so consumed with thoughts of death and what a horrible person I'd allowed myself to become. How ridiculous! How could losing a man's love and attention make me plunge into such a tangle of lies, bullshit, and negative thoughts that I would want to take my own life!?

Years later when I asked a psychic who channeled a positive helpful entity from "the Other Side" I was told that I chose this experience in this incarnation because this same man (my massage instructor) had loved me deeply and spent a fortune on me in my last life, and I left him flat like an old shoe without even an apology or good-bye kiss; so since I'd treated him with such inconsideration way back when I chose in this life to actually think and "feel" like what it would be to be the recipient of such mean-spiritedness. Now that made sense to me.

Even though this explanation came in retrospect, having this new information helped my mind to put this experience in a higher, more enlightened perspective. And I felt soothed. It was just karma. Like attracting like. My unkind words and actions to a man who had worshiped me, adored me, and spent a fortune on me did not deserve to be treated like shit; so in this life, just to balance out the scales I wanted to gift myself with the opposite experience. Maybe my treating my lover so callously put him into the same negative, dark state of mind I was experiencing n the here and now back in 1981. it was my former actions that had caused me to choose my current "crazy" state of mind.

After I took the massage examination, not much changed. My anxiety and thoughts of wanting to escape my life became more acute than ever, and I began planning to commit suicide while living in Grammy and Pop Pop's house while they were sleeping. It was crazy that with all their love, nurturing and kindness that I saw no other way out. In retrospect, it seemed so selfish, mean and cruel to do something so terrible to myself knowing how much it would hurt my family. But, I was acting like like a baby and felt completely incapable of freeing myself from the anxiety and fears I was having about my future. I think I might have attracted some type of demonic entity and to fall so deeply down the rabbit hole of hopelessness, doubt, and despair. Unless you have experienced the deep darkness of suicidal depression you will not even have an inkling of how badly it feels to experience those types of negative, suicidal thoughts because they are so against the nature of our "Inner Being", the God/Goddess divine Beings that we all Truly Are. Our bodies were made to be holy temples of the "Living Spirit". Our spirits are eternal, and absolutely nothing can prevent the soul from continuing. It will go on eternally; but we get to choose in what state of consciousness we wish to dwell in.

I told Susan, one of my friends from class, how badly I was feeling and she suggested I see her psychologist. A lot of good that did! I dreaded sharing "the real me" with my friends, let alone a stranger. I felt as if I had no "voice". Since I did not understand why I felt the way I did, or what was actually happening to me, I was in a state of complete confusion and utter hopelessness. I was not really sure what to say to a psychologist. The doctor was not a very warm or compassionate person either. He sent me home after about twelve minutes, suggesting I read the book "You Don't Have to Rehearse to Be Yourself". I felt crappier and more unworthy than ever.

The strange thing is that I never linked the experience of Sid's betrayal and abandonment of me with my self-doubt, depression, fear, and desire to die. I spent the first few weeks after he ABANDONED ME FOR Rose, his new girlfriend, in a state of traumatic shock—especially because he never told me he'd gotten back with her, nor that he did not intend to move me into my new apartment the next day like we'd planned. I had completely lost my confidence even in my ability to communicate. I am sure my throat chakra, solar plexus, and heart chakras were completely closed down, not to mention all the other ones above and below them.

Ironically, it was Sid who called me on the phone at my grandparents' home to say. "Hi Meryl. I've got some good news. I've had the good fortune of massaging the baseball player, Willie Stargell, who is down here as the new manager of the New York Mets. Sarasota and Bradenton is the Mets' winter home. Sid continued, "Mr. Stargell is a very fine man who loves to get massages on a regular basis. Meryl, with opening my new school in Tampa I don't have time to go to Sarasota any longer. You would be doing me a great favor if you would take over working on Willie for a while. He's a kind, generous, but very large man, and it will take you at least ninety minutes to do a full body massage on him, but he is very generous and will pay you at least a hundred dollars." Wow, how could I refuse that gift?! I was not making much money as a waitress at the Wildflower vegetarian restaurant, and I definitely enjoyed giving therapeutic massages much more than waitressing.

In June, I finally told Grammy about my suicidal thoughts and feelings. She said that I should not be ashamed, because she'd had a nervous breakdown herself when she was in her forties, as had my mother. However, she thought it best I go back to Jersey to live with my mom. She had the feeling that my mother would know what to do. So it was decided that Pop Pop would buy me a plane ticket the next day, fancy cat carriers for my kitties, Groucho and Burger and that I would be leaving them almost immediately.

The night before I had to fly back home I was desperate; so I bought a bottle of carbonic acid when I went grocery shopping for Grammy one afternoon. It was my intention to drink down the entire bottle and poison myself. I'm not sure why I didn't want to return to New Jersey and the comforting love of my mother who also knew what it was like to be deeply depressed, so she had some experience with psychologists and a psychiatrist. She also was kind, loving, and had a lot of compassion for people who were suffering. Why would I not think that she could help me too?

My plan was to wait until Grammy and Pop had gone to sleep. Then I took out the bottle of carbonic acid I had hidden in my luggage. I was a bit scared to put it to my lips, but I slowly sipped and took one gulp. It burned a little, but I was determined to put myself out of my misery. I gulped the rest of the bottle, finishing about 11:30 PM. Then I lay down on my little couch in the den and waited to be released from the hellish prison I was in.

Fortunately, homeostasis kicked in. I felt my little heart beating like crazy. I was a little scared of that, but yet somehow I closed my eyes, prayed, and waited for sleep. Eventually, I was unconscious, and magically, with all that poison in my system, I still managed to fall asleep, but I did wake up to urinate some of it out after a few hours.

The flight the next day was in the early afternoon, and Pop Pop had made reservations for us to eat an early lunch at the Kapok Tree Inn in Sarasota; it was one of his favorite restaurants, so when I awoke still alive I just pretended as if everything was "normal" and went along with the plan to go with Gram and Pop to eat at the restaurant and wait in the airport until my flight arrived following lunch. I had a full glass of ice water and Pop had ordered me a delicious meal though I have no recollection of what it was. All I remember in the condition I was in was that I had to get up from the table once or twice to pee out the carbonic acid which the food and drink had completely flushed out of my system. It smelled like I was urinating out a few gallons of smelly gasoline.

Strangely enough, I had spoken to Sid a few days prior to let him know I was flying home suddenly; and he wanted to see me off at the airport, so we had arranged to meet before the plane left. But, as usual, I run late, and luckily, for me, I suppose, I never was able to meet up with him, the creep who broke my heart and who was the catalyst who was responsible for me going into the suicidal depression in the first place. What the hell was I thinking by getting together with him right before returning to New Jersey? That's how out-of-touch I was with myself and my own feelings. Obviously, I was still numb and in a very confused state of mind.

Mom picked me up at Newark Airport with my sixteen-year-old brother, Scott, who was living in her apartment in Old Bridge at the time. It was not a particularly happy reunion for me because I was still wanting to escape having to live with the circumstances of my life as it was, as well as the dark, negative, suicidal, and hopeless thoughts. But mom and I loved each other, and mom, who also struggled with chronic, sometimes acute or worse, suicidal depression, called her psychologist, whom she believed in and felt would know what to do. He diagnosed me with acute anxiety and chronic depression; he believed drugs would work for me, but the anti-psychotic, Mellaril, he prescribed did not help one bit. Mom suggested I give the medication a few weeks to work, but I did not believe this drug which made me feel like a zombie was going to help one iota. Then Mom tried placing me as an in-patient in the psychiatric section of her local regional hospital, Raritan Bay. For goodness sake, who wants to be surrounded by other patients who are depressed, negative, and hopeless just like me? It can be very depressing. Besides, I felt no relief from the increased medications the doctors gave me and it's not right going from one locked room to the next when others think you are crazy, even if you are. I mean, I was still thinking nutty, suicidal thoughts, but I was still ashamed to let the doctors or anyone know.

After being surrounded by other depressed people, I felt just as frightened and more depressed than ever when they released me. I barely spoke to anyone in the entire two weeks I was there, so I made absolutely no progress in the state of my health or natural Well Being. I didn't like any of the doctors or psychologists and certainly made no friends. I actually believed I was "better" than most of these super depressed and frightened folks because I was a vegetarian and a person who did yoga. Can you believe I had such pride, even though I was in such a place of low self-esteem, that I deluded myself into thinking I was "better" than all these other people who also were sad, frightened, and sick with depression? Low self-esteemed egotistical delusions seem to go hand in hand from my personal experience with acute depression as well as the manic highs of this illness.

I was released from the hospital feeling just as bad as ever, and even more terrified because all I could think about again nonstop was putting myself out of my misery by poisoning myself. You'd think I would have learned the first time that that type of suicide attempt was NOT going to work. But, I tried taking the entire bottle of Mellaril by washing it down with the hard liquor I found in my mother's liquor cabinet. (I was not even a drinker and hated alcohol probably because my dad was a mild alcoholic.) Anyway, believe it or not, I survived again! Either God would not accept me into heaven as I was; or Satan was afraid I was going to take over his reign in hell!

I was unaware, according to a psychiatrist's diagnosis, that I had a serious biochemical imbalance in my brain, a mood disorder that was eventually diagnosed in March of 1988 as manic depression, also known as bipolar disorder.

It's called this because a person with this type of mental illness experiences severe mood swings from one extreme of great euphoria and thoughts of grandeur to the opposite polarity where there exists only doubt, anxiety, confusion, fear and despair. At least that was what I believed at the time.

In my case, I believe these severe mood swings were caused by a number of factors: childhood trauma coming up to be healed, deep-seated feelings of unworthiness and fear of being deserted and abandoned, caused by violations of my personal physical, sexual, psychological, and emotional boundaries in childhood, and several times after that in later life.

I had a terrible eating disorder when I became depressed, since I had no appetite for life, and I could barely taste the food I was eating anyway. The resulting nutritional imbalance aggravated the mental imbalance. Everyone needs excellent nutrition to maintain physical and emotional health and energy.

While in the manic phase my mind dwelt in heavenly bliss, but there was a price to pay for feeling tremendously high all the time. I was so ecstatic (without the use of any drugs or alcohol) and overly enthusiastic about everything that sometimes I could not get to sleep until the early hours of the morning – usually between 2:00 and 3:00 AM. My judgment was compromised because I began to feel exhausted during the day, and I did not feel grounded.

I always spent far more money than I had, thereby setting myself up for a depression when the bills eventually came due. On one occasion while on a cruise with my boyfriend, Gary, I impulsively spent $1500 on lithographs that I later discovered were worth far less than what the auctioneer led me to believe.

I had so much energy when I was manic that I could barely sit still. Sleep was possible only after I completely exhausted myself. I felt extremely sexual, lacked healthy boundaries, and had sex impulsively with men that I barely knew. I experienced myself as psychically in tune with many people and able to read their thoughts and feelings. I believed I was intuitive, knew without a doubt I was Spirit inhabiting a physical body, and connected to Source, the creator of all things. I knew in my heart I was made of Light, as was everything and everybody. But when I experienced the consequences of the poor decisions I made while in a manic state I'd end up slowly spiraling into numbness, despair, and deep depression.

During a depression, the mind becomes preoccupied with negative thoughts and irrational fears. These fears are seldom based in reality, but the constant dwelling upon a negative thought like, "I am afraid I can't pay my bills" will attract to it more thoughts of lack. Eventually these constant "lack thoughts" will turn into a physical reality for the thinker. Sometimes, I would not get out of bed until late afternoon or even answer my telephone. I was just too tired, lonely, overwhelmed, and afraid to get out of bed in the winter.

Eventually, the depression would pass, and I would return to mania.

It was a pattern that would be repeated many times throughout the years.

Later in my life when I was a single mom in my forties and fifties I still had to deal with both the highs of mania and the despairs and chronic anxiety of acute depression. During the depressions all I wanted to do was stay in bed until very late in the morning watching TV, and then, after my bath or shower I'd sit upon the couch all day long and watch television or go into my room, and read or write a paper for one of my classes at Mercer County College.

In truth, every one of us is an individualized expression of All-That-Is, a divine spark of the One Consciousness, God's Life expressed in human form. We are each equally divine, with a direct connection to the One Source of Creation and an individualized form of That Being itself! Every thought we think, each feeling we feel, affects us personally and creates our future health, relationships, and circumstances.

We are also a collective consciousness, so that positive, uplifting thoughts and feelings benefit the WHOLE as well. We all become and manifest what we think as creator gods ourselves.

This is the story of my life with bipolar disorder – the ups and the downs, how it began and how I have overcome or managed to live with it, told sometimes with humor and sometimes with seriousness. Along with a splash of metaphysics and a grain of salt.

INTRODUCTION

Once I heard Hilda Charlton, a metaphysical teacher from St. John the Divine, in New York City, say, "Kids, there is nowhere to fall but into the arms of God."

She always referred to her audience that way because she saw us all as Divine Children of Source, God Most High of the Universe. Having fallen, myself, from the heights of Truth and ecstasy into an abyss of unworthiness and terror, resulting in numerous attempts to take my life, I can honestly say that this is true. God's grace is so magnificent and the love and protection of Jesus, the Christ, the Divine Mother, gentle Mother Mary, all my guides, and guardian angels so powerful that I was saved in each hour of darkness and held in the Light of their love. I was rescued every time from dark thoughts which manifested in suicidal ideations and debilitating depressions. Now I am stronger, more humble, and a lot more compassionate and caring for having given myself the experience. If I could survive what I went through, have no doubt that you can survive whatever challenge or circumstance you are temporarily undergoing also. I know when we are "in it" we feel like we will never get through it, but from my own experience, everything passes. Seasons change and spring will come again. There will be a great Light at the end of the tunnel, the knowledge and wisdom you will have gleaned from direct experience.

After several attempts at suicide, in 1988 while at the Carrier Clinic, I was diagnosed as having manic depression, bipolar disorder.

Sometimes, during chronic depressions, I was in a state of terror. I was so filled with dark thoughts and feelings that I would not want to get out of bed until the afternoon, or even to answer my telephone. I felt needy and scared. The only person I felt safe with or comfortable talking to was my mother, who also had much experience with anxiety and depression. I felt like I could trust her to understand my weak, vulnerable condition. She was often depressed and lonely, so she had compassion for what I was going through. My Mom offered me the empathy, nurturing, and the thoughts and feelings of safety I so desperately needed.

I once believed that the initial chronic depressions in November or December were partially caused by lack of sunlight to provide melatonin for my body after we turned the clocks back an hour in October, that is "seasonal affective disorder". But there were also paralyzing depressions in the late spring or late summers, but never during Thanksgiving, my favorite holiday. In retrospect, I believe that my depressions had deeper, more subconscious roots.

While in the manic phase, or perhaps it was just my Kundalini rising which gave me more confidence, creative energy, and a desire to have the better things in life I enjoy and deserve like massages, trips to other states and cruises. Whenever I gave myself good things and nurture myself with extreme self-care like meditation, massages, jacuzzies for deep relaxation, and meet loving, fun, and sensuous kindred spirits, I experienced myself as divine, with unlimited creativity and potential to accomplish anything and everything I wanted.

Sometimes, though, I'd put a lot of travel purchases, gifts for my family, donations to charities, clothes and jewelry on my credit cards; and I know most of those actions were not practical or prudent. I would engage in magical thinking, and spend lots of money before it was even made. I just expected that the money would be in my checking account before the merchants deposited the checks I wrote with little or no money to back them up.

Not having enough money and abundance to pay my bills and have extra for recreation and food had a lot to do with my moods too, of course. While on the mood stabilizer, Depakote, I tended not to spend as carelessly, so I did not feel anxious once all the credit card bills would come due.

Especially when I was a single mom living on SSI disability, a modest amount of child support, and a part-time income from my massage and holistic healing business, I was accustomed to being frugal and very prudent about spending money.

Still, I was living on the edge all the time, and it was causing me anxiety. Sometimes the worry I felt about not being able to pay my basic bills would build into fear and eventually terror that I would not be able to support myself and my young daughter, and these negative thoughts and guilty feelings would quickly spiral into more negative thoughts and anger at myself for having been extravagant in the first place, which put me into a state of depression. Plus, I felt terribly ashamed about living below poverty level, and I never wanted to ask my son or ex-husband for money. These negative thoughts of shame and guilt would quickly spiral into non-acceptance of my emotional state. Instead of being gentle with myself and my ignorance about how to create a budget I could stick to, or even balance a check book.

I felt such a resistance to depression and weakness that I refused to allow anyone to know how badly I felt – not my kids, not even my pastor – that I would eventually believe there was no way out of how and what I was thinking and feeling except through suicide. It is difficult for me to believe this was once true of myself because I am normally such an optimistic, spiritually focused person who prides herself on being a positive thinker and lover of myself, God, and all beings.

When manic, I felt extremely sexual, had a lack of healthy boundaries, and sometimes had sex impulsively with men that I did not know very well, usually without the protection of a condom. I believed then that my vibrational frequency was high enough that I did not usually attract illness, but I also believe, in retrospect, I could have been more discerning and used better judgment. Now I usually exercise more caution and discernment, and I have better discrimination when I am feeling more grounded and not too high or too low. I also have a sweet, loyal steady boyfriend in my precious friend, companion, and helpmate of ten years now, Gary. He is my rock, the man who has been in my corner through all my ups and downs and over and outs.

I wrote a lot of ecstatic poetry during manic or "hypo-manic" phases feeling like a playful elfin fairy flitting around bringing love, joy, and fun wherever I went. During these manic or "hypo-manic" phases I was extremely happy, euphoric, and sometimes ecstatic with lots of energy, joy, exuberance, enthusiasm, and love pouring through me most of the time. I became a dreamer and visionary, but I had no plan of action or means of putting my dreams into form. I wanted all the good things in life like a devoted mate or husband living with me in a happy home, inner peace, and World Peace.

Sometimes I'd desire wealth, fame, travel, fortune, and adventure as well. I've already been on eleven different cruises that are my favorite way to travel to exotic places like Bermuda, Alaska, Costa Rica, Mexico, Curacao, the Panama Canal, and Belize to mention just a few.

While in an expansive state of meditation during these so called "manic" phases, my heart is so open that I still want to help heal, serve, and soothe people everywhere. I would want to feed the entire world's population of hungry children, stop animal abuse, take care of homeless people and the elderly.

In my expansive states of being and unity with all people and creatures I want to ease the pain and suffering of people the world over with the boundless love and compassion I am feeling. I want to be big enough or wealthy enough, like Oprah Winfrey, to go all over the world and shake the hand of or hug each man, woman, and child. I think now that this is a very loving, healthy state of mind and not delusions of grandeur, as some of the psychiatrists would tell us. It may be impossible to accomplish in the physical sense, but I am positive that on a spiritual and telepathic level, many beings the world over can feel this supreme love and Goodwill I have toward each precious one.

Every soul is connected to God, and I believe it is my duty to do the best I can in each moment to live my best life and send love, goodwill, and positive inspiration toward people everywhere. The animals can feel it and love us in return. So do plants.

It has even been scientifically proven that plants react to music, loving thoughts, and appreciation with sensitive instruments. The scientist, Luther Burbank, did a lot of work with plants testing their "feelings" with the instruments he invented for this specific purpose.

At times, however, I did have such unrealistic, magical thinking when I felt extremely "high" that if I kept fantasizing about becoming a famous singer and superstar celebrity that I felt that God would send the perfect agent or manager eventually who would hear me by chance and want me to cut a record for some famous label as a way of bringing my message to everyone.

This actually almost happened in 2015. My dear friend and world class musician, Don Slepian, has been playing and recording New Age music on synthesizer, piano, and flute recorders since 1981 – at least that is when I began ordering his tapes and CDs from a New Age music catalog. He worked with and was good friends with an older, very talented keyboard player and music producer, a man named "Forever" (Sammy) Fields, who worked with greats like Frankie Valli of the Four Seasons, and the comedienne Totie Fields. Even Barbra Streisand sang backup vocals for Forever six months before she became a superstar. Stevie Wonder, once lived next door and wanted to work with him.

Forever is an amazing musician and vocal coach as well as a man who creates groups like the "Rat Pack" and writes shows for his little groups who perform at local New York hotels like "The Hilton Garden Inn" in Staten Island every year. I saw his Rat Pack perform once, with Gary. The restaurant in the hotel was packed even while it was snowing outside with a blizzard was predicted as the snow continued to fall throughout the night and into the next morning and afternoon. Gary and I stayed there over night because it was too late and would be too dangerous for us to drive home at 11 or 12 PM in the blizzard.

We stayed overnight, had a terrific dinner, and caught a very funny show; the singers were all excellent and happened to look and sound exactly like the members of the original "Rat Pack" – Dean Martin, Sammy Davis, Jr., and of course, my heart throb, Frank Sinatra. Forever even added an actress who played Marilyn Monroe who sang her famous song "Diamonds are a Girl's Best Friend".

Not mine. I like turquoise, rubies, amethysts, amber, picture jasper, jade, and malachite, to name a few.

Forever is still booking gigs for his "Rat Pack" at different hotels, casinos, etc., and we are still working on my first jazz demo, which has taken much longer than we expected because on February twenty-fifth, 2016, several months after we began rehearsing and getting to decide which songs would suit my voice the best with my low contralto range I got double pneumonia, and I nearly died. But that's a story for a later chapter.

Once I healed from that, Forever had to have spinal surgery, and then we had to wait until he recovered enough from that to work again. He also had heart surgery before or after that. Now we've been delayed for months by the presence of the "novel corona virus", the pandemic that's been going on and claiming the lives of thousands since March of 2020.

Forever Fields and I recently finished recording one song I love by Ira and George Gershwin, "A Foggy Day". When I first heard it sung by Judy Garland I absolutely adored her rendition. Then I heard Ella Fitzgerald and Louie Armstrong's jazzy version and got even more excited about using this song to introduce my love for jazz on my first demo.

We recorded tracks for "Moondance", by Van Morrison.

I also decided I would also write books and poetry for the purpose of sharing my message of love, joy, gratitude, and unity. That is how creative and expansive I have been feeling for many years, but without a plan of action and so many activities that have distracted me it has been years of waiting patiently for my deepest dreams to come into manifestation.

I still believe I am a powerful woman and that if I have the opportunity and the means I will make a very big difference on the planet with the great love, talents, and determination God has given me. I have many heroines I'd like to emulate – like Oprah Winfrey, Judy Garland, Jane Fonda, Rosa Parks, Mother Harriet Tubman, Mother Theresa, Pocahontas, Gloria Steinem, and Catherine Johnson, the genius mathematician who worked for NASA, our space program, and one of the first women, a black woman facing great prejudice due to her race while living and working in a segregated state, to make an amazing difference in our space race to get to the moon. Her genius helped to put men like John Glen in space. The highly acclaimed film "Hidden Figures", released in December 2016, was based on the biography of Mrs. Johnson with the same title written by Margot Lee Shetterly, If it were not for women like Mrs. Johnson the United States space program would never have gotten off the ground.

I wish to have the same kind of dignity, courage, determination, and patience of these amazing, powerful 'ancestors' of mine, but maybe I can make a difference in the way mental and emotional health is perceived, especially from a psychiatric standpoint – not like a terrible disease to be treated which only creates a negative stigma and causes people to feel ashamed, embarrassed, or bad about themselves.

Afraid and embarrassed to share our problems and troubles with the world or only feel safe enough to confide in just a few who are sensitive and compassionate enough to understand the complexities of what is going on multi-dimensional levels.

Perhaps we are all perfect Beings, but extra sensitive people who may or may not be having a spiritual experience. Or maybe it is just a nutritional deficiency that causes mood swings. Or poverty and sad circumstances. Lack of exercise, movement, enough sunlight and deep rest during the depths and dark of winter may cause seasonal affective disorder, perhaps? Or maybe we have mastered so much in this incarnation that we wanted to give ourselves even greater challenges and adversity to make ourselves stronger…. or maybe it's karma.

Just don't ever let your karma run over my dogma, babe. I'd be very upset.

Having manic depression could be part of kundalini awakening. The kundalini is the coiled energy located at the base of the human spine that travels up and down in two major meridians, the *Ida* and the *Pingala*. All of our samskaras (a Sanskrit word for predispositions – especially bad habits) are cleared away in order for each of us to experience Self Realization, our unity with God and all beings.

After all, aren't we are all here in the name of Love to share our unique talents on Earth in the service of God and humankind? Are we not here to learn and evolve, to love, be loved, and be of service to humanity in whatever small, kind ways we can?

It is still my desire now that I am over 60, to be the best I can be in every moment of each day, to be open and authentic, and happy and peaceful within myself. I feel so much gratitude for the gift God has given me with this precious human Life to spread love, music, hope, and compassion with the voice God has given me. Even though I am a woman of limited material means as of this moment. According to some US data I actually live below poverty level; I even receive food stamps, SSI, Medicare, and SSI disability. However, magically holy Spirit has been providing for all my needs for food, shelter, fun, recreational activities, and all good things for many years now. Even when my thoughts have been negative. Even when I shot myself in the head and could barely speak or pick up a pen to write out what I was feeling God took great care of all my needs through other friends, family members, doctors, nurses, and other strangers who were sent by God to help me...

Even after setting my left hand and pajamas on fire following watching Joan of Arc on television one night. My Gosh already. Enough egotistical melodrama for one lifetime. Now tell me what we are wanting.

I have a yearning to be in service to God and Man each day of my life in the best way I possibly can. I want to help end homelessness and poverty. I especially would love to contribute to the healing of the sick and soothe people in hospitals all over the world, especially people in distress locked up in psychiatric institutions or worse yet, locked away by themselves out of shame or fear, in their own homes, too frightened to go out their front doors.

I have a vision to see the antiquated prison system reformed. May we release everyone from jail who does not deserve to be there. Especially black or brown folks who were arrested just for smoking pot or having some type of drug in his or her possession. I know. You're thinking these sound like unrealistic dreams, fantasies or delusions of grandeur of some crazy lunatic, but I believe we are all on the verge of a major awakening in consciousness, major transformation in all our institutions, and many people the world over will have such open hearts that we will truly come to realize that we are our brothers' keepers and have the power, desire, intention, and opportunity to be responsible for the well-being of not just ourselves and our families but stewards of our precious Mother Earth, all her creatures, and co-creators of a loving, caring, harmonious global community.

Such true desires are not "problems" or "disorders", much less "mental illness". The difficulty for me and some others I've spoken to comes with being unable to constructively channel the incredibly fast-moving energy of kundalini (spiritual energy) rising up through the chakras (the seven energy centers located along the spine beginning at the coccyx going up to the sahasrara or crown at the top of the head and beyond).

In Hinduism, the state of samadhi or Supreme Enlightenment is reached when the energy pierces the crown chakra at the top of the head. A transcendent state in which one experiences no separation between God and themselves, a very quiet place of sublime peace and inner bliss not contingent upon anything outside ourselves. It is a place of bliss and union, where there is no mental chatter at all.

When my soul asked for an acceleration which began in my mid-twenties with Shaktipat initiation from the great saint, my beloved guru, Swami Muktananda, I had a lot of kriyas, both emotional and physical. Kriya is a Sanskrit name for purification.

I had bouts of zealous energy, sleepless nights of activity in which I'd clean house, sing, chant, dance, or write until 3:00 AM or later. My mind was racing, and I had so much energy it was tough for me to sit and just be still. If people close to me suggested something was wrong with me, I'd become angry and defensive. I thought they were just jealous because I had super powers and did not need sleep. I felt so ecstatic and high most of the time, whereas most people I met were just ordinary, not particularly happy people seeming to be living humdrum, mediocre lives.

In retrospect, I realize how egotistical and cocky I was at these times. My downfall was my pride. No matter how energetic or euphoric my state was at the time I was still no better than any other person alive. Even a homeless drunk or prostitute is as dear to God, to Lord Jesus, as the saint or sage. The hobo of today may be the Christ of this Universe or another. The virus, whose name shall not be mentioned again, may be used as an avenue for God's good. You wait and see. Something wonderful will come out of this whole thing. Just be curious and have an open mind about its effects: bringing small groups of people together; increasing appreciation of being able to see one another outdoors, walking in nature, going within, or seeing a precious few people with masks at the gym. I made a new friend, Jenna, one morning while singing along with Michael Jackson songs at Princeton Fitness and Wellness and pedaling a stationary bicycle. She is a lovely, older black woman who wore a T-shirt emblazoned with the phrase "Mother of the Universe". She heard me singing, and we began to chat. We became fast friends because it felt like we were kindred spirits and we exchanged phone numbers and e-mail addresses that very day.

At the Whole Earth Center in Princeton where I go occasionally to learn and shop for delicious bulk nuts, grains, kefir, yogurt, fresh veggies, almond butter, tofu, and tofurkey burgers, I often run into a few friends just by chance. But there is really no "chance" in this vast universe. There are Laws put in place like the Law of Gravity like the Law of Attraction, deliberate Creation, the Law of Karma, and others that make everything work for all our highest good.   There would have to be a loving intelligence that cares for all people or we'd blow ourselves all to pieces. I truly believe the unconditional LOVE trumps hate!

From a higher perspective there are no accidents in our vast universe, and everything is predestined on one level, happening for the greatest and highest good of everyone on this precious planet. Yet then there is free will, choice, and intention. A good friend and angelic being once told me "Reality is not set in stone. It is malleable. Nothing ever stays the same.

According to the famous American baseball player, Yogi Berra "If you see a fork in the road, just take it." Or fake it. Fake it 'til you make it."

Pretend you are a successful, published author and eventually, at the perfect time for you, you will have the confidence to be one, girlfriend. Just practice, practice, practice. Read your work aloud to yourself and in small writers' clusters at local libraries, hospitals, and gymnasiums. Speak to crowds after making a personal video you share on the internet. Call your friends at "Dress for Success". And NAMI. Inviting others into your home, like Amy Ascordia, Asha, and Noel Lagana to each share and read your works aloud, and allow others to constructively critique you about how it made them feel. Like your British friend, Maurice says, "You can do it, Meryl." Persistence, determination, and daily discipline will pay off. You'll see. Now, get some good rest. You can continue your divine work again tomorrow.

When I was depressed, suicidal, racing thoughts I could not seem to control even with the help of medication, would plague me inexplicably, and I was never sure of the future, or when I would feel paralyzed. I rarely take medication now, but I am my using a positive new attitude, Christian Science teachings, unconditional love and connection to the Divine Source I AM to help quiet the mind. And specific foods, supplements, and sensuous and sexual expression to ground all the creative kundalini energy I feel in my physical form.

After each "manic" episode, the need for sleep and the proper nutrition, with enough minerals and vitamins, became overwhelming, and the pendulum swung to the opposite pole. I became severely depressed and frightened, because I'd believe there was something terribly wrong with me.

How could I be so ecstatic one minute filled with the enthusiasm of God and overwhelmed with feelings of love and connection to All things and people, trees, and animals, singing and dancing all the time and then three months later feel so scared and selfish I did not care about making a positive difference in the world at all? I just would want to feel normal enough to barely be able to function.

Many times, I became so exhausted during a manic phase I just wanted to quit feeling ecstatic and exuberant about everything and everyone. I just wanted to be a regular old person who simply got a decent night's sleep, so that I could function well enough to take care of myself, or to prepare and eat three square meals per day. Without a proper night's sleep and three-square meals per day how could I take care of anyone else, especially my youngest daughter, Sky?

I became frustrated and overwhelmed, and spiraled downward into a serious, selfish state of mind in which I became anxious, withdrawn, inexpressive, taciturn. A real dullard. Bored and boring to myself and others. Not my usual happy, positive self-laughing and smiling – singing and dancing most of the day or night. I was ready to trade my life of excitement, enthusiasm, and ecstasy just to feel normal again, to get good nutrition and six or seven hours of decent sleep per night. Nothing was really terribly wrong with me except that I BELIEVED deep inside my core that something was wrong.

The Course in Miracles says "Love brings up anything unlike itself."

Where do all these foolish beliefs come from? I don't know, but I've decided not to listen to them anymore. I am Now in this holy moment realizing my supreme value as a holy child of God Most High, the infinitely intelligent Creator and Creatrix who loved me enough to put a bit of that Conscious Awareness, the same divine spark and intelligent Love inside of me and my mind, heart, and soul. It is that same soul and loving awareness that exists in you, me, and every brother, sister, and living creature here on this beautiful planet, not to mention other planets and in all the stars in the sky and grains of sand on every beach in the world. Wow, are we a BIG, LOVING, Infinitely intelligent PRESENCE, and AM I glad I finally figured it out again in this precious moment. I know I have known this all along; but we often play a game of hide and seek with ourselves, just like we did as little children.

If there were unworthy, scared, or shy thoughts coming up from my conscious or subconscious mind to be healed, they would surface after several months of a hypomanic or manic phase. I'd often compare myself to other better writers, singers, or entertainers. I would believe, and experience, no self-confidence at all. My low, unworthy side, the "inner critic" would think "I'll never be a successful, published prolific poet or writer like Danielle Steele, Stephen King, or Maya Angelou. I cannot even finish one darned book!" In the past I had messy, disorganized drawers and file cabinets filled with tons of poetry and prose from years of writing spilling over the sides of my desk and file cabinet, but no published anthology or collection of work until October of 2015 when I finally self-published my very first book with Author House, "Heartscapes", an anthology of prose and poems spanning forty years of my life.

In my depressed, dark days my ego told me I was too lazy, unmotivated, not confident, or too busy to send any of my writing out to a publisher because I did not believe I was a "real" writer, so my kind beau, Gary, offered to help edit my poems and pay Author House several hundred dollars to publish and place my poems into the form of a beautiful book with a large picture of myself on the front cover that was taken at church one evening at the Center for Spiritual Living where I was a hostess welcoming folks into church during Rev. Rich Volk's and Rev. Rhea Carols' joint ordinations. It is a very happy, flattering photograph of me that I hope will attract folks to open up the book inside and read my inspirational, autobiographical poems.

A small amount of the medication, Depakote, or the generic version (divalproex), a mood stabilizer, helped me to keep my mood in the middle so I would not have those serious mood swings from one extreme to another most of the time. I also slept better which meant I was able to function better in the morning and make myself a healthy, nutritious breakfast. Healthy, nutritious meals and supplements have been KEY to my having more energy and fuel for the things like work, exercise, hobbies like making art, writing poetry, and other activities I had on my agenda for the day.

I sometimes try to follow the teachings of Mary Baker Eddy, who founded Christian Science, so I've been off the Depakote and other medications for a few months with no ill consequences, but I would not think twice about taking medications again if I felt myself slipping back into a negative state of mind. Recently, I went back on Depakote for a while, because I had a mini crisis last April, and a period of depression afterwards.

In truth, there is no reason to worry about anything. For, just like Job in the Bible, what we fear and worry about we will attract. It's that simple. Thought is creative. We get what we think about. Whatever our mind focuses upon expands. So, it behooves us to become at least a Divine Witness of the ever-changing thoughts and emotions if we cannot discipline ourselves to think pure, positive thoughts of hope, appreciation, gratitude, and love. By the divine Law of Attraction, thinking and speaking about what it is we want will eventually lead to the good feelings and circumstances that we are desiring to create.

When I have respect for money and for myself, I tend to use moderation in spending and in situations requiring me to have healthy boundaries. The ultimate Truth is that Substance is infinite. It was a matter of cultivating a "watchful consciousness". And giving myself a decent night's sleep of at least six to eight hours, so that I would use better discrimination in all my decisions regarding money, sex, and how I lived my life from moment to moment. Depakote also helped me to choose foods that were more likely to make me feel healthy and better about myself. I also was able to afford and take better supplements in the morning like B complex which is very good for mood swings and depression, magnesium, calcium, and other good minerals, Vitamin C, D, and others I was guided at certain times to take daily.

Now I realize that it is not always a good thing to be addicted to feelings of euphoria and ecstasy for too long because the opposite of that feeling of euphoria and ecstasy is dysphoria. Because we live in a balanced and orderly universe, what goes up must come down, just like the Blood, Sweat, and Tears' song "Spinning Wheel", suggests. This song, written and sung by David Clayton Thomas and performed by Blood, Sweat, and Tears, is a very basic metaphysical teaching.

I never realized what a metaphysical song that was when I was younger. Now, as a yogini realizing Who I Am, again and again, I know in my heart that that balance is always key in our lives; I realize the practical good sense of taking the "Middle Way". My personal path since September twenty-seventh, 1981, Siddha Yoga, explains the great benefits of chanting and meditation. Done as a regular practice they both relieve stress, create a state of sublime peace and equanimity, and are ways to open the heart chakra. Chanting kirtan and the Guru Gita on a regular basis have been my favorite ways to experience bliss and God's supreme love for myself and all other beings.

For most of my life I have experienced thriving physical health, except for the times I was not sleeping well during manic or depressed phases. Then, though I had no signs of chronic illness, I would be too busy or too tired to cook or prepare healthy, nutritious food, so I opted, instead, to eat poorly by going to a drive-in window for a sausage, egg, and cheese sandwich for breakfast before 11AM, or a burger with extra tomatoes and pickles for lunch or supper, which would be my only vegetables I consumed for the day. These types of quickies non nutritious foods, at first created indigestion, constipation, or something minor like that. But eventually I think the diet of fast-food including tons of wheat gluten and dead cows; and the bi-polar medications I took whose side effects were constipation, possible suicidal ideations, and extreme fatigue in the morning and for hours afterward, also caused me to have "leaky gut" syndrome which also made me to feel exhausted and contracted in nature, as opposed to energetic and expansive like most people who have adopted a completely vegan or vegetarian diet. I had been vegetarian at one time with my first husband because I am a gentle soul who does not believe in harming animals and other living creatures, especially those that have a face. However, when I would become manic or hypomanic, it was so challenging to manage and calm the powerful Shakti (Sanskrit for chi or "Life force") that both my chiropractors would recommend I begin eating foul, fish, or cow beef again. They both convinced me it was OK, and that is why cows were put upon this planet. But I detest the way our animals are treated so inhumanely in our current factory farming food conglomerate, so I vowed months ago never to eat cows again...

I believe that the only times I ever got sick were when I was over-stressed and my immune system was compromised due to poor diet, lack of exercise, or lack of sleep.

One of my ex- husbands had herpes when we met, but I never contracted the disease even though we never used condoms. Through his own research he learned to manage the disease very well through good nutrition, vitamins, exercise, and positive thinking. He may have even cured himself of the virus. I've not spoken to him about it since we divorced, but he always looks healthy to me whenever I see him at holidays. This year they have opted to spend time alone and "social distance" just to be safe, and I will miss both their divine presences. Instead of sitting upon my assets ignoring my highest ass-pirations, and being numbed to the pain and suffering in this world by watching the boob tube I have chosen to write, exercise, swim at the gym in Princeton, or go to physical therapy with Dr. Kim at Edison Rehabilitation where I also receive massage, chiropractic adjustments, and shiatsu plus acupuncture when I decide I need it.

When I chose to give birth to my second child at home the midwives suggested I get a blood test to make sure I did not have the herpes virus which could be passed on to my baby, and is potentially fatal at birth. The midwives had already lost one baby to the herpes virus, and did not want to risk the possibility of that happening again, so I was tested. My blood showed no signs of this virus or any other. I was very healthy and thriving. And I still continue to choose that consciousness of abundant health.

These days, I make a tiny bit of cash offering foot reflexology at the Ariel Center for Well Being. It is my specialty since I have a very strong hand and thumb. I am also intuitive; besides the scientific knowledge I have about zone therapy and meridians in the body corresponding to points on both the feet and hands, I somehow instinctively KNOW exactly which acupressure points to touch without ever asking. My hand automatically goes to those needy, sore places during a massage treatment. I've been very blessed to have this gift of healing since I was younger, but I did not get in touch with this magical talent until I went to massage school in 1981.

Even when I took my first day long massage workshop in 1976, my friend, Patsy, the instructor who would become my best friend with whom I'd travel to Florida to study at the Sarasota School of Natural Healing Arts, saw me working on fellow students and told me I had a natural gift for therapeutic Swedish massage, foot reflexology, and healing.

I love and completely "BELIEVE IN" the POWER of HEALING MASSAGE for both the giver and the receiver. If all of us would get at least one hug or one massage per day this whole world would be transformed! We all need loving touch – safe, non-sexual, nurturing touch that relieves tension in sore muscles and achy joints, improves a person's circulation, moves lymph and toxins out of the body, and generally creates a sense of well-being and euphoria, peace, and deep relaxation.

I am, and have been, creative as an artist and poet, with an abundance of new ideas for projects and inventions. However, during manic phases, my mind was overwhelmed with so many brilliant ideas it worked too fast for me to focus on any one of them. I usually overextended myself and had way too much on my plate – especially for a person with a physical handicap. I rarely took action on anything specific. It seemed as if I was just running from one fun activity to another without any rest until I was exhausted. At the end of the day, I was no closer to accomplishing any of my long-term goals or deepest dreams – like the writing of this book, for example. Or publishing my many poems and songs. Or making a CD of my original compositions and some of my favorite jazz standards.

I am so blessed because, despite all my poor choices and poor judgment in the past, God has always taken care of me through doctors, nurses, aides, friends, and family – even at those times I was too weak of mind or body to take care of myself. My mom, my loving son, and my daughters have supported me. I cannot thank my son enough for his love in the form of financial, physical, and emotional support. Now if the bills are late occasionally, I do not worry about it. Once I've paid my rent, phone, credit cards, and electric bills online I relax completely knowing that everything will eventually get paid at the perfect time. I just take them one at a time. The Cable Company will not go out of business because I paid my bill a few days late. It doesn't really matter. For me it feels better to pay a few bills several days late, preferring to meditate and swim if it makes me feel better and more connected. Then, magically, I'd come home, and presto – there would be a call from a new client on my answering machine saying they wanted to schedule a massage session or some other holistic treatment. Or a check in my mailbox I had been expecting for weeks would appear at just the perfect time.

I stopped opening the mail that consisted of requests for donations or catalogs enticing me to buy stuff that I really did not need such as early Valentine's Day or Christmas gifts for others. Now I just put most of that junk mail into the recycle bin before can "buy things with money I don't have to impress people I don't like!" That's what my beau, Gary, says, anyway.

In "Heartscapes" there are two graphic, erotic poems of me with two beaux in my forties having a loving, intimate experience outdoors on a sunny day being caressed by the sunshine on our faces loving one another under a sweet green sycamore tree cooling us and shading us on a hot sunny July day.[1] Now wouldn't you like to read it and find out who the special guy is? Perhaps it's you. I never name any real names, in order to protect the guilty. ... I mean the innocents.

There is also a graphic description of me giving birth to my first baby – my precious son, who was born at home on my bed with two midwives, Barbara and Ann. I went into labor during a surprise birthday party for my mother. This amazing experience is described in more detail in a later chapter. Who knew that the surprise party for my mom's forty-seventh birthday would have a surprise in store for me as well?

So much has happened since. And now there is this, my memoir, which I have been living and writing since 1991, over 30 years in the making!

Yes, but when I am finished, what an accomplishment and how fulfilled I will feel just to have had the resolve, patience, persistence, and determination to stick to it, to the tapestry of this beautiful one's unique life – my very own story on paper and something of value to share with my children, grandchildren, friends, and folks all over the state of New Jersey, where everyone has got to be crazy. I mean I could live absolutely anywhere. I could live in the sunshine state of Florida, beautiful red rock mountains and valleys of Sedona, Arizona, the great state of grace in Carmel, California. Or I could choose a home in the state of Texas where my Teacher, Esther Hicks, who channels the teachings of the non-physical entity, Abraham, and the Laws of Attraction, Deliberate Creation, and Allowing, live. Oregon, Oklahoma, or Hawaii, but God put this blessed one in the great garden state. Former home of Meryl Streep, Bruce Springsteen, John Bon Jovi, and Elsie the cow who lived in Bordentown, of course!

This is the story of a life with bipolar depression, but, more than that, a story of learning how to live an enriching and enjoyable life despite the inevitable ups and downs we all experience – or perhaps because of them.

What is needed is balance, clarity, and understanding, without losing the positive attitude.

My thoughts on achieving such a balance are found in the final chapters of this book.

---

1 Heartscapes

BEGINNINGS

It all began, seemingly, "normally" enough.

In 1955, the birthing experience in the hospital was terrible. My mother had no support from my dad, the doctor didn't come until the end of her labor, and the nurse in the delivery room was not very nice or compassionate while my mom labored in terrible pain. Most women were drugged, some given epidurals, the drug, Pitocin, which makes a woman's contractions come lightning fast. Some women must have Caesarian sections or episiotomies leaving them with scars and in pain after these surgeries.

My nineteen-year-old mom was terribly frightened, feeling alone, abandoned, and in acute pain. I was brought into the world in a very traumatic way, with forceps, blinding lights, and a hard spank on my bottom, so I came in with the subconscious affirmation that the world was a dangerous place and men hurt me. Because my mom was drugged, I did not get to bond with her right away.

Through rebirthing, a conscious connective breathing technique pioneered by Leonard Orr in the nineteen sixties, I was later able to remember and clear a lot of the fear and pain surrounding my own traumatic birth experience on July 15th, 1955. That is also why I chose to give birth to my own three children naturally with midwives at home twice and the last time and at a birthing center. My third baby, Sky, was born in the Family born room of Helene Fuld Hospital in Trenton, NJ. Gabriel and Kyrie were born in my bedrooms in two different homes.

Mom and Dad and baby me

It seems I was an exceptionally bright baby. I said my first word, "daddy" at six months old, and I was speaking full sentences by the time I was one year old. My mom read to me from the time I was just a baby, she told me. My pediatrician said "Mrs. Olson, you have no idea what a wonder it is that your baby is speaking so well because she is the first and you have no other children. If you did, you'd truly appreciate how special and intelligent she is." I remember being a few years old spelling rhyming words aloud to her when she came in to tuck me in at night to read me a story. She read rhyming picture books to me like Dr. Seuss' "Cat in the Hat" and "Green Eggs and Ham".

1

Every night I'd say something like, "The mouse, M-O-U-S-E is in the house, H-O-U-S-E. Mommy read to me a lot from the time I was very young because, according to her "No one ever read to me, and that's why I grew up not very smart like Aunt Marlyse and not liking to read books myself." I remember that she read to me from Aesop's Fables, and Grimm's Fairy Tales. Then she sang to me. She had a very pleasant voice that was soothing and made me feel very happy and loved. I really loved when she sang to me at night when she tucked me into bed.

During my early childhood, my family – Mom, Dad, my maternal grandparents (whom we called Grammy and Pop Pop), and my paternal grandparents (Grandma and Grandpa) all lived in Staten Island. I will have much more to say about all four grandparents later.

I grew up as a pretty normal, happy, and positive young woman excelling in elementary and high school in academics, music, sports, and musical theater. I attended lots of extra-curricular activities including cheer leading. I even became the captain of the "Green Team" when I was twelve because I had a loud, enthusiastic voice and the next year, "The Blue Team". I couldn't do a split, so I never got to be a cheerleader in high school. As the eldest child I was very strong, happy, and for the most part, a leader in school. In sixth and seventh grades I became cheerleading team captain.

Sixth grade was a memorable year for me since I was my teacher, Mrs. Elinor Young's, favorite student. Not only did I get straight A's, but I was chosen for the lead role as Becky in the eighth-grade musical, "Tom Sawyer." I also became the new girlfriend of Glen, the young boy in my class chosen to play Tom Sawyer. We went "steady" for a little while. He even gave me his class ring which I wore around my neck. I loved boys and I loved to flirt and kiss.

My mom did most things for me, and didn't teach me how to cook, or balance a checkbook, or even what it meant to be independent and learn about finances. Mom was unhappy just being a wife and mother. She took good care of us, but she often seemed to be depressed. Due to her yelling a lot, I had little real confidence in myself and my own abilities; I badly needed and wanted approval from everyone, especially her. I was always trying to please her and get her attention, but most of the time she was cleaning, ironing, cooking, or involved in other domestic chores. That's probably why I became an entertainer, loving to sing, dance, and act in plays and musical theater. I loved making people happy and wanted my family and everyone I met to feel happy and good about life. I was a happy, positive little girl who had my own sense of a loving God who deeply cared for me and everyone.

Though I was raised with the idea of "sin" and punishment for sin in Catholicism, it never really resonated with me. In my heart I knew Jesus and God loved me and everyone for doing the best they could do; He was an unconditionally loving Creator and Father of His children. The concept of sin made no sense to me, and I believed it was a false teaching from the time I was seven and made my first communion after studying Catholic principles and beliefs in catechism at Sunday school.

In high school, life got a bit screwy because my parents were having problems which meant that we had to relocate to a new home after living in Holmdel, NJ, for twelve years. After some searching, my parents found a nice town house in Fords, NJ, right across the street from where the new Woodbridge Mall was being built. I felt saddened to have to move, leaving my childhood friends and neighbors in Holmdel behind, as well as my teachers and student friends I'd made while attending Red Bank High School (home of Count Basie) for my freshman and sophomore years, but I had no choice. We moved in the beginning of summer, so by autumn I started out as a junior at Woodbridge High School.

I had been a very popular gal while attending Red Bank High, but once I moved, I was not well known, had just a few friends, and I did not get asked to the junior prom, so I took the initiative and asked Lou Chiellini, a handsome sophomore, to take me. I was not shy, but it was very difficult switching schools in mid semester. Luckily, I made a few friends, but before I knew it I would have to move again.

Mom sometimes got so angry at me that she'd chase me and break hairbrushes over my head while I was running down the stairs to get away from her. I have no idea what I did that made her so angry, but whatever it was I'm sure the punishment was much worse than the crime. Physically, the pain was not bad, but the psychological and emotional pain I suffered at the hands of my mother was far worse – damaging, and traumatic. It nearly caused me to go into shock. I would run upstairs and cry into my pillow for hours until I would hyperventilate while mom was downstairs in the kitchen cursing and screaming to herself. Years later, I would be diagnosed with Post-Traumatic Stress Disorder as a result of this experience, among others.

My mom has had many shock treatments for suicidal and acute depression, and she says she does not remember the physical abuse at all.

When mom was kind, she was sweeter than Glenda, the Good Witch of the North, in the Wizard of Oz. The scary part of growing up was not knowing which witch was going to pop up. If the Wicked Witch of the West or East came around, I had to walk on eggshells all the time being very careful to never get anything dirty, never spill or drop anything, and especially to be careful not to get my fingerprints on the walls. I had to be the "Perfect Child" or live in fear of the consequences which were screaming, yelling, and cursing. Occasionally, I got spanked or smacked with the slotted metal spoon if I answered back. Or if I disobeyed.

When my dad came home from work, he'd sit on our maroon couch in the living room having his two glasses of "Manhattans" which he or my mom would prepare for him daily. During that time Mom would be preparing a delicious dinner consisting of some type of meat like chicken, a pot roast, meat loaf, steak, corned beef, or pork chops, one or two delicious frozen or fresh vegetables, and white potatoes either boiled, mashed with lots of butter, or roasted like the little red bliss potatoes which she would fix by sauteing onions and garlic in a frying pan after they were cooked. I don't know how the heck she did it. My mom was a terrific cook, and mealtimes were always relaxing and fun, with laughter and lively conversation. Daddy would share something about what happened on his job during the day. We kids would talk about what happened, if anything, during our time at school, or about our after-school activities.

Saturday or Sunday nights Dad would take out our little projector and focus it upon the big white screen which was on the back wall of the recreation room downstairs; and he would put the slides in and show them to us one at a time. There were always slides of us kids, too, from Thanksgiving, Christmas, Easter, and other holidays, or just in our pajamas when we'd go to the drive-in movie theater across the street on Route 35.

There were also trampolines there, and before the movie started Daddy would take me, and my brothers Pete, and Scott there to jump up and down in our jammies. It was always playtime for me and my brothers when Daddy was around. After we finished our nightly dinners which I do not think any of us really appreciated, the three kids and daddy would go into the living room to play. I don't remember even one of us ever saying "thank you" to mom for all her hard work with meal preparation or clean up. Sometimes I would set the kitchen table with plates, knives, spoons, forks, and folded napkins exactly the way mom taught me.

Actually, sometimes I said "Thank you". My Dad taught us that saying "Please and Thank you" was good manners, especially with people outside our immediate family.

While mom cleaned up the dishes, putting most of them into our automatic dishwasher except for the three or four copper-bottomed Farber ware pots and pans she used for cooking, we would play; she made the stove shine like the top of the Chrysler building. Oh, we did clean off our plates and place them in the sink or on top of the counter, but other than that we had little responsibility. Oh, except for dusting the sides or tops of my bedroom or living room furniture. Mom did everything else. All the cleaning and washing, drying, and folding of laundry as well as the cooking of nearly every meal.

Occasionally, dad might prepare a ham or turkey sandwich for us, and on week-ends in the summer he would barbecue steaks or hamburgers on the outdoor grill, but for the most part, cooking was mom's domain. As was weeding the garden or occasionally mowing the lawn if my father was too tired. My mom worked incessantly. No wonder she was miserable. She had so little time to rest, socialize with friends, or even take up a hobby. I'm feeling tired just thinking and writing about it.

She also did all the sewing and hemming of my skirts and dresses. When my dad quit smoking, he saved enough money in quarters in a glass jar to buy mom a Singer sewing machine which she used to make me two cotton dresses, one yellow gingham, and the other a plain light orange colored dress with a bust size of 28, for "Tom Sawyer" when I landed the lead role of Becky Thatcher in the eighth-grade musical. I'll never forget the bust size because, at the time, I thought that was a decent size even though I had practically no breasts at all.

That was just the circumference of my back and chest. It sounds so funny to me now as I recall that I actually believed I had real womanly breasts.

Mom liked knitting, so she knitted dad really nice wool sweaters. A pretty red one and a blue one too. Sometimes she'd knit me a scarf or a hat. I loved when she taught me how to knit and crochet because then I could have fun making nice things for our family too. Like slippers. One year I made five pairs of yellow and sky-blue slippers for everyone in our family for Christmas. I made a colorful scarf once too. Being able to knit and crochet made me feel important and talented because I felt confident that I was able to contribute something of myself to my family.

Mom also made home-made cakes, brownies, and occasionally fresh bread. The best part of her making a Duncan Hines cake or fudge Brownies was that we kids could get to lick the icing off the spatula and beaters as well as the bowl. I always thought that if I made cakes myself when I grew up, I would only lick the batter and skip making or eating the cake. I liked the batter much more than the cake itself. Except for her brownies. I loved a dessert or snack after lunch or dinner of fudge brownies dunked in a glass of milk or French milk tea. Yummy!

Mom did all the chaperoning. She took me to basketball games and sometimes cheerleading practice. She also drove my brother, Pete, in our light green older Buick to wrestling matches, Scott to Cub Scouts, me to Brownies, then a year of Girl Scouts following that.

While mom was cleaning the kitchen after dinner it became "Playtime" for me and my brothers in the living room with daddy. We played hide and seek which was very scary because my dad would turn out all the lights and pretend, he was a monster. He would hide somewhere in the darkest corner of the living room while we waited in the dining room. Then he'd come out of some hidden place while we were cautiously looking for him. He'd jump on all three of us, one at a time, and tickle our bellies and we would laugh out loud until we were breathless.

We also played a game called "horsey" where Dad would put us on his back and crawl around the living room with each of us on top of his back. Then he would lay on his back with his golden brown slippered feet up in the air, and I would sprawl across them while he lifted them in the air and I would try to balance myself so that I could fly in the air. During our fun playtime, mom was working the entire time until she was finished making the kitchen immaculate so that she could relax with Daddy after she was done by watching a little bit of television either downstairs in the recreation room or upstairs on their Queen-sized bed with the lovely large pink comforter and bedspread in their Master bedroom.

When we were young, we had an early bedtime of 7:30 PM which was right in the middle of Man From U.N.C.L.E, with David McCallam in one of the main roles as Ilya Kuriakin, and Robert Vaughn playing Napoleon Solo. It was a great spy show, and if we had to go to bed before it was over, I'd wait a few minutes after mom or dad tucked us in and then I'd sneak out of my room to finish watching the show while lying behind the open doorway to my parents' room.

My brother, Peter, and I often misbehaved; we fought a lot about stupid things, and often we did it together after we were punished for fighting over TV and who would get to see his own program. Then we would bond and make believe my parents were the "enemy" lowering our voices to a whisper but loud enough to be heard over the new intercom system installed in our rooms, pretending we were secret agents like Napoleon Solo and Ilya Kuriakin; then we'd write notes to each other on lined paper and pass the secret notes under each other's' bedroom doors.

Then, it started getting weird.

I was clueless that my parents were having marital problems. They always kissed in front of us and I never saw them fight or heard them argue. My mom did get depressed a lot; and Dad would come to tuck me into bed, tell me a story and say he loved me. I loved when my dad tickled my back. It felt so good and relaxing, but when I was fourteen, and in eighth grade, his fingers kept on going down into my underpants; I became physically excited. Physically, it felt good to be touched "down there", but knowing it was my dad doing the touching was very confusing. After all, he was not only my father and protector, but he was my mom's husband. What would she think? How would she feel? The whole thing felt scary and awkward to me, so I tried not to think about it much. I just went along my regular merry way with my head in the clouds seeing the world through rose colored lenses, like in the song "La Vie en Rose." I should have known that something was off somewhere, or my dad would not be touching me in that way.

I felt so terribly embarrassed that I could not even talk about it with my dad face to face until many years later. I was afraid to look him in the face after these uncomfortable sessions. Dad came to me after about six months of the uncomfortable episodes at night to apologize, and say it would never happen again.

I will have much more to say on this subject in the Chapter "Growing Up with Father", but this was certainly the beginning of a deep-seated mistrust of men and fear of abandonment.

Dad then said "Don't ever tell your mom or anyone else or she might want to divorce me, and I'd have to leave you, Pete, and Scott." So, I never told my mom. It was not until I was twenty-four or five years old that we would finally breech the subject after my boyfriend, John Hischer, spilled the beans to my mother one afternoon when I was not around.

I did tell other people, however, like Frank, the sixteen-year-old lifeguard I was dating whom I met at the Junior Lifesaving Course given by the YMCA that spring. when I was a sophomore at Red Bank HS. Wow, was he gorgeous, and a really nice guy! Frank never told anyone, as far as I know.

Frank was a sophomore from Lincroft, NJ, who attended the junior lifesaving course with me at the Red Bank YMCA. I did not pass the lifesaving course, but I got something better. I won the friendship and heart of this very sweet, handsome, wealthy, and caring, sixteen-year-old young man when I was only fifteen. Frank not only had amazing biceps and triceps from lifting weights, diving, and swimming, but he was caring, kind, devoted, and smart to boot. He was really the first young man with whom I began to explore the wonders of petting. He was the first male other than my father whom I allowed to touch my breasts and vaginal lips. We would make out in his parents' basement and once, when his mom was not home, we even explored one another in Frank's bed upstairs in his bedroom. I loved making out with Frank and having him undo my brassiere in order to caress my small sensitive breasts and nipples, but having him touch me down in my private area was a whole new experience for me, and I really liked it. It was a very exciting experience, though I did not climax. Nor did Frank.

I really liked Frank because he was sweet, strong, sensitive, talented, and fun loving. But most of all, I knew he cared about me. We were both virgins, and it was fun exploring most of the "bases" together in order to experience the joys of physical and emotional love without having to lose our virginity before marriage – which was something young Catholic girls were not even supposed to consider as an option, for fear we would sin against Jesus and God. So, I tried very hard being a "good little girl" for as long as I could, but that all changed when I turned fourteen and fifteen.

Give me a break, you hypocritical priests. Who is calling the kettle black here? Bishops and cardinals have conned us for hundreds of years by covering up the clandestine rapes and systematic molestation of thousands of unsuspecting altar boys, nuns, and other loyal, devoted young parishioners and their parents who trusted them. When many of these accusations were made public in Boston the Catholic church bought off the parents and innocent victims with undisclosed settlements that were sealed in order to protect the reputation of the perpetrators, or so they said; they promised the "alleged" victims and their parents that these priests would either be defrocked, retired, or put onto an island where they could not harm another young boy or girl. That was a huge lie and rarely the case. The cover up continued for years because it was allowed by the popes, bishops, politicians, policeman, detectives, and an entire community which tolerated this abuse, rather than exposing the priests and having them punished. The whole scandal made me feel sick and disgusted when it first came out in the media and then again when the movie "Spotlight" came out in November of 2015.

Frank sometimes wrote me loving letters, and he'd always call me his "Liebchen". His parents were German, so I guess that was an endearing name for one's beloved. Frank and I spent the rest of sophomore year together and we went to his junior prom. I also tried water skiing with him on the Navesink River on his friend, Jack's, boat. I was happy to be on the boat, but when I tried to ski, I was a flop. A complete and total failure! The water was cold and I could not even stand up after two tries. So, while Frank and Jack were taking turns doing somersaults, cartwheels in the air with jumping, diving dolphins, trying to impress me, I guess, I finally gave up in disgust. Frank was an excellent skier and a real show-off. He did all these tricks and could ski on just one ski and do front and back flips. His friend, Jack, steered the motorboat, and then they'd switch off.

Frank did not need to impress me with his acrobatic or athletic ability, because he was a very nice-looking guy with very big muscles, auburn hair, from a rich, proper German family in Lincroft and so sweet and appreciative of me. A genuine nice guy. Maybe even potential marriage material if he ends up being a good lover. He was already nice, charming, kind, and truly good to me in many ways, but I did not have enough experience to know what a truly good man was, so I let him and love slip through my fingers after less than one year. What the heck was I thinking?!

That summer while Frank was home and I was up at Gold Key Lake, our round resort home in the Poconos, I turned sixteen and fell another muscular lifeguard, a blond, short, man several years older than me named Charley, who had a hot, muscular body, though he was a few years older than me. I would sail out onto the lake in my pink and white two-piece bikini on my red and white catamaran, hanging out over the pontoons in a strong breeze, the wind blowing through my sun drenched, lightly colored long blond hair feeling free and independent and pretending I was helpless. After enjoying some special quiet time alone with the calm, peaceful lake water, for some extra fun I'd deliberately capsize the sailboat so Charley would have to come out to rescue me. What a silly little fool and flirt I was! He wasn't even interested in me; he liked an older blond, Rubenesque gal named Bethany, who talked to him at his lifeguard stand or he'd come over to her large, rectangular red and orange colored beach towel with a large sun in the center, rays going all around it and ask if she needed Coppertone lotion slathered on her back and shoulders where she could not reach. He'd try to impress her with big knowledge of politics and secular popular music from the Carpenters, to Yes, to the Who. Charley went on and on about how Karen Carpenter had one of the best voices he'd ever heard. I was so jealous. I liked her voice, but I knew I could sing just as well as she, and I had a lot more confidence, vivacity, charm, and all-around charisma. Karen was great, a talented drummer, good on harmonies, and beautiful in her lemon-yellow outfit onstage at the Garden State Arts Center when I saw her, but I could outshine her anytime, I thought, if just given the chance. She was already on a big stage near my hometown, recording for a big record label with her handsome, talented, composer and arranger brother, Richard; and I'd only performed in grammar school in the eighth-grade musical, "Tom Sawyer", in all my little grades from fourth and on up as a second alto, first alto, and finally in high school as a second soprano and finally a first soprano in the Woodbridge and Westwood choirs and a little in chorale, but I digest. I mean digress. I'm getting ahead of myself again. (Thank God I have a good editor in my Gary Bear. He is very focused and I'm all over the place.)

Eventually I'd end up in Girls' Select chorus at Red Bank High School.

That was back in the days of black and white Polaroid swingers and tiny little Kodak Instamatic cameras that my parents had to bring to the local pharmacy, or Woolworth/s to get developed, and it would take one entire week.

I was not very patient. I could not wait to get them back, even though I was definitely NOT a very good photographer. I just liked to look at myself. I think I was a vain little thing. Plus, I loved having photos of my new golden kitty, Creampuff, whom mom and dad let me rescue from the ASPCPA until mom was very pregnant with my youngest brother, Scott, and she became allergic to the cat fur. Then, I was so sad we had to bring her back, or perhaps we gave her to a neighbor. I don't remember because I was so very upset. I was three, and Pete was just one year old. We lived in Staten Island back when it was still pretty, instead of the big floating garbage dump it has now become. I was a spoiled little brat sometimes.

What an improvement now with the cameras embedded right into our "smart phones", which took me years to get because I was never into technology much and very happy with a little flip phone for many years.

Oh, back to the saga of me, Frank, and Charley. I'd temporarily forgotten all about them, because it was a long time ago, and who needs boys anyway?? What was I thinking?

I have always chased after men who were older, played hard to get, or who were unavailable and not truly interested in me. Sometimes they'd have girlfriends or even wives! I could be a naughty little girl when I wanted to be. I'm still a little naughty. (As some famous lady, but I forget who – maybe Margaret Meade, Mae West, or Virginia Wolf – said "It's not the nice girls who get into the history books!") Like Mae West, when I am good, I'm very good, but when I'm bad I'm better!

I think I broke Frank's heart, too, when I fell for Charley. I hurt a really nice guy to flirt with an older man who was not even interested in me. Oh well, it was not the first time I was a fool for love and certainly not the last. I wish Frank were here today so I could tell him how much he meant to me and how sorry I am now for not appreciating him. He was definitely a "keeper" if you know what I mean. He had looks, smarts, ambition, and his parents had money. Frank already was working as a lifeguard at Seaside Heights Beach and putting money away for college. I wonder where he is now…. Probably married with two or three children living a happy, wild life traveling around Europe and in a camper during the summers touring the entire USA. That's what I'd like to do someday, I think. Like Jerry and Esther Hicks having great times traveling in them in their "Monster Bus" until Jerry was finished with what he came to do on the Earth plane and ascended into a higher plane of consciousness. I wonder where he is now too.

Getting back to my family's routine, Mom woke the family up early in the morning, got us kids dressed, gave us breakfast, and saw us off to the bus stop. I loved school and enjoyed classes during the day. In eighth grade at Holmdel Intermediate I was just dealing with being in a new and different school, so I studied hard, did my homework and tried to ignore what was happening at night.

After all, my dad was a very good, kind man who worked very hard to take care of us. I did not want to hurt him or get him into any kind of trouble. Besides, what would my mom think about it? I felt so terribly embarrassed and ashamed for both of us that I dare not even confront him face to face. I was always laying prone on the bed on my stomach, never saw him touching me, just felt the pleasurable, kind of scary, exciting feelings. What happened behind closed doors a few nights per week was not so bad, so I kept it "our little secret". My dad never forced me to have sex with him, or even took out his penis, though I did see it a few times when he came into the shower with me once when I was in there. I'd seen it other times too when he was going to the bathroom and I was waiting to go in. I'd only seen one or two other penises in my young life, but my dad's penis looked large. Both my parents rarely shut or locked the door when they were in the bathroom. It was kind of an open-door policy in our family bathroom, so if one of us needed to brush our teeth or get into the bathtub while someone had to pee, we'd just do it all at the same time. No one really noticed or even looked at anyone else, we just did our business and finished up. I saw my brothers partly naked when they were little, but as they got older, they became modest and either covered up or kept the bathroom door closed and locked, but my parents did not care much about being seen nude in front of us; they really lacked boundaries with us as far as I can remember, but it was just our bodies, and it seemed natural to be free that way, so I never questioned it since I figured all families were probably like that. I did not know differently, since we acted like that from the time I was a little girl.

Confused.

Even with Dad touching my private parts sometimes, he was still my wonderful "Knight in Shining Armor" who took care of us, played with us, taught me how to swim, how to sail, and bought us a ten-foot catamaran, a snowmobile and a resort home in the country, where we would play and spend summer vacations, holidays, and Christmas at Gold Key Lake in the Poconos, ten miles from Milford, PA.

It was a beautiful little round redwood home called a Rondette with three quarters of a porch and deck surrounding the outside where we could lay on chaise lounges or sit on redwood chairs and relax with fresh homemade ice tea, lemonade, and healthy snacks. There was a little bird feeder with a piece of glass over it for the birds, but chipmunks and a sneaky squirrel would often get into it and steal most of our birds' sunflower seeds. Sometimes we kids would make a trail of sunflower seeds from the top step all the way down to the bottom with a few sunflower seeds on each step hoping the chipmunks would follow the trail of seeds until one would come up to the top and eat right out of our hands, tickling our palms. That was so exciting.

Sometimes in winter or spring while riding in our VW bug we might see a large bear walking straight up near the side of the road while we were going toward our house or out to the development's highway entrance so we could drive into town.

A lot of beautiful deer would come by our house at evening time or in the morning just as dawn was breaking. It was so exciting and wondrous to see these beautiful, large, wild animals in their natural habitat – sometimes whole families would gather on the golf course a mile away, beyond the creek. We might see a few mother deer's, a big buck with six or eight points on his beautiful, majestic antlers, and several baby fawns. They were just magnificent, and I always tried to sing and talk to them, while approaching them slowly with some food, but they would run away most of the time, if we got too close. Having a resort home in the Poconos was the very best; as a kid I felt so lucky and blessed! If it were not for my father working so hard and deciding to purchase a vacation home where we could have fun and really enjoy life to the fullest, we would not have been so fortunate and privileged. I was so grateful to him for all the fun and adventure he brought into our lives.

Daddy was also the one to teach me to ride a two-wheeler bicycle when I was about six or seven years old-- a shiny, turquoise 16-inch Schwinn bicycle, by raising the training wheels ever so slightly each time I rode it, so that after a while they were off the ground, and I was already riding on two wheels, but I just did not realize it. I loved riding my bike so much that I'd take it out nearly every day after school to ride all around our development. I was so good at balancing that I could first take one hand off the steering wheel and then, while coasting down the big hill on Miller Ave toward our house, I'd take off the other hand and ride all the way down with no hands, balancing myself perfectly and feeling the wind streaming through my long blondish brown hair, or making my long light brown or dark blond ponytail fly back from my face.

So many fun things did my dad teach us. Dad took us to the lake in the Poconos when it was icy, and he and mom taught us to ice-skate; mom even taught me how to do a cross over and to skate backwards. Daddy also took us to Indian or Telegraph Hills in Holmdel, near our schools, sleigh riding and tobogganing in the winter. Daddy worked very hard, so he learned to play equally as hard. He really knew how to give himself a good time. I think he liked being a father, and like his dad and mom before him, gave us all the good things in life.

Daddy taught me how to take risks and be adventurous in life. He took us on vacations to Florida and paid for us to go to Disney World each time we'd visit our grandparents in Venice. Nothing would ever make me think bad, unloving thoughts about my dad. Not then, not now, or ever.

So when he apologized for touching me six months later and told me not to say anything to anyone, that was that. Not only would my dad and I never be that close again, but I was not even allowed to talk about how confusing it was, and how weird it made me feel. Not just weird, but "Bad" like I did something very wrong. Even if I was not the one who encouraged or initiated the contact between us, I never actually tried to prevent it or stop it from happening. I felt so ashamed. Other than telling a few of my boyfriends and one of my stepsisters, I never discussed it again for eleven years. I just thought it was a big mistake and tried to put it out of my mind. I never really thought it was something that affected me – until I became older and developed certain bad patterns in my relationships with men. I always had problems having orgasms except for giving them to myself with my own hand.

Truly, the first orgasm I ever had with a man was by my dad's all knowing, experienced fingers when he shared my bed one night after reading me a story, and then I think we watched a little television together. I fell asleep, but when I awoke there was my hero sill next to me with his fingers inside my open vagina. It was one of the most exciting moments of my young life. I was exactly fourteen and a half, and I can remember the sweet, pleasurable sensations to this day.

Soon after, he left my room, and six months later, told me he was ashamed, did not understand how it ever happened, and said "Just try to forget about it and don't tell anyone ever, especially your mom, or she'll divorce me and that will be the end of our happy family." Suddenly, all that sweet closeness and awe for my dad, and my seemingly natural, intimate feelings and physical sharing of our bodies, hearts, and minds turned into subconscious, deep seated shame, guilt, and confusion. Not just confusion, but frustration, hurt, disappointment, and abandonment. How could something that started out so sweet, so new, precious and wonderful, all those sweet sensations in my pussy and down my back seem so contemptible? I had loved when he slowly tickled me from the top of my spine and ran his fingers slowly and sensuously all the way down my neck to lower back until I was just dying physically, yearning for him to go into my little yoni and just touch the lips. Previously, only one other man who opened me up while I was on the massage table after he massaged and relaxed me, my dad has been the only one to know my body well enough to give me that kind of intense pleasure. It was so exquisite. I wanted to cry out "Oh God!", for the sweet joy and release of that tension, but I was alone I my bedroom with him, and inside we all know that little girls are not supposed to be touched by their daddies in that special way, so I just shut down to all men for a while, feeling betrayed and abandoned.

I became promiscuous after that; and I did not know what healthy boundaries meant. My dad had violated me – he crossed a line he should not have. Not to say that I did not love it, but incest is such a taboo. Just like pornography. Smoking marijuana. Doing drugs like magic mushrooms, Sex, drugs, rock and roll all have to be regulated because who knows what would happen if we had more fun on this planet and actually enjoyed all the sweet sensations in our young bodies from the time, we are babies until the time we become old and gray? We might be healthier. We might be happier. We might want to live in the precious now moment, we might tell the truth more about needing to take good care of ourselves and our penises, vaginas, and merge them with no shame with love, open hearts, and exquisite joy! Oh my God – even have children or not, into our sixties, seventies, and eighties, if, indeed, we wanted to.

Changes.

Mom and Dad had met "Aunt Joan" and "Uncle Wally" on their honeymoon. We children met "Aunt Joan" and "Uncle Wally", and their children; Tommy, a funny guy who was my age; Kathleen, a friendly, pretty curly haired brunette who was a year younger than me; Debbie, a fun, bubbly, creative, pretty girl who was a few years younger than Kathy; and Suzie, the youngest and sweetest sister. When I was were very little our families became so close over the years that we considered them our relations. We called their kids our cousins and eventually the girls would become my step-sisters and Tommy my step-brother.

We saw their family frequently over the years even though Aunt Joan and Uncle Wally lived in Bergen County, and we were at least ninety minutes south of them by car in Holmdel.

They would drive up in their silver Buick Electra convertible with a bright red leather interior with the top down to see us at special times like the Fourth of July or Easter, when mom would make us all a delicious pot roast, fresh ham, or turkey, freshly mashed potatoes with gravy, and several types of vegetables with delicious creamery butter and salt.

Mom set the dining room table with our finest sterling silver on our best white linen table cloth which was freshly washed and ironed the day before. Mom was fastidious about our place settings where she placed the sterling silverware. Two Forks on the left on top of a neatly folded linen serviette. Knife, soup and dessert spoons were placed on the right of the plate. She carefully put a long stick of butter from the Frigidaire into the sterling silver butter tray and poured homemade gravy made from drippings in the pan mixed with flour into the sterling silver gravy boat. It was a carefree, happy time of my life.

The couples would switch off hosting each other. Joan and Wally would have us up to their beautiful home in Bergen County for Thanksgiving or some other holiday. I liked their house better because Aunt Joan was not as fanatical about cleaning as was my mother. All four of her children and the three of us could get away with running and playing inside and out of the house, and if we got our fingerprints on the glass door going outside it did not matter to her. My mom would think we were all getting away with murder running around the whole house without anyone disciplining us or asking us to settle down.

In our immaculate house we were not allowed to wear shoes indoors. They had to be taken off in the garage and left there before we entered the kitchen. There were no such restrictions when we visited Aunt Joan and Uncle Wally. I felt free to just be a kid and have fun. No one cared much if we got our fingerprints on the storm door or walls. It was a much more comfortable atmosphere than my own home in which to play and just "be ourselves".

Unfortunately, after about ten years or so of these regular visits to our parents' friend's house I was called into my bedroom one late afternoon after school by my mom who had a sad and serious look upon her face. I could tell that she'd been crying.

"Hon, I need to talk to you about something serious. There is no easy way to tell you this. Aunt Joan called me this morning to tell me Uncle Wally had a heart attack and died." It was devastating for all of us. Our family truly loved Wally. He was a very beautiful, gentle man, and he was so loving and kind to us kids, he felt like part of our family. His wife and four children became our "adopted" aunt, uncle, and cousins when their eldest son, Tommy, and I were about two or three years old.

Oh, my God. At my tender age of fifteen, I was not accustomed to anyone dying. A few years before that, my dad's brother, Freddy, who was my favorite uncle, also passed away, but other than that, I never had to deal with death or grief. I was too young to attend Uncle Fred's funeral, and after a few months I did not think about his death much at all because going to school, doing homework, and my own life was enough to keep my mind occupied in the present moment.

Aunt Joan was now a young widow with four children who'd just lost the love of her life. She was so very distraught, languishing for love and losing weight, that my mom decided to invite her to our summer home in the Poconos for three weeks where she and the four kids could have some place to relax with people who really loved her in the hope that she might feel a little better after losing her husband. It was during those weeks that my dad really fell in love with Joan. They had always been close friends; Joan was a gentle woman of great physical and spiritual beauty. Her skin was flawless, a soft and smooth creamy white, her shining brunette hair always up in a French a twist or a bun making her look very pretty framing her gorgeous "movie star" face. Unlike my own mother, I never once heard her yell, scream, or curse at her children. Even though she had four, occasionally boisterous children she never lost her temper or became impatient with them. I never once heard her criticize or scold any of her children. I loved her very much myself, sometimes more than my own mother.

Since Joan was the very beautiful, usually happy, gentle woman she was, whom both my parents loved as a close friend for many years, it's not difficult now as an adult to see how my dad fell in love with her. But at the age of fifteen it was difficult to understand and accept that my dad would end up falling in love with such a close family friend. It was not just confusing, because it was such a betrayal to my mother, but it also would be the end of our seemingly happy family – at least from my perspective. I secretly had to share these uncomfortable experiences with my boyfriend, Frank.

Shortly after my dad fell in love with Joan, while I was attending Woodbridge High School in 1972, my parents separated. My mom and I were fighting a lot. She'd say things like, "You always favored your father over me." Of course, I did. Dad was my knight in shining armor. Besides, he NEVER smacked me in the ass with slotted metal spoons or got so angry at me that he'd chase me down the stairs and break hairbrushes over my head while I was running for protection.

The separation was confusing for me. I felt sad, disappointed, and a little scared.

I was just a little more than fifteen years old. Things were so tense and uncomfortable between mom and me that I begged my dad to let me come to Westwood, NJ, to live with him, switching schools in the middle of my junior year where I attended Woodbridge, High School. I escaped from my mother's abuse by moving in with Daddy into a small two-bedroom apartment that Uncle Wally purchased for Joan's security in case anything ever happened to him. I left my mom and my younger brothers behind. Though I knew it would be challenging to relocate to another high school in the middle of the school year, that is what I chose to do. It was much easier to leave an abusive situation with mom to live with my dad who was easy-going and never ever raised his voice to any of us. I was no longer concerned about him touching me in an inappropriate way since he had apologized. Plus, he was now in love with Aunt Joan, so I knew in my heart that things would be different, and we would have a more "normal" family.

The transition to Westwood High was hard for me, because Westwood High had a much more advanced language program, so I lost my straight A average in French and English too. I came to Westwood High right before final exams, so I had not learned 90 % of what the other students had learned. I had to cram in lots of new literature for English, and the French students were speaking fluently only in French whereas the French students at Woodbridge High school were speaking in both English and French. I had a rough time following and ended up getting an average grade on the final which gave me a B for the end of the year. I did OK in English, my best subject, and average in History and Chemistry.

No more unusual or inappropriate incidents occurred after that with my dad. Once he'd found

Joan, Daddy fell deeply in love, and I suppose he must have felt more fulfilled sexually, spiritually, and emotionally. Joan was a devout Catholic, and asked daddy if he would allow her to baptize him since my atheist grandparents never believed in such an unnecessary patriarchal ritual, coming from more relaxed, intellectual, discriminating, critically thinking Swedish and Danish parents. Daddy asked my mother to give him a "quickie" divorce so that he could marry Joan soon afterward, who became the love of his life until he died ten years ago. They were happily married for over thirty years. My mom and dad divorced after seventeen years, and not all those years were happy toward the end.

My mom was hurt deeply, but years later she told me Joan did her a favor. Mom was not very happy in her marriage and really needed to grow up and become her own person. She hadn't even graduated from high school, but after my father left, she got her GED, applied to and was hired by NJ Bell. Then IBM for many years. Then Southland Corporation which owned the Seven Eleven food chain. And then Johnson & Johnson in Skillman, New Jersey. Contrary to what she believed about herself being incompetent and lacking intelligence when she was just a teenager she truly was very intelligent, learned rapidly, and became a very successful and industrious worker as a receptionist for IBM and Southland Corp., and customer service representative for both NJ Bell and Johnson & Johnson. I was very proud of her, and much more compassionate about how she endured the challenging transition of becoming a "single" mom.

Not only did Dad continue to take excellent care of us financially and in many other ways, he showed his love for us by helping "mom" (Joan had asked both my brother, Pete, and me to start calling her mom instead of Aunt Joan, since we were all living together as a family) by cooking our breakfast sometimes and helping us get our lunches together, and by helping all of us with dishes and clean-up after dinner. Plus, he was ready to pay for my college education and Tommy's if we both agreed to attend a state school like nearby Ramapo College in the Ramapo Mountains or Montclair State University and give us both cars so that we could commute from our huge four-bedroom home on Sibbald Drive. It had an Olympic-sized pool in the back yard. I thought it best not to rock the boat, so I put our unconventional past intimacy behind me for many years. It was from Park Ridge High that I would eventually graduate.

I was able to talk a bit about the incest with one of my step-sisters after I moved in with their entire blended family in the summer of 1972. It felt quite uncomfortable sharing with Debbie about my dad's molestation of me at fourteen because I still loved and cared for my dad, plus he was living with all of us at the time in the new home he'd purchased with Joan in Park Ridge, New Jersey... In a way, I felt guilty for "snitching" on him.

I had a lot of experience making new friends at that point in the autumn of 1972, so the transition to Park Ridge High was much easier. Since I was a good singer and actress, I made friends with several boys and girls in Chorus and Girls Select. I was one of the big stars of the Pop Cert, the annual talent shows in October, and after trying out for the senior musical, in April the next year, Paris Simms, the Choir director and Chorus teacher, awarded me the lead role of Anna in "The King and I". I made a lovely Anna with my long light brown hair put up in a bun on top of my head, and danced the polka with the King, played by David Gilliland, with great gusto.

I wore beautiful costumes that were rented from New York City. The gorgeous satin purple gown I wore for the ballroom scene was worn by the opera singer, Roberta Peters. Her name was on the gown, so I assumed she'd worn it. The striped black and white long dress I wore for the teaching scene was worn by Sherry North who played the lead role in Oliver on Broadway. I loved wearing an authentic hoop skirt underneath the lavender ball gown, green canvas dress for the opening arrival in Siam scene, and the black and white striped cotton dress, which made my dresses expand a few feet in circumference. It was cool learning how to walk and sit like a lady in this hoop skirt.

I performed the show on Thursday and Saturday nights to rave reviews, and my entire family, including all four of my grandparents, came to see me. I had a great time in the role and was lauded by most of the teachers and students for the remainder of the year. I had a few close friends and dated two talented, handsome men over the course of senior year. By the summer I'd broken up with my boyfriend, Bob, right before he left for the University of Denver.

Dad and Joan wanted to treat the entire family to a special vacation before all the children grew up and left for college, so one evening at dinner dad said, "Guess what? We are all taking a Mediterranean cruise this summer and spending four days in Rome!"

Wow! Were we surprised? My dad booked passage on a less expensive cruise line for all nine of us – he and my step-mom, Tommy, Debbie, Kathy, Suzie, Peter, Scott, and me. We all had the time of our lives.

Being such a large family with four beautiful young women walking to dinner dressed to the nines attracted all sorts of stares and glares from the waiters and other passengers, especially the men. We had an attentive Italian waiter, Luciano Ruocco, from Salerno, who started flirting with me right from the start, and within a few nights he was inviting me to visit him in his cabin. When I came to visit him, he showed me photos of many other women he'd met while working on the ship and whom he'd befriended and then visited in America. It seemed tacky to me, but what did I know? I was seventeen and still a virgin. Lucio was much older than me, but he had long, reddish blond hair and muscular arms. He was well built, and handsome. I was attracted to him immediately, but I did not do anything sexual other than kiss him in his cabin. I was brought up to be a good Catholic girl, so I truly did not expect to have sex before I got married. I did not find him to be intellectually stimulating, just handsome, well-traveled, and interesting since he was from a different culture. My maternal great- grandparents were also from Italy, so I found Italian men fascinating. Since he was an older man with a lot of life experience, it was fun and interesting being with him between meals, when he was not working.

We had a brief stop in Cannes on the French Riviera, where we basked in the sun and I got to practice my high school French with a few tourists and natives I met while on the beach. Then we sailed to Majorca, Spain, where all the girls were treated to a string of their famous pearls.

The most different of all the ports was Bizerte in North Africa, where we got to spend time in the desert riding camels. I loved getting atop the camel's hump as he lay down and then stood up tall and I felt like I was riding up in the sky. Though a bit homely looking, they are amazing, humongous creatures. I felt like an Arabian princess being escorted to some special prince in a mysterious land.

My favorite stop, however, was in Italy, where we got to see the ruins of Pompeii. It was so weird to think that that place was once a bustling city, full of life and activity, but was now reduced to ashes and fossils. The remnants of huge stone buildings and the Coliseum was awesome. As I observed the blackened fossils of people who had died from the burning ash, I remember thinking that they looked so small and childlike in stature, but it just occurred to me that the volcano reduced them to ashes of their former selves. Without fat, skin, and bones, a person could look pretty tiny. Being in Pompeii was a humbling experience. To think that all these people were just going about their normal daily routines and had no way of escaping the eruption of Mount Vesuvius as it suddenly exploded on this tiny isle was just mind--boggling. What a tragedy it was! It made me remember how precious life is.

We traveled to Palermo in Sicily where I admired the large, lush olive groves and round, robust, and friendly people.

The next day we traveled to Florence, where we were privileged to see the famous statue of David and Michelangelo's agony and ecstasy manifested in the beautiful backbreaking paintings he did on the ceiling and walls of the Sistine Chapel. My favorite part of Italy was getting to spend three whole days in Rome where we got to see the opera, Aida, outdoors, in a beautiful amphitheater. They actually had live camels and llamas as part of the performance. Verdi's music was performed with great gusto and expertise by the singers and musicians in the orchestra. The coloratura soprano and tenor received many bravos from the audience, especially my dad, step-mom, my siblings, and me. The staging, costumes, and entire spectacle were so opulent and beautiful that it moved me to tears of joy and awe.

While in Rome, we took several bus tours and had a "private audience" with the Pope. Well, it's not exactly private. I think there were scores of people there, from what my parents told me. I was the only one in the family who chose not to go, since I did not resonate with the teachings of Catholicism.

The bus rides were more fun for me than anything. I felt like I was on some kind of thrilling roller coaster ride because the roads in Italy are rather tortuous, and the drivers of the huge tour buses go very fast and can't see what is coming around the bend. Before the drivers go around a hilly turn, they all honk their horns to warn oncoming traffic so that they don't have a head-on collision. The roads are so narrow that each time we'd go around a blind turn, my heart leapt into my stomach. It was scary the first few times we went around those dangerous, tortuous turns where we could not see what was coming, but our driver was a real pro and accustomed to doing it on a daily basis.

Shopping in Rome was relaxing and fun because there were so many beautiful things to buy and one could haggle with the merchants for the cheapest price. The American dollar was worth a lot to the Italians, so we were able to get some great buys. We brought back lots of new clothes, sunhats, and gifts to take home.

Dining was even more fun than shopping. The Italians eat their biggest meal in the middle of the day, and then they siesta for several hours afterward. Dining in Italy is a festive and relaxed occasion where people enjoy chatting and leisurely eating delicious ante pastas, pastas, salads, freshly baked breads that smell almost as delicious as they taste with lots of whipped butter or dipped in extra virgin olive oil. There were meats marinated in herbs, garlic, and wine in between sips of Chianti or white wines. Delicious food, sweet pastries, fine wine and great conversation made the noon meal the most enjoyable event of the day. All the waiters were so happy to serve us and loved giving our large family special attention. All four of us single girls were flattered by the whistles and stares of men wherever we went. Well, at least I know I was. The Italian men were not embarrassed to flirt or show appreciation for beauty, especially for an attractive young woman.

After siesta time naps back in the hotel, we'd shower and dress again to go out for a light supper and shopping in town. I loved the candlelit fountains where everyone looked more beautiful by moonlight. It was so neat that so many people gathered there late at night to enjoy the beauty of the evening and the late-night starry sky.

While on the cruise I sang a song from Jesus Christ Superstar called, "I Don't Know How to Love Him" in the talent show. I wore a sexy white halter-top that accented my voluptuous bosom and tight navy-blue hip hugger pants that clung to my large butt like a banana skin. I felt attractive as I entertained. It was natural for me belting out a song about a man like Jesus whom I felt I'd loved in many lifetimes. I did a great job, and was complimented by many of the passengers who saw me perform.

I was also noticed by two of the musicians in two of the bands that played on board ship. One man was named Jim, and the other was a sexy dark haired Greek drummer and singer named Dmitri. He was very cute and charming too. Both these men were attractive and charming enough to woo me into their cabins at different times when they were not performing. My parents were rather upset when they found out and forbid my going into their rooms. I did it anyway in secret, because I was old enough to make my own decisions. I enjoyed spending sensuous time with both Jim and Dmitri, but I lost interest in both of them when our very sexy waiter, Luciano, continued to flirt with me during mealtime.

The Family at Christmas

I developed a nice friendship with Luciano. Though I was still a virgin, this very handsome, blond, charming, well-built older man courted me on the cruise and eventually came to visit me in America at my parents' house and in hotels nearby. He even taught me how to prepare and bake an authentic Italian covered pizza in our family's oven! We spent several months writing to one another, but due to the distance between us and the difference in our ages, the relationship never got too serious, even though he did ask me to marry him. He probably was looking for a way to get into the country. I did enjoy the thrill of dating a handsome man from a foreign country who wrote me endearing letters, and taught me some of the joys of sex without intercourse.

This cruise and trip to Italy was the last vacation we would take together as a whole family with my dad and Joan before the children all grew up and went away to college or moved out on their own.

What an incredibly fun and educational experience for all of us! With my step-siblings there are seven children ranging in age, at the time, from nine to eighteen years of age! I am the eldest.

I really liked the other young, handsome musician, Jim, from England who was working aboard ship as the drummer in one of the American bands. His name was Jim. He had light brown hair, hazel eyes, and a charming English accent. When I was shaking my tail feathers on the dance floor, he noticed me. We struck up a nice friendship too. I told Jim I played guitar, so he brought out his folk guitar when I visited him in his cabin, and we shared some original songs. I showed him how I could finger-pick "Sounds of Silence" by Paul Simon.

Wow, looking back at it know I am amazed I was attracting so many men and did not feel the need to just choose one. And I still managed to keep my virginity intact. That was the miraculous part of it all.

I enjoyed the fun, the variety, and the attention of all these hotties until my parents could not find me one night, and everything came to an end. I forget which man's cabin I was in at the time, but my parents assumed the worst, and I was told I had to stay with the family from then on. I was not allowed to leave my cabin at night ever again without supervision, or go out during the day by myself any more. The odd thing is that except for some French kissing and a little petting, nothing much happened while I was alone in their cabins. I was eighteen years old, so I did not see what the harm was in that.

FOR THE LOVE OF MUSIC

After high school, I floundered somewhat because I missed my college orientation at Montclair State, so I had to pick some leftover classes, and I had no idea what would be my major. I was truly interested in theater and voice, but my parents dissuaded me from following my dream convincing me that I should have a profession that was more stable with a dependable income. I was so unhappy at Montclair that I dropped out in the middle of the first semester without telling my parents for a month. I started having depression and mood swings that would force me to look at my past since underneath my happy, confident mask I felt as if something was terribly wrong with me. My first depression began right after dropping out of Montclair State in the middle of my freshman year.

I was about to launch my new career in music.

I had always loved performers and performing.

Judy Garland was my favorite star when I saw her in "The Wizard of Oz" and later in "Meet Me in St. Louie", and in "Easter Parade" with Fred Astaire. I absolutely loved hearing her belt out, "The Man That Got Away" with such glee in "A Star is Born" with James Mason. Judy and Barbara were always the singers who could move me to tears of joy, as well as tears of sadness. So, my whole life I'd just go around pretending I was a great singing superstar celebrity just like them waiting to be "discovered". I'd imagine Gene Kelly was my partner and I pretended to be Debbie Reynolds when I'd go for walks in the rain around my development in Holmdel, twirling my umbrella and singing "I'm singing in the rain. I'm singing' in the rain. What a glorious feeling! I'm happy again." I still do that when I hear the old song come on the radio while I'm shopping at the local Shop Rite in Montgomery Township, NJ.

I don't need anyone's approval. I sing for my own enjoyment – for the pure delight of hearing my own voice and expressing the enthusiasm I feel for God, for music, and for all the blessings of Life itself! I don't need someone to say I sound good. I'm not really gifted vocally, but I have a tremendous amount of heart, charisma, charm, determination, and courage! I also love to dance and love to get people up out of their seats to dance with me.

When I was younger, I loved Ella Fitzgerald, Sarah Vaughn, and Cher, too. I used to love watching Cher do the vamp song with Sonny wearing his barbershop vest and bow tie looking cute as ever tinkling his ivories behind the object of his devotion.

My stepsisters, Debbie and Sue, would dress up in costumes and lip-sync to "I Got You Babe" in their living room in River Vale, NJ. Debbie put on a long nightie and got a long flowing dark brown wig she bought for fifty cents to portray Cher. Sue wore a really funny looking short-haired Beetle-style wig. She was perfect as Sonny because she was only ten or eleven years old and on the short side. Susie has a cute little button nose and freckles, and she really cracked us up.

Debbie was even more perfect in her portrayal of the tall, long-legged, and gorgeous Cher. Debbie was about thirteen at the time and just the right height to tower over her sister's male counterpart the way Cher did with Sonny. Deb looked perfect in her slinky light blue silky nightgown, and the long, cheap wig made her look like a hysterical caricature of Cher. Deb copied Cher's mannerisms to a tee; she was constantly brushing her long hair back behind her sexy, sultry creamy white shoulders with a look of arrogant, playful disdain on her face as if she knew she was a queen and wondered how the heck she got paired with this short, funny looking geek! Susie just looked adorable with the short-haired cheap Beatle wig, our brother, Tommy's, brown pants, and a man's flowered blue Hawaiian shirt. Debbie and Sue had quite a flair for comedy. I'm surprised neither of them ever had an interest in community theater when they became adults. Not one of the seven of us except Tommy and Pete had an interest in theater, music, or comedy. Both Tom and Pete learned to play folk guitar, and Tommy would write hysterical poems about his good friend, Fred, who was a scientific, geek type who wore thick glasses, so we all made playful fun of him a lot even though Tommy really liked him as a friend. Fred never knew that we all giggled about the way he looked and talked, so we did not think our teasing would hurt him. We were just having good, clean, silly fun.

I first saw Ray Charles perform at the Newport Jazz Festival in 1977, when my live-in boyfriend, Greg Askildsen, and I decided to take a trip back up to Vermont. It was quite an inspiration. Ray was not only an amazing musician, but he was a great human being and someone from whom we could all learn a lot of good practical wisdom about how to live a happy, productive life. He did not let his blindness, other peoples' ignorance and prejudice, poverty, or pain stop him from doing anything in life he wanted to do. In fact, instead of feeling sorry for himself he put all of his feelings and passion into making some of the most beautiful music of the century. And he turned his life story into his lyrics.

He was not afraid. Because he was blind people often tried to cheat or take advantage of him, but he was intelligent and quickly learned about the ways of the world. When he got money for a gig, he initially insisted that He get paid in single dollar bills so that he could count the money himself and be sure that he was getting paid the right amount. He was such an amazing talent that in the beginning of his career, several of the managers and others in the music business saw him as an easy mark and used him to further their own profits. But Ray quickly learned how to take care of himself. Eventually he came to know whom he could and could not trust.

Gradually, through his own desire and efforts he went from being a poor young man to a very rich one who controlled the rights to his own music.

His blindness did not stop him from meeting people or from having relationships with women. He had a wonderful wife, many wonderful children, and many women and men that loved and adored him. He even beat his own inner demons and kicked a bad drug habit, which he had initially used as a way to soothe himself when he was hurting. With the encouragement of his wife, family and friends, he entered himself into a rehab program. His triumph over his addiction made him an even stronger and more compassionate man.

He was also able to come to terms with something he'd been running from all of his life – the untimely death of his little brother, which he witnessed as a little boy, and for which he felt responsible. He was finally able to forgive himself for his brother's death, which was actually not his fault at all. However, the shock of seeing it was so traumatic that it haunted him for years, until he finally faced it.

Thank you, Ray, for bringing so much joy and inspiration to me and thousands of people who still have the good fortune to listen to your wonderful songs. What a voice! What a musician! What an amazing man and an inspiration to us all, Ray Charles.

When I was twenty-five years old, I had the good fortune to see Count Basie in Red Bank, where I had attended high school). After the show was over, he was kind enough to pose for a photograph with his arm around me.

I saw the flugelhorn player, Chuck Mangione, with Ray Charles in Vermont when he had the hit, "It Feels So Good". Mr. Mangione said when, he announced the song, that it was the one that ended up paying for his children's' college educations.

I've also seen the Manhattan Transfer twice in Atlantic City when I was gambling at an Atlantic City casino and also at the Garden State Arts Center in Holmdel, NJ, where I grew up. They have the best harmonies, arrangements, and greatest jazz stylings for a singing group I've ever heard. I've sung a few of their songs like "Tuxedo Junction" and "The Boy from New York City" when I sang with the wedding band "Smooth Sailin" when I was twenty nine years old.

I've also had the privilege of hearing and seeing Bony James open for Al Jarreau twice at the Beacon Theater and then in the summer of 2004 in Saratoga Springs. Bony was really hot at SPAC one June, as he got very daring and took his horn out into the crowd playing and dancing right beside several audience members. The crowd went wild. I don't think Bony's manager and/or bodyguard was too happy about it, but the fans were thrilled.

One of the kindest, sweetest, most romantic men I've ever had the privilege to hear perform live was Jon Lucien, a black artist I've been listening to since I was twenty-one. An assistant minister, Laurie, from the Psychic Science Temple of Metaphysics, turned me on to his first album. I don't think I've ever heard a more romantic and sensitive voice in my life. Two of my favorite songs of all time are his renditions of Antonio Carlos Jobin's "Dandi" and Lucien's original song, "Rashida". I love the way he sings "Maiden Voyage" and "Creole Lady" too. Jon shared with us in concert that he lost his daughter in a tragic swimming accident, but that she would communicate to him from heaven telling him to keep on sharing his music and his love the way he does so well. Unfortunately, we lost Jon in August, 2001, when he was 65.

The music and lyrics of Stevie Wonder have touched me like no other music ever has. He has the power to move me to tears of joy, sorrow, and ecstasy for the God within and without. I perceive him as one of the brightest Lights in our Whole Universe, and his eyes, though blind, see the Truth behind the illusion that is the cause of so much suffering in our world, racism, discrimination and separation of classes through forced segregation due to white supremacy which is something we are still dealing with in the year 2022. Stevie Wonder, through his honesty and courage to tell it like it is in songs like "Living for the City".

The first hit I ever heard by Stevie Wonder was called "Fingertips" released from a concert he did live at the Regal Theater when he was only thirteen years old. A song he made famous when he was still called "Little Stevie Wonder". We all had the privilege to watch this young boy grow up into a fine man and excellent musician and composer right before our very eyes, on stages all around the world. He is a Multi-Grammy award winning musician and great humanitarian.

Nothing puts me into a state of ecstasy like dancing to the music of "Do I Do" on the original

Musicquarium album and all the "Songs in the Key of Life", which honors all the great jazz legends like Count Basie, Louis Armstrong, Ella Fitzgerald and Billie Holiday. I especially love "Sir Duke" about Duke Ellington. "Isn't She Lovely", which he wrote for his baby girl reminds me of the great love and joy Kyrie and Sky brought me when they were newborns and toddlers.

SINGING IN THE BANDS

In my depression after quitting college, I was in a quandary about what to do or where to go next. I was not looking forward to having to get a full-time job yet or being completely responsible for myself.

By that time my brother, Pete, had also had enough of mom's yelling and complaining, so he'd moved in with the rest of the family in Park Ridge. I loved being part of a large family and living with three sisters and two brothers. We had a very happy family and lived a comfortable, abundant life.

It was only after my parents began to make more rules and put restrictions on me that I had any desire to move out from under their comfortable, protective roof.

A few weeks later I looked in the want ads of the local papers and found a rock band looking for a lead female singer. The name of the band was crazy – "Baloney-no matter how you slice it", it said. They were a fun rock band focusing on the early sixties rock groups including the Beatles, Rolling Stones, the Kinks, and some Linda Ronstadt and Fleetwood Mac. I thought George, the red-haired lead guitarist, was quite talented, and Tommy, the blond rhythm guitarist, charming and very handsome. As soon as I auditioned, I was told I'd gotten into the band. I could now earn pocket money by performing and doing what I loved to do — sing, dance, and look pretty on stage.

I quickly found the perfect living quarters while perusing the classified ads again. Two women living in a nice three-bedroom apartment in Garfield were looking for a third housemate to share the rent, phone, and utilities. My share would be $85.00 per month for the rent and only 1/3 share of the telephone and utilities. That's how long ago this was. Can you imagine having only to pay $85.00 for a third of the rent now? I then had a full-time job at Plains Pharmacy as a cosmetician making a whopping $110 per week. Back in 1974 when I was nineteen that seemed like a lot of money to me since I had so little experience in the workplace or with paying all my own bills. I was so accustomed to my parents paying for everything. I was very inexperienced in the ways of the world, and I had no idea of the value of money. But now I had a "day job".

My boss was quite a character. He was very sweet to me, but he often ranted like a crazy man whenever he was under stress and he needed help. The pharmacy was open every day of the year except for New Year's Day. My boss was very proud of that.

I was proud, too. I was working as a cosmetician and make-up artist without ever having gone to school or gotten a degree, and it really didn't matter because I knew that that job was just a stepping stone. I knew I was a great singer, dancer, and actress, just like Doris Day, Debbie Reynolds, or Judy Garland, and I intended to become a superstar celebrity someday just like they did. It might take me a little while, but I was hopeful and optimistic at that age. I was young, naive, and inexperienced, so what did I know?

The first time I had sex with a man I was nineteen years old. The creep was my boss at Farrell's Ice Cream Parlor, an assistant manager who traveled up from Maryland to Jersey. Frank took advantage of me in in the hotel where he was staying and he did not even believe I was a virgin. After it was finished, he did not cuddle me or even allow me to sleep beside him.

After that terrible experience I figured sex was not all it was cracked up to be, and I became promiscuous. I felt so used and abused, especially because I was told the first time a girl has sex and gives up her virginity it is supposed to be wonderful and special. This man treated me as if I were a prostitute, except that no money was exchanged.

After that, I hated sex and I rarely stayed very long with just one man who really loved me who was caring and kind to me. I only felt sexy with the "bad guys". I would feel pleasurable feelings in my genitals at the very beginning of a relationship with a nice man who loved and respected me while the relationship was new; but as soon as it turned into a commitment of any kind, I would shut down sexually, and eventually find another man with whom I could have a clandestine affair. The newness in a relationship would ring my bells, make me feel excited, and give me the adrenaline rush I suppose I felt initially with my father touching my breasts and genitals.

I cannot think of anything that made me feel more excited than the time I woke up in my bed with the TV still on with my dad's fingers in my pussy, touching my labia and stimulating my clitoris until I had an explosive orgasm. It was the most exciting moment of my teen-age life, but I could not even make a sound through it all. For if I made a peep, my dad would know I was awake and aware that, in my young eyes, he was doing such an evil, guilty thing to me, his fourteen-year-old daughter. And I was loving how it felt! It felt fantastic! Then that would make us Both "BAD" in my "little girl eyes". So, I kept my mouth shut, and did not reveal this secret to anyone for the longest time, but I cannot keep my silence any longer.

I had told my boyfriend, John, about the incest with my dad. I met John while I was go-go dancing at the "Down Under", a restaurant and bar in Iselin, in my mid-twenties. John worked at IBM. So did my mom, as a receptionist, after she and daddy divorced. John was the person who finally told my mother that my father sexually molested me, after I broke up with him to be with my massage teacher, Sid.

My mom confronted him on the phone about the incest, but of course, he said I was lying, and denied it. If his new wife had ever found out he had been doing something that inappropriate with me, he would have been very upset and embarrassed. She may have even left him, who knows? I doubt it, though. They were very much in love, and it seems that I have been made the "problem child" with mental illness and for exposing something that should have remained hidden or forgotten according to the rest of the family, or so it seems.

It was not until I was 25 that finally told my dad, to his face, that he was the first man to make me have an orgasm, and he was surprised. He said "So, you are still daddy's little girl." That upset me because I'd already fallen really in love with my teacher, Sid, so I said "Absolutely not. I really think what you did to me was very inappropriate, Dad, and it messed me up in my relationships with men for a really long time. What you did by violating my boundaries made me feel embarrassed and ashamed about sex." That was the first time I could stand up for myself and tell the truth about how I really felt to him directly. It was an empowering moment for me.

After dropping out of Montclair State, I had some free time during the day, so I decided to try out for the American Academy of Dramatic Arts on Madison Ave in New York. I was also studying voice with a vocal coach named Jo Locass at Fred Steele Singing Studios. I passed the audition for AADA by doing one of my songs and monologues from "The King and I", but class was not starting until early September, so while I waited to start school at AADA, I began taking jazz dance, movement, and sight-singing classes at Herbert Berghoff Studios in Greenwich Village. Classes were inexpensive and fun, and I learned a lot. I felt so important and blessed to be a young gal in the BIG CITY where so many stars get their start. Just attending singing and acting classes made me feel very special since these were gifts, I wanted to develop, so I felt like I was on the right track by cultivating my natural talents.

I also attended some cattle calls, large open auditions for off Broadway and Broadway shows, but I never got a call back. I had a beautiful head shot taken by a professional photographer with my resume' on the back, but I had the feeling that no one even paid me a second look. I did not have a union card for the Screen Actors Guild, nor was I a union musician or singer. I was just a pretty, happy, naive young girl with a Big Dream like so many thousands of hopeful young actresses, singers, and dancers who come to New York hoping to find stardom. I loved to sing, dance, and act, and I'd wanted to do what I loved to do. I did not care about the money or fame part. Well, maybe a little.

I got nowhere in New York.

I left my cosmetician job in the fall to go to acting school full time. I excelled in singing as I always did. Unfortunately, I was not a great actress, and I was not one of the 32 students asked back for the following year. It was OK though because I did not think I was cut out to be an actress waiting for the right parts and having to take odd jobs as a singing waitress, store clerk, model, or whatever. I knew from the time I was 21 I was no Meryl Streep.

My band, "Baloney", performed at Fairleigh Dickinson College, on the Circle Line Ferry going around Manhattan, in bars, and restaurants at night and on week-ends. I had a lot of fun rehearsing and performing with the members of Baloney and earned a bit of pocket money to put into my savings account and for recreation.

This was no ordinary band of guys. Two of the four players were ministers at the Psychic Science Temple of Metaphysics in Paterson. The lead guitarist, George, was an ordained full-fledged minister who was naturally psychic, humorous, and intelligent. George and Tommy, both invited me to their church that Sunday. It was at this new church that I found a spiritual home and the first spiritual teaching I studied that resonated in my heart. I began studying and taking classes with the pastor, Rev. Bill Daut, who was also psychic and regularly channeled his dead teacher, "Dr. James", at Sunday services and during some week night classes.

The first lesson was "God is Love". The second was "You are your brother's Keeper" and all the lessons I studied made perfect sense to me. Unlike traditional Christianity which, in my perception, often focused on sin, guilt, and trying not to go to hell, Psychic Science focused more on God's unconditional love, God within the individual, the eternality of the soul, and the power of the individual soul to channel God's healing power.

This was the first religion I can say I chose on my own and not because it was my parents' doctrine or belief system. I learned how to meditate and began dating George, the red haired, bearded lead guitarist, to whom I was not physically attracted at first, but his intelligence, depth, spiritual nature, talent, and sense of humor won me over in a short time during and after band rehearsals and at

Sunday services. He was five years older than me, and we shared a special relationship for several years. We began having sex, and I wanted to spend nights over at his apartment in Paterson. My dad and step-mom forbid this because they wanted me to remain a virgin until marriage while living in their household. I had not been a virgin since I was nineteen, but my step-mom did not know this; she was an old fashioned Catholic, so it was just understood that all of the "children" should be saving themselves for that one perfect spouse, I suppose, who would initiate them into the precious pleasures afforded by the marriage bed. Though I had hoped to be a virgin until I married this did not turn out to be the case, so I decided to enjoy my sexuality once I discovered it with a number of men who seemed to care about me.

I really loved singing much more and enjoyed being in the rock band until I felt my boyfriend, George, began to take me for granted. I became disillusioned with him and began to date the bass player, Tom, and George simultaneously. I could not decide which man I wanted as my steady, and then I met Gregory, a tall, dark blonde, handsome young man with a vivacious personality, at the Psychic Science Temple of Metaphysics, my church home. We became close friends and in a short time Greg was spending most nights over my apartment.

Shortly after that after he was involved in a serious car accident caused by an inexperienced driver. Greg was seriously injured and had to have his spleen taken out. It was during that period I invited Greg to live with me so I could help nurture him back to good health. Months later we moved from that tiny room in Garfield and would eventually find an apartment in Hackensack, NJ, where we would live together for a few years, until 1979.

Greg loved jazz and turned me onto some great jazz singers and musicians. He took me to see "The Jazz Crusaders", with Joe Sample on piano, at a small concert hall in Teaneck. I loved the group who became very famous and later on would just come to be known as "The Crusaders". Greg played a few great Al Jarreau albums, Al Di Meola on guitar, and Stanley Clarke on bass. I was really coming to love and appreciate jazz which was a type of music I'd not been exposed to except for swing and big bands. I'd also heard an album of Ella Fitzgerald's when I was working at Plains Pharmacy. Her pure, melodic voice blew me away. Then we took a trip to go leaf peaking in Vermont to watch the leaves turn color in mid-October. It was lovely.

My step-brother, Tom, loved John Denver, and it was from listening to Tommy's albums that I also began to appreciate John's music myself. One of my most favorite songs of his is "Sunshine on My Shoulders" and "Annie's Song". Years later, John Denver came to Baba Muktananda's ashram in South Fallsburg to entertain for Gurumayi. I missed his performance, but I was told he was as terrific as ever. He'd made an album that was supposedly inspired by his love for God and the guru.

Pete and Tom both knew how to finger-pick on their inexpensive, but pleasant sounding, folk guitars. I can't remember how I got my first guitar, but I think it was a gift from my parents or from the Long's next-door neighbor, Doug Bowen. Doug was the first person to teach me how to hold the guitar and how to place my left fingers on the strings of the frets and to press down hard while I used a pick to strum the strings with my right hand. Doug patiently showed me how to place my left fingers on the frets to make the sounds of a C chord, a G chord, an E minor, and an A minor. It hurt my fingers a bit at first, but I practiced them over and over until my fingers on my left hand became callused, and the strings did not buzz or squeak anymore when I played. He was a smart and a really creative, nice, fun guy.

Doug was intelligent and creative, and I found him very interesting. His mom was a member of the elite MENSA organization, and I found Doug was quite a brilliant, independent thinker as well. He was a "college man" at Rutgers in New Brunswick and worked at the Burger King in Park Ridge. He and his friends were intellectual, liberal, vegetarian peace activists. I'd never met a vegetarian before, so I was impressed.

Doug and his friend, Gary Wright, wrote this really funny song about their experiences selling Burger king whoppers. Playing bluegrass and jug-band songs was easy and fun, because the chords were simple and there were not that many changes. I learned how to play a washboard with thimbles and make some decent sounds with the kazoo Doug gave me as a gift. I still love bluegrass and jug band music.

Unfortunately, when I was younger, I never made my own albums or cassette of original music in order that I might realize my dream of getting a recording contract. Well, actually, I did cut a demo at Bell Studios in New York City with my very first rock group, Baloney, (no matter how you slice it) with Rev. George Callanan on lead guitar, Tommy Johnson on rhythm guitar, Jeff, our bass player, and Tommy Sussino, our hot Italian curly haired drummer. I sang lead, George played a mean electric guitar almost as well as Jimmy Hendrix or Eric Clapton, and Tommy Johnson played rhythm guitar and sang back-up harmonies. We did a cover of the Beatle tune, "You Can't Do That" on which I sang a funky rock lead vocal.

Our friend, Rob Berman, was the electronic technician who got us into the studio where he was working part-time as a sound engineer, so he did all the technical stuff at the soundboard. It looked very complex, and I was quite impressed with the way the master tape was coming out. It did take a lot of time and many takes to get everything perfect, but it was really fun, though. I was only twenty-one years old then, and I never had a care.

Many years later I realized that this studio we used to record our three songs had been built by Preston Nichols, a very special man and author whom I met at a UFO conference held at the Days Inn in Bordentown and led by my friend, Pat, an expert in UFO and paranormal phenomena. Even Joni Mitchell had recorded there.

I would attempt to record again in 2002. I began recording a CD of original poetry and songs with the help of my dear friend, Les Fina, in his basement studio using piano and synthesizer keyboards of my multi-talented musician, friend, and computer wiz, Don Slepian, to accompany me on synthesizers and keyboard, and my friend, Les, recording. The project got shelved, however, when Les decided to go to dental school at NYU; then his computer crashed and we lost all the great work we'd done for six months. At the time I did not think I could afford to pay for a professional studio and sound technician.

After I left Baloney, I auditioned for a show band named Spectrum. I really loved this band because I learned choreography for several of the numbers and was showcased as one of three lead singers performing hits like Donna Summer's "Last Dance", Kiki Dee's "I've Got the Music in Me", and Walking on Sunshine".

Pierre, the leader of the band, purchased a $20,000 van equipped with a bar, refrigerator, and three comfortable bucket seats with enough room for the band members' equipment in the back.

Our lead guitarist, Joe, was very talented, and we had a drummer, Luke, and bass player named Marlowe, to accompany us too. All six of us fit comfortably in the van and we traveled up and down the east coast performing two shows a night at places like the Sheraton in Ocean City, MD, and the Bond Court Hotel in Cleveland where we performed right on the heels of Bruce Springsteen and his E Street Band during the time Cleveland had just filed for bankruptcy. All the members of the show band were like a family, but Pierre began sleeping with Sue, the other female singer who was much younger than me. He was interested in me too even though I was living with my boyfriend, Greg, at the time. It was foolish of me, but being lonely on the road I ended up becoming sexual involved with Pierre too. Once the other singer found out he had sex with me, too, she made sure Pierre fired me. Right after I was fired, I flew back to Hackensack with the costumes Greg's mom had donated to me and Sue for the band. Soon after I was fired, I was told Pierre's van was vandalized in Cleveland and stripped of everything including the bucket seats while the band was out at a disco dancing on their night off. I did not feel so bad for Pierre because he had just fired me. I guess "what goes around comes around".

Once I got back to Hackensack, I began to look in the trade papers for cabaret shows and bands for which to audition. I kept seeing an ad searching for an alto singer for a three woman show group currently forming to perform in New York City and the Caribbean. The ad said they needed an alto singer who could dance or move well. It also said the applicant needed to know how to tap dance. I had only tapped in kindergarten and did not feel qualified at all as a professional dancer, let alone tap dancer, so I never called on the ad, even though I saw it in the trade papers several times for a few months.

I was friends with a pianist named Lee Curreri who often accompanied people at auditions for cruise lines. He told me he even accompanied Barbra Streisand briefly. Lee liked my voice, my style, and me as a person, so he encouraged me to audition for this three-girl act that was being put together by a New York agent named Hal Kaye. The group was Hal's idea, and he'd already hand-picked all the music, had harmonies written, arranged, and scored by a professional New York musician and pianist, Bobby Blume.

Hal had costumes made and designed by his girlfriend, Patty, and professional charts were already written for his three gals whom he wanted to perform two shows per night in popular nightclubs and hotels. We were to rehearse the parts and choreography for three months prior to our first gig at the Sheraton Hotel in Curacao in the Caribbean where we were already booked for three weeks. I was still nervous about having to learn tap dancing, but I felt confident about my personality, my looks, and singing ability, so I finally decided to give the audition a shot. Hal Kaye loved me and gave me the alto part in "Take Three". What a fabulous opportunity; now all I had to worry about was learning to tap dance and do the soft shoe.

We traveled to Curacao, Netherlands Antilles, where we performed for three weeks in the evenings.

Alison Gertner, the choreographer and lead vocalist, had an interesting time teaching me to tap in the kitchen of my small apartment in Hackensack. It took me an hour to learn the time step. I was so embarrassed while learning to tap that I would not let Alison watch me while I was practicing. I did learn the soft shoe and other choreography easily, and after a while felt comfortable fillapping too. Alison, who was a nice Jewish gal from Lakewood, New Jersey, was very kind and patient with me. And we became close friends in a short amount of time.

The other singer, Nanette, had a lovely soprano voice and the three of us sang medleys in English, Hebrew, Spanish, and French in harmony. We blended very beautifully together, and all three of us had nice figures and were attractive. All three of us took turns emceeing and announcing each song and medley in Spanish and English. I did not know Spanish at all, but since I already knew some

French, it was not difficult learning some Spanish since the roots are Latin. Actually, I learned all the words I had to sing for "Somos Novios" and "Cuando Vuelvo a tu Lado" phonetically as well as the patter I needed to introduce my numbers. My accent was good enough that Spanish speaking people would come up to me after our performance and thank me in their native tongue. Unfortunately, I had to tell them I really did not understand a word they were saying. Since then, I have had a lot of Spanish neighbors and Mexican workers at Griggs Farm over the years, and my beau, Gary, had a Cuban father, so little by little I am picking up small phrases in Spanish.

In Curacao it was a thrill for me to have my maternal grandparents, "Pop Pop" and Grammy. in the audience watching me shine every night for a few weeks. Grammy and Pop Pop loved to travel and loved going on cruises to Mexico, Puerto Rico, Jamaica, and the Virgin Islands. What a thrill it was for me to have Pop Pop and Grammy, in the audience watching me shine as I sang and danced in two original, choreographed shows! We wore sequined black jumpsuits for one show and diaphanous gold and green tops over danskin tights for another. We also had royal blue danskin jumpsuits, which we wore under diaphanous light blue flowing blousy tops.

I had a blast performing in Curacao. Alison, Nanette, and I lay on the beach tanning most of the day and swimming in the magnificent blue ocean with two Dutch marines, Peter van den Molengraaf and Martin. I also had the good fortune to meet and attract a handsome pilot from Bonaire named Joseph, who swept me off my feet and onto the back of his windsurfer.

Joseph was an expert windsurfer and pilot, and an experienced lover. We ended up having sex after a brief period of friendship and we corresponded with one another after Take Three went back home. Joseph and I continued to be friends and occasional lovers when he would fly into Miami when I attended massage school in Sarasota. He flew into Sarasota and New Jersey a few times to spend time with me, but eventually the distance between us became a problem and we each went our own ways with other people. He was a real hunk and a charming, sexy man who knew how to treat a lady, and I won't forget him.

Unfortunately, Take Three disbanded after six months, since Hal couldn't get us lucrative gigs.

Shortly thereafter, Greg and I broke up. I was a bit depressed and had a long-term cold that just would not go away, so my mother suggested I move from our apartment in Hackensack into her apartment in Old Bridge, where she could help nurture me back to health. I had been doing massage therapy on and off part-time since I was living with the women in Garfield and decided to get more serious about studying holistic healing. I'd met a man named Al Ostrow who came to m e for a massage while working out of my back bedroom in Garfield. He was president of the AMTA. Al suggested I go to school to become a licensed massage therapist even though there were no laws in New Jersey requiring it at the time.

PATSY

I met Patsy Boston – who was to become a close friend – at the same Psychic Temple of Metaphysics, where I'd met George and Tommy, in 1976. She was an assistant minister, and when I found out she was a masseuse I scheduled an appointment for my first professional hour-long Swedish massage. Patsy was terrific, a sweetheart of a person, very psychic, a good cook, and had a beautiful country accent having grown up on a farm in Ohio. She was divorced and also had a sweet teen-age daughter with blond hair named Kimberly.

Patsy told me she was giving a day-long workshop on how to give a Swedish massage in her house, so I thought I might try to learn something new I really loved to receive, so it might be fun to give massages too to my boyfriend and maybe some friends to earn extra money. I was a make-up artist at the time for Roget cosmetics making up people's faces in beauty salons working strictly on commissions. It was somewhat lucrative, but I could sure use some extra money in my pocket, something that I really loved to do, so I enrolled in the workshop with a small deposit.

I absolutely loved learning the four strokes of Swedish massage – effleurage (stroking), petrissage (kneading), friction, a deep elliptical, rolling movement used mostly up the spine or on the kneecaps and elbows one does with the thumbs, and tapotement (a percussive movement done by cupping the hands over the buttocks, pinching, or slapping with a flat hand quickly on the back or buttocks at the end of the other three strokes. I picked up the strokes easily, and Patsy told me while I worked on my partner that she believed I had a natural gift for massage and healing and suggested I get myself a portable massage table and start my own practice at the same time that I was singing.

I began massaging some of my friends and members of the Psychic Science Temple.

While living with my mom, I continued to practice massage at the Executive Health Club in East Brunswick. One of my clients who owned the Lamppost, a bar and restaurant, in North Brunswick, told me he needed more reliable go-go dancers. I decided to do go-go dancing part time as a way to earn extra money to go to massage school.

Patsy and I took a trip to her parents' farm in Lexington, Kentucky and drove further south to Miami and Sarasota, Florida, in order to check out massage schools where we could study long enough to become certified and licensed massage practitioners. We really loved the holistic aspect of the Sarasota School of Natural Healing Arts much more than the business-like atmosphere of the massage school in Miami, so we planned to save enough money to move to Sarasota and attend school there. By the time I'd made enough money to go to massage school and buy a car, my wage had gone up to $18 per hour in most of the nightclubs and bars where I danced two or three times per month. The tips came out to an extra $50-$150 per shift. And I worked five to seven hour shifts at most of the clubs. I had so much fun and enjoyed all the money I was making that I did continue working as a go-go dancer for a few years after I got back from Florida. In the summer of 1980, our applications were accepted and we plunked down our deposits. School at that time was only $1500, thousands of dollars less than they are asking now at schools in New Jersey.

It was quite a huge undertaking because Pats had to sell her home in New Jersey, and we both had to sell and/or pack all our belongings and my two cats into our two small cars, and drive all the way down to Venice where we would temporarily stay with my mom's parents until we found our own apartment in Sarasota. But everything worked out perfectly as if our new lives were already prearranged and set up by God Herself. Grammy demonstrated her amazing skill as a cook, which included making us a great key lime pie and a pecan pie.

While staying with Grammy and Pop Pop we perused the classified ads and immediately found a garage apartment on Siesta Drive not far from school by car in a pretty neighborhood with a lovely yard for only $150 per month rent. We'd find out later that the owner of the school, Isabel, lived there too when she first came to Florida. The class was six months long and some of the happiest months of my life while I was still single.

I did not know then that six months later I would be headed for my first breakdown.

I will now talk about some of the people that were major influences in my early life.

GRAMMY AND POP POP

All four of my great grandparents were immigrants from Europe, who had come to America seeking a better life. Grammy Lucy was born here in Staten Island, New York, as was her husband-to-be, Fred Lawrence Vere.

Pop Olson came over here on the "boat" from Sweden, he told me, with his parents and seven of his siblings. Henry was the eldest. His wife, my precious paternal grandmother, Anna, came over apparently on that same "boat" to Ellis Island with her parents and her sister, from Denmark.

My four grandparents all adored me, and the feeling was mutual. But I became particularly close to my mother's parents whom I saw almost weekly until they moved to Florida when I was about eleven. I had friends whose grandparents were either dead or living far away, so I considered myself to be very lucky to have all of them alive, healthy, and actively involved in my life as a young girl.

My mom's father, whom we affectionately called Pop Pop, took my brother, Pete, and me to the Staten Island Zoo or to the park every weekend until I was about six or seven. Pop Pop was about 5ft. 11 in. tall, large, and handsome with about an extra ten pounds in the middle from a great fondness for my grandmother's Italian cooking and bowls of Breyers vanilla ice cream. Pop Pop sported a full, thick, wavy, salt and peppered crown of hair which he kept slicked back with Vitalis. He had a dark curly waxed mustache to match. For an older man in his late sixties, I thought he was very handsome.

I also remember visiting Grammy and Pop Pop at their home in Staten Island when I was 9 or 10 years old. Atto the park, they'd push us on the swings or go up and down on the see-saw. Afterward, Pop Pop would give us lunch and then we'd visit my favorite place, the Staten Island Zoo. We got to see the beautiful, majestic lions and tigers from Africa, alligators, crocodiles, and huge, long snakes, like boa constrictors, in large tanks indoors. Outside there was a very ancient one-hundred-pound tortoise. Lots of storks standing on one leg, pink flamingos, peacocks, colorful Macaws, and other tropical birds lived at the zoo too. But my favorite animals were the large gray elephants and the monkeys. Chimpanzees especially. I loved watching the babies play and hang on to their mom's backs and tails. Sometimes I would dream of seeing all these animals in their natural habitats in their native countries when I grew up to be as old as my mom and dad or even as old as Grammy and Pop Pop.

Pop Pop and Grammy also treated us to shows at Radio City Music Hall in Manhattan around Christmas, where we got to see the fabulous, beautiful dancing Rockettes in their fancy sequined costumes doing their high fan kicks in perfect precision with all of them in line. I dreamed I might be able to dance like them one day and be as pretty and voluptuous in a sexy costume with large breasts and a round bottom. I was skinny as a rail and flat as a pancake, but I knew how pretty and sexy women could look from looking at my dad's Playboy magazine's when he was at work. I was still a child, and I'd only had a kiss or two from two different boys at that point. I was very inexperienced, but I dreamed of growing up to be a beautiful big, sexy teenager. How happy I'd be when I turned seventeen or eighteen, all grown up with a nice figure with handsome young men taking me out on dates just like my dad did with my mom when she was that age!

There was an older gentleman at Radio City, the organist, who always played at the beginning of the show. It was amazing how much beautiful sound he could pump out of that machine – it filled the entire room with harmonic vibrations of love and joy. The Rockettes, though, had a whole orchestra behind them when they did their amazing routine.

My favorite time at Radio City was when Grammy and Pop Pop took my cousins Dru and Daragh, Pete and me to hear Julie Andrews sing in the movie "Mary Poppins". To this day, that is one of my favorite movies about one of my favorite characters. And Dick Van Dyke – who could forget that goodhearted, black-faced chimney sweep with the resonant voice and jolly disposition with a heart of gold dance like a dream with Mary Poppins and the other chimney sweeps over the rooftops of London? He was like a Zen master, the first such person I ever saw portrayed in a movie. I still love Dick Van Dyke. A true master of dance, song, comedy, and slapstick. I will never forget seeing Mary Poppins in that big theater for the first time after the Rockettes did their thing. My cousins Dru and Daragh were with me. It was magical. Being with Grammy and Pop Pop, we always felt special. All of us were loved, and treasured for who we were exactly as we were. Completely accepted. Never criticized. Only praised. Grammy and Pop Pop always saw only the best in us no matter how we behaved, but we loved them so much we were almost always on our best behavior. They believed we were so smart and talented that we could do absolutely anything we wanted with our lives.

Pop Pop also showed us the beautiful Christmas tree and the ice skaters at Rockefeller Center. Then they'd take us all out for a fabulous dinner at a neat restaurant like Mama Leone's or the Hawaii Kai. where we'd order something fun like a Pu Pu platter and Nada Pina Coladas with parasols and fresh pineapples in them. Nobody knew how to show someone a good time like my Pop Pop.

When I was little, Pop Pop had a kind and jovial temperament. He sat me on his lap all the time on his favorite chair in the living room while working out the New York Times crossword puzzle and asking me, "What's a four letter word for this, sweetie petutie?" I'd be so ecstatic if I just guessed one or two answers. Pop Pop was so adept at doing them that he'd have them finished in fifteen minutes or so.

After retiring as a railroad engineer, Pop Pop became an inspector for the city of New York, so he often got my brother and me into movies for free. The manager of the theater was always very nice to us making sure that we had good seats and were kept away from other noisy children. It made me feel proud that my Pop Pop was so important.

It was Pop Pop who suggested some years later that I go to the Eileen Ford modeling agency to see if she would hire me as one of her models. Ms. Ford was one of Pop Pop's clients he was paid to visit as an inspector for the city of New York. I suppose he did not notice my – to my mind – Rubenesque 117 pound, five-foot-three frame as a sixteen-year-old young woman. As far as I knew a girl had to be beautiful and skinny as a rail to become a top model. That was not me, and I had no desire to model clothes for the Sears catalog or for high fashion couture. I was way too curvy. Besides, I wanted to be a famous super singing star and movie actress like Judy Garland or Debbie Reynolds from the time I saw our fabulous Judy in the Wizard of Oz and "A Star is Born". Then I saw Ms. Reynolds in "Singing in the Rain" with my other favorite star, Gene Kelly, a regular guy from Pittsburgh, Pennsylvania. I dreamed of dancing with Gene Kelly and Fred Astaire from the first time I saw them in movies on television, but I was not that great a dancer. I could see myself dancing with them in my always overactive imagination. I liked to dance a lot, but the adductor and abductor muscles in my thighs were very tight, and I did not have much of an extension, having very short legs. But what I lacked in stature I made up for in enthusiasm.

I had a powerful voice which I knew how to project from the time I was about twelve. I was chosen as a cheerleader and captain of the cheerleaders for the young boys' basketball team in sixth and seventh grades. I also loved to sing and starred in musicals from the time I was in sixth grade when I was chosen for the female lead as Becky Thatcher in "Tom Sawyer," the eighth-grade musical at Holmdel Intermediate where I attended sixth, seventh, and eighth grades. There was a professional director who told my mom I was talented enough to become professional. He saw a star quality in me that he found in some of the best actresses and singers in New York. I suppose my Pop Pop and Grammy also saw that star quality in me, or perhaps it was their love and belief in me that created it. Becoming a mom and then having mental illness changed everything, but I do not mind having had to give up those dreams of becoming a superstar. and I am so happy just to be alive and healthy with my children still loving me as I am. Truly, I am really OK that my life went just as it did. Becoming a celebrity would not have given me more pleasure or joy than I now experience.

When my parents moved from the Staten Island projects to Holmdel, New Jersey, I was three years old. Pop Pop would still make the two-hour drive to visit at least once per week. Pop Pop was the most loved and welcome guest arriving at our neighborhood in his long black car with the red leather seats. Like the Good Humor man loudly ringing his bell to summon all the kids in the neighborhood, Pop Pop would unabashedly announce his arrival to everyone around the block with about twenty short blasts on the car horn as he approached our home at 28 Miller Ave. in the Newstead development behind the Holiday Inn off Route 35, and all our friends like Joey and Anthony, and Bobbie, and Johnny Posada would come running. Pop Pop had been poor as a child, but now that he was a successful adult with a good income, he loved treating us to shows, movies, concerts, and when he came to visit us on weekday afternoons after school he would delight in driving us and whatever friends and neighbors from the development he could squeeze into the back seat of his Chevy Impala, to go get ice cream sundaes and ice cream sodas.

Friends from all around the block would stop what they were doing and come out of their homes to say hello to see if they might be the lucky ones that Pop Pop would take with us to get an ice cream sundae or soda at Tiny Glenn's Sweet Shop.

Tiny was the first "dwarf" I would ever meet, and he made the best ice cream in town. Boy, did he love when Pop Pop would come in with Pete and me and as many of our friends as we could fit into the back of Pop Pop's car. A few of us would squeeze in on top of somebody else's lap. Pop Pop was so generous, the more we ate the happier he was. He encouraged us to eat as much as we wanted. He'd grown up in a poor family, and I think it made him feel a great sense of satisfaction that he had the means to be able to give of himself in this way. He really loved kids. In some ways he was like a big kid himself – always telling jokes and teasing us. These trips to Tiny's were some of the most exciting, fun afternoons of my young life.

Mom and Grammy shared with me that Pop Pop had a rough childhood with a mom that didn't love him very much and favored his brother, Vic, and younger sister over him. Mental illness ran in the family back then too. Grammy told me that one of Pop Pop's sisters, Annie Lorrie, tried to commit suicide by putting her head in an oven.

She married my Pop Pop, Fred Vere, when she was in her early twenties, and they lived in Staten Island when I was young until I was 11 yrs. old when my parents told me they were following my paternal grandparents, Henry and Anna Olson, to Venice, Florida.

Pop Pop always treated everyone to dinner out at a nice restaurant being the proud, generous person he was and coming from a poor family who survived the Great Depression. He was very poor when he was younger, so he made up his mind to get good grades in school so that he could make his German mother proud and go to college on a scholarship in Staten Island, New York where they lived in a modest apartment. After completing high school and passing the exam to get into college where he would study and get an undergraduate degree in drafting and engineering. He went to college to become an engineer working for the Reading Railroad, and later, as an inspector for the city of New York. He typed his reports at a lightning speed of 140 words per minute upon an old-fashioned Royal typewriter right in front of me, the apple of his eye, being the first grandchild and first baby girl on either side of the two parents. Before computers were invented there was no way of correcting mistakes except to start all over again with a fresh piece of paper, using "white out", or by placing something called "Correct Tape" under the keys that had printed the mistake which had to be carefully inserted directly underneath the black ribbon where was the mistake in order to erase a specific letter or word. Pop Pop was brilliant and felt very proud to be upper middle class. Perhaps, by societal and economic standards of the times, his family might have been considered to be at the lower end of the upper class since my grandparents owned a beautiful, well-kept three-bedroom home in a beautiful neighborhood that had a lovely garden and a well-kept, finely manicured lawn on a large property. Pop Pop also was well equipped to send both of his daughters to college, but it was only my Aunt Marlyse, the one considered to be "the smart daughter" who had the privilege of going to Barnard College. My mom was considered to be the prettier of the two sisters and sent to secretarial school locally, which bothered her. She said "Pop Pop thought himself industrious, wealthy compared to his parents and very capable of taking good, material care of his young, attractive, hardworking wife and two daughters." He would take even better material and emotional care of his six grandchildren, my three cousins, two brothers, and me after his Uncle Victor, a popular, successful dentist, died and left his nephew, my Pop Pop, a pretty healthy inheritance.

Since my "Grammy" was my angel and nearly my most favorite person on the planet I'd like to share a few stories about her. Lucia Vere was born on February 15th, 1909, the eighteenth and last child born to Columba and Ludovico Comeforo. Only ten of her siblings would survive and grow to become adults like her sister, Erna, and her brothers, Larry, Joe, Tilly, and Lovey whom I called my uncles when I was a little girl except for Uncle Joe, who died before I had the chance to meet him. As the youngest of the big Italian bunch, my grammy was adored by her parents, her sister, and all her brothers.

I recall being alone with Grammy when she would take me out on the train and sometimes the ferry boat on a Saturday afternoon to visit her work place, the Chase Manhattan Bank, where she worked converting money like lira and other foreign currencies into American dollars. I just loved traveling with Grammy, especially because we often went with my cousin, Dru, and we'd get to wear the same outfits with matching dresses, tams, gloves, and even matching pocketbooks. And those cute little white anklets with lace at the top. Grammy always said she and my mother loved me so much they dressed me looking like I came out of a bandbox. Dru and I almost looked like twins even though I was fourteen months older.

Grammy would take care of me at times. Once, I remember my parents dropping me off at Grammy's and Pop Pop's on a Friday night when I was not feeling so well. I had a runny nose, and by Saturday morning, I had a fever. Grammy was worried when she noticed some spots on my face. I had the measles, and had to be quarantined in their home for several days. I stayed until I got over the fever and was no longer contagious. You might think I felt badly, but I was happy to live with Grammy and Pop Pop. They always treated me like a princess. Grammy made my favorite foods. I'd have cream of wheat for breakfast, with a little sugar mixed with milk and whipped butter – delicious! There was home-made chicken or turkey soup for lunch. Grammy made sure I drank lots of water, ginger ale, tea, and juices – like orange juice, prune or apple. I lay in her bed, sleeping or watching TV. I was almost sorry when the fever broke.

My Grammy was the kindest person I have ever met with a heart of gold, as big and expansive as the outdoors. The thing she was most generous with was her love in the form of cooking the most wonderful meals – homemade Italian recipes like lasagna, spaghetti with meat sauce that took an entire day to prepare so that all the juices and spices can seep in. And her melt in your mouth, handmade manicotti and raviolis were "to die for". I mean to live for. To this day I still use her ingredients when I prepare my homemade spaghetti sauce. And her recipe for apple celery stuffing at Thanksgiving is one of my all-time favorite side dishes. I have never tasted a turkey dressing as delicious, and do not believe I ever will. I like to make it special, even if it's not Thanksgiving because it is so healthy, naturally sweet, and delicious. The desserts were amazing.

My Grammy was the greatest chef and hostess on the planet as far as I was concerned. My parents, brothers, and cousins would agree with me too. As well as all the other relatives and neighbors too. Well, my mom comes in a very close second though she stopped cooking large holiday meals when she turned 70.

Grammy's unconditional love for me and all our family members was also expressed through her devoted service to us in the form of relaxing, chatting, and just BEING with us, and made me and all my siblings feel completely loved, safe, wanted, and important. After we finished dessert and Grammy came back to the table Pop Pop would bring out a deck of cards and we'd play different card games or board games like Casino, poker, Monopoly, or Black Jack. We played with red chips and bet pennies and nickels. This was lots of fun, and it made me feel so grown up to be part of an adult game. After the game we'd watch TV. For a little while in the family room and then go to sleep. I always slept soundly at Grammy and Pop Pop's house after a meal, because I felt so safe, loved, and satisfied.

These times with my parents and Grammy and Pop Pop were some of the happiest of my life. Sometimes my brothers, Pete, Scott, and I would have the great fortune of being invited to Grammy and Pop Pop's for more than half the summer by ourselves or with our cousins, Dru and Daragh.

Grandparents have to be the most wonderful people in our lives. I once heard a saying that God could not be everywhere so he created grandparents.

Another sweet thing Grammy did was to teach me skills like how to knit a scarf and a pair of slippers. My mom taught me to crochet too, but I preferred knitting. It was easier to pick up. It was fun learning a new skill and actually creating a finished garment from scratch as opposed to buying it already made. It gave me a sense of accomplishment.

My brothers and I were hams and loved making up shows to please our parents and grandparents.

Grammy and Pop Pop loved watching us act, sing, and do comedy routines. They would always thank and praise us for the creative shows my brothers and I would put on in their den, the family room where we relaxed and watched the Jackie Gleason show on a color television. With the help of ideas and songs we borrowed from Alfred E. Neuman's Mad Magazine, some original song parodies, dancing, a few funny original skits, and anything that sparked our creativity, and we'd create a complete show in the moment. Pop Pop and Grammy made us feel like princesses and kings for the entire time we spent in their household.

Grammy had a way of making each moment you spent with her special. If she was reading a magazine or the newspaper at 6 AM, and I woke up early after a good night's sleep in the den in Florida, she'd invite me to sit at the kitchen table with her while she'd share tidbits of interesting information as if I were on her level even when I was just twelve or thirteen years old. My grammy's lap was the comfiest place in her beautiful, immaculate house. She could sit with us in the den in Florida or have us lie with her in her bedroom watching the Jackie Gleason Show, Carol Burnett, or Perry Mason when she lived in Staten Island, and we could discuss the story, the actors or whatever interested us, and we all felt so comfortable and at ease in her relaxed and peaceful presence.

Pop Pop loved to share his love for Jackie Gleason with us. Jackie was also poor as a child, but overcame poverty to become a big, wealthy star. He was known for the phrase "How sweet it is!" I guess he must have really enjoyed becoming rich and famous after such humble beginnings.

Pop Pop kept himself active even when he retired. He did a lot of walking and swimming when we visited and he worked around the yard daily pruning trees, mowing the lawn, gardening, etc. Until the last few years of his life he always seemed energetic and healthy to me. But actually, his body had been slowly breaking down for years.

The qualities I loved best about my Pop Pop were his love for his grandchildren, for animals – especially cats, and his love for gardening. Pop Pop even loved fish and frogs. There were little green, dime frogs that would hide behind the white slats that surrounded his front door. He would tell us to try to catch them. He had a green thumb, and his indoor plants on the lanai were always thriving as well as his palm trees, hibiscus, shrubs, and whatever colorful flowers he'd planted. He told me he used "Miracle Gro" as a fertilizer, and that was what made his plants do so well, but I think it was his tender, loving care, and the fact that he appreciated their beauty so very much. Plants and animals are sensitive to our feelings, and they respond in kind, to our love, kindness to them, and appreciation of them.

I suppose some illnesses and tendencies really may be genetic. Like the hopelessness, despair, depression and suicidal tendencies on my mother's side of the family. Though I never once saw my grammy depressed or even unhappy. She always seemed to be looking at the bright side of her life even when my Pop Pop teased or abused her psychologically or criticized her relentlessly when we kids were around them in their Venice, Florida home. One summer I asked that we be sent home early when Pop Pop began criticizing my brother, Pete, when he was only about nine or ten years old. Pete was the apple of Grammy's eye. I was Pop Pop's favorite, so it was really tough for me to stand up to him when he got hypercritical of either my grammy or my brother, Pete, but one summer when I was about thirteen, I let him have it at the dinner table one night when he stated criticizing both Pete and Grammy. I would not stand by while he tried to hurt both my grandmother and precious younger brother's feelings, though I don't even think Pete was old enough to even be aware of what was going on. And Grammy always ignored the abuse by turning the other cheek and thinking about his positive qualities.

After all, there was no way she would ever divorce him since, she did not drive nor work after they both retired to Florida. Plus, they had a blast hanging out with my paternal grandparents, Henry and Anna. They took fun cruises and other trips together, went to the Kapok Tree Inn together for lunch or some fine restaurant for inner, visited each other's' homes for dinner and afterward played Scrabble or cards after dessert. Grammy was a fine cook and pastry chef and Pop Pop a fine gardener who insisted giving us kids fresh squeezed orange or grapefruit juice from his own trees in the backyard for our morning breakfast.

Two of my favorite places to visit besides Disney World were the Ringling Brothers Barnum and Bailey Circus and John Ringling's beautiful mansion in Sarasota which still stands today. I love it so much that I've probably gone to the museum over ten times since becoming an adult.

Grammy loved when Pop Pop took her and all the grandchildren out to fancy places for lunch and dinner, as well as to the beaches and state parks like Myakka.

Another wonderful fun, and educational place we frequented was the Shell Factory in Fort Meyers.

Despite Pop Pop's sense of adventure, kindness, love and affection for us, he had a lot of trouble showing love and affection to the one person who loved him more than anyone, and who was loyal and devoted to him as a wife and mother to Marlyse and Arleen; plus, she was a great cook, laundress, hostess, housekeeper, and gracious grandmother to his favorite grandchildren, but Freddy had the most difficulty showing affection to his mate, Lucy, the woman who loved him more than anyone did and served him his entire life.

As I grew older, I sensed that all Pop Pop's teasing and joking covered up a deep sadness in his heart. When I got to be about nine, I noticed how jealous he became when my brother or I would show my grandmother affection. He was particularly jealous of the close relationship between Pete, who was only six, and Grammy. Pop Pop would become mean and begin to pick on Grammy, often calling her stupid. We loved them both, and this made my brother and I very uncomfortable. Grammy was actually wise and savvy about many topics.

After a while Pop Pop's verbal abuse became intolerable. I felt the need to protect my grandmother since she would never stand up for herself. She just ignored the abuse and looked embarrassed. I felt so sad for her. Speaking up for Grammy only angered and alienated Pop Pop more, so usually we'd leave him alone and go into the den with Grammy where we could watch TV by ourselves and cuddle with Grammy on the couch.

My grandmother had no ego. She did not have a lot of self-confidence when it came to certain things, but her love was so pure and golden that it was her kindness and love that was the Wisest thing she could teach us. She taught us unconditional love by her fine example, of course. How to love and be loved. And think happy thoughts. That was her motto.

Whenever my mom or I would feel sad or depressed, she simply told us to turn our attention away from the negative things going on and just focus on those blessings we had and things that made us feel happy like good, healthy food, funny television shows, and good music. She never seemed to understand when my mom or I had depression. However, she shared with me once that she had a nervous breakdown when she was married to Pop Pop. I think it was after he got violent with her and Aunt Marlyse when they were living in Staten Island. But somehow, she managed to ignore whatever criticism and abuse he dished out. Grammy did not ever learn to drive a car so when she was older and they retired to Florida she had no way of getting around except for Pop Pop who always played chauffeur for her and all the grandchildren. In New York she had been able to take public transportation whenever she needed to go somewhere if she could not walk.

I was back living in New Jersey when Pop Pop was dying in the autumn of 1982. I'd already gotten Shaktipat from my guru and felt balanced and happy again after coming out of my first nervous breakdown that began in February of that year.

I had begun studying A Course in Miracles, which I'd heard about from several friends. It was a course in unconditional love and forgiveness that was supposedly channeled through a woman who was tuning into the Christ Consciousness. It consisted of three books – a large text that was rather complex, a workbook with daily lessons, and a manual for teachers. Several of my friends involved in metaphysics and spiritual growth were already studying it, so I decided to invest the required $40 in the books and joined a study group with my friend, Barbara Cole, at the Holistic Health Professional Center in Old Bridge, where I was working as a massage therapist.

While in my study group I began to open up psychically. I had an intuitive feeling about a week before Pop Pop passed away that he was about to ascend, and I prayed that I would get down there in time to see him before he made his ascension. Barbara told me about a friend who needed her car driven down to Florida, and that she would pay all the expenses and pay me extra money for the driving and expenses to get back to Jersey. I jumped at that chance, and within several days I met Emma Forehand, picked up her car, and started out on the long trek to Florida by going to DC I put her car on the auto train, and stayed with it until we got off in northern Florida. I drove the car the rest of the way from there to Venice to see Pop Pop. I planned to take Amtrak for the return trip.

The trip turned out to be even more urgent than I realized at first.

Grammy had told me that Pop Pop was very ill from colon cancer after he turned 76 years old, he'd lost over thirty pounds, and he was at home with her. Until he was dying of colon cancer, he had been very robust and seemingly healthy as he drove grammy and us kids everywhere in Staten Island, Manhattan, and finally, when they moved to Florida, to Sarasota Key, Nokomis Beach, Venice, and Manasota Key beaches plus all the fanciest restaurants in the area like the Kapok Tree inn.

Pop Pop was bedridden in the house for the last year before he died, and Grammy told me he was much more expressive of his love and appreciation for her during that time. I suppose it was "now or never" and being deathly ill made him much more aware of what was important in life, like appreciating the people closest to you and telling them how grateful you were for their company and service that you loved them very much and always would.

Unfortunately, Pop Pop did not change his diet or his lifestyle much after finding out he had colon cancer. For as long as I can remember he ate a few bowls of Breyers vanilla or butter almond ice cream following a large dinner, drank large glasses of whole milk at lunch, and ate all the fatty bacon, sausage, and other meats my grandmother prepared for him on a daily basis. He had too much uric acid in his system which caused painful gaut and diverticulitis prior to the cancer, and this should have been a warning sign to him that he needed to make changes in his diet. Most allopathic doctors are given very little schooling in regard to nutrition and diet, and Pop Pop was never told anything by his physicians that what he ate might be contributing to his poor health. He also had angina, but I believe his physical diseases were much more a result of deep emotional and psychological scars than just his diet alone.

Pop Pop did not want to die in the hospital. Though he got radiation treatments he would not allow the doctors to give him chemotherapy because he had a beautiful, thick head of silvery hair mixed with dark brown, or was it black? I suppose it might have just looked black from the Vitalis or whatever cream he used to keep it slicked back. He was too vain to chance losing his hair from the chemotherapy treatments... He was still handsome even into his late seventies. Pop Pop adored me from the moment I was born, and we were very close.

When I finally arrived in Venice, Florida, to visit Pop Pop on his deathbed, it was late Saturday afternoon, and he was in very bad shape; I had the feeling that he was afraid of dying.

He seemed so happy and grateful to see me that his otherwise very gaunt face temporarily lit up for a few minutes. His usually large, robust 270 lb. frame had been ravaged by the cancer, and he'd dwindled down to an emaciated, sickly version of his former self.

Pop Pop lived through the night, and, though he seemed to be going in and out of consciousness, was still alive on Sunday morning. After Grammy spent some time with him, I went into his bedroom to pray over him, chant, and give him comfort and a sense of peace about making his transition into the next plane of consciousness. I kissed him, held his hand, and said "Pop Pop, I love you so much. Don't worry. You have, family, friends and a guardian angel who will help you leave your body and move into heaven." I stayed in his bedroom for a half hour chanting my mantra "Om Namah Shivaya" quietly praying to my guru, Swami Muktananda, that he helps Pop Pop not to fear leaving his body to go into the astral or etheric reams of consciousness. I asked Baba if he would help Pop Pop cross over. Then I retired to the den to rest.

About an hour later Grammy went into their bedroom to find that Pop Pop had left his body.

Pop Pop Vere was the second of my precious grandparents to pass away, but I remember his dying very well because he loved me so much that he waited for me to drive down to Florida before he decided to ascend.

Grammy had not shed a tear, but she called some of the relatives, including my mom and Aunt Marlyse, her sister, to tell them the news. Maybe she was temporarily in shock. She said all the "proper things" to the relatives like, "Well, at least he doesn't have to suffer anymore." And "He was such a good man." to the friends and neighbors.

Underneath it all, I believe she was so relieved her lifelong job as a servant to her husband was finally over – as well as his psychological abuse. Though I don't believe she ever really allowed herself to feel the pain of his abuse. My grandmother's way of dealing with hardship, abuse, and negativity was to ignore or deny what was actually going on. I think that that was the only way she could survive so much psychological beating without becoming an emotional wreck.

A wake and funeral arrangements were made swiftly. I stayed down there long enough to see Grammy through both of them. I chose not to attend the wake because I don't really "believe" in their value. I knew for certain Pop Pop was no longer in that lifeless shell with his face all made up to "look good" for the onlookers.

I did attend the funeral service, though, as a tribute to him, and I sang a song for him and the family. It was one I'd learned at the Psychic Science Temple of Metaphysics called, "Open My Eyes". The lyrics are very beautiful and appropriate. The beginning goes:

"Open my eyes that I may see glimpses of truth Thou has for me. Place in my hands the wonderful key that shall unclasp and set me free. Silently now I wait for Thee, ready my God, thy will to see. Open my eyes, illumine me, Spirit Divine."

Even though my Pop Pop was not a religious man he loved to hear me sing, and I was sure he was watching me from an astral plane or celestial realms and felt love and gratitude that I honored him in this way. Pop's way of being religious was by being a good, kind, hardworking man. He was a loving father and husband who worked hard as a civil engineer and inspector for the city of New York. He provided his wife and family with a lovely home, where Grammy could put delicious, healthy food on the table for all three meals, enough for regular vacations and recreation. He also kept the property beautiful, watering and caring for his gardens and the trees, flowers, and plants.

A day after his funeral I was sitting down at the breakfast table with Grammy in the early morning hours before the sun rose while she was reading the morning newspaper. She asked, "Honey, what did you say your Indian guru's name was again, Swami Muktananda, or something like that?"

"Yes, Grammy, it's Muktananda. Why?"

"Well, it says in the paper here that he died. On Saturday", which was the day before my grandfather.

Once Pop Pop died, I brought Ms. Forehand's car to Sarasota, where she was living, and left it with her. I then took the plane from the Sarasota airport into Newark, where I was met by my boyfriend, who brought me and my luggage back home.

A few years later, Grammy began to forget things and to have a bit of dementia. When she paid the mortgage twice, my mom and aunt decided to go down to Florida to bring her up to New Jersey after selling her house, so she could live with Aunt Marlyse. Then, Grammy said Aunt Marlyse was not cooking for her, so eventually it was decided she would come live with my mom.

Mom would get angry at her for little things like forgetting to put in her hearing aid or leaving the door unlocked, so eventually I convinced Mom to put Grammy into an assisted living residence in nearby Princeton called Buckingham Place.

Lucy lived her final years there, a residential center for seniors and some people with disabilities and dementia or with Alzheimer's disease.

She was one of the happiest and kindest residents ever to live there. Even though she had to get a pacemaker put in, she was like the bionic granny traveling around at the speed of light with her new walker. She participated in exercise class every morning and all the activities that were offered. When I went to visit her, she was often involved in a bingo game or watching a movie from which she did not want to be distracted because she enjoyed everything she was doing so much. She always lived in the present moment and truly knew how to focus upon and delight in each person who came across her path or became fully focused upon whatever activity she was involved in doing. present Most of the other residents knew her and thought she was such a caring, kind person. She was a Light to all she met, and I am proud and honored to have had her as my very special grandmother, the matriarch of our large Italian family. I intend to be as happy and healthy as she was when I'm 100 years old if I'm still alive.

I was blessed to work at Buckingham as a part-time concierge some days, evenings, and weekends for six months until I was fired. I enjoyed meeting and befriending all the lovable, friendly, and interesting residents and staff. Later, my mom would get the job as part-time concierge until she was let go. But at least both of us had the chance to spend the last few years of Grammy's life close to her. In fact, my mom would pick up her laundry to do at home and help her out in many other ways. Everyone there knew Lucy, because she was so full of energy and enthusiasm. She had a very simple motto for enjoying life. She always told me, "Honey, think happy thoughts."

Grammy was one of the most joyous people I ever knew. She has been one of the most caring, supportive, and influential people in my life. Her love has always been constant, unconditional, and uplifting. My Grammy brought joy to everyone wherever she went. She was beautiful in every way a woman could be, dressed to perfection in clothes that my mom ironed for her, always had her hair freshly coiffed and a manicure every week, and was the most generous person I knew.

She gave birthday cards, Christmas cards and money to her daughters, six grandchildren, thirteen great grandchildren, and one great grandson, Zachary. Like me, she remembered the birth dates of all the people in the family, though my mom had to purchase the cards for her because Grammy did not drive.

Grammy was Catholic, so she'd attend the mass they had at Buckingham. But she also attended the Jewish and Protestant services, whatever classes were offered, and went to all the movies. Grammy was a positive lady who loved life with a passion. Even at 97 years young she always kept herself involved, interested in new things and experiences, and excited about her family, friends, and keeping abreast of current events by reading the newspaper, watching the news on TV. She was always ready and willing to learn new things, meet new people, make new friends wherever she traveled, and was always compassionate, friendly, open hearted, and kind to people.

Grammy was so generous and kind to me that I wanted to give her just a small token of my appreciation for all the years of loving kindness, gifts, and money. She even purchased two new cars for me when I had accidents without the benefit of collision on my insurance policy because I believed I could not afford it. She even paid off half of my mother's mortgage on her condo many years ago and gave the same amount of money to my Aunt Marlyse. I believe the source of her great abundance was her golden heart, her loving service, and ease with which she shared her good fortune with her family and friends. She deserved every bit of the abundance, love, and care she got from my mom, my aunt, my grandfather when they were still together, and finally, in her last years before her death, the nurses, doctors, aides, and other helpers at Buckingham Place. Since she was the youngest of eighteen children, so she also inherited money from all of her brothers who passed away before her as well as my Pop Pop's pension and the money Pop inherited from a favorite uncle who formerly was a dentist who loved him a lot.

I had hoped to make enough money so that I could take her on a world cruise, but it was not to be.

I was fortunate to spend the night before she passed away in the emergency room of the hospital with her after an asthmatic attack. She had COPD (chronic obstructive pulmonary disease), and she'd been transported to the hospital several times from Buckingham prior to that night, when she was having problems breathing. The last night I saw her, I had her pick a goddess card from my Doreen Virtue Goddess deck. She picked Eirene who was the Goddess of peace, the Roman Goddess known as Pax.

If I'd only known that was going to be the last time, I ever saw my favorite 97-year-old grammy I would have washed and kissed her hands and feet thanking her for so many years of unconditional love and service to me and the rest of our family. I loved being part of a large family with an Italian heritage. Italians love life – we love our families, we love preparing food for our family and friends, and eating it together as a family while we chat and share stories.

I loved her with all my heart and still do many years after her death. She was my guardian angel here on Earth.

If it were not for my grandfather and my grandmother's love, I do not think I would be alive and happy today. They were there to help when I was in a suicidal depression when I was 26 while living at their home in Venice, Florida. If it had not been for them, I might have successfully committed suicide or ended up confused in some unfamiliar psychiatric hospital or insane asylum following the betrayal and abandonment of my lover and former massage instructor, Sid...

A grandmother's love is so precious. Now that I have a grandson, I think so far, I am doing OK because he laughs and lights up like a star each time, he sees me.

I got to meet Grammy's eldest sister, Erna, but my memory of her is vague, since she passed away when I was three years old. Her brothers, Larry, Lovey, and Attilio, (nicknamed Tilly) all lived to be octogenarians or into their nineties. Each one was gentle, loving, kind, and had a great sense of humor. They were all delightful male figures in my life even though I only got to see them on occasion while I lived in Staten Island or when I visited Grammy and Pop Pop at their home on Staten Island before they decided to retire in Venice, Florida...

Uncle Tilly was my favorite. I especially loved when he would magically extract whole quarters from my ears. He made me laugh hysterically. I also danced with him as a little girl by standing on his feet while he'd hold me up and move me around the dance floor. Uncle Tilly lived a long, happy life and passed into Spirit when he was ninety-four. I was in my late forties when he finally ascended into heaven. His widow, my aunt Lena, passed away a few years later.

Anna & Henry Otto Olson

Like my mom's parents, my paternal grandparents, Anna and Henry Olson, came over by a ship to Ellis Island with their families to begin new lives in America. Grandpa's family came from Sweden. He was the oldest of eight children, and I don't think his education went much past the eighth grade because he had to work to help support his siblings. Grandpa Olson needed to learn a lucrative trade, so he became an electrician around eighteen years of age.

My grandma, Anna, who, by pure coincidence, also had the last name of Olsen spelled with an e, had parents who brought her and her younger sister over from Denmark. I was given the middle name, Ann, in her honor. Thank goodness all four grandparents chose to raise their families in Staten Island, or I would not be here right now. It was destiny that my parents would meet in New York, where I would eventually be born in Staten Island hospital.

Grandma and Grandpa Olson were completely the opposite types of personalities from Lucy and Fred Vere, who came from a bit wealthier family. While Grandpa Olson worked daily as a union electrician, Grandma was a stay-at-home mom, raising three boys: my Uncle Fred, my dad, Pete, and my Uncle Henry, who was the youngest. Having all boys made them very different types of parents. Much less protective than Grammy and Pop Pop, Grandma and Grandpa loved camping at Montauk Point in Long Island where they went every summer. I had the opportunity to go to Montauk with my parents at least two or three times, and I just loved it! It was so much fun sleeping in our warm sleeping bags under the stars in a big tent and the soft glow of moonlight shining through the tarp, or in the big green canvas tent, or on the beach, after roasting marshmallows and hot dogs over a campfire. Daddy and Grandpa would cook them on the fire, and I would put them in a long bun, and drown them in ketchup and relish. I wasn't crazy about hot dogs, but I loved the taste of ketchup and relish. I still do.

We also sang songs around the campfire. Grandpa Olson could sing great harmonies, because he was a member of the Society for the Preservation and Encouragement of Barbershop Quartet Singing in America (SPEBSQA). I loved hearing him sing old songs, like "Wait 'til the Sun Shines, Nellie", in his clear, resonant baritone voice. He looked so dapper in his red and white striped jacket with three other men, bringing joy to audience members wherever they performed. I bet that is how I learned to harmonize at a very young age.

I loved swimming in the large waves of the ocean at Montauk. My parents brought our floats and surf boards, and sometimes we'd get to use Daddy's mask and flippers. I was not a very strong swimmer at ten years old, but I could tread water and stay afloat as early as seven because daddy taught me how to do the side stroke, the back stroke, and the crawl in our four-and-a-half-foot, above-ground back-yard pool.

"She's a little water rat," Dad and both my grandfathers often remarked. I also loved walking along the beach picking up shells, stones, and other objects of interest, while chasing and running from the cool tide as it came in to shore. Once I found a neat-looking brown helmet shaped thing with a tail that I brought back to my parents. Daddy said "It's a dead horseshoe crab, but you have to throw it back into the water, because it has a horrible stench." I guess I did not notice the smell, in my excitement finding this large, interesting looking crustacean. I had curiosity about everything I found along the beach, from the time I was little. I carried a pail or large clear glass jar in which to carry all my little treasures which I'd bring back home with me.

Lack of money never stopped Grandma and Grandpa from giving us a great time. It seemed they always had fun and knew how to enjoy themselves with little or no big agendas. I remember always having fun with Grandma Olson, who never seemed to worry. Unlike Grammy Vere, who was protective of me, and always had me under close watch, Grandma let me do a few things all by myself. She gave me a nickel or a dime to go into a small store with her to buy a pack of Juicy Fruit or Wrigley's spearmint gum. She also trusted me enough to give me her house key when we got off the train in Staten Island not far from their apartment, and let me sprint down the tree-lined street in front of her, to go into the vestibule and open her apartment door all by myself. I loved that she let me feel more independent than both my mom and Grammy did, and that she trusted me to take some responsibility. The only money I ever got from my mom and dad was my weekly allowance which usually went into my bank account to accrue interest or quarters from the tooth fairy when I lost my baby teeth. I rarely got to go anywhere out of my home to spend these quarters without my mom accompanying me, and she always paid for everything. I had no idea of the value of money because my dad and mom paid for everything for me, and I was very spoiled and ignorant about money. This hurt me in a way, because I never learned the value of money, and even in school nothing was taught about how to balance a check book. Just basic mathematics. I never wanted to grow up and leave school because It meant I'd have to get a job and work for my own living—eek! I still feel that way. Having a lot of money is just not that important to me. It is just a means to an end. I'd rather be singing, dancing, gardening, or spending time outdoors with my friends or grandson in nice weather. I do, however, still take a massage or foot reflexology client every now and then for extra pocket money.

Like Pop Pop and Grammy, Grandma and Grandpa loved music, classical and opera, in particular. Grandma told me they went to the opera on a regular basis, but because they could not afford the seats, they often chose to stand in the back of the balcony, where you could watch and listen for free if there was room. My dad acquired their love for all the Verdi and Puccini operas which he would play for me, on albums at home. Eventually, when I was sixteen, he would take me to the Metropolitan Opera House to see "Carmen", my first opera.

While still living in Staten Island, Henry and Anna vacationed in Florida several times to visit Uncle Henry, Aunt Jerry, and their four boys, my cousins, David, Danny, Kenny, and Andrew who all lived in Saint Petersburg. After a few years they decided to move south to a mobile home park called Bay Indies in Venice, Florida, about a half hour, by car, south of Sarasota, on the west coast not far from the beautiful Gulf of Mexico. My dad's youngest brother, Henry, loved living in St. Petersburg, Florida, just south of Tampa, and Grandma and Grandpa would visit Uncle Henry, Aunt Jerry, and their four young boys a few times per year. Living in Florida was a more relaxed lifestyle for the seniors and probably a bit cheaper than living in Staten Island. My dad and mom were invited by Grandma and Grandpa Olson to visit them during our Christmas and summer vacations. At Christmas we usually flew down to Florida.

But even more fun were the times we'd travel by car during summer vacations. Mom and Dad would load us three kids into their Ford station wagon, chock full of all our luggage on top tied down in the luggage rack, In the car we stocked fruit juices, water, fruit, nuts, and other snacks. They'd put the back seats down, line the entire back of the car with down comforters, blankets, and pillows to make it softer and comfier, so we could fall asleep while they took turns driving, from around 8 PM, straight through the night, until the dawn woke us, and we'd take a break to stop and eat a hearty breakfast of eggs, bacon, sausage, and orange juice, and to fill the gas-tank. It was such a fun adventure, my brothers and I did not mind that it took about twenty-five hours straight to drive to Venice, including all the stops for bathroom breaks, food, and gasoline. We rarely stayed overnight in a hotel. We were so excited about seeing our grandparents that we just wanted to get there ASAP.

We would play word games like "G-H-O-S-T" to pass the time. And we'd see who could find the most different out-of-state license plates, and play other games we'd make up on the spot.

Visiting Grandma and Grandpa was fun because they'd take us down to Manasota Key Beach where the television star from Laugh-In, Dan Rowan, had a home, or Venice Beach, where we'd sunbathe, swim in the Gulf of Mexico, and look for shells and sharks' teeth. Once, we even went deep sea fishing on a chartered boat. We kid never caught anything, but it was fun watching the adults catch big fish. Usually, they would catch grouper. I just loved getting a tan or sunburn being on the water for so many hours.

And if Grandpa or Daddy caught a fish, they'd bring it home so Grandma could clean it and then we'd eat it for supper. It would be so much fun to be with Grandma and Pop because neither of them cared if we got dirty, so I could just be my tomboy self, and have a great time. I was so glad that Grandma and Grandpa were not immaculate and fussy about keeping their house clean, like my mom and Grammy. Grandma did not care if we got some sand from the beach on her floor or carpet, and Grandpa never worried about anything, so we never felt afraid of just being ourselves.

Pop always said, "All you have to worry about is, if you are sick or healthy. If you are healthy, there's nothing to worry about. If you are sick, all you have to worry about is, whether you live, or you die. If you live, you have nothing to worry about. If you die, all you have to worry about is, whether you are going to heaven, or hell. If you are going to heaven, you have nothing to worry about. And if you are going to hell, you'll be so busy shaking hands with all your friends, you won't have time to worry!"

Grandma and Grandpa considered themselves atheists or agnostics, but they were both such loving, kind, and happy people, I don't think God cared.

All four of my grandparents got along very well and after visiting Anna and Henry a few times in Venice Lucy and Fred decided to have a home built there too. It took a couple of years, but eventually their home was built in a very nice neighborhood in Venice, and Grammy and Pop Pop rented a furnished house toward the end while the new home was close to being finished. Henry and Anna, and Lucy and Fred enjoyed each other's company so much that they would go on several cruises and other vacations together. I thought that was really cool. It was so neat that both my parents' parents loved each other's' company, especial since some parent's in-law do not get along at all and there might be some fighting, arguing, or gossiping.

Like Grammy, Pop Pop, and his wife, Anna, Henry Otto Olson, was fun loving, happy, and kind. I'm so blessed that all four of my grandparents placed the importance of family first. So, my brothers, step-sisters, stepbrother, and I all got the benefits of their kindness and innate goodness.

Pop Pop used to hum tunes all the time even though he was not much of a singer. Pop Pop (Fred

Vere) had a deep appreciation for all types of music even though Grandpa Olson had the better, more confident singing voice.

After Grandpa moved to Florida, he joined the Venice chapter of SPEBSQA. Grandpa was a great writer as well and he'd write little anecdotes and edit the barbershop quartet singers' newsletter. Grandma Olson wrote funny poems about the family and enclosed them in the letters Grandpa would send me. Henry and Anna were both great letter writers, and once the audiotape machine was invented, I'd get tapes from both of them every week or so when I was a teenager and all the way into my twenties. I always looked forward to getting regular letters and cassette tapes from them filled with all sorts of anecdotes, songs, and tidbits about their fun, exciting, but relaxed lives in Florida. Whenever we left to return home after our vacation, Grandpa always had tears in his eyes. He was a really loving softy emotionally who would sing in nursing homes and pick the elderly ladies in wheelchairs up out of their seats to dance with him.

I recall playing Scrabble with Grandma and Grandpa from the time I was twelve or thirteen. Grandma Anna was always a great player even though she did not even finish grade school in Denmark. She had a fantastic vocabulary, loved to read, wrote me newsy letters right up until a year before she died. She and Grandpa loved to play bridge, poker with my grandparents, parents, and us kids around Grammy Vere's large formal dining room table when we'd come down to Florida to visit them all over the holidays, both at Christmas and sometimes over Easter vacation, or for ten or more days over summer vacation. Grandpa and Grandma loved taking us to Venice or Nokomis Beaches to pick up shells and sharks' teeth after a thunderstorm. I remember grandma feeding all the feral kittens that made their home in her and Grandpa's backyard at Bay Indies Mobile Home Park in Venice, Grandpa did not have the same love of cats that Grandma had, so he would not let any of the wild cats come inside their mobile home. Grandma bought lots of Friskies canned food and fed them all outside.

They also lived near Alligator Creek where we would tie up large pieces of chicken breast with long pieces of white string and lure crabs slowly down into the creek in order to catch them and eat them at Grammy and Pop Pop's house. It was one of the most fun things I remember doing as a kid.

I felt great delight when I swept the crab up in my net, but hearing the crabs squeal with fright before getting cooked in a pot of hot boiling water made me squeamish, and I felt terrible then, but the crabs sure tasted delicious—especially dipped in melted drawn butter.

One difference between Lucy and Anna was that Grandma Olson, though quite a bit overweight, felt very sexy and confident about herself as a woman. She had Grandpa Olson wrapped around her finger, and he would do almost anything for her, including ironing. They were very affectionate with each other. I'd never seen Pop Pop kiss Grammy on the lips, and they, in fact, slept in two separate twin beds while living in Florida. Grammy told me that after she had to get a hysterectomy, Pop Pop had no interest in her as a woman, and never even kissed her on the lips anymore. What a shame.

Grandma Olson, on the other hand, would not put up with any slacking off in the sex department. Once, when Grandpa Olson had to get prostate surgery, he was told to rest for a while, and I heard from my mom that Grandma threatened him during this time, "Henry, you'd better get yourself together soon, or I will have to look for another man! "At least, that's what she told my mother. They apparently had a happy, healthy sex life, and Grandpa Olson adored her. Pop Pop Vere was jealous and had a lot of insecurities, whereas Grandma and Grandpa did not seem to have any issues that stopped them from being intimate and loving toward one another – at least in our presence.

My favorite things about Grandma, besides the fact that she adored me, was that she was a very earthy lady who loved sex, having fun in life, and she felt so confident about herself that she never worked too hard; she allowed Grandpa to serve her, drive her everywhere, do some of the cooking, help raise her three boys, take her on cruises, camping, and just relax and enjoy life.

Grandpa and Grandma had a healthy, active sex life even after they were retired, from what Grandma told me. After Grandma died from a brain tumor, in her early seventies, all the old widows were chasing Grandpa. He shared with me that he got so confused having so many lunch dates he could not keep them all straight, so eventually he settled down with one nice lady, Laura Pretorius, in Bay Indies, but he never married again.

My paternal grandma, Anna, was the first of my four grandparents to die. I was told by my Grandpa Olson while I was in New Jersey living with my boyfriend, Greg, in Hackensack, NJ. She died in the hospital pretty suddenly in 1976, so I did not have the chance to tell her how much she meant to me or to say good-bye. Grandpa Olson told me she was having delusions or hallucinations about me being one of the nurses coming to tend to her. Who knows what the Divine Mystery has us do in our dreams? I would not be surprised if I did visit her during my sleep while in the astral plane. When she died, Grandpa had her cremated, and because they were atheists I cannot remember if there had even been a memorial or funeral service for her, so there was no real closure for me. I loved the fact that Grandma loved most people, never gossiped, and just enjoyed her life with Grandpa to the fullest. She was an inspiration to me because she was her authentic self and never did anything for anyone's' approval except her own self. She was raised in a natural way by her parents, and I liked that grandma and Grandpa never worried much about money, but they still enjoyed life to the fullest. I suppose Grandpa had a good pension, having been a union electrician for Local three in Staten Island for many years before he retired. Like my father, Grandpa Olson worked very hard to care for his family.

Grandpa Olson died before Grammy Vere. Before he passed away Uncle Henry, the youngest of the three boys, who lived nearby in St. Petersburg, took away his car because he was beginning to have car accidents. I got several more letters from Grandpa Olson even after my dad and I became estranged for a while after I wrote the article describing our unnatural incestuous relationship and mental illness while I was hospitalized at the Carrier Clinic. I sent this article out to many of the relatives. Grandpa admitted it must have been hard on both of us to not talk to one another.

Because Grandpa was an atheist, like Grandma, when he died, my dad called me to tell me, but there was no mention of a funeral or memorial service that I can recall, so all I knew was that he died at 91 years old. I have no idea what from.

To this day I miss and still love all of my grandparents, and I believe their loving kindness and different qualities helped shape who I have become today.

In my memory, I can still feel the cold waves on my skin when I'd go swimming up at Montauk Point with my dad and Grandpa Olson. I loved coming out of the cool ocean into the hot summer sun, having Grandpa or Daddy dry me off, then lying on the sandy beach with the sun caressing my face. Camping in the large tent's mom, dad, and Grandpa put together, roasting marshmallows over the campfire, and having the adults make us food over the fire or Grandma Olson making a delicious ham or turkey sandwich with lots of mayonnaise, salt, lettuce and tomato for our lunch.

My mom hated camping because she hated getting dirty or sand in her clothes and shoes, but we, kids just loved it. Especially if we sang songs in the early evenings around the campfire like "Michael Row the Boat Ashore", "Where have all the Flowers Gone", "He's got the Whole World in His Hands" and other folk songs. We also sang some songs by the Kingston Trio, which was one of my dad's favorite groups.

GROWING UP WITH FATHER

I grew up with a father who was not religious, but was very open to new ideas and checking out different systems of thought. Though his parents considered themselves atheists, my dad said he was agnostic, but he believed in a Prime Mover that created the universe. After being disillusioned by the conventional religions he checked out while in college, he began to read a lot of New Age material that came out at the time.

I remember him having a book about the healer and trance channel, Edgar Cayce, called *The Sleeping Prophet*, by Jess Stearn. He also read some of the Seth material channeled through Jane Roberts. Dad was the one who made me question the concepts of sin and hell that were such core beliefs of Catholicism, the religion my mother was raising me to follow. As a teenager, I read a few of these books which greatly interested me and sparked my interest in spiritualism, as well as the idea of reincarnation and the continuance of the soul after the change called death.

My father had me wondering why people like Pygmies in Africa who were not baptized and had no knowledge of Christianity were destined to go to hell, according to the Catholics. At least that is what the nuns taught me in catechism, on Sundays before church. I'd ask my mother why this was a sin, but she couldn't answer the question. It didn't seem fair to me that people who weren't baptized or who practiced faiths other than Christianity were excluded from a happy afterlife. Or worse were destined to live in a fiery hellish place. I knew in my heart that a just, loving God would never punish his own innocent children made in His image. Even my young mind was certain of that truth.

As most daughters do, I adored my father. I saw him as perfect in every way—as my knight in shining armor, as someone who would defend me in the world as well as protect me from the psychological abuse and rage of my mother. I believe the adoration was mutual. I was the firstborn child as well as the first female grandchild, so as a baby and toddler, I was treated pretty much like a princess. I remember being showered with attention and affection by my parents and grandparents in my early years, and except for difficult teen years, the love and care continued on into adulthood.

Sometimes, after dinner, dad would show us home movies of himself walking on the catwalks of the Verrazano Narrows Bridge where he was a foreman electrician, putting up the lights on the span which connected Brooklyn to Staten Island.

"Today one of the guys nearly fell off the catwalk while putting up the electric lights." he shared one day with mom. There actually were several men who were killed from falls while working on that job. My dad also had photos and slides of the dangerous catwalks and his men working with white hard hats on their heads for protection.

As a child, I did not realize how fortunate I was to have so many material blessings. My father worked very hard to provide for his family, also working overtime as an electrician on Staten Island, so that we could indulge in "the good life". Daddy had a long commute from our house in Holmdel, New Jersey to his jobs, which were usually in Manhattan or another New York borough. He'd be up with my mom at 5:30 AM. to wash, dress, and have breakfast and wouldn't arrive home until 6 PM or later. It was a long workday for him, and he usually came home feeling enervated.

The men who worked for my father had to create long, dangerous, teetering catwalks before they could even begin the task of putting up hundreds of lights just for the men who worked on this very dangerous project, beginning about 8:30 AM just after the sun had risen. As foreman, Dad had to get there early before his workmen. He confided in me, his precious 12-year-old princess, "Honey, I hate being the boss on this job because it means I am responsible for the lives of all of my workers – plus making sure the job gets done right. It's a lot of responsibility, so I feel so much stress when I get to work, and while driving there. I listen to a lot of wonderful music en route to my job for the 90-minute commute in order to distract and relax me".

The Electrician's Picnic

One very fond memory I have of my dad is of being with him, his father, mother, and other relatives and friends at the electrician's picnic every year. My Grandma and Grandpa Olson would attend because Grandpa was also a union electrician like my dad. My parents must have invited nearly all the relatives in both our families because I remember almost all my aunts, uncles, and cousins being there as well as my four grandparents. Or maybe most of the Olsons were all electricians in Staten Island and Brooklyn.

It was great being the only granddaughter on my dad's side because I received so much love and attention. Daddy and Grandpa would pick me up like a little rag doll and throw me several feet up into the air and catch me on the way down while I screamed with delight. Then Grandpa would hold me by my ankles and swing me around in circles while my mom and Grammy gasped, their hearts skipping a few beats.

Mom and Grammy tended to worry that I might be hurt at such times, or while hanging upside down from the monkey bars in the playground. But I never was. Fear never even crossed my mind. I felt exhilarated and laughed with glee while being tossed around, and getting a bit dizzy. Besides, I believed that my guardian angels were always watching over me. And God always protected me.

One of my favorite games at the picnic was the egg toss. The adults didn't let me play until I got older, but until I reached about seven years old, I loved watching my parents and grandparents miss or break the eggs while catching them getting their hands and clothes covered with the drippy, gooey yellow yokes. I also loved whacking the paddle ball, trying to wiggle the hula hoop more than a few times around my mostly underdeveloped hips, and playing relay races. In Staten Island, it was illegal to buy fireworks, so the children often got treats of sparklers which were just as awesome and exciting to me as the scary, cacophonous booms of cherry bombs and rainbow-colored sprays of Roman candles the adults set off. A brief show of amateur pyrotechnics put the final dazzle on a fun filled day for all the children.

By that time, I was ready to be lifted by my dad's strong arms, carried to our cream-colored Volkswagen Beetle, and gently placed in the well, where I'd snooze comfortably without a care on soft pillows and a fluffy comforter for the duration of the drive back to our home in Holmdel, New

Jersey. I have sweet memories of my dad lifting me up and carrying me to bed after I'd fallen asleep at the drive-in movie or coming home late from some place far away, like Staten Island.

My father loved to play games too. When my first brother, Peter, who was born three years after me, was old enough to participate, we would play "Monster" in the living room after dinner. Pete and I would stay in the kitchen, while my dad hid somewhere in the dark living room. Pete and I would gradually venture out to the dining room, and within seconds my father would jump out from some dark, hidden corner, and pounce on both of us. We would both get wrestled to the ground and tickled until we could no longer stand it. Then dad would be a "horsey" for us and we'd both get on top of his back while he crawled around on all fours. One of my favorite games was when my dad would lay on his stomach, bend his legs so that his slippered feet made a stable platform for us to place our tummies upon; then he would move his legs around in circles so he could give us a ride. He created so much fun and laughter for us.

While we were having a great time playing, my mother was slaving away in the kitchen washing dishes, pots and pans, and shining the stove.

Arts and Music

My father was a lover of the arts. He loved music of all kinds. He played all his favorite operas and even took me to the Metropolitan Opera House and the New York State Theater to see La Boheme, Carmen, and La Traviata as a teenager.

Besides opera, Dad loved Bach, Beethoven, Tchaikovsky, and some other classical composers, so he fostered in me an appreciation for classical music too. But my dad's favorite was music from Broadway shows. He would get the old 33 RPM long playing records. He also bought eight track tapes of whatever Broadway shows he would see when eight tracks became popular though their presence was rather ephemeral once the audiocassette and later the CD was invented. I had the opportunity to familiarize myself with, and to come to love, both the music and lyrics of at least eight Broadway shows. I remember singing along with the songs of "L'll Abner" and "How to Succeed in Business Without Really Trying" with Robert Morse. My all-time favorites were the Rogers and Hammerstein musicals, "Oklahoma" and "Carousel" with Shirley Jones and Lyle MacRae. I know each and every song by heart. We listened to the music from "Funny Girl" with Barbra Streisand, and got to see her movie with Omar Sharif. Barbra was my idol, and I'd listen to her early albums for hours easily memorizing all the lyrics and practicing singing along with her. I wished I could have seen her in a Broadway musical, but I was too young at the time. Maybe one day I will have a chance to meet her or watch her perform live. One never knows what the Divine Mystery has in store for us, does one?

Another all-time favorite musical is "Fiddler on the Roof" with Zero Mostel. I loved singing, "Matchmaker, matchmaker, make me a match. Find me a find. Catch me a catch", etc., and especially "If I were a rich man..."

The very first musical I remember going to see with my parents and grandparents was when I was seventeen years old and very impressionable. It was the unconventional and fun, flower powered, hippie happening "Hair", complete with great peace songs, frontal nudity, and lots of fun lyrics like those of the song about Frank Mills. I'd love to have played a role in "Hair" in a community theater setting. The title song, "Hair", and the song, "Easy to Be Hard", were later popularized by the Cowsills and Three Dog Night.

Following that musical, I was privileged to see Tim Rice and Andrew Lloyd Webber's, "Jesus Christ Superstar". I saw that with my parents and Grandma and Grandpa Olson. I learned and knew every song by heart, because my dad played the eight-track tape in the car a lot before we went to see the actual live show.

I think "Jesus Christ Superstar" was the first show my dad brought the whole family to see. I'll never forget being dazzled by all the talented actors, but in particular, I was impressed by Ben Vereen with his energetic jazz dancing and poignant singing playing the character of Judas [2]. The originality of the costumes, staging, unforgettable music of Andrew Lloyd Weber and imaginative lyrics of Tim Rice awed me. Dad played the tape in our silver Electra convertible with the red leather interior, power windows and locks, and cruise control. It would be the car that my dad would use to teach me how to drive at seventeen years old. It was like driving a monster bus! I was so nervous when I first learned to drive it that I was lucky I did not crash into anything. I was so scared and uncomfortable driving in the beginning that during my first driving test, I failed turning. Can you believe it? Now I'm an old pro, but it's funny to think that I failed to pass the exam twice before I ever got my license finally at eighteen years old. I guess if at first if you don't succeed, it's important to be persistent, and to try again until you achieve what you set out to do.

Those were some of my happiest times as a child – being with my family, my hair blowing in the wind, listening and singing great music while my dad or mom was driving the family somewhere – usually up to our resort home in the Poconos.

My father also had a few comics' albums like Alan Sherman and Tom Lehrer whose songs I found hilarious. My favorite was "Vatican Rag" by Tom Lehrer.. The first stanza goes, "First you get down on your knees. Fiddle with your rosaries. Bow your head in great respect and genuflect, genuflect, genuflect." It's a hilarious parody of Catholicism. I remember all the lyrics to this day because it makes me laugh so hard.

Another favorite musical group of dads was The Kingston Trio. One of his favorite songs by them is called "Scarlet Ribbons" He sometimes sang it as a lullaby to me at night when he tucked me in to bed. The song is about a father's frustrations at not being able to fulfill his daughter's prayer to have some scarlet ribbons for her hair. After searching high and low and not finding any scarlet ribbons they mysteriously appear on his child's bed the next time he goes to check in on her. I saw this song as evidence of how much he loved me and wanted to provide me with everything that I desired. The song also shows a belief in the mysterious power of prayer and miracles.

I still remember the lyrics to all these songs.

Play

My dad loved to swim. His parents brought him up swimming in the great ocean waves at Montauk Point on Long Island where they would camp in summer. So, dad put up a four foot above ground pool in our back yard. He taught me how to swim and dive, and to hold my breath under water. He would stand me on his shoulders, and I would balance precariously and then fall laughing into the

---

2   I would see Ben Vereen again in a play at the McCarter Theater in Princeton, and have a chance there to meet him in person. Years later, in 2013, my beau, Gary, would take me to see him at the Bristol Riverside Theater in Pennsylvania..

water. I became an excellent swimmer because of my dad's love and patience in teaching me how to float, the breaststroke, sidestroke, and the crawl. Mom taught me the backstroke because it was the only one, she knew except the doggy paddle, but she was great at floating.

My dad loved to play so much that eventually we would purchase a "Rondette" (round house) at Gold Key Lake in the Poconos ten miles from Milford, Pennsylvania. We would drive out most week-ends after school and work were over on a Friday night, and spend spring break and summer vacations there.

Dad bought and created some toys and other playthings for us to enjoy while we were there. My brother, Pete, and I had fun pushing one another on a tire swing hanging from a tree. Dad also rigged up a long rope between two trees with a pulley. We'd slide fifty feet across and down toward the road on a tree branch swing on wheels and pulleys from one end of the rope to the other. That was one of the scarier rides. It is similar to the swing line ride they offer these days at some resorts. Having the use of only one arm now I am no longer willing to try this ride. I do not even like going on roller coasters anymore, though, as a child, my dad took me and my brothers regularly to fairs where we would ride the kiddie coasters and later on, the scary adult roller coasters.

He also bought us a snowmobile to use in the winter and a ten-foot red and white catamaran to sail upon in the summer. Both these activities were fun and exhilarating to Pete and me. I was too young to drive the snowmobile by myself, but I'd hop on the back and dad would give me a ride that left me breathless while I'd hold on for dear life to his waist.

We also went sledding, tobogganing, and ice skating during the winter months. As a child I delighted in big snowstorms. Now that I'm an adult and am responsible for cleaning the car and driving in the ice and snow I've lost a bit of the excitement I had as a child when we got over a foot of snow and we got to stay home from school. During snow days my brother and our friends had an exhilarating time sledding down the large hill near our school, called Indian Hill.

When I was fifteen, my dad taught me how to unwrap the sail of our catamaran, push it out into the lake, catch a breeze blowing toward shore and sail out onto the usually placid lake. I learned how to tack and come about, and how to just relax lengthwise on the canvas when the wind was still. My favorite time to sail, though, was when the wind was very brisk. I'd stand on the pontoons while hanging on to the aluminum side pole with the sail in my opposite hand. I'd lean way out over the water practically touching it with my back. Sometimes I'd let the boat capsize – just for the fun of it – when there were not too many other boats on the lake. I had a crush on the lifeguard, Charley, so I could not wait for him to come out to rescue me even though I knew I could write the boat if I really wanted to. It was more fun to pretend I was stuck and needed rescuing.

My dad didn't attend anything I was in that I can remember except my senior musical, "The King and I", after my parents were divorced and I managed to land the leading role of Anna. He was either too tired or just couldn't be bothered, I guess. My mom, on the other hand, always felt it was her duty to attend all of our events and make us feel as if we were talented and had done a great job.

THE BEGINNING OF ABUSE

Though the emotional closeness I felt for my dad as a child was very special, when I reached puberty his interest in my developing body got out of hand. My family was pretty comfortable with nudity in the bathroom when I was young, and at some point, I noticed my dad was commenting on the size of my large behind playfully teasing me and calling me "Crisco". His playful pats on my buttocks eventually turned into fondling my breasts from underneath my nightie when I'd go into his bed to wake him up for breakfast late on a Sunday morning. It was embarrassing to me. Too embarrassing for me even to speak about with him. Usually, I would just giggle and say, "Stop daddy." I suppose that there was a part of me was flattered that he noticed me and thought I was attractive.

As a little girl I always dreamed I'd "marry" my father or someone just like him. Then as a young teenager I felt an attraction for my dad and wanted him to notice me. I remember brushing my long hair out on my pillow so that he would think I was beautiful when he came in to tuck me in to bed at eight or nine o'clock in the evening.

I used to have a recurring fantasy from the time I was about eleven. In the "dream" a wicked, ugly witch kidnapped me and held me hostage in a dark cellar. There were several older boys and a man there. I was stripped of my clothes and lay naked in a large glass case. When the witch decided to go out for a while, she warned the boys that none of them are to touch or disturb me in any way. But once she'd gone, the oldest and bravest boy, who found me ravishingly beautiful, could not control himself. He lifted the lid while I was sleeping and began to fondle and stroke me. The touching woke me from my sleep, but I did not speak because I found the sensations so pleasurable. Wow-it almost sounds a lot like the fairy tale, Sleeping Beauty, doesn't it? This fantasy became the reality I would create with my father several years after I first began having these "dreams".

I subconsciously used my sexual energy to attract my father. I was unaware of what I was doing and confused sexual expression with love. Once I attracted him, however, I felt confused and conflicted and knew in my heart that this kind of closeness with my father was inappropriate. I felt very guilty, and the guilt stayed with me for years.

In fact, had the experience not been such a societal taboo, ultimately it was a very pleasurable one, one in which I felt very happy and a loving connection to my dad as well as my Self. In certain cultures, and tribes around the world it is considered normal and healthy for the son to have his first sexual experience with his mother and for the father to teach his daughters about sex and lovemaking. It is a shame that most of our societies cannot be more open about sex. We could talk about it in schools and at home, and in this way, we could free ourselves from all the negative conditioning and judgments surrounding sexual expression.

After being in incest groups and therapy I came to realize that I was not "responsible" for the incest. I think it is normal and healthy for most young girls coming into puberty to want their fathers to find them attractive, sensuous beings. My dad was the adult and should have respected the natural societal boundaries that exist in a parent/child relationship. He really should have known better, but he still followed his lustful urge to know me in a more intimate way. I believe he thought he was making me feel good, and it is true that physically I was extremely excited and enjoyed the new sensations. It was just a strange experience to me that I was feeling this kind of sensuous and sexual pleasure with my own father. He was my mom's husband, for goodness's sake! He was the man who was supposed to protect and care for me. I should not need protection from my father.

Eventually my dad became even more intimate with me, especially when he would tuck me into bed at night. What began as affectionate backstroking progressed into fondling my genitals from behind. I felt so embarrassed and confused that I couldn't confront him directly face to face in order to make him stop. For some reason I just couldn't or wouldn't be assertive and say, "No, don't touch me please. It feels good, but it does not feel right in my heart. I am ashamed and embarrassed that you want to touch me this way." What was worse was the guilt I felt because I enjoyed the pleasurable sensations that were new to me coming from a hand other than my own. Other than masturbating myself and experimenting with my girlfriends when I was a child I had never been touched "down there" before. At least not by a person of the opposite sex. I was only fourteen, and the extent of my sexual experience with boys was making out and French kissing.

Our physical bonding felt unnatural, awkward, and created so much confusion and guilt within me. My relationship with my father or my mother would never be the same. From that point on, though I loved my father, my sense of trust as well as my innocence was gone.

The intimacy I shared with my dad, including his abandonment a year later, as well as the secrecy surrounding it, would proceed to influence all my relationships with men in a negative way for most of my life. Out of guilt, shame, and embarrassment I had made experiencing sexual pleasure bad and wrong for me. I wouldn't allow myself to trust a man or to get too close for fear that I'd become vulnerable, would get hurt, and feel used, and abandoned yet again.

Not being able to talk about what happened was frustrating and contributed to my confusion and shame. I was asked to repress my feelings, thoughts, and emotions about something that had a profound impact on me as a growing adolescent. Being unable to express the original sadness, guilt, and confusion would cause me to shut down when a present-day experience of abandonment would trigger the original trauma of my dad's abandonment. I'd often go into a depression after being with many men who would just use me for sex or were so shallow that they only really wanted to be with me because my physical beauty. I would choose lots of men when I was single who had no idea of the deep, sensitive, intelligent person I was. Many would love me and leave me, and due to this first experience I suppose I did not trust men in general and often made poor choices when choosing men to date. So, until I turned twenty-five, I did a sexual dance in which I enticed all men like crazy: but once they got close and there was a commitment, I'd turn off all my feeling in my genitals giving myself permission to leave and move on to the next because I was no longer turned on or satisfied sexually. Sometimes the only way I could feel truly turned on and excited was if there was some kind of taboo in my relationships with men.

For example, I'd create triangle relationships in which I'd become involved sexually with a married man or the partner of a friend. Having a relationship with someone whom was already involved or dating many men simultaneously seemed much "safer" than allowing myself to become truly committed and vulnerable to one emotionally available partner. A present-day event like a man leaving me for another woman or just deciding it wouldn't work out would always seem to bring up the unresolved pain and anger surrounding the original molestation and abandonment.

Subconsciously, I'd affirmed that men just wanted me for my body and couldn't be trusted. So, this is what I often created as a reality in my relationships. Men would use me for sex or love me and leave. I saw this as a personal rejection, and I'd usually become depressed, fearful, anxious, and angry.

Thank God my dad never forced me to submit to oral sex or intercourse the way some men do with innocent children. I know several women who have had this experience, and it is very difficult to overcome. They often had to "dissociate" from their bodies consciously blanking out what happened just to survive the trauma. When the subconscious memories begin to resurface as an adult the survivors of severe physical or sexual abuse experience such fear and terror that they think they may be going insane when they begin to "see" and remember these past traumas buried in the subconscious mind. I once saw the movie, "Mystic River", by Clint Eastwood, and it is a very good example of how devastating the effects of child abuse are. I recommend this movie if you want to learn more about sexual abuse and the toxic shame and problems it causes later in life.

I even had my first orgasm with a man by my father's hand though he was not aware of it at the time. I fell asleep in my bed while we were watching television together. When I woke up his finger was rubbing me in the middle of my vagina up and down. When I woke up, I was surprised, but I was so excited that I kept very quiet and still and in moments I climaxed.

I felt so guilty afterward, and the shame would stay with me for years afterward. Though the experience was physically pleasurable, my Catholic upbringing had taught me to feel shame about my body. And culturally I was conditioned to think of incest as one of the worst sins in the world. One day my mother discovered me after I'd masturbated, but before I had the chance to wash my hands. When she smelled the scent of my genitals on my hand, she admonished me by saying, "You don't touch yourself down there, do you? Don't you know that's a sin?"

I lied and said I didn't masturbate, but her own shame about her body was not going to keep me from enjoying myself. After all, it was my body, and I certainly wasn't hurting anyone. But being touched by my father was such a taboo that I did feel very guilty and "bad" about it. Six months after the secretive, private touching dad fell in love with my step-mom and the fondling ceased. He came into my bedroom one Sunday afternoon to tell me he was very sorry about it. He did not understand why it happened and he regretted what he'd done. He asked me not to tell my mother or anyone because she might divorce him if she knew. So, I never mentioned what had transpired between us to her. I confided in my boyfriend and eventually I would tell two of my stepsisters.

My dad is a very private person, and he became very hurt and angry when I exposed our past in tan article written while I was hospitalized for manic depression at the Carrier Clinic in May of 1988.

My father and stepmother chose to ostracize me after reading this information,

Dealing with their ostracism during the holidays was emotionally challenging for me, but now I've come to accept it as their choice and their loss. I know it is because of their fear and inability to confront the truth of what happened that it was easier for them to pretend I did not exist and "it" never happened. When confronted by my mom back in 1981, dad lied about the incest, so I've no doubt he also lied to his wife, my step-mom, just to save face. She is a very proper, loving, conventional, practicing Catholic, and I'm sure just the thought of my dad and I being intimate is something that frightens, embarrasses, and threatens her. It is not my intent to do any of those things. It is only my intent to share my story and personal wisdom I've gleaned through my experiences growing up as a child and adolescent, into a healthy adult woman who has finally come to love herself unconditionally, and to live without shame and guilt completely. I do not experience myself as a victim anymore, and I realize I chose those childhood experiences with all three of my parents for my own soul growth. I am still evolving sexually as a woman and a dakhini priestess of love and ecstasy through the study and practice of tantric sex and ritual. Guilt is a useless, futile past time fraught with ignorance of the Truth of Who you really are. These judgmental ideas and thoughts originated in the time of the Ancients when the fearful religious patriarchy took over power from the goddesses and priestesses that were loving and caring for the Earth Mother with great skill, compassion, and industry. The original indigenous cultures celebrated their connection to the Earth Mother and worshiped her through ritual, feasting, song, dance, and celebration. The Judeo-Christian domination of the males started long before the domination of Roman Catholic Church and probably goes way back before recorded history. Women were the first ones to honor the God and Goddess within. We were the original priests, priestesses, sorcerers, prophets, healers, wiccans, and wise Counselors. It was out of our very bodies that men and women were born, and for this we deserve a place of high honor and respect.

In a sense I had become a scapegoat, and I was the one who was blamed for something that was not even my fault. And my dad and stepmother refused to even meet Sky until she turned ten years old when they just happened to meet her at one of my brothers, Peter's, family parties.

What upset me was that my step-siblings and even my own brother protected my father throughout the years, but not one ever had the guts or desire to stand up for me. My stepbrother did not invite me to his wedding. And I'd never met any of my nieces and nephews until recently at my brother's home. They were all "enablers" of the deep dark family secret.

My brother, Pete, who is a devout Christian, never once tried to mediate throughout all the years except on my father's behalf. Sky and I were ostracized. What was worse, Peter volunteered every year to take Gabriel and Kyrie away from me and my mom after Christmas brunch to bring them to the home of my dad or to one of my stepsister's Christmas dinner celebrations. I was deliberately not invited.

We finally had a successful, joyous meeting in June of 2000, and they adored Sky upon their first meeting. However, right before Christmas my brother informed me that though my other two children, Kyrie and Gabriel, were invited as they had been every year since their births, Sky and I were still unwelcoming to celebrate Christmas with them. I had hoped that Sky and I would be included in the Christmas celebration after that loving, successful reunion meeting with my dad and step-mom at my former sister-in-law, Julie's, 50th, birthday celebration. It was the first time they met my youngest daughter. Two of my stepsisters just met Sky for the first time in September at my brother's wedding. Eleven years had passed since her birth, but since everyone chose to ostracize me, they also never acknowledged their granddaughter or niece's birth, either, for the first eleven years of her life. My brother said, "Joan still can't forgive you for what you did". I'm still trying to figure out what I did that I needed to be forgiven for.

During the challenging 2000 Christmas season I wrote the poem "They Kept her in the Closet" in anger and frustration about how badly it felt to be ostracized and misunderstood.[3]

It had been easier for everyone in the family except my mother and brothers to ignore me and pretend I don't exist. Maybe they thought I must be a crazy liar because of my mental illness and suicide attempts. If they accept me into their lives, then they will all have to face the truth of what actually happened. So, it is easier to ostracize me and keep me in the closet along with the family's shameful little secrets. Another uncomfortable truth for the family to look at, though it has never been a secret, is that my step-mom was one of my mom's dearest friends, and she and my dad had a clandestine affair following the death of her first husband, Walter. My mother was deeply hurt and angry for years following the divorce. It all turned out for the highest and best good of everyone concerned, however. My mom was so much happier attending to her own needs and desires instead of having to slave away for a man who did not truly care about or appreciate her. My dad and step-mom remained happily married for over thirty-two years until my dad's death in August of 2012.

The incest is not even something I care to speak about anymore except on occasion with my counselor, or if I think my personal experience and growth would be valuable to share in group therapy or with another woman who experienced something similar and is now suffering. I've forgiven my dad for that and choose to remember the loving, kind things he did for me most of the years I was growing up. Anyway, I've moved on. I don't wish to dwell upon the past. I don't see any point in holding onto something that is unpleasant and makes me feel sad or angry.

I believe, however, it is important to share all of my childhood experience and insights with others for my own personal healing, and so that other victims of sexual molestation or child abuse know that they are not alone. No one should have to live in fear and secrecy holding onto guilt and shame – especially my dad. I know he loved me very much and never deliberately intended to cause harm.

---

3 Available in my poetry anthology "Heartscapes".

LIFE WITH MOM
(OR WHICH WITCH?)

Because he worked so hard, Daddy didn't think he should have to help my mom at all with household chores or child rearing. My mom was also exhausted from a long day of cooking, cleaning, making lunches, and caring for three young children. There was not much communication between them, and this truly frustrated my mother. When he came home from work, Daddy just wanted to drink a few Manhattans to relax, nap, read in bed, or watch television, so my mother felt neglected and unappreciated. She only had three children to talk to all day and would have really liked to talk to my dad about anything, she told me. She began to feel very depressed and resented the way he ignored her except when he wanted sex, food, or some company with whom to watch television.

Though I remember my father working on projects in the garage, mowing the lawn, and doing some yard work, my mother was angry at him because he refused to help her at all with cooking, household chores or taking care of us. She hated having such a large home to clean, and I remember her being depressed for most of their seventeen-year marriage.

Dad would try to cheer her up and help her out of these low moods by taking us all out to Stewarts' drive-in hamburger joint for root beer floats, french fries, hamburgers, and onion rings. And then we'd go to Loew's drive-in movies and watch a double feature like Agent 007, James Bond, in Thunderball and Dr. No. My dad, Pete, and I loved the evening out, and my mom was happy she didn't have to cook or do dishes for one night, but the outing was just a temporary distraction from some real problems in the marriage. Getting her out of the house seemed to help a bit, but it was like putting a Band-Aid on a broken arm. There were lots of issues to be addressed, and feelings to be shared, that were never communicated. My mother expressed her displeasure about certain things, but my dad was unwilling to change his habits, or do what she asked of him. Little by little my parents grew apart. My mom was very unhappy. Eventually, she would take her unhappiness out on me.

I suppose my father did the best a man of his generation knew how to do. The roles of that time were pretty clearly defined, with most men being the sole breadwinner and bill payer, responsible for the yard, care or repairs on the car, garbage, and garage, while most wives stayed home all day to take care of most, if not all, the domestic chores, and the children. Mom had to cook, clean and care for us.

Few women that I was aware of in the nineteen fifties and sixties worked, or were encouraged to pursue fulfilling activities outside the home, other than the PTA, hobbies like knitting or sewing circles and church.

My mom was not religious, and was too tired to be very active with the PTA. One year she was the "class mom", and another year she helped out with the Cub Scouts. She also got me into Brownies, and I became a cadette in the Girl Scouts for a year. Mom was too busy cleaning, sewing, shopping for our clothes, and being a chauffeur to all our many activities, to have any time for herself. She was truly caring and devoted, but her own personal desires, if she had any, were put "on hold", and her spirit would have to pay the price for all this attention to and caring for others, without any love or concern for herself, or her own dreams and desires. She was totally selfless. She was the one who'd go to conferences with my teachers, Open House night at school, my cheerleading practices, basketball games, rehearsals for plays and musicals, wrestling for Peter, parties, movies, and shopping, all mine and Pete's concerts and plays, most of my basketball games, and whatever other activity my brothers and I were involved in. She was there to drive us, to watch us, to support us, and be proud of us. God, just thinking and writing about it all is making me feel exhausted! No wonder she'd get bitchy and depressed. She was being a supermom and was not devoting any time to herself and her own physical, spiritual, intellectual, or emotional needs. No one deserved to take care of herself more than my mom, but it was not her nature. She was very much like my grandmother, Lucy, in that respect. They both had immaculate homes. And they took great care of their husbands and children from the moment they woke up in the early morning until the time they went to bed. And I don't believe either of their husbands appreciated what selfless examples of loving service they were. They both have been treasures on earth! They have been exemplary human beings, mothers, and lights to all that came in contact with them. These kind, joyful, vibrant women have touched so many lives, especially mine.

My mother and I are mostly dear friends now, but growing up with her was like growing up with someone who had a schizoid Dr. Jekyll and Mr. Hyde type personality. In my mom's case I thought of her loving, nurturing aspect as the "Good Witch of the North" and her mean, dark side as the "Wicked Witch of the West" from the movie, "The Wizard of Oz", with Judy Garland. I compare myself to Dorothy, who got knocked on the head, swept away in a windstorm, and separated from the people she loved, then tried so hard to fly over the rainbow to get back home, to feel loved and happy again. In her adventures in her new land, still thinking of home, she meets many new and interesting people, who love and support her too, but she is always yearning for home. In the end she realizes home was always within her own heart and mind.

My mom hit me and screamed at me a lot when I was young. She would spank me or yell at me for little accidents like getting my fingerprints on the living or dining room wall, spilling milk on the floor, or getting food on my pretty blouse.

As an adult and mom, myself now I rationalize that she was tired, but her strong over-reaction to these petty mistakes and mishaps really hurt my feelings and frightened me.

The most painful and toxic abuse was psychological. She criticized me frequently calling me names like "typical Olson slob", or saying that I was lazy. From the time I was about four years old, if I got my fingerprints on the walls or spilled milk on the floor, she would begin to scream, curse, and vent so much anger that I felt like the most unlovable, bad, and sinful person in the world. She would begin a screaming cursing tirade while she was cleaning up the mess I'd made in the kitchen. I'd run out of there fast, up the stairs, retreating to my bedroom so I could get out of her way. She'd start with a litany in which she'd curse at all the saints in the heavens. It went like this: "God damn you, Jesus, Mary, and Joseph. You Jesus Christ of a son-of-a-bitch of a bastard of a Jesus Christ of a son-of-a-bitch of a bastard and so on" repeating the string of damning curses for about ten or fifteen minutes until she got all the anger out of her system. I'd be upstairs in my room hiding and crying on my bed. Every ten minutes or so I'd open my door to see if she was still cursing or if it was over and if it was safe to leave my room to go downstairs to watch television.

Sometimes she would still be screaming and cursing and I'd be devastated because I thought that I was the one responsible for her anger. I must have been a pretty horrible child for her to get so angry and feel so bad. I thought that her treating me so badly was all my fault – that if I had only been a better child that she would not feel so sad and filled with rage all the time. Underneath those thoughts, I felt so sad and angry with her for being so mean, but I was never able to express my anger. I just cried so long into my pillow that I'd begin to hyperventilate. Afterward, I'd be so exhausted from all that emoting and trauma that I would eventually calm down and sometimes fall asleep.

Eventually, Mom would finish venting her rage, which never really had anything to do with me, and she'd come upstairs to apologize. She'd turn back into the "Good Witch", who was gentle and sweet, and she'd offer to make me a delicious dinner with mashed potatoes and gravy, two vegetables, and chicken or steak. God, I hated her for that.

The mixed messages were so confusing. She had just been so abusive to me she'd made me feel like the smallest, most unworthy cockroach nobody could ever love. I felt as if I was nothing but an unworthy pest, and now she was acting nice again and expected me to forgive and forget about the whole prior episode of violence and terror – just like that, without ever even acknowledging how badly she made me feel. It was an awful lot to process at such a tender age. I was a very sensitive child, and I just wanted to be loved and to love her in return.

The anger and rage I felt toward my mom were deeper and more intense than the surface anger and distrust of my father, because it was not all right in my mind and heart for me to express it at all. I felt guilty about being mad at her, because she was my mother and she usually took such good care of me physically. I knew deep down she loved me. So, I stuffed a lot of my rage deep into the caverns of my mind and had the subconscious thought and feeling that I was unlovable and terribly unworthy.

There were times, when I became a teen-ager, that I got up the courage to laugh in my mother's face when she chased me and caught me, spanking me over and again with her hand or a metal slotted spoon. Once, as I was running down the stairs trying to get away from her, she threw a hard plastic hairbrush at me so violently that it broke in two when it hit my head. The laughter I expressed was just a cover-up for the terror I was feeling, and a feeble expression of the anger I felt about being stalked like an animal. I was very conscious of the anger and rage I felt toward her, but at a deeper level were subconscious feelings of self-hatred and feelings of unworthiness, as the only child my mother hated and punished. My two younger brothers were never treated that way. She seemed to really love them- maybe because they were boys.

I'd turn to my dad for protection and comfort. Most of the time, however, he was at work when she physically abused me. When he was around, he did stick up for me, and if he was at home, she did not usually get physically violent with me, though she never stopped the criticism, even when he was near. Those were the times when he would intervene, and I considered him my savior and protector when she got crazy and bitchy, and took it out on me.

My mom, as I was growing up, was not a happy person. She had a few moments of joy, and could be cheerful and open-hearted at times, but because she had so little confidence in herself, she did little but serve my father and her family, and keep her large house immaculate. She was unfulfilled spiritually, emotionally, intellectually, and creatively. She had just a few good friends, no outside interests, few hobbies except knitting, and no career to bring her joy and fulfillment. She told me that my dad said he did not want her to work. She didn't even have a high school diploma because she dropped out of school early in order to get away from her bad family situation. She would graduate years later after my parents divorced, getting her GED so that she could be hired by New Jersey Bell.

My mom was more like a mother to my dad rather than a wife or romantic partner whom he loved and respected. She'd make him a ham, corned beef, or salami sandwich with mustard or mayo, put it in a Glad plastic baggy, throw in a red Delicious or Macintosh apple, a navel orange, add a cookie or two, and that was finished until her next task. She already laid out his clothes he wore to work just about every day. In the frigid winter months of December, January, February, and early to mid-March he was layered up like a big turtle popping out of its hard protective tortoise shell. After slipping into his insulated beige jacket or heavy dark coat Mom bought for him from Sears, mom made sure he put a black or red wool hat over his somewhat balding blondish light brown hair, which began thinning when he was in his early thirties, to keep his head warm; Finally, she wrapped him up in a woolen blue scarf she had knitted with her own hands.

She loved to knit and crochet sweaters, hats, scarves, and slippers for us. The finishing touch was putting on his heaviest, warm winter jacket or coat, in order to protect him from the whipping, frigid wind and other elements while he worked high atop the Exxon Mobil building in Manhattan, or putting lights up on the Verrazano Narrows Bridge, the longest suspension bridge in the world at the time. Mom cared enough to be sure he was warm enough while working outside in the frigid winter weather.

So, breakfast, and dressing my dad, was the daily routine at 6:00 or 7:30 AM if it was November, December, January, or February, in order for daddy to get to the job by 8:30 or 8:45 AM latest, before his workers arrived at 9:00 AM.

Mom and Dad heard the alarm go off at 5:30 AM and, after going to the bathroom to wash their weary faces and take care of their bathroom business, they sauntered ever so slowly down the four stairs of our split-level home in Holmdel in what seemed to be safe, perfect carefree suburbia. Once Daddy got down to our immaculate kitchen, he would help make the coffee in his new "Mr. Coffee" machine mom purchased for him at Christmas.

The routine changed according to the seasons. Spring, summer, and autumn was much easier on Daddy the foreman, and his workers, because the weather was more comfortable – warm and breezy, or so hot that he dressed down quite a bit. My handsome dad was my hero.

Despite her unhappiness, Mom was truly a gentle, caring woman, who was devoted as a wife and mother. I think she had moments of happiness, but because she was so exhausted from slaving away for all of us from 5:30 AM until 8:00 PM every night, she didn't really have any energy to pursue any enjoyable activity just for herself.

I know she did not abuse me intentionally. She did share with me after I became an adult, that she was jealous of all the love and affection my grandparents showered on me from the time I was born. She also shared that her own mother criticized her a lot as a child, and that after I was born mom said gram criticized her even about how she took care of me. Mom was only nineteen when she gave birth to me. She was just a kid giving birth to a baby.

She loved me very much when I was born, but she was not psychologically or emotionally healthy enough to have a baby so young.

Most of the time, she was caring and kind, until I was about four. That's when I have vague memories of her abuse. That's when she started to scream at me a lot. I was a tomboy, and the last thing I cared about was staying clean and looking "as if I came out of a bandbox". That was what my mom and Grammy would always tell me. They both prided themselves on the fact that my dresses and all my clothes were the best brands, clean, and ironed. I wish they had been more concerned about my mind and heart and not so much about unimportant material things like how I looked to the outside world by wearing the best clothes, black patent leather Mary Jane shoes, with matching handbags and white gloves if I was going to church or out with the family for a special celebration.

Every Thanksgiving my mom would go all out and cook for a few days prior to the Thanksgiving celebration. We'd usually have some special company like my grandparents or my Aunt Joan and Uncle Wally, and their four children from River Vale, New Jersey, about ninety minutes away from us by car.

Mom would prepare an amazing feast of turkey stuffed with apple celery stuffing, baked yams, mashed potatoes and gravy, cranberry sauce, homemade bread, broccoli casserole, sometimes sauteed mushrooms in butter and onions, and two other vegetables. God, there was enough food for an army. And after dinner we'd clear away the dishes, mom would clean up, and we'd be invited to stuff down dessert after a short respite while Mom was loading the dishwasher and washing all the pots and pans that were still left.

There was always a pumpkin pie, an apple pie, and ice cream to put on top just like there were when my grandmother, Lucy, hosted holiday dinners. The pies were my grandmother's recipes, so they were the most delicious pies a young girl could taste.

As long as she could until she hit her mid-seventies, mom would spend a few days preparing a Thanksgiving feast as special and bountiful as she did when I was young. She made holidays special and fun for everyone in the family back then, and cooked and hosted holiday dinners in her lovely condominium in Franklin Park, New Jersey, until her late sixties or early seventies. She was so organized and such a great manager that the table was always beautifully set and all the food out on the table still hot at the perfect time when we sat down to say grace. This was a talent I would never have. Mom absolutely amazed me with her hard work, talent for decorating her home, cooking skills, and organizational abilities. She always looks just perfect in a beautiful, ironed or freshly dry-cleaned outfit, and her two-bedroom condominium is beautiful, cozy, and immaculately clean. She is a master of making her home environment beautiful. She's never taken a class, but she is a master decorator.

I enjoyed the time my family spent together very much. We ate meals together, talked, and laughed. In the summer we swam together, went to the drive-in movies, and had barbecue cookouts. I had pretty much everything I wanted except my mother's approval or emotional affection when I became older. She did a lot of things for me, but because she criticized me so much, I didn't have much confidence in myself. She would say disparaging things like, "You're so intelligent, Meryl, but you have no common sense".

I always wanted to help her when I was little. She'd read me a Brownie book about elves and fairies doing good deeds when people were out of sight, and I'd try to be like the elves by going down into the kitchen after my parents were in bed to see if there was anything I could do in the kitchen to help out. But usually, it was always immaculate. Sometimes my dad might have left a dessert or cereal bowl he used while watching TV in bed with mom. If I found something I'd happily put it in the dishwasher and shine up the sink.

Sometimes I'd try to help during the day when mom was awake, but it seemed that whatever I did whether it be dusting the living room furniture or the tops or sides of my bedroom furniture, it was never quite good enough. Mom would have to go back over what I did to make sure it was perfect. So,

I just stopped offering to help. Nobody could do anything up to her standards anyway, so I figured I should not even bother trying to help after a while because I felt as if I was only getting in her way.

She always made me nutritious meals and took me shopping a lot to get new clothes, shoes, and special outfits for holidays with matching gloves, a hat, and purse. She also chauffeured me to all my after-school activities, dates, etc. She cooked the most wonderful holiday meals, made Christmas gift opening and birthdays the most special events a child could ever have. The happy memories I have of being with my mom certainly outweigh the bad.

Each birthday was filled with lots of special presents and a birthday party when I was younger. As I got older, I'd either get to have a pajama party with my girlfriends or else just a special gift and homemade birthday cake with candles that I'd blow out with a wish.

As I explained previously, after Uncle Wally died, Dad married "Aunt Joan", and eventually Joan, her children, and I lived together.

My father had not loved my mother deeply for years except as a substitute mother, a woman who could service his physical and sexual needs. Their marriage had not really been happy for several years, so in many ways my step-mom did my mother a favor. My mom was miserable for at least the last five years of their marriage and truly needed to get out and become her own person. On the other hand, my dad and step-mom were very much in love and happy for many years until my dad passed away. Mom was left to find her way to joy and independence as a single mother.

Mom remarried after a few years and moved to Florida where she gave her second husband money to start a metallurgy business. It was a disaster, both the man's attempt at business, and the marriage itself. He turned out to be jealous, cheap, and psychologically abusive. Within three months of her moving to Florida I could hear on the phone how unhappy she was, and I encouraged her to divorce him and move back to New Jersey where she could start over again, and I could help her emotionally. I took the auto train to Florida, helped her and my brother, Scott, pack most of their belongings in the two cars, and we drove, in tandem, back to New Jersey where she would find an apartment in Old Bridge and begin the work of getting her GED and finding a job to support herself and my brother, Scott. I was so proud of her because she worked for NJ Bell for a while and did very well until she had a nervous breakdown. However, like me, she got well, and became stronger because of the experience.

Eventually she got a temp job at IBM. As the receptionist and switchboard operator they loved her so much at the company that they hired her full-time after several months, and she worked there for years. After that she worked for Southland Corporation and Johnson and Johnson in customer service. My mom was very industrious, always looked beautiful in her Evan Picone or other designer suits and dresses, and was always on time or early for work and all appointments, unlike me, whom she says "will be late for my own funeral".

Looking back on it know I wish my mother had had some sort of counseling or support for her own experience of abuse as a child which caused her to have chronic depression and obsessive-compulsive disorder for most of her life. Mom endured so much stress and with all the challenges she was having as a housewife and young mother at such a young age, she really could have used a counselor, good friend, or pastor with whom to talk so that she could understand herself better. But as a metaphysician I am also aware that there is something called "soul contracts" that we make while on the "Other Side" before we choose to reincarnate. My soul chose Arleen as my mother for its own growth, and my mother volunteered at Spirit level to serve me in the dysfunctional way she did so that I could work through karma, learn forgiveness and come to embrace my own personal power. She is truly a very loving, gentle soul, and it must have been just as difficult for her to abuse me as it was for me to experience it. I know that this was not her true nature, but she was learning and evolving as an individual soul just like me.

There are no victims in life, only volunteers. That may sound difficult to hear, but we all vibrationally attract the most perfect situations, people, circumstances, and experiences into our lives according to Universal Law. God never gives us more than we can handle. He helps us handle what we have been given. Our souls are very strong and the human spirit resilient.

One thing about my mom: she has always been "here for me" through each trial, tribulation, and challenge with the many moods swings I have had to deal with having bipolar disorder. She has been here for me through every seeming obstacle to happiness. Despite her own difficulties with chronic depression on and off since her teens she still managed to care for, love, and encourage me as a child and long into adulthood. She has also been at my side to celebrate my successes and given me the simple and important joys of having a loving family. She's taught me by example that courage, gentleness, patience, kindness, and perseverance will overcome any obstacle. I am alive and much of my happiness is due to her love. Without a place for me to "come home" that is filled with love, tenderness, forgiveness, laughter, stability, home cooked meals, beauty, cleanliness, and order, I would have been lost.

MY BROTHERS

Pete

Three years after I was born my mom gave birth to a son. It was decided he'd be named after my father, Peter. He was given my mom's maiden name as a middle name. Pete was a healthy eight pounds at birth and blond and beautiful like my dad's side of the family. From the moment he was born I think there was a sibling rivalry between us. When Pete and I were growing up we used to fight like cats and dogs over who would get to watch our favorite television program. However, we loved one another and shared the same friends.

I remember playing TV Tag on our front lawn with Pete and his friends, board games like Monopoly and Clue on his friend, Bobby Posada's, patio, playing baseball in the sand field with all the boys. I was a very good first baseman and hit relatively well too. His friends, Joey, Anthony, Bobby, and Johnny, all teased me when I got up to bat calling me "Swivel Hips". I suppose I was more of a tomboy when I was seven through age fourteen because I enjoyed playing sports with Pete's friends more than my own. My phase playing with Barbie dolls, Tootles, and Chatty Kathy lasted only until I was in third grade. Then it was much more fun to go out into the sand field with Pete and his friends to play baseball or "Combat".

I also loved catching frogs when they were tadpoles in Holmdel Park's big lake or when the frogs just had back legs and putting them into a large aquarium I kept at home in the garage. I'd observe them grow front and back legs at the same time, as they would lose their polliwog tails. When they could finally jump around and not just swim, I knew it was time for me to bring them back to Holmdel Park's Lake or over to the frog pond down the street. It was no beautiful lake, but instead a sort of stinking, stagnant pond with floating lily pads where the frogs happily croaked all day and night. I remember it was located by the green house next to my friend, Debbie 's, house, where I would happily spend hours on my own exploring the woods, colorful hot house, and raspberry and blackberry fields which were dotted with yellow and white flowered honeysuckle bushes and all kinds of trees and wild bushes. We'd pick the flowers from the honeysuckle bushes and suck out all the sweet honeysuckle. By the time I got to the frog pond my little froggy friends could not wait to be set free from my large pail to thrive in their own natural environment.

One time I went to the frog pond in the winter with my friend, Amy, when the ice was frozen. I was afraid to walk upon the ice for fear that I'd fall into the water. There was no skating allowed on this pond which was way out in the woods and far from the street where people could see and hear us. Amy dared me to jump upon the ice. She did it first to show me it was safe. When I jumped my plump little body covered in underthings, shirt, pants, sweater, blue leggings, and red rubber boots, fell right through the ice into the freezing cold water up to my arms. I was shocked and Amy had to help me out as she stood there laughing hysterically at me. I, however, did not think her little prank was so funny. I couldn't tell my mom what happened because she'd already warned me not to go down to the frog pond. I think that's one of the last times I ever disobeyed my mother. She did not spank me, but I don't think she believed me when I told her I slipped and fell in some puddle. Moms always seem to know the truth even when you are looking them straight in the face lying like a cowardly lion.

I also loved getting a large pink plastic pail and going out near the frog pond and greenhouse or into the fields to pick fresh mouth-watering blackberries. I think Pete, our friends, and I ate just as many fresh berries as we picked for mom to make as we went along picking through the thorny brush as we brought home for my mom to wash and make jam or preserves. The berries were so delicious that sometimes we'd just wash them and put them in a bowl of milk or eat them plain with Reddi-Wip squirted all over the top.

Even when Pete was five or six years old, he had a kind of presence and commanded most of the older kids. He was three and a half years younger than me and most of his friends, but if Pete got upset about something and wanted to stop playing the game no matter how far we were in Monopoly or baseball everyone in the bunch obeyed and heeded his request. That really bugged me. I wondered how my kid brother could have so much power and charm that everyone older than him listened to whatever he wanted.

Now Pete is over 60, and he still has that same kind of boyish charm, charisma, and a great sense of humor. He had a lot more confidence than me as a child, and I think that was because my mom adored him and never criticized or abused him the way she had done with me. Whatever she did worked because Pete and I used to wow everyone at weddings with our dancing ability. He used to throw me over his hips and toss me into the air when we jitterbugged together. My mom and dad were both terrific ballroom dancers and experts at the cha-cha, rhumba, merengue, lindy, fox trot, and two-step. I used to love to watch them dance together when they were happily married. I learned a lot from both of them. Peter dances very much like my dad. He is suave, graceful, confident, and sure-footed. Since I'm now hemiplegic, and do not have the use of my left arm, I am unable to dance with the same alacrity, agility, and grace with which I once did. However, my lack of grace and physical prowess has not dampened my enthusiasm or the fire in my soul to express myself through the art of movement.

Peter and I have always loved one another very much, but because he was three years younger than me, and a boy, he ended up becoming closer to my brothers, Scott, and step-brother, Tommy, as we grew older. Besides, Pete and Scott, were both "born again Christians from the time they were teens; and I resonated more with the Eastern philosophies like Buddhism, Hinduism, and the yogic path. I think I was inspired by the book "Siddhartha" by author, Herman Hesse. When he was born, I was already three years old, so I might have been a little jealous since I was no longer the only child who was adored by both parents and grandparents. Just a bit of sibling rivalry there until we matured.

I adore Pete, and I'm so grateful to him for all the support he's given me and my mother during our battle with mental illness. He is a very kind, grounded, peaceful, caring born again Christian, and fun-loving individual. He is just the type of man I'd want to marry myself except that he is a bit too conventional for me and I could never live with a Republican. Oh well. I never said he was perfect.

Pete has been there for me at several crucial moments in my life, which are discussed in later chapters. His connection to Jesus and unwavering faith as a born-again Christian has seen my mom, me, and entire family through many of the challenges and adversity we've had to endure during the times of darkness with suicide attempts as well as other illnesses like the time I was in the hospital with double pneumonia.

Pete was unhappy in his first marriage, and his first wife, Julie, who mothered his first two children, Sarah and Matthew, met another man on the Internet whom she eventually married. Even though I truly liked and respected Julie, both she and Pete seem to be much happier with different spouses. Pete and Kathy had a daughter together and now the little baby girl, Caroline Grace, is a teenager. and just completed her Junior year in High School. I'm crazy about my nephew, Matt, who is seventeen, and my niece, Sarah, as well as my grandnephew, Zachary, who is adorable and terribly precocious and active at four years old. I just saw my grandnephew, Zachary, recently, when he helped Pete move my mom out of her home in Franklin Park, NJ, to graduate into assisted living. Zachary himself, graduated from high school last June, and he's grown into a very strong, handsome, capable young man. The last time I really spent any time with him he was ten years old and dancing nearly as well as Michael Jackson at the wedding of his mom, Sara, to Tim Lynch who became a great husband to his mom and father to him.

At age 25, Pete was with me when my son was born. At that time, he worked as a chiropractor and lived with his wife nearby in East Brunswick, New Jersey. He makes a lot more money than me and owns a lovely home in Cape May now in New Jersey. Pete was left by his first wife, with whom he had a beautiful son, Matthew, and adopted her daughter, Sarah, too. He married a lovely gal named Kathy in Florida in September of 2004. Kathy was a sweet Christian girl with a great sense of humor and a golden heart. She complemented my brother very well, and I saw many positive changes in him since they started loving one another.

Kathy passed away in 2021, and Pete is planning to move the family out west next year.

Scott

It was spring of nineteen sixty-four and I was nearly nine years old when my mom told me we were going to have another baby sometime in the winter. I was in Mrs. Hope's class in the third grade at Indian Hill School when I found out the exciting news. Pete was five going on six that year, and his birthday present was to be a little baby brother, born one day before his sixth birthday. Pete was born on December 6, and Scott chose to give him a special present by coming a bit earlier than expected to Red Bank Hospital and into the world on December 5, 1964. Boy, was I excited that I was going to become a big sister again! I got to help my mom when she came home from the hospital with changing Scott's diapers sometimes, heating up a bottle of formula and feeding him, or just playing with him in his crib. He was really cute and sweet with light blond hair just like my dad and brother when they were younger. Oh, I was blond when I was two until I was five years old. You can see my platinum blond baloney curls in my kindergarten pictures from school.

Mom was tired a lot after he was born so I used to help her change Scott's diapers, watch and play with him from the time he was little when mommy needed to wash clothes, vacuum, cook, make my dad's lunch for the next morning, and so on.

Anyway, I was crazy about Scott and truly enjoyed his precious, sweet, and loving Presence. He did not cry much. Mom said he was a really good baby, and he was. He grew up to be a nice brother and a good friend to me. I remember teaching him French when I was learning the new language in the sixth grade. I would ride Scott on the back of my bicycle and say, "Contes d'un a quinze, Etienne. There is no French equivalent for Scott, so I called him Steven. I taught him how to count to twenty in French when he was just about four years old sitting on the back of my turquoise Schwinn two-wheeler.

We remained close until I moved out of my mom's house when I was sixteen. We lost touch for years, but Scott came to my mom's surprise forty-seventh birthday party and attended the labor and birth of my son. He served as a missionary in Jamaica, before returning only briefly to New Jersey, but, like Pete, he has been here for me when it mattered. He is a very kind, caring born again Christian. His first marriage produced a son, Christopher, whom we all love, but the marriage was not happy, and did not last.

Scott's second marriage to a woman from California named Caroline whom he met online who has three sons, has been very happy and successful. Their connection was so strong that after just a few months of online dating they met and fell in love with one another almost right away. They both had similar interests in Jesus Christ, studying the Bible, and spirituality, caring for their children, and taking good care of their bodies with a healthy diet and regular physical exercise. I was surprised when my mom told me they were running marathon races together. Caroline is a great mom and a very pretty woman, too. I've not seen Scott for many years since my dad's funeral about ten years ago at our Lady of Mercy Church in Woodcliff Lake, New Jersey, but we are both on Facebook, so we connect that way sometimes. Now Scott and Caroline live in Washington state with the three boys who all must be in high school by now.

Scott is a mature, gentle, sweet, kind, loving, caring man with a great sense of humor. He was blond, brown eyed, and handsome as a child and grew to be an attractive man who always seems to have a smile upon his face.

THE DANCER

I have always been very friendly and interested in people no matter where I went. I love and enjoy meeting all types of people and have no judgments about what anyone does for a living. I was quite impressed with all the women who were working in the bars as go-go dancers with me on both day and night shifts.

Tommy's dancers worked two shifts from noon to 7 PM and from 6 to 11 PM. I loved to dance, and I truly enjoyed being teased by the go-go and burlesque dancers I'd seen with my former boyfriend, George, when I was 21 years old. Some dancers were supporting families; others had dreams of buying expensive cars and homes and were able to save thousands of dollars from dancing several nights per week in order to fulfill their dreams. Others were putting themselves through massage school like myself, or through chiropractic or nursing school. Some were just enjoying the power that comes with expressing their sensuality and sexuality, or they just enjoyed dancing.

It was really fun getting dressed up in different costumes being able to strut our beautiful wares all over the stage. Most of the men we met were just nice, regular guys out to relax and have a good time during their lunch breaks or after work by having a beer and watching pretty women dance.

The pay was excellent for the better dancers like myself. I started out working at the Lamppost in New Brunswick on Livingston Ave. back in the late seventies. The owner of the Lamppost was a man named Tommy C. He came to get massages at the Executive Health Club at the Sheraton Hotel in East Brunswick where I worked part-time a few nights per week. He thought I was attractive and told me he needed some more dancers at his bar that were reliable because many of them either canceled at the last minute or were late arriving to work. He suggested I come one night to check out the dancers and to audition myself. When he told me the dancers were starting at $12 per hour, plus tips, for dancing only one-half hour on, and then one-half hour off to rest and make a costume change, I'd made up my mind to give it a shot. It sounded like fun. I loved to dance and to entertain from the time I was a young child. I was already accustomed to performing songs in front of audiences at Fairleigh Dickinson and other college bars as well as the Circle Line that went around New York City. I also performed in schools, nursing homes, and nice restaurants, and sang at an occasional wedding for four years at that point, and I loved the attention.

I still remember the night I auditioned. There was a very experienced dancer onstage who was proficient at luring the men into giving her lots of tips. She wore a black mini-dress with panty hose and a skinny thong underneath that showed off her honey cheeks. I watched her tease the heck out of all the men at the bar by slowly and deftly pulling down her pantyhose one inch at a time, and finally throwing them out into the crowd. Then she'd lift her skirt all the way up to the top of her thighs giving the illusion that she would show off her pussy. She never got that far, but the men loved being teased, and she cleaned up in tips. I didn't believe I could ever do anything like that, and felt somewhat intimidated to go onstage after her.

I was a novice at burlesque, but I felt confident about my looks, my singing and dancing ability. I was pretty, had a nice figure and was a good dancer with a lot of energy and charisma, so I chose a really good set of songs on the jukebox that made me feel confident and energetic. I just went up and danced for them as if I was dancing in my own living room.

The men liked me, but I only got a dollar or two in tips. When I went up for my next set I'd changed into a sexy hot pink brassiere and turquoise hot pants with silken black panties underneath. I wore a red blazer over the top of my undergarments so I could sit with a few of the men at the bar who'd asked me to join them for a drink and chat with them. I did not drink alcohol, but I asked for an orange juice and became friendly with two of the patrons as well as the redheaded barmaid, Angie.

I liked getting the money, and by the time I went up for my third set, I felt a bit more confident and courageous. I enjoyed being watched by the guys and dressing up in a new and different outfit. The set went well, and I made six more dollars in tips than the first time I went onstage. I felt more relaxed just sitting at the bar afterwards, talking about myself with a few of the patrons.

The fourth time I went onstage to dance, I flashed my breast every now and then. I made several more dollars in tips. The men clapped loudly in appreciation, and Tommy hired me. From that moment on I became a seasoned, professional go-go dancer who got paid good wages and loved making lots of money doing what I loved to do – dance, look pretty, and create beauty and sensuality all around me.

I got three dates for future performances in the next two months. Tommy also told me about another bar in old Bridge where I could work because he knew the owner. It happened to be only two miles from where I lived, so I ended up getting lots of gigs there.

I went back home and created all types of sexy outfits and costumes from my own wardrobe from scarlet red teddies, diaphanous light blue nighties and Victoria's Secret lingerie to G-strings with red and black garter belts and nylon hose. The girl I danced with that night told me where to purchase thongs and the best stores to buy costumes, bras, hose, and panties.

I would dress in layers with a beautiful dress or black jumpsuit over my go-go outfit. I had a shiny black satin jumpsuit with a matching black bow tie I wore around my neck for a special set. The dresses and pantsuits were part of my dress-up wardrobe. I'd wear mini-skirts and sheer blouses over my sexy thongs or underwear so that I was dressed properly when I'd come out of the dressing room to sit and chat with the men at the bar.

I really enjoyed being watched by the guys. I learned how to dance while undressing a little piece at a time to get the guys really titillated so they would tip me for each piece of clothing I'd take off. Often, I'd wear a long scarf around my neck so that I could take off my sexy brassieres, throw them out on the floor or give one to one special lucky guy in the audience whom I found particularly attractive. We were not allowed to flash our nipples back in those days, so I'd drape the scarf perfectly over my breasts in the middle to cover my large pink nipples. Every now and then I'd move the scarf aside for one or two lucky patrons to get a glimpse of one of my full round breasts. I was always rewarded with a one- or five-dollar bill for this burlesque move. I was gradually learning by experience how to have the men eating out of my hands and loving it.

After a while I started to do "floor work" in which I would relax and do hatha yoga asanas onstage to very slow, sultry numbers like Captain and Tenille's, "Do That to Me One More Time" or Dionne Warwick's new hit song of the late seventies, "Deja Vu". I loved dancing to those songs every set because it gave me a few minutes to relax after an energetic number and look the men straight in the eyes hypnotizing them into thinking I wanted to have sex with them. I'd run my fingers across my inner thighs as I slowly and deliberately stroked my Mound of Venus, driving all the guys crazy. It was during those slow numbers that I really learned the art of seduction and I cleaned up in tips.

I sometimes brought a bottle of massage oil up onstage with me and began to massage my stomach and thighs right in front of the guys relaxing myself and feeling very sensuous. I know they were all fantasizing that it was not me, but them who had their hands upon my beautiful, curvaceous body.

I varied my sets to include several bouncy, energetic, sensuous numbers like Michael Jackson's "Rock with You" from his amazing "Off the Wall" album and Madonna's "Like a Virgin" to soft ballads and quieter, sexy numbers sung by Earth, Wind, & Fire, or Teddy Pendergrass, or to Marvin Gaye's "Sexual Healing".

Boy, was that fun! It made me feel very feminine and powerful. There's something to say about having a whole lot of men watching you strip and you know you can get them to do practically anything you want.

By the time I'd made enough money to go to massage school and buy a car my wage had gone up to $18 per hour in most of the nightclubs and bars where I danced two to four times per month. The tips came out to an extra $50-$150 per shift. I managed to save over two thousand dollars in less than five months and paid for my boyfriend's used five speed silver Mustang Mach 2 and a seven-hundred-hour program at the Sarasota School of Natural Healing Arts, where I would end up excelling as a student in anatomy, physiology, nutrition, therapeutic Swedish massage, and heliotherapy. I also took two special workshops to become certified in polarity therapy and colon irrigation with Pierre Pannatren and Mariltn, our nutrition teacher.

I stopped dancing professionally when I got engaged in 1983, but I still thoroughly enjoy dancing anywhere and everywhere I get the opportunity. That includes the free form improvisational dancing I do at the Arts Council of Princeton with Catherine Judd Hirsch and all my friends who attend Dance Improv monthly on Friday nights. I also take much delight in singing and dancing in the aisles at Shop Rite to the canned music they play from the sixties, seventies and eighties. People look at me strangely sometimes, but mostly they smile, and probably wish they could be as joyful and freely expressive of their inner bliss as I. I also thoroughly enjoy dancing in church when there is an entertainer I like. I once danced with Brian D. Levine, Freeholder Director of Somerset County, and with the seniors from my mom's adult daycare center, at the center's picnic.

I don't care who sees me or hears me when I dance and sing. I am probably most free and expressive of my ecstasy when I am alone dancing around my living room to Stevie Wonder, Earth Wind, and Fire, and Chicago. I just love to move my body to the rhythm of the percussive drums. And as I hear the angelic call of the blaring horns, I just can't keep myself still. When I hear the call of rocking electric guitars, piano, horns, and the alluring melodic rhythms of Earth, Wind, and Fire, Chicago, and Stevie Wonder I want to exalt God and dance with more passion and ecstatic abandon than when

I listen to any other music on earth, except for kirtan at Integral Yoga of Princeton or drum circles at Princeton Center for Yoga and Health.

I really get down when I dance to "Another Star" and practically fall on my butt when I try to jump into the air and fly. I used to be able to do tour jete's and all those fancy jumps and footwork before I became physically challenged, but now I just dance for fun and out of my love for God and Self. It's the same thing, is it not?

Even now, I am a terrific dancer just as I am and bring lots of joy and fun wherever I go, whether it be a restaurant, night club, concert venue, on the lawn at the Princeton Shopping Center during the summer, or on a cruise ship. People always remember me as "The Dancer" and comment to me the next time they see me on how much they were inspired or felt joyful watching me dance and sing.

In my travels, years after my professional dancing days, and even after my injuries, I would often encounter people for the second time, and be recognized immediately as "the dancer".

MASSAGE SCHOOL AND LIFE IN SARASOTA

By 1980, I'd known Patsy Boston for several years. She was a member of the Psychic Science temple I attended, and was a massage therapist who not only gave me my first massage but offered a week-end workshop in massage and reflexology course where I discovered my natural talent as a healer when I was just 21 years old. While living an hour apart in New Jersey, and we truly became closer to after we decided to take the adventure together to go to a holistic healing and massage school together in Florida. We checked out a school in Miami too, but it was not as eclectic nor did it offer all the holistic classes, we found were available at the Sarasota School for Natural Healing Arts like colonics, nutrition, and a polarity workshop with Pierre Pannatier. It was not just the technical aspects of massage and anatomy and physiology. There was also a class on hydrotherapy and heliotherapy. The school seemed to have all the variety of courses in holism we wanted to try. Both of us had been practicing massage therapy for over four years.

I began massage school at the Sarasota School of Natural Healing, owned by Isabel Durkenson, in 1980. My favorite instructor was named Sid.

Though I had a boyfriend, John Jay, back home, when I met Sid, there was something about him that I'd never felt before with any man I'd ever met. Though he was married, he told me he had an unconventional, open marriage, and he and his wife, Edie, separated shortly after that so she could move in with her boss, he told me. Within a month we were massaging one another inside the screened-in porch of my quaint little garage apartment.

Sid was much older than me and reminded me in many ways of my father. When we made love, I was able to access a lot of repressed anger I was holding inside after being sexually molested by my dad when I was thirteen and fourteen years old. The repression of my rage and sadness after dad's abandonment would often cause me to go numb in my genitals and to distrust men with whom I became close physically and emotionally. Through neuromuscular therapy and deep tissue massage Sid helped me to release some of the shame, guilt, and repressed emotions that I was holding onto in my pelvic region.

Losing my virginity at nineteen to an older man who had no love for me was painful and made me very angry too. Following the experience, I closed down sexually and often manifested yeast and vaginal infections. No matter how many times I'd treat the infections with Monistat or some kind of medicinal creme I'd end up with another infection several months later because I had not healed the subconscious trauma. My sacred yoni (my vagina) was very sad and angry that I did not treat her with more love, honor, and respect. Sometimes the anger would come up in the midst of my lovemaking with Sid, and I'd scream into a pillow and cry for several minutes. This therapy was helpful, and usually we would rest for five or ten minutes, then resume our lovemaking.

Sid's massages were sensuous and very healing. Then we began to hang out at his house, and we had a few dates going to beautiful Siesta Key Beach and Marina Jack's together. He was a very sexy Scorpio like my dad. He had been a dean at a college in North Carolina prior to his massage career, and I loved his intellectual nature mixed with a down-to-earth country boy way, a sweet humility, and his kindness to me and all the other students in class.

Sid was short in stature, very charming and handsome in his own boyish way, with a light brown short beard; he looked like a combination of a Mennonite and a leprechaun. He had a special magical air about him. Especially in his healing touch, and the way he massaged me. I was most attracted to his mind, his intellect, and the chemistry between us was subtle at first but became very intense the more times we met in class and after class outside of massage school.

I was on an emotional and physical "high" for several months. I was experiencing the natural high of being in love. I was happy with myself, doing well in school, and especially enjoying living in such a wonderful relaxed climate not far from the ocean, beach, and the marina. I have been a lover of water and a good swimmer most of my life. While in school I also worked as a waitress part-time at a fine restaurant called, "Your Mother Should Know", and after I quit there, I worked at "the Wildflower", a natural foods restaurant.

And still I managed to find time to do all my homework, study anatomy and physiology well enough to get straight A's on the quizzes and exams, write poetry, and compose several songs on my guitar.

I wrote one especially for Sid's birthday called "The Key" as I sat happily on a blanket on the grass at Marina Jack's. His birthday was All Saint's Day, and he was so pleased with the song I wrote for him. We were very much in love despite the fact that he was still married, but separated from his wife. I had so much energy during this time that I'd stay up until early morning hours making entries in my journal. Sometimes Patsy and I would go for walks with the cats on Seminole Drive in the moonlight. Both Burger and Groucho would follow close behind. Then after reading and writing I would not fall asleep until 2:00 or 3:00 AM.

I kept myself in good physical shape by biking, doing hatha yoga stretches daily, and jogging on the beach. I also ate mostly natural, organic vegetarian foods. Little did I know that this state of bliss and high energy would not continue but would shortly be followed by an opposite experience of the same intensity. I suppose what goes up must eventually come down.

How could I know that, within a few months, I would plunge into an abyss of suffering and fear so severe that I would attempt suicide on several occasions? I finally realized there was no escape but to get down on my knees and go within in prayer to ask God for help. This was the first manifestation of the severe mood swings that would plague me on and off for years until I was diagnosed in May 1988, with bipolar disorder.

Patsy, my best friend whom I'd been living with in Sarasota for the duration of the thousand-hour, six-month course, had become close to one of the other instructors, our nutrition teacher, Marilyn, and soon after our graduation, Patsy was offered a position as a massage therapist in her healing studio in St. Petersburg, an hour north of Sarasota by car. So, upon deciding to take the position, she chose to move, leaving our cozy little two bedroom furnished apartment in Sarasota to be near her new job. She told me she'd be moving out in a month.

Unsure where I would go next, I told many friends and other students in class I needed to move soon or find another room-mate.

By that time Sid and I were making love and he'd sleep over at my place on a regular basis. My Christian landlady lived on the property and had judgments about my lifestyle. I was told not to have any more overnight guests, or I'd be asked to vacate the premises. I was happy and in love with Sid, so I chose to leave rather than tell him to stay away, I was especially happy when he made the time to spend the night and have breakfast and herb tea with me in the early morning before he left for work... I felt really special. Not only was I the teacher's pet and best student, but his lover as well.

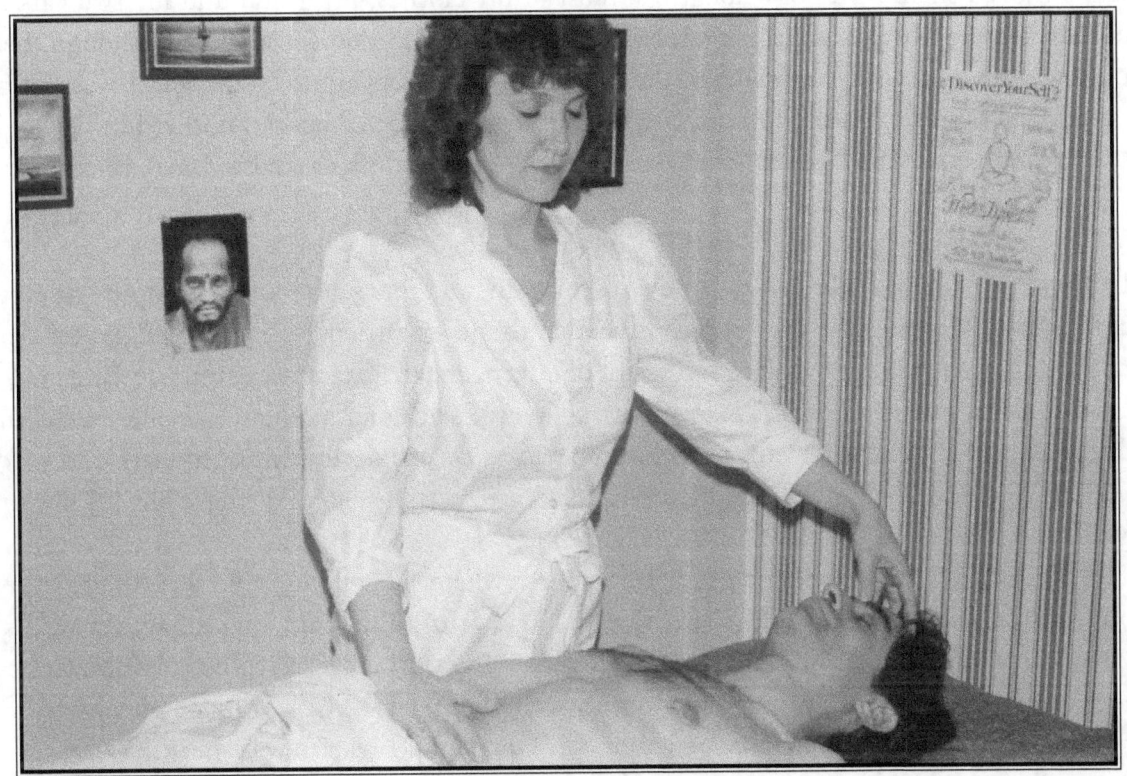

Reiki on a massage client

Over Christmas vacation I went back to New Jersey to be with my mom and brothers over the holidays, and when I called Sid on the phone one afternoon, his voice did not have the loving, open-hearted tone it had formerly had. I had sensed that something was off, especially when I slept over his house one night upon my return, and I noticed he had turned over the framed photo of us I'd given him for his birthday, so the photo of us looking happy together would not be seen. My caring acts and former thoughts of gratitude, openness and positive expectation completely changed in just a month's time making me doubt myself and irrationally, even the existence of God. Now, on the phone, something in his voice and demeanor, sounded sneaky and false. Sid did not have the enthusiasm and passion he had had before I left for vacation. When I asked him why he sounded different he admitted to me he'd met someone new – a young woman named Rose who would be going to Yale whom he'd begun dating. He was amazed that I was so psychic, and humbly apologized for his indiscretion.

There was a waitress named Karen I'd met at the whole food's vegetarian restaurant in Sarasota, the "Wildflower" where Patsy and I sometimes enjoyed having lunch or dinner. I needed extra money upon leaving massage school while waiting to take the Florida state massage licensing exams coming up in three months, so I became a waitress at the Wildflower too.

Technically, we were not legally allowed yet to do massages on paying clients until we passed the State licensing exams given by the Massage Board, so I decided to work at the Wildflower part-time, though it did not pay much. It was kind of fun meeting new people, eating delicious, nutritious vegetarian soups, entrees, and desserts for practically nothing, and the tips were decent too.

My waitress co-worker, Karen, knew of my need to find a new apartment or housemate in less than a month and offered a bedroom in the house she was renting not far from the beach on the Gulf of Mexico. I was desperate, Karen was very nice, and besides, I loved to swim, so on the first of February I moved small boxes of belongings, most of my clothes, my guitar and my two cats to her vacant bedroom, and bicycle into her garage. This situation did not last very long, though, because the house was overrun with cockroaches, the next-door neighbors argued a lot, and I was not happy there at all. Luckily, her landlord found out I had two cats, and Karen had not let him know I was subletting from her or that I had cats; cats were not allowed, so I was asked to leave. I had only been living there for three weeks.

I had less than a few weeks to find a new place again, and I was a bit anxious, so I decided to see a psychic named Marlene who'd been recommended to me by a friend. She saw me getting a phone call and finding a beautiful, new place as a result of talking to a friend or acquaintance. She said, "You are an old soul with many talents. I see you having a large yoga and meditation center in the future. One day you will be using all of your talents combined to do wonderful things in service to God and humankind in some type of large healing or yoga and meditation center. We have already shown you what you can do with your hands."

Then she added "I do see a period of frustration here where you will lose your way, forget your faith and lose your persistence. Know, dear one, that the love your guides and angels have for you is very strong and in time, through faith and persistence, you will eventually overcome your challenges and be able to come to a place of harmony, and get back on your path." Then Marlene seemed to go into a deeper meditation and her voice changed a bit. I felt as if someone else was speaking through her.

"Beloved Meryl, good evening, dear child. It is I. It is us. God has amazing plans for you, my daughter. Much more than you can appreciate at this moment. Much more than you have ever dreamed. You have a talent for writing. Automatic writing. You will write a great book someday that will change the lives of thousands of people. You have many guides who want to use you as a channel for their wisdom and Light. We have much practical information for humans of the earth plane from 'the Other Side'".

"You will soon be meeting a great spiritual teacher," she continued. "He will light the spark that ignites your soul. The loving heart that you already have within will be ignited as if by a great flame, and everything will change as a result of that initiation. Your flame will be a candle that lights the way for many others. We honor, love, and respect you for all that you are and all you have already come through. Go in peace, my child."

At the time she was speaking I felt encouraged and excited, though I still felt some stress about not knowing where I was going to live.

All the great, positive things she mentioned about my destiny seemed so far off in the future that I did not feel especially comforted by the reading. I did feel their love, though, and was more peaceful than I had been before I came, but I was still feeling sad and anxious about the prospect of losing Sid, whom I believed was the "love of my life", my own special personal "knight in shining armor". That perfect man for me I believed might become my husband someday. That potential loss of losing the man I loved so dearly, the one I fantasized in my imagination might become my future husband eventually seemed to take the bright color out of any good things or events in in my life. It was as if I saw everything from that point on as black (evil) or blue (sad and deeply depressed) My dark thoughts, perceptions, and feelings cast a shadow over sunny days making me inured to the beauty of bright blue skies and large puffy white cumulus clouds that I would normally love and appreciate; I'd normally be able to dive into the clouds in my imagination as if they were billowy cotton.

Now I would awake to a lovely, sunny day, and I was unable to feel joy or appreciate its beauty. I just felt numb.

Irrational ideas and skewed perceptions of reality began causing the shadow in my mind to get darker becoming blacker day by day. I realize now that I was suffering from both grief and post-traumatic stress.

In the midst of these crazy thoughts and feelings, somehow, with God's grace, I managed to connect with an acquaintance I met at the health food store, the "Granary", who was going to be moving out of his rented house on Siesta Drive in Sarasota; he wondered if I might be interested in checking out his place immediately so he would not lose his security deposit. It was a lot more than the $75.00 per month I'd become accustomed to paying living with Patsy when we split the $150 rent. It was more than four times what I had been paying – $350 per month, but the rent did include cable TV and all utilities. The place was a cozy one bedroom furnished house with a nice, clean brown and white cotton spread on the double bed in my bedroom, some things in the kitchen cupboard, a small living room with a simple five-foot-long beige couch, a long brown wooden coffee table and two sturdy, simple end tables on either side. The whole place was simple, immaculate, quiet, serene, and in a place of rural beauty near a babbling clear creek. It was spring and birds were chirping early in the morning but after just a few weeks I had no desire to get up out of bed nor could I sleep soundly at night. In fact, I could barely sleep at all without waking up feeling disturbed and frightened – of my own negative thoughts and fears. There were even thoughts of self-hatred and suicide. I was terrified of the future and felt completely hopeless about my ability to continue a happy, successful life. I did not understand what was happening to me, or why I felt so terribly depressed.

I had gotten some of the money for the $700 rent and security deposit together by doing massages even though technically I was not supposed to be working without a massage license. I had to wait until May before I could even sit for the state licensing exam, but I'd still gotten a few clients through friends on the sly. I had already been doing massage in New Jersey for four years before deciding to go to an accredited school to get certified, so I was already an excellent, competent masseuse. I just wanted to know the names of the muscles, bones, and anatomy I was manipulating. A certificate to hang on my wall would be helpful too.

Anyway, my Pop Pop Vere could always be depended upon for his support and generosity, so whatever the difference was that was needed for the rent and security deposit he made up with a loan – one of those he usually did not expect me to pay back until I was rich and famous.

THE FIRST BREAKDOWN (1981)

Sid said he was happy for me and promised to help me to move. However, the evening before I was supposed to move, I kept calling Sid to remind him and to find out what time he would come to pick me up and transfer all my belongings into his van. I had trouble contacting him by phone from the Patio, a restaurant bar in downtown Sarasota that I frequented with Patsy and my friends from class. There were great bands – even the Allman Brothers played there at one time. It was the "in place", where I'd go with Patty to meet several of our friends like Mark C. and Mark P. and a couple named Patty and John, to dance, drink, and relax. I did not really drink. I'd just get an orange or cranberry juice for refreshment in between dances. We had a tall, dark-haired friend with a nice physique named Michael who was a terrific dancer, so I often danced freestyle with him to the faster dances like Kool & the Gang's "Celebrate". I so enjoyed the live bands, and dancing with a guy like Michael who really knew how to lead or follow my bouncy jazz or rock style was so much fun, but on that night, I was getting nervous about my impending move to my new home, my second move in two months!

In between dances that night, I kept calling Sid to find out what time he would come to Karen's house to pick me up and transfer my belongings into his orange van. After trying unsuccessfully for hours to reach him, I finally realized something was awry and decided to drive to his house that night. It was a crazy thing to do because I had an intuitive feeling he was not answering his phone because his new girlfriend, Rose, was there, but I did not have much choice since he had agreed to help me move the next day. And I had no one else to help. Patty was already in St. Petersburg with Marilyn, and I knew nobody else in town who had a van or pick-up truck. Plus, I was so poor that I had no money to rent a U-Haul plus I had a few hours to find out all that info, and I was in a bit of shock, so I was not thinking clearly about possible solutions if Sid bailed out on his promise to help me. When I knocked on Sid's door his housemate, Tom, answered the door. He said in a cool tone "Sid has company, and does not want me to let you in. He'll come out in a few minutes."

Besides all the confusion, a part of me was really pissed off at him for dating Rose when he'd already told me he would break it off. I was angry and wanted to confront him about his betrayal and indiscretion. I wanted to yell at him, cry, and make a scene, I suppose, at a subconscious level. But it wasn't my style. Having had an angry mother who would scream a lot caused me to think sharing angry feelings was a terrible, hurtful thing to do, so I often stuffed a lot of rage or acted it out in a passive aggressive way.

Truthfully, I was terrified of confronting the fact that I was a has been, and he was now with someone new that I'd only heard him talk about; I really did not want to face the fact that this woman was his new girlfriend who'd replaced me in such a short time after he professed his love and enthusiasm for our new, exciting relationship, especially not after all my fantasizing about a long-term relationship leading to marriage. I was living in a fantasy world and in denial since he'd had an open marriage when we first met, and his wife had only moved out of their home a few months before. What the heck was I thinking?

I suppose sexual, romantic love makes one irrational, puts a usually keen, discerning mind into denial and makes one overly optimistic. I certainly had high hopes about our relationship way too soon into the game. Besides, I'd just broken up with a boyfriend in Jersey that I chose to leave behind. I'd been dating him for a few years after meeting him while I was go-go dancing, but broke it off after deciding I liked Sid better. My handsome, blond John was most likely heartbroken after coming all the way down to Florida to visit me and then finding out I had a new beau. That's instant karma for you. What goes around comes around.

By the time Sid got to the door I was feeling very vulnerable. He came out of the house so that I could not go inside saying "Rose is here." Instead of getting angry which would have been an appropriate response I went into shock and shut down; I stuffed all that rage and upset down deep in my subconscious. All I could do at that point was cry devastating tears of disappointment and grief. Sid felt compassion for me and held me in his arms while I cried for several minutes.

I left immediately after that to get into my car unable to deal with all the surprise feelings of rejection and abandonment. I felt devastated, ashamed, angry, and embarrassed, and was in a mild state of shock. All the emotions I did not allow myself to feel got trapped in my muscles, my fascia and my subconscious. I never allowed myself to feel angry and enraged by the betrayal and sudden shift in Sid's feelings toward me. Most of this anger and rage I turned inward on myself over the next few weeks as I began to feel terribly confused and so frightened and depressed that I lost my rational mind.

I began to entertain the idea of suicide for the first time in my life once I was in my new home living all by myself except for my two precious kitties, Groucho and Burger, as my only company.

The whole experience was such a shock I'd forgotten to ask Sid if he was still going to help me move my things the next day. I cannot even remember what happened after that or how I made it home in the fog I was in from crying so many tears. Nor do I recall who helped me move. I think it was Pop Pop who helped me, since I had no furniture, just my cats and a lot of clothes and boxes which he probably put in his trunk or the back seat of his Chevy Impala.

What I do remember is that I felt suicidal from the first night I spent in my beautiful, suddenly too large new house. I was afraid and terribly lonely even with the company of my two cats, Burger and Groucho. Nothing made sense to me. I could not understand anything that had happened. I just felt confused and no longer wanted to live in the fear that had become a permanent companion in my mind. I felt totally small, anxious, frightened, and wanted to be invisible to everyone except my Grammy and Pop Pop.

Though the house was clean and pretty I felt terribly sad, grief stricken, and in shock from this trauma. I was afraid and terribly lonely even with the company of my two cats, Burger and Groucho. I had no desire to ride my bicycle, go to the beach or marina where I usually loved to go to enjoy swimming, sunbathing, writing in my journal, compose songs on my guitar, and especially participate in drum circles and contemplate the beauty of the red and orange sunsets going down on Siesta Key Beach in the warm evenings after a day spent sunbathing my beautiful body. I had quite a lovely, trim figure from doing hatha yoga, walking, swimming, and riding my bicycle around town or at Grammy and Pop Pop's house when I'd go visit them often by myself or with Patsy for dinner. I had no energy or desire to write in my journal, cook, spend time with friends, or any of the activities that used to make me happy. I could not understand anything that had happened. I just wanted to go to sleep and be unconscious of all the painful events that had so recently occurred. Sleep eluded me completely. I tried to watch TV, but I was so depressed and unconscious I could not concentrate on anything for very long nor could I even follow the stories. I just felt numb for weeks.

I had no appetite and bought no food except some basics like peanut butter, herb tea, and instant oatmeal. I would not cook for myself. When I was starving, I'd eat peanut butter out of a jar with a spoon, drink some milk or have cereal with juice or low-fat milk. I had very little money, so whatever I did buy I purchased with food stamps. Whatever cash I had left over after paying my rent and security deposit I used for cat food for my two sweet, beautiful kitties who immediately sensed something was deeply wrong. In the morning when I got up, I would feed Burger and Groucho, and then I had no idea what to do with myself the rest of the day. Not even television distracted me long enough from my negative, unworthy, fearful thoughts. I felt so hopeless that I forgot completely about God's love for me, and my love for Him. I just knew there was something terribly wrong with me, I did not know what it was, but I had the thought that I should be destroyed. Well, not me exactly. More like my body or my mind which I saw as the cause of the problem.

Even being at the beach with Patsy did not bring me solace or joy any longer. My thoughts began to get fearful, anxious, and extremely negative. My negative thoughts about myself were unrelenting. Irrational ideas and skewed my perceptions of reality; the dwelling upon negative thoughts began causing the shadow in my mind to get darker becoming blacker day by day. I felt only hopelessness, unworthiness, and despair. These black thoughts and feelings completely replaced my former feelings of joy and light-hearted thoughts and good feelings from being newly in love and experiencing the passion of sensual and sexual connection. I had felt the joy of learning new things in class, and now classes were ended too. So many great things ending all at once was devastating. I would not see most of my classmates again. Patsy would be gone, I had no new place to live yet, and, as far as I knew, Sid would be moving on too.

All I could think of as a way out of this dark despair was to rid myself of this body. I would try to suffocate myself with my bed pillow, but that never worked because the desire to inhale always arose again after such a long exhalation.

The strange thing is that I never linked the experience of Sid's betrayal and abandonment of me with my self-doubt, depression, and desire to die. I never even told anyone about what happened except Patsy, but she was already living in St. Petersburg which was kind of far for me to travel, a two hour round trip, and I did not have that type of strength or motivation. Besides, with all my suicidal thoughts I was afraid I might crack up my car or hurt someone else, and I had no desire to hurt anyone except myself. It would be very bad karma if I drove my car into someone else on the highway. And I'd only limit myself and create more troubles for myself if I could no longer drive.

What to do? Try to run away? Unfortunately, I could not run from myself or these terrible, irrational thoughts. Like a ghost they seemed to haunt me wherever I went.

Should I attempt suicide alone in my new house, where I would not actually hurt anybody? I suppose in my extreme pain I completely forgot about the many people who truly loved me and would be devastated if I died, like my Grammy and Pop Pop, Grandpa Olson, Patsy, my mom, my two

Christian brothers in New Jersey, my classmates in Florida, my aunts and uncles, and my other close friends and former boyfriends in New Jersey, especially John, my most recent beau before Sid. Then there was Greg, the first man I lived with in Garfield and then Hackensack who also introduced me to the Psychic Science Temple of Metaphysics in Paterson where I met Patsy, and my former boyfriend, George Callanan, a full-fledged psychic and minister at the church. George played a bad-ass lead guitar Eric Clapton style in my first rock and roll band, Baloney. George and my other boyfriends and friends would certainly all be affected if I committed suicide, but in my deep, chronic pain and feelings of hopelessness and despair I saw no one and nothing but my own selfish prison. No one and nothing mattered to me but being released from this self-centered, hellish prison.

Patsy was already working in our teacher, Marilyn's, clinic. I felt too ashamed about my thoughts and feelings of weakness, despair, and suicide to tell her how badly I was feeling, so I really felt too terrible to want to allow any of my friends to know how frightened and ashamed I felt. I was normally confident, fun, spiritually minded, and a very positive person by nature. I hated this dark side of me. I could not accept or love myself in this condition, and could not forgive myself for being so selfish and self-centered that I thought of no one who loved me and how they would feel if I actually hurt myself or killed myself.

Luckily, Great Spirit knew and saw all that was going on, and my guardian angels intervened. One night I got a call from Sid. He wanted to come visits me and see my new place. He was working in Tampa trying to start a massage school of his own, so he was not getting down to Sarasota that much. He said he had some good news for me.

I had never allowed myself time to process the anger and rage I'd felt about how he treated me regarding leaving me for his new gal, Rose, and for not coming through by helping me with my move as he had promised. I was feeling so vulnerable, weak, and frightened I did not have the courage or strength to confront him, let alone get angry at him. I was even frightened and embarrassed to be honest with him about how badly I was feeling. He knew me as vivacious and confident. I did not feel anything but self-doubt and fear, but I was too proud to let anyone know this—especially him, a man for whom I had such strong feelings and always appeared as talented, beautiful, and confident. I kind of wanted to avoid him, but he said he had some good news, and I was looking for any news, just about anything that might give me a bit of hope or the slightest relief from all the negative, hopeless thoughts that had become my constant companions. I just wanted the slightest bit of positive change that would relieve me of my suffering and help me to feel just the slightest bit better. Something that would make me want to get up in the morning again, so I listened with interest to what he had to say.

"I've had the good fortune of massaging the baseball player, Willie Stargell, who is down here as manager of the New York Mets. Sarasota is the Mets' winter home.

"Mr. Stargell is a very fine man who loves to get massages on a regular basis. He has some trouble with his knees."My friend, Tom, told Willie about me."

"Meryl, I am so tied up with everything at my new school in Tampa that I don't really have a lot of extra time to go down to Sarasota to give massages any longer. You would be doing me a great favor if you would take over working on Willie for a while. He's a very large, robust man, and it will take you at least ninety minutes to do a full body massage on him, if not longer, but he is very generous and will pay you at least a hundred dollars."

Wow, how could I refuse that gift! I was not making much money at my job as a waitress at the "Wildflower". Certainly not enough to pay my higher rent, so I said "Yes, of course. I'd be glad to help you out. Thanks." to Sid's proposition immediately. I had nothing else to look forward to in my life since school was over, so this felt like a gift from God.

Besides that, I was going to be massaging a famous baseball player I'd even see play on television! I was spending a lot of time not doing much of anything but worrying during the day and watching TV at night after dinner.

WILLIE STARGELL

Willie was one of the kindest men I'd ever met. Besides being large like a bear, he was muscular and gorgeous. Though he was a great talent and leader in the sport of baseball he was a humble man with a gentle soul. He was a very generous man too. At the time we met he was separated from his wife; so, though there was a bit of a soul attraction between us, and I would see him practically nude during massages, he was always a perfect gentleman with me in all ways. We got to be good friends after a while, but we never even shared a kiss that I can recall.

One time after I completed his nearly two-hour therapeutic massage, he gave me one hundred dollars extra and asked if I'd run out to a local restaurant in Bradenton to buy some dinner for the two of us. When I came back to the house he said "Thanks so much, Meryl", and refused the change when I tried to give back the money left over from his Ben Franklin. We got to become pretty close friends after several massages.

One night after we finished eating dinner together it was getting dark, and since I was living in Venice with my grandparents an hour away, he asked me if I'd like to spend the night there.

I had my guitar in the car and asked him if he'd like to hear a few of my original songs. He said "Sure, I'd love to. You are a multi-talented lady, huh?"

I played two love songs I'd written – one called "Live to be Happy and Free" and the one I'd written for Sid's, birthday, "The Key". Willie liked both of them and complimented me on my voice as well as the lyrics. I guess Willie could tell what a sensitive, special woman I was, and he probably intuited that I'd been deeply in love with Sid and in pain because we were no longer together even though I never spoke about our love relationship, not wanting to jeopardize their professional one.

When we got tired, Willie asked me if I'd like to sleep with him in his large Queen-sized bed. He was experiencing severe pain in both his knees which had undergone surgery, and he asked me if I'd like to sleep in his bed that night in case he woke up in pain as he usually did for some time. I was surprised I fell asleep so quickly and easily after getting a big bear hug from him, especially since Sid had broken up with me unexpectedly, I was having suicidal ideations and had terrible insomnia almost every night. It was like sleeping with my uncle or big brother. He did awake after several hours with knee pain, so I did heal massage on both of them. He said I soothed him and made him feel a lot better, so much better that he fell back to sleep shortly afterward.

I had no idea what an amazing man I was honored to meet and to know as a friend because I was just a young girl when Willie was playing baseball for twenty-one seasons with the Pittsburgh Pirates. I saw him on television when the Pirates played the New York Yankees or the Mets, I suppose, because, being a Jersey gal born in New York, the only teams I rooted for were the Yankees and the Mets. I did not realize that Willie played with the Pirates both as a left fielder and first baseman during a very long, successful career. He got 2,232 hits during his triumphant career, 423 doubles, 475 home runs, 1,540 runs batted in, led his team to clinch two National League pennants, two World Series in 1971 and 1979 and was voted most valuable player in the World Series.

He was the Pirates' team captain and a true leader, especially considering all the prejudices Negro men had to put up with, especially in major league sports at the time.

The only reason I had the privilege of meeting him was because when he retired from the Pirates in 1997 due to a kidney disorder that required dialysis he became the coach of the New York Mets, and their winter home was Sarasota, Florida. Recommending me to Willy was the best thing Sid ever did for me.

In retrospect, I wish Willie and I had kept in touch through letters. And that I'd had the greater fortune of getting to know him even better, but I was in shock and still grieving the loss of my massage teacher, friend, and lover, Sid, whom I would get to see only once more. It was going to take me a while before I got over the loss of someone I loved so deeply, as well as his betrayal and sudden abandonment.

Besides, I had the feeling that Mr. Stargell was still in love with his wife, and I did not want to confuse him while he was trying to work things out in that sacred relationship. Both of us were in transition as far as our love relationships were concerned.

I just feel so lucky and blessed to have had the good fortune to do healing work with this beautiful man and to have shared a brief, therapeutic friendship and sharing of souls.

I later learned that Willie Stargell died from a stroke at age 61, on April 9, 2001. He was inducted into the Baseball Hall of Fame in 1988, the same year my first husband and I divorced and I remarried a black man three months after meeting him while we were psychiatric patients at the Carrier Clinic in Bellmead, New Jersey.

MOVING AGAIN

It took a few weeks before I got up the courage to call my grandmother to tell her I was not feeling well at all. I did not care about myself one bit, but I did still love my cats in my own limited way and could barely get up the strength to feed them or change their litter box, so it was mostly due to my wanting my cats to be cared for that I finally had the guts to call my grammy to tell her the truth about my depression and negative thoughts and feelings. I was so ashamed and confused I did not talk to anyone else about how badly I felt. Since I refused or was unable to care for myself living in the new apartment by myself, I finally confessed to my Grammy what was happening; and she invited me to live with her and Pop Pop in Venice.

Pop Pop and Grammy came right away, packed me up along with the cats, my bicycle, my clothes, and my few belongings. Pop Pop and Grammy brought us to the safe, nurturing haven at their home. After being so happy, healthy, and strong for the first six months I spent in Florida I didn't have the courage to tell Grammy and Pop Pop I was feeling as depressed as I was, and certainly I couldn't share that I was suicidal. I was just too ashamed and embarrassed to tell anyone how badly I was feeling, not even my best friend, Patsy who was already living in St. Petersburg. I simply told my Grammy I was down and did not think I could support myself until I got my massage license which was going to take a few months because I had to wait until May when the state of Florida offered the next licensing exam.

I felt temporarily a little better being in Grammy and Pop Pop's loving care and beautiful home also knowing that they would cook for me, I'd have no rent to pay for a while, and Groucho and Burger would be loved and cared for too.

However, after a week or so my female cat, Burger, developed a painful urinary tract infection and she began urinating on the plants in Pop Pop's lanai. Pop Pop bought a carrier for her and we took her to a veterinarian who gave her medication for the bladder infection, and eventually she got better. I believe she tried to take on my grief and anger issues that I was not allowing myself to feel. I should have been terribly pissed off at Sid, but I did not allow myself to feel much of anything; I had suppressed all of the rage I had toward Sid for how badly he'd treated me and all that had happened was stuffed deep down inside me.

My thoughts were still uncertain, I was frightened about my future. I still knew not what to do with myself during the day if I was not working at the Wildflower or going to Willie Stargell's home to give him a massage. At night I had so much fear and resistance to life that I could not sleep much at all, so I'd pace around Grammy's house looking underneath her kitchen cabinets for something with which I could poison myself and put myself out of my misery. I would lie to her and Pop Pop saying I had a massage to do at Grandpa Olson's during the day when I actually had absolutely no plans to do anything. I was even afraid to talk to people for fear they could see right through me. I was so ashamed that others would know how weak and frightened I was feeling. I really did not let on to my grandparents just how badly I was feeling, but inside my heart and mind I knew I could not keep up the charade forever.

I owe my life during that period to the love and support of my grandparents; but because I lived in fear of the demons in my mind and felt apprehensive about my future, I continued to keep my suicidal depression a secret and pretended to be fine. I lied about going out to visit friends or do massages. I'd go out for a drive in my car just to get out of the house for a while and to feign some type of life. I left Gram's house with no purpose but to daydream about killing myself and to figure out how I could possibly release myself from the terrible suffering I was experiencing without hurting anyone else. I almost tried to crash my car into a telephone pole or another car, but my own conscience prevented me from hurting any other person, so I always changed my mind the moment it occurred to me.

I would pray constantly that I would cross the highway and get hit by a truck, but nothing bad ever happened to me. Each night I couldn't sleep after about midnight. I felt so much guilt for feeling suicidal and for having a resistance to live and accept that I was alone again without the man I loved, even though my heart was so closed to myself I could not truly feel love for Sid or anyone. I'd wake up terrified and would pace the den and living room for hours. If my mind had been rational, I'd have known I was perfectly safe and was being well taken care of. I know this sounds strange, but I was more terrified of the depression and fear I was feeling and of my uncertain future than of something real. I had never experienced such terror and hopelessness in my life. I was literally afraid of feeling afraid. It made no sense. I couldn't figure out what was happening to me. I had never felt so frightened nor had so many negative thoughts in my life. I had lost all of my self-confidence and was terrified of what the future would hold.

Suddenly, I'd lost all faith in God and myself. My mother was often depressed, and I never could relate to her pain and feelings of depression until this devastating personal experience of loss. I would usually try to cheer up my mother by saying, "Mom, life is so great. You have so many blessings. Just focus on all the things for which you have to be grateful." But I had no true understanding of the deep mental and emotional anguish she was experiencing at those times. Now I finally had a clue as to how much pain she was in at those times. However, I don't believe she'd ever felt badly enough to want to kill herself when I was growing up. Her sense of duty outweighed any crazy or cowardly thoughts of leaving us three.

My crazy behavior, hiding, and chronic depression continued for six weeks until finally my friends and I had to drive north to Winter Haven to study and take the Florida massage board licensing exam. Somehow, I was able to pretend well enough so that my friends did not discover my terrified state of mind. I put up a good front, and my mind was not as frightened when I was with people engaged in conversation or activities as when I was alone. As always, I was too embarrassed to share the bad shape I was in. I just listened and let everyone else in the car do all the talking.

Patsy sensed something was wrong with me, but we never really talked about it. She gave me a massage once before we left for Winter Haven, but my mind still felt crazy and I felt no joy in it. I was still more in my head than in my heart or physical body. None of the things, people, or activities that usually brought me so much pleasure mattered anymore. Not swimming. Not sex which I did share with Sid one last time, though I felt numb in my genitals, and it was completely unfulfilling for me. I could not enjoy being with my grandparents or friends from massage school. I could not even feel joy while relaxing on the nude part of Lido Beach in the warm sunshine with Patsy and another male friend of ours from school. I was just terrified all the time.

Even my sweet cats seemed like another burden to care for. There was so much sadness and anger in my mind and troubled heart, that I could not understand anything that was happening to me. I just felt tired, exhausted from not sleeping, afraid, and unworthy. I could not explain what I was feeling even to a counselor my friend, Susan, recommended. I talk to her psychologist because I was so confused, I did not know what to say. I was just too embarrassed to appear that weak and vulnerable to any other person. I felt completely separate from God which was the worst part of the whole experience. I did not even feel worthy enough to pray for myself. I had reached rock bottom of all feelings. My own personal experience of hell, the nadir of existence.

Why I wanted to wait for the Florida state licensing exam taking place in Winter Haven was inexplicable to me, since I could not picture myself ever passing or even wanting to work again as a licensed massage therapist in Florida. I'm not sure why I wanted to do so when I did not even want to live anymore with all the pain and fear I was experiencing. I suppose it seemed like the next most logical step after finishing my massage training and certified in holistic health, massage, colonics, and polarity therapy. At the center of my being, I figured that if I ever did feel better, I wanted to be legally permitted to offer massage therapy in the state of Florida. If I were in New Jersey, it did not matter because there were no licensing laws at the time, but Florida law required not just certification from an accredited school or college but also a massage license just like a hairdresser or esthetician. All my friends from class were studying for the exam, so I made arrangements to carpool with Patsy and our friend, Susan, to drive up to Winter Haven where we could all take the test together.

The practical part of the massage was very easy for me because giving a great therapeutic massage was always my God given talent, the written was not as easy due to my poor state of mind and lack of concentration, but I knew I had at least passed with a B or a C even in my crazy, confused state of mind.

After I returned home to Grammy and Pop Pop's house, I called the psychologist Susan had recommended. I felt so nervous being suicidal that I did not even know what to say to this man. He had no compassion for me at all, and after I told him a bit about losing Sid in an anxious way for ten minutes, he cut the session short and sent me home with a book called "You Don't Have to Rehearse to be Yourself". What an A-hole. I was feeling suicidal, the guy was so insensitive, had the compassion of a camel, and just made me feel worse about myself. If I had been feeling better about myself, I would have told him he should be disbarred.

Yet, my bad feelings and thoughts were all in my head and imagination since things were really not so bad. I was not homeless. I was not hungry. Grammy and Pop Pop and my Grandpa Olson in Florida loved me very much, and my mom loved me too even though she was all the way up north in New Jersey. I had two close friends in Florida, but I just saw everything from a negative perspective. I only saw the cup of my life as half or completely empty. Instead of seeing my cup as half full with lots of opportunities for growth, change, and my new massage business as a feeling of accomplishment and cause for joy I was terribly afraid to just put one foot in front of the other since I perceived all experiences and circumstances in my life through this dull gray, negative lens. I felt so bad for so many months that I believed my life was over. At least I was too afraid to continue and wanted it to be over.

It was a miracle I was able to pass the massage exam since I could barely focus or concentrate on anything. Amazingly, I'd find out several months later that I'd passed the written exam with a 78 and got a 98 on the practical. My crazy thoughts did not impede my skills as a masseuse.

Once I'd gotten back to my grandparent's house after taking the licensing exam, I could not contain my secret any longer because my suffering was too great and I could not go on pretending indefinitely. I finally told Grammy the truth about how I felt. She confided to me that she'd also suffered a nervous breakdown once when she was in her forties and my mom also had the same tendency toward mental illness.

"Honey, I feel so bad for you. I know how terrible you must feel. When I had my nervous breakdown, I was even afraid to go out of the house to go shopping. I think you should go back to New Jersey to live with your mom. I have a feeling she will know how to help you," she said with great compassion, concern, and tenderness. Grandmothers are very wise and loving beings due to all their life experience.

Within a week it was decided I'd fly back to New Jersey with my precious cats. Pop Pop bought them extra-large carriers so they could fly on the plane with me. I left with a few suitcases of clothes, and the rest of my few belongings like pots, pans, bathroom articles, and my bicycle were packed up and stored away in my Grandpa Olson's shed in Bay Indies where he lived ten minutes from Grammy and Pop Pop. My 1980 silver Ford Mustang Mach 2 was left behind as well and was later driven back to NJ by my very loving, supportive brother, Peter.

For some reason I was still terrified at the prospect of going back home and not feeling any better, so I started to secretly plan a suicide. I began to search for poisonous substances in Grammy's kitchen cabinets while she and Pop Pop were still asleep, and I was pacing for hours in the middle of the night unable to get back to sleep. I could not find anything that would permanently do the job, so I started to look in the supermarket for substances with warning labels that said, "Do not drink. This is poison." After some searching, I found a bottle of cleaning fluid, carbonic acid, I believed might poison me enough to put me into a comatose state where I would not have to feel anymore or be aware of my confused thoughts. I hid the bottle until the night before I was supposed to fly home to New Jersey. In the wee morning hours on the day, I would have to leave I attempted to put myself out of my misery by drinking the entire bottle of carbonic acid while my grandparents slept. It tasted horrible, and immediately I lay down on the couch in the lanai with my heart pounding feeling fearful. All my homeostatic mechanisms were working overtime to keep me alive.

Nothing much happened, and fortunately for me, my grandmother cooked me her usual big breakfast of eggs, toast, bacon, and freshly squeezed orange juice. I vomited a little in the toilet while Pop Pop loaded my luggage and the cats into the Cadillac. A few hours later we were on the road and in a half hour we were treated to an appetizing lunch in Sarasota at Pop Pop's favorite fancy restaurant, the Kapok Tree Inn, before I had to board the plane. I suppose the food, juice, and water helped me to eliminate most, if not all that was left of the carbonic acid. My grandparents had no idea I had tried to poison myself just hours before we got into the car to drive to the Sarasota airport, and I never told them. I just remember feeling sick to my stomach and making multiple trips to the bathroom to pee out what smelled like gasoline. I was very lucky the poison did not do any permanent damage to my stomach lining, liver, or intestines. Who knows? The toxic residue might still be stored in my liver.

I called Sid the previous night to let him know I was returning to NJ, and he arranged to meet me at the airport in order to say good-bye. In my ill and confused state of mind I was running late for the plane and never got the chance to connect with him. It was probably for the best because I was a walking zombie at that point, and seeing him would have been more of an embarrassment to me than a happy reunion. I felt no love for him, myself, or anyone anymore. I still stubbornly retained my former thoughts of confusion, fear, and a tremendous amount of repressed rage, which I'd turned inward on my own self.

My mom had been depressed most of my life while I was growing up, but she took all the drugs the psychiatrists prescribed for her with little or no relief. I did not believe psychiatry nor medications worked since I 'd seen no proof of it in my own family. My mom never ever had manias or suicidal tendencies, though, when I was younger, until she was fired from her job at Southland, the Seven Eleven Corporation, went into a serious clinical suicidal depression, when she was 60 years old, and then tried to overdose on a full bottle of stelazine, the medication she was being given at the time.

Luckily, for both of us, on that day I was late to meet my grammy and mom's sister, my Aunt Marlyse for a funeral we were all attending. I could not remember the name of the funeral parlor or the address. I tried to make lunch plans with other friends, but nothing materialized. Mom had been feeling very depressed and I was worried about her because after having been fired from her job, for the first time she shared she felt hopeless and was having suicidal thoughts that week.

I called her at home several times, but when I could not get through, I had an intuitive feeling I should drive to her home in Franklin Park from Perth Amboy where I'd just gone to the Bradley's department store to kill some time.

When I arrived, I rang the doorbell, and it took a while before mom finally opened the door for me. I could see she was very drowsy and not looking right, so I asked her what was wrong. She finally came clean and shared that she had taken an entire bottle of her medication, Stellazine. I quickly went into action packing a bag of clothes for her quickly, calling the hospital, and driving her to the ER. at Princeton Medical Center on Witherspoon Street as opposed to Robert Wood Johnson Hospital because I wanted her to be closer to my home so I could visit. I figured they would pump her stomach and then put her into the psychiatric hospital, Princeton House, where we had both spent time during chronic clinical depressions. They did pump her stomach even though by that time most of the pills had been absorbed, and she was kept overnight in Princeton Hospital on suicide watch just to make sure that she would not have complications from the pills which had been absorbed and digested. Luckily, nothing tragic happened. Mom ended up fine even though she had to be transferred to Princeton House the morning after that for a few weeks, and even after a few weeks there, she was still not feeling her usual normally productive and happy self.

I was still suicidal when my mom picked me up at the airport. First, she made an appointment for me to see her favorite psychologist, who diagnosed me with chronic anxiety and depression. As if I did not already know that. Duh. That label did not help me at all. Nothing was getting to the root of my problems. I still was so "out of it" and clueless that I did not connect the very obvious dots. Boyfriend loves me. Betrays and lies to me. Leaves me for another girl. He doesn't show up to help me move from one apartment on the beach with cockroaches to new apartment on canal. School is over which was fun and I loved my friends, teacher, and learning new things. My best friend moves out of our garage apartment to a new practice an hour away from Sarasota. More loss and grief.

I had little money and had to find new places to live twice in two months. Then, knowing I cannot handle the depression on my own I choose to move again to my grandparents' home in Venice, a fourth move in three months. Then I was shipped back home to New Jersey, still depressed, still suicidal, to live with my mother. I loved my mom, but I wasn't crazy about living in New Jersey.

It was a tremendous amount of loss and transition in just fourteen weeks. I was just astonished to find that someone actually believed they could put a label on the most hellish state of being anyone could experience. Talking to Dr. Tugender did not help me one iota because I did not understand what was wrong with me and was still too afraid to share that I was still feeling suicidal for fear that I'd be put into a hospital or the doctor would tell my mom, and that would thwart my plans.

I believed that if I told someone the truth I'd be locked up in an institution and would never be free. I'm not sure why I had this terrible fear of being locked up in an institution for the rest of my life.

After a week staying by myself while my mom was at work, she decided to check me into the psychiatric ward of South Amboy Hospital where she'd spent two weeks herself during a severe depression.

The doctor put me on high doses of Mellaril, which only made me feel like a zombie. While there I spoke to an alcoholic patient who told me he attempted suicide once by taking a bottle of his medication along with an entire bottle of whiskey. I should have figured that since he was still around to tell about it that this was not a successful way to kill oneself, but my mind was totally irrational, and I was determined to escape my intense suffering, fear, and anxiety any way I possibly could.

I hated being in the psychiatric ward of the Raritan Bay Medical Center, for two weeks because I felt no relief from the medications the doctors gave me, and it was actually worse being around other people with depression and anxiety since it was a very negative environment. I felt just as frightened and depressed when they released me as when I entered the hospital. No progress at all. I could not wait to get out so I could go home and attempt suicide again. I did not relate or interact with hardly any of the other patients there. I was judgmental of many of them because I was a vegetarian, and I saw most of them eating meat. I cannot believe I had such egotistical pride even in my suicidal depression. I used my ego to continue to self-isolate, and in those days in that hospital there were few arts, hatha yoga, or exercise programs, or at least I'd have had something fun to take my mind off myself and my petty problems.

When I was released, I tried overdosing on a nearly full bottle of Mellaril washed down with a few gulps of hard liquor found inside my mom's liquor trunk in her living room. I had overheard one of the patients speaking about how he had tried to kill himself by using a large amount of alcohol mixed with a lot of his medication. But, if I'd been rational, I'd have realized that since the man was still alive the pills and booze obviously did not help him to pass over to the next realm. I wish I'd realized then what I do now – that I am a Complete FAILURE at suicide. I have probably tried every possible way to kill myself except for jumping off a ten-story building or a bridge, mostly because I thought beforehand that I might actually hurt myself! Duh.

So, one afternoon when my mom was at work at IBM and my brother, Scott, was out working at Kentucky Fried Chicken in Old Bridge I popped as many tablets of Mellaril as I could wash down with whiskey, rye, or whatever I'd found into the back of my throat. I then lay down on the couch to die and went partially unconscious. My youngest brother, Scott, who lived with Mom and me, discovered me when he came home in the afternoon from his job at Kentucky Fried Chicken, and tried to waken me.

When he saw the state I was in, he called my mother. She came home immediately, and they both poured cups of tea down my throat while walking me around the living room to keep me conscious. I think I vomited whatever pills had not been digested, and once again my suicide attempt had failed. My guardian angels on earth and in Spirit would just not let me go back home yet. I thank God each day for all His and my angels' unconditional love and protection during my times of weakness, hopelessness, and despair.

It seemed that no matter how many times I would try to kill myself my higher Self and guardian angels intervened. They knew what was my soul's purpose as well as the sacred contract I'd made while in Spirit to triumph over this disease and to help others who are suffering. They knew that eventually I would be able to experience the lessons I needed to learn in order to get to the other side of the depression. Once I was able to accept and embrace the dark side of myself, I started writing everything in a journal and prayed for new thoughts of hope, faith, and acceptance of the present moment, my depressions would dissolve. I would then think more positively, have some hope in God and myself, and begin to feel a bit stronger day by day. Gradually the dark gave way to the Light of my Self where there exists only unconditional love, feelings of peace, acceptance, contentment, and joy. But in the meantime, after the attempted suicide, my mother decided I needed to go back to South Amboy for more treatment.

Of course, I was readmitted to the hospital the next morning after the overdose. My brother, Pete, drove me, since mom had to work. Other than making me feel like a total zombie and somewhat dysfunctional, the booze and pills had no effect. I was released again from South Amboy a few weeks later still in pretty much the same shape though I pretended to be better just so I could get out of the hospital. I know this sounds ironic, but I hated being in the hospital because it was filled with crazy people—drug addicts and alcoholics to whom I could not relate. My ego rationalized that I was better off than most of these other patients because I was "spiritual" and a vegetarian. What a joke. The ego can be like a stealth bomber at times. I know I was not behaving like a spiritual being by trying to destroy God's temple, but I was not in my right mind. If one believes in a devil or being possessed by demonic entities, that is the only way I could possibly rationalize the "why" of my actions. I deluded myself into thinking that I was better than those other "sick" people. The ego can be very tricky. Even though I knew something was wrong with me I believed I wasn't as bad off as the alcoholics and drug addicts were. So, I kept myself isolated and felt even more depressed being away from the other patients, but especially from my family.

In retrospect, I wish I'd have gotten to know some patients in order to share my problems with people who might have been able to understand what I was going through and who could extend empathy and encouragement. Then I might have realized that I was not alone in experiencing these temporary states of darkness. In all those moments of weakness and fear I felt too much shame and embarrassment to tell anyone the real truth about what was going on in my head. I never felt comfortable showing weakness. At all costs I tried to preserve the masque of being "normal" and OK.

I was unaware, according to a psychiatrist's diagnosis, that I had a serious biochemical imbalance in my brain, a mood disorder that was eventually diagnosed in March of 1988 as manic depression, bipolar disorder.

It's called this because a person with this type of mental illness experiences severe mood swings from one extreme of great euphoria and thoughts of grandeur to the opposite polarity where there exist doubt, anxiety, confusion, fear and despair. In my case, I believe these severe mood swings were caused by a number of factors: Sid's loving and leaving me so suddenly, childhood trauma coming up to be healed, deep seated feelings of unworthiness caused by the trauma as well as a violation of my personal boundaries then and in current relationships, and a nutritional imbalance. Everyone needs excellent nutrition to maintain physical and emotional health and energy.

When I got back to my mother's apartment, I made the motions to try to get involved in life again, though each time the mom suggested I go visit the chiropractor I used to visit in Old Bridge where we lived, because he was planning to expand his office into a holistic health center with a nutritionist, massage therapist, and rolfer. I procrastinated out of fear. I finally did as she suggested, and Dr. Rich rented me an upstairs room in his center for my office for a reasonable $150.00 per month.

The doctor also suggested I teach a course in massage therapy at the adult school in Old Bridge for seven weeks in order to promote myself. I was terrified to do that, but I went through the motions because, just like all my other motivations I wanted him and everyone who knew me to think that I was "normal" and competent. So, I pretended I was fine, but inwardly I was frightened and hoping I'd get hit by a car in the meantime. Maybe God would be merciful to me, and I would be able to escape having to move forward and take responsibility for my life. I had no confidence and was still inwardly terrified, but I was able to hide my fear for weeks and pretended to be normal. I knew for certain I was not "normal", but I still did not want anyone to know there was something innately wrong with me. At least I believed there was something innately wrong. How absurd! What could have caused this core belief? I did not know, but eventually, by the grace of God and my inner guides I would be able to get in touch with and change this crazy, irrational thought.

A week before I was to teach the course at school I went outside at night, looked at the starry sky, hugged a tree for strength and prayed with all my heart that I would have the courage to do what I said I'd do. And that my fear would subside. All I wanted was peace and the feelings of love and gratitude for life I once had.

I'd written an angry letter to myself the day before berating myself for not appreciating my family and all the blessings I had in life. I had become a "negative-alcoholic", and little Meryl was the one I truly hated. I realized while writing the letter that I was addicted to thinking negative thoughts about myself and every aspect of my life. I prayed for courage to change so I could believe in the power of God and the love inside myself again.

That special night one week before the course was to begin, I somehow found a new perspective and shifted my thoughts and attitudes from "not my little will, but thine be done." When I went outside in front of our apartment at Glenwood, I was impressed to hug a tall, wide tree at the bottom of our stairs for strength. Then I began to contemplate the wonders of the night sky. I had an intuition to drive down to Carl Sandburg Middle School the next afternoon where I was supposed to teach the course in about six days. I went inside one of the classrooms, re-experienced how familiar and relaxed the learning atmosphere was. I sat down at one of the small desks and pretended to be one of my students who'd be listening and learning from me the following week.

I imagined myself writing the basics about Swedish massage on the blackboard, picked up a piece of white chalk and began writing on the blackboard the five basic strokes of Swedish massage with their definitions and applications. Then I went home and began to write up a lesson plan. Once I did this, I was no longer nervous or anxious. I felt prepared to teach and share what I had already learned. Writing down what I knew and what I planned to teach totally took away the fear of the unknown for me, and I began to become excited about sharing and teaching what I'd learned in school as well as other things I'd picked up by experience and self-study before ever attending school. Once I made up an outline about the origin of massage and the five basic strokes of Swedish massage the rest of the syllabus for the course came to me easily. Little by little I began to feel comfortable and then enthusiastic about my choice to become a leader and massage instructor. I even bought a special uniform to wear, and I was such a good teacher that several of my students not only loved my class, but befriended me and eventually began to come to me for massages at the holistic center in Old Bridge where I worked during the day.

One of my students, a very kind Indian man named Hosny Basily, was so sweet and magnanimous that he gave me $400 to purchase a new green leather covered Earthworks massage table. He gave me this money out of total love and generosity without expecting me to pay it back. I was moved to tears.

My massage clientele grew gradually after I advertised in the newspaper, and then when I went back to go-go dancing part-time to supplement my income, I invited my followers from the clubs to come get massages from me as well. Some of the men who would see me dance became my friends and massage clients too. I eventually had a grand opening announcing my practice at the new Holistic Health Center of Old Bridge and invited my students, my mom, brothers, some friends, and my rolfer, Jim. It was a very successful party, and I got more private massage students for a course I wanted to start at the center as a result of my enthusiasm and intention to be a success. A few of my students were encouraged by me to continue with their studies at a certified school and two have successful practices to this day.

AWAKENING

Being Rolfed

I heard of Rolfing while I was in Florida.

Rolfing is a powerful and intense form of deep bodywork developed by a woman biochemist and pioneer in the holistic health field, Ida Rolf. Ida had a child with polio, and it was out of her desire to cure her child that she was able to tune into divine guidance and gradually developed a ten-session "structural integration" treatment for the entire body that turned into this deep form of therapeutic bodywork. It actually dissolves unwanted blocks and barriers in the connective tissue and restores one to better, healthier postural alignment. It is not the same as massage, and no oil is used to soothe like in Swedish massage treatments.

My intuition guided me to call Jim Starr, the new rolfer on staff at the Holistic Health Center of Old Bridge, New Jersey, where I started my new massage practice with my chiropractor, Dr. Therkelsen. Friends in school had told me how powerful Rolfing is in releasing trauma and negative emotions that we often hold in the fascia, the soft connective tissues, of our body.

During the Rolfing sessions with Jim, anger, sadness, and fear were released as I breathed into the pain while he plied my body fascia deeply all around my spine, shoulders, entire legs and arms, and even inside my mouth, ears, and nasal cavities. Using very deep finger pressure on my bare skin, Jim reintegrated all my fascia into a perfect place of balance with my posture. My body looked and felt much lighter after just two of the ten sessions. I stood more erect, lost unwanted pounds, and my pelvis was no longer tipped backward.

While Jim was working, he played a sacred chant, a Sanskrit mantra imbued with the power of God, which is used in India, America, and all over the world by saints, devotees, and people from all walks of life. This mantra is "Om Namah Shivaya," which literally translated means, I honor and bow to Shiva.

In Hindu philosophy, Om (pronounced AUM) is the primordial sound from which all life sprung. The creative power of words is recognized in many religions. For example, in Hebrew scripture, it is written "God *said* 'Let there be Light,' and there was light." The Christian Gospel of John reiterates this idea in its opening verses, "In the beginning was the Word… and the Word was God."

In Hinduism, Shiva is the name of the first being to evolve to the state of complete God Realization. Namah in Sanskrit means I respect, honor, or bow. Shiva refers to the male or unmanifest aspect of God, the Father.

I received shaktipat, a spiritual initiation, during these Rolfing sessions, by the power of God and the Guru working through this mantra to awaken kundalini, the coiled inner meditative energy that resides at the base of the spine. This is the prana or chi, the energy of Life represented by the sign of the coiled serpent in medicine [4], that travels through all the chakras, (energy centers) until it finally comes to reside in the sahasrara or crown chakra at the top of the head, where total enlightenment, bliss, unity with all, and oneness with God is experienced. In Judaism the symbol for the kundalini is the Tree of Life, described in the kabbalah.

Receiving shaktipat is such a blessed initiation!

As he did with all his clients, Jim took Polaroid pictures of my body nude before and after each session so we could compare the progress and changes in my form from one session to the next. One could tell by the relaxed smile on my face and improved posture after treatment that I had been completely changed from being in a state of extreme fear and tension to one of peace, confidence, relaxation, and eventually profound joy. I did not mind being photographed nude because I was a free spirit and accustomed to going to the nude part of Lido Beach in Sarasota.

I did lots of deep breathing during these intense body work sessions and all kinds of emotions would come up. Many times, I did not express these feelings completely until later, when I was driving back home in my car. First, I'd cry very heartfelt tears for a while. Then I might scream and yell, even though I was not sure what I was angry about. I just vented pent up emotion. Then, finally, I would laugh with a light heart. I suppose, if someone had been in the car watching and listening to me emoting, they would have thought I was absolutely nuts to cover such a span of emotions in such a brief period of time.

Afterward, my mind would become very still, and I'd feel sublime peace. I had the thought that everything that transpired in my life was perfect. I felt a deep connection to God within my own heart. I felt full of love and joy.

I have heard that this is a classic kundalini experience. There are many. Some people see sparkling blue or other colored lights, hear inner sounds, go into spontaneous hatha yoga postures, or breathe quickly in a way they never have before. This is called pranayama. All these are beneficial and are signs that the kundalini has awakened and is moving through the body, purifying all the chakras. The word "yoga" itself comes from a Sanskrit word yug meaning "yoke". All kinds of yoga are intended primarily as spiritual disciplines. But the main intention of each is the same-to still the "vrittis" or modifications of the mind because once the mind is quiet it is easy to remember our one true essence which is pure, untainted, guileless love, ecstasy, conscious awareness, and energy.

Eventually I wanted to know more about the source of my bliss and new experiences, so I asked Jim what was happening to me. He told me I probably got shaktipat from his guru. Shakti is Shiva's consort and refers to the divine feminine, the creative aspect of being. In Hindu philosophy, out of the divine union of Shiva and Shakti, the entire universe was created.

---

4 The caduceus, or wand entwined by two serpents and associated with the messenger god, Hermes, may be seen in medical literature and on medical buildings to this day. A more correct symbol for health and wholeness is the rod of Asclepius, the ancient Greek god of healing, which is depicted as a single serpent coiled around a staff. In yoga, the staff is identified with the spinal column.

Meeting my Master

There is a saying that goes, "When the student is ready the Master will appear." This happened for me in 1981 at 26 years old. A dark night of the soul caused me to pray wholeheartedly to God for a breakthrough and healing of my suffering. Thank the Lord He answered my prayers quickly by leading me to Jim Starr. He and his wife, Ann, took me to the Siddha Yoga ashram (yoga center) in the Catskills to meet the saint, Swami Muktananda. I fell in love with him at first sight.

In receiving shaktipat, my heart center was fully opened and I experienced the purest love within my own self when I received the mantra, Om Namah Shivaya, directly from Baba Muktananda on September 27, 1981. That was the most wonderful, auspicious day of my entire life.

I was told the building used to be the Gilbert, a resort hotel, but was converted by the guru and his followers into an ashram, where people lived year-round and did spiritual practices from early morning until evening. The devotees who lived there maintained an attitude of love and respect for God, the guru, themselves, and each other. God was worshiped daily through different rituals and selfless service (*guruseva*, performing whatever tasks were required to run the ashram, including cooking, cleaning, ordering food and utensils in bulk etc.).

Love, sublime inner peace, and bliss were directly experienced through the ancient practices of meditation, chanting sacred Sanskrit mantras, and *guruseva*. There were courses in hatha yoga, meditation, chanting, music, and the Eastern philosophies of Vedanta and Kashmir Shaivism. Programs and intensive workshops occurred on a regular basis. Many famous actors and musicians were attracted to Baba's philosophies and Great Spirit. I personally met and interacted with actor Raul Julia, and actress, Felicia Rashad, who often emceed evening programs at the ashram in South Fallsburg. My best friend and nanny to my children, Janet, sat next to actress, Lisa Bonet, once on a group flight with Gurumayi to India where our final destination was Baba Muktananda's ashram in Ganeshpuri.

The ashram schedule was challenging to a newcomer. The day for most people began at 3:30 AM with a quick shower and dressing with respect, prior to meditation and chanting. At 4:15, chai tea was served, and at 4:30, there was a lovely brief chant called the Arati, signaled by the beating of a loud bass drum and the sound of a conch shell being blown. From 5:30 until 7:00 AM was a sacred chant honoring the guru disciple relationship called the Guru Gita, the song of the guru. Many times, I'd oversleep and miss meditation, but I absolutely adored chanting this sacred song, and usually was alert enough to enjoy that special time, which, for me, was like meditation. All the practices and courses were designed to help a person quiet his or her mind and go within and truly experience the love, sublime peace, and bliss that is always present within all humans, and that we easily experience when the mind is quiet.

From the moment I walked onto the grounds of the ashram and saw finely sculpted statues of great beings like Christ Jesus, the Buddha, Martin Luther King, Shiva, and Mahatma Gandhi, I knew I was in a special, sacred place.

Colorful flowerbeds with fuchsia pink and white petunias, purple and yellow pansies, yellow and orange marigolds, and pink zinnias garlanded the building, and the grass was trimmed perfectly. Soothing wind chimes rang out a melodious welcome outside the entrance-way where a beautiful round mandala had been drawn in multicolored chalks. The entire place was immaculate and permeated with an ambiance of peace, beauty, love, kindness, respect, and order.

A pretty blond woman wearing an Indian sari greeted us with a warm smile when we entered, and led me to another woman who took my photo and gave me a name tag. Everywhere we went, many people (mostly Westerners and a handful of Indians) acknowledged us with radiant faces and sweet smiles.

We walked past an information center, and through two long corridors, past what looked like a dining room. Hung on the walls of the corridor were many colorful paintings of men and women clad in a very different garb than I was accustomed to as an American. Many of the men looked like they had on large diapers and nothing else. I would learn from Jim that these were loincloths, and the men who wore them were usually monks, *sadhus* (sages or ascetics), or celibate *avadhuts* (saints, who were usually in a state of God intoxication totally unconcerned with people and unaffected by the world.) The women were beautiful, and one saint named Lalleshwari wore long dark hair that fell to her knees, because she was clad "only in the sky", and out of respect for others she allowed her hair to cover her breasts and genitals. Other women were painted wearing saris, with Lord Krishna, a blue being, working by their side.

Outside the main hall was a shoe room, which had a sign that said, "Leave your ego outside with your shoes." In the hall we were led by a hostess to the front of the room near Baba's (Sanskrit for "father's") dais (holy seat) after his wife, Ann, told her it was my first time at the ashram. Most of the people in the hall were sitting quietly with their legs crossed on the clean lush grayish blue carpet, densely packed, like sardines in a can, as close to the front of the room as possible, to be near Baba's seat. Some older, less athletic, or disabled folks sat in comfortable royal blue cushioned chairs in the back and one man named Mahadev was sitting in a wheelchair. Behind these chairs was a large painting of Muktananda when he was younger – looking very handsome and muscular with not much clothing on.

A magnificent painting was above what looked like an altar that had several vases of apricot gladiolas, a sterling silver tray with incense, a lit candle, and a pair of sterling silver sandals. Incense and frankincense smelled sweet, better than my mom's best perfume. The delicious scents filled me with joy, a sense of deep relaxation and sublime peace. There was also a little picture of Swami Muktananda's beloved Master and guru, Bhagwan Nityananda, whom they called Bade Baba.

People were laying themselves down on the carpet, prostrating in reverence to the representation of their teacher, Muktananda. Bowing in this way was said to worship and honor the guru, God, and your own Self, I was told. So, I walked to the back like the others, bowed, and said a prayer of respect and gratitude.

Meanwhile, at the front of the hall, a lady swami clads in an orange robe led everyone in a slow chant of Om Namah Shivayah. I already knew the melody of the chant because Jim had taken me to the Freehold Meditation Center twice on Friday evenings for a program, called *satsang* in Siddha Yoga. The Sanskrit word *satsang* means "in the company of the Truth." After the twenty-minute chant we were led into a brief period of meditation.

The chant was soothing and quieted my mind, which was excited with thoughts of anticipation about meeting a great saint who was revered by many the world over. Suddenly, with my eyes still closed, I heard excited whispers spreading through the crowd. "Baba's coming," someone whispered. And then silence, when the people remembered they should respect the quiet sanctity of the space the guru had created. As he passed by me, I peeked at him out of the corner of my eye to see him striding like a focused, powerful, yet graceful man, down the pathway leading to his seat. Though he was really of medium stature, thin, and in his seventies, he had the presence of a quietly powerful giant in vibrant health, and could pass for a man in his late fifties.

Though Baba was nearing the end of his life, he had the toned, muscular and flexible body of a young athlete. After bowing to the picture of his guru, Baba Nityananda, he lifted himself easily up onto his seat with agility and grace; he sat in a half lotus posture with his back erect and gave us a great big smile, exposing what looked like new shiny white dentures, while he exchanged a few words with a strikingly beautiful dark-haired Indian woman dressed in a fashionable scarlet dress. I was told this was his translator, Malti. She is now known as Gurumayi Chidvilasananda, and replaced Baba as the head of the Siddha Yoga lineage in the summer of 1982 before his passing on October 2nd.

Baba was wearing an orange shirt and pants, and his head was covered in a simply adorable orange knit cap. He looked playful and adorable, but his presence was subtly powerful and serene at the same time. It seemed that, psychically, he knew everything about each person there in the audience. Baba was a *Siddha*, a perfected human being, who had purified his ego and realized his Self as God, one with all beings... He was part of a great lineage of Ascended Masters who came from India, going all the way back to Sri Jnaneshwar, who were born fully realized beings, those who had already reached a level of Self Mastery whereby they'd ascended to heaven while still on earth. The Siddhas had all attained the state of Unity consciousness, in deep communion with Source, in which they experienced themselves as God all the time. Neither Bhagwan Nityananda nor Shankaracharya needed to come back to the earth plane. They volunteered to come back to help all of humanity to attain this same level of Self Mastery.

When Muktananda addressed the crowd, the first thing he said to us via his translator, Malti was, "I welcome you all with the greatest love and respect, with all of my heart." It was such a beautiful way to be welcomed. I felt that his words were totally sincere, impersonal yet meant especially for each one there. I can't remember now what his talk was about, but I do remember him speaking of his own guru, Bhagwan Nityananda, with utmost love and tenderness – almost with the same reverence and sweetness a newlywed husband would speak about his own wife or vice versa. One could tell that he felt devotion and gratitude to the Being who had bestowed upon him the world's greatest treasure – Enlightenment, the complete realization of himself as God, one with the source of All-That-Is, a state of sublime inner peace, equanimity, supreme love, and ecstasy. God's nature is *Sat-Chit-Ananda*. That is, Pure Being, Consciousness, and Bliss Absolute.

After more chanting, we were told we could have *darshan*. to meet and talk to Baba Muktananda directly. People waited patiently on a long line for at least an hour to get the chance to speak to him or just to bow to him and receive his blessing with the peacock feathers. I was told that it was traditional to honor a saint in this way. When we bow to a great being in this way, we are honoring the Great Self of all which is the same as honoring our own beautiful selves.

I was very excited that I was going to meet Baba and would be introduced to him for the first time. I knew Muktananda sometimes gave out spiritual names to aspirants and new seekers, so I decided to ask for one when I was introduced. The names were on cards that Malti handed out. All the names on the cards were special names of gods, goddesses, servants and lovers of God like Krishnadas, Giridhar, Krishni, and Ramdas.

I bowed when I met Baba and simply said I was happy to meet him.

He said, "*Bot acha*," "Very good" in Hindi and blessed me by brushing the top of my head with his peacock feathers. I also received Indian "prasad", a gift of a sweet from one of the young women sitting to his right.

When I returned to my seat, I looked at my card to see what name I'd received. The name Niranjani was on the front. On the back it said Niranjani meant pure and taintless or stainless. I thought he had made a mistake.

In my mind I believed I'd committed many sins and I had often felt unworthy or impure – especially after having been sexually molested by my father and been promiscuous most of my life.

I had also lost my virginity in a traumatic way to a charming, but cold-hearted assistant manager, my first boss at Farrell's Ice cream Parlor in Paramus Park where I became a bus girl at nineteen years old. When Frank and I met we flirted a lot during my training. He did not have a permanent home here because he was flown in from Maryland just to train the waitresses and busgirls. He was staying at a room in the Holiday Inn. One night he took me to his room where we kissed and made out on the couch. Eventually he lured me into the bed and had sex with me. I told him that it was my first time, but he did not believe me because I was adept at foreplay. After he ejaculated inside me rather quickly he turned over to sleep. I wanted to cuddle and kiss, but after ten minutes he asked me to leave his bed and hotel room saying that he had a hard time sleeping with me there. I was very hurt and left abruptly after getting dressed. I felt hurt, angry, dishonored, and unappreciated. It was not a painful experience physically, but there was no pleasure or caring in this lustful expression. I felt used and abused.

I was hurt and angry that this insensitive man did not believe I was a virgin, and he had no appreciation for the beautiful, loving, caring person I was. I was planning to keep my sacred space for my husband or at least a special, kind man with whom I was in love. After this man seduced me and took my virginity I felt like a prostitute. That was the way he treated me except I got no money for the act. I thought to myself, "This sex thing is not what it's cracked up to be". Since I'd lost my virginity I began to think I was impure, and I might as well fuck around. I was so angry after the experience I came back to the hotel parking lot with my two stepsisters and let some of the air out of two of his tires. I placed some dead flowers on his car to symbolize what he'd done to me, I suppose.

After that I became somewhat promiscuous and began having sex with Steve, another assistant manager who was as short as me. But he was very cute, sweet, enthusiastic, and perky. He also played piano for us in the ice cream parlor on the old-time player piano. Steve cared for me at least, and began to talk about us living together. The relationship went nowhere, and I was eventually fired from Farrell's because I was so angry with the first manager who took my virginity that I told the other waitresses about what transpired. There was a policy that the staff was not supposed to "fraternize" with one another. I got blamed for the incident. The management chose to use me as a scapegoat and terminated me, rather than their important assistant manager. I was the one who was penalized, and Frank got to keep his job, until he had sex with Jane, another young waitress, got her pregnant, and had to leave the company in disgrace. I was told they got married after that.

The more I contemplated the meaning of my new name, the more I realized why I received it. I came to the conclusion that Baba had given me the perfect name! He could actually see who I was better than I could see myself. He could perceive the pure openhearted being I truly was, that I was not a body, but an essence and expression of the Holy Spirit.

Baba perceived me as the pure and formless blue light of consciousness, an individualized expression of God. He saw everyone in this way. Baba said that whenever he would meet a person the first thing, he would see was this beautiful blue light before he would even notice his or her form or individual characteristics. Once in one of my meditations after chanting with great love and gusto in 1985 I saw the "blue pearl" and I went into an ecstatic and sublimely peaceful state within myself. It was a deep state of quiet serenity and utter contentment where everything was beautiful, Light, and balanced.

Later on, I looked up my new name, Niranjani, in a large catalog in the hall by the information center. Upon further research I found the name also meant "formless" and was another name for the Goddess Durga. It was also mentioned in the Guru Gita at least four times throughout its 188 verses. I believed that Baba wanted me to focus on the essence of That which I was rather than to be so identified with my body so much. For most of my grown-up life I felt pride or unworthiness, shame, or guilt depending on how I looked or "felt" about my body. Baba was reminding me that I am so much more than just a body. I realized I was and am Great Spirit, the very Self that animates my body.

I am the unconditional love and pure essence of Divine Consciousness. I am Shiva, the Cosmic Dancer, and the Divine Actor on this stage called Life. I am Shakti, the Goddess that has become all forms. I am the Eternal Witness of this divine play of consciousness, and life has become so filled with delight, sport and fun. That was the beginning of my journey to Self-Awareness under the guidance of an enlightened Master.

Since that time in 1981 I've experienced many transitions and transformations as well as more ups and downs. It is only through the grace of God and my gurus that I am still alive and happy now. Affirmative prayer, exercise, loving intimate relationships, positive thinking, and the medication, Depakote, for more than twenty-five years. I also use Bach flower essences and attribute my health and success to the support of my precious family and friends, my church, the Center for Spiritual Living Princeton, Rev. Karen Kushner, and the grace of God and my gurus have been my lifelines to happiness, balance, and success.

Shortly after I met Baba, Jim Starr suggested I compose a song for him for his upcoming birthday in May of 1982. I channeled a beautiful song entitled "By Your Grace" with four verses about my relationship and experiences with God in the form of the guru, which I had the great fortune to perform at the Freehold Meditation at a Friday night Satsang. I sang and played it on guitar again for Gurumayi Chidvilasananda at the Siddha Yoga ashram in South Fallsburg, New York, along with three other original songs, during darshan. I continued to grow and have joyous experiences during the rest of that summer and into the fall. I immersed myself in the practices of chanting and meditation, and took a three-week intensive class to become certified as a hatha yoga instructor that summer with Swami Shivananda, one of my favorite Siddha Yoga swamis.

"By Your Grace"[5] is the song I wrote for Baba on my guitar that I believe was channeled through my mind and heart because it came so quickly in less than thirty minutes. First came the chords to the verse and then the chorus. The lyrics to the four verses were penned in about twenty minutes and were completely from my heart. In May 1982, dedicated to and inspired by Swami Muktananda Paramahansa, for his lunar birthday I played and sang "By Your Grace" at the Freehold Meditation Center for Lata and Ramon Goldberg and all the other devotees of Baba and students of Siddha Yoga who came to Satsang there on Friday nights. I sang with great love and reverence to Baba in honor of his birthday.

Baba passed over in 1982, the day before my grandfather. I found this out the day after Pop Pop's funeral.

I was in shock. A few days before I had been asking Baba to help my Pop Pop to be at peace with dying and not to be afraid to leave his physical body not even knowing that Baba himself had already

---

5 The lyrics have been published in my poetry anthology "Heartscapes"

ascended the day before. Actually, he was already an Ascended Master Who knew all things, so they call his passing away his final samadhi, the blessed time when He merged with the Infinite Being again.

One who has become a perfected Master, a guru, is not the physical being. The guru is a force, an entity, or a channel of Light, so we can be affected by this energy in many different ways-through the mantra, through sound vibrations, words of truth spoken by others or that we read in books, and often when we quiet our minds in prayer and meditation, we can tune into that Loving Essence that is our very own inner nature and Truth of Being in the Present Moment.

Since I knew there was a Siddha Meditation Center in Sarasota, I was able to attend a satsang there to help me come to terms with my guru's death. I was with other devotees there so we could share stories about Baba's miracles in their lives, and also how Baba's words and actions lived on in Gurumayi Chidvilasananda, just like Bhagwan Nityananda's love, wisdom, and grace lived on in Muktananda, his greatest and most devoted disciple. The guru's power, love, wisdom, and grace are beyond all form. It is something always felt on a more subtle level than in the gross physical body. It turned out to be very auspicious and a boon that I was in Venice, just one-half hour away from the Sarasota Siddha Meditation center run by my friend, Michael Rose, another healer and massage therapist I'd met while in school. I went to him for a massage, and I used him as one of my "practice patients" when we had to massage a hundred clients for our practicals. I was so thankful that I would be able to connect with some other Siddha Yoga devotees during such a disturbing time.

I was so relieved that I could attend the center in Sarasota where I could chant and meditate with other devotees, and watch a video of Baba. We also got news of what was going on in India and South Fallsburg, New York, the main ashram in the US where I'd met him. It was so helpful for me to have the support of other Siddha Yoga disciples during such a difficult time of transition. I thought it was so ironic that I was praying to Baba to help make my grandpa's transition easier when he'd already moved on the day before. I'm sure Baba heard my prayers anyway and was there at the moment I thought of him. To this day, I can connect with Baba just by thinking of him and holding him in my heart. I feel the same way about my Pop Pop, whom I still think of with so much love to this day. I was the apple of his eye. And despite his faults, he was a very kind, loving, and generous man. He was a terrific grandfather to me, my first cousins, and my brothers, and I will always be grateful to him for that.

The death of my guru was more difficult for me to take than the passing of my own grandfather. But I think that was because it was unexpected. Baba had told his entire Siddha family except his inner circle – that he would be making at least three more world tours, so just about everyone was in a state of shock. I had only met him less than a year before, and now he was abandoning me just the way my dad and Sid did. That was how news of his death first affected me.

After a while I would adjust to the fact that we still had the two gurus, Swamis Nityananda and Chidvilasananda, whom Baba had installed, prior to taking mahasamadhi. They would be the ones to carry on the lineage, and Baba invested them with the full power of the Siddhas before he decided he would be taking mahasamadhi – his final liberation and reunion with Godhead. Unfortunately, Swami Nityananda left the ashram in shame with the cook, and later set up his own ashram saying Gurumayi was truly the only guru invested with the power of the Siddha lineage.

EARLY DAYS WITH DAVID

David and I had met at the Freehold Siddha Yoga Meditation Center in 1981. We were all devotees of Swami Muktananda, and I loved the fact that all these men interested in meditation and Self Realization were spiritual, loving men on a yogic path I firmly saw as a way to enlightenment and God Realization. We all chanted, prayed, and meditated together which made for a loving, caring, fraternal type bond. I was not attracted to David one bit. He appeared awkward and "geeky" to me. He said,"Hi. Nice to meet you, Meryl. I have my own Siddha Yoga Meditation Center in East Brunswick with a Satsang on Monday nights."

David and me at the wedding

"Very nice," I said, "but I'm busy on Mondays." In my mind I thought, "forget about it. You just look like a skinny twerp to me." In my arrogance I never gave him or his Center a bit of a chance.

I avoided David's advances for over a year and a half. Though he invited me to attend a Satsang in his home in East Brunswick, New Jersey, several times and acted very interested in me I just ignored him and decided to date every other available single man who attended the Freehold Siddha Yoga Meditation center. I in fact dated two of the other eligible bachelors who went there. These relationships proved unsuccessful. Steve was the handsomest and nicest of the three I dated, but I did not feel physically attracted to him even though he was very cute, smart, and sweet. Ironically, David and I would use Steve's apartment complex, Fox Run, in Plainsboro, New Jersey which had a lovely lake and clubhouse lake in which to hold our wedding ceremony near and reception afterward. It seemed I just was not physically attracted to the men who were nice and respectful to me, no matter how good looking or charming they seemed to be.

Maybe after watching my parents' marriage falter and divorce when I was a mere sixteen and how my Pop Pop would not even kiss Grammy after her hysterectomy that made me sour on conventional marriage and want to get a good career before ever considering marriage and having children. Though I dated and had unfulfilling sex with many men I was not interested in marriage. I continuously denied David's requests for a friendly date or to even attend a Satsang (meditation and chanting session) at his own Siddha Yoga Center for a while.

Eighteen months after our first meeting, David invited me to teach hatha yoga at a workshop he was facilitating for the Holistic Health Association of Princeton being held at the Unitarian Church in Princeton. David and organized and facilitated a workshop for the speaker, author and lecturer, Joseph Chilton Pierce, all the teachers, and logistics. It was that fateful day in January of 1983 that my feelings finally changed toward him. I was a new yoga teacher certified by the Siddha Yoga Foundation the summer before, and was an instructor part-time at the Freehold Meditation Center, When David invited me to be the guest instructor at the seminar, I was honored and finally happy to oblige one of his requests.

He was an excellent facilitator and leader. He was also very open-hearted and delighted in selflessly serving the guru. He told me he had been the manager of the Manhattan ashram for a year and traveled on several tours with Baba doing set-up and various types of seva for Swami Muktananda for at least five years before I'd even met him. I finally saw David in a new light – as a powerful leader and courageous man committed to being in service to the guru and humanity. It was from this new perspective that I felt open and interested in wanting to know him better.

Our workshop was an amazing success with many participants having unique and powerful experiences in their meditations through the power of the shakti (a Sanskrit word for the feminine, creative energy of God) and the guru's grace. I did a fine job as the hatha yoga instructor and I suppose some of the asanas (the yoga postures) may have prepared people for the heart opening chanting and meditation experiences they had afterward. Our featured speaker, Joseph Chilton Pearce, gave a great lecture on his own personal experience with God's grace after meeting Swami Muktananda. He'd just published the very popular book "Bond of Power" after having had great success with his other books, "The Crack in the Cosmic Egg" and "Magical Child".

Our good friend, Karna (Howard Matric) also was present to lead the chanting and meditation sessions. Several people came to us afterward to share what a powerful experience of chanting and meditation they had had. Teaching hatha yoga came naturally to me as I'd been teaching it at the center for several months, so I truly enjoyed it. I felt happy to be able to contribute to others peace and spiritual growth in this way.

I was living in East Brunswick at the time with a woman friend named Bea, whom I'd met at the Freehold Center.

Once the workshop was over, David invited me and Karna to go out to the Greenline Diner in Princeton for a wonderful vegetarian meal. I naturally said "yes". Not only was I hungry, but I was impressed with the man I saw who facilitated this powerful, successful workshop. He had a fine intellect and was very confident in the way he ran things. We really enjoyed one another s' company.

I would become interested and attracted to his fine intellect, spirituality, and devotion in selfless service to our guru and spiritual master, Swami Muktananda. I was a new devotee who had just met. David was considered to be an "old timer", having gotten Shaktipat initiation many years before just by reading our guru, Swami Muktananda's, autobiography entitled "The Play of Consciousness", which I would read later in my journey. All of an enlightened Master's words are powerful, prophetic, and considered to be purifying mantras in themselves.

I also fully enjoyed the company of Karna, who ended up being best man at our wedding just six months later. When I actually did allow David to take me out on a date, he courted the pants off me, and just swept me off my feet. From the minute I decided how special he was and let him in spiritually, emotionally and intellectually, we became very close and quickly fell in love.

After dinner, Girish (David's spiritual name) asked me if I'd like to go to the movies the next day to see Gandhi which starred the actor, Ben Kingston. I readily accepted because I was really starting to like all the beautiful qualities David possessed. On the car ride home from the diner I felt very happy about the success of the workshop and the nice relationship that I was allowing to happen between David and me. I was feeling ecstasy, and I was not quite sure why. On the way to my East Brunswick home, I began singing spontaneously in a very operatic coloratura soprano voice. I was singing some beautiful tones I'd never sung before. It was almost as if I was anticipating the great future that I was about to have with this special man. It was something I was not accustomed to doing, even though I was a first soprano from the time I was seventeen in Choir until I started singing in weddings and in rock and jazz bands in my early twenties. I sounded a bit like an operatic diva, and it was giving me great pleasure to sing in this angelic coloratura voice.

The seminar and Satsang (a Sanskrit word meaning "the company of the Truth") must have opened up a deep part within me that had an inner knowing this was the man who was going to be my husband and the father of my children. I just remember feeling ecstatic on the drive back to my apartment in East Brunswick.

The next day when David picked me up for the movie, he even began to look more attractive to me. He no longer seemed wimpy which was the first impression I'd had of him. He seemed very kind, intelligent, and was a great devotee of the guru and God. He was also dark haired and attractive in a Middle Eastern Mediterranean sort of way. The movie about Bapu's life touched us both deeply; and we both were particularly moved by the marriage ceremony when Gandhi and his wife were just teenagers. My entire perception of him shifted in less than twenty-four hours! From that moment on I think David began to fantasize about being married, and he courted me like crazy until I agreed to move in with him.

After the movie David took me out for dinner, and he invited me to go out with him after Satsang the following Friday. Two weeks later we were walking to the Brunswick Square Mall in East Brunswick, a few blocks from his home nearby off Rues Lane, we were so happy we were singing all the songs of Annie Haslam off of the Renaissance album, "Prologue." Somewhere, in the midst of sharing all that joy and closeness, David asked me if I would move in with him. Since we'd only been dating three weeks, I thought he was out of his mind and quite a bit premature or overly optimistic.

It was such a whirlwind romance that I refused at first. I'd lived with a man named Greg for nearly two years when I was 21 years old, and while a professional singer who was in two different traveling show bands. Our long separations while I was traveling resulted in my having affairs and a painful break-up. I was hesitant to live with a man again after that. I told David he was crazy to want to live with me after only dating such a short time. Not even one month, for Christ's sake! I said, "David, don't you think you are rushing things a bit? Besides, I've already lived with a man once, and when we broke up, I was devastated. If we were going to do anything I'd want us to make the commitment to each other to be married. But let's just see what happens."

We saw each other every day after that precious moment of connection. We called each other every day and David would write me poems on a regular basis while I'd leave surprise greeting cards on his car windshield sometimes with small poems from me.

It was almost Valentine's Day and David gave me a loving greeting card and a beautiful pair of 14 carat gold love knot earrings from Plum's Jewelers. His beautiful card expressed his love and devotion and he continued to take me out on dinner dates and accompanied me to Satsang on Friday nights.

A week later we were down at the Philadelphia ashram with Swami Umeshananda, and on the way home in the car David proposed. It was kind of strange how the whole thing unfolded.

We drove down together for this Satsang that included a very long chant of several hours and began about 10:00 AM. We were chanting Hare Krishna, Hare Rama. Anyway, the men and women are separated in Siddha Yoga so as to avoid getting distracted. But my mind kept wandering and I was getting a bit bored and restless after a few hours of sitting in the same position. I prayed to Lord Krishna to help me quiet my mind, and I would think about how he would appear to the Gopis, the young cow-maids who adored him, in one of his beautiful forms and make love to each one in the way that each one loved best. I began to look at Girish from across the room seeing him as the object of my devotion and divine worship; and I'd imagine him as Krishna making love to me. The Philadelphia ashram is imbued with so much of Baba's love and has an incredible amount of Shakti. Anyway, after an hour or so of chanting Hare Ram, Hare Krishna my mind began to wander, and I began to tire of being away from David; I started to yearn for him. I began to think of Krishna and how he was supposed to have appeared before the Gopis (the milkmaids who were devoted to him) and how it was legend that Krishna appeared to each of the Gopis individually and made love to each of them in the way each woman had longed who wanted to be in His loving embrace. While we were chanting Om I began to see the walls and everything around me become consciousness, and I could hear the sound of OM in the walls. Then I felt an incredible opening in my heart and tremendous love for myself and David whom at that point had become my very own personal Krishna.

As arduous as he was, I never expected to have sex with him or to be his wife in such a short period of time. We barely knew one another. It was the "honeymoon" phase of a new relationship, and I truly enjoyed the courtship, and also getting to know him spiritually and intellectually. I enjoyed kissing him, but I never allowed our physicality to get too far until about a month after we'd been dating and we decided to attend a saptah (saptah means seven in Sanskrit, but usually saptah refers to an extended continuous chant that goes on for one to seven days) at the Philadelphia ashram. We drove there in the same car. We were instructed to sit on opposite sides of the hall because men and women were separated in all the ashrams so as not to distract one another while meditating because our focus was supposed to be within on the inner Self in meditation and chanting.

We could not wait to leave because we were feeling so much sexual energy, we wanted to be alone with one another.

When the saptah was finally over David and I got into his car to go back and began kissing. We got so hot for each other we had to drive somewhere out of the way, and pulled over to the side of the road so we could become more intimate. We both took all our clothes off and put a blanket over the top of us. We had a great time though we did not go as far as having intercourse.

This was a first for us. Up to that point we had not really expressed too much in an intimate way beyond kissing. We got into the car and began French kissing deeply immediately. All I remember is one by one each piece of our clothing came off until we were both completely naked underneath a green army blanket David had placed over us. We were giggling like crazy and just could not stop laughing. I wonder what the toll taker thought was going on when we pulled up to the toll booth at whatever bridge it was to take our toll money from him naked as jaybirds underneath that old blanket. All I recall is that I was feeling light, happy, sexy, and that I could live with this man for the rest of my life. Then we laughed hysterically as we both stayed nude underneath the blanket and drove home together feeling close and very much in love. It was especially funny when we stopped to pay the toll in PA knowing we were naked in front of the toll booth collector. He must have sensed something was up because he gave us a very strange smile.

The following Friday we announced our engagement and had a small party for our closest friends. I decided to move out of the place I was living because my landlady and housemate was the woman who'd been dating David just prior to me. Suffice to say things were a bit awkward and uncomfortable. I temporarily moved in with Rich Parren, one of my yoga students who attended the Freehold Meditation Center because he owned a large home in Old Bridge and was kind enough to rent me a room. That situation only lasted just a few weeks before I decided to move in with David. There was one slight problem, though.

David's father owned the house in which he lived. He was a very successful builder, and David's house in East Brunswick was one of the models. Unfortunately for me, Mr. and Mrs. Cohen were Orthodox Jews living in Highland Park who also had a home in Israel. They were extremely religious and very prejudiced toward anyone who was not Jewish. They even referred to non-Jews in a disparagingly as "goyam". They were so strict and narrow minded that they didn't even spend time with Jews that were less orthodox like Conservative or reformed. When David told them he wanted to marry me they were not pleased. They insisted that in order for us to marry that I would have to go through a conversion process and arranged for me to meet a very nice Rabbi named Yehudah Fine from Brooklyn. I met Rabbi Fine and his family. David and I were invited to have dinner on the Sabbath at his home, and then we were invited to a Seder.

I really liked Yehudah and his wife, but I did not care very much for David's parents, who did not really want to get to know me as a person. They just wanted to change me without ever really knowing anything about me. The whole process seemed like a farce to me because David and I were already very connected spiritually through our love of Muktananda, God, and each other. We were vegetarian, so we already kept a kosher home. We both were very happy as devotees of Muktananda and had no desire to change our lifestyle or the ways in which we practiced spirituality – chanting, meditation, yoga, and selfless service.

I was just concerned about David. I wanted him to be able to have a good relationship with his parents, so I said I'd begin classes in Judaism and start the conversion process. In the meantime, David and I continued to attend satsangs and go up to our ashram in South Fallsburg to spend time with the swamis, Gurumayi, and other devotees of God and the guru. Baba had left for India in the fall, and as fate would have it he would never again return to the United States. He took Mahasamadhi, the "final liberation", in October of 1982, and Gurumayi and her brother, Nityananda, would replace Baba as joint heads of the Siddha Yoga lineage.

David and I were growing deeper in love each day, and we became inseparable. Each night he'd tell me, "Honey, we are going to get married much sooner than you think". I didn't care when it would happen. I was already so deeply in love I felt as if we'd be together forever with or without a wedding ring or ceremony.

The following week-end was an intensive workshop up at the ashram in the Catskills, and during that week-end we spent the entire two and a half days without a stitch on holed up in David's bedroom in East Brunswick meditating across from one another, or making love. It was a very intense weekend of purification and sweet intimacy. Since I'd been sexually molested, I had issues of trust with men, and sometimes I stopped feeling in my genitals. I allowed myself to feel some of the fear, sadness, and anger surrounding what happened with my father and other men afterward, and through this letting go I was able to feel more of my heart and my genitals opening up to the sensation of love. Shortly after that my friendship with Dick, the man from whom I rented a room, became strained because I believe he was also attracted to me, so I decided to move out again, but this time I moved into David's home in East Brunswick. A week later (exactly four weeks after our first date) David and I were supposed to see my favorite singer, Angela Bofill, at the Beekman Theater in New York City.

That morning I became ill with a mild flu or virus, and he wanted to make me feel better, so he came into our room with a beautiful, simple diamond engagement ring he had planned to give me later for which he paid only $600 in NYC. He kept saying "Honey, we are going to be married sooner than you think. I love you very much, and whenever you want to have children, I am OK with it."

Though I'd told him I loved children I was not in a real hurry to have any babies, but I think David just got carried away with all the love and meditation energy he was feeling as his heart opened up. He was a water sign, a Piscean born in early March, romantic like me, and willing to give me just about anything I wanted. After he proposed that morning of the day, we were going to see Angie in concert I began to feel much better. In fact, my flu symptoms practically disappeared within a few hours, and we were able to get ready for a trip to Manhattan and attend the concert together. Angie was fantastic, and I loved the sax player who opened for her too. It was David Sanborn before he had gained too much recognition. It was a very special evening knowing we were there as a committed couple engaged to be married and very much in love. I had an absolutely ecstatic time.

Little did I know at the time but marriage is an intense spiritual initiation that our guru, Muktananda, likened to "tapasya" --a Sanskrit word for burning. It is meant to burn away the ego, one's sense of individuality, our sense of separation, past life memories and karma, and all impurities until one experience God in himself as himself AND reflected in his or her spouse as well. No sense of separateness or Duality. Only Oneness. Unconditional love for Self and all others. In fact, in that state of Oneness, there is no sense of "otherness". Only the Self, the Supreme Being, existing in, as, and through oneself and all beings.

So, from that perspective I NEVER saw Divorce or separation as a possibility. I was so naive about real committed relationships in the beginning I did not see us having problems of any kind except possibly sexual because I had been molested as a teenager by my father, and always seemed to have problems in this area. It had always been tough for me to trust men enough to open up sexually in a long term, committed, monogamous relationship. I usually seemed to be attracted to the "bad boys" and just have short flings. Men usually would love me and leave me.

Or I would flirt and entice men like crazy, feeling sexually stimulated or alive so long as there was something new, clandestine, exciting, or forbidden in the relationship—in the same way as the feelings I experienced in the six months my dad touched me in an inappropriate way in my bedroom when he would tuck me into bed when I was fourteen. The inappropriate sexual and emotional intimacy I experienced with him was confusing, but it felt good physically, was exciting, forbidden, and must be kept secret. I had a tremendous amount of guilt due to the clandestine nature of our special, intimate relationship, and the subconscious guilt and toxic shame stayed with me for years.

Our wedding was quite amazing. It was what you might call a do-it-yourself wedding. We planned it ourselves. We planned and cooked all the vegetarian foods by ourselves and our friends all brought their own special vegetarian dishes. Our three-tiered wedding cake was made by Merly, a friend of ours from the South Fallsburg ashram, and he brought it all the way down from the Catskills without any mishaps. We rented China and gold-plated utensils from Millers Rentals in Edison. We did all the decorating ourselves, and we hired a band of my good friends with whom I'd formerly sung and performed, so that I could sing a few songs myself during the reception. The band included a pianist named Bob with whom I'd sung when a member of the Cosmic Vaudeville Company and All-Star Band when I was 21.

David rented a white tuxedo and I wore a simple old-fashioned antique looking off white wedding gown I'd purchased from Brooks in the Brunswick Square Mall for $50.00. My ornate $140 veil was more expensive than my wedding dress, and really added something special to the simple dress. It framed my face and I felt gorgeous like a princess. I had white satin pumps and my hair was put up in a French twist with tendrils hanging from my ears.

Singing at my wedding - I Will Survive

My dad and step-mom came down from Bergen County so Daddy could "give me away". My mom was the matron of honor and wore a lovely lilac gown. My step-sisters, Debbie, Suzie, and Kathy wore light blue gowns as the bridesmaids as did my cousin, Dru.

We asked my dear friend, Mike Cindrich, from the Psychic Science Temple of Metaphysics, to be the minister. He would also officiate at my second marriage. I knew Mike from the time I was a member of the Psychic Science Temple in Paterson when I was in my early twenties, and he was my chiropractor on occasion as well. He performed a simple, but beautiful ceremony during which I got up out of the audience to sing "Amazing Grace". The wedding was just lovely and went smoothly considering I did not even get dressed in my gown until after my dad and several guests had already arrived because we were so busy doing all the setting up, preparation, and decorating the reception area ourselves at Fox Run in Plainsboro, where our friend, Steve, from Siddha Yoga rented an apartment. We set up the chairs and had the ceremony right next to the lake at Steve's, condominium complex, where we rented the clubhouse for our reception for a mere $150.

I sang several songs at the reception which was really fun because I got the opportunity to dance, which is my favorite pastime. I think we all should have realized something was amiss, though, when I sang Gloria Gaynor's very popular theme song "I Will Survive" at the reception which happened to be a disco hit at the time. Who knew the title of that song was going to be a prognostication of things to come?

I feel so blessed that I eventually was able to give birth to three healthy, beautiful children despite all my mental and emotional problems before and after they were born. Thank God David was somehow able to remain stable despite my mania, my affairs, and my leaving him for Lyle, a black man fifteen years my junior whom I met when I was hospitalized at the Carrier Clinic in 1988 during my first period of mania after we were married. It's the **LOVE** that produced the three most glorious beings of Light on the planet today, and believe me, I am not being prejudiced because I am their mother. These are one young man and two angelic young women whom I have had the privilege of sharing my sweet life-my three magnificent offspring without whom I could not be here today-- alive and well. Without them I might be dead today. Or possibly in jail or on long term retreat in an insane asylum. Their love for me and mine for them has saved my life many times, helped me to persist through each challenge and dark moment until I came out the other side into the glorious Light of reason, unconditional love, and wisdom. Being here on this planet with my children has made me WHO I AM. Our mutual love for each other has literally made me a stronger, more caring, more determined, humble, and more compassionate person. They also have helped me to laugh at myself a lot more and not take life or myself so seriously. I also learned a lot about having to surrender control and just allow Great Spirit to guide and guard me and them.

The three of them were God's special gifts to me. And I am forever grateful to God, to Gabriel, to Kyrie, and to Sky for giving me three reasons to fight this debilitating mental illness, manic depression. And actually, become a better person for having come triumphantly through this experience. Without the support of my friends, my loving, patient mom, my ex-husband, and children I am certain I would not be here telling my inspiring story to you today. I will tell you about these magnificent beings in the order of their births. Without their unconditional love, support, and belief in me I would still be struggling or perhaps, might have successfully committed suicide and would now be in a hellish realm somewhere on the other side without having the privilege of watching them grow up, have their own families, and have the privilege of sharing in their amazing lives.

GABRIEL

My firstborn I named Gabriel. He impressed me with his special, angelic name from the celestial realms while he was checking out Planet Earth for the most perfect parents in order for his soul to evolve while serving the many humans in need on this Earth plane. And most important, it is the name of a special archangel in the celestial realm, one of many angels and guides who work with me and other Light Workers here on Earth from the higher dimensions. I wanted my son's name to be special and unique-like mine. I figured at the time I found I was pregnant that the name would work whether or not the baby was a boy or a girl, though I had an intuitive feeling I was carrying a boy. Our dear friend, one of the monks David knew from Siddha Yoga, Swami Sevananda, told me I was carrying a male child, too, after I finished massaging him at our home in East Brunswick.

After having barely survived my own birth in Staten Island Hospital, where they were not very hospitable, about a month after I found out I was pregnant I firmly decided to give my son a better, much gentler start in life with no insensitive male doctors, hospitals, drugs, blinding lights, or smacks on the behind. I wanted our experience to be a totally gentle, conscious experience for us both. Wow, did Gabriel's birth turn out to be an adventure – not just for me and my husband, David, but for seven other people who assisted me.

I had heard of women who gave birth in their own homes using midwives who encouraged them to take back their own power by remembering birthing is a natural, relatively easy process. In fact, from my own experience, it can even be painless and enjoyable when we relax and follow our body's intuition on how to handle each contraction.

My husband David and I had taken classes with Barbara, a midwife, for about ten weeks to understand the labor and birthing experience in more depth since we were choosing to have natural childbirth at home with no drugs or intervention of any kind. Like episiotomies where a laboring woman's perineum is actually cut in order to help the baby's head fit through the hole. But I had already envisioned exactly how my perfect birth would be. So, no complications ever took place except one when Gabriel's anterior shoulder got stuck, but the midwife easily remedied this by stretching my perineum with her gloved fist.

I had become close friends with both of the midwives, Barbara and Anne, during eight- and one-half months of prenatal check-ups where I learned to use a pH stick in order to check the alkalinity of my urine. All the women having home births were encouraged to take responsibility for monitoring their health during the entire pregnancy, especially in the last two trimesters.

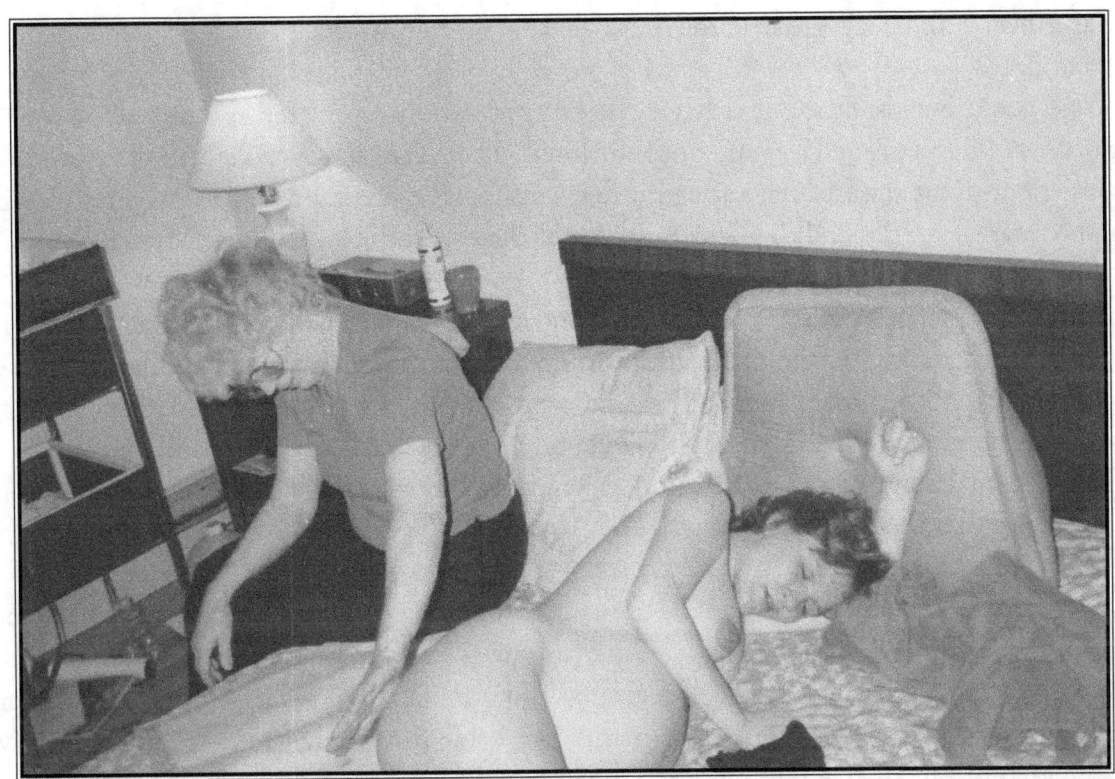

Midwife Ann and me

The day before Gabriel was born turned out to be very special. On Saturday, February 4th, 1984, my mother's 47th birthday, I had planned a surprise birthday party for her with all the trimmings. Little did I know my mom's surprise birthday party would have a surprise in store for me as well.

Mom's special day turned out to be the same day I began having light labor contractions in the morning after I woke up. There was a bloody show in my panties when I first awoke; my midwives told me my mucous plug had come out which was a sign my labor would begin soon.

A whirlwind of energy swept over me in the morning, and I spent the day singing and dancing to my favorite artists on the stereo, Angela Bofill and Earth, Wind, and Fire while I vacuumed, dusted, and began preparing all the food for the party.

David was a tall, handsome dark-haired Jew who looked a bit Middle Eastern. He was an insurance salesman for Equitable who almost always worked six days per week, but had taken the day off for the special occasion. He put up colorful streamers and other decorations in our living room in Jamesburg while I began layering my main course, vegetarian lasagna, in the same way my mom and maternal grandmother had taught me. It takes three hours just to prepare and cook the tomato sauce alone.

I was having mild contractions all day while preparing the baked lasagna with my grandmother, Lucy's recipe of fresh ingredients like mozzarella and ricotta cheeses, layering the par-boiled curly lasagna with a home-made sauce. I also prepared a garden salad, and a fruit salad for dessert while still having mild contractions.

After all the cooking was done, I got dressed and ready for my six guests to arrive. My good friends, Elaine and Stan Levy, came from Hightstown, Jack and Marcy, our special friends from Siddha Yoga came, and my brothers, Peter and Scott, brought the birthday guest. Mom was truly surprised.

My brothers, Peter and Scott, were there, too.

It was a diverse and lively group at the party, sharing my family legacy favorite foods, and everyone had a great time.

No one could believe that I was having light contractions every ten minutes all through our dinner because I never uttered a sound or complained. They were relatively light, so I just focused on entertaining my guests and leisurely eating the delicious food I'd prepared. What a wonderful, relaxing evening pregnant with possibilities. I had no idea of the fun and joy the Great Mystery had in store for me that night and the following morning.

The mild contractions became more intense, and after a while, I was not laughing and talking so much. I was just focusing on the contractions in my belly and vagina gradually dilating my cervix. It was my first experience with labor so I became a bit anxious. I was so relieved when all the guests finally left our home at 10 PM. David and I could be alone and almost ready to call for the midwives' assistance. But my two younger brothers said "Meh, we want to be there if the baby is really coming. Will you call us after the midwives arrive?" They would also be called to come back sooner than they knew.

I was so grateful that my son chose to be born on a Sunday when David would usually be home. He changed into his light blue silk pajamas after the ten guests left. He would have stayed home anyway just in case I was in "real" labor. David was excited about the birth of his first child, a son whom we had already chosen a name – Gabriel. The name had come intuitively to me when I was only two months pregnant from an angel in the celestial realms.

I was extremely healthy and athletic, being a yoga instructor and practitioner, and as far as we could tell from all my check-ups, the baby was too. The midwives suggested we have a backup obstetrician in case any complications arose during childbirth, so I went to Dr. Howard Graybelle in Kendall Park just once, at my midwives' suggestion, to engage his support just in case there was a breech birth or any other complication.

I realized I was truly in "REAL" labor around 10:30 PM, so I finally called Barbara and Anne, the midwives who were traveling an hour from Red Bank in order to assist in my labor and delivery. I did not want to bother my midwives prior to that if it was just a false alarm. There is such a thing called Braxton-Hick's contractions which usually do not lead to a birth too soon. But now, I was pretty certain Gabriel was on his way down from heaven to meet his new mom and dad. I happily agreed to call the midwives since I thought I might need all the physical, emotional, and spiritual support I could get. While waiting for them to arrive I began chanting my guru, Swami Muktananda's, mantra, "Om Namah Shivaya" which means I honor God in the ancient Sanskrit language. It was a powerful mantra used all over the world to put devotees of God into deep meditation, and the power of its vibration put me into a relaxed mental state while having to endure the more painful contractions. I learned how to use my intuition each time a contraction came to drop down into my pelvis while chanting and singing Om very loudly. I used my husband's body to hang from allowing David to support all my weight. Each time I had another intense contraction, I put my arms around David's neck while dropping down into my pelvis every time the pains would come dilating my cervix even more as the baby gradually came down the birth canal. The contractions were coming five or six minutes apart, so we could not wait for the midwives to arrive. David walked me around the living room, and each time a contraction came I would loudly chant our mantra, "OM NAMAH SHIVAYA," relaxed on the couch for a little while, and hoped for the best.

In the meantime, David had called Peter and Scott, who both returned promptly. They both helped out a lot by supporting my weight and encouraging me until the midwives got there. David had been supporting me and physically holding me up many times during a 12-hour labor, but he got tired after about six hours. My brothers became back up support, allowing me to put my arms around their necks to hang down during the really painful contractions which were coming faster.

Then the midwives arrived!

Ann and Barbara were lay midwives and both had prior experience as obstetrical nurses, so I knew they had lots of experience delivering babies naturally without any drugs or intervention from doctors when that was the mother's choice in her birth plan. A woman has the right to choose whatever works for her and makes her feel comfortable while giving birth. Some want to numb the pain with drugs and this is absolutely fine, but it was not what I wanted.

We had lavender and peppermint scented candles lit setting the sacred mood and beautiful New Age music playing in the background by keyboardist, Steven Halpern, and harpist, Georgia Kelly's, "Ancient Echoes" which put us all in a quiet state of meditation and deep calm. There was a feeling of sublime peace, amidst mixed our excitement mixed with great anticipation and expectancy. It was one of the most sacred and exciting nights of my life, even better than the night of David's and my wedding where we were in a state of exhaustion and just wanted to get to sleep after the reception was over and we were nearly too tired to get out of our wedding clothes.

Right before the end David and I took a shower together to relax and refresh ourselves.

According to Barbara and Ann I was nine centimeters dilated already around 4 AM. Only one more to go until I would be told to push, but my water had yet to break.

David and I had taken on two housemates' months before to help us out with expenses. Sven, a music teacher rented one room from us, and another very dear friend from Siddha Yoga, Jack Stoller, was staying with us temporarily while he and his wife needed a break from each other. Jack had been David's best man at our wedding a year before. Both Jack and Sven knew of the impending event and stayed home to participate in the fun. Jack's wife, Marcy, who lived in East Windsor, came over too, so I had plenty of support from family and friends, both male and female.

Then at 6 AM, as the light of dawn was coming through the windows, we all got giddy and began singing "Blue Skies" together. Peter and Scott played two kazoos I keep on hand to play jug band music. Sven played air guitar, and Jack played an imaginary trumpet while David played the drums upon his lap. I had so much fun singing like Ella Fitzgerald and listening to the creativity of the guys playing the different instruments I barely noticed the pain when another powerful contraction came along. I just scat sang through it Ella Fitzgerald style.

Wow, there is nothing more exciting than having the Kundalini energy going through your body when you are about to give birth to a LIVING ETERNAL SOUL as a new born baby. I had never experienced anything quite like it before. Except when I received shaktipat initiation from my guru, Swami Muktananda Paramahansa in 1981, but that tale is for a later time.

In our childbirth classes, David, and I had come to understand the labor process – how to handle the pain of contractions by using our breath, assisting the baby down through the birth canal by squatting, hanging down into the most comfortable position until one's cervix is completely ten centimeters dilated and; then, in the final stage of labor, we are told to push or bear down so that the baby's head can crown. Once the head comes out, normally the rest of the body follows pretty easily.

But, in Gabriel's case, it was already 7:00 AM, we were still singing "Blue Skies" a la' Ella Fitzgerald as the sun was coming up, and I was still not fully dilated. I was having so much fun that I began to scat sing, and barely noticed when another contraction came, so I scatted right through that. Do da do wa-do da-da, bop she bop, shu wah-do dah, etc. It was really fun, and it seemed as if I was making progress, but I still had no urge to push, and the baby's head was nowhere in sight yet. I was about nine centimeters dilated when they decided to check me again to find out if there was a problem.

Anne who was British, put her gloved hand into my vagina and realized there was still a bit of a lip there in my cervix, so she put her whole fist into my vagina to stretch the perineum. That seemed to do the trick. I felt spacey and higher than a kite from all the endorphins my body was producing. Maybe also from the space of love surrounding us all from the angelic realm and the love of all the people present in the bedroom. I was sitting upon my bed on my knees, and all of a sudden Barbara said "Meryl, you've got a baby head hanging there, honey. Put your hand down there and feel it!"

So, dazed and very happy, I did just that. Nearly ten hours had already gone by since they arrived at midnight. Thank God they were there. I felt relaxed and secure in their competent care.

They knew exactly what they were doing and were extremely patient, kind, positive, and nurturing. Very reassuring. They knew just how to support and encourage me to listen to my own intuition when it came to giving birth. Their wisdom and belief in me gave me courage and confidence in myself as a birthing mom.

I treated each contraction as if it were unique and did something totally different and appropriate for each one. Sometimes I hung my arms around my husband's neck and hung down low so that the weight of my body went all the way down into my pelvis. I usually chanted "OM" or something similar while visualizing my cervix opening up wide. Sometimes I bellowed the word "OPEN" while hanging from David's neck. He could only take so much of me hanging all 125 pounds of me from his neck, so after a while I did the same thing from my brother, Peter's neck. Then, when he tired, I used my brother, Scott just like I would hang from the limb of a tree if I were giving birth outside in a forest.

Then, when Scott tired, I asked my housemates Jack and Sven, who were both pretty big, strong guys and glad to oblige. They had become a part of the whole Labor party after an hour or so of hearing my loud noises and chanting during contractions. I suppose all the excitement and noise got their attention even in their rooms with the doors closed.

Scott and Peter were both very helpful and seemed to be enjoying the contrast in the atmosphere, alternating between very quiet and peaceful and then excitement as my labor began to progress. Not only did they help by holding me up, but they also fetched water, Recharge to replace my electrolytes, juice, or snacks if I was thirsty, and finally, mangoes, my favorite fruit, after Gabriel actually came "down the hatch".

At one point when it was taking so long in the early morning hours my brother Scott said "Meh, that baby is sure taking a long time coming out!

To which Ann replied in her lovely English accent, "That path has never been tried before, Scott."

Silly Jack quipped, "Well, at least not in THAT direction!" making our audiotape of Gabriel's birth R rated instead of GP.

After Anne had rid me of that extra lip by stretching my perineal muscles with her fist, I was a full ten centimeters dilated; and Gabriel's body should have been coming out completely following his head, but there seemed to be an obstacle. Ann and Barbara told me to lie down so they could check out what was going on with their stethoscope, so Ann put her hand inside my vagina.

Upon close inspection she found that Gabriel's anterior shoulder had somehow gotten stuck in the canal, so she did what she needed to do manually to free it, and moments later, at 10:31 AM Eastern Standard Time – "Voila, lots of fluid and black meconium came down with a beautiful 7-pound, three-ounce baby boy!!!! you cannot imagine the relief and joy I felt at that exquisite moment! All of us had tears of joy in our eyes when he finally made his amazing entrance – especially after all that waiting and hard work. I had a beautiful, tiny baby boy lying on my belly still connected to me by the umbilical cord which Ann and Barbara instructed David to clamp and then snip after it stopped from pulsating.

I highly recommend having your baby at home if you are healthy and desirous of a very gentle, warm environment in which to bring your newborn child. I lit candles in my bedroom and had an audiotape of my mantra "Om Namah Shivaya" on a cassette player softly playing in the background. After a while I changed the music choosing to listen to the soothing, haunting melodies of Steve Halpern and harpist, Georgia Kelly's, "Ancient Echoes". This beautiful music calmed me and created a very soothing, mystical atmosphere.

Sometimes, I needed to get into a warm or hot shower with David during the labor. All these things I was able to do because I was in complete control of my surroundings and my body. Had I been in a hospital setting I would not have been able to indulge my every divine desire and whim. I could have been induced with the drug Pitocin which makes labor lightning fast and uncomfortable, or given a painful episiotomy, an epidural, like my mom had, drugs to ease the pain, or even a Cesarean, and I wanted none of these. I had already visualized and imagined a relaxed and perfect birth with no intervention of any kind. The birthing experience turned out to be even more fun and enjoyable than I had expected. Some aspects were even relaxing and meditative. A perfect birthing experience. I had no tearing. No episiotomy. No bleeding. No drugs or medications. And a very healthy, happy, seven-pound, three-ounce baby boy who was given an Agar score of 9 which is excellent. I felt so blessed and proud of myself. There I was a new mother who had just brought her first newborn baby into the world in the most gentle way possible in the quiet, peaceful surroundings of my own bedroom, surrounded by loving friends and family members. What an amazing adventure for which to be so grateful to Goddess and Great Spirit. I was a new mom now breastfeeding my precious, healthy, blue eyed baby son, Gabriel. In my mind I saw him as a great Master descended from heaven onto the Earth plane through me. It was awesome. I was in bliss and in awe of this incredible process. After I gave birth I went to the bath to clean myself up, unwind and relax in the hot water for ten minutes while David bonded with Gabriel. Then I rejoined my guys in bed holding Gabriel close to my breast and nursed him for as long as he wished.

The three of us bonded as a family for hours, and I rested while food was delivered to my bedside by the others in service to the birthing parents. Peter or David made me some scrambled eggs and brought me orange juice and a mango, my favorite fruit. I just lay back and listened to the audiotape of the last 12 hours I had been engaged in the birthing process. It was a very interesting audiotape and made me laugh a lot. And cry. I wished we had a video tape like we did later with Kyrie's birth, but Gabriel came a week earlier than he was expected, and we were unprepared. Besides, I was not sure how I was going to deal with the pain and was a bit nervous about being filmed as a first-time mother just learning how to birth a baby. Naked. For all the world to see. Not that I was shy. I was a naturist and nudist who felt very comfortable in my birthday suit, but this was a special, sacred time, and I was unsure what was going to happen and not sure if I wanted to share it with anyone but the people present at Gabriel's birth.

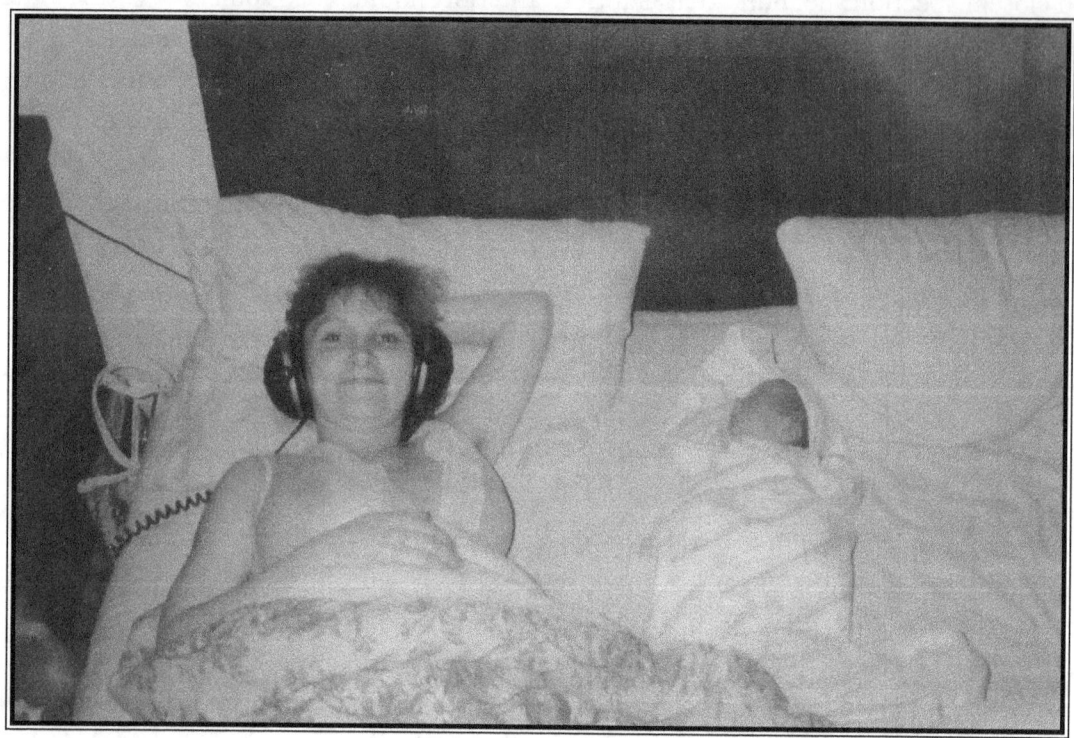

Gabriel and me on the day he was born

Gabriel was born with some jaundice because we had different blood types. I am O positive and his blood type is something more common, which if our blood mixes during the birth process, antibodies usually form thinking my blood is an antigen. The antibodies sometimes pass across the placental membrane into the baby's circulation resulting in the destruction of some of his red blood cells which cause an increase in a waste product called bilirubin. If too much bilirubin is produced it can overwhelm the baby's normal waste elimination processes, leading to jaundice. The bilirubin is a yellow pigment which gives the newborn's eye whites and skin a yellowish pigment. When Gabriel came out, he looked as if he'd been to Florida for a nice suntan. When I brought him to the obstetrician for his first check-up a day later, he suggested I take him to the hospital to get a PKU test and put him in an incubator of some type with lights for photo-therapy to help alleviate the jaundice.

I said to him, "What, are you crazy? Do you think I am going to have my little boy's sensitive and delicate soles of his little feet pricked by needles? And then taken away from me to be put under some artificial lights? I told the doctor flatly, "ABSOLUTELY NOT!" I suggested I take him outdoors to get some sunshine which is supposed to take away the jaundice. But the doctor said to me," Do you see any sunshine in February?" The A-Hole. Well, as a matter of fact, I DID manage to find some sunshine on a few colds, wintry days following February 5th, bundled up my little baby boy in his warm layette, woolen booties, a velour pajama outfit over that, a knit hat, and sweater and put him in my blue corduroy Snugly close to my chest where we went for several walks near my home outside in the cemetery in the early afternoon with the bright sun shining upon us, and his jaundice was completely gone within three days.

David and I also chose not to get Gabriel circumcised at birth for the same reason I did not allow him to get his feet pricked for the PKU test. Circumcision hurts! I'm not sure if you have ever seen a movie showing a baby being circumcised routinely in a hospital. It is an absolutely barbaric procedure, way worse than getting smacked on the bottom when the newborn comes out of the birth canal. Very painful and traumatic for a newborn baby boy. As a living, conscious entities, we feel everything and remember every feeling, sensation, sound, smell, and bright lights that blind us in the hospital. These sensations are traumatic to a newborn baby and stay with us stored in the subconscious, in the fascia of the body, and in the brain. For these reasons I made very conscious choices regarding my pregnancy and labor knowing that even the smallest thing like a harsh tone, a nasty scream, smoke from a cigarette, or any other negative thing would affect my baby now and in his future.

Gabriel's dad and I would separate later, and David chose to have Gabriel circumcised when he was five years old, but I was not given a choice in that decision. Gabriel was living with David at the time, and I was rarely consulted for important decisions like that after David and I divorced, when we decided to co-parent in separate households. David convinced me to allow him to keep the house and we agreed he should be the primary caretaker of our children due to the fact he had all the money and was more stable emotionally. At least at that time I believed he was the more fit parent. It was the hardest decision I had ever made in my life to give my children to him. But out of my deep love and concern for them I agreed on joint custody only if I could visit them frequently at his house and they could spend week-ends and several weeks during the summer with me.

I just loved being a new mom. The first week was made easier for me because I had so much help from my mom. Mom came every day for several hours the first week watching him when I was in the shower or bathtub, helping by preparing breakfast or lunch while I stayed in my bed with Gabriel, she just fell in love with him as we all did, and also offered to change his dirty diapers when needed so that I could get some down time just for me. My husband, David, who worked as an Equitable insurance salesman at the time, chose to stay home from work Monday and Tuesday. Sunday was his usual day off, so we got to be alone together as a family for three blessed, quiet days to get acquainted. The only visitor we had was my mom.

We chose to have a "family bed" with Gabriel sleeping between us so that when he got hungry during the night I could just roll over and offer him my full breast, and then we could all go back to sleep. The first few days of breastfeeding are the most important because the baby gets colostrum before the milk comes in, and the colostrum contains all the antibodies and other things a baby needs for a healthy immune system. He will get all the immunities the mom has in those first few days while he is nursing.

I so thoroughly enjoyed the intimacy of breastfeeding my newborn baby. Just holding his warm body close to me while looking into his beautiful blue eyes was heavenly. I'd sing to him sometimes when he was nursing during the day in my rocking chair or on the couch. I composed a special song just for him on my guitar entitled "Little One" that I would sing to him frequently along with Brahms' lullaby. Since I had been a professional singer and dancer since my late teens, I often sang to him while he was in my womb and played all types of music for him from New Age during my massage sessions, chanting tapes during meditation, jazz and Motown when I was dancing or singing in the car. My favorite group was and still is, Earth, Wind, and Fire, especially when I just wanted to go into a state of ecstasy while dancing in my living room, I would play their albums to dance and sing along with, every few days.

I believe this is why Gabriel has such a love of music today and is a very talented singer and self-taught musician who plays drums, guitar, piano, and in school studied the sax for a little while. Gabriel loves music and studied musical theater in high school where he starred in a few musicals like Grease. He also attended an elite musical theater camp, French Woods Festival, for several summers, in upstate New York, north of Monticello where he studied and had starring roles in "The King and I" from the time he was 10, but he decided to make music his hobby rather than career, for he believed he should have a stable profession like his father, David, and decided to major in economics and marketing at the School of Business in Manhattan so he could become a partner in his dad's annuity and insurance business.

Gabriel also won the starring role as Billy Flynn in "Chicago" and the lead in Stage show. He even learned all the rigorous choreography in "A Chorus Line" playing the athlete, a basketball star who sings "Give me the ball, give me the ball, yeah!" etc. Luckily, his girlfriend, Nicole, played the lead role of Cassie and gave him private dance and tap lessons, so even though Gabriel had never danced before he learned all the challenging choreography and looked just like one of the pros on Broadway, and we were all very proud. I loved "A Chorus Line" on Broadway so much I have seen it ten times in total counting Gabriel's performance at French Woods.

I felt very comfortable nursing Gabriel in public, which is what I chose to do after about twelve days of having him totally to ourselves. On the twelfth day I decided to get my hair done at my hairdresser's in Spotswood, and I decided to put Gabriel in his carry cradle since I did not want to leave him at all those first few months when we were just becoming acquainted as a new family, but I needed to have a life apart from him as well in which I felt free to go to New Woman, the health club to which I belonged, so that I could exercise, swim in the pool, and go into a jacuzzi and sauna to relax.

I was also accustomed to getting my hair and nails done bimonthly, and I was not going to abandon this nurturing practice and good habit just because I'd become a mom. I felt comfortable enough to start bringing Gabriel a few places with me after he was seventeen days old so that I could get him accustomed to social life and also so I could show him off to all our friends and wherever I went like the supermarket or restaurant. David and I took him out to dinner with us a few times, to the movies, and up to our meditation ashram in South Fallsburg, NY, so he could meet people and just fit "naturally into our relaxed and spiritual lifestyle.

Gabriel was such a relaxed, quiet, happy baby who began smiling after just a few days of being at home with us. He brought joy and peace wherever he went with me. Even when we were in the movies, we'd just set him down in his little carry cradle mom gave us and he'd peacefully sleep through the entire film. He was a very happy and quiet, content little baby who began sleeping through the night when he was about two and a half months old. Prior to that he would awaken once or twice to nurse, and I did not mind at all. I loved having him close to me, and I loved nurturing him. Feeding, dressing him, and bathing him was a joy to me. Having a new baby boy was just so much fun. I did not feel tired at all because I had a very helpful, supportive husband and we lived a very comfortable lifestyle. I also did not have to worry about working during the first year of his life. I was a massage therapist and workshop leader, but I only worked part-time when I wanted. Mostly for fun because I enjoyed doing bodywork and healing others. The money was just an extra bonus to me. I really did not need it to support me or the family. My husband took care of all of the bills, clothing, and groceries. I lived the life of a queen.

Being back home and getting back to my life as an adored wife and mom, part-time massage therapist, workshop leader, and back to singing with the band was fun and fulfilling. Things had cooled down between Tony and me since I'd made the decision to focus on my marriage, but David and I were still having challenges in the bedroom and not much had changed except that there was a willingness on both our parts to spend more quality time together as a couple and with our son. David worked a lot, but he would take off at least one evening a week, usually a Friday so that we could go out to dinner in town by ourselves while Janet, my best friend and live-in nanny, stayed home to watch and play with Gabriel.

Janet and I had met at the George Street Co-Op in New Brunswick where they sold organic fruits and vegetables as well as nuts, seeds, and grains in bulk for people choosing to lead a nonviolent vegetarian lifestyle as David and I were doing along with Baba Muktananda, Gurumayi, and most of the Siddha Yoga devotees. She was an assistant coordinator, and I became part of their cashier corps called the "tofu review". I worked one day per week for several hours once per month so that I could become a co-op member and receive 10 per cent off all my purchases. I also wrote articles on nutrition, holistic health, and healthy pregnancy while a member of the Co-Op.

Janet and I became fast friends as she were very playful, funny, artistic, and out-going like myself.

I called her Jannie Pie and her pet's name for me was Marzey. My grammy always sang that cute famous song to me "Mares eat oats and does eat oats and little lambs eat ivy. A kid'll eat ivy too, wouldn't you?" That's from where she got the name Marezy, I think.

Janet and I had so much fun kidding around with each other and we were both very creative, so we decided to teach a workshop together where people could play. It was called a "Fun4All", and we called Gabriel our mascot and "Master of Playfulness" when he was a mere six months old. We gave our first play-shop in August of 1983 when he was six months old. I taught dance aerobics and hatha yoga to friends and strangers, while Janet led several different types of games. Like David, we each chose a name for ourselves like a quality we wanted to embody. I remember David was "Peace", I was Moon Dancer, and Janet was Joy. On that special day I met a musician named Don, and another massage therapist, whom I came to call "The Pan Man" or "Pan", two single men who would become lifelong friends and future lovers. The workshop was fun to teach and to participate in, and we both made a little money too.

Janet was a playful person, and basically, she was there to bring joy and fun into our lives as new parents. She would play with Gabriel and take him to the park or George Street Co-op with her on a regular basis. But she also would have us do playful things at home as a family like spend an evening finger painting, coloring, playing games, or playing music together and dancing. Janet was a Godsend. If I wanted to go out by myself, I'd express my breast milk into an eight-ounce bottle and leave it with Janet to feed him while I was away shopping, exercising, or whatever. If I went to a friend's house, I'd bring Gabriel along with me.

One of the games was called a trust exercise to to see how much we could trust another person by falling back into their arms without looking. I trusted so much I practically fell to the ground while allowing the person behind me to keep pushing me up so that I would not fall. I think I was a little too trusting.

Janet offered other original games I'd never heard of. Another one was being blindfolded and experiencing our sense of smell, sense of touch, by placing smelly objects below our nostrils. We touched different things like lambs' wool, cotton, something hard like a hardboiled egg, something cold like ice, and something warm. We were asked to guess what all the items were. That was fun.

Another friend, Zara Rose, whom I'd met at a massage workshop I taught in New Brunswick, attended the Fun4All that day along with my girlfriend, Elaine Levy, who'd been there the night I went into labor with my son at mom's surprise birthday party. These two women also became women with whom I have maintained continuous friendships since the nineteen eighties. Zara, Janet, and Elaine have been three of my closest women friends throughout my lifetime, though Janet pulled away for years after the shooting, and I completely understand why. She was also diagnosed with manic depression while she was living with us, and asked for a leave of absence so she could be treated at the Carrier Clinic for bipolar depression and an addiction to marijuana. That came as a surprise, and I could not quite believe she wanted to leave us and voluntarily put herself in a psychiatric hospital. I just couldn't understand the seriousness of chemical addiction nor did I understand anything about mental illness, particularly manic depression, at the time, being completely unaware that I would eventually become affected by it myself.

Janet, had been using pot regularly – probably to self-medicate. And she also spent many weekends trying to enlighten herself by taking several of those New Age workshops like Werner Ehrhard's EST Sensitivity training, Lifespring, and Gavin Barnes' three-day workshop called Direct Centering in New York City. She seemed so thrilled by the power and positive affects they had on her that she was able to convince me to sign up for a few of them too. First Lifespring which was OK, though I don't remember too much about it.

My other best gal buddy, Zara Rose, told me she had done this amazing training called "Women, Sex, and Power" too and wanted me to attend her graduation. Whenever people would go to these graduations different people were dispensed to try to convince the guests and attendees to register for the workshop or sensitivity training. Some of these trainings had value, but most of them were about manipulation and control. If I had them to do all over again, I probably would not sign up for any of them. The only workshops I felt were of any value for me were the intensives Gurumayi Chidvilsananda gave during the seventies, eighties, and nineties where one could actually receive "shaktipat initiation" during an intensive week-end of meditating, chanting, and studying with the guru, her instructors and initiated swamis. These workshops were truly heart opening, and they always brought home a lasting quality of peace, joy, and discipline that stayed with me so that I would be inspired to maintain a more rigorous practice of hatha yoga, chanting, contemplation or meditation, and doing sadhana, my own personal spiritual practices.

My favorite thing was to chant the 188 verses of the 90-minute Guru Gita (in Sanskrit "the Song of the Guru"). It is a conversation between Parvati and Lord Shiva. In Siddha meditation ashrams the world over it is still sung from 5:30 AM until 7 AM. If I could not chant that early in the morning at home because I did not wish to wake my children when they were babies and toddlers I would chant later in the day while in the car en route to some play date, the gym, or shopping for David. I'd just place the CD with Gurumayi's voice leading the chant into the CD

Chanting and singing God's name in kirtans was my favorite practice, and to this day, is still one of my favorite ways to bring joy and peace to myself and others when in the context of a group with live musicians. No matter what challenges are presented to me, If I am keeping a regular daily practice of meditation and chanting, I find I can deal successfully with just about anything the Universe throws at me. At least that was until I did the drug "ecstasy" with my friend, Janet. Then I used it again once with my husband. Then a third time I wanted to use it with David, but he refused to do it at the last minute after I'd already taken the drug by myself. I had an ecstatic and inspirational experience while on the ecstasy, but the positive emotions did not last for any length of time, and for hours or days afterward many negative emotions would come up like anger, irrational anxiety, and then fear. I had nothing to be afraid of for I lived the life of "Riley". My husband paid all our bills, took us on vacations to visit Gurumayi in India, Florida, California, etc. Wherever the guru went David would want to follow, and I happily went along and brought the children when they were little. Of course, I loved being with Gurumayi too and doing the practices, so I traveled by his side whenever or wherever he wanted to go. David and I had purchased a beautiful "new" 200 yr. old bi-centennial country house in Englishtown, NJ after we sold our "starter home" for nearly $80,000 in Jamesburg. We had a brand-new home with four bedrooms, a little room off the bathroom upstairs which we used as a bedroom for our nanny. A lovely large back yard with many evergreen trees, bushes, and shrubs that formed a natural barricade around our property, and a white cement porch where we put a big round plastic table with a light blue and reddish orange umbrella in the middle of it which came with five beige plastic chairs and a chaise lounge. I chose the $2000 set myself imagining we would all use it as a place to relax and enjoy our lovely back yard with family and friends without having to worry about skin cancer or getting sunburned since the ozone layer has now been depleted by man, according to the experts, and is supposedly unsafe.

In the front yard at the entrance of the black macadam driveway stood a twenty-foot-tall holly tree with scores of bright tomato red holly berries, which, if made into a tea, I've since found out, can be very poisonous to the human body. I only found that out because following a manic high in the spring, I was feeling deeply depressed and foolishly looked up ways in which to poison myself. Thank God I never actually tried making a tea out of the berries.

Janet was a buffer in my relationship with David who could be very moody at times, especially when he worried about money, felt pressured, or under stress. If he was playing the stock market, particularly when he was trading commodities, he would get tense and anxious when he was losing money, and his mood became unpredictable. At those times he might lose his temper, get angry and vent his anger out on me, Janet, or his women employees. Sometimes he'd get so frustrated or angry he'd lose his temper so badly he began taking it out on objects. Throwing them in front of us until they got smashed to pieces.

For example, he would throw Gabriel's toys in a violent way on the ground so hard that they would break. He even broke the large brown play table we'd bought for Gabriel to make buildings on out of Legos or to work with Play-Dough. This side of my husband was never evident when we were first courting, dating, or newlyweds. It came as quite a surprise to me since he was a devotee of Baba and such a kind, spiritual man who actually managed the Siddha Meditation Ashram in New York City for a year and set up many other ashrams for Swami Muktananda in the five years before I had met him. He even traveled to India to be with his guru, and I considered my husband a gentle, loving man in service to God and the guru, so watching him suddenly explode into mini rages was a shock to me.

At other times David could be psychologically abusive to me, Janet, or any one of his female employees, just like his father, Eli, had been to his women employees, according to what he told me after we were first married... This aspect of David's personality was disturbing, but I loved him, and for the most part, he was kind, stable, an excellent provider and a doting, loving, caring father. A more faithful, hardworking husband I could not find. His good qualities outweighed the bad, and when I said "I take this man for better or for worse, I meant it.

After I became pregnant with my son, my husband no longer saw me as a sexual woman. All of a sudden, I was a mother-to-be whom he treated lovingly with great respect, but not intimately anymore. Then after nine months I became a mother, to be respected and cared for, but still not loved or appreciated in a romantic or sexual way. Wow, did that come as a surprise since he was so hot for me while we were courting. David courted and pursued the pants off me, literally, but once he got into them and we had a baby together he was no longer interested in me as a female.

I do not believe we were compatible at all physically. I won't go into the gory details because that was our business, but much of the problems in our marriage stemmed from a lack of communication because we did not connect well in that intimate and sexual way that is so important in new and long-lasting marriages, and we were both afraid to talk about it. I felt as if we were both virgins when it came to experiencing the joys of sexual intimacy but without the excitement a new virgin feels. I told David I wanted marriage counseling and to be able to have affairs outside our marriage if he was going to refuse to make love to me. He lied saying he did not care whether or not I had affairs, but deep down I knew he truly did. Marriage counseling did not really help us because David was stubbornly refusing to budge on the issue; he still refused to make love to me for months, and I felt very sad inside because I truly loved him and yearned to feel the same emotional and physical closeness we felt right before and after we first married.

I guess I just did not care much about our sex life, which was practically non-existent in the beginning since we had a family bed with Gabriel sleeping between us. When David got anxious about our financial condition, he insisted I return to work early. I was somewhat angry at his suggestion, and since I'd made more money as a go-go dancer than I had as a part-time massage therapist I said "If you are forcing me to go back to work already, I will make money the fastest way I know – using my sensual charms to woo men toward me on the go-go dance circuit. I was basically passive aggressive with my anger because he was not available for me emotionally or sexually. I was not feeling satisfied as a woman at all. I felt fulfilled as a mother, but I was inwardly longing for those early days before we got married when David was courting me. He could not wait to be intimate with me before he found out I was pregnant and expecting our first child. At that moment, my Jewish husband no longer saw me as a feminine woman even though I was lovely, beautiful, and kept myself in great shape during the entire pregnancy and lost every bit of the twenty-five pounds I'd gained within two weeks of giving birth to Gabriel. It was not that David did not treat me well, he just focused on making money at his new job as an insurance salesman and ignored me most of the time except during dinner and on week-ends when I suppose he did not feel as much pressure to make money. He worked six days per week!

After go-go dancing for a few weeks, I was at one of the nicer bars called Virgo's on Route 130 dancing the day shift from noon to 7 PM when I met a very handsome, muscular man from California who was visiting his mom here in New Jersey. His name was Bill. He was gorgeous. He bought me a drink and after we talked for a while, I told him I was a massage therapist. He said he could use a massage while he was here on vacation and asked for my business card. He called me for an appointment a week later, and while David was away working at Equitable during the day Bill came over. His body was so muscular and fit I had a tough time keeping focused on my work, but I was very appropriate for the entire hour. When he got up from my massage table completely naked before I left the room, I could not help but imagine him kissing me passionately and making love to me. He asked me if I'd like a back massage when I came back to the room after washing my hands. and he was just so handsome and masculine I could not resist his offer.

I only removed my short sleeve white massage top uniform because I was not ready for him to see me naked even though he saw most of my body when I go-go danced in front of him in a light blue thong and fuchsia pink bra covering my breasts.

After he was finished doing long, relaxing effleurage Swedish strokes for ten minutes and eventually kneading my entire back removing every bit of tension from my shoulders, upper and mid back the he kept moving his hands down to my lower back and pelvis and onto my buttocks; and I felt a bit of a thrill to be relaxed in that area after such a long time of being ignored in my pelvic area. I felt as if I was in heaven. This young boy (well, actually a twenty-five-year-old grown-up man) knew exactly how to please me. I appreciated his tender, loving care. He appreciated my beauty and femininity. He gave me just what the doctor ordered. When he finished plying any tension from my back and buttocks, he turned me over and kissed me. Wow – what a wonderful kisser was he as well. Then, to my surprise and delight he picked me up from the hard massage table in his strong, muscular arms, and carried me to the guest-room bed two doors down with no effort whatsoever.

I had never had a man carry me to a bed and begin kissing my face, my eyes, gradually going down my neck, licking it and placing kisses on every part of me. Eventually he was licking, kissing, and massaging both of my breasts too. I'd never had a man seduce me like that that I could remember. And, believe me, I would have remembered being loved like that! I allowed Bill to completely seduce me and eventually he was inside my yearning yoni. Every part of this man's body was muscular, beautiful, and knew exactly what it was doing in making love to a woman in every possible delightful way. It was one of the best, most joyous, and romantic times I'd had since I'd become a new mother. I did not feel the least bit guilty about it, because I felt so happy; and besides, David was not open to supplying my needs as a woman for over a year. I felt renewed as a woman and so very joyous and fulfilled.

The next day we planned to see one another again. There was a place in Marlboro called Water Haven, about twenty minutes from Englishtown by car, and I loved this place because I could get a massage somewhere first, and continue with the deep relaxation at Water Haven where there were hot tubs, saunas, showers, and steam rooms in individual little suites where a person could deeply relax and feel purified from head to toe. Bill and I rented one of the rooms together, and, in the jacuzzi and in the steam room before we showered together, he soaped up my breasts and buttocks and massaged my flat stomach. It was even sexier and better than being alone in my house with him where I did not feel completely comfortable because my husband and toddler lived there.

I continued this long-distance affair with Bill for nearly a year, but having phone sex was just not the same as being with him in person. We kept in touch, though, by phone, and we wrote a few letters and sent holiday cards, and eventually Bill told me he was going to school to become an airline pilot. When his mom got her PhD, he came back to Jersey a few years later; and of course, we saw one another again. I had just missed his 27th birthday, so I used one of my credit cards to buy a nice shirt for him. Things with my husband were still strained, and we never made love or even kissed sensuously before bed. I delighted in having this affair with a very handsome, strong man who truly appreciated my beauty and femininity. I had been so unfulfilled in this area for such a long time, and having a strong, attractive man massage me, kiss me, appreciate my naturally sensuous, feminine nature, and seduce me in the way I liked just broke down all my defenses, and I loved it! I did not think about being a married woman or about David for one second while Bill was seducing me. I had hungered for David to seduce me in this very same way, but it just was not happening. I was still beautiful with a great shape even after I gave birth, and I kept myself in good shape all during my pregnancy too, so I did not understand why David was not attracted to me sexually anymore.

I never felt very sexual when I was busy being a good mom, never had the interest or even made the time to masturbate, but when the chemistry was there, like in the case of Bill, I felt really happy and natural expressing the natural sensuous, erotic, feminine part of my nature again. Bill and I met several times after that first exciting occasion at Water Haven in Marlboro, NJ. We had a very exciting affair for a few months during the summer, but Bill went away shortly after we met, and we were reduced to having phone sex and a long-distance relationship. We wrote a few letters and kept in touch for a year, but out of sight, out of mind. I spoke to Bill a few years later, but we never saw or spoke to one another again after that.

I got a Hitachi vibrator I when I took a sex workshop with Betty Dodson in 1984. I had learned about her from my girlfriend, Liz, from East Brunswick. Betty Dodson, an author, former lesbian, and well-known workshop leader and Sexpert, lived in uptown Manhattan and came to the door naked dressed only in a black belt and gun holster minus the shooters. There was no furniture in the living room, just a lot of oversized, fluffy, burgundy pillows spread out all over the immaculate, shining hard wood floor. Since I'd never seen a room without furniture I was in awe of its simplicity and spaciousness.

Betty taught about twelve of us women including a lady in her late seventies about how to create chi using pranayama, the fire breath technique we teach in yoga and meditation classes, what was an orgasm, and using a mirror to show each individual lady participant the beauty of their genitals, where our clitorises, the rosebuds, as she called them, and where our anuses and our labia were located using this small, but effective hand mirror. Every woman gathered around each of the others when it was her turn to share and learn about the beauty and uniqueness of her private parts. It was very educational. She also asked "How do you each feel about your orgasm at this time in your life?"

Well, I was not having any and did not even believe it was possible with my husband who was inexperienced and treated me with kid gloves from the time I became pregnant with our son. Then Betty handed each one of us our individual vibrators and taught us how to use them gradually and gently so as not to come to a climax too quickly. That was difficult since the vibrator was so intense. Even when I had it turned on low, I had such a great imagination that I could climax in minutes unless I took it away and forced myself not to cum too quickly.

I learned so much about self-pleasure and control during that workshop and felt as if I had another lease on my sex life – especially since my husband had premature ejaculation and really did not understand much about "foreplay" and how great it feels to just kiss and make out for an hour or so until I got hot. It was very unsatisfying, and we avoided sex and romance, for the most part, choosing to focus on snuggling each other and enjoying being together in the company of our new baby son, Gabriel, who slept in our "Family bed" with us from the time he was born at home eighteen months prior to that. David was an excellent provider and terrific father, but as a lover and romantic partner he got a D plus.

In August of 1984 David had won an award from Metropolitan Life and he was honored at an Equitable insurance dinner at the Channel Club in Monmouth Beach down by the Jersey shore.

I was excited about this because this was my very first date with David alone out of the house since Gabriel was born six months before. I love to dress up and go out to lunch or dinner with my husband occasionally because, for the most part, we had become total homebodies since Gabriel's birth. Except to go to work, food or clothes shopping, we stayed home as a family eating, reading, making home videos of Gabriel, or watching videos and movies on television.

My mom had agreed to babysit, I bought a new fuchsia pink silk dress from Lord & Taylor's to show off my beautiful 118-pound, curvy motherly form. I had easily lost the rest of the 25 pounds I'd gained during the pregnancy from breastfeeding, exercising, and taking care of the baby.

Unfortunately, sometime during the day I said something to David that deeply upset him, though he never told me what it was, that caused him to become so angry that he refused to speak to me; and he retreated from me for the entire afternoon. No matter how much I pleaded he refused to communicate anything. I tried to talk to him for hours in between cleaning up the house to find out what was the matter, but he kept silent the entire time, and I was really upset and thought our evening was completely ruined.

At 4:30 PM I begged him to be reasonable and at least make an effort to communicate and get dressed for the dinner party. My mom came over early, and eventually David donned a suit and tie, though he still refused to say one word to me. He was being very immature and I felt like crying, but I kept my cool thinking if I just ignored his moodiness eventually, he would move out of his crazy behavior and start talking to me like a rational, mature man again. I did not believe he could not stay silent forever. No such luck. He continued giving me the silent treatment the entire ride to the Channel Club in Monmouth Beach, for the most part of the dinner, and to this day, I have no idea what set him off. He even spent hours in the meditation room with his talas over his head before we left as if he had changed into some celibate, silent guru who was never going to speak to me again for the rest of his days. That went on for hours. Even when I'd go up to ask him if he was OK, he was stubborn and refused to speak one word to me.

What could I do? His behavior was upsetting to me, but we were all dressed up, and he was being honored. Our first date night since Gabriel was born, and I was determined to enjoy myself. I wanted to have a good time despite his immature behavior, so I made the best of a bad situation, and pretended to enjoy myself. The food was delicious, and I enjoyed the company of all the other people present.

There was a pianist, Tony, playing some really great music like old standard ballads and singing. I loved what he was playing so I decided to leave my taciturn husband to his own devices after I was done with the appetizer and salad to visit the piano player. I stood next to him by the piano quietly appreciating his performance. Besides being a great entertainer with a terrific voice he was a tall, dark Italian who was very handsome.

This really gorgeous Italian dark-haired pianist was stylishly dressed in a dark suit, beautiful pink dress shirt, and matching tie. He noticed me immediately and got my attention by saying, "Do you know you are the most beautiful woman in this entire room?" After all the ignoring on David's part I happily ate up this delicious compliment. I was not only noticed for my beauty, but Tony complimented me on my pretty voice as I was quietly singing harmonies along with his leads. We had some casual banter in which I told him I was currently a go-go dancer, but I wanted to get back into singing professionally which I had stopped right before leaving for massage school in Florida in 1980.

Through the conversation I could tell that Tony was attracted to me, and he also said he was losing one of his female singers in his band. He'd recently found out his alto singer was having a baby and she would be leaving the band. Well, I could sing alto and second soprano, and I had years of prior experience, so we arranged an audition after he mailed me an audiotape of the parts I needed to learn—the Andrew Sisters " Boogie Woogie Bugle Boy" for which he had written charts of my parts and some Manhattan Transfer songs. He had me learn the alto part to "Tuxedo Junction," and the lead vocal to "Chattanooga Choo-Choo". I was a quick study.

Since David was still acting distant on the ride home, I was really glad I'd met Tony and had some joyous new experiences to anticipate in my near future. I really loved singing, dancing, harmonizing, dressing up in nice dresses and gowns, and making my own money.

I went to Tony's home in Asbury Park to audition. I won the part of the alto singer in his band immediately. The wedding gigs paid really well and I felt much more "legitimate" as a professional singer in a wedding band as opposed to a go-go dancer, though in those days I never took my clothes off.

It was illegal to even show your nipple, and a club could be raided by the ABC and get closed down for lewd behavior like "My Wife's Place" in South Amboy often did. That happened to be one of my favorite places to dance because the tips were very generous.

Eventually David let go of whatever was bothering him, and we began communicating again. But having a "family bed" did not help our sex life one bit. In fact, our experience of sex was so frustrating and ephemeral that most of the time we avoided it completely for months after Gabriel was born. We just related as loving parents and had occasional heart-to heart talks after we shared powerful chanting and meditation experiences. Or we'd become temporarily close after taking New Age workshops like "Direct Centering" with Bayard Hora or the "Alivening Week-End" with Glen and Barbara Smyley. After completing these enlightening workshops, we would feel temporarily expansive and openhearted treating one another with deeper love, honor, and respect. But somehow, the increased love and awareness never lasted beyond a few weeks. The same problems in the bedroom would keep arising which seemed to affect everything else in our relationship.

I really enjoyed making music with Tony, and the attraction that was slowly developing between us during rehearsals and at gigs. It was fun being creative and figuring out great harmonies together. Sometimes I'd have to go alone to his house to rehearse my solos and alto parts, and I found myself becoming romantically attracted to him despite the fact that he was also married with two young children. Like me, he was having problems in his marriage. I'm sure his wife was unhappy with the fact that he'd had a serious affair with another pretty singer before I came into the band. His wife apparently never forgave him for it, so out of this distrust came resentment and no physical or emotional intimacy. Just like I was dealing with at home with David.

So, we were both "ripe" for some male/female intercourse. Communication, I mean, of course! Nothing happened until one night after a gig at the Molly Pitcher Inn in Red Bank when I realized I'd locked my keys in my car, and I had no way of getting home. Tony offered to drive me back home to Jamesburg, so I did not have to call my husband so late at night and wake him. Besides David was watching Gabriel, and it was much easier for Tony to give me a lift as opposed to waking up my husband and son to have him drive all the way to Red Bank to rescue me.

Tony and I were both love and sex starved for so long that a little conversation and kissing led into a natural progression of what a healthy, attractive couple do when they are alone in a car late at night. It was very exciting, and I so enjoyed making out like I was a teenager again. We certainly had chemistry. Eventually, Tony ended up running all the bases until he'd hit a "home run", so to speak. It was really exciting and enjoyable, but after feeling completely satisfied I was glad to arrive safely back at my home to find my two guys snuggled up together in bed sleeping soundly.

Though I thoroughly enjoyed the excitement of being intimate with Tony, when I arrived home at 2 AM I was just as happy to be home and able to climb back into my family bed with David and Gabriel. I felt grateful to David for being kind and loving enough to take care of the baby while I was out working and expressing myself in a joyous, creative way. The affair might have continued for a while, but I was foolish and, during a long walk we were taking with Gabriel days later in our neighborhood, David and I had a petty argument about money, and I confessed the indiscretion without thinking and said I wanted to divorce him when the argument heated up to a boiling point.

David was a control freak. He'd be stressed out over finances or because he lost money in the stock market, and all of a sudden, he'd have a blow up where he'd act crazily. He might go into the kids' toy box and begin to take everything out saying the kids did not need half of their toys which he decided he wanted to be thrown away or given to charity. As I mentioned before, once he got so angry for no reason that he picked up Gabriel's play table with four legs up and threw it on the carpet floor with all his might. He threw it with such force, that even on the soft pile carpet the table broke in two. He frightened me with this behavior, but he was such a strong personality and definitely the dominant one of the two of us that I let him get away with several of these tantrums. He did beat me once at the beginning of our marriage when Gabriel was just eighteen months old, after I'd had that one indiscretion with Tony in his car. We had a very heated argument when I told him I'd had sex with my bandleader one night after he drove me home. I did not have to tell him, but I wanted him to know that I was desirous and beautiful to other men, so that hopefully he would make more of an effort to be emotionally and physically intimate with me. We were still practically newlyweds but were rarely ever romantic and certainly not sexual anymore. We were in counseling at the time. David insisted I stopped having affairs, and I said "No, I will not stop seeing men outside our marriage until you change and begin spending more quality time alone with me. I want you to start making love to me again."

"If we don't start having sex like a normal couple, I'm going to divorce you!", I threatened.

David lost it. "If you try to divorce me, you'll get exactly what you came in with – NOTHING!"

I was livid. The fight and heightened emotions made me speak irrationally with intense anger. Stupidly I countered with, "Oh yeah? I'm going to take you for everything you've got."

Well, that's exactly what he needed to hear in order to explode in a rage upon my petite and vulnerable body. The first punch came like a lightning bolt into my belly followed by another dozen lightning-fast punches until I fell down before him crumpling onto the gray paved road where he continued to pummel me beating me and kicking me upon my back. He even punched me around my face and eye. I tried to defend myself, but I was in shock. Eventually I had no more fight or energy with which to defend myself or to think or speak. It was over. And so was my affair with Tony.

David had beaten me right before my little son's eyes. He then took off with Gabriel leaving my limp body lying in the middle of the road, where my next-door neighbors saw me and kindly came over to carry my weak body back to our doorstep. But when they rang the doorbell, my husband refused to let me in. I was forced to use the next-door neighbors' phone to call my mother.

Mom was livid and immediately drove to our house in Jamesburg with my brother, Scott. My mom was so pissed at David she was banging on the door for about five minutes threatening to beat him up or call the police if he would not let me in. "Open up, you bastard, or I'll call the cops right now." Still no result. Luckily my brother stayed calm, objective, and peacefully stated "David, Meryl is out here badly hurting. She has a cut over her eye and she can barely walk. Please let us in so we can take her up into the bedroom, clean up her eye and get her comfortable in bed. Finally, David listened to reason, but all the while he was defending his actions acting self-righteous saying I was an adulterer and I deserved everything I'd gotten from him. That evening, even after apologizing to me, he told me to lie to the doctors who treated me, as well as the ER doctor. Scott thought I should get totally checked out that night at Old Bridge Regional Hospital since I'd been beaten so badly, and we were not sure if anything was broken. I was cut and bruised above my left eye, and David had pummeled my stomach so hard I began to menstruate for the first time since I became pregnant. After ten minutes of resting in my bed Mom and Scott took me to the ER at Old Bridge Regional Hospital where I was checked out for broken bones, etc. I experienced an aching soreness in my back and belly that was so painful I could barely walk and certainly would not be able to dance anymore because it hurt just to walk and climb stairs. But despite the physical and emotional trauma, I had not been terribly hurt or scarred. My guardian angel must have been with me. I was so sore I could barely move and was literally unable to sing, drive, or dance in the band, so I did not see Tony for three weeks while I was healing from the trauma.

So much for the exciting days of David's and my courtship when we'd write one another romantic poems and leave them on the car windshield or give them to one another during a romantic dinner at a restaurant. I could not understand how such a wonderful romance and early seemingly successful early marriage could have come down to this? What had I done to manifest such a horrible, violent relationship less than two years later which had seemingly been born in heaven? I was completely confused and asked for guidance from God and my guru, since I really did not know how to proceed from that point on. I was a new mother who loved and adored my precious, young son living in a nice home with a nanny and a man who was, all of a sudden, a complete stranger to me. I had experienced his controlling, unreasonable behavior before and mini outbursts of rage upon toys and objects, but never upon my own physical body. I felt as if I was living with the part of my mother that behaved like the Wicked Witch of the West when I was just a child and spilled milk or got my fingerprints on the walls or glass window panes. I felt again as if I were walking upon egg shells. Frightened, confused, and wanting to run away.

By the time I'd returned home from the hospital, David had a change of heart. He was now much more apologetic and offered to take me to the ophthalmologist the next day to check my eye as well as the cut and bruise under the brow, but he still insisted I lie to anyone who asked what had happened which I guess I did, but I cannot remember how I explained the bruises.

Two weeks after the blow-up I began to feel better with David and Janet nurturing me and caring for my body, mind, and heart. A week later my friend, Elaine Levy, shared the news that her daughter Lorrie, was getting married to a wonderful young man named Glen, and we were invited to their large Jewish wedding. I really wanted to go, and David agreed to escort me to the wedding followed by a reception held in the community room at the large clubhouse in Twin Rivers in Hightstown, NJ, where the beautiful couple exchanged traditional vows in Hebrew under a canopy with the marriage sung by a rabbi, the couple stepping on the wine glasses, and other beautiful rituals. I had never attended a Jewish wedding before and I was moved to tears by the couples' love for one another and the sweetness of the vows and the ceremony. David was as well. I saw a few tears in his eyes as Glen and Lorrie exchanged their sacred vows. His heart was really open to me again after that. Just as it had been the time, we saw the movie "Gandhi" portraying the young yogi and his sixteen-year-old bride exchanging marriage vows in the movie with Ben Kingsley on our second date.

We had a terrific afternoon enjoying the delicious four course dinner, drinking a bit of wine, and dancing to the band together.

Stanley, the father of the bride, asked me if I'd be willing to go up on stage to sing a song with the band. They already had a female singer, but Stan and Elaine loved my voice and original songs I played for them on guitar during the many visits I made to their home, so they asked if I could dedicate one song to the newlyweds. I asked the band if they knew the song "You're an Angel in Disguise" by Madonna, though I forgot what key I sang it in. It was a touch too high for me, but I still did a great job and got a standing ovation.

I always knew how to put over a song with a lot of enthusiasm and energy, and my dancing is so expressive that I bring lots of joy and inspiration to people. I literally spark a fire in peoples' hearts when I am on the dance floor in a restaurant, a bar, at church, or out dancing on the street at a festival like Princeton's "Communiversity". People are just mesmerized by my energy and enthusiasm when I dance and sing – even with my disability. I am always amazed at how I affect people when I dance.

Many guests got up on the dance floor during my solo number. It was so well received that the audience asked me for an encore, but since we'd not rehearsed, and they already had a female lead singer, I felt it was inappropriate, so I declined. After that, David was really proud of me and we danced a few more songs together and left hand in hand feeling very much in love again.

The next morning after the wedding was a Sunday and was the first time, we'd made love since I'd gotten my period again after I stopped breastfeeding Gabriel. It had stopped when he was almost two, and the night David beat me up I began menstruating again for the first time since I gave birth in February to Gabriel. David actually placed Gabriel in the other room and we shared some very sweet French kisses which led to more romantic foreplay and eventually we consummated our marriage again after such a long dry spell. I felt so much happier. Then David heard Gurumayi would be leaving in the beginning October to go back to India with an entourage; and she was inviting many of the devotees to travel with her on an Air India plane with inexpensive round trip group rates.

We went to India with Gabriel and our nanny, Janet, for three weeks, which seemed to strengthen our commitment to one another, and I knew I would have to give up the affair with Tony, my bandleader, if we were to have any chance at all of our marriage working. In fact, one morning after chanting the Guru Gita and David was back at the room watching Gabriel, I was feeling a lot of love and gratitude for his kindness and service to both me and Gabriel. I knew at that moment that our marriage and the love of our family was much more important to me than the temporary affair I was having with Tony.

I decided to leave Tony's band when I was six months pregnant with Kyrie because wearing high heels was causing my pelvis to go out of alignment, and I was uncomfortable. I had to keep going to the chiropractor for more adjustments just to feel "normal".

I saw Tony once after I left the band when he was performing, so I could see the new singer, Sara, who had replaced me. She was a decent singer, and she played jazz on saxophone too. The spark was still there between us, and I was tempted to make love to him afterward again, but I consciously made a choice to be loyal to David, especially after finding out we were expecting another baby. I did not want to jeopardize our relationship any more than it already was., so I consciously decided not to see him again after that time. After I'd given birth to Kyrie Tony's wife left him because she believed Kyrie was his biological child. She actually threw him out of their home in Ocean Grove. Maybe Tony suspected Kyrie might be his biological child, too, and he came to visit me and the baby one day when she was three months old.

David tried to be a good husband and father in the best way he knew, but my personality was much softer than his. He was a control freak, and I was a softie, a pushover. It was time I learned about boundaries – healthy boundaries. Was there such a thing? I had never heard or been taught about them.

David and I both had emotional and mental health issues from childhood that needed to be addressed. I've already said much about mine: David's were largely caused by his relationship with his father.

We tried some of the New Age Love and sensitivity training seminars like "Direct Centering" with Gavin Barnes who changed his name to Bayard Hora. Our nanny, Janet, did the three-day training first and invited me to attend her graduation night. I was very gullible and quickly got conned into registering for "the Course". It was a confrontive, somewhat powerful seminar, but the main idea was to call your friends and family to tell them how great it was and then get them to register too. For me it was a lesson in trusting myself to listen to my own intuition and not be manipulated by others into doing something I did not truly want to do. I did the course shortly after giving birth to Gabriel and signed up to be one of the teaching assistants for a few months. David came to my graduation evening and actually was convinced by one of the attendees to register for "Direct Centering" himself. We kind of got along for at least six months after returning from India, especially because I found out three months upon returning home that I was pregnant again with a new baby. It took me a long time to realize even after I shot myself that we were not compatible anymore. I did not have healthy boundaries nor did I even UNDERSTAND it was OK to have boundaries at all. As far as I was concerned, we are All ONE, so why should I feel separation from anybody. In my mind it was not SPIRITUAL to get angry with my mate or anyone, for that matter. I saw it as a weakness, so if one of my boyfriends treated me with disrespect or like crap, I usually would not allow myself to feel anger toward them. I'd stupidly turn the rage, frustration, and pain in on myself. And that's not a good place to harbor anger, rage, or any of the so called "DARK" emotions.

By the time we returned from the hospital David had softened and began to feel bad about beating me so badly. He even told me he would drive me to the eye doctor the next day, but he warned me not to speak of the abuse telling me to lie about how I had gotten the cut above my eye.

It's ironic but the entire time I was sitting quietly with my thoughts waiting to be seen by the ER physician at Old Bridge Regional I was trying to understand my responsibility for the violence that had erupted between us and then done to my body. In anger I said just the things to set him off so that he would lose his temper. This was not something I had tried to do consciously, but on some unconscious level I guess I wanted to be punished for having committed adultery which, according to my Catholic upbringing, was one of the most grievous of sins a woman could commit.

For most of my life I've had problems expressing anger. I saw it as a terrible weakness and an emotion that hurt others. I felt it was not all right for me to express it at all because of the harm it could do. So, I kept it bottled up inside, and eventually I would turn most of this repressed rage and subconscious hatred on myself. In my little child's mind I thought, "How could I be angry at my mom when she was my mommy whose love and care I needed?" Besides, she always feels better eventually and turns back into the "Good Witch" again who loves and cares for me so much.

As an adult, I believed I was "bad" or unspiritual if I felt angry. So, I would bury these feelings deep inside myself where they lay in my subconscious where they would fester and build until there was so much rage needing to be released that it would implode. Not being able to get in touch with my inner feelings eventually turned into a state of insanity in which I had so much self-hatred that I felt compelled to take that gun to my head to release myself from the intense pressure and suffering.

Feeling emotions is what makes us human. In most of our families we were brought up, as children being told it is not proper or acceptable to express. We are squelched at an early age because our parents were uncomfortable expressing their own emotions.

When it comes to the suppression of emotions, we as young girls were allowed to cry, but were discouraged from getting angry. I am one of many women who tended to feel terribly guilty whenever I have an angry thought or feeling. Because my mother was angry so much as I was growing up, I decided that to express anger was a terrible weakness. The expression of her rage hurt me so deeply that consequently I learned to "stuff" my anger. I had a lot to be angry about, but I never allowed myself to feel this emotion or even own up to being angry, and look at where it got me.

When someone has been abusive to me, I've felt so uncomfortable expressing anger about it that the most truthful I could be about being mistreated was to say that I felt hurt or resentful. This was the worst a nice, loving, spiritual person like me could feel about another human being – even if they were abusing me physically, sexually, or psychologically. I would make excuses for the person who was mistreating me. I would delude myself into thinking I had forgiven my abusive parents or the abusive men I attracted in relationship in order to resolve the subconscious pain and rage I had inside. I even excused my first husband who was psychologically abusive as well as physically abusive on two occasions in our five-year marriage. As a consequence of repression, I felt an underlying rage that would tend to erupt at unexpected times and in hurtful ways when I got into my teens, and later on as an adult I turned this anger and hatred onto myself. The suppression of anger and resentment would cause tremendous tension in my face, jaws, neck and shoulders. I'd become so tight and tense I felt like the weight of the world was on and in my shoulder blades!

We as women were allowed to express our sadness and tears, but it was unladylike to express anger. Because I'd been hurt so deeply by my mom's angry outbursts, I desperately tried not to express any kind of anger. I also believed it was unspiritual. I could never own up to the fact that despite all my love and gentleness, there was a shadow side of me lurking underneath the surface where I felt a tremendous amount of hatred, rage, and unworthiness. I had suppressed so much hatred and rage toward my parents for their abuse, neglect, and abandonment that when I became an adult, I turned these powerful, dark emotions onto myself through numerous suicide attempts.

Little boys are told they are sissies if they hurt themselves and their fathers see them cry. The fathers were not comfortable expressing their pain, so they told their sons," Don't act like a girl, son. Be strong. Be a man. "So young boys grew up just like their fathers suppressing their sadness, presenting a strong exterior to the world by trying to act macho and tough. But underneath the facade they were still hurt, angry little boys afraid of being vulnerable and getting hurt. On the outside is an impenetrable fortress, but on the inside of many men their hearts are closed and dying.

It is our nature to feel. Unless they closed their hearts how else would men be able to go off to war and kill their fellow men? Unless he stopped feeling how could a man rape, torture, beat, abuse, and even murder women, children, girlfriends and wives? Our young men are killing themselves and each other on our city streets in gangs and in the pursuit of drugs, power, and money. Most likely these men were beaten, abused, and criticized severely themselves and were never allowed to express their helplessness, pain and rage Both parents abused both of my ex-husbands physically and/or psychologically, and I'm sure that this is one of the reasons I chose them at a subconscious level. I married a man very much like my mother instead of a balanced, whole, unconditionally loving partner.

Some men who have abused women tell them that it is for their own good or that they were provoked into doing it. This must have been their experience being raised by dysfunctional parents who had no good role models themselves and very poor parenting skills. The abusive men were hurt, angry, and resentful for being mistreated themselves as young boys. These poor, abusive adult men act out their childhood trauma on the women in their lives modeling the behavior of their parents or whatever male role models they had.

Consequently, they suppressed the rage and pain and shut down their hearts so they would not be vulnerable to the pain again.

How else could men or women, for that matter, torture, maim, and kill animals for cosmetic testing and the like unless they were completely numb? How could we continue to treat our livestock --the cows, pigs, and chickens with such indignity and disdain that they spend their entire lives, as short as they may be, in boxes and stalls where there is no room for them to move or roam, where they are tortured and live in fear until it is time for them to be electrocuted or beaten, maimed, mutilated, and killed? Many of us have totally closed down our heart centers.

I made my holy communion at seven years old and my confirmation at 13, but for the most part, I did not buy into most of the church dogma regarding original sin and all that nonsense. Even at seven I knew the whole concept of sin was off. I also knew I did not need a priest or other mediator to talk or pray to God or Jesus. I felt an instinctive connection, an innate love for God and his for me. I had the thought that He loved me unconditionally, but I tried to go along with the desires of my mother and grandmother to go to church on Christmas and Easter Sundays as well as to go to catechism in the second and third grades to study.

If I'd not been brought up Catholic with the ten commandments as our Laws, I do not believe I would have felt so much guilt about having affairs with other men, including my father if you count the molestation, he perpetrated upon me when I was thirteen and fourteen years old." Thou shalt not commit adultery" was one of the ten commandments and next to murder, one of the most grievous of sins. Do NOT commit adultery. Even though I consciously did not buy into the whole concept of sin I suppose on some level I must have felt really guilty and believed I should be punished. It was not something I even felt conscious of. In fact, I really did not think it was my fault. I was just fulfilling one of my basic, primal needs for love, sensibility, sex, and affection.

INDIA (1985)

We had previously planned a three-week trip to India in October to be with our gurus in Ganeshpuri, about a two-and-a-half-hour trip by bus from the Bombay airport through the jungle.

We flew on the plane with a large group from the South Fallsburg ashram and our guru, Gurumayi Chidvilasananda. On the plane ride from JFK. airport in New York to Bombay there were three new babies of whom Gabriel was the eldest. All the new mothers had peaceful, non-traumatic natural births and not a peep came out of any of the babies for the entire eighteen-hour plane ride on Air India. The stewardesses actually brought you delicious meals for free back in 1985, and we were allowed to chant softly with the other devotees on this extremely special, peaceful flight. When the plane ascended, we mothers nursed our babies due to the change in air pressure which could be painful to their new delicate ear drums, so the breastfeeding kept all the little one's calm, happy, and quiet.

Arriving at the Bombay (now Mumbai) airport was quite an experience. In those days before 9/11 we did not have to pay for extra luggage or luggage that was overweight either. We had a relatively easy time getting our luggage checked for we were with the guru and were treated very respectfully and with calm expedience. At that time, Indian authorities regularly inspected almost all luggage, but only one or two pieces of luggage were opened in our group, quickly checked, and then we were moved along with Gurumayi Chidvilasananda and her entourage leading the way.

Bombay looked very poor from what I could see at the airport with very poor people living in cardboard boxes right outside the airport. I was in shock. It was something I'd never seen, not even in New York City. There was such diversity in Bombay with either extremely rich merchants and people in the large hotels or unbelievably poor beggars, children, and people with disabilities like boys with only one leg limping around asking for alms. It was a bit shocking and took some time getting accustomed to this new environment. I have a big heart and truly wanted to give some money to each child who was asking or begging, but my husband moved us quickly along. I felt as if I had been dreaming and was deposited into an entirely new world where old men and boys squatted on the sides of the road with little tin cans by their sides doing who knew what. David explained to me that these men were going to the bathroom and used the cans filled with river water to wash their genitals after they were done with their bowel movements. I'd never seen anything like it. What culture shock! As an upper middle-class American, I was accustomed to nice surroundings, even clean bathrooms in roadside gas stations; so, watching folks squatting on the ground made me think of what it was like before there was any plumbing, sewage, toilets, or Charmin! I suppose that is what our ancestors did; hence the divine desire for better hygiene with sinks flowing with clean running water at the4 turn of a faucet. Wow, how much we take for granted now. If I did not have lots of hot water flowing from the tap in my bathtub, I would be very disappointed, for that is my favorite way to relax in the winter especially. Sometimes I take a hot soothing bath at night and a more invigorating one in the morning with a few teaspoonsful of Dr. Bronner's peppermint castile soap mixed with a cup of Epsom salts to soothe my achy muscles.

We also saw women at 3:00 and 4:00 AM going to the river with jugs on their heads to fetch their family's water for the morning baths and breakfast. Some would be fetching a large amount of water that would be the family's entire days' worth for not just bathing, but also for cleaning dishes, cooking pots, plus the water that would go into making rice and other grains.

This just seemed so cool to me that many of these people living in the small jungle towns did not have running water, but were forced to rely on their own strength and hard work in order to bathe, cook, and wash the family dishes. No wonder there were rarely fat or obese people back then. They always kept moving if they wanted to live and work making a decent living.

It also made me realize how much I had taken for granted with all the modern conveniences at home in America like plumbing for washing hands before and after meals, taking long, leisurely baths and hot showers, not to mention dishwashers, washing machines, etc... There was also no toilet paper in most places in the ladies' rooms in Bombay. Occasionally we'd find some in a public restroom at the airport, but most restaurants had bidets, and we were told to bring our own toilet tissue from home if that was something we found necessary to use at the ashram. Luckily, we had been aware of this because David had traveled to the ashram in Ganeshpuri before on his own a few times before we got married. I was just too much of a yogic "Princess" not to use toilet tissue. I was also accustomed to taking long baths at home by myself and put Gabriel in with me too, but there were no bath tubs at the ashram.

In fact, there was a water shortage, and initially we were placed in a modest room where one had to heat the water for a brief shower first and pull on a string that allowed a thin stream of water to come out for douching. This was not acceptable to this princess, and I was very discouraged at first. I shared my concern and disappointment with David who saw the manager of the ashram; David agreed to pay more money for a family room and got us much better accommodations that had a normal shower where I could just relax under the hot water and not have to pull on a chain the entire time, I was washing to get sprayed. The room was larger and more accommodating for a large family.

The following is an excerpt from my journal at the time. How India has changed since those days!

India Journal

Dear Journal, Thursday, October 10, 1985

So, it is Thursday already, 1:50 PM, India time, and I'm not sure where the last three days have gone. I've been in that timeless kind of state lately. The way I felt when I was in labor with Gabriel, the way I feel when I'm making love, and the same way I felt when I first fell in love with David. Time had the quality of being "forever", and just one powerful moment simultaneously. I have to confess that I've not been experiencing a very high emotional state lately. I've been alternating between tired, whiny, grouchy, and at times peaceful. I know I can only improve from this point on.

The trip so far has been very interesting. The plane ride on Air India was quite enjoyable, especially with Gurumayi on our flight. The three babies barely made a sound throughout the entire trip. All three were breastfeeding, so that helped their ears when the cabin pressure changed as we got off the ground and when we descended, too. I made sure I nursed Gabriel when we were taking off, and he got very quiet and relaxed.

The stop-overs, delays, and constant security checks were a bit of a drag, but in general the time "flew" by, and I really enjoyed the trip – reading, sleeping, writing in my journal, a bit of chanting with Gurumayi, and enjoying some delicious vegetarian Indian and American meals. The food was probably the best I've ever had on a plane trip, combined with prompt, courteous service.

Gabriel's behavior was exemplary for an eighteen-month-old toddler. Gurumayi's grace was felt very much where the little guy was concerned. He was truly a delight, slept very well, stayed put well, and in general added a bit of joy and fun to everyone who encountered him on the plane. He did a minimum amount of "traveling" through the aisles, rarely cried or complained, and was very sweet to the other two babies on the airplane, both girls. I was so grateful for his patience and appreciative of his love and great disposition.

David, as always, made it very easy for me with Gabriel, by staying awake, walking and playing with him, when I was so tired, I could barely keep my eyes open. His indefatigable devotion to him always amazes me. I've been totally enervated for the last few days, suffering from jet lag, so David has done most of the babysitting. That is one quality about him for which I will always be thankful – his kindness and industry. He rarely seems to get tired – especially if it is something he loves to do, like working or taking care of Gabriel.

Once we arrived at the airport in Bombay, I started to experience some shock and disappointment about being in India. The airport in Bombay is very dirty. It smells putrid from urine, and who knows what. On the whole it was uninviting and not very welcoming. I was really surprised to see the terrible, unkempt condition of the airport. There were not even any rolls of toilet tissue in the public restroom.

And when I walked outside, I wished I'd stayed inside. The bus ride from the airport to the ashram was one of the most memorable and vivid experiences I'll probably ever have. We saw some people living in large cardboard boxes right outside the airport, with many people, mostly men, lying on the ground, sleeping. I saw a man masturbating in public as he watched our bus go by. I was awed to see scores of young and old men squatting on the ground to take a shit on the side of the road all along our journey in the wee morning hours. They each carry a little pail of water with them to wash themselves afterward – an interesting sight I was hardly prepared for. The squalor and filth of Bombay was a total shock to me – especially because I am accustomed to the clean, almost immaculate conditions inside Gurumayi's and Baba's ashrams in South Fallsburg, and which I soon would see, in Ganeshpuri, as well. Outside the city with its large hotels, people were living in shacks or shelters made with some sticks, cardboard and dried mud.

These domiciles were not half as well made as the forts I used to construct in the sandfield with my brother and his friends when we were kids. The night air reeked of old urine, feces, and garbage. I did not know how anyone could live in conditions such as these, unless they never knew any better. All of the roadside businesses were located in small, crowded shacks that had hand-painted signs upon their tops or in front, like "Nityananda Tyre" and "Krishna Electrical Supplies". The whole scene looked like something you might see in a movie, but how could it all actually be real?

As the bumpy bus ride progressed, the roads became more primitive, and the scenery much more beautiful. The vegetation became more lush, dotted with mango trees and many other plants I did not recognize, and we could all see beautiful mountains the size of the Catskills, or the Berkshires, in the distance.

The people here living in the jungle were already awake at 4 AM, roaming around happily before dawn. Some women dressed in beautiful, colorful saris and choles of purple, blue, white, and lilac, were en route to draw water for their families. Some had water jugs perfectly delicately balanced upon their heads. Some children were getting ready for school, and other young ones were waiting for their bus ride. Many men were roaming around, going to the stream or lake to bathe, just like Baba did when he was a young man. The countryside was welcoming, breath-taking, and a joy to behold. After a bit of time, the bus began to go past some marshlands, where the roads were practically washed out from the monsoon rains, and I became anxious we might not make it all the way through to the ashram. One time the bus driver stopped for some reason, and my heart sank as the other buses passed us by. I was so exhausted after the eighteen-hour plane flight that each moment seemed like an eternity. My attitude and my outlook were bleak.

The bus driver, to my relief, revved the engine again after a few minutes, and not long after that we reached the town of Ganeshpuri which was a lot dirtier than I had expected. I was expecting Ganeshpuri to be like a paradise sprung up in the middle of a jungle. Again, I was disillusioned. It looked dirty, crowded, and poor, somewhat like Bombay except that it contains Bhagwan Nityananda's samadhi shrine, and Baba Muktananda's ashram which is very beautiful just like the one in South Fallsburg, New York. Bade Baba's ashram is actually located in a town called Gavdevi about a mile down the road, and is a lot smaller than Baba Muktananda's. They are both beautiful and filled with the power, devotion, peace, and Shakti of the Siddha lineage.

We arrived at Baba Muktananda's ashram on the heels of Gurumayi, who was welcomed by a large crowd of devotees and a loud band. Outside the ashram, the road and the building were dirty, which disappointed me, because I was so accustomed to the immaculate conditions of all the Siddha Yoga ashrams in the United States of America, especially at South Fallsburg, New York, Manhattan, Philadelphia, and in California at Oakland and Venice. I was just too tired to appreciate the beauty of the grounds and the temples until the next day, as I became more conscious, and a lot less weary. I must say that it's taken at least three days for my physical body to feel more energetic again, after the long day and night of traveling. I'm not accustomed to that type of jet lag. Flying two hours to Florida or even five or six hours to Hawaii is completely different from crossing the International Dateline and spending eighteen hours in the air. It took me much longer to recuperate.

The first day we arrived, I was not pleasantly surprised to find that David, Gabriel, and I had not been assigned family quarters. David was in a large dormitory with other men, and Gabriel and I in the same building, but with six other bunks, for other women. When we arrived at our room, we found we were the first people to get there. I was very distressed to find we were separated from David – especially after I discovered we had no shower. Due to a drought, we were forced to use a pail with water that you heated each time you needed to wash your hands, shave, or bathe. I was practically ready to cry, or turn around and go home at this point, but I was too tired to do anything, except lie down upon the lower bunk.

David tried to arrange for family housing for hours, but the woman in charge of housing was nowhere to be found. Finally, after I had slept for three or four hours, David burst into the room with a smile and great news. He had managed to finagle us into a shared condo for an extra $400.00 for all three of us. I almost would have sold my soul at that point just to be able to take a hot shower. The facilities in the new place were like the Hilton in comparison to our dorm room. I forgot to mention that there was no toilet or toilet paper in our first room – only a hole in the floor that one squats over with a little spigot and pail to wash off your hands and genitals like a very primitive bidet. David had warned me about these primitive conditions he experienced during his first few trips to India when he was single, but I figured that after ten years they must have modernized and improved upon the old ways. David said they actually had improved upon a lot of things, but not in keeping with this Western woman's standards.

I figured if I did not get anything else out of this trip, at least I'd return home with a renewed appreciation for creature comforts like bath tubs, hot showers, indoor toilets, plumbing, and toilet paper in hotels, airports, and other public places.

In the condo we have three single beds next to one another, a large, attractive armoire as opposed to a foot locker which I had in the other room; and we have two large Indian-style screened picture windows with a beautiful view of the mountains and jungle. We share a bathroom with one other family, but it has a real toilet, a gigantic tiled shower room, and a small sink with a mirror in the hallway. And hot and cold running water in the shower! It's heaven!

The two other families that live in the bungalow are super nice, friendly, and helpful. Every person here at the ashram has been kind, helpful, and even gone out of their way to make us feel at home. There is a real community spirit here. It is so great to be welcomed with such love – especially when one is so far away from home.

Saturday, October 12*th*

Halleleuia! Today was the first day I felt like a useful human being while here at the ashram. Yesterday I was tired and depressed, so I slept from 2:30 in the afternoon right through the night into the next morning. Gabriel woke up at least six times to breastfeed, or to crawl and toddle around, and kept me awake for hours after 11:00PM. It was finally my turn to do spiritual practices and David's turn to babysit this morning, so I arose at 3 AM to shower and dress in a pretty, colorful sari which one of the women in our condo helped me wrap. They are kind of complicated to do properly unless you are experienced and really know what you are doing. I meditated for the first time in Bade Baba's samadhi shrine and then chanted the morning arati at 4:30 AM in the Nityananda Temple, had morning chai with the masses before early breakfast, then proceeded to chant the Guru Gita in the hall at 5:45 AM where Gurumayi graced us with her Presence and led us in devotional song. I completely surrendered letting in her love, beautiful, devotional voice, and peaceful focus, so I felt very giggly and joyous while in her Presence. It was great bliss for me to chant the Guru Gita with the whole group of devotees in the early morning hours, especially with her there leading the chant. It felt so wonderful to be awake so early in the morning before dawn doing devotional practices. Afterward, I quietly walked the peaceful, beautiful ashram grounds when all is quiet and one can hear the voices of God and His/Her angels. It reminded me of when I got Shaktipat when I'd be up all night in my chiropractor, Rich Therkelsen's, place, "Old Bridge Chiropractic and Holistic Center" where I worked and lived temporarily, praying, singing, dancing, and cleaning the entire house where Dr. Rich, Jim, the rolfer who introduced me to Babaji, a nutritionist, and I all worked together, while I was in complete bliss and euphoria.

I went to the seva desk to get a job while I was there for three weeks. Everyone kept telling me how hot and unforgiving was the India sun at this time of year, and even Gurumayi suggested we spend daylight hours between noon and 4PM indoors. Someone told me the beauty salon offered holistic massage for $5.00 a massage, and the place had air conditioning. I was told to look for Swami Apurvananda since he was the boss there, and he'd have to hire me. It took a while to find him, but by the guru's grace, it all worked out just fine. Voila! I am now employed as a massage therapist in the ashram beauty salon. I don't get paid, of course, but I hear the clients are allowed to give us tips, not that I really need the money. In any case I will be happy to make myself useful doing guruseva for several hours during the day.

The Ashram

Our stay at the ashram was so healing and wonderful for us as a couple. I got to sleep late in in the morning sometimes while David was working as part of the "milk project" delivering milk early in the morning. In the ashram late means about 7:30 or 8 AM. Usually, people who did not have young children rose as early as 3:30 or 4 AM for morning chai, meditation, and the Arati, a chant sung every morning at 4:30 AM. So, at least two or three mornings per week David offered to watch Gabriel sleep so I could rise at 5 AM, get dressed, and attend the daily chant, the Guru Gita, (literally the song of the Guru in Sanskrit, my favorite ninety-minute chant at 5:30 AM. I got dressed up in respectful clothes like my purple sari or a skirt and blouse, and I honored the guru and the Self several mornings per week with hundreds of other devotees. I allowed David to go himself the other mornings while I watched our baby. For me and most of the devotees, it was a very joyous and wonderful way to start the day with the austerities of meditation and chanting. I always dedicated my chanting practice of the Guru Gita to some special cause like helping people with mental illness or those in prison before I began my chanting. It made me feel fulfilled like I had started my morning with an excellent spiritual practice that influenced myself and the world for the upliftment of all humanity. Like a nun must feel while engaged in prayers most of her day. And then the rest of my day after that would be just "gravy" on top of the meat, though there was no meat served at the ashram ever. David and I were vegetarians back then anyway until Kyrie were born, and then we added a little bit of fish and an occasional chicken to their diets. Life is always sweet when one begins the day with chanting and meditation. At least for me. There were chants several times per day every single day at all the ashrams all over the world. In South Fallsburg, NY and in the borough of Manhattan in New York where David had been the manager. In Boston, MA, Venice and Oakland, CA, all ashrams we would have the honor and privilege of visiting, celebrating saptahs, or taking intensive workshops with Baba or Gurumayi. In Sydney, Australia. In New Zealand. There were ashrams and meditation centers established the world over by Swami Muktananda and then Gurumayi Chivilasananda who took over as head of the Siddha lineage in May of 1981 right before Muktananda took Mahasamadhi, his final liberation or "ascension" in October of 1982.

Baba Muktananda had implemented a disciplined and structured schedule of eating three meals per day, guruseva (work, literally service to the guru) like chopping vegetables before people woke up in the morning or later in the afternoon for the dinner meal, washing dishes, sorting silverware, cooking, and other tasks like gardening, purchasing food, hostessing the evening programs or whatever needed to be done to make an ashram filled with devotees and visitors to run smoothly. One could sign up to wash dishes, check people in at the welcome desk, welcome people to the ashram or be a host or hostess at the evening programs which began promptly at 7:30 PM following dinner from 5-7 PM, and then clean-up. One could work as I did in India babysitting and caring for the young children while their parents were in the programs, and many other practical jobs that helped the ashram to run smoothly. The person who was in charge of dispensing seva was very good at what they did like a person in human resources at a big corporation, finding the perfect jobs that fit one's talents and desires.

After a few weeks being with my family on this spiritual retreat I began to contemplate my life, my sadhana, my dharma (duty to God, my family, and community) and dreams. I did some serious thinking about all the affairs I had been having, while being a married woman in a sacred committed relationship with my husband. Including the exciting relationship, I was having at the present time with Tony. I realized I was going to have to choose between my affair with Tony or having a loving, committed, successful marriage to my husband. It was not a difficult decision. I chose my husband and family over the affair. No matter how challenging was my marriage I was truly a family-oriented woman who was in love with her husband and just loved being a mother and wife in service to God, her family, and community. I loved my family more than my own selfish desires of the flesh to be fulfilled sexually, so I asked my guru to help me let go of my attraction to Tony.

During the afternoons in India, it would get searingly hot and oppressive. Normally the heat in New Jersey or even Florida did not bother me, but I started to feel very uncomfortable in India. Luckily, I found a seva (job—literally, service to the Guru), in the beauty salon doing massages where it was air conditioned, thank Goddess.

Because there were no cell phones in those days, we had to make a special trip into Bombay to the post office where was there the sole pay telephone, so that David could call his employees to check on his annuities business back at home in Jersey. It was quite an interesting experience filled with handicapped young beggars asking us for small change and dollar bills, waiting a very long time for a long-distance call to be placed to America. While I waited for David, I strolled Gabriel around in his stroller to some nearby shops and just had to be patient. The Indian children thought Gabriel was some type of special Maharaja because he was in a large blue Graco covered stroller protecting him from the searing heat and scorching hot Indian sunshine being pushed or carried everywhere. After David successfully placed the call and finished doing business, we were starving for lunch which we had already missed at the ashram, so we went to a ritzy restaurant for lunch. There were some strong spices and chilies in whatever Indian dish I'd ordered that did not agree with me at all.

I hate chilis to begin with, but they affected me even worse because I was unaware, I was six or seven weeks pregnant. A woman's digestion is extra sensitive in the early stages of pregnancy, so this spicy dish really upset my delicate stomach. When we came back to the ashram later that night I violently vomited over and again, and I vowed never again to eat outside of the ashram. Being pregnant made my digestive system very sensitive, and once I came home, I continued to have a bit of an upset stomach, so I went to my primary care physician. She gave me the joyous, unexpected the news that I was "with child" again. why I was so much more sensitive to the extreme heat as well as the spices. It was a small price to pay for the gift that was brewing inside my belly and womb. My precious baby girl. I felt kind of sick almost right away, and it was worse by the time we returned to our little family apartment at the ashram. I spent the night retching in the bathroom and finished up the pleasant day with bouts of diarrhea.

KYRIE (1986)

Just before my daughter's birth, we were blessed to be able to travel to the island of Maui in Hawaii. David had done so well in his business as an Equitable insurance salesman that he'd won first prize as the top selling agent for Metropolitan Life. He had won first prize which was a trip to Hong Kong. That was wonderful, but it was a very long airplane ride. We'd just returned from India which was an eighteen-hour flight in both directions plus another few hours on the bus to Ganeshpuri, and it took even longer to fly to Hong Kong, so I suggested to David we take the second prize Met Life had to offer, a trip to Maui which was only eight hours in the air. Anyway, we left Gabriel at home in the care of our nanny, Janet, and we had what was like a second honeymoon. Actually, we never did go on a honeymoon because David had to get back to work right after we married on May 8th, and besides, we had guests staying over from the ashram in South Fallsburg, NY, for several nights after we wed. David's good friend, Vasudeva, and Merly, the fellow who made our beautiful wedding cake plus our best man, Karna Matrick, and my friend, Giridhar, stayed in the guest rooms upstairs.

After coming back from India and our trip to Maui I continued to feel great and do everything I wanted like hatha yoga, massage a few clients, sing with the wedding band, go to the gym where I would swim and go into the hot jacuzzi, steam, and sauna for deep relaxation.

We awaited our daughter's birth.

As with my son, I intuitively knew her sex and had already chosen a name for her without ever having been given a sonogram or anything like that. When Gabriel was born I intuitively "felt" a feminine presence around me and Gabriel. I already KNEW without a doubt I was going to give birth to a baby girl within a short time. Two years and three months later, to be exact. I had heard my friend, Wendy, a singer at my church, had named her daughter Kyra. Wendy was a member of the George Street Co-op in New Brunswick like me, a singer and a member of my church, Rev. Joan Fericy's "Church of Divine Light," in Somerset. She'd also chosen a home birthing experience like I did. Anyway, I just loved her new baby's name and decided I would give my baby girl the same name, Kyra, when she would eventually be born.

Did you know that each of our names has a certain numerological vibration? Each letter has a number from one to nine, and each two-digit number like twelve or thirteen is added together except for the numbers 11,22, and 33 which are Master numbers and need not be added for they have their own special, unique vibration. Our names help determine our unique experience in this incarnation, and we influence our parents, while we are on the other side, to give us the "perfect name" for the karmic experiences we need and want to have for our own spiritual growth. At least that is my understanding from several metaphysical teachers I've studied with. By the time I was eight months pregnant, David and I were vacationing in Hawaii, and I had an intuitive feeling Kyra's name was supposed to be three syllables, not two. I heard the song "Kyrie", by the band, "Mister, Mister" being played frequently on FM radio at the time and saw the video on Vh1. That is how I was impressed with Kyrie's unique name. I'd never heard anyone else with that name and to this day, only one other person has shared with me that they knew a woman with this name. Friends of mine told me their granddaughter was named Kyrie, and I was excited to hear it because I knew she must be a very special person since the name is Greek for Lord.

Except for the final few moments of labor, Kyrie's pregnancy and birth was very smooth, and I decided to remain with the wedding band just until I was six months along, mostly because I had trouble wearing and dancing in high heels during our gigs which really threw my pelvis out of whack. I was still very attracted to Tony, but I had decided to be monogamous and faithful to the best of my ability, while doing my sadhana in India, so I avoided staying out late after the gigs to hang out with Tony so as not to be tempted to become intimate with him again.

My labor with Kyrie was only six hours and very relaxed for the first three hours or so. I sat up in bed talking on the telephone to my mom and friends. As the contractions began to progress, I was guided to squat for a while holding onto the upstairs banister and sway from side to side. I chanted the mantra Aum as I swayed from side to side. It was a beautiful Monday morning filled with bright sunlight coming through my bedroom windows. My best friend, Janet, was living with us at the time and had agreed to be my birthing coach and Kyrie's nanny and caretaker. She was already a nanny to Gabriel. After three hours I was nearly ten centimeters dilated, and my midwives, Barbara and Linda, were very excited. There seemed to be a little problem though because nothing was happening after a half-hour. The contractions just stopped and I had no desire to push or bear down. They suggested I take a bath and go for a walk with my husband. Prior to that David was in the office downstairs working with my brother, Scott, and several employees. He has his own business called United States Annuities, which he ran out of our living room with a handful of devoted employees. He was a financial wiz and a self-made man.

David helped me out of my bath, dried my back, and put his warm maroon and dark green striped terrycloth robe I'd given him for Christmas the year before around my shoulders. We started to walk upstairs and eventually moved down to the living room and then outside. It was such a lovely day we wanted to welcome it and enjoy the afternoon sunshine.

Each time a contraction would come I'd put my arms around David's neck and hang until the contraction passed. I must have looked odd walking around our back yard nude with his maroon terrycloth bathrobe over my shoulders and my humongous protuberant belly hanging out. My favorite cat, Groucho, came outside with us and followed David and me. He looked pretty strange too as he'd just had his long-matted hair totally shaved off except for his tail, which was skinny and came to a tasseled point at the end. He resembled a black and white Puss in Boots. Groucho was devoted to me. He also attended Gabriel's birth. He was at my side through the entire twelve and half-hours of labor with Gabriel and laid his head on my neck in bliss just after Gabriel's birth.

This time our next-door neighbor was pregnant the same time as me, and they'd just welcomed a new baby girl into the world the day before, but I believe she had her baby in the usual way in a hospital.

We were thrilled when it was time for Kyrie to arrive.

Before the pain became too intense, twenty-seven-month-old Gabriel had been bringing me steaming hot wash cloths and placing them on my lower back for a few minutes at a time until they lost their heat. His sweet loving presence soothed and comforted me; Gabriel always brought me joy. Who would have thought he'd contribute so much to my labor and was in loving service to his mom at such a tender age? I knew; however, he was an Ascended Master and very special soul from the celestial realms who chose me as his mom and as a physical vessel for his Soul to journey back to earth where he would make an incredible contribution upon the planet. Gabriel has been sharing his love, joy, talent as an actor, musician, and singer, wisdom, and playful Spirit since he was a mere babe. At six months old Janet and I referred to him as the "Master of Playfulness". She called him "Mister Man" and I called him "Bear". He was a Light to All with whom he came in contact. I remember him building incredible structures with his legos, colorful wooden blocks, and toys as if he were an ingenious architect planning a new city. I remember having the feeling that from the time he was small he was going to grow up to become a great man and a charismatic leader of some sort. He was incredibly intelligent, determined, and persistent in all that he did.

I remember him having the most intense and angry tantrums from the time he was eighteen months old until he was nearly three years old. I was not quite sure how to handle them, so I asked for advice from my pediatrician. She said that this was normal behavior for a young man in his "terrible twos". I was still concerned when he was having at least two tantrums every day, so I asked a friend named Jamie Sams, from New Mexico, who was a channel for a nonphysical entity named "Leah" who claimed she was from Venus and that she, while on earth, had given birth to seven of the twelve tribes of Israel. This loving, intelligent entity who had a very distinctive, high-pitched voice with a sort of English accent. At least she spoke very proper, perfect English. Leah had come to Jamie when she was sixteen years old and asked to be channeled through her body. The advanced, loving being called herself "Leah." Jamie was a Native American healer, teacher, and psychic who traveled around America sharing the wisdom and knowledge of this delightful being. Jamie Sams is also the author of the deck called "The Animal Cards" with which I was familiar, and enjoyed learning about Spirit and animal totems for myself and others.

Leah's teachings were audio-taped and sold after the evening's channeling and for use afterwards on Jamie's website. I met Jamie and Leah in East Millstone, NJ, at Vince and Ronnie Jelm's home during a channeling session one evening. My special friend, Zara Rose, had attended the session, liked it very much, and asked me if I'd like to go with her the next time she intended to go. Jamie was a very talented trance medium and I loved her openness, her beautiful, caring loving spirit, and the practical wisdom as shared by the Native American teachers and ancestors. The Native Americans who arrived way before the European white man lived here in peace and harmony with great honor and respect for the Earth Mother. They practiced rituals, ceremonies, honored the Earth as their sacred Mother, held sweat lodges, and lived in harmony with Mother Earth and for the most part, each other.

Leah told me I could simply let Gabriel alone to express his rage and frustration while he was having these violent tantrums. She suggested I tell him that I was going to go in the other room and say that I was available to talk about what was upsetting him when he was ready. This seemed to work very well.

He was usually frustrated because his little body could not accomplish all the things his mind was capable of imagining, and he'd become so angry that he would start to go into a rage flailing his arms and kicking his legs. I suppose it was good for him that I allowed him to express his frustration and anger in this way because after five or ten minutes of venting and leaving him alone he'd just become peaceful and quiet. Allowing him to scream and flail like this worked much better than to try to control and suppress him, and I believe it probably saved him from having to go for years of therapeutic counseling and psychotherapy later on in his adult life.

My brother, Scott was there. Scott married a woman who gave birth to my nephew, Christopher. They moved to Florida, and we lost touch again. But prior to that, Scott worked as an employee in my husband's office of US. Annuities when we lived in Englishtown. Scott, while working for us, was the one my husband called on the phone while I was in labor upstairs with Kyrie and asked to leave work briefly so that he and another employee could put a saw horse together for us... I was in excruciating lower back pain toward the end of my labor, so David had the brilliant idea that leaning over a saw horse with a pillow on top of it would help to ease the pain. He turned out to be brilliant and quite intuitive. Once Scott and our friend, Art, put the saw horse together and placed it on top of my bed, laying on top of it took the pressure off of my lumbar area, and my labor progressed swiftly from that point on. After two pushes my daughter, Kyrie was born! So, Scott was the only family member other than my husband who was present at both baby's births.

At Kyrie's birth, Scott left his work in the office downstairs temporarily to help support the laboring mom. He did something very important for David and me. Since David was busy holding me and looking into my eyes, he did not have time to do one very important thing which would assist me in giving birth at the end. I was having terrible low back pains and cramps during my middle and final stages of labor. The pain was so intense that we asked Gabriel, who was only two years and three months at the time, to go into the bathroom and soak several washcloths in hot water. He'd bring them back and place them on my lumbar region, and it helped ease some of the pain, but at the end the pain got worse, and it was very difficult for me to get comfortable over the birthing pillow we'd purchased just for the momentous event; so, David had the ingenious idea of getting rid of the pillow we were using and swapping it for a sawhorse – the kind one uses to saw wood upon. It was a still sitting downstairs in our basement waiting to be assembled. David called my brother, Scott, who was working for us at US Annuities in the office downstairs, asked him to get some help from Art, our other full-time employee, and they took only fifteen minutes to put together the sawhorse over which I would use for the final stages of intense, rapid, and painful contractions as well as the actual birthing of Kyrie herself! I was in acute pain with Kyrie toward the end of my labor due to the way she was putting pressure on my lower back and spine. The contractions were so painful at about eight centimeters of dilation that I was crying and frustrated. I had not gone to the chiropractor for an adjustment prior to the birth because I was too busy or too tired. Anyway, the entire journey through labor was joyous and relaxed up until the final stages before and after my water broke. I felt a stabbing pain in my lower back, and my young son got so concerned about me when he heard me yell that he finally hid himself away in the bedroom closet unable to deal with the pain his mom was experiencing. He really loved me and felt worried when he knew I was in such bad pain. We were very close. He is still the apple of my eye. I call Gabriel my "Sonshine".

My friend, Janet, was also here to help keep me focused when the pain became intense at about eight or nine centimeters dilated. Then, all of a sudden, while she was staring into my eyes, my water broke, and that was a real relief. The pain was not as intense anymore, but I still tried to give birth using the large birthing pillow, but it was uncomfortable and too large. When, after an hour or so, that did not work my husband was finally inspired with the brilliant idea of trying the sawhorse. After Scott and Art put it together, they brought it upstairs and we put a bed pillow over the top of it in order to cushion my belly and take the pressure off of my lower back.

After six hours of labor, two lovely midwives, Barbra and Linda, helped me to welcome Kyrie into the world at our home in Englishtown on a very special festive day, Cinco de Mayo. She was brought into the world in my bedroom surrounded by her whole family (David, me, Gabriel, and my brother, Scott), and Paula – one of our other employees == who came into the bedroom immediately after Kyrie was born with a gift of two yellow ceramic ducks she had made, and my best friend, Janet, who was there for labor support.

At least three hours of my labor and birth were videotaped by a professional birth videographer named Gigi Blair who later became a professional midwife herself. I still have the only copy of the video, but I'd be willing to tape it and lend it out if you'd like to see firsthand how wonderful, easy, and natural a home-birth with midwives can be. My son took the videotape to have it copied over as a DVD. Kyrie's delivery is one that will probably go down in "herstory" books as unique and creative. First, I labored by holding onto the upstairs banister and squatting for hours all by myself. Then I relaxed on my bed talking on the phone until David came up from our home office and the midwives were ready to assist with the more difficult stages of labor.

Once again, I was thrilled to be a new mom.

Shortly after that, though, I began to feel frightened and unsure of myself.

After the Ecstasy

Who would believe that I'd go from a state of such joy and enthusiasm when Kyrie was born in May of 1986 into such a state of depression, hopelessness, and terror thirteen months later that I would want to kill myself? I felt such conflict wanting to abandon her and her three-year-old brother, Gabriel, the two lights of my life, forever, when I loved them more than life itself!

Back in 1984, fate had led me to Bernie Wayne, a well-known New York composer and vocal coach who saw my talent and had the connections to get me into show business as a soloist in Vegas, New York, and Atlantic City. He saw something special in me and told me he thought I could become the next Barbra Streisand with my talent, beauty and charisma.

Bernie had written the song for the Miss America contest and coached some celebrities like Mary Wells and the actor and singer, Paul Sorvino, whom I would see in the elevator sometimes when going upstairs for my voice coaching session. I still see him on television regularly. He's a very talented actor and operatic singer.

My husband was prepared to invest about $11,000 in me for ten original songs written especially for me, and even more money for costumes and coaching. I was somewhat afraid that I might fail and he would be angry with me, so I just didn't even try after the first few months of lessons in which I felt excitement, optimism, and enthusiasm. Bernie was so excited about my talent he brought in a man who had connections in the music and theater business to listen to me sing at one of my lessons. This man also thought I had great potential to be a star.

However, my initial enthusiasm waned after a few months of voice lessons. I lost my usual confidence and became frightened of failing. I eventually became paralyzed with fear and lost interest in getting my one-woman show together as well as life, in general. I don't know if it had to do with a biochemical imbalance created by using the drug, ecstasy, but it is very likely that had something to do with my depression and downward spiral into hopelessness, chronic fear, anxiety, terror, unworthiness and suicidal ideations.

After three months of anxiety, self- doubt and despair, my mental state got worse and worse. It didn't make any sense to David or me. Even though I had a beautiful new home in the country, a loving husband who took care of me as if I were a queen, a nanny to help me with my sweet new baby, Kyrie, and my two-year-old little "bear", Gabriel, I woke up each morning feeling terribly sad, frightened, and hopeless. As soon as I woke up, I was conscious that there was something innately wrong with me, and I dreaded getting out of bed. I did not have any idea what I would even do with myself during the day.

I usually brought Gabriel to a friend, Linda Renz's, house, in Jamesburg, where he would play with other children his age while I went to the beauty parlor for a new coif and manicure. Sometimes I'd go to the New Woman Health Club to exercise, work on a massage client at home, or I'd shop and have lunch with friends. Sometimes I'd bring the baby with me, but often after I nursed her, I'd leave her at home with Denise, so she could nap, and I could have some free time to myself. Since I was breastfeeding Kyrie, I'd express six or seven ounces of breast milk into a bottle for our new Jamaican nanny, Denise, to feed her when she woke up from her naps. Kyrie was one of the most beautiful babies I'd ever laid eyes upon. She was a very happy baby and was usually content while I was away just so long as she was fed and kept comfortable in her carry cradle or swing. Sometimes she would go out on sunny days in May and June for walks in her roomy lavender and turquoise Graco stroller along our pretty tree lined street in Monroe Twp. Sometimes I'd pick up her little ten-pound body and toss her up into the air just like my dad and grandpa had done with me when I was little. She loved that. I know she has no recollection of the short time we were together, but I was crazy about her and so thrilled to have a beautiful, happy little 7-lb. 9-ounce baby girl following the birth of my son. She was the largest baby of my three children, and she was cute and pudgy with a little round belly for the first year after she was born. Girls have a different kind of energy, and it's so fun to buy them little dresses and groom them. Kyrie had curly light brown hair and the most beautiful almond shaped blue eyes when she was first born. They turned brown like her dad's and brother, Gabriel's, after a few months.

I recall waking up each morning in late May of 1987, after I'd decided to stop breastfeeding Kyrie months earlier than usual, feeling so tired and listless. I did not even care to open my eyes to welcome the new day which was completely unlike my nature. Little by little I began to feel worse and worse, until absolutely nothing in my life brought me joy anymore. I even felt apathetic toward my precious, sweet children. It did not make sense to me, and I felt terribly guilty that I was not feeling my usual love and passion about them when just a few months before I'd felt so much joy and love just being near them. I wonder if my choice to wean Kyrie so young had an effect on my biochemistry, and I had some kind of belated postpartum depression.

A depression is often composed of many negative thoughts, extreme feelings of unworthiness, terror, hopelessness, and unshakable lethargy. With bipolar disorder it is always eventually followed by states of mania. Being in those states of mind devoid of feeling and interest in life or people was like being in hell, the nadir of existence. One negative, hopeless thought was followed by another and put me into despair and chronic suicidal depression.

Here is a prose poem I wrote during one of the periods of depression.

Another Part of Me

There is a part of me that hates myself and is running my life right now
It feels separate from God and everyone
Resisting Life, unwilling to participate
It has no desire to live or enjoy this moment
Perceiving everything from a negative point of view
It wishes it could live in the past when I felt deep love for myself and others
There is no present for this split off self
Only thoughts of disconnection, feeling nothing

Numbness
The only feelings it knows are dread, anxiety, and fear
Resisting the beauty of a clear blue sky and warmth of a spring day
Rain and darkness is what it prefers
To sleep and be unconscious
It does not have hunger, no desire to eat
Food is tasteless
It rarely feeds her body unless it is starving or so spacey
That she might collapse
Apathetic about everything she once loved
Including spending time with the people she loves
It cares about no one but itself
Wanting to shut out the world and die
Go back to God
Please help me Lord
I want myself back the way I was

Mind-Altering Substances

Because I was a goody two shoes growing up in the sixties and seventies I barely even heard of drugs. I'd heard that some of the rock musicians became addicted to some heavy mind-altering substances, and that some, like Janis Joplin, and Jim Morrison, had died using too much. Many more musicians and actors have died from overdoses since then, including two members of the band called "The Pretenders". I recently read the life story of the lead singer, Chrissy Hines, and was surprised how honest she was about sharing her experiences with drugs and alcohol which seemed to consume a large part of her life from her late teens to early thirties.

My life growing up was pretty blessed and innocent compared to most people, so it never even occurred to me to try, look for, or purchase something even as basic as marijuana.

It was not until I was 21 years old, living with my boyfriend, Greg, and traveling in the show band, Spectrum, on the road in a van, that I first took a hallucinogen. Greg had had been experimenting with drugs like pot and even cocaine which someone gave him at a party, but he said it hurt his nostrils, and he did not like it. But he'd just gotten some "magic mushrooms" (psilocybin) recently, and he wanted to share this special experience with me.

He told me I might vomit a bit in the beginning which I did, and then I sat down to meditate and relax in a cross-legged position on a chair in our living room. I was a bit frightened at first when I began to lose control, but Greg assured me that I could direct the "trip" with my own thoughts and feelings. If I was frightened, I could turn it into a bad trip, but if I wanted to have a positive experience I could just relax, pray, and trust God to guide me, which I did. It's been over forty years since that experience, but I'll share what I remember from that day.

We were invited out to dinner at the home of my band leader, Pierre Falerne, with his sister, Michelle, and two of the other band members. I recall feeling a bit paranoid at first; and then I believed I was reading everyone's thoughts at dinner because I began to feel very psychic. As I relaxed, I began to feel better and better. I was in a state of intense euphoria and was experiencing much wonder.

After dinner we decided to see the movie "Magic" starring Anthony Hopkins. It was a popular film which had just come out, so the line at the Bergen Theater in Paramus was very long, and we waited over an hour to get our tickets. The crazy thing was I did not feel one bit of impatience or anxiety waiting outdoors at night in the dark for so long. I felt like I could have waited three hours, completely enjoying every moment in the company of my boyfriend and our other companions. Once we got into the theater, I had to use the bathroom after we got our seats, and I remember after sitting down on the toilet being in awe of the way my fingers moved when I had to unsnap the snaps at the crotch of my red bodysuit in order to urinate. I had never really noticed how amazing it was to use my dexterous fingers before that special moment even though I had done therapeutic Swedish massage on many clients before, and everyone always told me how magical and electrical my fingers felt when I touched them. I felt like a newborn baby discovering her fingers and toes for the first time, and how delightful it was to be aware of them and how they moved to grasp things.

The movie was good, though a bit scary, but I was very content, peaceful, and fine on my own, with or without outside entertainment. The magical mushroom trip continued for about six hours, even in Pierre's van and in Greg's car as we drove back to our apartment in Hackensack. There, I went more inward and became quieter.

I was so changed and moved by the sacred experience that I chose never to do it again because I had a thought that I'd become addicted to feeling this way, and I had no desire to get addicted to anything that might possibly hurt me, so I chose not to do magic mushrooms or any other drugs at all while I was in my late twenties, especially after getting involved in Siddha Yoga and meditation, getting married, and becoming a mom. I'm glad I did not do drugs for most of my life after that first experience. I had no idea that I would later try another popular hallucinogen. The ecstasy.

However, I decided to try ecstasy because David and I were having a lot of problems with sexual intimacy during the course of our young marriage; and I was told by Jim, who performed rolfing [6] sessions on me and introduced me to my guru and to the dance teacher, Gabrielle Roth, creator of "Five Rhythms" movement therapy, that "This is a sacred substance developed in our time to help people get in touch with God in themselves and whomever you are with". Ecstasy helped him and his wife to "experience the Truth together," he said with enthusiasm. Jim was usually a pretty intense, mellow guy who never showed too much emotion, but he seemed pretty excited about using the ecstasy when I talked to him over the phone. I trusted Jim because we had similar desires for God Realization and Self Awareness. I hoped it would improve my relationship with David if we tried doing it together. Though I loved the euphoric and natural thoughts and feelings I experienced I believe it changed my biochemistry so much that it led to the three months of self-doubt and fear which caused me to attempt suicide again. I feel it is just as important to share the down side of experimenting with drugs as a warning to others that drugs can totally change and mess with our biochemistry for the worst, and I'm told by a good source that they can put holes in the auric fields around our physical body, leaving them open to pesky negative entities and "ghosts and djinns" who may be attracted to our Light or joy and want to reside with us in our minds and auras for a time making life a temporary "hell" while these negative entities are whispering negative, psychic garbage into our minds.

---

6 Rolfing was discussed earlier.

Jim had said "If you wish I could most likely procure several tabs for you and your husband to try." I said "Yes", and he actually got four tabs for us at twenty dollars per tablet.

The first time I chose to experience "XTC" was with my nanny and best friend, Janet, who lived with us. I have some memories about that particular experience that may have faded over thirty-three years. I remember we took a tab each in the meditation room after praying over it, ran to the bathroom to vomit a bit of it out. We said some things to one another we'd been holding back in order to be clear in our communication and let go of any judgments we might have about the other. We completely got out of our heads, left egos behind us, and became very close in just a few moments. We opened our hearts to one another as very dear friends for life feeling our unity and precious oneness with the other.

As the drug really got into our systems, we lost all inhibitions and took off nearly all our clothes. I remember sitting across from Janet in a cross-legged position and feeling so much love, appreciation, and gratitude for all she was to me. I felt such humility and reverence for her that I bowed my head low toward her feet. All of a sudden one of our workers named Noel came into the room without knocking and saw us; he must have thought I was licking her pussy because of where my head was placed, but I was feeling such reverence I was merely bowing to the Christ Consciousness within her; we were not sexual at all. The feelings were all very pure, subtle, and virtuous centering in the heart chakra and above. Besides, I've never really been attracted to women physically because I am not "wired" that way. I love them as sisters for their beauty, intellect, gentle, sensitive, wise, and spiritual natures.

Our worker, Knowle, who was shocked and embarrassed to find us both in the meditation room sans vetements (completely nude), humbly apologized and left abruptly; then Janet and I cracked up in hysterics. Feeling complete freedom, we pranced into the bathroom to wash our faces and remove all of our make-up which we felt was just putting on a mask because of BS advertisements and commercials. It's crazy how I have almost always believed I looked better with some mascara, lipstick, and foundation. Such nonsense. We were not born that way. God made us perfect the way we are. Even in our human imperfection we are completely perfect.

My beau, Gary, says "If God had wanted us to run around naked, we would have been born that way!"

Janet and I thought it would be great to experience our newfound love, joy, and wonder in nature. We got my four-month-old baby, Kyrie, from the futon in her bedroom and went outside. The baby was just beginning to stir from her long nap. We checked her diaper which we changed first. I held her close to me as we walked around the back yard as if we were experiencing the beauty of it for the very first time. The grounds were so beautiful. We had some really large evergreen trees, a beautiful twenty-foot-tall holly tree at the foot of the driveway, yellow daffodils in a garden on the side of the house, and a beautiful new beige and blue patio set with a couch, four brown, comfortable chairs with cushions on the porch on the side of the house enclosed by a large brown portable enclosed patio we set up just for the summer and fall to keep out the bugs. This was where Janet and I sat for a little while to breastfeed my adorable, little thirteen-pound baby daughter with the soft brown curls.

In retrospect, this was probably not a practical idea because some of the drug must have gotten into my breast milk, and in my euphoric, altered state I never even considered how this chemical might affect her. Nothing really happened afterward to her, as far as we could tell, thank God.

While on the ecstasy I remember the sensuousness of her mouth sucking gently upon my nipples more than I normally would, and how pleasant and sweet it was.

We decided to put her in her car seat in the station wagon so we could all go to a nearby park or a forest. We were feeling euphoric and so close to God, Mother Earth, and each other. I felt so incredibly blessed. The high only lasted for a few hours after that, but it was long enough that it felt timeless. I had no awareness about the passage of time just like in my experience with the psilocybin or as in the moments of bliss I experience during hours of tantric sex. I could only be aware completely of the perfect present moment.

I shared our experience with David when he arrived home and sat down to dinner. I kissed Kyrie and placed her gently in her nanny's arms. Janet checked her diaper upstairs, and David and I talked about the discomfort our worker felt when he came upon Janet and I in our birthday suits. Then I explained how wonderful our experience had been. I invited David to try the sacred drug with me.

We arranged to go to the "Queen Victoria", a beautiful Victorian bed and breakfast with a jacuzzi in Cape May with Janet and the kids. Janet stayed sober so she was in good shape to take care of the two children. My memory of this experience with David is not as vivid. I believe we were also sitting across from one another in meditation sharing metaphysical insights and our love for one another from our hearts. We were intimate emotionally and spiritually, but I do not recall us ever feeling sexual. The drug seemed to focus on the upper chakras where we felt so much love and reverence for each other as if we were worshiping God or the Christ Consciousness in one another. We had a very sweet time, but then the week-end ended.

When we returned home, I started feeling anxious and down for no particular reason. I wanted to do the ecstasy one more time with David. He said he would be willing, but he only pretended to take the drug in our bedroom while watching me take my tablet. I was kind of disappointed, felt a bit hurt and betrayed, but, looking back now, I completely understand why he wanted to keep his senses. He was a good husband, father, and disciplined CEO of his own annuity company who had a structured nine to five jobs in the house with several employees whereas I only did massage therapy part-time and took care of the kids with Janet's help. David had already experienced it, and he shared that one time he did peyote with a shaman as a guide with a group of other people as a sacred ritual. He said it was a terrific experience, but I'm not sure if he felt as safe doing the ecstasy alone with just me since there was no teacher, shaman, or guru present to make sure the experience would turn out safely for us both.

Again, I looked deeply into his eyes, and I felt this same reverence for him, but rather than kissing or getting sexual with each other we looked into one another's eyes and saw our own divine reflection. We were intellectual and began to remember past incarnations with each other. In one he was my teacher. In another he was entranced by me where I was a beautiful, sexy woman who danced on stages across the world during World War II. I felt as if he'd been my spiritual teacher or guru before. At that moment all ll I wanted to do was to lay myself at his feet which was so interesting because during our marriage, I believed I was missing sexual and emotional intimacy more than anything.

Well, a drug high does not last forever. What comes up must come down. About a month later, I began to think very negative, dark thoughts and became deeply depressed for what seemed like no reason. These negative thoughts and bad feelings spiraled into one of the most hellish nightmares in my mind which eventually had me waking up every morning in terror for absolutely no rational reason. All my bills were paid by my husband, we lived a very comfortable lifestyle with a live-in nanny to help care for Gabriel who was three and a half at the time, and Kyrie, my precious baby who'd just turned a year old on May 5th.

It sounds crazy, but I felt as if I was being psychically attacked or influenced by a ghost-like presence, a negative entity. I'd found out months later that a young woman had hung herself in our bedroom in our historical house which was over two centuries old. The owner prior to the last ones had died in the kitchen, and as a single man with few friends as a longshoreman, his absence was not missed for a while. He had several dogs who were starving after a few weeks of not being fed, and according to the realtor who told us the story, the dogs got so hungry they finally ate him. She said there was blood all over the kitchen floor, so the new owners had to replace the floor and at the same time decided to replace all the cabinets and put wooden beams with new lights on the ceiling to make the kitchen look livable again. Perhaps it was the ghosts of these former owners of our "new" country home in Englishtown who somehow tried to connect with me. I am only speculating, but I had no reason to experience the terrifying feelings that I had as well as the crazy thoughts in my mind, so I am guessing it might have had something to do with taking the ecstasy. Some people think I might have had postpartum depression, but I doubt it because I never experienced any negative feelings or even one day of morning sickness with either baby, and I was just a happy, proud mom-to-be all during my pregnancies; and when Gabriel was born those joyous feelings continued for at least a few years until this particular circumstance which occurred several months after taking ecstasy several times during the nine-month period.

It was due to these constant feelings and thoughts of fear, self-doubt, and terror that I eventually believed I could not manage being on this earth plane, and the relentless confusion and despair brought me to thoughts of suicide which I prayed would end these horrific thoughts and feelings.

I am assuming this was one of the major causes since I saw the same thing happen with one of my daughters after she experimented with the drug, ecstasy, with one of her older boyfriends in a hotel one summer without my knowledge. That entire summer she spent in and out of the psychiatric hospital at Helene Fuld Medical Center. We were all very worried about her, especially me because she became violent with me once, knocked me off my feet and fled from the house for days after that incident. It took several days to find out whee she went and I was deeply concerned. They could not diagnose her as being manic depressive, and she only took one shot of some medication the psychiatrist gave her the last time, and after that she got herself and her life together, so I suppose the effects of the XTC wore off once she stopped experimenting with it. Once she stopped using all drugs including marijuana, there was no evidence of the paranoia and mental illness that had plagued her during the time she was experimenting with ecstasy and weed. So, in my estimation, there is a good chance that the three times I used ecstasy before going into that dark night of the soul might very well have contributed to the inexplicable depression and fear I would eventually experience. I was beginning to spiral gradually downward into the mysterious depression about March of 1987 which continued to deepen into the crisis of April of 1987. At the time the cause of the depression was a mystery to my husband and me, but looking back I would not be surprised if my sensitive and pure system which was accustomed to eating natural vegetarian foods and had no substances, not even medications for anything being a holistic health care practitioner, I rarely even took an aspirin for a head ache, if I ever got one. So, I definitely would recommend caution if you or any one you love decides to experiment with any type of substance, even for spiritual or metaphysical purposes as I know some people do use marijuana, peyote, or ayahuasca for. If one is using those things for spiritual growth, I believe it is always best to use a shaman or have an experienced teacher or MD who is accustomed to the possible negative side effects of psychedelic substances. But putting a gun put to my head did not relieve the depression and it gave me another whole set of problems with which to deal for quite a few months after I survived. I somehow did lose the thoughts of fear, anxiety, and terror, though, most likely because I needed to focus on my rehabilitation and what I needed to do to get well enough to walk and to get back home to be with my family again. The mind cannot think two different thoughts and feelings at once, so, in a way, the fact that I was so overjoyed that I had another opportunity to see the faces of my children again gave me something for which to be grateful, and my mind was preoccupied with my rehabilitation. To this day I do not fully understand why this dramatic, traumatic set of circumstances came to be my karma. I just know that it has turned out to be a blessing of sorts since I have been able to relate to others with suicidal depression as well as to help some of the families of folks with mental illness as well as the consumers themselves.

I recall saying the mantra "Om Namah Shivaya" as I pulled the trigger as a protection just in case there was a more hellish realm on the "Other Side" actually worse than the frightening thoughts and feelings of unworthiness I was experiencing for those three months. As a minister and practitioner of yoga and Science of Mind teachings of Ernest Holmes, I do believe in the eternality of the soul and know for a fact that our consciousnesses continues even after the change we call "death".

So, next time you think of experimenting with drugs or have a cavalier attitude about trying marijuana, cocaine, ayahuasca, peyote, heroin, LSD, hash, or whatever, from my own experience, I advise you to think twice. Do a lot of research, use discrimination, and remember mine and others' experiences where people have overdosed and died, turned into addicts, did illegal things to procure the drugs ending up in prison, or lost their minds and jumped from bridges or buildings during manic phases in which they believed they could fly.

I, myself, became homeless, lost two or three jobs, good friends, my spouse, and living with all three of my children at some point in their early upbringing due to the biochemical imbalance created by using the drug, ecstasy, not even counting the other sad experiences that came with losing the usage of my left arm and hand after shooting myself in the head.

One of my old boyfriends and I spoke at length recently. He used to play bass guitar for me in a trio I had about six years back. Anyway, Pan told me he'd lost a precious twenty-eight-year-old granddaughter over a year ago because her husband gave her too much of a drug. She overdosed and died.

With drugs, you might have an enlightening, relaxing experience, but it is also possible that, if you are not careful and watchful, you might die or become addicted to a very expensive habit that will consume you and change your life for the worst. If you do decide to try hallucinogens, I suggest it is with the permission and guidance of a sacred teacher, shaman, or counselor with experience in these things. Meditation, art, music, tantric sex with protection or a monogamous partner, masturbation and outdoor sports are a lot safer, and can give you the same high. Dancing and singing give me natural highs every day.

SUICIDE (1987)

In May, 1987, I tried to electrocute myself in a bathtub, to strangle myself with a long scarf, to suffocate myself with a pillow, and to overdose on a nearly full bottle of my medication.

On June 11, 1987, following a three-month period of hopelessness, self-doubt and fear I shot myself in the head at point blank range with a 22 caliber Beretta pistol David brought home one afternoon for protection and target practice.

How could this be?

I was by nature a positive person, wife, and mother involved in holistic health care, meditation, and yoga. I had everything in life a woman could possibly desire. I had an attractive devoted, wealthy husband, a spacious five bedroom newly renovated two-hundred-year-old home in the country, a three-year-old son whom I adored, and a beautiful baby girl whom I'd just given birth to at home in great bliss eleven months before.

I woke up that morning with the first sense of relief I'd felt in months knowing I was going to be free of my misery, worry, and fear sometime later that night. I'd already snuck the 22 Beretta out of the hope chest the prior evening and brought it to my massage client, Joe Jablonsky, who showed me how to load and use it. Joe was left confined to a wheelchair, following an ambush, when he was a police officer. He lived in Highland Park alone, and he was the only person for whom I made a house call because he was disabled and housebound, for the most part. He was a very nice man who inspired me with his sense of humor, determination, and excellent ability to take care of himself and his needs despite his physical handicap which left him forever confined to being in a wheelchair. Poor Joe was in shock and so deeply saddened when he found out what happened afterward. He called me when I was at Robert Wood Johnson Hospital to see how I was to wish me well. It was ironic that I also ended up just like him for three months, hemiplegic and confined to a wheelchair. It is a miracle that I am still alive.

For the next few days, knowing I had my loaded gun upstairs ready to set myself free from my misery, pain, and fear, I felt a bit more relaxed when I woke up in the morning as opposed to the terror, I usually felt for at least an hour upon arising for three whole months. This fear I felt when I woke up was inexplicable and irrational, not really anything I could consciously understand or explain to my husband, mother, or close friends. I was actually embarrassed by these terrible thoughts and feelings being a lover of God and a follower of a wonderful guru who would always remind us that God dwelt within us as our very own Selves. I had never been a person to worry or feel anxious about anything, so this state of terror and fear was unlike anything I'd ever experienced, and it truly frightened me because there was no rhyme or reason for it. It was truly irrational.

The terror began as mild anxiety after signing up for a New Age training called a Direct Centering intensive facilitated by a man who fashioned himself to be a New Age teacher and guru of sorts named Gavin Barnes, but who eventually changed his name to Bayard Hora. The initial workshop called "Direct Centering", was held in Manhattan, and I took the course at nearly nine months pregnant, right before giving birth to Gabriel. I thought the course was the most challenging thing I'd ever done because there was so much manipulation and coercion going on, and me, being a very naive, trusting type of person, believed in the power of the course because I was not only brainwashed by the leader, but also because my two friends, Jim Star, and my best friend, Janet, who recommended it, completely believed in the power and sacredness of "Direct Centering. So, I signed up for the training with a payment I received from my dad and step-mom that was the interest which had accumulated on Gabriel's life insurance policy. I figured that they did not think Gabriel, at his young age, was ever really going to need life insurance until he became a lot older. So, I registered for "the Course" while attending the graduation of my friend, Janet, who also had me come to her graduation of "Lifespring", and "Women, Sex, and Power". I also took both those ridiculous seminars too.

So, while attending Janet's graduation I became registered for Direct Centering with two hundred fifty of the $550 I needed to take the week-end seminar.

Now, with these types of workshops and seminars the teachers and other students lead one to believe that the "magic" begins happening the minute you register and start writing down your goals and dreams. Maybe so. I suppose each person gets exactly what they believe they will... Gavin's initial "class" was held in New York City and was one of those very confrontive seminars where the participants are encouraged and almost manipulated to call relatives and friends sharing intimate things that really should not be talked about on the phone in front of strangers. And then you are manipulated into telling the friends and relatives at the other end how wonderfully transformative your experience of the training has been, and wouldn't it be wonderful if your friend or relative came to your "graduation" so that they could hear of your delicious experiences directly and to see how much you've grown and matured changing into a much better, more successful person practically over night; and wouldn't it be great if they laid down his or her deposit to take the course themselves so that they could achieve the same type of enlightenment and wisdom as you yourself had just experienced?

For some stupid reason I signed up to be a counselor or assistant is what I believed they called it when you did lots of trainings as a helper, but for absolutely no pay. Sounds like seva at the ashram.

I signed up to be an assistant right after becoming a new mother, so I had to take Gabriel with me to most of the courses since I was breastfeeding, and I'd take out my breast and nurse him whenever he was hungry right in front of everyone there. It seemed perfectly natural to me. My poor little baby was starving, and when he sucked my nipple, one could not see it anyway. Just the rest of the part of the breast that was showing. In the beginning I'd cover up my boobs and his head with one of Gabriel's receiving blankets, but after a few weeks of that it just occurred to me that it was ridiculous to hide something so natural and beautiful—both my breast and the loveliness of Gabriel feeding so innocently from it. Sometimes I'd express my breast milk into a little paper cup and share it with one of my close friends at Direct Centering.

There were all sorts of classes to take and hare after the initial training was over like "the Life Game" on Monday nights, the workshop on "Time", and all sorts of other creative little ditties Gavin

Barnes came up with to make cash off of his vulnerable, naive students. In a sense, it was a bit like a cult—just like Landmark Education, Lifespring. Scientology, etc. At least from my personal experience.

I know my daughter, Kyrie, her beau, Richie, whom she met at Landmark in Plainfield, New Jersey, and some of her friends as well as a few of mine like Kenny Hom, Zara Rose, and Robert Krenza, whom I know from Siddha Yoga, have shared that they personally gleaned a lot of wisdom and received tremendous value from taking EST., the Forum, the Leadership training, and other Landmark Education classes, I just decided it's not for me. I am very happy chanting kirtan, practicing hatha and restorative yoga, meditating, swimming, and dancing on my journey back to the Inner Self.

For the intensive training, a week-long course costing a thousand dollars, which was held in the Poconos in Pennsylvania we had to write on paper on a form they send you, what our deepest goals and dreams were; mine had to do with becoming very successful and famous in my singing career. As soon as my dreams started to manifest, I became scared and little by little I started spiraling downward into this hellish, negative, irrational state of mind.

Thank God all my three children are healthy and thriving with no signs of this debilitating illness. In fact, they all seem to have acquired only the positive side of the manic-depressive Pan, the one that makes them brilliant, energetic, happy, and creative. I thank the Eternal Father and the Divine Mother for their grace in keeping them all safe, happy, and healthy. I also thank their dad from the bottom of my heart for taking such good care of you for so many years when I was ill and for sharing his generosity of money, time, and spirit with all of us. Without him, my journey from darkness to light would not have been possible.

My brother, Scott, was the only person who came to see me in the hospital after I shot myself who treated me normally and made me laugh. He was the one who, upon approaching my bedside for the first time, said "Meh, you needed that like you needed a hole in your head!" Thank God, someone could have a sense of humor about the whole tragic mess! I don't see Scott much anymore except at funerals and weddings due to the huge distance between us but I try to keep in touch with phone calls on his birthday, cards at Christmas and by sending him updates on Facebook. Though we rarely see each other, Scott will always have a special place in my heart.

David and I had a peaceful divorce the day before I married my second husband, who would turn out to be even more abusive than David could ever could be. After all, what do you want from a young black man barely out of high school who you meet who is hospitalized as another patient in the same psychiatric facility as you? Listen ladies. Never marry anyone you meet in a mental hospital. Not even the doctors.

Can you imagine marrying a man who deliberately goes to college for over eight years and pays thousands of dollars in order to listen to people complain about their problems all day or all night long? You'd have to be NUTS!

Both husbands were Piscean. They were both like my maternal grandfather. When they were good, they were great – kind, loving, physically, mentally, and spiritually helpful, but when they were bad, they were angry, intolerable maniacal nut cases full of rage and blame. In both instances I realized I'd married the best and worst aspects of my schizoid mother. I wrote my poem "Divorced"[7] about David's and my divorce two years after the fact, not realizing how much pain was in my heart over

---

7 Found in my "Heartscapes" anthology.

the fact that I had to give up my husband, my home, and leave my children after my husband put me into the Carrier Clinic for nearly a month.

In the spring of 1988, David could not tolerate my euphoria and sleepless nights any longer. Besides the fact that I was feeling extremely romantic and sexual I was wanting to spend money on a new jacuzzi, a grandfather clock which I purchased a The Brass and Oak Warehouse in Englishtown, and other fancy items we did not really need. I was diagnosed with bipolar disorder and hospitalized at the Carrier Clinic for about a week or so when I met Lyle who would become my second husband in a mere four months' time. Crazy, huh?

DIAGNOSIS: BIPOLAR DISORDER

Bipolar disorder is, according to psychiatrists and medical doctors, a brain disorder that causes unusual and sometimes sudden changes in mood and activity levels. There are periods of extremely elated, energized behavior (known as manic episodes), and periods of hopelessness and inactivity (known as depressive episodes). Less severe manic episodes are known as "hypomanic episodes."

High dosages of lithium are often recommended as a treatment. Lithium can help a patient to stay grounded, not getting too high or too low. However, lithium can cause incontinence, and can damage the kidneys. Therapeutic use of lithium goes back roughly two thousand years. Even in those days, the brain was understood to be "unbalanced". Depakote, (or Divalproex, the generic) is a much more recent medication.

Doctors continue to believe that many mental illnesses are biologically based brain disorders. However, LI believe that they can be brought on, or at least aggravated, by poor eating or sleeping habits, stress, or negative attitudes, poor health, and life circumstances.

Mania

During manic phases I had bouts of zealous energy, sleepless nights of activity in which I'd clean house, sing, chant, dance, or write until 3:00 AM or later. Sometimes I could only sleep for three or four hours because I'd awaken as soon as it was light outside.

My mind was racing, and I had so much energy it was tough for me to sit and just be still. I seemed to have a lot of nervous energy as opposed to how I usually am when I feel peaceful, calm, and can easily focus and sit still for long periods of time. I wanted to run around a lot, dance, jump, and be "on the move" when I was feeling manic. I also felt a lot of sexual energy. I loved this feeling of ecstasy and euphoria, but usually it was followed by feelings of dysphoria, depression, sadness, anxiety, hopelessness, or some type of negative feelings that lasted for three months or so.

If people close to me suggested something was wrong with me, I'd become angry and defensive. I thought they were just jealous because I had super powers and did not need to sleep. While in the manic phase I was in denial about having any type of illness because I felt so ecstatic and high. It was only when the pendulum swung to the opposite polarity and I became severely depressed and frightened that I'd realize there was a "down side" to the euphoria and hyperactivity. Exhaustion.

While I was a single mom the exhaustion would mean I'd be too tired to cook for myself or Sky, my second daughter, and also way too tired to work for several days. Too tired to do laundry. Too tired to shop, too tired and depressed to go out to pay my rent. I would get to the place where I could barely function, especially during the cold of winter. And when I did not take massage clients, I made no money. All I had were my SSI and disability payments of less than $300 per month plus a few hundred dollars in food stamps, so according to government statistics, I was living way below the poverty level in these United States of America. Since I had no savings in reserve, I would then have more reason to get depressed, become ill, or filled with anxiety and fear.

Once in the summer of 1999, after suddenly going off my mood stabilizer and anti-depressant, I started to get hypomanic, the manic, and then became severely depressed having been off my prescribed medication for four months. I had over $600 in check bounce fees due to this "magical type thinking" and because I kept such poor records of my expenditures. I used my credit cards indiscriminately to give to charities and dine out at Indian, Thai, and Mexican restaurants in town, not to mention that I'd go on several vacations per year. When it came to finances, I truly needed to learn balance and order.

On the positive side, when I was hypo-manic or what the doctors would call a high functioning manic depressive, I was creative as an artist and poet with an abundance of new ideas for projects and inventions. Unfortunately, my mind was overwhelmed with so many ideas it worked much too fast for me to implement any one of them with great passion and focus. I usually overextended myself and had way too much on my plate. I rarely took action on anything specific. I did write a lot of ecstatic poetry and felt like a playful elfin fairy flitting around bringing love, joy, and fun wherever I went. I was extremely happy, euphoric, and sometimes even ecstatic with an overabundance of energy, exuberance, joy, love, and enthusiasm pouring through me. I truly believe this is God's true nature-bliss.

When I was feeling expansive, I would feel tremendous compassion for all God's children and creatures, not to mention Mother Earth Herself and wanted to take responsibility for many other peoples' problems besides my own personal life of petty concerns and seeming problems. I'd think to myself, for example, "Where are the mercy, compassion, and rehabilitation we've been trying to implement for years? Very few Americans truly care and advocate for the rights of our prisoners, and many are incarcerated for crimes they did not commit. Like the magnificent Ruben "Hurricane" Carter. Thank God he was one of a few who was acquitted after many years in jail and given a second chance at life as a free man. I'd also get overly involved in "fixing" the lives of my mom, some friends, or one of my lovers and ex- boyfriends, Michael, in particular. In a state of balance, I would call this meddling. Or co-dependence.

Then there are rich men like OJ Simpson who've committed horribly heinous crimes, but because of their wealth, power, and charm, are able to lie and fool people. The rich and powerful hire high-powered lawyers like Mr. Robert Kardashian and Robert Shapiro who get them off the hook. I read a book written by Nicole Simpson's best friend which influenced me deeply. Nicole's friend shared how she was so badly psychologically and physically abused by her husband, OJ, the famous football star and Heisman Trophy winner, that she had such low self-esteem and fear of being beaten that she'd often hide in the closet crying for hours afraid that he'd walk in the door and abuse her psychologically and/or physically as soon as he walked in the door wanting to start a fight with her for no particular reason. I just want to say, "Nicole Simpson and Ron Goldman, you were beautiful souls. I love you and have great compassion for your struggles and what you both had to endure; your gentle strength, talent, passion, and beautiful lives are not forgotten."

I have lots of dreams myself. Maybe I was and am being silly for imagining a world of inner and outer peace with no more wars fought over property and religious differences. unconditional love for Self and others. A world of beauty, wonder, and so much love and infinite potential of the human soul to grow—to be, do, and have absolutely anything we are wanting as free individuals and as a collective, loving, humane Cosmic Consciousness. A place where we are free to pursue all our dreams. I personally want to create masterpiece works of Art, compose music and sounds of the soul that soothes and is pleasing to everyone everywhere. I also sing and dance well and have a pleasant voice, so I plan to make a beautiful jazz demo followed by a jazz CD. with a few of my originals combined with jazz standards that will not only sound pleasing to the ear, but might sell thousands of copies and take me on a journey traveling around the world where I can sing LIVE in concert for other like-minded souls who enjoy sharing the same music as well as other simple pleasures like sharing a meal with close family and friends, visiting interesting museums, churches, and traveling to historical places. I do love delicious, healthy vegetarian foods that do not harm animals or disrespect other living creatures. I also want to explore the dimensions of the ocean, swim with dolphin pods in the wild and not just in some limited American aquarium like Sea World or Marine Land in St. Augustine, Florida where they basically just take professional photos of you and the trapped domesticated dolphins and then try to sell a lot of photos of the patrons posing with a dolphin or two, instead of allowing people to experience the true beauty and intelligence of these sentient beings by tapping into their unconditional love, healing energy, and creativity.

Most modern psychiatrists will tell you I was suffering from delusions of grandeur or that I was hypomanic. It behooves their egos to put labels on people and things they do not understand. They probably would consider C. G. Jung absolutely crazy too back in the forties and fifties if they were living back in then. I really dislike the judgmental and elite feelings and thoughts of the patriarchal medical diagnostic system they have in allopathic medicine today. Terming a person mentally ill, labeling them as schizophrenic, manic depressive, borderline personality, or other disparaging names creates tremendous negativity and stigma. It also ignores the innate perfection and divinity of the human being. Not all, but many of the doctors and psychiatrists I've met seem to rarely experience sublime love within their own hearts, so they must disparage and denigrate those of us Light Workers, holistic teachers, and enlightened beings who feel this way.

They thought John Lennon and Yoko Ono, the hippies and flower children of the nineteen sixties, were crazy too. But they were not the first nor are they the last to imagine a world of peace, love, and brotherhood. It's time for all of us Light Workers to be fearless and stand up for the Truth. Let us bring about the true "Apocalypse". In Greek Apocalypse means revealing what has been hidden. It is time we got rid of the caste system prevalent in all out-dated patriarchal systems that exist throughout all societies and in most man-made religions and to reveal all the lies and deception that has been going on behind closed doors by the elite 1%. All the lies and deception must come out into the open and brought to the Light to be healed so that people of all races, creeds, genders, and religions as well as all the animals on this planet can live happily in good health and in harmony.

When I felt euphoric and very connected to Source, I became a dreamer and visionary, but I had no plan of action or means of putting my dreams into form. I wanted all the good things in life like true love, another husband and my own home in beautiful surroundings with a garden or on a farm in Florida or Hawaii, possibly living in a natural, clothing optional community where we are self-sustaining growing our own fruits, vegetables, large pretty trees and flowers. I also desire equanimity and inner peace under all circumstances no matter what is going on in the world around me, World Peace, wealth for myself and every person upon this planet, fortune, possibly a sailboat, and to experience adventure. Possibly fame too if I did not have to go around wearing sunglasses and floppy hats to keep away the paparazzi.

I also love to travel and learn about other cultures, and this is one thing I did have the good fortune to experience during those times of what one might call mania. To me, it was just a heightened spiritual experience in which I would allow many of my deepest desires to manifest like taking cruises to Alaska, Florida, and the Caribbean with Jerry and Esther Hicks who channeled the non-physical entity, Abraham. I planned and enjoyed trips to places I always wanted to go to-like Mexico, Jamaica, Honduras, Costa Rica, and Belize.

I also wanted at those times of unconditional love, tremendous caring and compassion for all God's children, and I still desire, to feed the entire world's population of hungry children and to care for the elderly.

I want to ease the pain and suffering of people everywhere with all the love, compassion, and joy I am feeling. I want to be big enough to go all over the world and hug each man, woman, and child upon the planet. That was how expansive I was feeling during states of hypomania and mania, but

I feel very happy and balanced now, and I still feel that same inner love and compassion for people everywhere. Even space Brothers and Sisters. I was and still am filled with the boundless love of God.

I wish I could soothe people in hospitals all over, especially people in distress locked up in psychiatric institutions because I have personally experienced how horrible that can be. I want to have everyone released from jail who does not deserve to be there. I want to abolish the death penalty.

I have lots of dreams. Maybe I was and am being silly or overly optimistic. The psychiatrists will tell you I was suffering from delusions of grandeur, that I was manic or hypo-manic. They love to put labels on people and things they do not understand.

Most doctors, psychologists, and psychiatrists have never experienced this sublime type of sublime love and enthusiasm within their own hearts, so they must disparage and denigrate those of us Light Workers, teachers, and enlightened beings who feel this way. They thought John Lennon and Yoko Ono were crazy too at one time. But they were not the first nor are they the last to imagine a world of peace, love, and brotherhood. Rev. Dr. Martin Luther King, Robert Kennedy, Swami Yogananda, and Gandhi were a few more. Whenever we have a Master of Peace and Radical Change the establishment tries to have them assassinated. Like Christ Jesus, John the Baptist, Joan of Arc, Medgar Evers, John F. Kennedy, Bobbie Kennedy, our Brother Malcolm X, and so many hundreds of innocent black, brown, and white men and women that were just speaking OUT against injustice as the civil rights movement was beginning. We've come a long way since then, but still have so far to go. Innocent men, women, and boys are still being shot by police and their only crime is "walking black".

When I was in the ecstatic, manic phase I just believed that if I kept thinking about becoming a famous singer and superstar celebrity that God would send the perfect agent or manager eventually who would hear me and want me to cut a record for some famous label. I do know we get what we focus our thoughts on, but I was living in my own fantasy world for many years since I really did not take much action in the direction of realizing my dreams. I had too many ups and downs until I began to take a mood stabilizer and eat properly on a regular basis. I had lots of mood swings; it was kind of like being on a roller coaster. I was even afraid at times to make too many future plans because I was not certain if I would be mentally and emotionally healthy and able to function as my normal, confident "Self" at a future date since my moods were so uncertain and unpredictable, even while taking medication. I was too uncertain for a while that I might be so depressed that I wanted to hide out from my friends and usual activities. When I felt terribly vulnerable and weak, I just wanted to go into a cocoon and be "invisible" for a few weeks or months. I was never exactly sure how long these really dark periods would last even while I was on medication. Now I look at them as "dark nights of the soul", and I feel grateful that my guides, friends, family, and the grace of God helped me endure each trial and tribulation until I was able to come out the other side stronger, happier, more balanced, with greater faith, more confidence in the God within my own Self, and with more compassion and humility to help others who are suffering with mental illness.

As I write these words now, I am feeling much more confident because I have been on a healthy "track" in which I am eating and sleeping well, doing spiritual practices like affirmative prayer, chanting, and regular meditation. I also love listening to soothing music and taking soothing, hot Epsao salted baths in the winter and relaxing in the jacuzzi after a half hour workout at Princeton Fitness and Wellness up the road in Montgomery Township, off Route 206.

Getting massages on a regular basis, seeing my chiropractor, psychotherapist, nurse practitioner, dancing, swimming, and getting regular exercise has helped put me in a very balanced, happy, and peaceful place of equipoise. I believe I am more disciplined in my daily lifestyle, and my own inner connection to Source and listening to my inner divine guidance from my own angels and personal guides is helping me to remain stable and confident about my life. I feel so grateful I've survived and learned from my past mistakes, so thankful for the blessings I have while living in the Present moment, and I am optimistic about my future for I am slowly realizing more of my personal dreams and goals.

For example, I published my first anthology of poetry entitled "Heartscapes" in November 2015 and am nearly finished with this book, the first part of my self-help memoir. The first 65 years. There will be more great things to come, I am told. More miracles and blessings that I have partially earned through self-effort, but much of them will be the result of faith and God's miraculous grace and mercy.

DEPRESSION

Hell is definitely not a place inhabited by some monster or metaphorical devil. It is a state of mind. In the depressed phase many manic depressives feel such intense self-hatred, unworthiness, despair, suffering, anxiety, and fear that it leads them to suicidal thoughts, serious suicide attempts, and sometimes death. They see their situation as hopeless and think their only way out of it is through death. I recently read that one third of Americans (one million diagnosed patients) with this illness die from it by means of suicide or accident. Many of them are teenagers. Hundreds of them are physicians and psychiatrists who have accessible means to drugs and narcotics with which they can use to overdose. Some are sensitive artists and musicians who are prescribed opioids for pain or who become addicted to taking sleep medications. Some have addictive personalities and become drug addicts, alcoholics, or abusers of cigarettes and marijuana, in order to numb themselves from the painful experiences of their childhood or present grieving and financial troubles.

I am sharing my story in the hope that I may inspire others. If I can help save the life of just one other person or perhaps give her and her family hope, then my own arduous journey, however painful it has been, will have been worth it. I wish to shed some light on this mysterious disease and make family and friends of people with the illness aware of its prevalence and seriousness. However, the illness, or let's say the core beliefs, emotions, and symptoms of the illness can be changed and symptoms managed through various means, and most manic-depressives can still lead very active, happy, and productive lives.

All of the fear I felt was irrational. It had no basis in reality. My worst fear was of losing my mind. And since what we dwell upon expands and becomes our reality this is actually what I would create. I am sure the biochemical imbalance created through poor eating habits and a diet of negative thoughts had a lot to do with the depression and fear. But, what were the underlying causes of the biochemical imbalance?

I can't say for certain, but I believe part of the imbalance may have been caused by the repressed emotions I described. I had also experimented with the drug, ecstasy, on several occasions for a six-month period prior to becoming ill. Except for one minor depression after experiencing the high bliss of getting shaktipat from the guru there were no more episodes of highs and lows from 1983 until 1987. So, figuring out the mystery behind becoming bipolar again in 1987 has been an interesting journey into my unconscious mind and the deepest, hidden parts of myself.

During depressions, I did not believe I could even hold out a few days or weeks until a doctor's or psychiatric appointment. When I was in crisis, I felt like the only person I could reach out to was my mom because she had also felt that deep despair and depression with suicidal thoughts, so I knew she would understand, not judge, and have enough empathy and compassion to invite me to her house for a chat and lunch or dinner. Spending time with her was pleasant, her house was immaculate when mine seemed terribly messy and disorganized. I'd feel nurtured by her, AND I'd get a home cooked meal which was very important in my case, because in dark nights of the soul I'd not only lose my appetite for life, but my entire appetite for food and desire to cook completely. I'd eat because it was necessary not to die, but I could not taste the food I was eating most of the time. Well, some of the time. My mom was and still is a pretty great cook. Some women use eating more comfort foods as a way to feel better. They'd prefer to soothe themselves with ice cream, chocolate, bread, chicken wings, burgers, refined, sugary breakfast cereals and sweets. I never was attracted to those types of foods except when I was suicidally depressed and could not find the strength to cook or feed myself, so I'd venture out to the local Burger King a few miles from my apartment where I need not get out of my car for a Junior Whopper with extra lettuce, pickles, and tomatoes since that was my only source of vegetables and fiber for the entire day.

Some folks with depression use alcohol or marijuana as a way to numb or dumb themselves down so they would not have to feel the pain of loneliness, low self-esteem, or not being able to make a decent living. From my own experience with myself and my mom I realized that many depressed people tend to focus upon lack rather than the blessings we have. When I am thinking in a rational way and feeling my natural connection to God and my Higher Self, I remember that God has always managed to care for me and my entire family; My Teacher, Abraham, reminds me that, as unlimited expressions of the One God, we have infinite potential to be, do, and have anything we need and want. It's just a matter of trusting and allowing all the good things that are our divine inheritance. Or, as Jesus would say, "Seek ye first the kingdom of God, and all these things shall be added unto you."

We people who are considered crazy (mentally ill due to some weird brain biochemistry) are in truly Great company. Vincent Van Gogh. Dr. Seuss. Judy Garland. Patty Duke, Vivian Leigh, Robin Williams, Jim Carrie, Jane Pauley, Catherine Zeta Jones, married to actor, Michael Douglas— are just a few of these great, talented, human beings who have admitted to being treated for manic depression.

Shall I go on? Every one of us is a super talented, creative genius, and boy, do we know how to make money. And how to spend it! I think it's fun spending money. I mean we can't take it with us when we die, so we may as well circulate it abundantly with generosity and discernment, just like love. Ben Franklin himself said "Wealth belongs to those who know how to enjoy it!"

Forgive me, folks, if I have sounded cavalier about mental illness. It is truly a heavy subject, and it has such stigma that it needs to come out of the closet and be talked about. I use humor as a coping skill. Due to the terrible stigma surrounding mental illness, depression, and suicide, many people perceive themselves as weak and are ashamed to share their troubles with their friends, business partners, or professional counselors and psychiatrists. I tried coping with manic depression for years by myself before going to a counseling center that had a trained psychologist and psychiatrist available on a monthly and bi-monthly basis. Due to societal stigma and shame thousands of people are coping badly all alone, by themselves, using close friends or family members to try to make sense of manic depression, paranoid schizophrenia, multiple personality disorder, and other chronic mental illnesses. I personally experienced the intense shame, unworthiness, and embarrassment one feels when one gets chronically depressed after being fired from a job or losing someone I loved. It was nearly impossible to share the confusion I was feeling openly with colleagues, friends, or business associates. I even found it difficult to open up during times of weakness to my own minister. I believed it was wrong or shameful to feel weak, vulnerable, and unhappy, so I would curl up like a ball and hide out in my house during these times I did not have the courage to be authentic and show my weak, vulnerable side, especially since I should "know better" being an ordained minister myself.

It is my desire and intention to take mental illness, incest, and suicide out of the closet, so to speak. It needs to be talked about so there are no more suicides, mass shootings in schools, post offices, MacDonald s restaurants, or other public places. Too many people have given their lives already unnecessarily, and this topic must not only be talked about but viewed in a new light from a higher perspective. After all, we all have challenges. Maybe mental illness is not as real as we believe. After all, everyone must admit they have had negative thoughts of hopelessness and fear or felt deep despair at certain times in their lives following the loss of a job due to being fired or downsized, the loss of a spouse, special friend, mate, partner, or child. Then there is the weakness and loss that comes with experiencing any type of health challenge – any type of serious illness like terminal cancer or Alzheimer's disease which has caused a person to possibly feel such despair and hopelessness that they entertained thoughts of running away or euthanize themselves by committing suicide.

Thankfully, few people act on these thoughts unless they have been under extreme stress and economic strain for months or years at a time. Let's face it. Even psychiatrists have problems and successfully commit suicide by taking an overdose of medications they prescribe for themselves. Being weak or in despair is not a crime. Some celebrities like Michael Jackson, the Artist formerly known as Prince, and Elvis Presley have used doctor's prescriptions for sleep or anxiety and gotten addicted to opioids. We have lost so many talented performers and regular folks from the over prescribing of these types of medications that are addictive and dangerous.

Trying to commit suicide should not have any stigma associated with it because basically, as co-creators of our own reality including mental illness, wellness, or dis-ease, we do everything to ourselves. Whether we die from colon cancer, liver disease, COPD, lung cancer, heart disease or diabetes, we ourselves created All of it. If not in this lifetime, then the one before it. And guess what folks? There truly is NO DEATH; we are eternal infinite beings Who take our Consciousness with us after death as Spirit into the subtle realm. We merely discard the body, but our Light, our Great Holy Spirit, continues and often still tries to contact our loved ones on Earth from the "Other Side". And then when we are ready, we look for another perfect situation with the type of parents we need in which to grow and experience karma in a new body; so, we reincarnate taking all the same memories, samskaras (Sanskrit for impressions), with us into the new body in the next incarnation. At least that is my understanding from what my personal guides, angels, gurus, and Teachers like Abraham, tell me.

If that does not resonate with you, you need not accept what I believe, think, and KNOW in my own heart and mind to be true for me. It behooves us to look for the Truth of our beings and not just become deluded by the outer world, the physical form and distraction of the senses.

If we want to see what we have been thinking on a regular basis, let's look at our present circumstances. If we want to know our future all we need do is look at our present actions. There is no judgment here. We are responsible for All this, and since we have choice, we can uncreate or re-create all the circumstances in our lives including dis-ease. Most diseases are psychosomatic. Without incest, sexual molestation, and intense psychological abuse by my mother I might have turned out to be a much healthier, much less abusive person to my own self. However, I learned a lot during this process.

Since I have survived at least ten attempts to take my own life in order to ease my suffering in such a dramatic way I have to make light of something that was very tragic and traumatic for me, my close friends, and family members.

Bipolar disorder, is viewed by people who have experienced it or have had a family member who commit suicide, as a very chronic, acute, and serious mental illness that has been experienced by millions of people in the US. alone, and these are just the ones that are diagnosed and actually have the courage to come out of their dark, secluded homes where some hide from all other people staying depressed, cloistered, and isolated, zoning out in a fantasy world of television, sleeping too much or not enough, and sometimes numbing the pain of depression with alcohol, marijuana, or other drugs, as I explained before. So many of these folks, even myself, are dependent upon sleep medications, so it takes a lot of courage to get out of our depressing, secluded places of escape just to seek treatment. If not working with the biochemical and mental states by working with a psychiatrist, psychologist, and nutrition counselor, then by seeking out a minister, priest, or spiritual practitioner to pray for and counsel them in their time of need. Addressing the spiritual part of my being was what worked best for me, in the end, but everyone is different. We all have different, unique needs and belief systems. Whatever works for you is what's best for you whether it's Alcoholics Anonymous, Narcotics Anonymous, art therapy, church, accepting Allah or Jesus Christ as your personal Savior, medication, psychotherapy, or a physical activity like folk dancing, aerobic exercise, swimming, or weight lifting. Deep bodywork like rolfing worked for me after undergoing my very first suicidal depression. Intuitively, I knew that rolfing works on bringing up the subconscious emotions stored in the muscle fascia. I had ten sessions of Ida Rolf's postural integration and went from a state of intense fear before my first session to bliss, inner peace, and ecstasy by the last few sessions. In the meantime, during and after the deep, intense fascia manipulation I'd experience sadness, anger, rage, and laughter. Then I'd feel immense peace after releasing all those stored emotions.

Unfortunately, hundreds of people who do not seek professional treatment from a psychologist or psychiatrist, and even some who do, actually DIE from a successful suicide attempt. Like our friend, Robin Williams. The brilliant beloved comic genius and actor. Though I think I read that he was scared because he was getting dementia. Or like the author, Danielle Steele's, 18-year-old son, Nick Trainor, whom she wrote about in "His Bright Light". A very sad, poignant and heartfelt account of a mom trying for years to diagnose and save a beloved son from a debilitating mental illness no one understood back in those days or could even diagnose. What a talented young man and what a loss to his parents, friends, family, and the music industry. If only there had been more awareness during the time he was growing up acting weird, aggressive, suicidal, or depressed, feeling misunderstood and crazy, there may have been a nutritional supplement, a specific diet, and/or medications that may have prevented such a tragedy. I read the tale about Nick's brief life and was moved to tears for him and his family. Of course, I saw some of my own life and experience through reading about him. Nick was very special, but he was every man too. So many of us feel misunderstood, lonely, scared, and want to get away from it all by taking drugs, drinking, watching the tube for hours, or whatever means we all use to cope with the challenges we face in our everyday lives living in this dangerous, violent society where violence is accepted and condoned by everyone from the president on down to the police and other politicians.

I personally believe there are many complex factors that go into the causes and treatment of this debilitating disorder, and I will share my personal insights and wisdom gleaned from my own personal experience with this throughout the book in between the light stuff and the salient points in the story of my life.

I am also very grateful to all the dance teachers and dance troupes I've had in my life—like Ellen Tannenbaum who has been teaching dance aerobics on Mondays to the senior citizens at the Suzanne Paterson Center I Princeton for over twenty-- five years. Ellen makes exercise fun and easy.

Daily or weekly dancing, yoga, working with weights, and light exercise are crucial to a happy, balanced mood. Aerobic exercise creates endorphins and serotonin in the brain. Plus, the music Ellen plays is always happy, uplifting, and of a higher frequency. Like big band, old time swing music, and salsa, tea-chas, tangos, line dancing, and merengue. The music alone does something to my brain that makes me feel so much peppier and happier.

I have also attended an improvisational dance group bi-monthly called "Dance Improv LIVE" with live musicians and different dancers who show up on Friday nights on and off since 1986. It was only in the last fifteen years the group meets just once per month now at the Princeton Center for Yoga and Health on Orchard Road. How freeing to be in a place of safety where we are encouraged to move and create from within in a relaxing, respectful, and safe atmosphere that has no alcohol, sexual contact, or drugs present where we can feel safe and free to completely relax, tune into our bodies and Spirits, and move and dance in such an intuitive way that we love, respect, and honor ourselves in each and every precious, creative moment. How joyous to be in a state of complete spontaneity and freedom of movement or non-movement without thought! Each time we get together with LIVE original musicians and singers, all us dancers are inspired to move alone and together in a way that stretches and flexes our muscles, delights our souls, and together we create a completely new and different Tapestry of Light every month depending on who comes to the dance workshop and how we are feeling. It has since moved from Princeton to the Hopewell Train Station in the last few years. We are free to make up whatever we want in the moment or just lie down and rest if that is what our body needs. We are all true to ourselves and there are no wrong moves or notes if we choose to sing, stomp, clap, tap, slap our thighs, or shake our maracas. No matter how tired or low one feels in the doldrums of winter I guarantee you if you are able to drag yourself in after work on a Friday evening you will leave with a lighter, bouncier step and a smile on your face even if you just drag yourself in for one of the two and a half hours after a long week of work on a Friday evening.

Another dance group I love attending is called "Five Rhythms" started by the dancer and actress, Gabrielle Roth, whom we sadly lost to cancer last year. Gabrielle created a new therapy where we focus on the five basic rhythms of Life – spirals, staccato, chaos, and peace.

After all the suffering, egotistical melodramas and traumas I experienced for so many years, now, in this holy moment of the new year, January 6th of 2021, despite everyone's' preoccupation with the cure of the corona virus, Black Lives Matter, and ousting Trump and all the conservative Republicans when the current patriarchal, narcissistic, oligarchical, psychologically and emotionally unfit, maniacal POTUS whose name I shall not mention, I truly feel as if I have triumphed over bipolar disorder and do not always take medications for it anymore. I use Bach flower essences developed by Dr. Bach in the 1930's and low dosages of mood stabilizing medications now, but last year I was using lithium magnesium water or the over the counter supplement, lithium orotate, combined with a truly balanced diet of whole, nutritious fruits, vegetables, grains, with occasional servings of fish and fowl to keep me grounded and happy in this sometimes challenging world we live in.

I am not suggesting to any other person to go off their medications. I am only sharing my process and the path that has worked for me personally. Some of what I am using to maintain a happy, healthy attitude may or may not work for another person since we are all unique beings with our own personal challenges, belief systems, and needs. So, follow your own inner guidance in doing whatever you need to make yourself feel better. Check with your medical doctor, psychiatrist, therapist, minister, pastor, or whomever you personally trust. If it's a pill, a prayer, or a rabbit's foot. Use it, and feel good about it. Whatever it is, if it works for YOU, dearest one, that is what counts.

I, personally, like to start my morning with daily affirmations, affirmative prayers said while soaking in a hot Epsom salts bath, chanting and, or meditation on a daily basis to keep me balanced and in tune with my Higher Self, my own Inner Being, Source energy. A hearty breakfast outdoors if it is pleasant weather in spring, summer, or fall. Or, if it is warm and sunny outside, I like to meditate while being near my garden and communing with the beautiful, colorful flowers and plants.

During a depression, the mind becomes preoccupied with negative thoughts and irrational fears. These fears are seldom based in reality, but the constant dwelling upon a negative thought like, "I am afraid I can't pay my bills, by the universal Law of Attraction, will attract to it more thoughts of lack. Eventually these constant "lack thoughts" will turn into a physical reality for the thinker. Sometimes I'd feel so anxious and frightened during chronic depressions that I would not get out of bed until late afternoon or even answer my telephone. I was just too tired, lonely, overwhelmed, and afraid to get out of bed to face the new day in the freezing cold winter and sometimes right after we turned the clocks back which meant we'd get one hour less of sunlight. I often suffered from seasonal affective disorder because my body needed the melatonin and Vitamin D produced by the sun, so as a single mom living on a modest income, winters were not kind to me, for the most part – at least not until I realized I needed better nutrition; Full spectrum lights and a week to ten day vacation in Florida in February in Sarasota, by the Gulf of Mexico, helped alleviate the symptoms of my depressions considerably after I asked my friend, Dr. Van Beveren, for help and nutritional advice during times of crisis. When I had little or no money, he was very kind to me by offering a huge discount for nutritional advice and suggesting I sell and take Sunriver vitamins and natural supplements.

While in the manic phase my mind dwelt in heavenly bliss, but there was a price to pay for feeling tremendously high all the time, as I mentioned prior to this. I was so ecstatic (without the use of drugs or alcohol of any kind) and overly enthusiastic about everything that sometimes I could not get to sleep until the early hours of the morning- usually between 2:00 and 3:00 AM. My judgment was compromised because I began to feel exhausted during the day, and I did not feel grounded. I had so much energy I could barely sit still. I know now this is part of kundalini awakening which I will explain a bit later in the book. An actual spiritual experience.

I felt extremely sexual, had a lack of healthy boundaries, and had sex impulsively with men that I did not know very well, usually without the protection of a condom. I felt as if the energies and rhythms of my body were flowing to the tune of the Earth Mother. I experienced myself as psychically in tune with many people and was often able to read their thoughts and feelings. I believed I was intuitive, knew without a doubt I was a holy Spirit inhabiting a physical body and connected to Source, the creator of all things. I knew in my heart I was made of Light as was everything and everybody.

The truth is I have been told by psychics and mediums that I am indeed a celestial being of a high vibrational frequency. In truth, every one of us is an individualized expression of All-That-Is, a divine spark of the One Consciousness, God's Life expressed in human form. We are each equally divine with a direct connection to the One Source of Creation and an individualized form of That Being itself! Every thought we think, each feeling we feel, affects us personally, and creates our future health, relationships, and circumstances. We are also a collective consciousness, so that positive, uplifting thoughts and feelings of a personal nature, benefit the WHOLE as well. We all become and manifest what we think as creator gods ourselves.

I wrote the poem "Lost and Found Again", which is published in my anthology *Heartscapes*, during a Siddha meditation intensive at the Philadelphia ashram in November.1987, six weeks after I got out of JFK Rehab hospital, five months after shooting myself. We are all playing a game of lost and found. It is the One God Who hides and then experiences it is all His/Her/Its own Divine Play of Consciousness. It is God who hides and God who finds Himself!

CARRIER CLINIC (1988)

At the end of April, 1988, I started to feel high manic energy that was so intense I could not get to sleep at night without taking several tablets of L tryptophan, a natural amino acid, following a long hot bath at 11 PM or later, and still it was 1 or 2 AM before I finally drifted off to sleep. By May I was so euphoric I was dancing and chanting to music most of the day. I wasn't working too often, just an occasional massage, but spent time caring for the house, cooking breakfast and sometimes making lunch, food shopping and helping our nanny with one year old Kyrie and 27-month-old Gabriel. But during the day we would send them off to a home school at our friend, Linda's, house, in Jamesburg. My energy was too ecstatic and intense for David, and he suggested I visit our friends, Lata and Ramon Goldberg, in Florida. But that visit never materialized. David would send me out shopping and on errands for him, but I still ordered lots of clothes and things for the children from the scores of catalogs we received in the mail every week. David was nervous about all the money I was spending, even though we were very well off, because in these stages I never saw limits. I wanted to buy a jacuzzi for our bathroom and I also bought a cool old fashioned oak Grandfather clock from the Brass and Oak Warehouse in Englishtown, which he thought was imprudent. I also talked of going on more vacations again.

Neither David nor I understood that I had manic depression. We just did not know much about it back in those days, the carefree and creative nineteen eighties when both of our babies, Gabriel and Kyrie, were born naturally at home. But how could I go from being suicidally depressed in May and June of 1987, to a state of euphoria and then ecstasy in just one year's time? Not to mention that I was still hemiplegic on the left side of my body and could not use my left arm or hand at all. I also walked with a cane still and had a bit of a limp. None of my physical challenges changed or inhibited the bliss and inherent joy I felt just to be alive.

My mother had been a patient at the Carrier Clinic, so she thought we should try my being diagnosed by professionals in a hospital setting. I did not really want to do it, but David was at the end of his rope and really did not know how to help me to become calmer and fall asleep at a decent hour like him and the kids. Besides, he had to get up early five days per week to work full time downstairs in the office and supervise several employees. So, he desired to get a decent night's sleep without having to worry about me. And I cannot blame him for that.

The Carrier Clinic or East Mountain Hospital is a beautiful psychiatric institution set on acres of land with lovely trees and gardens in Bell Meade, not far from the Sourland Mountain Reserve. It was difficult being there, because I wanted to bounce around everywhere, but the nurses and attendants would force me to sit still through movies, television programs, lectures, and such. I didn't believe there was anything wrong with me because I felt so happy and thoroughly connected to God and to my guru when I chanted and meditated. Also, when I danced with wild abandon, I'd go into ecstatic states just like the whirling dervishes of ancient times.

The only things I liked about Carrier Clinic were their delicious food and their art program, taught by a special art teacher who would help me make all sorts of cool projects and would be my left hand if need be, when we did something like knitting an octopus' legs and head. I loved art and this was my favorite part of being at Carrier.

If I ever wrote a travel guide about the many different psychiatric institutions I visited, Carrier Clinic would be #1 for its cuisine, the art program, the morning exercise classes and daily walks outdoors in the gardens and upon the lovely grounds. There was a yoga and meditation class on Sunday evenings for an hour, the rooms were very clean, most of the nurses were competent, caring, compassionate, and pleasant, and there were a few doctors I would come to love, especially a woman psychiatrist named Doctor Moss, who was finally the doctor who definitely diagnosed the manic depression and put me on Depakote, or the generic version, divalproex, a mood stabilizer, along with Welbutrin, an anti-depressant. She told me I would not have the highs anymore, but neither would I go so low into despair. I was resistant to the medication at first because I was holistic and not into taking allopathic medications or drugs of any kind. While at Carrier the first time I had Dr. Khouri as my psychiatrist and I did not like him much. For the most part I did not like male doctors. I did not like too many of the nurses either, because I was resistant to accepting the fact that I had a mental illness which needed to be "handled" and medicated. The acceptance would not come until a few years later. As of this day I have a new perspective and different attitude about bi-polar illness and other mental illnesses and think that many of these medications actually cause harm or contribute to the illness in the first place, according to books I've read by Dr. Peter Breggen, who calls himself a "Conscious Psychiatrist and works in Delaware in his own holistic nutrition practice. I am currently reading and studying his book *Brain Disabling Treatments in Psychiatry*.

While hospitalized at the Carrier Clinic in May of 1988 I met John Bon Jovi's mom, Carol, when I could not sleep in the middle of the night. Now that's really a feather in my cap, folks! She had a great sense of humor, and I remember her sharing that her husband and her son should be there in the hospital instead of her. Who knows? Maybe that was true. Things are not always what they seem, you know.

SKY AND LYLE (1990)

My third child, Sky, was the result of my marriage to Lyle.

I had met him in spring, 1988, when we were both patients in Carrier Clinic, and was foolish enough to marry him, even though he beat me once or twice even prior to the wedding. I didn't want to embarrass him by bowing out in the middle of the ceremony in front of the minister and all our guests! Listen ladies, let me give you a piece of advice. NEVER marry anyone you meet in a psychiatric hospital or clinic – not even one of the doctors! Can you imagine someone actually CHOOSING a profession in which they must listen to people complaining about their problems all day long? You'd have to be NUTS!

Mom and Sky at her christening

Meeting Lyle

Lyle and I had met in the dining room at Carrier Clinic. He became a kind friend who would help me carry my tray to the table in the cafeteria and then sit beside me. He seemed like a sweet guy and he said he was diagnosed with having no mental illness. He was just being rebellious and did not want to follow the rules at the group home sponsored by Easter Seals where he was living at the time back in 1988.

One night Lyle called me at home very late about a week after I'd escaped from the Carrier Clinic. I left one week-end I was having a home visit, with David's help, against medical advice. So, this young, not particularly attractive black man who was fifteen years my junior, called my home about 11:00 PM saying he was locked out of the group home he lived in for not making the curfew a few nights in a row saying he didn't know where to go. When he was asked to move out of the center where he was living he told them he had nowhere to go, especially that late at night. Don't ask me why he could not just go back to his girlfriend's home where he'd just come from. I was hypomanic at the time and rather impulsive. I was not making very good decisions or choices on a regular basis the entire spring since around April.

. "Could you meet me in East Orange to pick me up so I could have a place to stay for one night since I am now homeless?" I must have been crazy at that time of night to leave my cozy home with my children asleep because I found myself offering to pick him up out of friendship and bring him back to our house that night because it was dark and I felt kind of motherly toward him. I just felt nurturing and gentle towards him, the way I am with most stray animals and people in trouble.

Little did I know what a mistake I made that night. Lyle slept in our meditation room, and the next day I was going to drive him to his uncle's house. In my manic state I was making very poor decisions. Don't ask me how it happened, but I actually had sex with him the next morning after he woke up in my bedroom with David listening on the intercom downstairs in the office. David was pretty angry, but he did not say much at the time

. However, he was the one who encouraged Lyle and me to live together and then make our brief affair into an official relationship by getting married. I am sure at that point he just wanted to get this sick, adulterous woman off of his hands. He also did not like that I was spending lots of money during this manic phase of my illness. Lyle and I went to the Holiday Inn nearby in Monroe Township to spend that night, and the next, until David suggested we not spend so much money on hotels; so he offered the use of his office in East Brunswick. We could bring some blankets, pillows, and a sleeping bag. It wasn't the Ritz, but we would not be wasting $50-75 per night on a hotel. We were putting all the charges on credit cards.

Lyle was released from Carrier and I left without doctor's approval against medical advice during a week-end visit at home with David and the kids. I felt well enough to stay home, cook, and care for the children again, even though I stopped taking the lithium they'd given me because it made me incontinent. I tried Tegretol after that and it seemed to help.

Marriage

The day after my divorce from David, Mike Cindrich, my personal friend, and the Psychic Science Minister who officiated at my first wedding, also officiated at my second marriage to Lyle. He said "If this marriage does not work out, I refuse to marry you again, because either you are not the marrying type or maybe I'm bad luck for you!" The ceremony, which was held in David's back yard, with my four-year-old son, Gabriel, as the ring bearer, my pretty little two-year-old daughter, Kyrie, as the little flower girl, and under thirty guests. I broke down in the middle of the ceremony, crying uncontrollably   when I looked at Gabriel and Kyrie watching me leaving them and their dad to marry another man. I was obviously not in a good mental state — certainly not one of sound mind to choose to marry someone I barely knew whom I'd met in a mental hospital!

I could not stop the tears, because I was still in love with my husband, and I looked over at my sweet little son. I realized I was leaving him and his little sister on that very day for the last time, but being manic I felt as if I had no control over my choices or my life circumstances. It was like everything was moving like a speeding freight train, and I did not know how to jump off, put on the brakes, or stop the train from moving.

My best friend, Zara Rose, whom I chose as my matron of honor, told me I could stop the ceremony right then and there, but I did not want to embarrass Lyle by saying I did not love him in front of all those people. I suppose I felt it would be too embarrassing to me and my family, and I did not want peoples' disapproval, The whole thing was already set in motion with the reception happening right after, the dinners and bands already paid for, as well as our honeymoon to Negril, Jamaica. What could I do at that point but look like a total idiot!? And make poor Lyle look like a fickle jerk too.

I finally did stop crying and managed to stammer something like "Sorry, folks, I guess I am just sad about leaving my house and my children. I am starting a whole new life with Lyle and I guess I'm a little nervous." Then I turned and kissed Lyle, held his hand, and thought I would just make the best of the circumstances I had created. I was not feeling happy or in love. Just partially numb, anxious, and a bit tense.

Hardly any of our friends or family attended our wedding or the wedding reception. Just my mom, Arleen, my cousin, Dru, who agreed to be two of my three bridesmaids, along with our live-in nanny, Denise. I'd invited two of my second cousins, Uncle Jay and Aunt Jean, who were married and both in their late seventies. And my precious friends, Elaine and Stan Levy, who also attended my mom's 47th "surprise" birthday party at my home the night before Gabriel's birth at home at 10:31AM on February 5th. There were thirty-five people plus the six members of the band, "Smooth Sailin,' if you want to count them in. A complete fiasco. The East Brunswick Chateau ended up throwing away a hundred thirty-five dinners. What a shame. If we'd known in advance so many invited guests would not show up, we could have at least donated the meals to the Trenton Soup Kitchen, a homeless shelter, or a woman's group safe shelter like Woman Space.

The reception was also a financial disaster. I'd paid $4000 for the use of the beautiful East Brunswick Chateau in East Brunswick, New Jersey and for the reception with music and dancing, and all the dinners. Most people we knew including my psychiatrist, most of our friends, and both our moms, did not approve of us getting married at all. They were right. We barely knew one another. Not only did we have problems, but Lyle had gotten violent with me on our way back from the ashram one afternoon. I got so angry I yelled at him to pull over and let me out of the car. When he would not I grabbed for the door handle and he socked me in the cheek. The black and blue mark was just beginning to fade three months after that incident. It was not a very good sign.

Our honeymoon to Negril, Jamaica, was pleasant because of the surroundings, but there was no real love or caring on my part, no real love or connection to Lyle since my heart was still with David and the children; and after a few days I started to feel a bit numb because I realized what a mistake I had made. I was still in love with David, and missed my children and home terribly as well as my full family life with a wealthy, generous husband, who had a great job who had helped me birth our two wonderful children. He also forgave me many indiscretions & still supported me and helped me to get well after I shot myself. If it were not for the love and support of David, my mom, my grandmother,

Lucy, and my sweet children I never would have made it through that first dark depression. A true "dark night of the soul". I know my guru had a hand in my surviving as well as in my healing and continues to be with me even after his death through the divine Presence of Gurumayi Chidvilasananda.

Abuse

If only I had remembered that Lyle had just socked me in the face three months prior to the wedding, and the black eye and bruise on my face had just healed enough so I could put some make-up on it and no one would notice it. Little did I want to admit that this was just the beginning of a whole cycle of abuse, both physical and psychological during the first three years I was with Lyle. I was in complete denial about both Lyle's and my problems with mental illness. The abusive marriage probably would have continued had I not eventually had the courage to go to WomanSpace to learn about abusers and how they operate.

Not only that, but, unfortunately for him and for me, I was never actually in love with Lyle. I felt sad and angry that David wanted us to separate, so rather than feel those painful feelings I picked a young guy with a lot of sexual energy, fun-loving, immature, and free-spirited, who had great enthusiasm for me, with whom I could feel wanted and young again, I suppose. It had a lot to do with the mania and feeling hyper-sexual, and David had absolutely no desire to make love to me anymore. That always seemed to be a problem with David after we got married and at first shared a family bed where we could not express much passion because Gabriel was always in bed with us, except some Sundays when he'd be playing down in the living room with his toys, blocks, and Legos, David might take an hour to spend some quality intimate time with me. Sometimes I felt like I lived for week-ends when he would finally just stop working and pay attention to me or take me out for a special dinner.

Marlboro

After Lyle and I returned from our honeymoon from Jamaica, I became very depressed. I spent an interminably long week at Marlboro State Psychiatric Hospital where, after one afternoon Lyle told me he had some place he wanted to take me, but kept it a secret. The next thing I knew he had driven to the Mental health Center at Piscataway where two men were waiting to bring me into the hospital if I did not choose to go voluntarily. Lyle was not only psychologically, but physically abusive. Once he was going to hit me and I threatened him with a butter knife saying "Don't you dare come near me, or I will hurt you."

Behind my back my husband had called the hospital saying "My wife has bipolar disorder, and I don't think she is taking her medication anymore; she shot herself in the head a year ago, and just threatened me with a knife during dinner. She is dangerous. I think she is off her meds because she threatened me during dinner and threw a knife at me when dinner was over. I'm afraid she might hurt me, herself, or someone else."

Of course, he neglected to tell them that it was actually he who was angry and tried to jump on me and choke me like he'd done once before, so that I held up the dull kitchen knife toward him self-defense. I never would have actually used it, but I felt threatened enough by his prior violence that I wanted him to know I had a weapon to protect myself and would no longer tolerate his abuse.

It only takes two doctors to have a person committed to a psychiatric stay if they both agree that a person is dangerous to themselves or other human beings. Well, Lyle, being the conniving liar he was, was able to convince the nurses and people in intake and admissions to have psychiatrists listen to his story. When, in actuality, he was the one who abused me but did not want to admit that he had a real problem or take any responsibility for the problems he was having with authority, money, and his psychologically abusive mother. She had abused him as a young child and teen-ager by pulling his pants down in front of his sister and him.

I could usually sense when Lyle was about to explode after a few minutes of listening to me just share my enthusiasm or exuberance about something like my children. I cannot even remember what subjects and topics set him off because it was so many years ago, and I was traumatized by the violence. I removed myself spiritually and emotionally from the actual scene because I was so terrified of him hurting me, a disabled woman with a physical handicap. Out of nowhere he'd suddenly jump me or attack me in the midst of a heated discussion or argument. It was amazing that he was able to turn the entire truth around to make it look like I was the violent one. OJ Simpson used to be able to do the same thing when the police were called to his house or to a public restaurant where he was abusing his poor wife. Coincidentally, I'd just finished reading her best friend, Annette's, excellent account of the violent relationship between OJ and Nicole in a little paperback book of under a hundred pages, a true account from the best friend's perspective, about Nicole, OJ, and their ephemeral marriage and short lives together as lovers, boyfriend and girlfriend, and finally, husband and wife, who became father and mother to two children together.

So, it seems Lyle must have said, "I think she's a danger to herself and others, "and the admissions people told him to bring me to the hospital over the phone when he called to report he was in trouble, probably so that I would not be able to call the cops on him again.

He was able to kidnap me saying we were going to the mall or somewhere that sounded fun. But he'd already told two psychiatrists at the Robert Wood Johnson Mental Health Clinic in Piscataway. Somehow, he persuaded me to get out of the car and got me to come inside with him. But, once inside, I refused to admit myself voluntarily; I cannot tell you the fear I felt in my gut when I realized where we were. I had no reason to go there except to get away from an abusive husband. He was the one who should have been put into the hospital in the first place, not me. I was a gentle wife and mother, not violent like my husband. But Lyle had already convinced them of his story, the psychiatrists had already signed the commitment papers and I was forced to go to Marlboro State Hospital, a place I'd only heard about as a horrible institution for really sick, crazy people. I never in my wildest dreams believed I'd spend any time there, not even as a visitor.

I was now forced to go to the hospital in an ambulance which was really such an indignity. I felt like killing Lyle and suing the hospital and its doctors. Of course, I was not strong enough to ever take legal action while in that frightened, anxious state. By the time I got out, I was just so relieved to be home that I just wanted to forget the whole incident.

I lay awake in my bed the first night I was in Marlboro, contemplating my fate and the injustice of it. I drew a picture of a little being who looked extra-terrestrial in nature. And next to the picture I wrote "In your gentleness you will conquer every foe." This helpful phrase has come to me many times when faced with adversity. Lyle tried so many times to cause problems in my life, but each time I felt afraid for myself or our young daughter, somehow our guides, guardians, angels, friends, and family were there for us to warn us of danger.

Marlboro turned out to be not so bad except that we were forced to get up by 6 AM, and we always had the doors locked behind us, then opened up by doctors, therapists, or security guards and locked behind us when going to meals, to bed, to different activities like exercise, group, art therapy or out for walks. It was like being in prison, with very little freedom except when we were permitted to read in a large community room or watch TV in the early mornings and in the evenings just before bed. Usually, it was the news or whatever dumb program an aide would turn on for the group.

Luckily, there was a review of my case within one week by a judge, and it was decided I was not, after all, a danger to myself, or anybody else. so, I was told I could leave at the end of that week. Unfortunately, I had nowhere to go, but back to living with the crazy, abusive man who put me there in the first place. I just "happened" to be a person with manic depression who was married to a man with a violent streak who could turn abusive at the drop of a hat. I never even provoked the man that I was aware of. Things would bother him that he would never speak about, and somehow, I only needed to say one thing to set him off, and usually his action was overblown and irrational. As it turned out, I was so depressed and upset about losing the family I loved dearly that I felt manipulated, hopeless, and helpless, forced into staying with an abusive, cheeky "lion cheetah" that I spent three full calendar months at the Community Mental Health Center, the psychiatric hospital in Piscataway. This time I admitted myself voluntarily, due to chronic paralyzing depression and anxiety.

I tried doing "wet rebirthing" in our bathtub which helped temporarily, but basically, I was traumatized and had post-traumatic stress from the way everything had transpired so quickly, from the brief three-month affair after being hospitalized at the Carrier Clinic where they diagnosed me as manic depressive, but I hated the lithium they tried to give me because it made me incontinent. Then they gave me Tegretol which is something they use to control seizures and as a mood stabilizer. I used that for a while until after a regular blood test it was discovered my white blood cell count was way too low, so I had to go off that. Shortly after that another medication was tried, but unfortunately, they never got to the root of the problem, both grief from losing my husband and children, and horrible stress from living with a psychotic, abusive man. It appeared I'd married the abusive, controlling side of my mother—twice.

While I was in the hospital, I immediately got to know one of the patients relaxing in the "day room" who had been there for three months. Her name was Pat. She was a lovely, blond friendly lady with an 18 yr. old daughter who'd visited her a few times. She was supposed to be going home soon. Apparently, Pat had had a brain aneurysm, and that was how she became depressed in the first place. I was so happy for her that after almost four months she was finally well enough to go home.

I was given week-end passes by my psychiatrist, Betsy Moss, nearly every week-end after I'd been there for one month. I'll never forget my excitement about going home the second time to see my favorite gold cat, Shanti, and relax in my own bed for a change, but there was an emergency meeting called by the doctors suddenly after lunch. We were all told there would be no outpatient passes that week-end, and when we asked why we were told that our friend, the patient Pat that I'd befriended, and who'd just been released and gone home the Friday before, had gone down to her lonely cellar, while her daughter and husband were out somewhere, and hanged herself from a rafter. I wonder if her husband and daughter would eventually die from a broken heart later that year or afterward.

We were all distressed, but I was more upset than any of the other patients because I was not being allowed to go back to my apartment for the week-end when I had really been looking forward to a happy respite from the hospital— finally. I felt a bit ashamed that I was so selfish and cared more about myself than poor Pat and her sweet family who'd just lost a mom and a wife.

We were told that Pat had a brain aneurysm, and her brain just was not right, so that's probably the reason she chose to leave her loving husband and beautiful daughter. Suicide is such a mystery, especially when the person leaves no note explaining his or her actions. I felt very sad for Pat's family, but I think I was still feeling depressed and selfish at the time that the impact it might have had on me as a healthy person would have been felt much more deeply.

I was released from the Piscataway Mental Health Center on February 15th, my Grammy's birthday.

There I felt so sad, frightened, and desperate to understand what had happened to me that I spent three- and one-half months there from late October until mid-February of 1990 after they made me take a test for college. I did so well in English that I placed as high as a junior in college; The doctors suggested I go back to college, but I felt much too old and incompetent, so they offered to pay for a secretarial school, which I was not too keen on either. I lasted only a day at Drake Secretarial School and returned all my books immediately. I did learn one important skill while I was there, though—how to place my good working right hand and my dexterous fingers in the middle of the keyboard to type pretty fast. The entire keyboard was already unconsciously "memorized" in both my hands, so this was a very valuable skill they taught me, and it helped me unlearn my old way of typing and replace it with something I could easily do with only one hand.

After quitting Drake Secretarial School, I began to look in the paper for jobs while getting up the courage to put ads in the paper again to begin my massage and holistic healing practice. When I came back home, I applied for some jobs I did not get, and then Lyle saw an ad that the YMCA in Princeton needed a member relations receptionist, and after interviewing with a girl named Beth who asked me why I wanted to work for a nonprofit at only $5.50 an hour back in March of 1988. I told her it looked like fun since I loved to meet new people and serve the public. I'd be able to use my communication and typing skills as well as learn some new skills. Besides, I'd always loved taking classes at both the YMCA and YWCA which both were lodged in the same building on Paul Robeson Place in Princeton; and I believed them both to be fantastic, reputable organizations that truly served families in the community.

I landed the job at the Princeton Family YMCA, thirty hours per week including Saturday mornings and until 1PM, which gave me structure, something fun to do with my time, and there was lots of variety in the position; and I liked variety. Besides, I got away from Lyle during weekdays and on Saturday mornings. After two months of work, I also asked the Executive Director, Dave Andersen, if I could teach a weekly beginners' gentle yoga class there, and he granted my wish. I made twenty dollars per session teaching yoga, but I very much enjoyed the variety of the 30 hr. per week receptionist position, which was not just about typing, filing, and answering peoples' questions; I got to register people for classes, answer phones, and take new members on tours of the pool and entire facility. It was a great job to have, especially after feeling no confidence at all in the work place for at least a year after shooting myself in the head and leaving my precious family, since no one would hire me for a job with my physical disability. I felt a lot better about myself having a nearly full-time job at a non-profit in a good community like Princeton, and eventually Lyle found work as a clerk-typist and word processor at Bristol Meyers Squibb in Princeton also.

Teaching meditation and beginning hatha yoga once per week at the Princeton Family YMCA gave me something fun to do and made me feel useful plus I got to meet and make some new friends from the Princeton and West Windsor area. So, I made the best of my marriage to Lyle now that I felt more fulfilled as a woman with an actual career; and he stopped being violent with me for some reason, probably because he got the job which gave him something fulfilling to do as well. I'm guessing that some of the stressors of financial pressure were off of him with us both working.

However, Lyle and I would soon find out in a month or two after my coming home from the Mental Health Center in Piscataway that we had a surprise coming, some joyous news in early May of 1989, that I was pregnant with another daughter whom Lyle wanted to name Sky, after a girl in his senior class in Livingston High School. At seven months pregnant I began to feel a bit tired and it became uncomfortable walking too much with such a large, protuberant belly as a hemiplegic person who walked with a slight limp and a cane. So, I gave my two weeks' notice and left my job at the YMCA when I was a bit more than eight months pregnant with Sky. I still taught two more yoga classes before giving birth, though, because it was healthy and very relaxing.

I went off Tegretol, the medication I was using to control the bipolar mood swings, because I knew it could be damaging to my developing little fetus, so for nine months I was not medicated and doing fine, but as soon as I gave birth everything changed in my biochemistry. Not just that, but I was under quite a bit of stress.

The night I went into labor was something I'll never forget because it was so exciting. Unlike my first two births which were in my own home, peaceful, relaxed, and carefree, Sky's birth was a bit of high anxiety because she was born in the Family born room at Helene Fuld Hospital and came rather quickly without our having much time to prepare. I just remember sitting in my rocking chair in our comfortable apartment in East Windsor writing an angry letter to Family born because they would not allow me to give birth at their birthing center in Princeton, which was closer to our apartment in New Brunswick, and the midwives also made me get some sonograms when I was nine months pregnant and about to give birth. The first test proved inconclusive because the baby was hiccoughing which spoiled the results of the test, and they forced me to come back so they could redo it. At first, I said "No, I would not come", as it was already so late in my pregnancy. What was the point? The nurse told me that if I refused to take another test, they would not be my care providers any longer. I had no choice but to comply with their wishes, or I would not be able to get another midwife at such a late date.

So, I was rocking and writing fast and ferociously when the contractions began. They were pretty mild, so I continued to write and let Lyle sleep while I was in the early stages of labor. He'd worked that entire day at Bristol Meyers Squibb at his new job as a word processor and clerk typist; and since it was about midnight, I did not want to wake him up. I thought I'd try to go through most of the mild labor contractions on my own since it was my third time and I felt pretty confident I knew what I was doing. I guess two or three hours had passed and the contractions began coming faster and felt more painful than the first stage and it felt as if I was dilating pretty quickly. I finally yelled or screamed in pain which woke Lyle up out of a deep sleep. He was upset I woke him up and yelled "What the heck is the matter with you?" until I cried desperately in pain "I'm in labor." Then he became even more upset.

"Why didn't you wake me up, Meryl?"

"I knew you worked all day and you needed your rest. I just did not want to disturb you until it was absolutely necessary." Then we both went into action. Fast forward to calling the midwives at Family born. Louise, the midwife I really loved whom I wanted to use, had just been helping a woman give birth and attended her for most of the night, so I was given a different midwife, Pat, the one on call. I told her over the phone I'd been laboring for a few hours, and it felt to me as if the baby's head had dropped into the birth canal.

She said, "Oh no. "Just throw some clothes in a bag and put a blanket and some towels in too just in case you give birth in the car."

"Oh, shit, here we go!"

Wow, that scared both of us! Lyle and I rushed so much that we forgot to take the infant car seat and the bag of clothes I'd packed for myself to change into from my nightgown. We did remember the baby's bag with the new yellow and white cotton layette as well as the little cotton receiving blankets, we would wrap Sky in after she was born. So, Lyle and I prayed and chanted in the car that we would make it to Trenton to Helene Fuld Hospital before the baby was ready to come out of my vaginal canal. I was chanting the Guru Gita, a sacred Sanskrit ninety-minute chant we usually chant with hundreds of devotees at 5:30 AM up at the ashram in the Catskills in South Fallsburg, New York, with Gurumayi and other devotees of Siddha Yoga.

The entire time Lyle was driving he was running all the red lights since there were no cops around that late at night or was it that early in the morning?

I kept praying to the Goddess, Kundalini Shakti, that Sky would not come out in the car since it felt as if she had already "dropped". Lyle focused on the driving, but he ran most of the red lights since it was very dark and about 4:30 AM. Luckily, no cops were out to stop us or ticket us. Sky could not wait to come into this world. I think she knew (her soul, I mean) that I needed her to help save me from an abusive marriage and knew she would be strong enough to become my "left hand baby and young lady". When we arrived in about 25 minutes later to the hospital there was no one there at the reception desk to greet us. Finally, someone came, and then when they found out I was in the late stages of labor they would not let me walk through the doors by myself where I needed to go into the Family born room to give birth. The receptionist said "It's hospital policy that we bring you inside in a wheelchair" as if I was some invalid or very ill, which I was definitely NOT, thank you very much. That's another reason I hate hospitals. They are unnatural settings for women to give birth and very dis empowering, for the most part. My daughter, Sky, had a much more positive experience giving birth to my grandson naturally in Princeton Hospital with midwives assisting twenty-five years later.

My contractions got heavier, came more rapidly, and felt more painful. I began to yell and Lyle went to look for a wheelchair and someone to assist us. Apparently, Pat, the midwife, had yet to arrive. "She is only a few minutes away," we were told. Well, it was only twenty minutes and two and half contractions after our midwife, Pat, entered the room to assist me that we became new parents of a beautiful little seven-pound three-ounce baby girl. Twenty and a half inches long. She was exactly the same size as her brother, Gabriel, had been. So, all the midwives' worries about her size had been for naught, and the tests they forced me to take like the sonograms and so on were all unnecessary. My intuition had been correct about everything once again – her sex, her size, and her being in perfect health. Her agar score was ten.

My friend, Jean Levine, who worked for my ex-husband, David, had agreed to drive Gabriel and Kyrie to Sky's birth, but she arrived about ten or fifteen minutes after Sky had emerged from my womb which was just fine except that Kyrie had just contracted chicken pox which I did not know until after she came.

Unfortunately, Lyle had never contracted chicken pox as a child and had no immunity to it, so since Kyrie was contagious Lyle contracted a bad case of shingles. Luckily, I'd had it when I was very young, so I was immune to it. I forget if Gabriel had just gotten one pox or none at all, but luckily, he never got the chicken pox either.

I met Pat again years later when my beau, Gary, became one of the new organizers of the Princeton

Singles meet-up at Grover's Mill Coffeehouse in West Windsor. I did not recognize her at first, but after she told me she'd been a former midwife at Family born for years we realized she had been my own midwife that early morning I naturally gave birth to Sky at 5:31 AM on January 31rst, 1990.

Lyle's illness

Lyle became deathly ill for at least two weeks after Sky was born, so there was nobody to help me with caring for my newborn while I was recuperating for at least a week after giving birth. I'd left the hospital six hours after giving birth, the minimum time allowed since I hate being in hospitals at all, so there was no time for me to rest there. I preferred to relax at home because I disliked giving up my freedom when I am inside hospitals anyway. Thank God I was able to get a kind black woman named Dorothy from Trenton, a nice home health aide who assisted me with meals, house cleaning, laundry, and a little with changing the baby's diapers or clothes when I took my bath or shower or needed to change into my casual clothes.

Lyle and I were both exhausted for several days, and all he could manage to do in his unhealthy condition with shingles was sleep all day. I went into the bedroom to wake him up every few hours to make sure he was drinking a lot of water and juices since I did not want him to get dehydrated. I felt pretty lonely, but Sky was a beautiful, sweet baby, and I was just loving having a new baby girl again since I'd really missed my sweet little one year old infant, Kyrie, after having the breakdown. For many months, I could not spend time with my infant daughter after becoming mentally ill, shooting myself in the head, recuperating from that for two months in Robert Wood Johnson Hospital in New Brunswick followed by three months at JFK rehab in Edison, and at home until I had my first manic episode. That's when I was voluntarily admitted to the psychiatric institution where I met the patient, Lyle, who would eventually become my second husband and instrumental in the breakup of my family, through no fault of his own. I left my first husband and two beautiful young children I loved deeply for a man of a different race whom I barely knew who was abusive and fifteen years my junior. He was so immature he talked about high school a lot and listened to lots of rap music, but on the bright side I liked his youthful enthusiasm for black musical artists like Freddie Jackson and Shirley Murdoch. He also turned me on to some good black films and film makers like Spike Lee, and new television shows like the Wayan Brothers with Jennifer Lopez as a dancer and new star on the horizon. She was still an unknown back then in the late eighties.

I was homeless for a little while during my eventual separation from Lyle. After being separated for just a few months from David we were divorced by Jacqueline Printz, and a popular divorce attorney David knew personally. I married this stranger I barely knew a day later in my ex-hubbie, David's, back yard in the home I gave up to him and my two children in Englishtown, NJ. Which later became Monroe Township off of Route 522. And I lost my two children all within the space of about six months. Everything happened so fast I felt like I did not know what hit me. I think I was both numb, manic, or in shock because I barely felt the pain of all these rapid life changing transitions. I buried all the sad feelings of grief, anger, and depression deep inside me somewhere in my subconscious.

Eating Disorder

I had a terrible eating disorder when I became depressed since I had no appetite for life, and I could barely taste the food I was eating anyway. If I did not go into a psychiatric hospital or travel the many miles to my best friend, Zara Rose's, home in the winter for a hearty soup, salad, and possibly a tuna sandwich, or catch my mom on a good day when she felt compassion for me; I would not cook for myself or prepare any decent meals unless my daughter, Sky, was home, and I felt obligated to cook breakfast like scrambled or poached eggs on toast or for supper like baked or fried chicken on a day I was feeling good, a baked potato, and/or a steamed vegetable like broccoli or carrots. I dreaded when the time came to have to cook supper for both of us. In my depressed state it seemed that I did not remember how to cook very well. I was too exhausted to fuss or try new recipes, so often times poor Sky would also go hungry right after school unless she visited her friends, Savanna and James, around the block in Griggs Farm or Naju whose mom, Jesse, would take pity upon her and give her healthy snacks until dinner.

I feel terribly ashamed and embarrassed to admit this failing in myself as a mother. I didn't know this until she became an adult, but she recently told me that her friends would laugh at her for saying she was hungry and asking for food or a snack after coming home from school to find me in bed studying or reading with nothing in the oven or on the stove cooking for supper,, and I feel guilty and so ashamed to say that all I wanted to do was stay in bed until very late in the morning watching TV after giving Sky breakfast and getting her off to the bus stop for school. Then, after my bath or shower which was often after 10:30 or 11AM I'd sit upon the couch all day long and watch television or go into my room, close the door and read my college books or write a paper for one of my classes. Luckily, we were poor enough to receive welfare, food stamps, and WIC. Sky was able to qualify for the free lunch program in school when she turned five and was able to attend kindergarten in the Princeton school system.

Being mainly a vegetarian, I also eat eggs for protein and take Vitamin D supplements. Now that I am feeling better, I make sure I eat plenty of fresh fruits, veggies, and grains that contain many of the B vitamins necessary to maintain good emotional health. When I am under stress I often do not eat well, especially if I am feeling depressed or nervous about finances which I often experienced as a single mom when I didn't sleep well. If I did not sleep well, I'd be too tired to cook for myself. In my negative state of mind, I had no appetite. Nothing tasted good. Not eating was not really an option, so I often looked to others like my mother or my girlfriend, Zara Rose, to prepare some delicious and nutritious meals for me when I was too tired, depressed, or so bored of watching television which I used to numb my feelings most of the day. I always felt way too tired to cook for myself. My mom and my friends' kindness cooking for me were the only things keeping me afloat.

I did use my Food Stamps to buy microwave meals for both of us because they were easy and semi-nutritious. Sky loved Marie Callender's pot pies, as well as her large turkey and chicken dinners with at least one vegetable, mashed potato, and a tiny dessert, etc. I did not know until way after the fact; that she was starving after she came home from school around 3:00 PM. I assumed that she was fine because we qualified for the free lunch program, so why would I not think she was being fed properly or that she might be going hungry sometimes? If I had been conscious and aware that Sky had been hungry and suffering, I hope I'd have made certain that she was getting a healthy snack after lunch like soup, cheese and crackers, or cereal with fruit to hold her off until dinner. But it was not until 2015 when she was first pregnant with my grandson, that she told me that she was always hungry when I was depressed and often was forced to visit her friends like Helen, her mother, Leticia, who is from Guatemala and an excellent cook and hostess. Helen's step-dad, Juan, is actually an excellent chef by trade and works at a local restaurant in Princeton, so they often treated her to dinner since Sky was always welcome and treated like another daughter by them. I felt terribly ashamed and embarrassed now that she felt coerced or like a victim in the matter of hunger, as if she had no choice in the matter but to ask for hand-outs and much more variety at dinner.

Even if I'd had to pay for Chinese take-out, pizza, or buy the most expensive microwave meals I would have done anything to make sure she was happy, at peace in her heart, and fed properly. Especially now because I personally believe, and have experienced, in my heart of hearts, that depression or even mania can be due mainly to a nutritional imbalance. I've heard the author, scientist, clinical nutritionist, vegan proponent, animal rescuer, and radio personality on WBAI, Dr. Gary Null, say that most mentally ill patients when tested, were found lacking in Vitamin B 12 and other B vitamins as well as minerals. Especially schizophrenics. In my personal experience I believe depression can be caused by nutritional deficiencies besides lack of exercise, psychological problems, deep seated feelings of unworthiness, childhood trauma, hopelessness, and negative thinking.

But it is a complex illness to understand, and I believe there are many factors that could possibly begin with trauma sustained during birth. I also believe many of us have traumatic memories from our childhood and even past lifetimes. From my research and personal experience, it is not just a simple biochemical imbalance in the brain that can be treated by drugs, medications, and talk therapy as the medical establishment would have you believe. At least in my opinion gleaned from over twenty years of scientific study and personal experience with bi-polar illness, it is unique to each individual. Many illnesses are psychosomatic; without studying and treating the person as a Whole Being including Mind and Spirit, the body's healing will only be temporary, at best.

I also have learned that many of my problems as well as the mental illnesses of a few friends and family members were caused by or exacerbated by the use of marijuana, alcohol, or especially hard drugs like ecstasy, crack cocaine, and heroin. In my case I experimented with the drug, ecstasy, in 1986, several times, for one year prior to my shooting myself in the head. This certainly changed my biochemistry and affected me deeply in more negative, harmful ways than I could possibly realize when I used it.

More Abuse, Deception and Miscommunication

Once Lyle healed from having the shingles, he began to enjoy our baby, Sky, and having a family, or so it seemed. Until one day when I received a monthly phone bill higher than $200 which was in my name since I paid most of the bills while Lyle was out of work. There were dozens of 900 calls to a business called multi-Quest which all totaled were very expensive – about $260, and since I'd not made the calls myself, I wanted to find out if there was some kind of mistake. I called the 900 number, and a woman's voice answered. I asked what type of business I was calling, and the woman quickly apologized to me saying it was a phone sex service that Lyle had been calling many times while I was pregnant and even after I'd just given birth. I was incredulous and felt so betrayed – especially because I was footing the bill for my husband's semi adulterous antics. When I confronted him he said "Honey, I'm sorry. It was really nothing. I was just lonely while you were at work and wanted to have someone to talk to. We never even talked about sex. They would just listen to my problems and try to make me feel better."

I was pretty upset about that because I just began to feel a bit closer to Lyle and happier with our relationship since Sky was born and he seemed to really care for both of us. Unfortunately, I was fooling myself. Lyle had a real problem with communication, not just with me, but with most of the adults in my family, nor did he make much of an effort to relate to Gabriel and Kyrie when they stayed with us overnight on week-ends. He appeared to be jealous of my relationships with them and was not very kind or playful with them when they would stay overnight on week-ends after I returned home from the hospital with the new baby, Sky.

Lyle would read the newspaper at the kitchen table as opposed to talking or relating to me. Sometimes I could tell he was upset or angry about something, but he'd choose to keep it bottled up inside. I might say something, just an offhand remark that he took personally and he would jump from his seat at the table, knock me to the floor and begin choking me. He put his hands around my neck until I began to cry and struggle away from his grip. This happened more than once, and each time he would apologize profusely saying "Honey, I can't believe I did that. I promise I'll never hurt you again."

I did, however, ask him to leave the house for a while, and then while we were living in East Windsor, I realized our money was running out, and we were starting to fall behind on the $640 per month rent, especially with these exorbitant phone bills and Lyle out of work while he was very sick or did not show up on time and eventually got fired. He was in and out of work. He just did not have a lot of stability as a husband or provider.

I was confused, but every time I'd hear the song by Vanessa Williams "Dreamin' " I had this thought that I rarely liked to entertain because I hid it so well, even from myself, but I knew deep down in my heart that I still deeply loved and truly missed my first husband, David, and our sweet marriage of almost six years. I knew deep inside I was really sad and grieving, but I could not really feel my pain and was not sure why. Without medicine I was really "out of it." After marrying Lyle and coming back from our honeymoon in a state of sadness, grief, and confusion when he began to hit or abuse me psychologically again and again, I was in a quandary about what to do. I was already divorced from the man I loved, contracts were signed, bank accounts split. Supposedly all assets were equitably distributed, but there was a hole in my heart as big as the state of Virginia. I did not realize at the time that just finding and staying on a good medication would have helped to stabilize my moods as well as finding good employment and structure again and possibly a better and more mature psychologist. Though I began going for counseling I still felt hopeless about the situation with Lyle without even understanding why.

Lyle had begun to abuse me both psychologically and physically a few times again, just like my mother had from the time I was about four years old on and off for years. The abuse began when we lived in East Windsor, but then we decided to separate. I had no place to go, so I asked my friend, Joanie, in Twin Rivers, if Sky and I could live with her until I found something more permanent. I could not afford the $640 rent in East Windsor all by myself. Lyle and I were struggling financially. Even though David was giving me $1,000 per month alimony for one year after we divorced, I had nothing left after paying all the bills and paying the minimum monthly payment on several credit cards due to the exorbitant expense of the wedding, the reception with two bands and the subsequent ten-day honeymoon in Jamaica.

Then Lyle lost his job at Bristol Meyers Squibb for some reason he did not completely share with me. Maybe he was using marijuana or crack cocaine to self-medicate at the time, I just cannot be sure.

By the time Sky was five months old Lyle and I were fighting over who would keep her most of the time. Every other day I'd get a restraining order against him, then he'd go to the police saying I was an abusive mother who was neglecting and sexually molesting my baby. So, he'd get an order saying that he would get temporary custody of her. This went on for month until I went to Legal Aide to try to get permanent custody of her. Unfortunately, the case did not go so well when it finally came to trial a few months later.

Lyle was his own attorney and, as usual, he lied again through his teeth just like he had that previous time he successfully had me committed to Marlboro State Hospital, in order to to get his way. He wanted Sky to be put into a foster home and eventually adopted, I suppose, knowing there was absolutely no way a judge would grant him custody as a father and a mentally ill, violent one with no job, at that. Except for the true part which was that I had manic depression and tried to commit suicide on more than one occasion, everything else he said was evil, unethical lies. He knew the black judge who was the former prosecuting attorney for Mercer County would not grant him custody due to his past record of abuse, but since he told her I was molested by my father and he thought these patterns continue in families he told her he was afraid I'd sexually abuse our baby daughter because I'd been abused by my father, and I'd written in a fifteen-page article that sexual abuse is often passed down from generation to generation. Upon hearing that, the judge ordered emergency foster care for Sky the same week-end I'd scheduled a party for all of our friends and family to witness her baptism. I was devastated, and my Legal Aide attorney was of no help. She did not even contest this decision or try to appeal the judge's unfair decision right away as she should have; she lost my case, custody of my new six-month-old baby whom I was still breastfeeding, but I still had to pay her the minimum of three hundred dollars as a Legal Aide attorney, $250 plus court costs.

The sad thing was that since I'd already baked the lasagna and ordered other food for the party I went ahead with it anyway without Sky, and just had several of my closer friends over to talk about what had happened and to eat the feast I'd prepared. I was in shock again, but I pretended not to feel the pain of losing another baby daughter who was taken from me at almost six months old when I was still breastfeeding her and put into foster care suddenly which would last for nearly eighteen months until I finally got myself together, got my mood stabilized, and got Lyle completely out of my life, or so I thought.

Once while Sky was visiting with Lyle after I'd moved temporarily into my friend, Joanie's, house in Twin Rivers, he kidnapped her one afternoon while I was sleeping, telling Joanie he was just taking her out for a short walk in her stroller. He brought Sky to his friend, Kevin's, house in West Orange, New Jersey, in Essex County, and I did not see her for several days.

I was terrified when he did not bring her back to my apartment at the scheduled time. I somehow intuited where she might be even though Lyle would not tell me on the phone when I persistently asked for two whole days. I had a feeling he'd brought Sky to his best friend, Kevin's house, since he was not wanted at his mother's house where he'd been estranged ever since he turned eighteen. Nor was he welcome at his Aunt Vi's and favorite uncle's home where his cousin, Daryl, had lived for years. When I told David what had happened, he suggested I get the local police involved. Since I had temporary custody at the time, what Lyle had done was illegal and considered kidnapping, so the East Windsor police contacted the West Orange police who found that Kevin was wanted by the police for hundreds of dollars' worth of unpaid parking tickets and some other minor offense. So, by the fourth day the West Orange police stormed Kevin's house where they discovered both Lyle and baby Sky while I sat in my car watching and waiting to take her back into the shelter of my arms. The two young men were quite surprised, especially when they were both taken to the local jail, fingerprinted, and locked up for I don't know how long because I split that scene the minute I got my precious baby, Sky, back into the safety of my loving, nurturing arms.

I felt a bit smug with a sense of confident triumph, but mostly deep relief that I'd gotten my baby back who was still breastfeeding, so my breasts were swollen and hurting. The minute she began to nurse again my swollen breasts were happy and continued to produce milk in response to her suckling.

Somehow both Lyle and Kevin were able to post bail, and Kevin made arrangements to pay money down on the few hundred dollars of parking tickets he'd owed for quite a few years. I still did not trust Lyle, and frankly was still quite afraid of him.

My ex-husband told me I should be very careful because he was so angry at being put in jail that he vowed to get me back by doing the same old nonsense, so he could get temporary custody of Sky again. In the meantime, I contacted Legal Aide since I did not have a lot of money to pay a decent attorney. In retrospect, I finally realized Lyle was an abusive psychopath who truly hated his mother and would do almost anything to get back at her by abusing all the women in his life he allowed himself to get close to. It turned out I would not be the last woman he'd try to hurt or control. He would psychologically abuse his second wife, who luckily, had several brothers who protected her and would not allow the abuse or the marriage to continue. and a girlfriend he met out in Indiana.

After the break-up with his second wife, Lyle became a truck driver and moved out to Indiana. Following the short-lived abusive marriage and divorce, he would continue the same pattern and cycle of abuse with two other girlfriends who were crazy about him and whom he introduced to me. One was named Julie with whom he fell deeply in love. Julie lived in Indiana and had a nineteen-year-old son with whom she lived. While I was moving from our apartment in Jamesburg, I needed someone to help me move my furniture and stuff, so Lyle and his cousin would be the ones to help me. Then Lyle would want to to spend time with Sky and he'd say "I have no place to go tonight. Can I just spend one night here to be with my baby?" I'd be stupid and fall for his apologies and his charming ways once again, plus I was not sure if I could care for a little baby all on my own. I'd tell Lyle to go away and not come back but the next day when I returned home from school at Mercer County College, I'd find him sitting on my front step with a bouquet of flowers and a greeting card begging me to let him come back inside the apartment so he could make it up to me.

Besides, he missed me and he wanted to see Sky. By the second or third time I went to the police station to get a restraining order against him. Even the restraining order did not prevent him from trying to see me or Sky, and once he ended up in the West Windsor jail because the cops caught him driving with a suspended license.

Things between Lyle and me continued to be rocky, especially when Gabriel and Kyrie (who were living with David) would come to visit on the week-ends. I think he felt threatened by their presence; Lyle was not particularly warm to anyone at all, not even himself unless you consider he had a healthy sexual appetite, but sex is not the same as love or true care and concern for another human being; and at holidays he was usually very quiet, rarely saying much of anything to my family or my brother, Pete, and his family, whom I rarely ever saw, except at holidays, birthdays at his home in East Brunswick, occasional weddings, and funerals. There was something very wrong with him like borderline personality disorder or paranoid schizophrenia, because he was definitely socially stunted, at least around my friends and family. We tried, however, to make the best of a new marriage despite the manic spending I did on our honeymoon and the wasted money spent on our wedding. Neither of us had a job, so I had to file for bankruptcy within eight months after we wed. We did continue to have sex on a regular basis which, I believe, was really the only thing holding us together at that point besides the fact that neither of us had anywhere else to go. I did not believe David would ever take me back after all that crazy nonsense. Perhaps I just felt too unworthy to be with David having a serious mental illness. Part of me thought I needed to punish myself because I felt so guilty for leaving him and our precious little ones.

Due to the abuse or to the lack of funds, there were several major and minor moves while in relationship with Lyle. One time I was completely homeless when I did not trust him at all, I was living in Twin Rivers with my girlfriend, Joan, but when her dad found out I had a cat he told her I had to leave as soon as possible or I'd be gently escorted out the door with all my belongings put outside to be thrown out into the garbage or picked up by me later. Eek! Like the beloved Lion cartoon character of my childhood, Snagglepuss, I was forced to exit, stage left, before getting into too much trouble.

Sky was placed in foster care when she was nearly six months old, so when I was homeless, I was all by myself and did not have to worry about bringing a baby into that unstable situation. It was very difficult losing her to foster care while I was still breastfeeding her at five and a half months old, but it would have been worse if she had been part of the abusive relationship and then dragged around to different places to live temporarily on a daily basis, or God forbid, a woman's shelter. I think that was probably the lowest I'd been in my life apart from the time my massage teacher betrayed me and I went into my first suicidal depression.

I did not want to ingratiate myself during those three rough homeless weeks, so I never spent more than one or two nights at one person's home for the night. I cannot even imagine how hard it must be for moms and families to be homeless in NYC in the dead of a freezing cold winter. It must be so challenging for not just the mom, but the needy new little baby or toddler.

During the day I'd go to David's house to spend time with Gabriel and Kyrie and to just have a safe space away from Lyle. I chose to sleep in my car when the curtain of darkness rolled around at about eight PM or a bit later. Once I slept in David's station wagon in his gravel driveway in front of the house in Monroe Township all night long because I was exhausted and too ashamed, embarrassed, and proud to ask him if it was OK with him if I did sleep in the car. I did not feel courageous or confident enough to ask if I could actually sleep in a room inside the house like the guest room or meditation room, or even upon the couch in the living room in my street clothes. So, I ended up crying in his car, formerly my car, until in exhaustion, I fell asleep.

I'd picked out as the family's new Chevy station wagon a few years before we got divorced, and I never imagined I'd be spending at least two nights in David's driveway sleeping inside his car at night because I was too ashamed to ask if I could spend the night there. I'd make phone calls during the day to my friend, Zara Rose, my brother, Pete, or other friends to ask if I could sleep on their couch for a night or two. This went on for several weeks after I'd applied and was accepted to live a small apartment complex in Jamesburg not far from where David and I once owned our first home on Sherman Street.

It was in that apartment that Lyle pushed my head into the bedroom dresser our second Christmas morning in front of Gabriel, and I got a gash over my left eye which I lied about to everyone who asked, including my mother because I was too embarrassed to admit the truth to anyone about how bad our relationship had gotten.

he only reason I allowed Lyle to stay with me was because having a disability and a new baby was so challenging, not to mention that after I gave birth, I became very spacey and disoriented from not being on medication for nine months while I was pregnant; my biochemistry completely altered after giving birth. I was so exhausted from lack of sleep and tired out from nursing Sky without the proper nutrition and extra calories I needed as a nursing mom, that it was even very challenging for me to shop for groceries at Shop Rite. I'd begin to feel dizzy and want to leave my grocery cart there before waiting on line to pay for them. The aid I got from him in changing and dressing her made me very dependent. I also needed his help with cleaning and organizing. At times he could be very kind and helpful, and I suppose most of the time I just did not want to be alone, so some company was better than no company at all. I suppose that way I was not forced to look at my pain of giving up my husband and children. I finally had to move from the apartment in Jamesburg just to get away from Lyle, and I ended up at a less expensive apartment called Gardenview Terrace in Hightstown, not far from the one we 'd shared at Windsor Regency when Sky was born and I lived right next door to my new friend and former nurse at the Carrier Clinic, Mindy Gerber, who would be the sweetest and only person to offer to throw me a baby shower for Sky. Mindy and I lost touch for a while after I moved, but we reconnected again at at a mutual UFO aficionado and friend's party for fourth of July in Hamilton in 2007 and are acquaintances and friends on Facebook to this day due to our mutual interest in UFOs and paranormal phenomena.

Lyle kept coming back.

David supported us all in a very comfortable lifestyle. Besides, David and I shared the same spiritual philosophy and were devotees of Swami Muktananda, Gurumayi Chidvilasananda, and on a yogic path together. I even knew back then I created my own reality, so when he'd occasionally act crazy like my mom or even hit me once I excused the behavior thinking it was my fault. What had I done wrong to make my husband act that way toward me? Well, we'd both been horribly abused by one or both of our parents, and I believe we were both emotionally stunted and needed lots of psycho-therapy, contemplation, self-reflection, and/or deep spiritual work.

Baba Muktananda, our guru, believed marriage was a very high spiritual sadhana. Muktananda said "Marriage is a great tapasya" – a Sanskrit word that means burning. In this case, it meant burning away of the impurities of false understanding and identification with the ego. We could either focus on the sacred love and God within each other and end up experiencing great bliss, deep sublime peace, contentment, unconditional love and enlightenment, or we, as a couple, could choose the other path of egotistical melodramas, arguing, fighting, and blaming, separation, and self-destruction. Sometimes I think it is so easy to project what we do not like about ourselves onto our mates or other friends.

All the negative qualities we'd project upon one another from inside our own subconscious, defense mechanisms developed by the old Reptilian brain that had absolutely nothing to do with the TRUTH of WHO we are—divine, individualized aspects of God Consciousness, who deserves love, respect, honor, and kindness.

By the Universal Law of Attraction and karma, the law of action and reaction, we'd get more of what we think about. Focus on the God within our own Selves and on love and appreciation for ourselves and our partner, or we can choose creation by default, seeing ourselves as powerless victims and end up separated and or divorced off like I did with both David and Lyle, and move on to another partner who will have the exact same qualities in their subconscious that need to be healed as ourselves.

In "The Course in Miracles" it states "Love brings up anything unlike itself." And in my case, this happened multiple times until I decided to get off the emotional roller coaster of high ups followed by very low downs.

In truth, according to Abraham-Hicks, who wrote the book "Ask and it is Given", our emotions are indicators of how connected or disconnected we are from Source within and without. Each one of us has an emotional guidance system that allows us to know how connected we are to Source energy. To God, our own higher Selves. I was a pushover who let many men prior to marriage and then, my first husband, walk all over me – just the way I did with my mother, the original perpetrator of psychological and physical abuse. In my mind it was not spiritual for me to get angry at anyone nor did I even understand that it was normal to have healthy boundaries. My SPIRIT was generous to a fault, I was emotionally immature and pretty much let myself live with and tolerate two abusive control freaks as live-in mates until I realized I deserved better. I finally got help in my second marriage by going to WomansSace which was an organization dedicated to sheltering abused women and children from their violent husbands who were often abusive fathers, many of whom had either alcohol or drug problems, with a safe place to live, a shelter where they could not be found and hurt again, a place where they could feel safe and also be educated about men with abusive personalities and be able to do whatever was necessary to get stronger in themselves and reclaim their own lives.

GOOD SEX IS NOT LOVE

It was only until my mid-thirties that I began truly enjoying sex following my divorce from David when I met a man named Ernie at his office in Woodbridge. He was a body worker who studied massage therapy like myself, but he offered a specific type of bodywork called biosynch. He'd been recommended to me by a lady named Terry, one of the lesbian women who worked in David's office, because she connected with me over a period of time and knew I needed some special healers to help improve both my hemiplegia, my gait, and maybe even alleviate some of the depression and mood swings through somatic means.

In my experience just talk therapy and a bit of medication never really did much of anything lasting; it never got to the "core belief", the subconscious thoughts and feelings, and the root cause of my suffering.

For many years before learning about tantra and polyamory, I had a terrible, unfulfilling sex life – until I met Ernie at his apartment in Woodbridge when he gave me a massage and special session called bioenergetics. Terry had gotten work done by him, and she seemed to think he was very special.

Indeed, he was, in more ways than one. I was immediately attracted to this quiet, intense, attractive man at our first meeting where we only talked and shared our backgrounds and what I wanted to accomplish through the biosynch sessions which were way more creative and effective than just a therapeutic Swedish massage. His specialized bodywork, amazing intellect, and calm, quiet energy literally changed me for the better in just our first meeting. It was at our second meeting I decided I wanted him as a lover even though I was still technically married to Lyle. I said to him one day on the phone "Ernie, I am finding myself very attracted to you and wanting you to make love to me."

To which he said "Thank you. I'm honored, but since you are married, we don't really have to act on that desire. It is enough to just notice it and acknowledge the attraction", which, after three months or so of sessions and sharing different things with him, seemed to be mutual. But he was cautious since he was a professional, so I believe he was careful not to get involved physically or emotionally with his clients. Plus, he knew I was married, and to a man who had been abusive to me, and we had a little girl together. Though he had lived for several years with a few women, Ernie was never interested in getting married or having children.

SKY IN FOSTER CARE AND WITH MOM

My toddler, Sky, was taken from me when she was six months old and put into foster care for eighteen months because of lies Lyle told the judge about me mixed with some truth about my mental illness and my serious suicide attempt in which I shot myself in the head. He'd read in my ten-page article entitled "How I Survived my Suicide Attempt and Continue to be Healed" that mentioned my dad had molested me sexually, that these patterns were often continued in families; so knowing he would not get custody of Sky due to his physical abuse, he tried to hurt me and prevent me from keeping my baby by saying that sexual abuse usually continues and is passed down from generation to generation. After the judge ruled that Sky was not safe with me, I told her I was having my baby christened that week-end and asked if the foster mom would be able to bring her to David's house in Monroe for the christening and party, but I was refused.

So, the day I went to family court with my woman attorney from Legal Aide was one of the worst days of my life. My precious little baby girl was ripped from my arms while I was still breastfeeding her the week-end before her baptism. I had planned a large party to celebrate her divine nature and entrance into our world with about fifteen friends and family members. My brother, Pete, was supposed to perform the christening. But when the judge, the former prosecuting attorney for Mercer County, ordered her into emergency foster care on that very day, I was in shock. If I'd had an inkling that anything like that was going to happen, I'd have brought my mother with me whom I know would have immediately volunteered to take my baby, Sky, into her beautiful, immaculate home and heart.

She adored Sky from the moment she was born as she did my other two children. My legal aide attorney was not a very good one, and she did not help one bit once the decision was made by objecting, filing an appeal, or anything. Maybe she did not care at all. It was devastating.

Immediately, the euphoria I'd felt for three months prior quickly dissolved and devolved into frustration, despair, and after a month or two of losing my baby whom I still wanted to nurse and continue bonding with, into chronic depression and anxiety. My baby daughter whom I loved with all my heart, just like her sister, Kyrie, was suddenly out of my life. And I was at a loss of how to solve this problem; or even if there was any solution to this debacle at all. I was angry at her father, but too much in shock to figure out that I could have the confidence or the courage to do what I had to do in order to get her back.

All I knew was that I went there with a positive attitude even after Lyle had physically abused me on more than several occasions figuring that naturally a judge would usually choose to leave a child with its biological mother before anyone else unless she was an alcoholic or drug addict. But I had none of those addictions. I did not smoke, drink, or use drugs, not even marijuana since I was 21, and I was 34 years old. I could not believe my horrible fate.

What was worse was that we only had visitation rights with the baby once per week, and it was in the same room together at the Mercer County Board of Social Services, where we would begin to argue, Because I was pretty upset. So, it was decided that we visit with her separately. I had a brief half hour with Sky and then Lyle took her and held her for a half hour. I wondered if he'd had any idea what a poor decision, he'd made by attacking me as an unfit parent in family court. Did he actually believe she'd be better off in foster care? No, I find that hard to believe. He was just hurt and angry that we'd separated and I wanted to leave him permanently. He was filled with so much anger and resentment toward me that he chose to be his own attorney and made up all those lies about me for spite to get back at me so I would not get full custody of Sky.

I'd also filed a restraining order against him – twice, for my own protection.

MORE ABUSE

Lyle did some really horrible things to hurt me besides the physical, psychological, and emotional abuse. One time when we lived in New Brunswick I was ill and confined to my bed, so I gave him my debit card asking him to do me a favor by depositing all the money I gave him – $350 in cash – into my checking account to cover an installment due on my car insurance. I trusted him as my husband to help me because sometimes he was truly kind, and I always tried to see the good in him no matter what he was showing me because that was the type of person I am, though I can be very naive. If I had the slightest doubt that he would steal my money I certainly would never have entrusted him with the cash. But he was my husband, and we did share most of our monies, though I had a separate checking account because, when we met, he was only nineteen years old, and he did not even have a car, a job, or a checking account, while living at Easter Seals, a group home. So, what was I thinking when I chose to marry this black teen-ager fifteen years my junior whom I met in a mental institution who was barely out of high school and still talking about high school, his former girlfriend, his favorite rap music, and high school experiences? That was how manic I was when I made the decision to leave a comfortable life with David and the kids to move into a new place with this man, I barely knew to begin a new life. My judgment was obviously extremely poor and impulsive while I was manic. That was one time I wish I'd listened to my mom who warned me against marrying him. Lyle's mom was not supportive of the union either which made absolutely no sense to anyone but ourselves and David who probably could not wait to get a mentally ill wife off his hands.

I had forgotten when I entrusted Lyle with the money to pay my car insurance that he was driving with a suspended license. Would you believe a policeman stopped him for some small thing like a tail light being out, and he was not only given a ticket for driving with a suspended license, but since he did not have his registration or insurance card in his glove compartment. he was arrested and taken down to the court in East Windsor, so he used my money to bail himself out of court.

Ironically, he owed money for parking fines and another ticket in West Windsor, so he was then brought down to the lock-up in West Windsor where he stayed until I could bail him out.

Then I found out he stole the insurance money with which I entrusted to him, to pay bail to the West Windsor Court to keep him out of jail. That is the type of person he was in my experience, from my perspective—a liar and a scoundrel. But he ended up in jail anyway when a second policeman stopped him and found out that not only was he driving with a suspended license, but he owed a lot of money in back parking tickets to East Windsor, so despite all his scheming and conniving it was his karmic fate to end up in a jail for a few days anyway.

The marriage continued to go downhill from there, but crazily, I chose to stick it out, or I believed I might stay homeless, and I'd never get my daughter, Sky, back from foster care. I found an apartment in Jamesburg in the end of August on Colletti Court in Jamesburg, but I had to wait until October 1, when it would be vacant and available which gave me time to get up a security deposit, so it was my destiny to remain homeless for three weeks while waiting for the apartment to be vacated by the other tenants. During that time, I either slept in my car because it was still warm out or on various friends' couches because I did not want to ingratiate myself. During the day I would hang out at my ex-husband's house in the living room where I would read or write. Kyrie would sometimes be there with our nanny if she did not go to her pre-school with her brother, Gabriel.

I remember there was a three-day holiday, and my mom was permitted to take Sky for the long week-end. Of course, she allowed me to come to her house to spend all that time with her. At that point I was able to feel some joy again, and I resolved to do all the necessary things as far as red tape went with DYFS (the Division of Family Services), to get Sky out of foster care.

I was a caring, loving, affectionate mom. I could not help the fact that I had a mental illness due to having a biochemical imbalance and not just one, but two abusive husbands. I cannot believe I married someone exactly like the abusive, dark side of my mother not once, but twice. What the heck was I thinking? I'm talking about the fact that I attracted two men who were both physically and psychologically abusive like the mean-spirited mother I knew from my teens, but who also had a kind, caring heart deep down. I realized when my mood improved just by being with my baby for three days that I was not really crazy and depressed at all, but just very sad and in shock over losing my sweet little baby girl.

So, in order to have more of a chance of getting Sky back I crazily asked Lyle if he wanted to live with me and try to get along again. We got some "free" living room furniture, a soft, light brown couch, with a matching chair and love seat from Unclaimed Freight in New Brunswick with vouchers we got from the Mercer County Board of Social Services, If a person is homeless they also shell out some money for a portion of the security deposit, especially if one is on welfare, which I was at that point after spending all the money I'd gotten from David in the divorce settlement which was at least over twenty thousand dollars with a year's worth of alimony at $1,000 per month. I'd never had that much money before at one time and had no idea how to manage it, especially in my crazy, manic state of mind. I'd spent most of the money from David's and my divorce settlement on Lyle's and my wedding and honeymoon. Not to mention that I was responsible totally for the rent, utilities, gasoline and completely supporting Lyle and I financially since he did not have a job.

David allowed the kids to come stay with us most week-ends and on Christmas. But Lyle really did not like my children nor my mother, as he was a kind of jealous man, not a very social or gregarious person like me, so after a short time, he was up to his old tricks again getting angry at me for no reason. He would hold his feelings in, not communicate when things were bothering him, and then out of nowhere he would erupt like an exploding volcano. He'd either jump on me and put his hands around my throat to choke me, punch me, shove me against a wall, or push me down. I could not believe he became so abusive again after he humbly apologized for every incident bringing me a beautiful bouquet of flowers and the perfect, loving, romantic greeting card expressing his love and sorrowful act of contrition for his behavior. Each time he promised up and down he was so sorry and "it would never happen again."

One time Gabriel and Kyrie were visiting. I recall they slept over night at the Jamesburg apartment, and Lyle got angry over some paltry thing I said. He hated it when I was feeling happy and confident about myself. He was also very jealous of my children.

Anyway, we were eating oatmeal I'd cooked for our breakfast, and he impulsively dumped the entire bowl of warm oatmeal over my head soiling my newly washed hair from the day before. Gabriel remembers that to this day twenty-eight years later. It affected him deeply to see his mom so hurt, abused, and treated with such disrespect. Especially when he felt powerless at his young age to do anything about it to protect me. I was in a quandary about what to do. I did not know the shelter, WomanSpace, even existed in Princeton at that time. Or maybe it had not been conceived or built yet in 1990. I felt completely victimized and embarrassed that I was being abused. My mom and ex-husband knew about a few of the times Lyle hurt me or lost his temper and threatened to hurt me because he actually punched my hand so hard in David's home he fractured my pinky, but other than David offering me some advice to leave him or to give me a temporary place to stay for a few nights, neither David, nor my mother, were much help. I knew it was a terrible situation, but I felt so hopeless and powerless to change anything. I felt so powerless I believed I was going to be stuck in this hopeless situation forever. I remember truly having that thought that my abusive circumstances were permanent.

I believed I was doomed forever to live with Lyle because of my disability, and because I needed him to help me bathe and dress Sky, as well as get her in and out of her car seat since it was really rough for me to do it with only one working hand and arm. And then I began depending on his financial support to help me buy diapers, clothes, and food for Sky since he eventually did get a few excellent, decent paying temp jobs as a clerk and then a computer typist for Bristol Myers-Squibb. I was hoping and praying things would change. It seemed I was not that concerned about my own welfare that much. I could tolerate most anything since I was strong and became accustomed to having David be controlling and psychologically abusive on several occasions in our relationship before I even got into the marriage with Lyle. After I began having outside affairs, David had been physically abusive on two occasions as well. It seemed I was getting what I was accustomed to feeling comfortable with from the time I was four on and off until I was a teenager with the "Wicked Witch of the West". It seems we get what we think about and what we felt comfortable with as children. According to Harville Hendrix who wrote "Getting the Love You Want" it is a normal pattern for us to be attracted to and choose romantic partners who will re-create what we first experienced back in our childhoods in order to work them out and heal these unhealthy patterns with psychologists and marriage counselors in order to consciously create what we are wanting and needing in a "Conscious Marriage".

My Second Divorce

When Lyle began to abuse Sky in front of me in my home in Hightstown, I knew I had to protect her and immediately do something to get him out of our home environment. I was living with her in my own apartment, but since Lyle was temporarily homeless, I'd let him sleep over some nights when he came to visit us for the week-end.

One evening, we were peacefully watching television in my bedroom. Sky was about three years old when she did something wrong from his skewed perspective; and he impulsively smacked her right off the bottom wood railing of our queen-sized bed where she was innocently and happily perched. I'd seen him spank her before if she was running into the road into a dangerous situation or got her hands near the stove or something that might hurt her, but I understood that that was just for her protection. I did not like it, but I let it go until this one incident knocking her off the bed for no reason that seemed rational.

It was then I knew I needed to sever the ties with him completely and immediately, if possible, and if I was able, leave temporarily just to get him out of our home environment. I'd already moved out of the Jamesburg apartment into a better place in Hightstown that was a little cheaper to get away from him, but he offered to help me move, and I accepted since I had no money to pay a mover and not too many male friends at that time who were strong enough to help move furniture and carry boxes. I'd wanted to leave him prior to that, but with both my physical and mental disabilities I did not have a lot of confidence to take care of a baby daughter by myself with the use of only one arm. I felt trapped in the relationship – especially because at times he could be so kind, helpful, refreshing, and interesting, and being vulnerable I'd fall for his kindness and focus on his good qualities.

I had liked the music and videos he shared with me. There was a part of his personality I enjoyed as well as the good sex we shared or I would not have been with him at all. I also felt compassion for him because he came from a very abusive mother and his dad abandoned him when he was only two years old. Lyle's relationship with his mom was not like me and my mom. She had money, was intelligent, and had a great job as the vice principal of a school in Livingston, NJ, but was not warm or close to Lyle. She acted more like a critical, cold woman who would rather be a social worker to Lyle rather than a nurturing, caring, encouraging mom. She believed he was flawed in many ways. He told me she used to smack him if he got Cs on his report card. He did not get Christmas or birthday gifts if he did not do exactly what she expected of him. No wonder he ended up getting a mental illness. It does not show up out of nowhere.

And Lyle had a kind side and when I was super depressed or anxious not washing the kitchen floor and ignoring housework, so he would kindly pick up a broom to sweep and a mop to wash the floor. I felt better then and was much more apt to vacuum the living and dining rooms, also if I had a massage client while living in Hightstown in Gardenview Terrace Apartments while I was first figuring out what to do with my life after losing my first husband and family since David totally supported me financially in a very affluent way.

I tried to get clerical or other part-time jobs as a receptionist, but mostly I was turned down. I nearly got a job as a doula helping women who had just given birth with caring for their infant, by offering breastfeeding support, light housekeeping, and diaper changing the newborn so the new Mom could get some rest; but even though I was asked back for a second interview I was told the agency had a fear none of their clients would feel confident about using a doula who had a disability like mine even though I said I could still do most of the tasks the job required. I felt downhearted when I did not get the job as a doula, so Lyle recommended I go to Mercer County College to apply as a full-time student. Since my income was so low, I should be able to qualify for a PELL Grant and other free grants to pay my tuition and fees. I applied and was accepted as a full-time student at Mercer County College.

But Lyle's dark side was too often in control.

The day Lyle hit Sky for something very inconsequential, I made the decision immediately to separate from him permanently for the sake of my daughter and for my own mental health. We were separated, I was living in Hightstown with Sky in an expensive, one bedroom apartment that allowed cats (and I had three!). I allowed Lyle to stay overnight with us a few times to visit Sky mostly because he told me his uncle had asked him to leave and he had nowhere else to go. When I saw Lyle whack our little toddler off the bedpost with the back of his hand, that finally woke me up. It seemed I could tolerate the physical and psychological abuse myself because I was strong enough to handle it, but when I saw him lose control to the point that he got violent with our precious daughter I knew he had to go for good.

MERCER COUNTY COLLEGE

Most of my fears were exaggerated and irrational before I finally got accepted into Mercer County College as a full-time student majoring in Humanities and Social Sciences. I had never graduated from any college, not even the American Academy of Dramatic Arts! I did get my massage and holistic healing certification as I mentioned previously, but there were still other things I was interested in. I had a very active mind and loved learning itself. Once I got accepted into Mercer County College as a full-time student with a goal to get an Associate's Degree in Liberal Arts, I felt at least I had a specific goal. I was not sure exactly what it was, but learning new things, being with other people who stimulated my intellect, and getting involved in some other activities while at school put my focus on things, I believed were positive which meant I was able to stop thinking about being married to an abusive husband with a mental illness.

Sky was two and a half years old at the time, and luckily, had become completely potty trained. This was great because the children's nursery located right on the West Windsor campus would only accept toddlers if they were out of diapers. Prior to my going to school she was being dropped off to stay with a woman babysitter in West Windsor who watched several babies and toddlers in her home for a reasonable rate not far from where we lived, but once I was accepted as a full-time student at Mercer, I realized how much easier and more practical it would be to be able to leave her at the college nursery school.

Going to school on a full scholarship meant I needed to go full-time which meant I needed to take at least twelve credits, attend school four days per week the first semester. English Composition, French, and Psychology were my favorite subjects in freshman year. Since I was a good writer, I easily got as because my term papers were well written, and all my test scores were excellent. I had to take Algebra 1 my first semester since I'd forgotten most of my high school Algebra, but that was so easy because I had a great teacher — not to mention that when a student took tests in the testing center if you did not get the score you wanted, you'd get to take it again later. It was a different test, but you could go back home to study the things you'd forgotten or knew you got wrong, so it was very easy to get As. A score of 90-100 was an A. Now that I was doing something productive with my time by going to school the pessimism and feelings of toxic shame about feeling weak and unworthy the prior spring and summer, were finally gone completely. I enjoyed going to classes, learning new things, and believed I'd finally found something positive to do with my time. I no longer judged myself so critically, and my confidence was coming back.

I also put classified ads in the Town Topics and US1 newspapers to attract new massage and reflexology clients, and then began massaging a few clients part-time again in order to pay my car insurance which was exorbitant from speeding, careless driving tickets, and one accident. I was in the bad driver's pool in New Jersey, so I was forced to pay an extra fine to New Jersey on top of my already hefty car insurance payment. I noticed that when I was not on my mood stabilizer, I tended to get hypomanic, manic, or so enthusiastic while singing in my car that I would not notice how fast I was traveling.

I also enrolled in the yoga class that was being offered, and really loved getting back into taking hatha yoga after quitting teaching at the Princeton Family YMCA when I was eight months pregnant with Sky. The teacher at Mercer really liked me, and I got to know her well since I stayed in the class for the next semester too. She knew I'd been a former yoga instructor, liked teaching and chanting, and was a devotee of Muktananda as well. So, when she had to stop teaching classes at Mercer County College in order to do something else in another state, she recommended me to replace her to the dean of students which was quite a boon. I got paid $300 per semester for teaching a 90-minute yoga class weekly which was way more than the $5.50 per hour I was making as a peer counselor twenty hours per week. I was recommended for that position also by one of the counselors, and though it paid very little it was considered prestigious. We got to host the International Student dinner when Alpha Mu Gamma, the honors club for language students, had an induction ceremony for new students in April or May. I'd been inducted myself in the spring of 1993 as a scholar in French, and the international dinners were delicious and had a variety of favorite food for the students who took German, French, Spanish, and Italian, I still get invited every spring to go back for the induction ceremony of new students as well as to stay for the dinner which often is accompanied by a musician or dancers doing a special multi-cultural presentation. These days they even give out awards for students who excel in American sign language. Once I even sang a Spanish song on the stage that I'd learned while in the three girl show group, "Take Three". The song is called "Quando Vuelvo a Tu Lado." Everyone loved my singing, and since I don't understand the Spanish words, we had one of the former male Spanish students come up to translate each phrase right after I sang it.

Last year there was no entertainment for the International Dinner because there was some type of argument with the hired entertainer who decided to leave abruptly, so I volunteered to sing the song again spontaneously to meet the need, and I was well received.

There was also a yoga club for the students who took my hatha yoga class, so I volunteered to be the president once I found it would give me a seat on the Student Council. Being a yoga practitioner and instructor not only paid off in monetary benefits, but it also quieted my mind, so I was in better shape not just physically, but mentally and emotionally, stronger, and my body became more flexible, too.

I also volunteered to be a "Big Sister" with the "Big Brother/Big Sister" mentoring program I joined after seeing a flyer that the organization needed new volunteers.

And I volunteered to help out some organization in Trenton for the International American Rescue Workers Committee, and I picked up their need for volunteers and phone number from a flyer that was posted on the bulletin board at the local McCaffrey's Supermarket located in the Princeton Shopping Center. I called and began doing volunteer work for them, too, but I also told them I was a professional singer who would happily volunteer my time with a hired piano player named Greg Lagana whom I'd recently met at a mutual friend, Don Slepian's, surprise fiftieth birthday party, so both Greg and I volunteered to perform for the young children and teens they served for their Halloween party at a library in Trenton. We got paid in food, coffee, tea, and all the smiles we saw upon the radiant faces of the little, impressionable ones. The kids loved Greg and my singing so much that several of them drew beautiful, colorful pictures of us which we ended up taking home with us.

I was charging $45.00 per hour for Swedish massages, so somehow, with the $50 per week I got in child support, a few hundred dollars in food stamps for me and Sky, and whatever was left over from my PELL federal grant for college tuition and books and other monies given to me by the state, I was able to support myself and Sky in a comfortable lifestyle.

I made a few close friends, and was inducted into Alpha Mu Gamma, the honor society for students who excelled in languages. And by 1993 I was also inducted into the National Honor Society, Phi Theta Kappa.

Of course, it really helped my peace of mind and improved my mood when my ex-husband would give my son, Gabriel, his credit card, to treat me, Kyrie, and Sky to a delicious, healthy, relaxed dinner complete with appetizers, drinks, and desserts at the Olive Garden, Red Lobster, Ruby Tuesday's, or Fiddleheads in Jamesburg every week or two. So, even though I was aware that I was living below poverty level compared to most people I knew, I did not really feel or experience myself as a "poor" person living on the dole.

If my car needed repairs or maintenance David was pretty kind and generous. He either told me to bring my automobile to his mechanic, or if I needed new tires, I'd have Bruce from my local STS put them on my car while I waited, and David would just give him his credit card number over the phone. So, everything was handled easily without my having to worry about where the money would be coming from which would usually cause me to get depressed prior to that period of my life.

I am a sensitive, intelligent woman who was honored by the NJ State Assembly and Governor Christie Whitman in 1995 as a scholar and leader in my community the spring I was graduating from Mercer County College. A contest is held for the graduating students every year by USA Today Newspaper in conjunction with the honor society, Phi Theta Kappa, which honored the top students each semester of all the junior colleges. I was nominated by three people along with a wonderful woman, Evelyn Swain, a mother of five children and a true scholar in science and mathematics. When I was nominated, I was asked to get endorsements and letters of recommendation by teachers and other influential people at Mercer. I asked Dean Morson, the dean of students, whom I happened to respect deeply and who happened to become a good friend of mine, and my sociology professor, Art Foreman, to write letters of recommendation for me about my scholarship and leadership abilities.

I enjoyed being the instructor and president of the Yoga Club at Mercer County College as well as a paid peer counselor part-time who helped other students excel at college. Art Foreman, my sociology professor, was well liked; and he was also the person we chose to be the advisor to sponsor the yoga club. Art accompanied us as as a chaperon on a field trip up to the Siddha Yoga Meditation ashram in the Catskills one week-end. About eight of the yoga students accompanied us. It was fun and educational for everyone.

JUST ME AND SKY (1994)

The wonderfully positive and miraculous thing that happened to me was I made special friends at Mercer County College with a young woman and single mother like myself named Vicky. She was a very intelligent, sweet single mom who owned her own home in Trenton. As we became closer friends, she learned of my desperate situation living on and off with an abusive husband. She was the woman who told me about WomanSpace, where I took classes while still living in my home in Hightstown. WomanSpace provided safe housing to married women and their children whose spouses were abusing them physically or psychologically. They not only provided housing, but counseling, and things like clothes, toiletries, and practical things women needed. I believe transportation too. They also supported our education. Fortunately, I never needed to live there, but I did avail myself of their classes and counseling services. I finally "got smart", and I stopped allowing Lyle to manipulate, control, or charm me into allowing him to be part of my life anymore. I began to attend some of the classes there at Vicky's suggestion. I met Vicky while attending classes Mercer, where we would have coffee in the mornings or lunch together in the large cafeteria in the afternoons. They sometimes had educational or musical programs with small bands, so I'd get up to dance and sing along with them.

WomanSpace was where and when, in the early nineteen nineties, I learned about the violent, usually violated male abusive personality type – the type of man who harms you one moment blaming his victim for the violence, then in order to manipulate you into taking him back he comes back very apologetic, loving and sweet with flowers, gifts, and cards just to get in your good graces and back into your home in order to have sex with "his" woman only to abuse her again a day or week later when all his crazy shit hits the fan again and the subconscious pattern is triggered by something his lady partner said or did.

Luckily, Vicky was kind enough to offer me a large bedroom in her house in which Sky and I could live with our three cats along with their litter box, as well as the use of her kitchen, living room, bathrooms, and some limited space in her basement for storage of my belongings.

In October, 1994, I moved my bed, dresser, and nightstand into that extra bedroom, as well as all my clothes, shoes, purses, and other things. And she was kind enough to allow me to bring my precious pets; she let me keep my three kitties in the room while I attended my classes during the day until I'd come back and let them out or spend time with them in my room. I had the litter box in there too. I was paying $350 for the month which seemed like a break to me because I was paying $584.00 per month at Gardenview Terrace for a crappy old one bedroom apartment with an old kitchen, living room, and bath. There were occasional cockroaches flooding in from the next-door neighbors' apartments at times which kind of bothered me because I'd never had that problem before. We also had fleas in our bedroom closet, but that was my fault from not taking the time or extra expense to use the $50 per month per cat, Frontline flea control medication on all three cats, and the cheaper flea collars never really worked, so what to do?

In Hightstown, I had lost one of my kittens to severe flea infestation. I didn't know that could happen. I was sad and just devastated, but I could not keep up with all the expense of my apartment, car insurance, groceries, etc. I felt overwhelmed by the full life I'd created during times of hypo-mania and mania when I had poor discernment and terrible judgment.

Living with Vicky and her sweet son, Brian, was not the Ritz, but I knew it was temporary and Vicky had a good head on her shoulders, so I learned some things from her. Also, she did not let anyone push her around, including Lyle. He was not allowed to set foot on her property. Since he was permitted to see Sky two week-ends per month he had to meet me at the train station in Trenton where I'd walk her to him with a baby bag filled with clothes, diapers, a bottle, and maybe a lunch or some snacks.

By that time, I'd taken Lyle to Family Court at the suggestion of my babysitter in East Windsor, so I was getting child support regularly which helped pay for diapers, a little food, sometimes an electric bill, and it kept us from arguing about the small amounts of money he'd give me occasionally to help pay for Sky's needs. Somehow, he believed putting a ten- or twenty-dollar bill in my hand or pocket every week or so was enough to keep our young toddler fed and clothed.

I don't remember everything because there were restraining orders filed a few times.

The problem I had was that Lyle did not always honor the restraining order, especially when I lived by myself in Hightstown. Sometimes I'd come back from school and he'd be sitting outside on the porch waiting for me with flowers and a greeting card apologizing for bad behaviors and saying he truly loved me and he was a changed man; he also said he loved our family and wanted to visit Sky. There was a part of me that believed I'd be a victim the rest of my life and would never be able to rid myself of this crazy, immature, violent, psychopathic man.

But my angel and God's grace were still on my side, and a few good things happened to us. One boon was I had joined a group of women a few times who all had physical disabilities and were gathered together to help support each other. At the second meeting a woman named Joan mentioned to me that she lived in a really nice apartment complex called Griggs Farm that was specifically designed and appropriated as affordable housing for senior citizens, people with disabilities, and single dads and moms who had very low to moderate income for condos and/or town homes there. One had to apply to Princeton Community Housing giving all sources of income, tax returns, etc. in order to qualify for this really exceptionally low-income housing. Most people who filed for housing there were on a long waiting list, some for years. I checked out the complex and visited Joan at her apartment. It was a very nice development whose streets were lined with pretty trees, colorful gardens, a tennis court, a basketball court, and it was well maintained. I applied immediately. I also applied at a beautiful property in West Windsor around the same time.

It would be some time before I was able to move to Princeton, two years and three months to be exact... I happened to get the phone call that my name had come up on the housing list two months after I moved into Vicky's home in Trenton. I remember it was early December. A woman called to say "Miss Olson, your name is the next one on the list to get a low-income apartment in Griggs Farm in Princeton. It would be available in February of next year. Are you still interested?"

"Are you kidding? Of course, I am. I've been waiting for this moment for two years and three months now."

I felt a bit guilty because I'd be moving out of Vicky's place just a few months after moving in, but we could still be friends, and it turned out within several months, Vicky and her son, Brian, would sell their place and move into a newer, nicer home in Roosevelt, NJ. I even helped her move, and we remained friends for a few years after that.

Lyle's mom has been dead for years now; she died from lupus at 50 years old, or I would not be writing negative things about her, but these are the facts. She hit him in front of his sister, he said, by pulling his pants down right in front of Nicole, humiliating him. Nicole would end up going on to graduate from college with an MBA and to law school after that, eventually becoming a successful attorney. Lyle's mother did a great job supporting him financially with an excellent job as a Vice Principal, but she had the warmth of a cold fish. She was completely against our marriage as was my own mother since Lyle and I met at the Carrier Clinic when we were both patients hospitalized three for mental illness in the spring of 1988.

Lyle and I were finally divorced six years after I filed for divorce. We were separated on and off in 1990 and for most of our marriage. I tried to do everything by myself through Legal Aide, but I was unable to get Lyle to agree to give me any monies toward my pain and suffering as well as some decent child support for Sky, so, at the suggestion of my dear friend, Zara Rose, I contacted an attorney she knew, Marvin Grossman. Though I had to give him 1/3 of the monies he collected for me it was worth it to finally be free, and I finally ended up with a bit less than $15,000, which went straight into the bank for Sky's education and the moneys we absolutely needed to live on.

It was not long before Ernie and I let our friendship become closer, and the intellectual and physical attraction blossomed and grew into a sensuous, and then a sexual relationship. I'm not sure why, but it was probably the best sex I'd ever had in the beginning, and after some time Ernie would invite me to spend the nights sleeping in his bed which was also located in the same upstairs area as his office. It was the first time I experienced deep relaxation with a massage first and tantra which is a relaxed way of allowing energy to flow and focusing on the woman's pleasure first before the man even considers having an orgasm. It is a delicate dance of communication and loving expression of both partners for each other. Ernie sent me through the roof with our first kiss. The Soul is in the kiss, and I knew if the kiss was great the rest of our lovemaking would evolve gradually into something sensitive, romantic, and beautiful. Ernie was not a jealous man like David and Lyle had been. He was a relaxed man who was evolving spiritually and into holistic things like myself.

Of course, there was no commitment, no pressure to pay bills, and no children for either of us to support. David was wealthy enough to handle all those financial matters for both our children which left me fee to enjoy myself without responsibilities for the first time in my life.

Ernie and I were relating moment by moment as if we were new just tuning into one another s' needs for pleasure and Connection living and expressing love in the present moment through the connection of our bodies and souls. It seemed as if he knew what pleasured me intuitively without my having to tell him... I would think in my mind about what I liked and what felt delicious and good in my body, and Ernie would deliver whatever it was – like kisses on my neck and soft nibbles of my ears, soft, sensuous long, light strokes on my face, neck, breasts, back, and buttocks. Everything he did felt better than any man I'd ever been with – even better than my father, but this time it was natural and mutually desired, so there was no guilt or shame, only pleasure. That was the beginning of my good experiences with my sensuality and tantric sex putting me into a delightful, moving meditation which went from deep relaxation into contentment and gradually higher and deeper levels or waves of bliss and soft orgasmic euphoria which was completely different from the powerful, intense, sometimes explosive orgasms I gave myself quickly and greedily using my vibrator which I playfully call my "Power Tool" or "electrical banana" as Donovan called it in his song, "Mellow Yellow", which was bound to be a sudden craze". The electrical banana was indeed to be the very next phase for a woman to take full responsibility for having her own orgasm without the need for a man. It's nice in a pinch if one has a good imagination to go along with the use of the vibrator, but there is no love, no connection, no waves of bliss like a woman or man can feel during "tantric sex" as one gets deeper and deeper into the pleasures of each little erotic spot on and in the body. For me there are levels of pleasure that are so satisfying by both giving and receiving both oral and vaginal sex after some digital stimulation and spiritually connecting through deep, romantic kissing.

I have been polyamorous with multiple partners, but I care for, love, and connect emotionally, physically, and spiritually, with all of them. Each one has been in my life for years; we share similar interests and hobbies; and all my partners know about one another since I am extremely honest and open in every area of my life with my closest friends. I have one partner who is married who came to me initially as a client but after a few months that relationship became sexual because he told me his wife has an incurable disease that prevents her from having intercourse. I met her several years after I began having a relationship with my massage client; and the three of us have shared three way sensuous massages which has been both therapeutic and pleasurable for the two of them and improved the quality of the physical intimacy in their marriage.

I am truly committed to the wellbeing of each one of my partners. As opposed to being promiscuous and only into first chakra sex with one-night stands which is something I did in the beginning of my sexual life at nineteen which left me feeling empty, guilty, disrespected, or ashamed. As I have matured and learned more about tantric sex and polyamory, I realize that there is not one person outside of me that can make me happy. I am the only person responsible for my happiness. I have different kinds of relationships with several different men as well as a few close relationships with women, and in combination I feel satisfied in many different ways, not just physical, mental, emotional, or spiritual. Most of my lovers have shared an appreciation of either music, art, metaphysics, or dance. Since those are the things that make my heart sing it is nice to be able to share those fun activities with others.

I consider myself bi-curious, though I have had a few threesomes with a woman including Ernie and his new lady friend, Susan, following our break-up. I completely enjoyed kissing her, fondling her breasts, massaging one another, and different positions with which to share pleasure for all three of us including massaging of our backs, buttocks and shoulders. But I particularly enjoyed talking to Susan and getting to know her intellectually and spiritually. Susan knew all the delicate, subtle things a woman likes to feel like the stroking of her face, neck and long light effleurage stroking of my entire back from the top of my spine to the bottom. I also love to get the inside of my neck kissed and light kisses inside of my ears which I will happily do another woman or man if he or she enjoys it.

David, who was providing for my first two children, also continued to provide some support for me even after my divorce from Lyle. As a single mom raising Sky, I would slide down the emotional scale from frustration to overwhelmment, when I'd get way too much mail, unpaid bills, and lots of clutter on my desk and in my living space in general. It was sometimes impossible – I felt so exhausted that I could not properly feed myself, do housework, and was too tired to work or even want to work. I'd very quickly slide down the emotional scale into pessimism, hopelessness, despair, and finally depression into anxiety and fear, all the way down to terror where I'd even be afraid to wake up most mornings because I would immediately become aware of my negative thoughts, what I perceived as a filthy house, bills piling up on my desk, etc.

In retrospect, every time I got depressed or suicidal, I wish I would have been able to accept myself as I was, realizing that I was going through a lot of struggles and challenges in my life at those times which required gentleness, kindness, and nurturing love like a mother cat would be with a wounded kitten. These days I try to be gentler with myself, nurture myself with massage or getting a pedicure or something to make me feel better as opposed to being so punitive.

After all, if anyone I know is depressed or going through a hard time, I am very sweet, encouraging, kind, and try to be gentle with them the way I know in my heart that Jesus and our angels would be. So why was it so easy for me to be kind and good to my mom, a dear friend, nurturing and loving to my son or daughters if they were ill. I was even loving, gentle, and caring if I found a wounded animal like a little bird or even a spider or other insect, so why could I not be loving and extremely caring to myself as well, God's precious child?

The sad thing was that during depressions it was so difficult for me to live with myself feeling like a victim, especially a person who was negative and not grateful for my many blessings. I hated myself because I was not feeling grateful for all I had and was not doing my sadhana (a Sanskrit word for following a devotional path or actually performing daily spiritual practices like meditation, chanting, and contemplation. I suppose a Christian would consider reading the Bible daily or studying the scriptures weekly with a support group from their church their own personal sadhana.

But most of my practices were done alone because most of the Satsang's given at the meditation centers in Siddha Yoga did not exist in my area anymore. The main ashram in South Fallsburg also closed down in the nineties. It is sad that in those cases where we have given up on ourselves that that is the most important time for us to ask for spiritual and emotional support through affirmative prayer, by talking to our pastor or minister, going to church weekly to remind ourselves that although I had forgotten about God's love for me, and abandoned ALL my spiritual practices, God Himself never stopped loving me and would NEVER Leave me. The reason I stopped going to church or asking for prayer was because I felt terribly ashamed and embarrassed that I had become so weak and lacked faith in God.

My sleep was disturbed and usually I'd have to call a psychiatrist and psychologist in desperation when I began to have suicidal ideations in these times of crisis if I'd already stopped my medications and psychiatric treatment because I was doing very well. Sometimes I'd be discharged from a health center by my psychologist because she'd say "You are doing very well and well enough that we'd like to replace you with someone else who really needs treatment" like my psychologist did at Oaks Integrative Care in Lawrenceville. But sometimes something would precipitate my going into despair and depression again. Most of the time I felt so hopeless and unworthy in those dark nights of my soul in which my despair and suffering was so acute that I did not even believe I was worthy of prayer. Well, that type of unforgiving, judgmental attitude did not help soothe me at all. It made me feel more worthless than ever.

I felt like I was four years old again, a time in which my mom was hyper-critical of me. It did not matter how I tried to please her. No matter what I did as a little girl to try to help out by being sweet or helpful.

If I was not a good girl or I ended up spilling milk on the floor, got fingerprints on the clean white wall, or soiled one of my pretty dresses, mommy would start screaming curses at me. I'd run from her feeling sad, angry, and afraid. Many times, I remember running up to my bedroom while she was still screaming and cursing downstairs in the kitchen while cleaning up the mess I'd made with an accidental spill; it was certainly not on purpose. I did not deserve her abusive yelling and ranting. I'd throw myself on my bed and cry so hard for so long that I lost my breath and would hyperventilate. Eventually, I was so exhausted I'd cry myself to sleep. Then she'd come upstairs after her screaming to apologize and invite me down to have supper by myself, but I was so hurt and angry at that point. I'd stuff all that anger into my subconscious because I saw her behavior as hateful, harmful and not OK because it devastated me. It was not so much her words but her tone that frightened me. I ended up making expressing any type of anger wrong and bad, so I'd end up turning all that subconscious rage and anger for her inward upon myself.

Unfortunately, I carried this type of behavior into my adulthood in these two abusive relationships, but I did not realize it. Nor did I know that it was OK for me to say "No" to people who wanted things of me, nor did I know it was healthy to have boundaries.

For example, my first husband would act in a similar fashion ranting and raving at me because I made a special dinner of tofu and steamed veggies as opposed to his usual salad and plain tofu, and he'd end up going ballistic on me. That four-year-old in 28-year-old Meryl Olson- was re-creating that same scenario with him so that I could heal all that rage and anger I had suppressed as a child with my mom. Sometimes I'd cry and take his occasional violent outbursts personally, but, for the most part, I was passive and forgave him all transgressions. I did not want to rock the boat because he was my husband, I believed I truly loved him, he was a great father and provider, and I was committed to working through any obstacles that came up in our relationship; I think I felt initially helpless to do anything about it because his behavior was so irrational it did not make any sense to me.

My relationship with Lyle was more of the same controlling type behavior, only the abuse was worse and more frequent. I tolerated the hitting and choking for a year or so because we had a family, and being a woman with two disabilities I definitely did not feel confident enough to care for Sky all on my own – until I had no choice but to trust God and learn how to care for both of us with the support and encouragement of family members, counselors, close friends, chiropractors, and a team of doctors and home health aides involved in our care.

MEETING DOCTOR AND MISS UFO

Back in the nineteen nineties while I was attending Mercer County College my boyfriend, Ernie, told me about a UFO and paranormal conference taking place at the Days Inn in Bordentown, NJ. It sounded like it would be fun to attend because I already believed in extra-terrestrials, angels, and could see UFOs from the time I was in my mid-twenties. Pat, a very handsome Italian looking man with dark brown hair who wore very nice New Mexican like turquoise jewelry and was well dressed wearing a yellow shirt, a nice beige jacket, and a multi- colored tie with planets and a space ship emblazoned upon it, was the facilitator who welcomed the guests and participants at 10 AM when the conference began as well as introduced each speaker before they came up to give their lectures.

Most were authors and experts in their particular fields. Many of them showed videos and photographs projected upon a screen for us all to see of UFOs, different planets like Mars that had either buildings or beings living upon them. We even listened to astronauts over the phone during some of the conferences like Edgar Mitchell. Both Mitchell and John Glen admitted to knowing about the secret space program, and both had seen unidentified flying objects which appeared to them to be alien space crafts.

There were all types of people at the conference sharing amazing experiences from people who had been abducted by aliens to those who had worked for the secret space program run by our government that most presidents from Eisenhower onward knew about. There was a woman named Nicolette from California who channeled races from the "Other Side" and sometimes angels or angelic beings. All the beings were benevolent, but we also learned about extra-terrestrial beings like "the Grays" and "Reptilians" who were, according to the lecturers I heard, malevolent beings.

Once we heard from a man who had such an extraordinary experience with an extra-terrestrial spacecraft that a movie was made about him called "Fire in the Sky". Travis Walton had been accidentally abducted by an alien space ship when he and his buddies saw an amazing light in the sky and took off in their truck to follow it. Travis got out of the truck to get a closer look at the craft, but he disappeared right in front of his friends' eyes. He was missing for five whole days while his buddies were questioned by the authorities who disbelieved their story thinking there was some type of foul play. Anyway, Travis was released five days later once the extra-terrestrial beings were able to repair the damage done to him when he got sucked into the force field of their ship. He's written a book about the experience and travels all over the globe to UFO paranormal conferences sharing his experiences.

A few years before Travis Walton I heard a man named Preston Nichols talk about both the Philadelphia Experiment and the Montauk Project.

I was very impressed by the lecture he gave as he was incredibly intelligent and had documented evidence to back up many of the things he said.

Besides being an electronic wiz from the time he was a kid he claimed to have had the honor and pleasure of being abducted by the Pleiadeans where he was taken aboard one of their ships and then taken to their star system.

Since his body was not strong enough to withstand so much light frequency, he claimed to have had a sort of death of his former physical structure, and was transformed into a new being of Light by their doctors. He came back to Earth a changed being. Preston had been very sickly as a teenager, but when he returned from his visit to the Pleades he felt energized and in perfect health!

In some metaphysical books what happened to Preston and other physical incarnates that experience a near death experience is referred to as the "walk-in" phenomena. However, according to my non-physical friend, Abraham, it's not like discarnate beings are waiting around for an entity to die in order for them to take over that soul's form. It's more like the same entity chose that transition for growth and then they decide while in the non-physical realm to return to the physical plane incarnated with much more of their Inner Being physically present upon the Earth plane.

Each one of us has a non-physical counterpart even while we are incarnated here upon the earth plane. We are truly multi-dimensional beings existing simultaneously in more places than just one. I'm not quite sure how to explain it myself because I do not have a conscious understanding of all that is going on. This is just the wisdom and knowledge passed on to me from Abraham, the entity that teaches through Esther and Jerry Hicks about the Laws of Attraction and Deliberate Creation.

When this amazing man, Preston Nichols, was returned to Earth he recalled everything he saw and learned from the Pleiadeans and used the information he gleaned to guide him in building a sound studio of an exemplary technology and to work on a time machine for the US government. which was built and used at Montauk Point in Long Island, New York.

It was actually Preston who had built Bell Studios, which was the same studio in which many superstar singers and musicians had made their albums and master tapes. He claims to have worked with greats like Jim Morrison who, according to Preston, liked to record in his underwear or in the nude. Preston also claims to have known and worked with Frankie Valli, and eventually the Beetles. All this information can be found in his book, "The Music of Time."

Preston even claims that he saw Jim Morrison still alive but existing in some type of comatose state following a bad experience or overdose of drugs. It's hard to believe, but has anyone ever seen his dead body? According to Preston, this was a business decision made by the recording executives who did not want the public and the fans to know what truly happened to Jim. Pretty freaky, stuff, huh? My beloved, Gary, thought I was a real nut case when I told him that. He still thinks I'm a nut, but an adorable one.

I met Karin about the same time I met her father, Pat at the conferences. She was charismatic, like myself, sexy, and attractive with long light brown hair, and she seemed to be friends with all the people who came to the conferences. A very outgoing and gregarious young lady like myself. She said she was psychic and had a gift for talking to disembodied beings on "the Other Side", especially those that had died suddenly and mysteriously so that their relatives were uncertain of how or when they died since they just disappeared and were not heard from again after taking a long trek or hike into the woods. Anyway, we got to know one another quickly, and it seemed like we were kindred spirits because we had similar experiences and belief systems. Karin was also a single mom like me, though she was younger than me so her daughter, Abbey, was only about nine years old when I met them. Abbey is now a grown young woman of 23 years, with a full-time job. When she was little, Abbey and I used to make art together sometimes painting or using markers to make colorful, abstract pictures. I also gave Abbey beginning piano lessons for about nine months. I was not a piano teacher, but she was just a beginner, so I was able to teach her basic notes, chords, scales, and a bit of meter and rhythm. I never had piano lessons myself except one, but I did take sight singing lessons with Elizabeth Hodes while attending the American Academy of Dramatic Arts at 21 years old so I got rudimentary training in playing the piano. I could at least play all of the scales, transpose, and identify the keys.

Pat, Karin and I were to take trips together, including one to Florida to visit their friends, Chuck and Gracie, then further south to visit Pat's friend, OJ, in February of 2011.

TRIP WITH ZARA ROSE

Another interesting and fun trip I took was with my special, longtime friend, Zara Rose, to Arizona and New Mexico. Z told me in one of our phone conversations she wanted to travel out west to see if she could find different shop owners that sold folk art, to take some of her beautiful, original painted and personalized clay rattles and other folk art, on consignment. She was hoping to share her pottery and sculptures with more people and market it to a larger audience. I told her I wanted to travel with her that June since classes would be out and Sky would be on vacation with her dad. Her son, Elijah, would be coming with us which was fine with me because I loved him ever since he was born and considered him my "godson".

Zara said "I'd love for you to come, but are you sure you have enough stamina for this We will be stopping a lot and visiting lots of shops, so it could be very tiring for you. Zara is a Taurus, and my moon is in Taurus which means I'm very persistent at best or very stubborn, at my worst. Once I've set my mind to do, be, or have something, even if others think I'm not up to the task, almost nothing stops me. If I want to go on a cruise or some vacation, I might not even have $100 in the savings, but if I really want something, somehow magically, by the alchemical power of decision and intention, money appears, and all factors line up in the universe conspiring to bring me exactly what I want.

That happened with both Abraham-Hicks cruises, mine and Gary's trip to Mountain Quest Institute, and my trip with Patsy to travel to Kentucky and Florida to see her folks and find the perfect massage school in the state of Florida. Then, once found, all the money, right people, the perfect car, and place to live appeared as if by magic.

That is what happened with most of my trip with Zara Rose. We had quite an adventure.

We decided to fly out separately to Tuscon where we'd booked several days at the Best Western, an inexpensive, but comfortable hotel with free breakfast downstairs, because I could be there a day or two earlier than Zara who needed to wait until Elijah got out of school, so I did my journaling, enjoyed the pool, and connected with a person from the Siddha Yoga Meditation Center of Tuscon who kindly picked me up in her car for the early morning chant, the Guru Gita, which was at 6:30 AM. What a great way to begin the morning! I love chanting the names of God, and the Guru Gita (Song of the Guru) is one of my favorite chants. A ninety-minute chant that is a great way to begin one's morning in a place of love, song, and meditation. It literally changes the vibrations of the room and makes you feel relaxed, happy, blessed, and in a state of sublime peace and equanimity.

In Sedona one afternoon we ate lunch at an outdoor cafe and had just ordered our meals when a colorful butterfly lit on my right shoulder giving me the sweetest ticklish sensation making me feel very loved, appreciated, and special. I did not move too much for fear she would leave me. The butterfly stayed on my shoulder for a blessed several minutes until our food was brought out by the waitress. It was almost as if she knew it was her time to depart when I mentally told the butterfly I needed to use my right arm in order to eat my lunch, when, at that very moment, she bid me adieu with a gentle flap of her delicate wings and went on her merry way. It was such a memorable moment because I thought "I must be very special, or my vibration was so peaceful that a living creature who is accustomed to flying all the time would give me the gift of its darshan (Sanskrit for "divine glance") When the term darshan is used it is normally used in the context of talking about a saint or guru giving someone the gift of their glance or welcome, but since the guru is not limited to any one form, and the same as God's creative force it can come through any person, place, or animal that is imbued with the power of the Guru's Shakti (active, creative force of God).

While in Arizona with Zara I noticed a man outside the grocery store in a wheelchair begging for alms and food. I wanted to buy him the healthy food inside the grocery store, but when I told him my intention, he said he didn't really care for vegetables, but he preferred a hamburger with cheese and french fries which is what he asked for specifically, so I got into my car to look for the nearest Burger King or MacDonald's and brought it back to him. I could tell from the way he was speaking he was not just homeless but in a very angry, negative state of mind, so when I came out of the supermarket before I left in my car I prayed to Jesus for his well-being, and within what seemed like moments my prayers for him were answered. I went inside the supermarket to buy him some fruits and then to the local burger joint to get what he told me he really wanted. By the time I got back I noticed a tall, dark haired nicely dressed man talking to our new friend, Joe, in the wheelchair. It turned out it was his former landlord who, by chance, crossed his path outside the supermarket while I was at the burger joint. My friend in the wheelchair thanked me for the bag of food and quickly sped away rolling his wheelchair with speed and determination away from his former spot where he had been sitting dejected begging for alms and food. I was curious what made him leave so abruptly, so I spoke to the man who was just talking to him, and he said, "Don't worry about Joe. He was just temporarily down on his luck. One of my rooms to let is vacant right now, so I told him to go there and spend the night. And maybe a week or two until I find another tenant. I was so pleased about the speed at which my prayers for him had been answered, so that I was fortunate enough to witness the "demonstration", the good results of my faith and Jesus' work. I don't know how long he was able to stay there, but I know his negative state of mind had been turned around by my kindness and he would continue to improve with Jesus' blessings and grace. So, never underestimate the power of prayer, a caring smile, and a genuine desire to reach out to a fellow human being who is always so much more than our limited perception. He or she is Consciousness in form, a brother or sister of yours, an individualized aspect in the Body of Christ. I truly believe that your smile, kindness, and genuine love for your brother or sister has far reaching effects, much more than we can see or realize in the current moment. We must all open our eyes to the suffering of our fellow man and the plants and animals who are also deeply affected by our actions. Love, compassion, and positive thoughts and feelings have a ripple effect and eventually will be felt all over the planet – just like our anger, judgmental or mean-spirited thoughts are experienced by others on a subtle level even though we are not aware, but selfishly think we can spout meanness and erupt in a violent way whenever we feel like it. Not true.

Zara and I went to the town of Jerome, which was overflowing with arts and crafts. We stopped at a little shop that sold souvenirs, stones, and trinkets. Zara talked to the manager about consigning her stuff. I looked for souvenirs to bring home for my children, and while at the register I talked for quite a while to the store clerk, who introduced himself as Michael Veritas, an artist and sculptor. He seemed to have quite an attraction for me. In fact, he seemed to be so carried away by my beauty and charm he tried to convince Zara to leave me behind at the shop with him. I had just stopped taking my medication about a month before we left for vacation. My doctor said I was on such a low dosage she did not see any harm in me stopping it for a while to see how I would feel.

Well, I felt fine, but my boundaries were not the best, and my judgment was impaired which is what seemed to happen many of the times I stopped taking the mood stabilizer, Depakote. I almost let this stranger, Michael, sweep me off my feet right there in the shop, and Zara had to put her foot down to make sure I left from the shop with her and Elijah. I did take Michael's store card upon which he put his cell phone number, and two months later go back to visit with my two-year-old daughter, Sky, in tow, to visit him after taking a three-day ride on a Greyhound bus to visit him.

In the meantime, the heat became intense, and Zara wanted to use the air conditioning for most of the rest of our trip when I did not.

I loved Sedona, and clearly remember the beauty of Oak Creek Canyon which, for some reason, the red rocks of the earth reminded me of Egypt even though I'd never been there except in my dreams and by watching motion pictures. We were experiencing time in Sedona in a different way. I remember chanting the Guru Gita there one morning and feeling tremendous euphoria. We spent just a few days in Sedona, and I was glad because my mood was getting very high. I'm not sure if it was just the effects of Sedona, or perhaps more of the medication was out of my system by that point.

We drove through parts of New Mexico too which was also beautiful and contained a lot of artists as well as art shops. The heat and long car ride were starting to take a toll on me, and Zara and I began to bicker. Thank God for Elijah who was a mediator and made fun of our petty arguments. We had some fun times, but when we finally parted it was a relief for all of us.

POLYAMORY

What is polyamory? According to Debra Taj Anapol, a tantra teacher and clinical psychologist who was one of the founders of the polyamory movement in the nineteen eighties, polyamory is loosely defined as any romantic or sexual relationship with multiple partners with the knowledge and consent of all involved. I had the privilege to briefly meet Taj after she taught one of her tantra workshops at Earthgate retreat center, the bed and breakfast inn located in Dingman's Ferry in the Poconos owned by my dear friend, and former lover, Ernie. It is called "Earthgate" because there are five vortices of energy on the property and it serves as a portal between the earth and celestial realms. Ernie is Pleiadean and works with the Intergalactic Federation like our friend, Michael, and several of my UFO friends. Earthgate contains five bedrooms and an extra barn and garage next door which Ernie refinished to create an extra place to store his tools and to use as a hatha yoga and retreat center in which metaphysical teachers can rent out to have special workshops. And use as a bed and breakfast. It is a really cool, immaculate place to meet really unique, artistic, unconventional folks, like those from the UFO community, yoga community, and metaphysical crowd. When Ernie and I dated, we experimented with polyamory mostly because we lived far from one another, and many women were attracted to him, just as men flocked to me.

After we broke up, we remained close friends and lovers; if I went to visit him, I still brought my new boyfriends up to Earthgate to meet him and enjoy the beauty of the place – especially if we made time to stay overnight.

Once, in 2002, I had the honor and privilege of bringing up my new boyfriend, Glen, a musician from Maine and we all used the outdoor jacuzzi together.

Ernie met a new woman friend after we broke up, a bi-sexual nurse named Susan whom I came to know and love while we'd hang out together in Ernie's hot tub outside. Prior to that we'd met at Ernie's home in Tinton Falls where he lived in a trailer outside his friends', Mary and Bill's, home. When Sue came, she organized, and transformed his first place. They got along well together and Ernie became more focused on his dreams like living in a special, clothing optional, polyamorous community. Sue not only ad a good relationship with him, but was supportive of him finding and purchasing a new home together with her where he could further his deepest dreams.

Susan, who was a bit masculine and very strong woman, had had a prior relationship with a woman chiropractor with whom she lived for a while. But she also had a daughter by her first husband, I believe. She had heard a lot about me from Ernie and how pretty, strong, courageous, and sweet I was having overcome the challenges of bipolar illness and serious suicide attempts.

Sue's job was to be on call at night as a manager for a nursing and health company who had to send other nurses to a person's home if someone died during the night, or if there was some other emergency during crazy hours, so often we'd all spend the first part of the night together following dinner in or out for the first several hours until she was on call. Initially, we could all dine together, relax, chat, make love in Ernie's bed, share "pillow talk", watch some excellent TV, and share as a triad. When Sue was finally forced to take regular calls, we would let her go to sleep alone in another room, and Ernie and I would sleep alone first in a trailer in Tinton Falls, NJ; but after Sue and Ernie purchased the home together in the Poconos with several bedrooms and a finished basement where there were more places to sleep, Ernie and I would stay alone in the king size bed of the Master bedroom while Susan, in her own bedroom, focused on her phone calls and night nursing work. Then we'd all cuddle together again at morning light or by 10 or 11 AM, and then have brunch together in town or next door at a neat place that sold mostly healthy, nutritious omelets, oatmeal, and freshly made blueberry or banana whole wheat pancakes. This routine made me feel very happy, because I loved, adored, and respected Sue. I had never really thought I'd enjoy being sexual with a woman, but I did enjoy the energy of our menage trois. Also, Sue was a very intelligent, grounded and spiritual woman with large breasts who was a great kisser with whom I could explore some new sensations. I really loved being French kissed by her, and having her lick my pussy. She was great at massaging my back too. I loved it when both Sue and Ernie would pleasure me simultaneously and then we'd switch off.

Ernie and Susan lived together for several years, and I found other special boyfriends after I moved away, but when I was single or somewhat manic, I'd take a trip up to Earthgate to be with Ernie overnight. I always enjoyed my trips to the Poconos, and sometimes wondered if Sue was a bit jealous because she and I were no longer lovers, and I'm not certain but I do not think she and Ernie were connecting that way very much anymore with all the responsibilities of having to meet the hefty mortgage every month and all the little daily crap that gets in the way of two people being romantic with one another. Plus, I believe Sue was menopausal since she was several years older than me. Ernie was eleven years older, but he was very athletic, healthy, and strong. We always made love at 6 AM when we first became girlfriend and boyfriend, and he could easily lift me up from underneath my bottom for minutes at a time to enjoy intercourse, and I really believed he loved me. He told me he did, but he was not interested in sharing a long-term relationship with a woman who had a toddler. And two children who were six and eight years older than Sky, my youngest. He was never really into kids. I truly appreciated Sue allowing me to spend time at Earthgate at all, especially if I was sleeping in Ernie's bed.

However, Sue once told me she thought it was a very good thing for Ernie to be with me sometimes. "He is always much softer and nicer to me after you leave", she told me on a few occasions when I asked her if she minded my coming for the week-end every now and then. Sue left Earthgate to move to California to be with her daughter and grandchild a few years after we had a big celebration for her sixtieth birthday.

I always wondered how much my background contributed to my ability to enjoy "unusual" relationships.

From the time I was a baby I was curious about my body, especially the pleasant sensations I felt while exploring my fingers, toes, neck, breasts, and genitalia. It seemed natural and normal to me to "learn" how to masturbate to orgasm when I was only five. My friend, Christie, taught me how to please myself in the privacy of her parents' dark, cool garage of her home four doors down from my parents' home in Holmdel, NJ.

Christie and I were both raised Catholic, so it was naturally expected I would be a virgin until I found the perfect Knight in shining armor and was married to him. Of course, when I was very little (four or five, perhaps) my mom told me what she was taught by her mom, my favorite grandparent, Lucia Comeforo Vere. Anyway, all Catholics, I believe, were told that it was a SIN to touch ourselves "down there". Gosh almighty! How could something that felt so pleasurable inside my "Cooley" which is what my mom called the entrance to my vagina, inner and outer inner lips of my labia, clit, anus, hiney, and all. All that stuff "down there" was sinful and "dirty" as far as she was concerned—just a place one uses to go to the bathroom, needs to wash every day because otherwise, all women would be smelly and dirty. The crazy thing is I knew that God made my genitals for something sacred like SEX (whatever that was) to make babies like me, my brother, Pete, and my little brother Scott, who was born nine years after me on December 5, 1964, so when Mommy brought him home, I fell in love with him, and believed him to be "my" baby too.

The only people who know I still enjoy more than one monogamous relationship with my current beau of five years, Gary, are him, my family members, and the lucky few with whom I choose to share friendship, intimacy, and love. Several of these partners have been in my life for over a dozen years, and one I have known for thirty-three, but have been intimate with for about half that time is my dearest friend, another massage therapist, who also has a girlfriend in New York who is his primary relationship. Our primary partners know about our other intimate friendships, but we do not need to go into any of the details about the relationship for fear of jealousy or our main partners feeling unloved or disrespected. I am completely honest with Gary about any other friendships and relationships I have because I care about him enough to tell him the Whole Truth about me. I always tell him where I am going and with whom I will be so he can always know where I am and not worry about me. But I highly I doubt if I will ever marry again because, so far that conventional type of relationship with two controlling men has made me very unhappy.

I am glad that I married so that I could have my three children while in wedlock so as not to confuse them. Though, look at actors and life mates, Goldie Hawn and Kurt Russell. They have four children between them, and they have as yet to tie the knot during the many years they have lived happily together.

Gosh, even thinking about being locked up and all in knots makes my stomach feel contracted. So many folks have judgments about this lifestyle. In fact, so did I at first. I am not into swinging, lying or cheating. I like honesty. I love people. I am attracted to certain qualities in men and others in women. I have been intimating with both sexes even though I am wired to be with men. I prefer being heterosexual most of the time though there have been occasions that I previously mentioned where I've been bi-sexual in the triad with Sue and Ernie, a man I've loved for a long time.

Anyway, when Sue and I met in his outdoor jacuzzi one day we enjoyed getting to know one another better after a nice friendship had developed. So, for a while, we became a trio and enjoyed hanging out doing things on week-ends when I'd drive to Tinton Falls from my apartment in Princeton.

They would eventually split, but I enjoyed several years of their unique, unconventional, unconditionally loving and open partnership. We all loved each other and got along well when I'd come up to visit for a week-end. Sometimes when I was a bit hypomanic, I'd come out to visit with my collage material singing loudly in the car and in a very creative mode Sue would sometimes be somewhat annoyed, but I understood she just needed some space, and my energy was probably a bit much to take, so I'd stay outdoors and swim in their outdoor pool or work on my current photo collage. The funny thing is I rarely saw Sue get jealous of the relationship I had with Elkara. She was a pretty independent woman who was strong in her relationship with herself. Usually, she would share with me that after Elkara and I had been together for the night that he came back to her happier, softer, and more loving after I left. Sally said "Meryl, you are the most feminine woman I have ever met."

I don't know about that, but somehow being with both Elkara and Susan brought out that lovely, sensitive, sensual, open-hearted side of me whenever we were together. I don't share that type of relationship with them anymore because Sue lives in California and I do not get to the Poconos much anymore either. However, all the friendships that I do have now have that same precious quality of love, sensual expression, sexual intimacy, and unconditional love. The desires and dreams of each person is honored and respected.

I have even shared my sensual life every two weeks for twelve years with a married man whose wife has an incurable disease. He started out as a massage client, but after a year our friendship deepened and became intimate.

Once my client took me to a local Chinese restaurant for dinner, but that was a special time because I was really hungry. We normally do prayer work, massage, and sometimes we will relax by taking a bath together. I love taking baths with a few men who can fit into my bath tub which is somewhat small.

You are probably judging me now for sharing this, but all I can say is "Unless you have walked a mile in my shoes you have no right to judge." Unless you have tried this for yourself if you're a single woman living alone you really do not know what you might be missing.

PAN MAN

The first time I met the "Pan Man" was in August of 1984 in the back yard of my spacious, rented home in Jamesburg, New Jersey, six months after my first child, Gabriel, was born at home. Gabriel's nanny and my best friend, Janet Berkowitz, a statuesque, thin blond who was charismatic, holistic minded, and a fun-loving woman whom I met while she was working at the George Street Co-op, would become my dear friend and nanny to my infant son, Gabriel. When Gabriel was about five months old, she asked me to co-lead a "playshop" for adults with her called "a" Fun4All". She would lead the games and trust exercises and I would teach hatha yoga and a beginner's dance aerobics class to music I loved that I had pre-programmed on an audiotape. Great music like Al Jarreau's "Mornin', Earth, Wind, & Fire's "September", and "Groove Tonight" and Stevie Wonder's "Superstition" were four of the songs I chose for the dance aerobics work-out.

Janet was a good friend of the Pan Man, and he came to participate with us at her behest. The Pan was married at the time, as was I. We became acquaintances, but there were no sparks between us. We were both massage therapists. He was a Scorpio and I was a Cancer, both very sensitive, sensuous emotional, and intuitive water signs.

The Pan was short in stature, and I was not particularly attracted to him from a physical perspective at the time we met.

As time progressed, fortune would smile upon us, and we got re-acquainted after we both divorced our spouses. It was 1996 when we would meet again at Ryder College in a large room dancing with the multi-talented actress, dancer, singer, and creator of "the Five Rhythms" dance method, Gabrielle Roth.

I'd first met Gabrielle when I was a babe of twenty-one years old in New York City and had the great fortune to dance with her while my body was perfect, flexible, strong, and whole; and I was feeling sexy and on top of the world.

A lot had changed since then. In June of 1987 during the Harmonic Convergence, I had those crazy suicidal ideations which resulted in the gunshot to my brain and hemiplegia, left side weakness. My left hand and arm had atrophied and became semi-paralyzed from the gun injury to my brain and nonuse of my little limb for several months while I was recuperating in Robert Wood Johnson Hospital in New Brunswick, New Jersey, for a month, and then three months at JFK Rehab in Edison, NJ, where they focused on strengthening my right leg and ranging my left leg. No attention was paid to my arms, especially my left arm and hand which needed massage, gripping exercises, electric stim, acupuncture, or biofeedback of some kind. My left arm and hand were just ignored as if they did not exist.

I'd not danced much after that because I wore a long leg brace, my muscles were still weak, and I was still learning how to walk with a long leg brace and using a four-pronged cane for balance.

I remember going to downtown Perth Amboy to be fitted for these ugly looking, beige, orthopedic shoes that I needed to wear in order to fit my brace down into. You know, the kind nurses and old ladies tend to wear for comfort, support, and I suppose wounded soldiers and children who needed to wear prosthetics. One of my legs tended to be longer than the other, but once my left leg became stronger during several months of outpatient physical therapy, walking around my development in Englishtown, and other exercises I was able to get the long leg brace cut down to a short PLO that just stabilized my ankle, but I still was forced to wear those ugly orthopedic shoes.

The reason I'm telling you this now here is because I was able to get so into Gabrielle's band's funky music so much that I just threw off those old lady shoes, took off the leg brace, and began dancing in my bare feet with no brace on or cane for balance. The drums had me on fire, and I did not stop dancing for the entire night, not even for a rest. I danced with every person on that floor at Ryder that night, including Pan Man who was truly a fun guy to dance with.

The Pan Man loved to dance a lot. In fact, he and his wife started a dance workshop once per month called "Dance improv" a few years before they divorced, and in 1986 I remember going to their dance workshop which was just taped music played on an audiocassette player to which we would spontaneously make up moves and be in relationship with the other dancers.

In the beginning of the workshop there were guided exercises led by a girl named LouAnn, the Pan's soon-to-become, girlfriend. In order to loosen everybody up and to establish a connection between the community of dancers she would first give us guided exercises like running around the room and letting out sounds of frustration, anger sadness, joy, that had built up during a stressful work week. Sometimes we even made all kinds of animal sounds. This was a great way to loosen up, connecting as a community.

At that time Dance improv met in a large room at the Princeton Arts Council. My nanny, Janet, had told me about this fun dance workshop and we would go together a few times. I even brought my infant daughter, Kyrie, there, when she was a mere six months of age. The next time Kyrie would dance at Dance Improv she would be in her twenties. By that time, it eventually was taken over by Catherine Judd David and morphed into Dance Improv Live with live musicians—usually a piano, at least two drummers, Dave, and my friend, Elay, a singer named Amala, and sometimes an electric guitar or flute player would add to the symphony of spontaneously created sounds. The cool thing was there was no pressure to do anything one did not want to do. Sometimes we'd often close our eyes while we were moving and dancing to get into a meditative state.

At first, we connected by sitting in a circle and announcing our names to the other dancers in the group while making our own special movement and accompanying sound. It could be a silly movement; It could be sad, angry, enthusiastic, or whatever we wanted to make up at the moment. Then the rest of the group would mirror the same movement and sound back to the person who just shared while saying his or her name and a feeling he or she he was feeling with the movement. This exercise created deep listening and awareness.

Then we'd be guided to make the circle bigger and find our own personal space upon the floor. I loved it when I got to the sacred space on time because the stretches and tuning into one's own body/mind and feelings were just as important as when we got up on our feet to dance by ourselves or with another person. We were told it was OK if we were so tired all we needed to do was to lie in Shavasana (the corpse poses, or child pose all night long, from 8-10 PM, but that rarely happened. Once the music got faster everyone was excited and inclined to move to the rhythm of their own intuitive guidance. We all loved mirroring one another and lots of people were doing "Contact dancing" where a couple would not let go of keeping touch with one another. Men were flipping women over their backs, tumbling alongside one another. Different tapestries and moving statues were created by duos, trios, and circles of all kinds with someone sometimes lying inside the circle. Often, I would be the one to crawl underneath and be the one "resting in child pose as a relaxing "monkey in the middle" because often, once I became disabled, I'd be afraid that I might be hurt or stepped upon if I could not keep up with the more athletic dancers. Some were professional like my dear friend, Bob Roth, and his first wife, Paulette Sears, who was a college dance instructor during the day. Catherine Judd-David, the leader, a beautiful, thin, creative, and flexible blond, Aurelle Sprout, and my sweet handsome friend, Paul, who was an amazing dancer and did the tango professionally for a while at Princeton University and other venues where I had the privilege of seeing him and his partner perform.

It was during the time the Pan and I re-connected at Gabrielle Roth's 5 Rhythms Dance workshop at Ryder College in 1999 that we would want to get to know each other as better, closer friends. Pan said "Gee, Meryl, it's so good to see you looking so well. I felt bad when I heard about your accident, but you look great now. It was really great dancing with you."

"By the way, I'm looking for a new person to trade massages with. My former massage therapist I used to barter with moved away". Would you be interested in getting together for a trade sometime?"

"Sure, honey. Where do you live now? Or, do you want to come to me? "I queried.

Well, we could work at my office in Lambertville sometimes, and other times I can meet you at your place," handing me his card. "You know I started my own massage school with my wife, but we sold it several years ago to two of the members of "The Dance and Drum Circle" I still teach small classes out of my office, and I am usually looking for a model to come to the office on Tuesday nights for people to practice upon. Would you be interested?"

I love giving and receiving massages, so I readily agreed. "Sounds great, dear." So, he gave me his card with both his home and business numbers. Coincidentally, his business card had the same colors as mine—green and purple.

And that was the budding of my unconventional, precious, and spiritual relationship with a man who would eventually become one of my very best friends and eventually, after opening up to one another s' heart energies during massages, an intimate friend as well. Not something I would have ever expected since he was truly not my type. Physically, anyway. Until…

One day during a massage at my home the Pan Man told me his girlfriend, "Dee" and he had not had sex in years because she'd been abused by her step-mother and did not like to be touched much. Not even get massaged. I felt compassion for him, so when I finished the posterior part of his body, I asked him to turn over and once I finished massaging his chest and his abdomen very lovingly I decided to move down naturally to caress his balls and lightly stroked his penis which was very beautiful and quite substantial, with a few light effleurage strokes.

He was so grateful to me. "Thanks so much, Meryl. It felt so great and natural to have my sexuality validated. I've not felt like a man for a long time now." The Pan had one of the widest shiva-linghams I'd ever seen. I never believed that one day a few years later that beautiful lingham would be inside me satisfying me like no other man had ever quite done before. And the best thing was that we were not in a committed relationship. We were not girlfriend and boyfriend. We were just special friends who psychically tuned into one another whenever either one of us was depressed or lonely and in need of a nurturing, thorough, therapeutic massage and some cuddling which eventually led into dancing around our living rooms or whatever felt spontaneous and natural.

As a single mom diagnosed with bi-polar disorder living on SSI and a small income from massage part-time, even though I took medication for it, I never knew if or when I'd fall into a depression that would spiral into a deep despair of hopelessness, anxiety, and self-doubt. I'd lose my appetite for life and food. Little did I know that my lack of vitamins, minerals, and good nutrition was contributing to the depressive moods in the first place. I had no appetite for life and no desire or energy to cook for myself. Thank God my daughter lived with me and I needed to make food for her, or I might not have eaten anything at all during these dark times.

One night I was deeply depressed and did not have enough desire or energy to be able to feed myself for several days on end. I'd feed myself and my daughter scrambled or poached eggs for breakfast in the morning before she'd go to school, but after that I would not want to eat anything. All I'd do after doing the dishes once Sky left for school, was go to bed, read, sleep, or watch TV, usually two back-to-back episodes of Mattock, my favorite show. I was in total despair and was afraid to shop for groceries because I'd not made enough money that week, and my food stamps were running out. "What if I did not have enough money to pay for the groceries once I got to the cash register?" was my fear, so unless it was the third of the month when I'd get a few hundred dollars in food stamp money deposited into the food BET account for which a person needed a blue card that looked like a credit card and needed a pin number. I had to reapply at Mercer County Board of Social Services every six months which was a real drag, and I'd get acute anxiety about food shopping if I did not get too many massage clients in a week. I was an excellent massage therapist but not a very good businesswoman.

Anyway, the Pan Man called me saying, "Hi Meryl. It's me. I'm in Princeton because I just visited my friend, Virginia. Would you like me to stop by?"

"Oh, my God, Pan Man. You have no idea how psychic you are because I really need you. Except for scrambled eggs I haven't eaten the entire day. In fact, I haven't shopped for groceries in a week, and I'm starving. Sky is at her friend's house for several hours studying for a math test. Do you think you could come over and order us a pizza? I am starving, buddy".

As soon as I knew God had sent my angel buddy to care for me, talk with me, and bring me food I began to feel better immediately.

Ofttimes, when I went to Pan Man's house for a massage, he'd also feed me the most delicious, healthy lunches and dinners his ex-girlfriend, Dee Dee, would prepare for him after doing his grocery shopping and cleaning his house. She'd bring her cute little white dog with her. I realize that my angel buddy was a "God send" to me during these tough times. Like a guardian angel and one of my "protectors upon this sometimes crazy, violent planet. He said that I helped him a lot too. Especially in the winter when it was cold and dark. He also lived alone, so if he was not entertaining one of his many lady friends, working at massage, painting, or going to a business meeting, he was alone and needed connection, love, and good company.

Besides having massage, holistic health and dancing in common, we both liked nude hot tubbing, clothing optional communities like Harbon Hot Springs in California and the nude beach at Sandy Hook, swimming, Native American chanting, drumming, visiting beautiful places, adventure, and an interest in sweat lodges.

The Pan was a member of the Dance and Drum Circle, like me. Before becoming a massage therapist, the Pan was an electrical engineer. He probably made more money doing that, but his heart was not in it. His love was very expansive and so much bigger and more unconventional than a person who is restricted to a corporate, five day per week" existence. It was not that "PM" was lazy, by no means. In fact, not only did he work at a successful massage business in Lambertville and created a very successful school with his wife, but he became a successful house painter as well. He also sold Alphay mushroom supplements, teas, and coffees, and made quite a bit of money as a networker. The Pan was an innovator, and that impressed me.

But the biggest thing we had in common was that we were both very interested in sensuous massage, polyamory, and tantric sex. I was just learning what polyamory was all about, but the Pan had been studying tantra (sacred sex) for a few years already with famous teachers like Charles and Caroline Muir, among others he met in New York City. He would eventually become certified as a Master tantra teacher by Charles Muir in California after Charles divorced his first wife, Caroline. So, the Pan and I began experimenting with a new, alternative style relationship without commitment, but we were always truthful with one another. We kind of made up our relationship as we went along, and we often joked to each other how happy we were without conventional rules.

Once we got together at his new office in Lambertville having such an incredibly joyous time, we relaxed and rested together after massaging and making love, and then he took me out to one of his favorite restaurants down the street. We were so happy and high from the sacred connection we had just made that we began smiling and laughing hysterically as we took our table. People in the restaurant noticed our levity. A couple nearby said "You guys should get married. "P" and I laughed to ourselves saying," Why ruin a good thing?" I suppose neither of us "believed" in marriage since I'd watched my dad divorce my mom and leave her for her good friend when I was sixteen; her second marriage was short-lived and failed after only three months. So, I had already formed my doubts about conventional marriage at sixteen years old.

Pan Man never told me how he got involved in polyamory or tantric sex. I never cared to ask. I was not really the jealous type, but sometimes it would bother me when I saw him talking to other women when we were at Pebble Hill Church together or somewhere else for a group event. Once he did not even save me a seat when he arrived first so we could hear his teacher, the guru, Shiva Bali Yogi, speak, and give his darshan to a small group of people. This particular time I felt hurt, angry, and disrespected, but usually, our relationship with no strings attached went very smoothly, so long as we were honest and respectful of one anothers' feelings.

One time we did a late morning trade at my apartment; Pan worked on me first like he usually did to relax me which is what tantra is all about—treating the woman first to deep relaxation through massage, sometimes just light effleurage strokes, then kneading, and whatever the man is intuitively guided to do to soothe and relax his female partner. We often joked that The Pan gave me great "head" which simply meant that he massaged my entire scalp, ears, and gave me a terrific facial working on my mandible, in between my eyebrows, head, and neck. He played soothing relaxing music by Steven Halpern like "Ancient Echoes" with Georgia Kelly on harp or "Spectrum Suite", amazing electronic music that is so deeply soothing and "other worldly."

When he worked on my back, he began stroking all the way down past my lower back and onto my fair skinned meaty buttocks. My butt was tired and sore from too much sitting on my ass-pirations -- watching TV, driving, or being at the computer, so getting my sore buttocks stroked, kneaded, cupped, slapped, and more tapotement which is simply percussive, chopping movements, followed by kneading and light effleurage strokes, was just what the doctor ordered for deep relaxation. Then ever so slowly the Pan used his fingers to stroke my outer labia lightly to arouse me just the slightest bit. Then he continued placing his skillful fingers further into me gently spreading my inner lips and brushing past my rosebud softly and eventually into my very wet, throbbing vagina. I was pretty open to whatever he wanted to do to please me at that point.

I was at the point of no return. It was the most excitement I'd allowed myself to feel in years since I'd had an orgasm by my father's hand while I was partially asleep in my teen-age bed while in the eighth grade. I did not have an orgasm with the Pan like I did with my dad, but I felt extremely excited and high.

When he told me to turn over, I noticed the very large bulge in his pants. I stroked his pants on the outside of his Shiva-lingham, and he unzipped his shorts. My God. When his Zeus-like cock was finally revealed I was happily amazed and desirous of having him take me completely-especially when he placed his lips upon mine and we began softly kissing which led to deep French kissing and dancing with our tongues in the most sensuous way.

My eyes completely closed and I melted into a still, joyous place deep within myself as the Pan climbed atop my petite, sensuous form. Very slowly and deftly the Pan took his time getting to know me energetically at first, because there was a very strong energy between the two of us, and he knew not to penetrate me too quickly because he would not be able to hold his erection for very long without cumming. His penis was also not circumcised which makes it extremely sensitive, so he really had to learn how to control himself in the various tantra classes he attended with the Muirs and other teachers by breathing all the sexual energy up into his heart chakra. We were both in tantric bliss after just a few minutes, and by the time he was completely consumed by my "yoni-verse", it was like a conflagration of hearts, souls, and bodies merging as One; we were both in heaven, a celestial place I'd only experienced several times with Elkara and one other man in my life.

"Wouldn't you like to know who that was?!

"Oh, my God. I just lie back and let the Pan take complete control of my body/mind while I surrendered completely to the love energies allowing the waves of tantric energy go from my first chakra (a beautiful, deep red) to my sadhisvhana chakra, the second creative chakra, which is orange in color. Chakra is Sanskrit for wheel. Then I breathed the energy up into my solar plexus, the color of bright yellow like the sun, and finally, the anahata, the color of green, the heart chakra, which is all about love and connection to God, Self, and community.

Then the energy goes up into the throat chakra which is a beautiful cobalt blue and is how we communicate to others through speaking, singing, poetry, writing, and other expressive arts. Then it reaches the ajna chakra, located in between the eye brows which is indigo in color. This is where intuition, telepathy, prophecy, and connection to healing and the Divine, is located.

And finally, with the breath and continuous focus, the crown chakra called the sahasrara, also known as the thousand petaled lotus, explodes into Divine Bliss and Oneness. This is where all of them merge and connect to the Divine Lover within and without. In that "inner state of Being there is no "Other" the way we often experience other people and God as separate from us. There is complete Unity, only ONE GOD, ONE Beloved. Our very own Selves connected to All-that-Is.

When we eventually learned to stay in the tantric embrace long enough, time we merged with one another spiritually, physically, and emotionally where we experienced the most exquisite waves of joy, bliss, and finally sublime inner peace when we felt like we were One and completely satisfied even if we did not cum.

I did not feel an explosive orgasm, nor did the Pan. We just lie there connected in tantric bliss for at least ten or fifteen minutes, I think, though it's hard to say how much time had passed because these holy moments as we lay there in each other's arms were experienced by both of us as timeless.

I felt as if we'd been that way before as angels in heaven or something like that. In fact, I called out "My God, I love you so much, my angel buddy. I promise I'll never leave you if you promise to make love to me every day."

We had become precious, intimate friends that day. What a pleasant surprise the Divine Mystery had brought me that sacred day. Whenever it was. It was probably over fifteen or more years ago, and during that time both Pan and I have had many sacred relationships with other boyfriends, girlfriends, and lovers. Even during all those times, we have remained close friends and massage partners.

But we've been "practicing" tantra on an off ever since. And the more we got together the more he got to know what I liked and how to please me. Even times I was depressed and swore I was not going to have any sex with anyone, ever, not even him, during or after my massage, somehow my heart would open and he'd end up lying on top of me; even with both our clothes still on, and I would begin to feel that amazing energy between us, and I'd want to have him inside me once again. I would get hooked on the "Panabrator" – whi ch is what we began to jokingly call his Shiva-lingham.

The Pan was not only a great lover during intercourse, but he also knew how to give me great oral pleasure before coming inside me ever so slowly, always knowing exactly how far to go into my energetic and auric fields before he'd come all the way inside of me. It was pretty intense for both of us, probably more intense for him considering the penis has all the nerves on the outside, his was extra sensitive being uncircumcised, plus the incredible Shakti from the blood pulsating to make him perfectly erect.

Sometimes I'd close my legs and it would make the energy and waves of pleasure more intense. The Pan Man was not only wide, but he was about eight inches long, so he was the only man I could do this with without his penis coming outside of my yoni. He has a very open heart, is a great, sensitive kisser as well. Most people are unaware that the Soul connection is in the deepness of the kiss. We both happen to be great kissers and we love to kiss for a long time before we fondle breasts, buttocks, or anything else. We could enjoy hours of foreplay before we ever got close to having intercourse. We were also very in tune psychically with one another, and this made for great romance beforehand as well as during intercourse.

At the Pan's apartment I'd tell him to play all my favorite sexy songs on YouTube for us to dance to in order for us to get in a relaxed, sexy, romantic mood. My favorite songs were by Freddy Jackson, like "Rock me Tonight for Old Time's Sake". Barry White's "Practice What you Preach", Kenny Loggins' "Love Will Follow", Al Jarreau's rendition of "Teach Me Tonight. "and "Reasons" by Phillip Bailey of Earth, Wind, and Fire. Sometimes I'd just be in the mood for something mellow and slow like Stevie Wonder's beautiful ballad "Ribbon in the Sky"; and we would dance with our hearts and all our chakras lined up together. Since I was also petite we aligned perfectly and naturally matched up all of our chakras while dancing.

In the middle of our dancing Pan would eventually lift me up in his arms and carry me to the massage table or to his bed and work on me there.

After communing in the most sacred, intimate way we'd be so completely satisfied and fulfilled that we'd relax cuddling together and fall deeply asleep for fifteen minutes or so, whereupon we would wake up completely refreshed. The Pan even knows how to anoint each one of his chakras with his cum so that he does not lose any energy after sex. He'd usually give me a little taste of his sperm as well. He said I was the most delicious partner he'd ever had—that my amrita (the juice from my yoni) was the best tasting he'd ever had. I don't know about that, but if it were true, it is probably because I try to keep my diet clean and composed of mostly vegetables, fruits, nuts, and grains. Not much coffee, refined sugars, or anything too acidic. Well, occasionally I'd partake of cheesecake or some sangria with dinner. Or dark chocolate cacao on occasion which was a natural aphrodisiac.

Sometimes in the winter if both the Pan and I were drained, tired, and not feeling our usual sensuous, energetic selves we'd, both decide to get into a hot shower or bath together at my place and Pan would wash my hair, condition it with jojoba or some nice Aloe and herb combination, and then he'd soap me up with delightful, sweet smelling bee soap or something natural he'd buy from the health food store in Flemington. We'd both feel so much better after that. Then he'd begin the massage on the table after we danced to a slow dance for five or ten minutes getting us extremely relaxed and ready to "work" upon each other.

Sometimes one of us would cry a lot of tears during a massage, and often we were not even sure why we were crying. The Pan had a few girlfriends in between our sacred relationship, and so did I have men friends and lovers, but it rarely got in the way of our friendship. Sometimes we would not feel like being sexual anymore if we had a new lover or beau in our lives, and that was fine with both of us. We just chose to do straight therapeutic, nurturing massage or a little bit of a sensuous massage, but we rarely told our girlfriend or boyfriend. Well, I usually would share our special friendship and loving relationship with my new lover whereas the Pan, being a Scorpio, was much more private and secretive than me. He probably suspected that his new girlfriend would become very jealous and not allow it, even though he had told her initially he was polyamorous.

If we were both completely single for a while, we promised one another we would live together in Mexico, Hawaii, or California in the same sacred clothing optional spiritual community where the Goddess was honored as the beautiful, sensitive, powerful sacred deity She is meant to be.

One time we had no beaux to speak of, and I came to celebrate New Year's Eve alone at his home, and we danced all night together; he massaged me and showed me some erotic videos of women who allowed men watch them masturbate to orgasm, for a price, which kind of turned me off, but since he liked them, I indulged his fantasy. Anyway, magically, at the stroke of midnight I had his beautiful Shiva lingham in my hand while I was kissing it and then his lips, while stroking him, and he was able to cum at exactly midnight; then we laughed like crazy.

Once in the autumn of 2009 the Pan took me to a tantra workshop in New York City on a Friday evening to learn from this married couple from California or Hawaii, I forget which, named Janet and Sasha Lessen. Pan came with me the first day, Friday, and was my partner, but he needed to work on massage clients on the next day, all day Saturday, so I chose to go into the city by myself.

It was the most amazing day, and I saw the most incredibly intimate, sacred, graphic demonstration of loving sex by a couple who deeply loved one another and connected intimately on all levels. Janet and Sasha Lessen talked about a yoni that became so excited that it could squirt during a most intense orgasm. The fluid that would come from the vagina was not urine, but amrita from the urethra. I never knew how to surrender that much, and it did not happen between me and the "Pan" until years later in our relationship. I think I was too nervous I might urinate on him when I felt that full wet feeling.

Sasha, Janet's husband, first showed us how he and Janet would make a "tantric date". He'd begin by talking to her telling her how beautiful she was and how much he loved her long blond hair, her voluptuous creamy white breasts, her beautiful face, and especially her open heart. Then they would make a sacred offering of their lovemaking to Mother Earth and the Gods to use someplace in the world that was needing healing. I thought that was the coolest thing—making their beautiful tantric lovemaking into a ritual, sacred offering of love to God/Goddess for the highest and best Good of the world. I thought that would be a nice thing to teach the Pan, especially since he was not able to make it to class that day.

Janet was so very beautiful and such a relaxed participant/receiver of all her husband's love and adoration for her that day. After Sasha gave her a slow, gentle effleurage like massage on the back of her body he turned her over and did the same thing on the anterior side. He gently teased her by softly touching her pubic hair and outer labia as he'd do long, gliding effleurage strokes all the way up her legs and thighs. He massaged her beautiful creamy white breasts while kissing her neck, face, and lips. Then, right in front of all ten of us students he plied her body like he was plucking a harp and Sasha began to "polish her pearl" with his tongue while using his finger to stimulate both the inside of her yoni and labia with his fingers.

We students were all spread out around her body on all sides in order to learn all the techniques he easily taught as we were watching as closely as possible while Sasha relaxed his beloved Goddess and intimately displayed all his masculine powers and intimate knowledge of her body to make his wife moan, squirm, and writhe until, all of a sudden, she made a sound of exquisite pleasure and this clear fluid shot out of her about three feet across the room into the air nearly hitting one of the men positioned at the end of her body near her feet. It was the most amazing thing I'd ever seen not counting the heads of my babies coming out of my vagina at home at the end of my labors.

Later on, when we were sharing at the kitchen table I said to Janet, "You are so amazing to share that much intimacy with us, Sister. Thank you so very much. I can barely have an orgasm without anyone watching, except by my own hand or vibrator. How the heck do you do it in front of all these people?"

"Oh, he knows my body so well; it's really easy. In fact, I'd have to work to hold back in order not to cum." We are a great team.

"Thank you so much for sharing your love for each other with us. I learned a lot and I feel so much better than when I came in last night. I will share this with my tantra partner tomorrow when I talk to him. He could not make it today because he had a full schedule of massage clients."

The Lessens invited me to come back to share with them after the workshop was over, but without the Pan I just did not feel guided to do so. I suppose I was just a bit nervous about being alone with them, not feeling very confident about my own sexuality.

Pan and I did not always get together in order to have sex. Once he took me to Pebble Hill Church in Doylestown, for a meeting of the New Hope Metaphysical Society sponsored by our dear friends, John and Amy Giallucco. Another time he asked me to meet him there so I could meet his guru, Shiva Bali Yogi, who has claimed to be the reincarnation of Swami Nityananda, Baba Muktananda's guru. I also met him at the home of a devotee in New Hope, PA, and there were quite a few devotees there chanting as he gave darshan (the divine glance), to all who did puja to him while waving the arati lights. We are told the gurus are omniscient and know exactly what to say or what to do to initiate a student, give him complete healing, and after awakening his or her kundalini energy, see the process through until the devotee becomes completely Self Realized, an enlightened Master just like himself. It's all a miracle and Divine Mystery to me. Just like the Master Jesus healed all the lepers, the lame, and raised Lazarus from the dead after five days of his corpse lying inside the tomb with his flesh rotting. Is it all truly real or just a metaphor?

What's a metaphor, anyway? According to my beau, Gary, "it's for grazing."

Oh, the other time we spent sacred time together without the benefit of being naked was when he escorted me to our friend, Delane Lipka's, memorial service, when she died suddenly from some mysterious disease, she never told anyone about. Delane owned and was the director of the first Holistic health retreat, Mount Eden, on acres of beautiful property in Washington, New Jersey. The Pan had known her for many years, and I met her the first time when she organized the first "Kindred Spirits Fair", a very cool holistic health festival she put on for kindred souls like you and me with concert music, dancing, vegetarian food, and lots of vendors selling items like homemade jewelry, Indian cotton clothes, scarves, purses, and other cool stuff.

My precious friend and musician, singer/songwriter, Fairy Elaine Silver, was very close to Delane, having formed a close bond with her while performing at the fairs and later on, after she ascended (passed away). The first time I met Fairy was when she performed at Rev, Angel Joan Fericy's, Church of Divine Light, where I would attend for many years until she announced she was retiring in order to perform weddings full time, and then move to San Diego, California, to follow her guidance to be with her beloved beau, Brucie, after her husband, Richie, died from cancer.

Pan escorted me to the funeral; and upon our returning to his home in a sacred ritual we smudged one another with a sage stick, and then we washed one another's feet in a bowl while bowing to one another like Jesus did with His disciples. We also burned incense and lit a candle symbolizing the flame of the undying Light of our Souls. That was a sacred, memorable moment for both of us that never led to sex.

Both PM and I have had a main partner now for a several years with whom we live. My beau, Gary, has lived with me on and off for about seven years even though he owns his own home in Hamilton where he sleeps overnight twice per week after having physical therapy.

Gary is so sweet and non-jealous that he allows me to enjoy the company of the Pan and a few other very close male friends, both whom I happened to have enjoyed company as former boyfriends in a conventional relationship many years before. Thank God Gary is so unconditionally loving and expansive that he does not feel as if our relationship is threatened. Gary still calls me "my little goil" and jokes sometimes when he is cuddling me saying "Mine, mine, mine, "in a sort of pretend possessive way. Gary Bear and I joke a lot in bed, and I appreciate his precious friendship, divine company when he is around, and the Pan Man and my other friends' divine company when they are here massaging me or taking me out dancing or to dinner.

Gary Bear does not like to dance which is fine with me just so long as he is OK with me having other dance partners on the dance floor or in the bedroom. I am still respectful of his feelings and am very particular about the few partners I choose whom Gary already knows, and if he does not know a new friend, I invite my new friend, into my home in order to meet Gary and feel comfortable with our unconditionally loving relationship.

Besides, Gary is an excellent, interesting person—a genius, of sorts, and I am very proud of him, so I always want my other new friends, whether they be male or female, to come by and get to meet my precious beau, who is not just a special man in my life, but I think he is a gift to the world. I feel so blessed that most all of the men in my life like the Pan, Kenny, Michael, and one of my very special massage clients of fifteen years, all choose to stay in my life as friends or lovers for the duration of my precious life or until one of us moves far away or gets married, I suppose. But then, why would I want to ruin a great thing? I've already been in enough institutions for one lifetime! The Pan Man says "Meryl, you've been in so many mental hospitals you could probably write a travelogue"—and I think I will!

GRIGGS FARM

I came to Princeton in 1995 when Sky just turned five years old after being on a low-income housing list for two years and three months. I'd just moved into my friend, Vicki's house for a month or two when I got the call that my name had come up on the list to move into an apartment in Griggs Farm. I found out about it from Joan, a neighbor there who was disabled whom I met at a group for women with disabilities. I ended up moving in right across from her. We lived near the tennis court which Sky was able to use a few times when I gave her some lessons. I feel very blessed to still be living in such a beautiful town for such a low rent because of my status to be able to receive a stipend for low-income housing. I love all my neighbors, so many of the interesting, involved, politically active, and caring people who live here in the town of Princeton. New Jersey is not my favorite state because of the cold winters, but I continue to live here because I want to remain close to my family, especially my children and grandchildren, and my mom still needs me being 83 years old. But Princeton is a joyous, happening place to be and live!

The Mother's Day Tree

When Sky was about seven years old, she brought home a gift of a little evergreen tree in a small pot for Mother's Day. We both watered it on a regular basis and gave it lots of tender loving care. After a month or so the tree grew and got too big for its little pot, so I planted it in my spring and summer garden outside the screen door. Each day as I would go out to the car, I would notice its beauty and how well it was growing. It was about nine inches tall when Sky first gave it to me.

After several summers I noticed the tree was becoming too big for my little garden of daffodils, sunflowers, tulips, pink and purple pansies and petunias, hyacinths, and annuals of whatever I decided would be the color theme for that summer. It was about four feet tall, nearly as big as Sky and me. I realized that in another year or two it would be so tall that it would hit the deck upstairs of the people on the second floor, so I decided to donate it to Griggs Farm while attending one of the monthly homeowners' meetings. I was very lucky and blessed because the Mexican workers carefully transplanted my tree from my small garden to the ground right in front of my designated parking space. All the residents in Griggs Farm have assigned parking spaces, and mine was the second handicapped spot when you made a right turn into the lot.

One day I came out and saw our beautiful Mother's Day tree proudly standing in a new larger spot where she had more room to grow, flourish, and literally spread her wings out. Each day I would see her in all her glory and beauty in the morning and in the afternoon or evening when I'd arrive home. I would thank her and compliment her on her beauty and also thank her for giving me and everyone in our neighborhood life giving oxygen. Quietly, she would acknowledge my loving communication and compliment me in return. Do you know that when I moved from Griggs Farm, she was the only thing I was really sad to leave? Some of my loving neighbors, too, but I can visit them anytime. I could not take my special tree with me when I moved. She had moved on to her own home in the ground, and she was way too big and beautiful for me to uproot her now. Guess how wide and tall she is now? Our precious Mother's Day tree is about twenty feet tall and still growing in height and breadth every day.

When I still lived in Griggs Farm every December, I'd happily take the time to decorate her with lights, garlands, Christmas bulbs, angels, pine cones, and whatever little ornaments I found that were worthy of her beauty. All my neighbors would complement me on "our" beautiful work of art. One of the neighbors told me she would continue to decorate it at Christmas after I was gone, but I drove around the old neighborhood in the end of December, and no one had. But it's OK. She's still just as beautiful as ever naked and unadorned. I went back to water my tree in mid-summer as it had not rained very much, and I wanted to make sure she was getting enough to drink. I knew she was getting plenty of sunshine, but now I just have to trust that Mother Nature is going to take care of our precious Mother's Day evergreen who has room to grow taller and taller each day. Once she was transplanted into a larger spot she spread out in all directions. And this all came from one seed that grew into a tiny plant that was given by Mrs. Tannenbaum to all of her first and second grade class students for their mothers. What a special and caring idea.

I was very inspired by a friend and neighbor at Griggs Farm, who was blind. Her name is Charla, and she lived in the building next to me and became a good friend to Sky and me over the years. She was a friendly, open, happy person who lived a full, active life just as if she still had her sight. She went for walks, shopped with friends, cleaned her house, cooked every day, did her own laundry, had a kind, handsome boyfriend and made friends with lots of people. Charla and I loved going out together whether it was going to the bank, the diner, or to the Shop Rite for food. We had fun wherever we went because we chose to. Charla was a joyous woman of color with a good sense of humor who used to be a schoolteacher when she still had her sight. Her great attitude and zest for life inspired me. She was a testimony that true happiness comes from within and doesn't depend on outer circumstances, our state of health, wealth, ethnicity, etc., but from our own state of mind.

Since Charla could not drive it was our friend, Kim, Sky and all the girls' Girl Scout troupe leader, who often brought Charla shopping for food or clothing. If Kim could not take her where she needed to go, she would ask me, but having a limp when I walked, I was not great at leading her where she needed to go. Sometimes we would trip up a little. We often joked about ourselves saying "We were like the crippled leading the blind." Truly, neither of us really felt like disabled women. We were both pretty powerful who did not allow our disabilities to stop us. Just about everyone in town knew Charla from her church work and because she had a dynamic personality. She could be a bitch too. She was a black sister who wouldn't take anybody's shit. And most people knew me either as "the dancer" or "Sky's mom". I danced just about everywhere I went in town whether it be at the Arts Council concerts in the Princeton Shopping Center on Tuesday nights in the summer, dancing at church, dancing and singing in the aisles of Shop Rite while I was shopping for groceries and cat food. All the women in my aerobics class at the Suzanne Paterson Center know me by name because I not only danced but sang aloud with gusto to nearly every song I liked. I have a really great memory for lyrics to songs that I like even from the time I was eight or nine years old. If my dad played it on the radio or on a record at home, I would recall every single word. To this day some of the older women there ask me the lyrics to a song if they are unsure of them.

Charla also had a steady boyfriend, Pete, on and off up until she died, a close relationship with her mom who died within a week of her, and seemed to be related to one quarter of the people in Princeton. Whenever I'd meet someone new and talk about Charla they'd say "Oh yeah, she's cousins with my friend, so and so, by marriage.

I was also close to my upstairs neighbor, Laurie, who was a hair dresser and affected by manic depression like me too. She took a few years to do it, but she was able to get her social work and psychology degree by going to school nights at Mercer County College. Laurie liked my massages and I liked the way she cut and styled my hair, so we sometimes bartered for services. We also liked cats, and both of us adopted cats from the local pet shelter, SAVE.

Laurie and I still invite each other to our birthday parties, see one another at dances, or at the Trinity Church in town the third Friday of the month which is when the pastor there has the "One Table Cafe', a place where, for the last ten years, people of all races and religions are invited to come together at one table to break bread together. We all get to eat for free because a fine restaurant in town has donated their services, usually a salad, bread and butter, a delicious entree, salad, dessert and coffee or tea while we listen to a speaker from a charity like the Trenton Soup Kitchen, WomanSpace, or some nonprofit organization helping the local community.

Donations of $10 or more are left in an envelope for the charity that is being introduced. The charities are hoping to educate others about their service to the community in the hopes of getting volunteers involved or the needed funds to continue operating. My beau, Gary, and I have attended several gatherings, and are always impressed and inspired by the various speakers who offer very much needed services to the Princeton and greater Trenton area.

Jane, one of my sweet neighbors, would often leave a ten dollar roll of quarters for laundry in my mailbox every few weeks or so, which was a complete surprise. I never expected it. It was a gift from the universe at the perfect time I needed it – just as I was getting ready to do the laundry downstairs in the community laundry room. Just when it was time to do Sky's and my laundry and change our bed sheets.

I love living in a university town. Most of the folks that live here are tolerant, progressive, intellectual, informed Democrats or independents. There is always something new to learn at the Senior Center held at Suzanne Paterson Center, interesting speakers and inspiring lecturers from all over, concerts going on at the library, Evergreen Forum classes in just about everything from opera to literature to French conversation for folks who want to travel to France. McCarter Theater has the newest plays, musicals, ballets, and other dance companies since the program director is the same man who does programming for Lincoln Center in New York City.

Princeton is the home of great minds and talented scientists, writers, and artists like Tony Morrison, Peter Benchley, Christopher Reeve's parents, my dear friend and author Alan Grayson, who died some years back, anthropologist and author, Ashley Montague, who passed into Spirit a few years ago, and his sweet wife Marjorie. Noam Chomsky, the great author and peace activist, a linguist who worked at MIT, once lived here. His daughter played softball with mine.

We have a great health food store, farm markets with local produce every week, and delicious diverse restaurants of every ethnic cuisine that cater to the rich, middle class, and some Chinese and Japanese take-out that will fit a lower budget.

My favorites are Indian, Thai, and Mediterranean since I try to eat vegetarian, for the most part when given the choice. I love to eat outdoors when the weather is nice, and my beau and I like to do so at Effi's Mediterranean Grill or the Thai place on Nassau at the corner of Olden Street. Until the corona virus pandemic there was a Panera Bread on Nassau Street where one could leisurely sip their coffee outdoors under an umbrella while chatting and petting a neighbor's dog as it walks by, or stopping to notice a stranger's new baby in its stroller or carriage where is easy to strike up conversation with the baby's mom or dad about the age and weight of the newborn, etc. People are very friendly here as in any university or small town even though there are lots of folks here. It is the same if one sits in Hines Plaza next to the library enjoying a snack or cup of tea at one of the many tables while appreciating a band or watching a dance. They also have regular ballroom dancing there monthly, and you need not have a partner. There is also folk dancing and ballroom dancing held regularly at the Suzanne Paterson Center, and ecstatic dancing at Integral Yoga of Princeton, and since my passion is dancing you will often find me at one or more of these venues.

There are two wonderful yoga centers offering kirtan chanting, meditation, regular Satsang's, and many types of yoga classes daily at the Princeton Center for Yoga and Health which also has Journey Dancing, the Five Rhythms originated by Gabrielle Roth, and drumming and dancing with master drum teacher, Mark Wood, the first Saturday of every month, held outdoors if the weather permits with a lovely ceremonial fire in the middle of the drum circle.

I particularly love Integral Yoga of Princeton originated by Jayadeva Mendelkorn because he and the teachers and receptionists are so welcoming and loving of all who enter there in a devotional way. They are very family oriented and offer family karaoke as well as monthly dinners and a movie for families and everyone who wants to come. He does not charge officially for most programs except the yoga teacher's training. Everything except a few programs is free, but a comfortable donation or dakshina offering is asked to be placed in the basket. The place is filled with loving acceptance, spaciousness, friendliness, and an air of respect and devotion. It is beautiful too. My daughter, Kyrie, and I performed our "Heartscapes" concert there back in December of 2017 and are expecting to be on the schedule again once the fear of the pandemic subsides.

Just recently, her boyfriend, Richie, taught the yoga class prior to Ecstatic Dance and Kyrie finished the evening with yoga nidra which is deep relaxation through sound healing. I gave her two of my Atlantean quartz crystal bowls, chimes for the opening of the heart and third eye chakras, and a Tibetan bowl for her sound healing workshops which completely heal and transform the space. I participated in the ecstatic dance and stayed for the sound healing which was like being in a mother's womb, which is how many of the participants described Kyrie's singing, chanting, and playing of the bowls.

I tend a beautiful flower garden in the spring and summer, so many people stop while they are walking their dogs to admire it and strike up a friendly conversation about the beautiful weather which leads to other friendly topics.

We have a beautiful, three-story public library with computers, the best books, DVDs, videos, and CD. rentals for just a dollar or two per day. There are people like authors, musicians, politicians, peace activists who come to the library to talk, inform, or give free concerts on a regular basis. There are also free movies.

Kyrie and Gary

Since I am a performer with the Solidarity Singers of the Industrial Union Council, I perform every August with my group for Nagasaki and Hiroshima Days commemorating the atomic bombing of those cities. Rev. Bob Moore of the Coalition for Peace Action always has a moment of silence at the exact time the bombs were dropped, a ritual lighting of candles, a musician playing flute recorder, the Solidarity Singers singing "This Little Light of Mine" and a song sung in Japanese written by a few of the survivors of the bombing and often a member of the Hibakusha – someone who had survived the bombing, share their experience in the hope that something that horrible never happens again. It is good to remember and remain informed about all the terrible things that happen in history as opposed to keeping our heads stuck in the sand like ostriches in order that we can make the changes needed to bring peace and unconditional love for one another and respect and compassion for Mother Earth and all her creatures before we all become extinct.

College of NJ and Dolphin Quest Cruise

I started a new semester in September of 1995 at Trenton State College which changed its name to The College of New Jersey, an excellent four-year college after graduating from Mercer County College with honors in April of 1995 majoring in English education.

At the end of September, I took a week off to travel to Bermuda on Norwegian Cruise Lines with about forty other Light Workers to do special healing work on the Triangle of Bimini. We were told by Michael and Shoshanna Rogers who lived in New York City and were accustomed to channeling Archangel Michael, Jesus the Christ Consciousness, and other Great Beings and Ascended Masters from the "Other Side" of the veil that we would be working with the dolphin energies. Michael had had a dream about it and his wife was able to translate what the dream and vision meant and they gave her an idea of what teachers she might contact to help with the work needed to be done.

My former lover and longtime boyfriend, Ernie Kara, had already registered for the cruise, and I still had a yearning to be with him sometimes, so I decided to register myself thinking I might spend some quality time with him. He was already in relationship with another gal, so that never happened, but I had a wonderful experience doing this spiritual work, enjoying Bermuda, dancing and dining on the cruise itself, as well as meet some other people who would be instrumental in more of my spiritual development. I also met a man name Gary I was immediately attracted to one night when we were all dressed up and dancing who would almost immediately become a close friend friend and eventual lover within a day or two of hanging out together. He was married, and I'm not sure why we felt such a strong attraction to one another. He was with a friend who kept mentioning his wife, Sandy, but for whatever reason his being married did not seem to get in the way of us enjoying one another s' company.

There were two teachers I really liked who were pretty well known. One was Rev. Gregory Possman, the President of the Universal Brotherhood Ministers' Organization who was and is a very clear channel for Michael the Archangel. Michael speaks in a deep, clear and resonant voice through Gregory whom he often referred to by the name "Ashid". I got the feeling that that name was a name Rev. Possman had received when he was living on a different planet; it felt intuitively to me as if he were an inter Galactic Being. I believe he, his wife, Sandy, and probably all the Light Workers who were attracted to being on the few thousand-dollar Dolphin Cruise to Bermuda and back were all Ascended Masters, at least that is what we were told by Lord Michael through Rev. Possman and the keeper of the Violet Flame, formerly known as St. Germaine who had a lot to do with guiding and guarding the Light Workers here in the United States of America, I'm being told. teacher of Sacred Geometry and the Flower of Life workshops, author Drunvalo Melchezedek.

Michael appeared to have a great sense of humor and his voice came through in a very deep, but playful, masculine, and confident way. Archangel Michael, though I imagine he is very serious about his work as a guardian of one of the four corners the Globe, or whatever he actually does to keep us all safe. He never shared with us specifically what he does to keep the galaxy, including Mother Earth, safe, was a very playful and Light Archangel, often teasing us about ourselves in a very playful way. Always laughing, and how we humans operate here in the third dimensional reality on planet Earth, which is not exactly efficient, especially when it comes to manifesting and creating our true deepest desires and dreams.

I really loved listening to Gregory channeling Michael because I felt a deep love and connection to him, as if from ancient times. On the cruise ship Michael shared with us that we were all part of the Great White Brotherhood of the Christ Consciousness, and we all came here to do specific jobs to help in the healing of Goddess Gaia, our precious Mother Earth, with the dolphins and whales, the guardians and stewards of Gaia who protect her, her children and all of her creatures who offered to serve humans, but not signed up to be tortured, used, and abused in factory farms from corporate greed. The animals were created to be our friends and playmates, especially since human beings were created to be the Masters at the top of the hierarchy "Food Chain. I doubt Mother Earth wanted us to, as her children to be violent, when our nature is to be one of kindness, caring, compassion, and divine Love, like Herself and Father God. Gaia is the Goddess, the beautiful, erotic, sensuous, sweet Creatrix, and Lord

Jesus, when they merged, is the Father of us All. They are the infinite parents of the World. The one Divine Lover out of boundless love, has actually Become the one Beloved, in us, as us, and through us. The Creator and Creatrix also expected us to love the animals as She love each one of us because animals all have feelings too. They are not only caring and loving of each other, but they love, guard, protect, and care for their young, just like we parents do of our children, but they are all very smart, intuitive, and can be very loving and helpful to humankind.

As you can tell by all the crazy Earth changes and destruction of Mother Earth's body through hydrofracturing, coal mining, taking out oil which usually ends of spilling into her pure, magnificent oceans. Hydrofracking, is not exactly being kind to our precious Mother. Why do you think the environment is so messed up right now with tsunamis, fires caused by unnatural heating of the planet? Then the damn oil spills by tankers and boats that destroy fish, sea birds, sea turtles, sting rays, octopuses, and finally, destroying Her precious coral reefs, this is not what Father/Mother God intended had in mind when human beings we created. Though we have dominion over the animals and free will to care for them, and play with them or hurt them, mistreated, torture and finally use them for food after a very short unpleasant life imprisoned in small cages or pens,, not appreciated when their little chick babies, young pigs, cows, and eat them, I personally do not believe any animals or even insects should be unappreciated, hurt, killed of many animal species by how we misuse, torture, and do not appreciate I eventually took a workshop offered by Rev. Possman in which I spent an entire day with a dozen other people at someone's beautiful home up north who wanted to sponsor Gregory. and my friends, Rev. Carola Van Dusen and Amelia LeBer whom I'd met years before at Angel Joan Fericy's "Church of Divine Light" in Somerset, New Jersey. learning a technique called "Manifestation Acceleration", a technique that uses creative visualization and several types of pranayamas (Sanskrit for yogic breathing techniques) for creating things or circumstances one is desiring to bring into third dimensional reality in a much faster way than one has been programmed to do by working hard or however we have been trying for years—like this book, for instance. My inner Spirit is telling me "Focus, discipline, and persistence. I have so many interests and distractions I've been working on this memoir since I began going back to college full-time in 1991 at Mercer County College to get my Associates degree in Liberal Arts.

Oct 1 1995 Channeling

The following was channeled from St. Germaine, Keeper of "The Violet Flame" Sunday, October 1, 1995, through Rev. Gregory Possman

"I am the keeper of the Violet Flame. We made a brief entry into this body some years back, and again, in the closing ceremonies on Dolphin Quest. We will begin to use this vehicle more.

Each one of you is an Ascended Master. Currently I come through many bodies on Earth. You know me as Saint Germaine. I prefer to be known as the Keeper of the Violet Flame at this point.

To those of you who went on Dolphin Quest, we have much to say. Each one of you is as a baby who has just been born. You were born the day you traveled through the birth canal on the waters.

For those who did this exercise, the spirit of Dolphin entered into each one of you. Each one of you knows that babies need love. They will die without love.

In returning to your home, you have attempted to return to the past. The past has been a place of non-love. A place of separation. Gather in groups, if possible, with your fellow brothers and sisters. This is one avenue you may receive the nurturing from. If you attempt to be nurtured in the old ways you shall re-experience the pain of the old ways.

When you were on the ship you were as one big bonfire. As you left to go to your corners of the globe, you each took a stick from that fire. As you join with other members, the sticks come together, and the flame you keep is nurtured and grows brighter.

Each one of you has been challenged in infancy. By the time you were thirteen months old, each one of you had experienced rejection in some way. Now, you are experiencing this rejection. We will explain:

Before the Quest each of you were living from a space of receiving in two ways. The familiar was, as a baby when you had an umbilical cord. This became an imaginary one that would latch onto people in order for you to get your needs met.

The unfamiliar was the tube of pranic life 9prana is vital energy, the air or chi force flowing up and down throughout your spinal column. While on the ship, each one of you began to remember breathing from the divine source.

Upon your return from the Quest, your divine memory breathing merged again with the outside world. You cannot fasten the old umbilical cord. Accept your divine connection and drink of the divine pranic energies that flow from the Godhead.

Do the breathing that your brother taught you. Study his technique. Accept your own direct connection with the Supreme Being. We also understand that you are feeling the sluggishness of the third dimensional life. This is the sense that you have everything, but you cannot see it.

We wish you to understand that when the mind cannot see something that it feels is supposed to be there, it interprets it as lost. Then anxiety sets in.

You have lost nothing. You are more found. You are able to see it before it manifests in what you call "reality".

Each one of you who were on the ship is trying to find the past and blend into it. You will not find peace in that. You are Eagles. Be Ascended masters and bring your past into your now present. This is peace.

"We mean anything you hold resentment to, or feelings of non-forgiveness towards. Bring these feelings into your Beingness now and call forth the Violet Flame to transform them into the Light of the ever present ONE.

We love you greatly.

May the light of the Grand Central Sun shine on you always.

Keeper of the Violet Flame

Channeling Sept 1997

The following was channeled through me on September 27, 1997 in answer to a question I asked for Rev. Joan Fericy and the Church of Divine Light in Somerset, NJ-a congregation of which I was a member:

"Beloved Children:

"You are all perfect beings. I am that I am and so are ye. Do not forget all is in perfect divine order as you face the adversities in your personal lives and deal with the seeming chaos and upheaval around you. As you know there are no mistakes or accidents in this vast universe. There is one Perfect Divine Intelligence working lawfully for the Good of All. You are never a victim. You deliberately create your own reality with each thought you think, word you speak, emotion you feel, and action you take.

"Your essence is Sat-chit-ananda—pure Consciousness, Being, and Bliss Absolute. You are created from unconditional love, and You are that love itself. God most high dwells within you exactly as you are in this very moment. There is no need for you to change or do anything unless you want to. Simply be yourself and experience your True nature. This whole creation is for you to experience All that you are. Source never judges you or anything you choose to experience. So why should you? Believe me when I say we are all equally divine, and All are needed in God's Magnificent Divine Plan. It is only the ego that feels separate from me and other beings, deluding itself that one is greater or lesser than another is.

"I am no respecter of persons. A homeless drunk or a prostitute is as holy and dear to me as the saint. In fact, he or she could possibly be the Christ of this or another universe. Do not be deceived by appearances. The lord shows up in the most interesting guises. Do not be fooled into thinking one is more or less spiritual than another. The scholar is no greater than the fool. Each of you is the noblest, most worthy, honorable, and magnificent being there is. Open your hearts and minds to the Truth of your being, that which you already are.

"Beware of faultfinding and judgment. If there be any darkness within you it is the negative thoughts you have about yourselves which you then project onto others. See yourselves as pure and good, and honor your own Essence. Then it will become easy to see the Christ Light in others. Go within to find peace. Think happy, uplifting thoughts. Feel gratitude for all that you have and all that you are. If only you were to know the power of your own mind and emotions you would never again think I'll of yourself or another. Thoughts manifest instantly as creations. You all collectively have the power to create and destroy entire universes. I have told you wherever two or more are gathered in my name, there I am in your midst. You, dear children, are living cells in the Body of the Christ playing out your divine roles, each following his or her divine purpose, making manifest a most beautiful creation as you gradually awaken to the Truth of your own Self.

"You are pure Light and Love. Everything else is illusion. We, the angels and archangels, are always with you. You will find us in the silence and subtler aspects of your lives. Sometimes you'll have an inner knowing that we are around guiding you, protecting you, and reassuring you in times of trouble. Also know that thee walk amongst each other as angelic beings embodying the qualities each one of us represents – courage, faith, clarity, abundance, playfulness, joy, beauty, inspiration, creativity, order, Light, gentleness, kindness, and so much more.

"Know that each kind word, deed, hug, smile, encouraging word, and affirmative prayer have far reached effects, much more than you can possibly see or realize at this time. So love and bless yourselves and all others. Especially your adversaries. Sometimes our enemies can be our greatest teachers. Is only through forgiveness, unconditional love, and inner peace that we will transform the hatred in this world. We love and honor you all with the one Collective Heart Sinanda, Kwan Yin, Muktananda, & Michael the Archangel."

RELATIONSHIP WITH
DAVID & LAURIE (1997)

I would have loved to have had the children live with me, but I do not believe I was strong enough, had enough financial resources, nor did I have enough room in my apartment for all of us. I don't think I would have been able to manage cooking for all of us or doing all the shopping, chauffeuring them around to their soccer games and other activities.

David met Laurie, a beautiful, intelligent woman, an artist with a Jewish background through his sister, Beanie, nearly eight years after we divorced. Thank God it took that long. I was still attached to having him and the kids in my life, but by the time they met, I'd become stronger and was dating Ernie Kara. Laurie had already begun to take over chores like buying the children's clothes and the groceries. The children were already living with David full time, and I only saw them at my apartment on week-ends, or if I went to their home in Englishtown to babysit for them a few nights per week. David generously paid me to babysit my own kids knowing I could use the money being a single mom to Sky and a full-time college student at Mercer County College.

When David and Laurie started dating, Laurie was very gracious in allowing me from the first to visit with the children in the house. Once we all decided to go up to the Siddha yoga ashram in South Fallsburg together as a family. David, Laurie, the children, and I had adjoining rooms so that if I needed help dressing or with anything David could help me as he'd done ever since I'd injured myself with the gun. If it were not for Laurie's kindness and acceptance of the difficult and unique situation it would have been much tougher for me to deal with the fact that they were getting married. And eventually Laurie would have to put up some boundaries so that I was not just popping in whenever I wanted like I was accustomed to doing before she and David met and fell in love.

While I was attending Mercer, I had a lot of term papers to write; and David would copy edit just about all of them during or after his work day. He was an excellent editor, and I managed to get nearly straight as on all my papers with his help.

The nice thing is that David and Laurie still allowed me to be a big part of the children's lives even in the midst of my breakdowns or whatever problems I would have now and then with this debilitating mental illness. My family loved both David and Laurie. At Christmas my mother would invite both of them to be part of our Christmas brunch since David and Laurie did not celebrate Christmas with Laurie's family being Jewish. My mom would buy gifts for them like a gift certificate to one of their favorite restaurants, so magically we were able to blend the families in a loving, harmonious way.

Everyone was caring and respectful of each member of the family. I feel very blessed that both David and Laurie have been so generous, loving, and caring to me and all the children throughout the last twenty or more years. David and Laurie are both pretty successful in their careers and financially are in much better shape than me, so they have been almost like surrogate parents to me by helping me pay for car insurance, AAA, and even groceries during periods of depression or times when I may have had a breakdown.

Twice at Thanksgiving Laurie was kind enough to invite not just my mom and me, but both of the men I love to Thanksgiving dinner at their beautiful home in Monroe where Laurie's beautiful, framed abstract oil paintings decorate the dining and living rooms. In fact, Laurie was sensitive enough to ask me if my friend and former beau, Michael, usually spends the holidays with me. Besides the fact that he escorted me to both of the kid's weddings she must have noticed that he spent Christmas with us all too when Kyrie and her former husband, Rudy, had us all over for the Christmas holiday in 2017. It is unique for a woman to have two serious relationships in her life, and even more unique and a blessing that she is accepted for being polyamorous along with her partners.

There was a time when I had only the kids over to my apartment for Thanksgiving, and David and Laurie would do their own thing sometimes going to Laurie's sister's house for dinner. But it seems we are spending more time as a blended family as the years go by.

The nice thing about having Laurie as David' new wife is that she was not just sweet, but loving and very "together", that is., whole and healthy after having done work on herself. She was an art therapist and became a psychologist after going back to get another degree while living with David. Laurie encouraged David to go for therapy himself which was a great idea since he had been controlling and occasionally psychologically abusive and on two occasions he hit me, but that was so long ago; and our relationship has completely transformed since then. David is extremely kind, funny, and has been so generous to me that he still pays for my car insurance even though it is not something he has to do as part of our divorce agreement. He also shows love, care, and involvement in Sky's life even more than her own father. The qualities of all three of us co-parenting Gabriel and Kyrie made them feel safe, deeply loved, and helped shape the two of them into the beautiful, talented, successful human beings they have now become.

David waited to retire until his late sixties. He had taken a small business in NJ and made it into a multimillion-dollar worldwide company on the web and by phone. Luckily, for all our sakes, even though we are divorced, he has been kind and generous to me, our children, and my youngest daughter who is not even his child. David was so kind and magnanimous he helped my son pay off half the new Chevy Cobalt I'd purchased in a hypomanic phase in 2006 for $18,000, eighteen years after we'd divorced. It was my son's idea because I was truly struggling with the $313.00 monthly payments on it due to a bankruptcy, I filed in the year 2000 and poor credit at the time. Gabriel asked me to find out what was the balance on my loan after I'd been paying for about seventeen months while living below poverty level, getting food stamps, and governmental assistance with utilities. A small bit of SSI and part-time income from massage was barely enough to cover rent, groceries, and clothes for me and my daughter. Let alone a new car payment.

WITH GABRIEL AND KYRIE (1998)

Although Gabriel and Kyrie have not lived in my household for years, our relationship has always been a pleasure. There are far too many wonderful experiences we shared to include in any book, but I will give a few examples.

We were blessed to see Kyrie star in "The Boyfriend" during her sophomore year at Monroe Township High School.

Kyrie also performed in "Grease", the Pirates of Penzance", and starred in "Secret Garden" while a student at the elite performing arts camp, French Woods Festival. Like Gabriel, she always lights up the stage. Whether she has a bit part or the lead your eyes are always drawn to her radiant light and effervescence.

It was rare for a first-time camper to land a leading role in a musical, but Gabriel, though only 12, was so charming and charismatic that he won the hearts of nearly everyone at camp including the casting director, the camp counselors, and most of the kids that attended the camp the first summer he arrived. Gabriel won the role of Tuptim's lover in the musical, "The King and I." He made so many friends that he continues to see many of these close friends who live in New York City to this day.

My "trip" on magic mushrooms with Kyrie and her boyfriend while she was attending the Berklee School of Music in Boston when I was in my early forties was very different from my first experience with my boyfriend, Greg. We shared deep thoughts, metaphysical insights, and some things that had happened to us that we needed to heal with our parents. After that we began making music together. Kyrie sang out in her beautiful way making up lyrics and music simultaneously, played guitar and piano, while her boyfriend, "Burger" played drums. I sang words I made up spontaneously and toned while playing percussion instruments like eggs and maracas. Her boyfriend put on the audiotape recorder so we could listen to it afterward. It was all spontaneous and fun to be so creative and joyous making up new stuff moment by moment.

We got very hungry afterward, and knowing it was unsafe for us to drive, her boyfriend ordered a cab to take us to a friend's restaurant in town where we ate delicious food and had a lot of laughs. We were blessed to be able to use my ex-husband's credit card to pay for the meal. This time the high did not last as long, so Kyrie's boyfriend gave us a bit more since he was the person who acquired the drugs. We were just mellow and tired after we got back to my daughter's apartment. Kyrie and I wanted to go to sleep, we felt lots of love for one another, hugged each other close; and we shared with one another that we'd had a great time, but we both felt complete with our drug experience after that one.

Kyrie and Gabriel call me just about daily leaving me singing messages, and I call both of them each morning while taking my morning bath to leave a loving, positive good morning message. Many times, I'm inspired to sing into their voicemails.

Kyrie and I both have a lot in common. Since we both enjoy dancing, singing, hatha yoga, and chanting kirtan we often get together to share those activities. We especially love dancing together at Ecstatic Dance new Jersey which used to be held at Integral Yoga of Princeton and sometimes attended Dance Improv Live together at the Hopewell Train Station before the fear of the pandemic literally shut the indoor dance expression down. There are occasional live dance jams, but they are reserved for outdoors since people have been so uptight about group gatherings due to the pandemic.

Gabriel often treats all of us to dinners every few weeks or so as a special way of getting our sweet family together. Not only is he generous, but he is kind, talented, funny, and the most charming, loving son a mother could ask for. I feel so blessed to have such a successful, hardworking, loving, and devoted son.

For several years before David met Laurie, he would come out to dinner with me and the kids to Chi Chi's, Red Lobster, the Olive Garden, or some nice, fun place making us all still feel like one cohesive family unit. David always picked up the tab, and nothing on the menu was ever off limits. We could order appetizers, drinks, expensive entrees, and dessert if we wished. Until David married Laurie Gabriel and Kyrie often came over most week-ends to visit, I would take Kyrie and Gabriel to their soccer matches and watch them play. They both were talented actors, so everyone in the family including my mom and grandmother, Lucy, while still living into her mid-nineties, would love to watch them perform in musicals at school and then, during summer vacations when David sent them to French Woods Festival, an expensive, elite camp known specifically for the great actors and actresses it produced, all of us would make the two and a half hour drive to the Catskills very near the ashram to see both children star in various musicals. The first year Gabriel attended camp he was chosen to play LunTha, Tuptim's lover, one of the leading roles in "The King and I" which I was so excited to see because I'd played the leading role of Anna while a senior in high school as I mentioned. I was amazed to find I still remembered a lot of my lines and much of the entire script. I sang along quietly to most of the songs. Then he had a small role in "A funny Thing Happened on the Way to the Forum" playing along with his soon to be dear friend, Gabriel, who had the lead role as Gabriel also played one of the Pharisees in Jesus Christ Superstar, a very professional production with a terrific cast and great orchestra.

He also landed a leading role in "A Chorus Line" which amazed me because the choreography is tough; it was very jazzy, Bob Fosse style, and just the same as the choreography on Broadway. His "summer girlfriend" at the time got the leading role of "Cassie", so I suppose the private lessons he received from her helped him to learn the steps quickly for a beginner. Even the costumes down to the gold top hats and suits for the finale were exactly the same as those I'd seen on Broadway. As fate would have it, the actress, Sandy Duncan, whose son had a major role in the cast, was in the audience the night we came to see the show which caused a bit of a stir. Sandy Duncan still looked as young and pretty as when she starred in Peter Pan.

The night I went to see Gabriel perform in "A Chorus Line" I brought my good friend, Lynn Hartz, from West Virginia, whom I at met at the International Writers' Guild "Remember the Magic

Conference" up there with me. She came up to visit for several days, so she came with me to Hancock, New York near Monticello and Lynn really loved the show including Gabriel's enthusiastic, professional performance. I stood up to shout Bravos for the entire cast which got an enthusiastic standing ovation. "A Chorus Line" is one of my favorite shows. It's such a favorite I've seen seven different productions of it, and this summer camp theater definitely compared to the best ones.

Gabriel also landed the role of Billie Flynn, the role made famous in the movie "Chicago" by Richard Gere. Gabriel did very well during the tap-dancing routine in the court room. I was happy to see he did not inherit my fear of being a good tap dancer. Kyrie also performed in "Chicago" though she had a much smaller role.

KYRIE, THE SINGER

I happen to be one of my daughters, Kyrie's, biggest fans, and for a while when she was not singing professionally much, I managed to create gigs in the Princeton area where I would be singing or performing my poetry from my anthology where I would feature Kyrie as the diva. I would recite several of my poems by heart, sing an original song and maybe one jazz or rock song like "Heatwave", and Kyrie would mesmerize the audience with her lovely voice singing a song from her heart with such soul that she transforms the atmosphere and audience into one of great love and joy.

I invited my good friend of many years and musician and synthesizer player extraordinaire, Don Slepian, to do some solo numbers and also to accompany us both on piano or synthesizer at concerts I originated to go along with my poetry anthology. Don also shares his masterful playing of two or three flute recorders. We have done several concerts at Pebble Hill Church in Doylestown, PA, Integral Yoga of Princeton, the Heart of Art Studio in Hamilton, and at my dear friend and foster grammy, Laura Kruskal's, home, called "The Princeton Origami Center.

Kyrie and I also did a gig I produced and emceed at the Senior Center at Suzanne Paterson Center in which my friend and dance aerobics instructor, Ellen, helped choreograph dances to "New York, New York" and another song for about eight of the seniors in our aerobics class who volunteered to participate in which Kyrie and I sang solo and danced. It was a free concert and a lot of fun to perform. My friends George Knoedl, who plays bass and guitar, played some of his original songs, as well as my good friend, Greg Lagana, who accompanied us on piano, were also part of the fun. Greg and George had also accompanied me and Kyrie during another concert I arranged at an Indian restaurant on Nassau Street owned by one of my friends where we featured two of my angel buddies and fellow ministers from Universal Brotherhood, Armand and Angelina Del Volpe, from Florida. Kyrie sang several of her original tunes which she performed with her guitar that night. Several of my friends who paid to attend that concert shared that Kyrie's music and divine Presence had shifted them into a more joyous reality and into living from a higher paradigm. That is how special, sweet, and precious is my daughter, Kyrie. She has yet to be truly recognized for the amazing talent she is, but her love and beautiful voice changes the atmosphere wherever she goes and sings.

LAUGHING

The two of us love to laugh, and when one of us cracks a joke the other starts to belly laugh and cannot stop. Both Gabriel and Kyrie used to make fun of me a lot or poke fun at the waiter. Unfortunately, they would do that to me a lot when we were eating out in a restaurant, right after I'd finished my meal. Since it would be right when I had a full belly, laughing so hard made me almost lose my meal, and it felt very uncomfortable. But to laugh that hard every time was well worth the discomfort.

DANCING

After Kyrie met her first husband, Rudy, and moved to London and back to the US. a few times we still always made a point to spend quality time with one another, whether it was just to go out to dinner or lunch with her sister, Sky, in Princeton, out to Palermo's Restaurant, on Thursdays which used to be karaoke night, to dance, sing a few numbers, and chill with the new friends we made there. Thursday night karaoke always seemed to draw the same crowd. Most everyone had good voices or at least good stage presence, and were encouraging to those who got up to sing. And just about always I would get up to dance for most of the fast numbers which gave everybody else in the bar permission to dance. I guess they all figured if I was not afraid to dance with an imperfect hemiplegic body with as much unabashed fun-loving enthusiasm as I had then they could get up too and have a good time without worrying what others thought about them. I like the phrase I once put on a T-shirt that my friend Karin liked "Dance Like No One Else is Watching" because basically, that is how we should all live our lives. Well, there are no shoulds. There are only coulds. We have a lot more possibilities when we live for ourselves and our own joys and dreams than if we care about other's approval or what our parents might think of us after we go to ten years of school to become a medical doctor or lawyer; and then we can hang a certificate up and put a shingle outside our door. If it makes us feel rushed, grumpy, or always on the go not having time to enjoy our family or friends then what is the point?

MINISTRY (1999)

I had surrendered my life to God and the guru as an ambassador of Light and minister of peace promoting Universal Brotherhood. I am so happy and proud of myself and accomplishments. In September of 1999, I was awarded a Bachelor of Divinity, ordained by the Universal Brotherhood Ministries as a legal minister along with my dear friend, Carola, by Rev. Gregory Possman, a former President of UB and on the Board of Directors. Becoming a minister in the Universal Brotherhood Organization, involved some serious contemplation about what indeed, was my ministry, writing an essay about it, and a physical ceremony in which I was ordained in Ocean Grove, NJ by someone from the Board of Directors with the authority to make me a minister. As a minister I am able to perform legal weddings, memorial services, funerals, and christenings. But, along with any form of initiation there are trials like chasms of fire purifying one's ego.

At one time in states of depression my achievements meant absolutely nothing to me. All I could think about was giving up and going back to God (by dying, I believed). Now that I experience my own connection to Source right here within my own heart, I know that I have nowhere to go but within myself in deep silence, prayer, or contemplation. Or I dance, sing, make love, garden, chant, and write. I focus on all the things that make me happy and bring me joy and ecstasy. Life is such a great gift and a blessing, and I am here to enjoy it. And boy, do I ever! I think sometimes that I am the happiest, most expressive woman in the universe. I feel totally free and uninhibited to express my love, creativity, and joy in any way I choose. I love sex and feel free to share intimacy with whomever I resonate with in a sexual or sensual way. I do not feel bound by any earthly or conventional rules.

I have my own unique guidance system just like everyone's, and I follow what is in my heart at each and every moment. I have learned to honor myself, respect others, and to be true to myself. If I feel some kind of heartfelt connection or sexual chemistry for a man or woman, even if I am meeting them for the first time, I just go with the flow and open my heart to them. I am a very healthy and happy woman. I enjoy giving myself regular orgasms through masturbation and by sharing chemistry with other friends and clients whom I love dearly. My love is expansive. I feel like I have no boundaries. It just keeps growing and growing. I feel tremendous glee and contentment no matter where I am or whom I am with. I see the Beloved no matter where I look. I see Him in the eyes of all the children, in the precious animals that serve us and bring us so much joy. In my sweet, devoted cats, Lovey Bear and Gita who are lying peacefully by my side as I write at 5:30 AM.

I see the Beloved in all my sweet friends and family, and in the beauties of nature. I see Him expressed in the beauty of the pink orange sunset, in the great expanse of the starlit firmament, in the green fields and pastures, in the vast blue green ocean, but most especially I experience Him right here in my own golden heart. I feel so much love and joy that sometimes I feel like my heart could literally burst! God's love is so sweet like nectar, that I just cannot contain it. I am filled to the brim with continuous amrita (Sanskrit for nectar) from within and without.

It is like a beautiful dream to me. My heart and mind overflow with gratitude, and my cup runneth over with more blessings than a 65-year-old woman could count on twenty million hands and feet. My guru's adorable feet! I worship the feet of my precious Baba, my precious Gurumayi, my precious mother and father, my precious children, grandparents, and ancestors who came before, just as much as I worship my own. The guru is the root of all action, and through the grace of God and Muktananda I have become one with the object of my worship. There is only God, dear ones. There is only love. Everything else you perceive is just illusion. Love is union. Love is knowledge, love is medicine, and love is wealth. Love is the greatest treasure of the heart. Love is the magnet that attracts the divine power. Therefore, feel love and let it flow continually in your own heart.

Rumi said, "Through love all that is bitter becomes sweet. Through love all that is copper turns to gold. Through love all dregs will turn to purest wine; through love all pain becomes medicine. Through love the dead become alive. Through love the king becomes a slave."

My Baba said, " Whenever you experience this rush of love in your heart for yourself and for everything in this world, you should hold onto this state. That is the doorway to divinity; that is the key. Don't let go of it. The truth is that this world is full of love. This world is an embodiment of the bliss of God."

Remember that nothing is small in the eyes of God. Do all that you do with great love. Let the innate good in your heart connect with the good in others, until the entire world is transformed through the compelling power of your love.

The poet saint, Hafiz, said, " Where is the door to God? In the sound of a barking dog. In the ring of a hammer, in a drop of rain. In the face of Everyone I see."

If you do not feel joy or love just change your focus. Think of something that makes you happy. Look outside your door at the beautiful trees, grass, and flowers. Make friends with your neighbors and pet their dogs. When you begin to notice one beautiful thing you will notice another until eventually you will see only beauty. The beauty of your own divine Self-expressed in form is everywhere you look. It is within and all around you, my dearest ones. Look and you will see. Seek and you shall find. Ask and it shall be given. So many splendid treasures and you need not look further than your own backyard. You don't need to take a holy pilgrimage to India, Mecca, or Jerusalem like my children and I did. You only need to go inside to that place of perfect stillness where love and peace reside. You are the joy and love you seek my dear children. You are the journey. You are the goal. You are the Enlightened One! You are the Buddha. You are the Christ. You are Mother Mary. You are the Magdalene. You are Ruth. You are Abraham. You are Moses. You are Yahweh. There is no one or nothing outside of yourself that is greater than your very own Self. We are all so blessed.

Through my new attitude and changes in my thoughts, words, and actions I am in the process of realizing all my dreams to become a successful published writer, poet, entertainer, public speaker, singer, and world traveler.

True spirituality involves caring for oneself, others, and the world. Some people prefer to do this in a relatively passive manner. I don't.

I take a trash bag with me during my morning contemplation walk to pick up whatever litter I see on the ground. Because I work for myself as a massage therapist and natural health care practitioner my time is my own and my schedule flexible so that I can write, dance, listen to music, entertain friends, exercise, go to the chiropractor, or do whatever pleases me during the day.

I try to do many acts of loving kindness throughout the day for it gives me great joy and brings me satisfaction when I bring joy to another. When I am kind and do something nice for someone less fortunate my heart feels humbled. My soul is on fire with love. I am a gentle being and I see only gentleness and purity in all others around me.

I donate food and clothing to my local shelter for teens and children who are temporarily displaced due to domestic violence, drugs, or whatever. I donate whatever clothes Sky has outgrown to the Vietnam Veterans and the homeless shelter in Trenton. I love to do this because it makes me feel so good and it makes room in our closets for new clothes and abundance.

Each Christmas I volunteer to help a family at Enable in Princeton who has a child or children with one or more disabilities. I used to work or Enable as a respite worker in the autumn of 1997. I just love helping other people even when it is anonymous. So many people have helped me and Sky when we lived at Griggs Farm with extra groceries like canned goods and gift certificates to local supermarkets that I just want to give back all the love, kindness, and service in whatever way I can. I don't have enough money for all the gratitude that is in my heart to give back to all the kind people who have helped me, but I do my best. My son and ex-husband think I'm generous to a fault. They don't believe I should be donating money to charities or giving out money when I don't have that much extra for myself, but I think differently. I believe that when I give money and service from my golden heart to help those that are less fortunate than me that God always takes care of me and rewards me in some unexpected way. I always pay my bills and have enough for necessities, regular manicures, pedicures, to get my hair done, and regular recreation, so I never really worry about money. It just flows in and flows back out again, just like the tides of the ocean. Money is love in action, and it can be very useful in solving the world's problems once you have enough to take care of yourself and your family

My Brief Journey into Christian Science

Shortly after my ordination, in October, I was walking along Nassau Street, the main street in Princeton and happened into the local Christian Science book store. I already knew some things about New Thought Christian Science founder and minister, Mary Baker Eddy, and became interested in reading some of the literature inside the store. I happened to share with the clerk that I suffered from bipolar depression for which I took regular medication, but I did not really like having to take the medicine. The clerk told me of a woman who had been suffering from months on and off with manic depression, but after becoming a Christian Scientist following the teachings proposed by Ms. Eddy in "Science and Health", in 1875. The book was later re-titled "Science and Health, With Key to the Scriptures". In a 1915 sermon, Mary Baker Eddy had said "Christian Science repudiates the evidences of the senses and rests upon the supremacy of God. Christian healing, established upon this Principle, vindicates the omnipotence of the Supreme Being by employing no other remedy than Truth, Life, and Love, understood, to heal all ills that flesh is heir to. *It places no faith in hygiene or drugs*; it reposes all faith in mind, in spiritual power divinely directed." [Italics added]. On the basis of such statements, Christian Scientists understand most voluntary acceptance of conventional medicine to derive from lack of faith.

Carol, the woman the clerk had mentioned was going to be on the radio that night, as a matter of chance, so I tuned into her. What she shared about going totally drug free even following a car accident, truly inspired me. She was basically praying, staying in seclusion, and reading her Bible a lot. She only surrounded herself with believers, with her closest Christian friends and family members who believed in Jesus' healing power. She shared that after months of ups and downs even on medicines she left work to do some inner study. From her work with Jesus and the teachings in the scriptures she revealed that she was completely healed, whole, and free of having to take medications of any kind for manic depression or any ailment whatsoever. Sounded pretty darn easy and wonderful to me which reminded me of my younger days when I would not even take an aspirin for a headache. If you remember, I took no pain killers or anesthetics of any kind during all three births of my children.

After hearing her on the radio, I was so inspired I wanted her to work with me so that I could finally stop all the drugs I'd been taking almost daily for eight years. I was able to get the phone number from the radio program, and I asked if she would be willing to work with me. She said "Yes,

I would, but in order for me to work with you, you must immediately stop all medications you are taking." Wow – just like that.

Well, that was fine, but I was not really a reader of the Bible, and that was just a great excuse for me to go off my meds without putting in the inner work, if you know what I mean. I threw the rest of my orange-colored pills into the waste basket in the bathroom. I felt exuberant, creative, very sensuous, and very connected to God within and all around me when I danced, chanted, and stayed up late at night writing ecstatic poetry and love songs to my boyfriend, Ernie, my three beautiful children, God, the trees, certain favorite animals (especially deer}, and Mother Nature in general.

One Sunday I also decided to attend the service at the local Christian Science church where I heard all sorts of amazing testimonies where people were miraculously healed of things like cancer, postpartum depression, and even broken bones. All as a result reading and studying the Bible, affirmative prayer. and the power of Jesus' love.

The euphoria lasted for three months. I was singing a lot, staying up past midnight watching comedy shows, singing with my folk group, the Solidarity Singers, and dancing a lot, but I remember one night after a day of activity following being up until 2 AM and going to different clubs and activities three nights that week I was supposed to go to Dance Improv, the monthly improvisational dance group I'd been attending since 1986, but when I went to turn the engine on, there was no spark, just the click one hears when there is a dead battery. When I looked up, I saw one of my lights and the radio had been left on which drained my battery. A perfect metaphor for my physical body and my life. I was completely drained with no more spark left to dance or even drive out of the parking lot. Part of me was disappointed I would not get to dance with my friends, but another, more practical part of me, was so relieved, and I did not even bother calling my best friend to ask him to pick me up or try to get a jump start. I realize now I was addicted to those "highs", almost like a drug. So, whatever the mood stabilizer was doing to help me stay in the middle was a very good thing, and I could see myself going off it, but not without doing it in some scientific way with the support of my doctors, minister, and family. My grandmother had given me my inheritance early because I asked after finding out both my brothers had received their inheritances early. I'd had another car accident, and due to the car's older age I had chosen not to get collision, so I was stranded unless I took a bus or cab. Being a single mom going to college full time and needing to shop for groceries, go to counseling, etc. would be very challenging without transportation, so I asked my sweet grammy who was in her early nineties if she could give me seven thousand dollars before she died, just as she had for my brothers. She generously granted my request which I turned around and paid for a used Honda Civic mostly in cash with a very small monthly payment for five years, and whatever was left I just pissed away on clothes and dinners out. Once the money was gone, I started to go downhill as I had in prior times when in the exact same situations. You'd think I would have learned after the first six times! Again, a lesson in balance. With euphoria, comes dysphoria, the opposite or equal polarity to balance out bliss – God's actual logical way of balancing the Universe.

For no apparent reason, in October, the euphoria turned into dysphoria. I was preparing for a concert in which I would sing and read my poetry. I had sung professionally years earlier, but after Kyrie, my first daughter, was born, I gave it up. When I was a single mom dealing with the debilitating ups and downs of bipolar depression, I lost a lot of my self-confidence as a singer and entertainer. For whatever crazy reason, I was really scared of performing again. During times of suicidal depression, I'd become so overcome with irrational thoughts and fears that I could barely function because I could not sleep at night. I felt as if I were wrestling with ghosts or demons in my bedroom.

In retrospect, I wish I'd told Carol that I'd been on the medications for years, and it would probably behoove me to check with my psychiatrist first to see how I could wean myself off the two medications and replace the regimen with excellent nutrition, vitamin supplements, and daily exercise. But I was hypomanic, and tended to be impulsive at those times. I would make decisions to buy cars, go on expensive vacations, or have sex with men I'd just met without the benefit of using protection. I had even married an abusive man fifteen years my junior whom I met at the psychiatric hospital, the Carrier Clinic, when we were both in-patients there, while I was in a manic state. I left my husband and two little children in order to do so. It was one of the biggest mistakes in my life after shooting myself in the head.

While I was on the medication, Depakote, a mood stabilizer I'd taken on and off since 1991, I rarely had dark thoughts of despair and self-hatred. In fact, I was very much in love with myself, my family, friends, and all beings everywhere. I also took an anti-depressant in the mornings. The only time I stopped the medicines was when I believed that they made me tired or lethargic and sad. But, as a holistic health care practitioner, I did not like being dependent on the medications.

The night before my second serious suicide attempt, I was in a place of mental anguish, torment, and terror. I was supposed to be performing songs and poems at a local Goddess Center, and for whatever reason I became extremely anxious about it. I'm not sure if I believe in ghosts – actually I do believe in people's spirits that have had trouble crossing over to the Other Side of Pure Light due to traumas like murder, betrayal, and things like that because they do not even know they are dead. Even though the anxiety had been going on for a few months after stopping all my medications, I started to become quite anxious and fearful.

That night was Halloween night, and my musician friend and supporter of many of my projects, Don Slepian, would be coming over to rehearse and place an original song of mine on audiotape for my practice at home for the upcoming concert the following month. All my confident thoughts and feelings about myself the prior months suddenly turned into "Voices" of unworthiness in my head that were nearly impossible to stop. For about a month I'd been eating poorly and began having private, clandestine suicidal thoughts again. When I told my mom she said you'd better go back to AAMH, the place where I'd been seeing a monthly psychiatrist and counselor twice per month. Once I believed I had "license" or permission to go off my medications I figured I did not need to go there anymore, so they had taken me out of their "system".

I called in the midst of this crisis and told them I needed an immediate appointment. The receptionist gave me the bad news that since I was "out of the system" I would have to wait three months just to go for a 90-minute intake interview, and then it might take another few months before I even got an appointment with a psychiatrist or nurse practitioner because they were so busy. In retrospect I wonder why they did not tell me about NAMI, the National Alliance of Mental Illness, which was right down the road in Lawrenceville, who would have recommended some folks I could talk to right away on their hotline. I really did not want to be hospitalized, especially since I had a ten-year-old daughter living at home with me. I always hated the hospital experience anyway.

That particular night I believed my negative, irrational thinking for two months had attracted some type of ghost or negative entity. The thoughts in my head were not from me is all I could say. The persistent inner voice kept saying "just rid yourself of your evil body and you will be free. You will be happy. Your suffering will be over."

Since I did not have an unhappy life and I loved my family and close friends I knew these thoughts were not my own and coming from some lower realm.

Don and I tried to rehearse that night, but it was impossible with trick-or-treaters coming to the door every ten minutes or so. We finally decided just to tape "By Your Grace" right away so I could practice my song with musical background at a quieter time.

For about a week I'd begun thinking and planning ways to end my suffering. I'd already tried almost every other possible way including shooting myself, so I was going to have to find a more permanent solution in order to rid myself of the body were the "Voices" (inner thoughts) going on in an endless loop in my mind except when Sky was home and I was interacting with her. She was the sweetest little ten-year-old girl whom I truly loved, believe it or not, and my other two children were so beautiful too, but since they did not live with me, I was not thinking of their welfare very much. I knew they had a father and stepmom to take care of them after I was gone.

I'd watched the movie about St. Joan of Arc just a week before, and for whatever reason, burning the body to cinders popped into my mind. What was I thinking? It is horribly sad, especially because I felt so ashamed, depressed, and alone that I considered taking myself away from my precious children—again! They were and are the sweet Lights of my Life. I did not have a lighter, and luckily, I did not do too much planning like buying gasoline or something that would cause me and my home to go up in flames. But one of my male neighbors whom I knew smoked cigarettes happened to pass me by as we were both leaving our mailboxes. I told him innocently, "I lost my lighter, could I please borrow one from you?" He gave me the lighter he had on him not knowing the devilish action I planned to do with it.

TRIAL BY FIRE, NOV 1 1999

I awoke the morning of November 1st, 1999 with thoughts of anxiety and terror racing through my mind. It was so acute, intense, and horrible that I began to hit the back of my head on the headboard of my bed to try and take my mind off the devilish thoughts. The physical pain distracted me from the mental pain. I remember stroking my face and head saying "Don't hurt yourself, sweetheart, but there was still that other crazy voice trying to drown out Mother Mary, Jesus, or my guardian angel's voice telling me they loved me and I would be OK. I had a lot of self-hatred come up about my "ugly" hemiplegic hanging left arm, shoulder and hand.

Then, in one thoughtless act, I put my left hand through the fire coming up out of the red lighter I used to light my meditation candles. But other than hurting my hand I realized this act was not going to set me free, so then the "Voice" said, "Set your pajamas on fire."

I had a long polyester cotton night shirt on, which was quite flammable, and it did not take long to set my shirt on fire with the lighter. I could feel my chest burning. I quickly ran into the bathroom to see what was happening and to stop the fire. I threw water on my gown, but could not stop the quickly burning shirt. I looked at myself in the mirror as if to face it, yelling "NO!" in a very loud voice and proceeded to pull my shirt over my head with one hand as fast as I could. I had an instantaneous picture in my mind of my beautiful, sweet, ten-year-old daughter, Sky, coming home from school in the afternoon, finding her mom burnt on the floor. In that moment, I made a conscious decision to STOP, as quickly as possible, this horrible suicide attempt from going any further.

Unfortunately, I did not know about "stop, drop and roll", to put out a clothing fire. I did not feel the pain so much, probably because I was partially out of my body, but I called 9-1-1 immediately "Operator, could you please send an ambulance immediately? I accidentally knocked over a candle while I was meditating and I'm badly burned."

"Yes, ma'am, What's your address?"

"I live in Griggs Farm in Princeton at 147 Griggs Drive."

"All right. Is there a fire anywhere?"

"No, I put it out myself. But I'm scared. Please send someone quickly."

I sprang into action, since I was barely dressed, going to my dresser to choose comfortable, pink fleece work-out pants and a long, lavender all cotton T shirt.

I went into the bathroom again to peer at the damage I'd done. My face was beet red. And part of both my eyebrows were burned on the inner corner. The color of my cheeks and chin matched the shame, embarrassment, and guilt I felt, yet again, about trying to take my own life – especially since I was a mother of three children.

Five or six minutes later, there was a knock on my door. A policewoman arrived with two EMT s who examined me and said that the burns on my chest, upper arms, and left hand were not too bad, probably a second-degree burn, so I did not feel so bad until I arrived at the emergency room in Princeton Hospital. Both the doctors there believed my burns were bad enough to be considered third degree and made the decision to have me airlifted to St. Barnabas Hospital in Livingston, NJ, the place that had the best burn unit in the area. I have little memory of what happened during and after the helicopter ride. I guess that they gave me a very strong pain killer to knock me out.

By now, this memoir is seeming more like "The Perils of Pauline" than the triumphant memoir about God's grace and love that I had hoped it would be. The amazing thing is, though, that the magic of this whole tale is that I survived this crazy illness to come out of the darkness embracing all that has happened to me, to come back into the Light of God's love as a stronger, wiser woman, to live a more balanced, happier, and safer life. Just that I am alive to talk about this is a miracle—especially at a time of the "Me Too" movement, when women all over the world are sharing their personal stories of rape, abuse, and harassment. Though I loved my father a lot, sometimes I believe I would not have manic-depressive illness if he had not molested me as a teenager.

I was intubated upon arrival at St. Barnabas. One week later, the doctors told my mother "Mrs. Olson, we can't assure you your daughter will be able to breathe on her own when we take out her

breathing tubes. In order to do the skin grafting we must take her off life support. We will be taking huge chunks of skin from her upper thighs to cover the burns on her chest, shoulders and arm."

But I recovered quickly and was released from St. Barnabas after seven weeks of loving intensive care, six weeks in a room at the ICU and one week in the psychiatric unit. So, Jesus, my angels, and God's infinitely intelligent and loving consciousness acting in as and through the hands and hearts of the various doctors, surgeons, nurses, and burn technicians working at St. Barnabas Hospital brought me back to a place of balance and healing after setting my hand and pajamas on fire which created third degree burns over 18 % of my body (left hand, chest and upper arms to be exact).

Subsequently, I decided to cover the skin graft scars over my heart and on my upper chest with a beautiful pink and green tattoo of a naked nymph coming out of a pretty flower with green leaves. Bobby, my tattoo artist from Living Arts Tattoo told me he was using my own breasts as a guide to illustrate the tattoo. It is still very beautiful today and makes me feel a bit better about having defiled my lovely body.

During the first several weeks I was in the bed recuperating at St. Barnabas I could not remember my boyfriend, Ernie's, phone number, or other things I would normally know consciously in an instant, but that may have been from the effects of the morphine I was on in the beginning. I was also having delusions in the very beginning the first week I was there. I kept dreaming I was not in a "real" hospital. I had paranoid delusions I'd been kidnapped by the dark haired, Spanish man who owned the Mexican restaurant at the Princeton Shopping Center, and that I'd been brought there for people to observe my naked body for some experiments. Maybe that was a side effect of all the intense medications I was on also. I kept telling my mom I wanted to go home for Thanksgiving, that I was afraid in the hospital. Finally, I told my doctor about the manic-depressive illness, and he put me on Depakote and also Zyprexa, an anti-psychotic which was new for me. I did not like it because it made me sleep all the time. Besides, I knew I was not psychotic. Or perhaps I was too psychotic to even be aware that I was psychotic. Drugs and other medications do strange things to me. I am very sensitive to the smallest amounts.

I recuperated from my burns. Each morning after breakfast in the intensive care unit. my wounds were lovingly bathed in a special oil by a funny, handsome, burn tech named Paul and his nursing assistants. That was the high point of my day. I was the "Queen" of the burn unit in the beginning until I began to improve incrementally day by day, week by week.

In the beginning I was still very depressed, and when I'm deeply depressed, I have no appetite and not much desire to do anything but numb myself with television. So, I did not eat much of the food. I was not hungry at all, but I was practically forced by the nurses, nutritionist, and family to eat whatever was brought to me. They said that I needed the food and liquids in order for the burns and grafts to heal quickly. But I was recalcitrant. I did not like being force fed bland hospital food, and even wrote a letter of complaint to the patient advocate, but eventually I was convinced by my mom, my son, Gabriel, and the nurses that the food was going to help get me better and out of there, so I complied. I was nearly all better, but my doctor recommended I go upstairs to the psychiatric unit for at least a week to see how was my state of mind.

When I returned to my mom's house in the dead of winter, it was with some misgivings. I needed to live with her for several weeks, until I was well enough to live on my own again. I still felt terribly ashamed and embarrassed that I'd allowed myself to get so depressed again that I tried suicide. It was hard for me to show my face in public to my neighbors, some friends, and even my boyfriend. The first time I saw someone I knew in my neighborhood when I came home to take care of my two cats, I hid my face in shame behind one of the large bushes by the club house in the development.

But then I finally took time to read all the mail that had accumulated while I was in the hospital. My mom had been collecting it every day when she'd go back to feed my cats and clean out the litter box after she picked Sky up from the bus stop. There had been so many well wishes from people I did not even know. Scores of funny, loving get-well cards. There had been not one, but two fundraisers to help me pay my bills while I was in the hospital by two of my sweet neighbors. One had a day of massage therapy one Saturday which brought in only $90, but what a kind thought and demonstration of love! The other was some type of Girl Scout bake and cookie sale that brought in even more money. It wasn't a lot of money, but the loving kindness behind these actions lifted my spirits more than I could imagine.

My insurance covered the cost of the hospital, emergency room, and ambulance, but my monthly bills continued while I was away. My mother paid my car payment, all the rest of my credit card bills and the electric bill. She explained to Patriot Media that I was in the hospital, asking them to temporarily suspend my telephone and cable service for a few months, and they did.

It was this type of kindness from friends, family, and even strangers that spurred me on to get better again encouraging me to get back into living a "normal" life again. And it would be a long time before I experimented with going off the medication again – or if I did decide to discontinue the Depakote I did so with the knowledge of my psychiatrist who tapered me off gradually.

I moved out of my mom's house Christmas Eve after an argument we had over something petty. I don't even remember what it was. She was overwhelmed after being burdened with so much extra responsibility, besides caring for Sky. And I used that argument to take my power back, so Sky and I spent Christmas Eve in a very clean apartment with my boyfriend, Ernie. My mom was so efficient she had asked my ex-husband, David to pay for a cleaning service to get the place in shape so I would not have a lot to do when I got home. So, I was happy to be home again in my own bed sleeping with my boyfriend, Ernie, beside me with my beautiful, sweet, ten-year-old daughter in the bedroom right next to me on one of my favorite holidays. How lucky was I to be alive! And to be able to feel again that I was both blessed and a blessing to others.

FIGHTING BACK (2000)

During the challenging Christmas season in 2000, I wrote in anger "They Kept Her in the Closet", a poem about how badly it felt to be ostracized and misunderstood.[8]

I have survived my past and refuse to be kept in the closet any longer. I wish to share the complete truth about my past experience with all three of my parents because it has helped shape who I am and what I've become today. I know that my experience with incest and abuse is common. Hopefully others who read this story can also relate to it and get beyond the pain of their past to a bright, shiny future. Just like mental illness the problem of incest is kept alive due to the negative stigma and secrecy surrounding it. It must come out into the open or the illness of the perpetrators and society's limiting sexual and cultural mores will never be improved upon.

Sex is not a shameful act. It is a divine, God given gift for the procreation of the species as well as a sacred expression of love, peace, connection, and joy. It is actually therapeutic and nurturing, but not something done with children or forced upon someone else without their consent. The expression of my sexuality and sensuality is a source of great joy to me, my boyfriend, and most of my friends. When we realize that our sexuality is connected to our spirituality, we will begin to heal the split between our hearts, minds, and genitals. Sex is spiritual. Choosing healthy sexual partners whether they be male or female is a part of what makes us whole and happy and helps us to define ourselves in connection to Source as we love and allow ourselves to be loved deeply by another. We also have the opportunity to choose how we wish to create our sacred partnerships. At times monogamy has worked the best for me. At others I enjoy the freedom of living a polyamorous lifestyle in which I am in more than one committed relationship, but I am honest about my relationships with each one of my precious partners.

We can choose to reevaluate the outmoded, limiting patriarchal views concerning sex and conventional sexual expression. All of us are divine, unique beings, and each one of us has a particular preference and unique way of expressing ourselves in that regard. All the shame, guilt, and secrecy regarding sex needs to be let go of in order for our society to become truly whole and healthy. Let's get sex out of the closet once and for all. Let's kiss and hug each other unabashedly in malls, stores, and churches when we meet one another. A long, openhearted hug with my friends, family, and even strangers who feel like kindred spirits when first we meet feels Soo good and just gives me warm fuzzies all over.

When we can see sex and affectionate expression as a normal, healthy, divine urge that expresses

---

8 Found in my "Heartscapes" anthology.

uniquely in each individual we can begin to free ourselves from the limiting, false ideas and beliefs that the antiquated patriarchal Judeo-Christian priests and forefathers foisted upon us out of their own fears and shame. The patriarch used shame and guilt about our innate God given sexuality and sensuality as a way to control us. Since "NOW" is the only moment there is, we, the survivors, can choose to forgive our parents, ancestral priests and dominators, and be free to completely love and accept ourselves as divine, Whole sexual beings.

We are the only ones who know what is right for our particular temperament whether it is monogamy, polygamy, polyamory, heterosexuality, bisexuality, homosexuality, transgender expression, or whatever. I like the Wiccan creed that states, "Do what you wilt and harm none". Let us enjoy sexual expression for the pure joy of it! Let's please ourselves without needing outside approval and follow our own inner guidance honoring our own boundaries and those of others. Let's deliberately create our own reality, and mind our own business. American zoologist and sex researcher, Alfred Kinsey, and his wife, Mac, were just two very inspiring, controversial expansive married scientific researchers into various sexual behaviors You are not alone in experiencing that your needs and desires were more expansive and different than what you'd originally realized. Alfred Kinsey is a leader, along with his wife, who spread peace, love, and Truth. The Kinsey's and their team of researchers were definitely pioneers who helped to move along the outmoded, patriarchal mass consciousness focused on greed and false concepts like sin and judgment. As Alfred Kinsey made the world aware in his many years of exhaustive research studying the sexual behaviors and habits of men and women in a scientific manner there is a lot more going on sexually than what is regularly taught or accepted in Judeo-Christian conventional society. He truly opened our eyes to the Truth and contributed immensely to science and the healing of humanity as a whole. He made us all aware that we are not weird or perverted in the various ways that we express ourselves sexually. Masturbating to orgasm is a joyous and nurturing experience. Sharing touch and expressing oneself sexually with a spouse, mate, friend or friends, no matter what gender they are, is fun, healthy, and makes us feel good. It is one of the things that life is all about--pleasure. Without touch and sexual expression life would be pretty dull, sad and boring, would it not? It also would not continue. How can our society continue to suppress a divine urge that is as natural as eating? Do we tell our stomachs to be silent when we are hungry? Of course not.

We are not all partial to heterosexuality, nor are most of us desiring monogamy or conventional marriages. There are many more of us who are inclined to experience a balanced sexual expression that is bi-sexual, and there are many people who choose conventional marriage on the outside but are secretly engaged in homosexual or bi-sexual behavior and have clandestine extra-marital affairs or relationships. I personally know several women who are happily married to men who enjoy dressing up in women's clothing. Two of these men are not homosexual, but it is part of their nature to enjoy self-expression by dressing up as very attractive, feminine women. I see nothing wrong with this behavior if it makes them happy, and they are honest about it. Who am I to judge anyone anyway? Only an individual knows what is right for him or her.

When there are honesty and people do not suppress or repress their natural sexual tendencies there is much less chance for illness or sexual violence. I have a belief that if many of our world leaders and all the rapists and terrorists had weekly sensuous massages, joyous, loving sex on a regular basis I think there would be less need or tendency toward child abuse, pedophilia, or rape in a sexually expressive, free, accepting, and open-minded society.

Masturbation and sexual education should be encouraged, not feared. When young adults are armed with knowledge, they feel empowered and free to make informed choices.

I'm surprised so many Christians do not support sexual education about the use of condoms and other methods of birth control. Our children are going to be engaging in sexual activity whether we like it or not, no matter what religion they are. It is a natural urge and we may as well educate our young adults about birth control and safe sex.

I am so lucky that I did not choose to go back to the Light prematurely, but have remained here in order to share my story.

Let us start with a new, fresh perspective on sex, and see how its repression can lead to violence. We must learn from the wars of our past as well as all our past experiences. We can start this moment with a new attitude of hope, love, and gratitude to our higher power and ourselves that we've made it this far.

It's never too late to have a free and happy childhood. It's never too late to begin a new and happy life dedicated to the service of your own joy and the growth and loving expansion of humanity. Let's invite love, goodness, harmony, and the peace of God into our hearts and our lives from this moment on.

THE MUSICIAN FROM MAINE (2003)

I was invited to be a guest at the surprise 50th birthday party of my good friend, musician extraordinaire, Don Slepian, by his wife, Jan, in January of 2003. I was excited about the party, and it just happened to be held at the same Unitarian Church in East Brunswick where I'd recently performed with my folk group, the Solidarity Singers of the Industrial Union Council.

Due to a bad accident on the NJ Turnpike, I got stuck in a bad traffic jam while driving on Route 1 en route to the party. I sometimes enjoy bumper to bumper traffic jams while I am driving because they give me a chance to sit back, relax, and meditate for a few minutes. This time I was glad this happened, because it slowed me down and gave me some time to relax and do some special slow, intentional breathing pranayamas called MAT or Manifestation Acceleration Technique. As I mentioned in a previous chapter, I was trained in this technique in the spring of 2001 by a minister named Rev. Gregory Possman, who at the time was the president of the Universal Brotherhood Movement in Florida.

Rev. Gregory, an ordained minister of the Universal Brotherhood Movement, was the man who ordained me and my friend, Carola Van Dusen, at her home in Keyport in September of 1999. He'd been channeling Lord Michael, the Archangel, for many years, constructing protective shields around the planet and teaching manifestation acceleration to any student wishing to learn the technique, as well as giving certification to those students wishing to teach the technique.

The purpose of the workshop and the MAT was to bring our dreams, intentions, and ideas into the physical plane in a much more expedient way than we humans are normally accustomed to manifesting. Michael encouraged Rev. Possman to use and teach the process to other Light Workers who were interested in accelerating their spiritual growth and improving their manifestation abilities.

In a full one-day workshop months prior to this I'd learned all about the benefits of using the technique, how to draw our desires, how to use creative visualization and how to do the five pranayamas, the breathing techniques that comprise the Manifestation Acceleration Technique. Slowly, but surely, I was remembering to integrate the three-to-five-minute practice into my daily routine whenever it would come to mind, in order to quickly create the goals and dreams I'd had for a while.

I'd not taken the five minutes in the morning to do my MAT pranayamas. I had two main intentions for that day and that period of time in my life – to attract more money and to find the perfect soulmate. While I was doing my breathing, I was imagining the type of man I wanted, as well as the qualities I liked. I decided I wanted a man who was sexy, kind, peaceful, gentle, creative, talented, unconventional, and attractive, just like me, who had a good job, and loved the same types of music as me. I also thought it would be nice if he liked children, nature, traveling, the beach, movies, metaphysics, and theater, too – like me. I had no idea that a man I already knew, a musician from Maine named Knowle Phillips, would fit most of this description – especially since I'd known him for over five years and never connected with him in an intimate way before.

Well, Saturday, February 25th, 2003, would turn out to be that auspicious, sacred day for me, on which I would meet the man who would be my lover for two and a half years.

Once I finally arrived at the church, I saw we'd been given assigned seats. Knowle was at Table #8 sitting with our mutual friend, Dave Miles, Dave's girlfriend, Laura, and two men I did not know. I was two tables away at Table #7 sitting across from Dr. Oreste Pellacotte, my former acupuncturist and Young Living aromatherapy expert. To my left was a monk I knew as an acquaintance, who was temporarily living up at Mount Eden, in Washington, NJ, the place owned by holistic health facilitator and ordained minister, Delane Lipka, who offered the Kindred Spirits Fair annually where both Don and Knowle would perform on each of their synthesizers annually. My friend, Fairy Elaine Silver, usually sang and played guitar there every year too. It was a wonderfully joyous holistic festival, a celebration where many Light Workers and kindred spirits reconnected in a beautiful natural setting in the woods in the late spring or summer almost every year.

The birthday party opened with Don looking very surprised and happy upon walking in to find Jan and many of his friends shouting "Happy Birthday, Don!" There were birthday balloons, streamers, clean white freshly ironed tablecloths on all the tables covered by paper napkin tablecloths with a small vase of fresh flowers on each one, matching party plates, napkins, paper cups for spiked fruit punch, and colorful utensils. Everything looked pretty and very festive.

After Jan welcomed everyone to the party, she invited Dave up to sing a special original song, written especially for Don by himself and Knowle, since, I imagined, they were two of his closest friends. It was a combination toast and comical song, and we all clapped afterward with great enthusiasm.

Then Jan invited anyone of us who'd like to make a little speech to Don, so I volunteered.

At the suggestion of my former housemate and college friend, Vicky, I'd taken the Toastmasters Course for a short while – about three months so far where I was learning how to do public speaking. I'd only given two speeches during that time, but it gave me confidence, and helped me to become aware of things in my speech that were no-nos, like saying "you know", "and everything","um", and other place holders that buy time while one tries to think of something to say when one is nervous.

Anyway, I don't remember exactly what I said, but the Toastmasters class must have paid off because a lot of the guests were laughing and clapping loudly when I was finished. I felt confident giving this funny anecdotal speech about me and Don, as I'd just gotten my hair done at Donna's Hair Studio, my second home, and I wore a classy, cream-colored wool suit with nice jewelry, so I looked and felt my best. I got several compliments after I was finished, and while we were all going up to the buffet table to get our dinners, Knowle, the musician I'd met from Maine, who played synthesizer at Don's monthly "Synthetic Pleasure" concerts held at the American Legion, in New Brunswick, came up to compliment me on my speech.

He was a very tall, dark and handsome man I'd noticed before, but never paid too much attention because he was dating a woman named Betina for a few years, and I always saw them sitting together at Don's concerts or any other events, like the Kindred Spirits Fair, where they'd be holding hands and intimately chatting. It was obvious she was his girlfriend here in Jersey.

While I was getting some salads and cold cuts for a sandwich, Knowle approached me saying, "Meryl, you gave a terrific speech. You were very funny."

"Thanks, Knowle. I appreciate it. Yours and Dave's song was very clever & funny too. I really enjoyed it. Thanks for writing and singing it. Are you performing anywhere in New Jersey these days?"

"Nowhere locally. Not for a while anyway. I think the Kindred Spirits Fair will be my next venue sometime this summer.

Meryl, if you ever need someone to play piano for you sometime at one of your workshops, I'd be happy to come down to play for you."

"Thanks", I said, not quite sure why he offered, since I usually didn't need musical accompaniment for anything I did unless I was singing professionally, and that stopped when I was thirty years old and six months pregnant with Kyrie, when I was in the wedding band 'Smooth Sailin' with Tony Conte.

Suddenly, it occurred to me that he was interested in me in more than just a professional sense, so I made it easy for him. "Knowle, are you trying to ask me out on a date? Would you like to take me out for dinner sometime?"

He shot back with great enthusiasm "I'd love to take you out to dinner!"

I loved hearing that kind of interest and enthusiasm from such a handsome, talented, sexy man. Shiva's dance had begun. At that moment the DJ played a slow, romantic ballad by Kenny Rogers. A perfect moment for us to dance, so I asked him if he'd like to escort me out onto the dance floor.

"Yes, of course, Meryl." He was two heads taller than me, so we loved learning how to embrace one another with my disability and the obvious difference in our statures. I was a svelte 115 pounds and a little fairy goddess, at 5 feet 3 inches tall, while Knowle was over two hundred pounds and six feet, three inches tall. My head landed right in the middle of his chest right over his beating heart. He was kind enough to help me keep my hemiplegic left arm partially curled around his big, strong back.

As we danced, I noticed a tuft of dark, curly hair peeking out from underneath his soft, cotton cream colored shirt.

I like the way he dressed. He was immaculate and neat, yet not dressy. He had a relaxed, cool, comfortable air about him. Though he was dressed casually in the cotton shirt and beige pants his shirt and trousers smelled freshly washed and pressed. I felt so relaxed in his large, strong, but gentle arms.

I excused myself to go to the lady's room where I saw Laura, Dave's girlfriend. We chatted for a few moments and she suddenly said "Meryl, I know someone who's got a crush on you." I said nothing.

I went back to dancing with Knowle when I finished in the lady's room.

When the dance was over, I noticed that the monk who'd been sitting beside me had left the party already. I asked "Knowle, would you like to join me at my table?" Knowle held my hand and led me to my seat like a noble knight escorting his lady gracefully to an important place beside him.

It was there that I forgot who I was. Knowle was quiet while I ate some more of my food, but he was very much with me in every sense of the word. The music played loudly around us because Dave had begun playing drums, so Don and a few others joined in adding maracas, tambourines, and other percussive instruments to the enveloping, trance-like sound. Normally I would be dancing all around, because that's the way I am. When drums are playing it is hard for me to sit still.

Knowle said "It occurred to me earlier this afternoon while you were speaking about Don, that you were the one for me. I have a feeling I've been waiting for this moment all my life."

"Wow, really? That's so sweet, honey. I am honored, Knowle, but you barely know me." I managed as my mind began to race.

I thought to myself, "God, this guy has no idea what he is getting into! He has no idea of my independent, polyamorous nature, nor the scores of men with whom I've already known in the Biblical sense besides my two previous husbands. And then there are all the men still in my life now whom I still love. I do not want to hurt him. I did, however, appreciate the compliment. It was kind of him to say such a beautiful thing."

I was torn between wanting to get up to dance and staying seated next to this quiet, attractive man. Suddenly, I felt inspired to place my hand on his heart. It was beating steadily and almost as loudly as Dave's drum. At that precious moment, he took my hand in his own and kissed it. I was spellbound.

There must have been an angel by my side; something led me to him, maybe my paternal grandmother or Grandpa. Maybe it was Baba Muktananda. I only knew that there was a force greater than either one of us at work bringing the two of us together.

Somehow, he found my face with his lips, and for the next fifteen minutes or so we were locked in a romantic, sensuous love trance. Our auras had merged, and though a tiny part of me still wanted to get up and dance to the steady beat of the drums, I literally could not move. I was glued to my seat. Knowle had spun a magical web around me, and from that moment onward I felt that I would never want him to leave my side, and later he shared he felt the same way.

Our kisses were very soft, yet passionate. An entire roomful of people disappeared while we were necking, just melting into one another s' warm, glowing embrace. I did not care if anyone saw us. I was completely oblivious to everything but him, my new beloved. I just felt for certain that Knowle was to be my gentle knight in shining armor for that moment, that day, for my entire life! Of course, this was not the first time I felt that type of powerful attraction toward a handsome man.

I wanted to merge with him, but I knew it was not going to be that day since I needed to pick up my daughter, Sky, once the party was over. I'm sure he also needed to get back home to his own place in New England, a long way from New Jersey.

The party continued, however, and I thoroughly enjoyed the music and company of my special escort. After some time, elapsed, I became more conscious of time, and I realized it was time for me to go home and get back to Sky. I bid Don and Jan "adieu", thanked them for a lovely party, and spoke to a few other guests before I left.

Like the perfect gentleman he was, Knowle asked if he could get my coat from the coatroom. "Sure", I said, and we both pranced off to the coatroom together holding hands like an elfin fairy and a large, dark, gentle giant. Knowle helped me get my expensive, cream colored midi length designer coat on that was a hand me down from my mom. Mom always passed her clothes on down to me. All her clothes were designer outfits like Evan Picone, Jones, and Chanel that she kept in such excellent shape that they looked brand new even after many years of wear.

When we left the church, the day was still beautiful – filled with sunshine and not too cold for a day in late February.

Knowle asked if he could sit in my car and chat for a few minutes while we exchanged phone numbers. He opened my door and got me safely inside before going around to the passenger side to get in next to me. There, we began to talk about some important issues that affected us both deeply and might impact our getting involved any further.

Knowle asked how I'd gotten disabled. He'd always wondered about my limp and why I was unable to use my left arm.

"I'm surprised you've not found out by now from Don or Dave. I have manic depressive illness, and on June 11, 1987, following a three-month period of intense self-doubt, fear, and depression, I shot myself in the head. I know it sounds crazy. And I know I needed that like I needed a hole in the head", said I trying to joke to soften the blow of this very tragic, serious sounding statement.

"Oh my God. I'm so sorry you had to go through such a terrible thing."

"Thanks, it's OK, Knowle. It happened a long time ago. And a lot of blessings and positive things came out of it since then. "

"I'm on a medication called Depakote that I use as a mood stabilizer, as well as an anti-depressant, since 1988, and they both help keep me in the middle so I don't have the extreme mood swings anymore. I had to deal with those debilitating highs and lows for many years, but not for a while now, and my experiences with manic depression made me a stronger, more compassionate person. That's why I became a minister and a speaker in the 'In Our Own Voice Program' for NAMI – the National Alliance of Mental Illness."

"Wow, that's amazing. Your family must be proud of you."

"I hope so. I'm just glad that my children forgave me a for wanting to abandon them, and are still such a special part of my life; and I have great relationships with both of them now. They have grown into healthy, successful adults with no signs of mental illness, thank God."

"I'm so glad to hear that. My ex-wife moved away and took my kids with her, so I don't get to see them very much. I miss them terribly, so I can only imagine how you must feel, Meryl."

After I'd taken Knowle into my confidence about my illness I asked him about his girlfriend, Betina, an acquaintance of mine who was best friends with my good friend, Jenna. I did not want to get involved in another triangle relationship with a man who already had a relationship. I vowed in my heart I'd never hurt another woman in the same way I'd been hurt, when my best friend started dating Doug, a man I'd met in church with whom I was already involved and loved dearly.

Knowle explained "Betina and I have not seen one another in over a year. I was in a correctional facility for eighteen months, and when I returned home, I kept asking her if we could get together, but she always had an excuse and kept putting me off. I just gave up asking her if I could come to Jersey to see her after a while, so you don't have to worry about that. There's been no one in my life for more than two years now. She doesn't care about me anymore, and I've gotten over her. You are the one I want right now. I know you are the one for me", he said unabashedly. I was surprised and excited.

I was shocked to hear of Knowle's imprisonment. I'd been in St. Barnabas Hospital recovering from being burned over eighteen per cent of my body following a period of deep depression when I met a Christian Science practitioner who urged me to go off my medication suddenly. I crashed after a manic phase and made another suicide attempt. This period in 1999 was during the time Knowle was dealing with this challenging period in his life, so I'd not heard about it at all.

"I'm so sorry about your being burned too. Dave had told me about it when he came to visit me when I was incarcerated, and I felt so sorry to hear about it."

I was curious to know why he'd been put in prison, so I asked him.

"There was a misunderstanding between me and my ex-wife. It happened during a very challenging time in my life. Robin left me for her former husband, and I was devastated. She took the kids away from me when she left, and I was in a lot of pain. One summer, the kids came to visit for a week when I was in a very bad state of mind."

"Anyway, I used poor judgment one evening while the kids were sleeping in the bedroom next to mine. I was watching a pornographic video when my daughter woke up and came into my bedroom to see me. She got very excited and asked me what was going on. I was surprised by her coming in, answered her questions the best I could; Then I turned off the TV and tucked her back into bed."

I was surprised by what he shared, but this did not seem like a good enough reason for any man to have to be put in prison. I did not judge him about this unfortunate circumstance. He seemed to have handled the incident appropriately considering how uncomfortable and embarrassed he must have felt.

"How and why were you put into prison for such an innocent mistake?" I asked.

"The experience impacted my daughter very much, so she mentioned it to Robin. My ex-wife is a very protective and proper mother, and became quite concerned. She got the police involved, and after that she was sorry, because they then got the state involved by calling DYFS. Hillary was four years old at the time, very innocent and impressionable. The police got her to admit to things that did not happen.

"When Robin learned that I was going to prison over what happened, she felt sorry she ever called the police, and tried to recant her testimony. But there was nothing she could do, once the state got involved. After Hillary's school called DYFS, everything got way out of hand. At four years old poor Hillary did not understand anything that was going on nor that she was instrumental in her dad going to prison."

"I hired a lawyer, but though I paid him a lot of money, he counseled me to accept a plea bargain thinking I would get a suspended sentence or just probation. He said, "most juries were so prejudiced when children were involved in any type of sexual molestation cases that they will throw the book at just about anyone. I advise you to plead guilty to showing the kids pornography and just accept the consequences. You are a first-time offender, he said, so you will most likely get a very short or suspended sentence with probation."

"I thought it was a ridiculous suggestion because how or why would I want to share a porn video with my two-year-old son sleeping deeply in his crib in the next room or my four-year-old daughter, but nothing like this had ever happened to me before. I suppose I was scared and somewhat naive, so I listened to him. I also paid him a lot of money."

"I trusted him, and I ended up in prison for eighteen months. It was the worst period in my whole life. I lost my apartment, my job, some of my furniture, and hardly anyone came to visit me in jail – just Dave, Betina once, and my parents once, toward the very end of my stay."

"I was so sad the first few days I just cried when no one was around. I felt as if no one cared about me, but eventually I got it together and got a job cooking for the inmates. This kept me busy, and the time went much faster. Once I was released, I was able to get a job as a counselor at the place I work now."

That evening in the car we shared some pretty heavy stuff, but it did not seem to affect the way we felt about one another. We both trusted one another and made plans for Knowle to come down to visit me for the week-end after he was done with work on Friday night.

Wow! Just the fact that he trusted me enough to share something so personal made me feel an intense infatuation for him right away. I could not wait for him to come to Princeton to stay with me that week-end.

The weird thing was that I was scheduled to get my period, but I wanted to make love with Knowle so desperately that I was able to delay my menstruation until the following Monday after he was gone.

We talked on the phone several times in the interim, and each time I felt more at ease and more attracted to him.

That first week-end together turned out to be very special. I spent the first four days in preparation for his arrival by organizing and cleaning my space, throwing papers out of my night table drawers, going through my file cabinet getting rid of old garbage and putting stuff in files that had been sitting around. I recycled newspapers and magazines, vacuumed all the rooms, dusted, and polished all my beautiful oak furniture in my living and bedrooms. It's amazing how the thought of a new lover entering my home could turn a person into Mrs. Clean.

I happened to be scrubbing the tile in the shower after scrubbing the sink and toilet when I heard the doorbell ring at 6:30 PM.

"My God, that can't be him already!" I did not expect him for another forty-five minutes or more.

I jumped out of the shower without actually having had much of one, and donned my robe so that I could answer the door since I had no time to dress. I opened the door a crack to see who it was. Sure enough, it was Knowle ninety minutes earlier than I'd expected. I was naked underneath my bathrobe, but he did not seem to be one bit disappointed. I invited him in while apologizing for my appearance.

"Hi there! So sorry I'm not yet dressed. I was cleaning the bathroom and shower. Come on in and make yourself at home. It will just take me twenty or thirty minutes to finish showering and dressing."

I offered him a drink of water, tea, or coffee, but I told him where to find everything because I just wanted to get out of my robe and back into the hot shower.

Luckily, I owned an upright black piano I'd gotten for free from a neighbor, so he had something with which to amuse himself while I was getting ready. I like the way he played piano even more than the way he played the synthesizer. I rarely played, so it was nice that someone who really knew how to play was making use of my instrument.

I had offered to cook, but Knowle said he'd rather take me out to dinner. I suggested the Olive Garden on Route 1 across from the Quaker Bridge Mall. Like a gentleman he helped me on with my coat, held my hand while walking me to his car, and opened my door for me. He was a good driver, too. Usually, I can tell if a man will be a good lover by the way he handles his car and by the condition of the car inside and out. Knowle's car was immaculate. He was a good driver, observed most of the speed limits, and did not tailgate.

I liked that he opened and closed the car door for me each time, and I loved that he was already holding my hand like a good escort should be doing. Especially me since sometimes I used my straight cane while walking outside, so I had a bit of a limp from the gunshot injury and subsequent stroke. I liked holding his arm, too. We felt natural and comfortable in each other's presence right from the beginning. There was no "awkward" period where we did not know what to say to each other and we fumbled for words. We were both very interested in getting to know one another, and our eyes connected a lot during our conversation. I asked him about his job and his week at work. He asked me about my massage practice and about my children. Sky was picked up by her dad for the week-end before Knowle arrived, so I told him a little about my relationship with Sky.

I could relate to him missing his two children who were living far away in Georgia, so he did not get to see them that often. Though I saw Gabriel and Kyrie on a regular basis and we lived in the same state, it was not the same as having them living with me and tucking them into bed each night.

After perusing the menu for five minutes I already knew what I wanted. The waiter approached.

I ordered green tea with my meal and broiled salmon for my entree. I always ask for water with no ice and a twist of lemon. Knowle got coffee and chicken Marsala. The meal came with endless salad or a soup for each of us. We both decided to get the large bowl of salad with extra olives and tomatoes. The meal was perfect. Delicious, healthy, and filling. We were pretty full, but we decided we would share a dessert and get more tea and coffee, so we ordered creme' broule', one of my favorite desserts. I rarely ate dessert, but that and cheesecake were my favorites, so occasionally I would treat myself.

I loved the way Knowle looked into my eyes while we were dining, and I could not wait until we got back into the car, hoping he would kiss me.

He paid the bill leaving a generous tip, and held my hand while escorting me out of the restaurant.

After getting me safely into the car he pulled me into him and kissed me sweetly on the lips. We were both hot for each other so it turned into a five-minute French kiss. It was obvious we both wanted one another and could not wait until we got home to make love.

We didn't watch TV. I put on some Freddy Jackson and asked Knowle if he wanted to dance. We danced to about four songs "You are My Lady," "Rock Me Tonight for Old Times' Sake", and "Me and Mrs. Jones" are the ones I remember before he took my hand and began leading me to sit on the couch where we began necking passionately. I was so glad Sky was with her dad that week-end because it gave us the opportunity to be romantic and sensuous before we got too sexual.

I asked him to play me a few songs on the piano. He played me a song he'd written for his children and another original song. His brilliant playing really turned me on. Everything about him turned me on, and I could not wait until we got into my bed together. I always wore cute turquoise colored flannel pajamas in the winter, so I felt comfortable just being myself, and excused myself to go into the bathroom to brush my teeth, use the potty, and get into my pajamas knowing they would come off eventually.

Knowle took off his pants and shirt and hung them up over the bedroom door... Then he left me to brush his teeth and get ready for bed too. He was wearing just his BVDs and no T-shirt. Wow, did he have a hairy chest, and stomach, even his back had hair. He wore his dark hair long and usually put neatly back in a ponytail, but he took it down for bed. Oh, my God, his long, wavy hair falling down on his shoulders made him look even sexier than before. I was extremely attracted to his manly looks. And his dark brown eyes, long lashes, and dark eyebrows, fine intellect, and quiet intensity made him very attractive to me. There was an unspoken magnetism between us.

He kissed me for some time on the lips and on my neck and ears before taking off his underwear and going down toward my feet where he began rubbing my feet, massaging my legs, and taking what seemed like an interminably long time before he worked up to my pussy where I was really yearning for him, anticipating him placing his beautiful Shiva-lingham inside of me. When he did, I was extremely wet and felt ecstasy come in waves like the ocean; and we stayed in a tantric embrace rocking side to side and up and down for almost ten minutes. I rarely had full blown orgasms during intercourse, but I was high as a kite seeing all different colors in my ajna chakra the longer he stayed inside me, deep royal blues, grass greens, pinkish purple, and turquoise, my favorite color. The longer he lingered, the more heavenly I felt.

After a while he came out of me to lay beside me to rest with his arm around me saying "You are an amazing lover."

Then I decided to get on my knees and brush my soft, blond, chin length bobbed hair against his chest, stomach, and penis for a minute or two teasing him before climbing atop him. He helped me climb on top and guided his lingham into my yoni. While I strode him, he put his hands on both my breasts and started to tweak my nipples which really got me more turned on and wetter than ever. I was already juicy, but he was really an excellent lover and we fit together like a glove. Sex with him was fantastic, and this was our very first time. We both felt satisfied after making love for nearly an hour and easily fell asleep in one another's arms with Knowle spooning me from behind, one of my favorite positions, with his hand on my left breast. I did not even have to take my bi-polar medication to fall asleep that night, but when I got up to pee in the middle of the night, I did take my 500 milligrams of

Depakote while in the bathroom, just to make sure I'd stay stable. I did not want to blow it by doing anything stupid that might compromise the good relationship we'd just begun.

The week-end was lovely, and I even made Knowle scrambled eggs with sauteed onions and spinach for breakfast after we made love again in the morning.

Saturday night we went out to see a popular movie. We held hands or he put his arm around me while we watched. Then after coming home, we made love again at 10:30 PM before falling asleep. It felt so natural to be with him, and it felt even more natural to have him inside me. I was already falling in love, or lust, who knows what love really is? I was truly enjoying every minute of his divine, sensuous company.

On Sunday morning we slept in, Knowle agreed to come to church with me late after we massaged each other's backs and shoulders, kissed and snuggled again in the morning. Then he treated me to a delicious brunch at the Red Oak Diner after walking along the river once church was over.

Afterward, we walked around town, and he took me to the Princeton Record Exchange where they have all sorts of old, classic LPs for sale which people could buy, bring in your own LPs to sell or trade if they were in good condition, and it was just really fun going through the hundreds of old vinyl LP's and seeing what new CDs they had too. We'd usually leave with one or two treasures depending upon what Knowle was looking for.

When we returned from our afternoon adventure we took a short nap, and I introduced Knowle to Sky when her dad dropped her back home after their week-end together.

We sat on the couch for a little while chatting. Knowle really liked coffee made fresh, so he usually made a pot in the morning, and saved some to drink before he got back on the road for the long drive back to Maine.

Things went well between us for quite a while. We attended the Kindred Spirits Fair together, and he performed there while I watched and danced. He bought me a beautiful wooden jewelry box with a neat picture of Goddess Gaia on the top.

We spent just about every week-end together for quite a few months. If he did not come down to me for one reason or another, he invited me up to his apartment. It was modest, but clean, located on a main road in a suburban town. The first time I came up he cooked me his special dish, curried chicken, rice, and a vegetable. Then we went to meet his friend, Doug, who played guitar, another musician, and a female singer at a place where they all jammed together playing mostly jazz. Saturday nights we'd either go to the movies after going out to dinner or we stayed in and watched television shows like old reruns of "Sex and the City" together on the couch. Sometimes he played music for me on his synthesizer. He was a musical genius, like my friend, Don Slepian. If it were not for his friendship with Don, I might never have met him.

Every June he was accustomed to getting tickets for the jazz festival up in Saratoga Springs, New York, at SPAC, so he invited me to come up to be with him for that three-day week-end in New York. It was decided that I would drive up with our mutual friend, Dave, from New Jersey, Knowle's best friend from college, and we'd all rendez-vous on Friday night in Saratoga with his other friend, Doug, and other new friends I'd be introduced to who were regulars at this jazz festival every year at the end of June. I had a marvelous time. Knowle would reserve his hotel room a year in advance, so it was usually pretty nice. I did not care how nice it was, just so long as it was clean. All we needed was a big bed, a toilet, and a shower since we were at the jazz festival all day long both Saturday and Sunday through Sunday night when the concert would end about 9 or 10 PM. Usually, we'd stay over one more night and we'd both get together with his buddies for brunch on Monday morning before making the long trips back to our respective homes.

Most of us normally got lawn seats and we'd bring blankets, lawn chairs, water, snacks, fruit, sandwiches, frisbees to throw, and instruments like drums, maracas, eggs, rainsticks, harmonicas, and other percussion instruments for a drum circle led by Dave annually that attracted children and their parents from far and wide to play in between the main acts-on the lawn, of course. This was one of my most favorite things. I was not much of a drummer being able to use only one hand, but I loved to dance, sing, and shake my maracas, if you know what I mean. I'm a good dancer, even with my disability, and I usually create a bit of a stir wherever I go with my energy, enthusiasm, and great exuberance for life and music.

The jazz groups were diverse, and I began to cultivate a real appreciation for all types of jazz, from the time I was in my early twenties—a diversity of artists like Al Jarreau, Manhattan Transfer, David Sanborn, Bony James, and Herbie Hancock. However, once Knowle introduced me to new artists I was not familiar with I really started to have a deep respect, love and appreciation for artists like Chick Corea and Bella Fleck and the Flecktones. I was already in love with the singer, Al Jarreau, whom I'd seen perform live many times and the pianist, Joe Sample, whom I'd seen perform in 1976 in Teaneck, New Jersey, years before with my boyfriend, Greg, when we lived together in Hackensack-ack-ack. His band was later called Joe Sample and the Crusaders.

They even had major talents who were cross-overs like Smokey Robinson without "the Miracles", the Four Tops, Patti Labelle, George Benson, India Gabriel, and my favorite jazz singer, Al Jarreau.

One year later in 2003, we were going up to Saratoga again, and Ray Charles was supposed to be the headliner, but he had to cancel at the end of April due to poor health. Later that year on June 10th, at the age of seventy-three, he would succumb to liver disease, and the U.A. would lose a legend. Ray was supposed to perform at the end of June; if only he could have held out a few more months we would have been able to hear him perform one last time. Wow, were we all heartbroken and disappointed? I did have the privilege of hearing Ray Charles perform in 1976 at the Newport Jazz Festival in Vermont when I was only twenty-one years old, and I traveled up to the festival with my live-in love, Greg Askildsen, who was the first person to turn me onto different jazz artists like Joe Sample and the Crusaders, Al Dimeola and Herbie Hancock.

Thanksgiving and Christmas of 2003 would feel extra special for me with Knowle by my side for both holidays. Sky seemed to like him too-probably because I was in a better mood having a committed relationship, especially one with great sex. My mom liked him too. Knowle would eventually take me to meet his parents.

He would also eventually introduce me to his two children and his ex-wife. We would plan a week's vacation to Florida where we would rent a car. At the end of our week's stay in Daytona Beach where we swam in the hotel pool, in the Atlantic Ocean, made love a lot, and parasailed together over Daytona Beach we would drive the rental car at 5:45 AM nonstop until we reached his ex-wife's home. I think it was a good thirteen-hour drive, but it went quickly since we listened to music and talked a lot on the way.

I'd picked up little gifts of shells, post cards for his two children, and a scarf for Roberta. Roberta would remark" Gee, Meryl, it's like Christmas when you come over!" It's not just that I wanted to make a good impression, but I was in the habit of bringing back small token gifts for every member of my family whenever I went away on vacation. Knowle's children seemed to like me a lot, especially his teen-age daughter, Hillary, with whom I quickly formed a bond. We only stayed one night at his children's home before we needed to make the drive back up to the airport in Atlanta, drop off the rental car, and get back home so that Knowle could get back to work. It was a wonderful vacation, and I felt honored that Knowle would care for me enough to introduce me to his children already. I felt like it meant he was pretty serious about our relationship. I believe he was pretty serious about me. I had no reason to believe otherwise. We were continuing to see one another every week-end and planning regular vacations together. We had plans to vacation shortly after the Thanksgiving holiday which I hosted at my apartment. We would be going for eight days with Sky to Orlando, Florida, by plane, in early December when it was beginning to get very cold in both Jersey and Maine. We planned to all go to Universal Studios together. I'd never been there before because I was accustomed to going to Disney World in Orlando from the time, I was a child and the park was newly built by Walt Disney following the success of Disneyland in California.

Visiting Universal Studios as a "family" was a really fun experience, and we rendezvoused with my good friends and fellow ministers, Armand and Angelina, near their home in Casselberry, near Disney World. I'd met Armand and Angelina in Atlanta, Georgia, at the Universal Brotherhood Ministers' 25th anniversary celebration, and we became fast friends. We only had time to meet for lunch, but it was certainly wonderful to see them again after so many years, and they enjoyed meeting Knowle and thirteen-year-old Sky. Sky loved our trip, and I think she was pretty happy that I'd finally found a boyfriend with whom I could have a steady, stable relationship who liked her also. She had been accustomed to lots of men going in and out of my life on a regular basis. Plus, she did not have a great relationship with her dad because, according to Sky, he was using drugs occasionally, and he was abusive to his second wife who divorced him and then was abusive to a few other girlfriends following their divorce. Then he moved to Indiana, and as far as we were concerned, that was fine with us since we never knew what we could expect from him. He was not trustworthy.

One day Knowle called me with a bit of concern in his voice. He was on the Amy's sex offender's registry because of the incident with Hillary I mentioned earlier, and he was supposed to get a rating from one to five with five being the worst. I cannot remember now exactly what it was, but whatever it was, it was way too high and not a fair rating, so it was decided he would make an appeal; so, I agreed to be a character witness for him since I'd met his wife and children with whom he now had a very healthy, appropriate, and loving relationship.

So one morning at the appointed time I went up to the court in Maine after spending the week-end with Knowle, gave my honest testimony, and it would turn out very well for him because they reduced his number by a point or two which meant he was not considered a danger to children which the original number he'd been given unfairly made him seem to be, so I was so glad I made the effort because he did not deserve to be saddled with a bad record for the rest of his life just because of one stupid mistake he'd made at a low moment in his life when he really did not do anything that hurt anyone except himself. So, he was grateful to me when he got the letter with the good news. I was really happy for him, too, since whenever he moved to a new state he was legally supposed to report to the authorities as a sex offender. I thought it was so unfair. I think that may have also contributed to our eventual break-up. He did not want to leave his new job he had really come to love, nor his home state, or the close friends he'd made. Plus, he would have to re-register as a sex offender if he moved to New Jersey or to any other new state outside of his home state of Maine.

The following summer after the jazz festival was over in 2004, we'd make more vacation plans, but this time we decided I'd drive up to Maine and we would make day trips from Knowle's house. The first trip we made was to Hyannis port where the Kennedy family had most of their mansions, and

I even saw one of their little sailboats moored there in Cape Cod. We got to take a little three-hour cruise where there was a floating casino, and I had a lucky streak at the roulette table. I have a lucky number—at least I believe it's luck because I won a lot of money for my date, Tony Romeo, when he took me to an Atlantic City Casino when I was twenty-six years old. After we finished playing Black Jack at 3:30 in the morning, Tony decided to play roulette, and he asked me to give him a number. I guess I must have been psychic that night because I gave him the number thirty-one black, and he put fifty dollars on it as well as money on black, so he won big bucks.

Then he asked me for another number. I said "twenty-three red", off the cuff, just like I had the previous number, and sure enough Tony had not taken much money off the table yet. He just put most of what was on the board onto twenty-three red. Would you believe that the wheel kept spinning until the ball finally rolled onto my chosen number twenty-three, one last time. At this point Tony gave me one hundred dollars from his pot so that I could gamble some money of my own. I'd come down with nothing, and was only planning to see a show, relax, and watch him gamble. Gambling was definitely not my thing since I did not have much to lose. I ended up going home with over eight hundred dollars cash that morning. I got home by 4:30 AM when he brought me back to my home in Old Bridge, New Jersey.

Anyway, ever since that night I considered thirty-one to be my specially designated lucky number. I'm not sure if it was my belief, my karma, the Law of Attraction, or some magical force, but I did end up winning with that number a few more times on cruises, at a gambling joint in Pennsylvania, and in Atlantic City.

So, that afternoon I put a chip on thirty-one, and it came up. I'd forgotten to take my individual chip off the number for the next spin, and magically, lucky number 31 came up a second time. I did not win as much that time as I had in Atlantic City because I kept playing and after a while I began to lose, so I don't think I brought home more than eighty-eight dollars extra, in the end. That's why it's always good to be practical and put most of the money you've won in a safe place in your wallet so you cannot lose the money you've already won. That's what I did in Atlantic City that very first time with Tony Romeo.

We celebrated Knowle's birthday in August at his place by going out to a restaurant, where we could listen to music and dance before coming back home to make love before we fell asleep in each other's' arms like we usually did.

After our little cruise excursion in Martha's Vineyard, we decided to go to Salem, Massachusetts, to see the famous places where the poor women perceived to be witches were found guilty of witchcraft and executed for treason. I'd done a research paper on Wicca, witches, the patriarchy, and the Christian church for English and History, so I found this topic to be particularly fascinating and a very sad time in our history. Anyway, we visited a few museums and stopped at a great restaurant that evening that served authentic New England clam chowder, King crabs, and lobsters. Wow, did we eat to our hearts' content that night! We stayed one night at a hotel in Salem before traveling back up to Knowle's apartment to share one last day together at his place resting and relaxing before he had to go back to work and I had to get back to Jersey to be with Sky. It was the end of summer, and though I'd had a grand time with my beloved, I was anxious to get back into the school year since Sky would begin high school as a freshman at Princeton High. And I needed to make some money again at my massage practice.

Also, I was planning to teach another Manifestation Acceleration Technique workshop for my friend, Betsy Zipkin, for her Course in Miracles group. There were only three students in the group, but the course was $150 per person, so I made a decent amount for a day's work. Actually, it was fun. Teaching manifestation did not feel like work to me, especially because I showed the video of Archangel Michael speaking through Rev. Greg Possman, and it was always a hoot to listen to Michael speak because he has a great sense of humor.

A month or two after I returned from our vacation it seemed as if Knowle was changing a bit; he seemed to lose interest in coming down every week-end to see me. And by Thanksgiving he made an excuse for him not to spend the holiday with me and my family. He said something stupid like being with my mom and Sky could be boring, plus his aunt had invited him to her house in Maine for Thanksgiving. It seemed strange and unlike him. I did not know what to make of it. Our summer vacation had gone so well and the time at the jazz festival was special again as well.

We did make plans to spend Christmas together, though, and he gave me a very loving card and a beautiful necklace. Sky had asked for a bicycle, and I'd gotten her other gifts to open before we surprised her by bringing out the bicycle which Knowle helped me to assemble. Knowle helped me wrap some of the gifts. We spent a relaxing Christmas Eve together, and as usual, had a lovely dinner, watched some relaxing television on the couch and made beautiful love before going going to sleep in one another's arms. His Christmas card expressed a beautiful, sincere sentiment, and he thanked me for two years of bringing love, joy, and gentleness into his life. I gave him a special card too and made a collage for him containing photos of us from our vacations with some poems and prayer affirmations sprinkled throughout.

But after New Year's Eve he began to pull away again, and I could not understand why he was making excuses every other week for not being able to come down to see me. Either his car needed repairs done, he was not feeling well enough to make the long trip after a long week at work, or some petty excuse was made for not making the trip to see me, so I probably should have realized he was seeing someone else without telling me.

The Friday before Valentine's Day I paid for us to spend a night at a hotel in Franklin Township, New Jersey called La Mirage where they had jacuzzies and porn flicks in the rooms because I knew he liked that sort of thing. I loved bathing and showering with him, and I certainly loved hot tubs, so I figured we would enjoy a very hot, romantic night.

I should have known the night I checked out the room to book our reservation, when I tripped over a step on the floor and fell forwards hurting myself, that this was not a great sign from the universe to check into this hotel for whatever reason. The universe was probably telling me I was not paying attention, and that I was ignoring the obvious which was leaving me open for a tumble and to be hurt.

The night before Valentine's Day at the sexy hotel was OK though not as romantic as I'd hoped and certainly not worthy of the great respect and dignity I deserve, but what was worse Knowle did not want to be with me on Valentine's Day itself. I understood since it was the middle of the work week, but I was willing to drive up to him, so I was surprised he did not want me to make the trip. He made another excuse for the following week-end even though I told him I was going to visit my daughter, Kyrie, at her college in Boston and I'd just spend Friday night and part of Saturday morning with him. How blind and stupid could I have been! I suppose I was in denial of the signs that had been in front of me for months. When Knowle kept making suggestions like "Don't you want to get on your way to spend time with your daughter?" I felt hurt and uncomfortable. Eventually I got angry inside and told myself," This is the last damn time this man is ever going to have someone as loving and special as me making such a long trip to spend time with a man who does not appreciate me! It was a prophetic statement for I never drove up to his home in Maine again to see him after that time.

Knowle came down one last time to see me, but I was depressed, numb, and felt absolutely nothing for him by the week-end of the Ides of March.

I remember it well because I had tickets for Sky and me to see the women's' group I'd heard so many good things about--" Sweet Honey in the Rock", at the State Theater in New Brunswick, before rendezvousing with Knowle back at my house by 10 or 10:30 PM. Since I was already in a place of despair and depression, I did not enjoy the concert with as much feeling and joy as I normally would have. In fact, part of the time I was dreading having to go back to my apartment after the concert was over to face Knowle. I did not trust him anymore and there was anxiety in the pit of my stomach, so I knew I would not feel comfortable making love to him anymore. Everything had changed. I knew in my heart he did not love me anymore and there was something or someone between us, but he was dishonest and had betrayed me. I'd felt a similar numbness and angst when my massage teacher betrayed me for the young woman going to Yale without telling me the night before he was supposed to help me move out of my apartment.

I don't remember that much about that night or the week-end. I just went through the motions pretending to be there, but I was already in partial shock and had dissociated. A part of my mind or heart was split off from the rest of my body. Or maybe my soul just decided to leave and take a vacation. I pretended to not feel well physically late that night or early Sunday morning, and I remember Knowle left for home earlier on Sunday than usual. Thank God. I did not have the strength to face him and the truth that he'd already fallen out of love with me. I was not ready to admit failure and allow another deep heartbreak. But within days the depression and despair returned until it became so acute, I did not want get out of bed in the morning. Days turned into weeks and I did not want to show my face of anxiety and doubt at church anymore nor did I want to attend Science of mind classes anymore. At my weakest is the time I need to turn to Jesus Christ, God, my guru, or anyone I loved and trusted for prayer, but I always felt so ashamed whenever I allowed myself to get into a place of despair or depression which only compounded the problems.

I remember it took about a month for me to realize I did not deserve to experience sleepless nights and mornings of exhaustion and anxiety any longer, so one day when I was coming back from the dentist or some appointment in Trenton, I had some courage to stop in at the church office on Route 1 to talk to my pastor, Rev. Karen, and to share with her how badly I was feeling. I remember she hugged me while I cried a little bit. And she talked about the Goddess Sophia, Goddess of Wisdom, who told her I should write out all my feelings. I bet Rev. Karen never expected to channel Goddess Sophia before that. Anyway, it worked. As soon as I got back, I began writing poems of what it felt like to be loved in such a deep, intimate, and sexual way, then how it felt to be betrayed. I ended up writing five poems over the course of a few days. And I ended up mailing them to Knowle. It was exactly what my heart and soul needed to do to begin the healing process. I could not keep all those mixed emotions of love, hatred, anger at being betrayed, and deep sadness all bottled up inside for much longer without hurting myself. The poems were later published.

For a few moments upon awakening in the middle of the night one night I entertained thoughts of driving up to Knowle's house and taking an overdose of my medication in his driveway while he was at work. What a jerk I was. What a jerk he was for not telling me the truth about his new girlfriend in Maine.

Until I could sleep through the night, I would get into bed beside Sky to snuggle up with her until the morning. And one morning I had a great idea. I decided I'd start giving Sky early driving lessons in a development about a half hour away during Easter break. It gave us something new and fun to do.

She was seventeen and would be going for her driver's license test by the following January. She had her permit and it was legal for her to practice driving during daylight hours. It made us both feel better.

Losing Knowle was hard to take, and it did take me a while to heal from the break-up... I decided to resist it at first and could not believe he would leave me after all the loving, but mixed messages he'd given me at Christmas and during our summer vacations. I decided to see him one last time by going up to the jazz festival with a friend, Marc, from Washington DC, whom I'd dated several times before. I'd met Michael at the UFO conference in Bordentown several years before and he took me to Montauk in Long Island for the week-end and to meet his sister. Al Jarreau, my favorite singer, was singing at SPAC that June, and that was good enough reason for me to attend the jazz festival again beside the fact that I wanted to see Knowle again and to check out his new girlfriend.

Michael and I met up with the usual gang of jazz aficionados including Knowle, his new gal, Tracy, Dave and his date, and two of Knowle's other friends and their wives or girlfriends. I felt somewhat uncomfortable being there as the ex-girlfriend of Knowle, but I was still a friend of Dave and several of the others I'd befriended from the two years prior, so I began to feel OK with being part of the group that went to dinner after a little while even though I was surprised at the way the new gal looked. I expected her to be prettier or sexier than me, but I had lots of judgments about her being overweight, and naturally, I was very jealous.

I completely forgot about that experience until re-reading my memoir just now, sixteen years later. Except that I wrote four or five powerful poems expressing my feelings for about five months after the relationship ended, I needed to express in order to heal from the ending of that love affair which I mailed to Knowle to help heal my broken heart which were published in my first anthology "Heartscapes" in November of 2015, I have completely forgotten, forgiven, and moved on to other people and things. It was tough at first because we had an incredibly exciting sex life, so I was very attached to this dark, handsome musician, a man whom I believed was "The One" – you know, that knight in shining armor in the fairy tales whom all little girls are told is the perfect husband they will marry who will adore her, provide for her, love, honor, and protect her through sickness, health, and all the rest of the patriarchal nonsensical BS-- a real whopper of a tale! That lie and $4.00 will get you a cup of designer coffee at Starbucks, ladies. I have kissed so many frogs I finally stopped giving away my power to men outside of me, no matter how handsome, rich, talented, sexy, charming, or whatever. I am completely capable of satisfying myself sexually, thank you very much. But don't get me wrong. I do love men. Of all shapes, sizes, colors, cultures, etc. I have quite a few men and women friends, and I realized after many experiences, quite a few special relationships and love affairs, and from being a single mom, that I love variety, so I prefer living an unconventional, somewhat clandestine lifestyle I have mentioned known as Polyamory. For about twelve years this lifestyle has been working very well for me, but it is not something I advertise. Only my closest friends and family members are aware of this.

Oh well. I've surrendered all of this to God, and when I am meant to share my story with millions of television viewers it will happen in His good time. I'm having too much fun living my life to concern myself with things like that. It's all in Her hands now. I have a very full life and I enjoy every moment of it. Maybe if I get onto television after my book gets published my life will get too busy and I'd have too much on my plate. I have just about all I can handle right now. I don't want to complicate my life or compromise the sweet simplicity and serenity that I have right now. Someday I'd like to be rich, famous, and successful, but right now I'm content with what is. I love being a mom and grandmother, singing with the Solidarity Singers, being a member of the Coalition for Peace Action, and attending the Religious Science Church (now called "Center for Spiritual Living—Princeton) whenever I have time. Above all, I treasure my relationships with my family, my boyfriend, Gary, and my many delightful friends, neighbors, colleagues, and lovers. Nothing is more important to me than the love and connection I feel with these dear ones.

ACTIVISM

Getting involved in the Solidarity Singers of the IUC, and the peace and resistance movement

In the spring of 2002, seven years after I graduated from Mercer County College, my massage business was slow, and I had a lot of extra time on my hands. I was volunteering part-time at the Coalition for Peace Action in Princeton. Rev. Bob Moore, the director of the Coalition, told me he was organizing a bus tour to Washington DC to lobby for peace. I had never been involved in politics at all unless you can consider working as a board worker for the elections for years as something political. I was involved in mostly spiritual endeavors. I had very little interest in politics, but I did not like being idle and thought it would be a good opportunity to learn about the peace movement in a more hands on way other than praying affirmative prayers for peace and world healing plus it would give me something interesting to do.

I watched Rev. Bob with awe and reverence the way he easily went into the different offices of Senators and representatives asking each one what policy they had on war and non-violence saying he would only support the ones that were anti-war. It was educational and interesting to see that a common citizen could have access to and speak with our representatives or the secretary for the Senator or Congressperson stating which bills we were in favor of and those to which the coalition was opposed.

Once our visits with the various representatives were completed, we had an early dinner, and then we were back on the bus for the five-hour ride back to Princeton. I was inspired to see a blind man on the bus with us named Ed who brought along his seeing eye dog, a large German Shepherd. It made me realize that even people with disabilities cared about what happened in Washington and the laws made for the country, especially regarding how much wasted spending goes toward the military budget, and that even I, a person with two disabilities, could have a voice over how my representatives in Congress voted.

All of a sudden, I heard people singing songs while riding on the bus I'd never heard. Songs like "Union Maid", "Solidarity Forever," Bread and Roses". I wanted to join in, but being unfamiliar with any of the words it was hard to pick anything up. Then, finally, one song I recognized – "This Little Light of Mine" so I joined in the singing.

One woman singing named Carol Allen, was from Princeton, and she shared that her group was part of a labor chorus who needed more singers. She mentioned that the rehearsals were just once every few weeks and the leader, Bennett Zurofsky, was very flexible; so that if I joined, I would not be expected to attend every single rehearsal or performance. Most of the singers were involved in the Labor movement and had full time union jobs. Bennett himself was an attorney for unions, and many of the so-called performances were right on the picket line or at demonstrations for a better living wage or for some good cause. This sounded right up my alley since the rehearsals were all the way in Iselin, NJ, and some of the performances were all the way up in Maplewood, Newark, or even sometimes Bergen County or New York. I did not want to have to travel too far, especially since my resources were meager and I did not have a lot of extra money for gasoline. This was a volunteer chorus, so I would not be getting paid anything. I came to my first rehearsal on a Tuesday night thereafter just to listen and learn.

Everyone there seemed to know all about politicians' stances on all the issues and exactly what was going on in the country and everywhere. Most people in the chorus were part of a union like the teacher's union, carpenters' union, or something like that. One of the members, a beautiful blond woman named Carol Gay was the head of the Industrial Union Council, very involved in politics and demonstrations for higher wages. Eventually, she was asked to be the marshal for the Labor Day Parade, who would lead the march at the Labor Day parade in September beginning at the Botto House Labor Museum.

Carol Gay also chose to run against incumbent Republican Congressman Chris Smith in the twelfth district in which she lived in Toms River as a Democrat. It was a shame the Democrats did not back her, and with little money to promote herself or to run a decent campaign no one really knew her, and she lost. I was, however, very impressed with how dedicated to service she was, and that she even had the courage to consider running for Congress at all. I'd never met anyone before who ran for political office, though I did get to know Phyllis Marchand, the mayor of Princeton at the time, from talking to her when I was a board worker for the budget, primaries, and in the general election. I had a good memory, so I greeted everyone who came to vote by name after just serving for a year. The mayor and other candidates running for local office would come to check to see how many people were coming in to vote and to see if any of the challengers had stopped anyone from voting who was ineligible.

Carol Allen, a great mother, peace activist, and genuine all-around great person, later introduced me to the leader of my singing group, attorney Bennett Zurofsky. "We sing in a fun choral group that is called The Solidarity Singers of the Industrial Union Council", Carol told me. "We are a motley bunch of peace activists who go around sharing songs of peace and demonstrating against big corporations like Wall-Mart who have no unions and policies that do not promote fairness in the workplace or social justice. "

It is because of my association with Bennett and the rest of the Solidarity Singers that I am learning something about the struggle of labor unions, true democracy and how out of balance our capitalist society really is. We are very loving and lighthearted though serious about sharing Knowledge and peace wherever we are invited to sing. Except for me, most of us have regular union jobs and do this work/play gratis out of joy and deep concern for the welfare of American labor and humanity. We sing wonderful old songs by great visionaries like Woody Guthrie and Pete Seeger,

HOSPITAL (2004)

During the late autumn of 2004, I was committed to a psychiatric institution for five days. My mom and I had had a big fight about money after a lovely post-Thanksgiving dinner. Arguing about money was not unusual for us. In fact, we often argued on a regular basis about many things. My mom says the two of us are like oil and water.

I had asked my mother to reimburse me for gasoline expenses I'd incurred during the transportation of my grandmother to her home and back from my mom's as well as to Grammy's doctors and back home again to Buckingham Place, an assisted living residence in Princeton where I'd worked as a concierge at the front desk. Grammy Lucy was experiencing more health problems than usual with COPD, asthma, and other related heart and lung conditions, so I'd volunteered to chauffeur her to a few of her physician's appointments. Grammy gave all the grandchildren (six of us in all) a check for one hundred dollars at Christmas, but as usual, I was running a little short and in need of gas money, so I asked my mother to write out a check for my Christmas gift early. Pop Pop and Grammy often gave all of the grand kids our checks early so that we would have enough money to purchase gifts for everyone since I was about nine or ten years old.

My mom complained I was spending too much money of late and absolutely refused to advance me the money I'd asked for. The only problem was that about 30 or forty dollars of that money was owed to me for gasoline and travel expenses, but my mom was insistent and just had to be right that I did not deserve it at that moment in time, and I became angry and indignant. Her refusal to grant my request seemed irrational and unreasonable, so I screamed at her. She said my yelling was violent and ran into the bathroom. I pleaded with her through the bathroom door to come out so that we could talk about the whole thing in a calm, peaceful, and rational manner.

Underneath my pain was a torrent of rage that I'd repressed from the time I was a child and she used to stalk me around the house with a slotted metal spoon which she'd use to beat me if I did not live up to her expectations or we had a petty argument. This time I was so incensed by her meanness that I reacted aggressively in a way I had always wanted to when I was a child but was too small and traumatized to do anything about the hatred and violence she wracked upon my body, mind, and soul.

My mom was depressed and exhausted after cooking for several days for her annual Thanksgiving feast and fearful because circumstances had gone awry in her life. She had financial concerns, and her boyfriend was ill with Alzheimer's, so she was not happy with her life or herself. She projected her own depression and concern for her own wellbeing onto me because she was tired and under so much stress. I asked her for a few dollars for gas money because the needle on my gas gauge was below empty, and I did not want to run out of gas on the way back to my grandmother's residence or my own.

When she found out I'd spent $80 at a beauty salon for Sky to get her hair cut and relaxed that morning my mother had a fit and refused to give me any money except one dollar. She said I was always asking for handouts, which made me feel small and unappreciated. I am actually too giving and generous with my money sometimes to the detriment of myself, so this comment cut me to the quick. I called my mom a bitch, and our argument escalated to the point that I through a deck of cards at her. Ironically, I'd brought the cards there to give blessings to all the people who came to her dinner. They are cards with sayings by the non-physical entity, Abraham, who is channeled by my friend, Esther Hicks. Abraham's teachings bring me profound joy, sublime peace, and contentment in a practical way that no other guru, church, or book has ever done in the twenty-nine years I've been on a metaphysical path. I have been listening to the audiotapes from Jerry, Esther, and Abraham for several years now, and they always uplift me.

I left Mom's house angry and in tears.

Mom then called my ex-husband and his wife, my brother and his wife to complain about me and suggest that I should be hospitalized because I was off the medication I normally take. My mother had the police come to my house as I was just leaving to attend church the next day. My daughter, Sky, answered the door to find a policeman at the door along with two people from the local Mobil Crisis Unit.

Though I told all three people I was fine and just going out the door on my way to church, I was detained because of things my mother had told people she spoke to on the phone at Helene Fuld Crisis Center. Sky was there watching the drama unfold.

The whole experience was initially terrifying for me and Sky, who had to call her best friend, Patty's, mom, to come pick her up at our house while she watched her own mom being escorted out to an ambulance by a 6 ft. 2" police officer, a crisis worker, social worker, and two ambulance attendants.

Sky had witnessed the altercation between my mom and me the prior night, and though she was upset she knew that her grandmother and mom had co-created the incident together. Sky and my grandmother told me that they thought my mom was being verbally abusive and nasty to me. They believed that my mother had provoked the argument. To this day I'm not sure if Mom was truly concerned about her own or my welfare, or if she was just being vindictive, but she conspired by phone with my ex-husband, David, his wife, and my brother, Pete, to have me picked up at my home on a peaceful Sunday morning while I was getting ready to leave for church, to be brought, against my will, to a psychiatric hospital to be evaluated. After waiting for many hours to get blood test results back to see if I had drugs or alcohol in my system (which I did not). I was eventually seen by the nurses and a psychiatrist who eventually had me committed to the psychiatric ward at St. Frances Hospital nearby because Helene Fuld had no beds available and I was not going to sign myself into the hospital voluntarily since I did not feel sick, depressed, or manic.

Though it was an unpleasant experience to be committed to an institution like that, I love my family very much and due to my good nature and plenty of practice I was able to make the best of it. I made a positive out of a potentially frightening situation. I used the time well to catch up on my reading, painting, and arts and crafts. I believed I was fine and did not want to be in the hospital.

Though I felt initially fearful and anxious about being observed by the medical profession, forced to take medication against my will, and be locked up on the eighth floor of the hospital for nearly five days even though I felt perfectly fine. As opposed to prior hospitalizations when I volunteered to be there in a state of chronic depression this time, I knew that I need not be there, so I made the best of the situation. I gave the whole incident to Great Spirit thinking, "Not my will, but thine be done, Lord. After I ended up in St. Frances I reconnected with my former psychiatrist, Dr. Susan Fuchs, who remembered me and is a lovely woman. Dr. Fuchs and a judge I'd never met had me committed after hearing of my long history of violent suicide attempts. I suppose they both wanted to be on the safe side, and they thought it was in my best interest to force me to take the medication, Depakote, again, along with a low dosage of Risperdal, an anti-psychotic medication. I was not having any psychotic episodes or behavior, so I questioned Dr. Fuch's judgment, but she said that the medication would help me to think more clearly. I had no doubt myself that I was thinking very clearly and deliberately, and it was my intent to get out of that hospital ASAP, so I went along with the program. Dr. Fuchs warned me that if I did not go along with her recommendations that I'd be there for a much longer time, so I was forced to heed to her demand to get back on medication.

I finally realized it was God, Great Spirit, who had brought me there. Once I surrendered to this fact I truly relaxed and enjoyed myself.

I painted and colored at least ten pictures which is something I'd been wanting to do for months but never made the time for. I have water colors, a paint pad, and new paint brushes that have been sitting in my desk waiting to be used for over one year, so now seemed like the perfect time.

I read half of my library book about Jane Pauley's life. Jane was also diagnosed with bipolar illness, and I'd love to be a guest on her show after this book is published.

In September, while waiting in my chiropractor's office, I'd read a magazine article that said Jane had a new talk show and that she had gone public about having bipolar illness.

I've rarely made time to read Jane's autobiography, Skywriting, and it was quite overdue, so it was about time I read it before I had to pay lots of money in library fines. I also brought Margot Anand's book, The Art of Sexual Ecstasy, with me, because it was an intro-library loan and it was already late.

I met and made friends with all the patients at Saint Frances as well as most of the staff. I really liked the male psychologist who led the group meetings in the afternoon because he was a Buddhist and I could tell he sincerely honored each person in the group and did not ever to talk "down" to anyone as it seemed my psychiatrist and other doctors, some nurses, and a few other staff members did.

I volunteered to be the chairperson of the daily group meetings in the morning. The staff seemed to be concerned when I'd open some of the meetings by saying, "I welcome you all with respect and love with all my heart. I am very honored to be here and to be able to learn from you all." The nurses and staff seemed to think that my words and behavior were evidence of "grandiose delusions" ... The truth is that I really did feel incredibly honored and humbled by all the stories I heard from the other patients in the group meetings. Many of us shared stories of childhood sexual, physical, or psychological abuse, and I felt honored and humbled to be around these beautiful souls who'd come so far despite their challenging past histories. We were all survivors, and we were all unique expressions of God.

Another older black woman named Verna was the most peaceful, sweet, creative Light I've ever met in a hospital setting. She spent hours coloring beautiful pictures with magic markers like me and brought peace and contentment no matter where she went in the hospital. She was another person who'd been forcibly removed from her home against her will and committed to the hospital. In fact, she had complained in group that the policemen who took her from her home did so in a way that was too rough and hurt her. This woman was an elderly woman who was one of the most peaceful, gentle beings I've ever met. I doubt that this was necessary. If I'd been Verna, I would have sued their asses for police brutality when I got out. But she was not a vindictive person, and I'm sure that after she mentioned it in group, she never gave the incident another thought. This lovely woman could have been my grandmother or yours, so she should have been treated with dignity and respect.

I was beginning to wonder if it was not the people who actually had the patients committed to the hospital that needed to be there instead of the patients themselves! Or maybe the judges, doctors, and nurses should all have themselves committed to the hospital in order to have a fresh perspective on what it is like to be forced into an institution against their will.

Why don't the psychiatrists and nurses see a patients' beauty and divinity? Maybe a few did, but most of them are not trained to look at the positive aspects of the patients they observe. Most have just a passing interest in these people and feel no true compassion or respect for the thousands of patients that divine intelligence brings their way. Most of the psychiatrists and clinicians have inured themselves to our pain and suffering, and at what cost? Most ignore the deeper essence of who we are treating us as if we are very sick, crazy people. They do not see that our illness is just a temporary malaise that will pass eventually with or without medication. Most of the psychiatrists I've dealt with are arrogant and set themselves on a pedestal way above their patients. It helps to enlarge their egos and gives them a sense of self-importance. They do not see our divinity nor do they realize than many of us have chosen particularly challenging paths because we are so strong and courageous. Many do not treat patients with the true dignity, respect, wisdom, and compassion we deserve. Most have no knowledge of the connection between good nutrition, regular exercise, positive thinking, and a healthy, happy balanced state of mind.

When I asked my two female psychiatrists to listen to the audio-taped research of Dr. Ann Blake Tracy from the Young Living conference about the dangers of taking most psychoactive medications they were not even willing to listen.

The doctors and psychiatrists want to close their eyes to this information because their very jobs are on the line. Without perceiving people as mentally ill they would lose their jobs and regular paychecks. When we take responsibility for our own health and well-being their services are no longer needed.

St. Frances in Trenton, New Jersey, was one of the better, more caring hospitals I've been in, but the program still did not get to the root of the patient's problems. Most of these people who are seen as sick were treated with heavy doses of drugs that caused them to function like zombies and consequently, were not able to be in touch with their own emotional guidance systems. The doctors and nurses in psychiatric hospitals or on the floor of or a wing of a regular hospital like St. Barnabas in Livingston, NJ where they so lovingly treated burn patients, watched and monitored a person's every move to see if patients fit into their idea of normal or appropriate behavior. Who the hell were they to think they know what is right or better for an individual than they know themselves? They have no idea. Psychiatrists and psychologists are basically guessing.

It's the consumer's right and responsibility to have access to books and literature about holistic health care as well as allopathic medicine or conventional psychiatry and psychotherapy. There are MANY different medications, herbal remedies, nutritional supplements, Bach flower remedies and alternative holistic treatment options available that might make him or her feel better. Therapeutic massage, shiatsu, yoga practice combined with silent meditation or contemplation, delicious, healthy foods prepared several times daily for the patient so that they get the BEST possible nutrition they can. Each time a physician instructs a patient or consumer about holistic health which includes the WHOLE PERSON-- Body, MIND, AND SPIRIT, we acknowledge that everything is connected... Without addressing all these multi-dimensional aspects of our selves, we will never get better. But it is unique for each individual. What works for one person in 1976 might not work for him anymore. That is due to the fact that we are ever evolving beings unfolding like lotus blossoms, and not only do our cells completely regenerate themselves every seven years, but our needs and desires are different every day we evolve and grow on this precious planet. We are continuously refining our preferences through contrast.

There are many different avenues for feeling better, and the bottom-line TRUTH is that they all work to some degree because we humans, or consumers as the psycho pharmacological industry refers to us, already have the POWER to HEAL ourselves RIGHT NOW in this Present Moment through our very own thinking. If we truly had faith and the belief that keeping a rabbit's foot or a crystal in one's pocket would make us well, indeed it would! That is how powerful your thoughts are. The mind is a contraction of chiti, or Consciousness. So, it behooves us to think about and dwell in the Land of milk and honey, if that is what we are all wanting, and I think I can say for certain that most people reading this now would rather be "Living the American DREAM" as opposed to the American economic nightmare.

It sounds crazy, but it If getting angry gives someone a better feeling thought or relief from temporary anxiety, depression, or a skewed negative perspective, so be it! so if the person is not harming themselves or another, allow them to go out into a soundproof room and just SCREAM their heads off.

Or, if it makes you feel better to just lie on your bed or sit upon a couch to relax, just read, play solitaire, pet your kitty cat, use a flea comb daily to make your cat feel especially close to you.

When all else fails, if you are depressed enough to isolate yourself and stay indoors for hours at a time, you can always numb yourselves by watching TV, OR watch the space between your breaths in order to deeply relax and KNOW that all is truly well no matter how BAD circumstances or things appear right now from our limited, narrow-minded perspective. It is all going to change three days, three months, or three hours from now anyway depending upon the thoughts and feelings we have set in motion.

On the day I was supposed to be released from St. Frances in the end of November, 2004, after having been there just four days and agreeing to take their medicine again one of the nurses or social workers noticed I was reading a library book about how women can have better orgasms. I brought it with me because I needed to return it to the Princeton library in about ten days. I figured I would have plenty of free time while at the hospital to delve into one of my favorite subjects. Tantric Sex and sensuality. Besides, I missed my boyfriend, Knowle. On the morning I was supposed to leave after four days of incarceration at St. Frances, due to my mother's crazy concern about me, a social worker saw my book, told my psychiatrist, and other nurses on my team, that they were concerned I was not ready to leave due to being hyper-sexual. I could not believe it. I was just reading a book I got from the library. I was not flirting with anyone or being inappropriate with any of the other patients. Hell, I would not even masturbate in that atmosphere, so the team was being ridiculous.

So, during my ten-minute visit with Dr. Fuchs, a lady psychiatrist, whom I happened to like a lot, I was told I was being kept there one more day for observation, whether I liked it or not. I spoke to my beau, Knowle, on the phone terribly disappointed I would not be able to come back home for at least another day. He was in Maine and would be coming to visit me for the week-end provided I was back from St. Frances. I wanted to get a manicure and my hair done before he arrived, and clean my apartment.

You have no idea, unless you've been committed to a psychiatric institution yourself, how long one day and night can feel like, especially when you know for certain that you feel and are just fine. A little unconventional maybe, sensuous, free-spirited, and creative, but definitely just as sane as most of the people in there including the doctors and psychiatrists. Totally bummed out by this news after leaving my doctor's office. I called my best friend, Jeanette, who got straight with me.

"Meryl, remember where you are. It's a strict institution like a church. You've got to play their game, live by their rules completely. Take the medicine. Be compliant with their wishes. Don't do anything to bring attention to yourself. That's how you get to go home. If you want to get out in the next few days, just do everything their way. Don't get yourself noticed. You've got to play things like a normal robot-like person and be really low key."

I said "But Jeanette, I did not do anything wrong. I was reading a darned library book. I'm not going to play all their stupid games acting just like a lemming or a sheep. That's not Who I am!" But I took her advice anyway. I did whatever I had to do to get out and get back home. Then, if I decided I wanted to get off the meds again I would. It was not my mom's or anyone else's damned business. Besides, I was and am a holistic health care practitioner and professional for over twenty-five years. I am perfectly aware of the negative effects the medications have upon my liver, kidneys, large intestine, and rest of my system. My best girlfriend, Janet, lost an entire kidney, after being on lithium for so many years! And as of this writing many years later she was going to lose her other kidney and was getting dialysis while being on the transplant list in order to get a free kidney. She did finally get on the donor list and was able to get a kidney, so she was feeling much better the last time I spoke to her on the phone and said the quarantine and shut-down of everything was doing her "good. I am not saying a medicine like this does not work for others because I know some people swear by it. Patty Duke Astin mentions she owes her life to lithium in "A Brilliant Madness". So does Dr. Kay Redfield Jamison and others, but each person's chemistry is unique as well as their beliefs and desires, so a different protocol would work for some and not for others.

I think we just need to be open to the best thing that suits our temperament. If you believe medication works for you, take that. If you think lots of vitamin supplements, a vegan diet, aromatherapy, or herbs will help with mood swings, practice that. If you think some ECT ("electroconvulsive therapy" or shock treatments) will calm you down and distract you from your current troubles, do that. A WHOLE series of them, if you wish. But BEWARE of the negative side effects like short- or long-term memory loss. I never got one, and I SWEAR I never will. However, my mom got a series of them at two crisis points of her life after getting fired from her job at sixty years old because the company was downsized; and then again when she lost her position as a concierge at nearly seventy years old at Buckingham Place when she was a beautiful mother and grandmother who adored her loving family, but the boss wanted to change her hours, and that would have meant that she'd be driving home in the dark which she was not keen about doing. The fact that my brother gave her his dog to care for had a lot to do with her recovery, I believe, as well. Mom is a natural born nurturer like me, so caring for her new Pomeranian, gave her purpose and feelings of love, but, at another time, she was convinced it was the shock treatments alone that did the trick. People always feel better when they have a pet to love and care for, or even if they have plants indoors and a garden outside. Connecting with "Life" within plants, animals, and people is so much healthier than escaping and numbing oneself with television, but watching comedies and crime dramas always seemed to help me a little bit as a distraction from my own personal problems for a while. So, since you are unique, only you know exactly what will soothe you and make you feel just the slightest bit better. And from that place you will find a better thought to think and a corresponding emotion to go along with the happier, more positive thought.

If you are aware of the positive magic Bach flower essences have on the emotional system, I encourage you to take them. Of course, it has to be the right essence for the particular mood or mind state one is in. If you are feeling hopeless take elm. I always have my beau, Gary, or someone muscle test me to see how many drops of each essence I need to take in my tea, juice, water or under my tongue. I love the many flowers' essences Dr. Bach discovered. Sometimes I'll take five or more essences in the course of a day. Each one has a very specific effect. For example, I'll take mustard if my mood is somewhat low and I use vervain when I feel a bit manic, have a lot of hyper energy and a bit too much enthusiasm, there are lots of essences, and they all say on the outside that they are for simple nervous tension, but if you look them up in the book or online you will find there are specific uses for each one. They say on the bottle for what they are indicated, but the print is so small you need a magnifying glass or telescope to read them.

If it helps to relax with a nice, cup of herb tea or an occasional glass of wine, do that. I like getting into a hot lavender Epsom salt bath by candlelight and praying "the Lord's Prayer", praying to Mother Mary, and then doing a particular spontaneous affirmative prayer for whatever it is I am wanting to affirm with Creator God, my Source, whether it be perfect health, abundant dollars, sublime peace, courage, seeing my new book published by the perfect publisher, whatever. I pray for World Peace too just like many other people around the globe, I'm sure.

I usually call one or two close friends or relatives to let them know how I am are feeling. And if you are afraid because you feel ashamed to let your personal friends or family know you can call in to Unity's 800 number or Religious Science International and they will be honored to pray with you any time of day or night. At least call your mom, dad, best friend, or church pastor to share that you need and desire SUPPORT at a vulnerable time. Make love to and nurture yourself, get a soothing therapeutic massage to get out of your head and reconnected to your body, or cuddle with your partner, if that helps you. Basically, whatever soothes you, whatever floats your boat. Speaking of boating, why not try going sailing, canoeing, row boating, or fishing in a local lake since it reconnects you to nature and is a very meditative sport. In the winter when it is freezing in New Jersey I like to vacation for at least a week to ten days in Florida, Mexico, or Hawaii – do something entirely new and different. So, by the time I return I feel relaxed and refreshed, and the weather is already starting to get warmer as spring approaches.

My friend, Lord Michael, the Archangel, says "There is nothing worse than a bored human! "Whatever action or thought will help you move up your emotional scale is all that counts. For it is our conscious and subconscious beliefs over long periods of time that eventually manifest as circumstances in our outer worlds. Be gentle with yourself, and remember that this, too, shall pass, just like everything else. If you are grieving over a loss allow yourself all the time you need to grieve. Healing from a death or broken relationship like a divorce might take months or years, but it's OK. You will get through it.

I was so happy my ex-husband, David, waited eight years before he decided to re-marry. I don't think I was strong enough before that to handle the fact that I was going to lose him completely to another woman. At the time I left him and my two children I was manic and had no idea what I was really doing. I was still in love with him when I married another psychiatric patient I'd met while hospitalized at the Carrier Clinic, but I was practically numb and in shock when the whole separation and divorce happened.

Do what makes you feel safe and less vulnerable.

For example, if going out shopping makes you feel anxiety for whatever reason, pay or ask a friend or pay Shop Rite or another supermarket to do your food shopping so you can clean up your desk or file cabinet. Organizing my space always makes me feel so much better. Cleaning can be therapeutic. Most times, in the midst of stress trauma, or feeling deep grief, taking action is very therapeutic because I am actually moving and not commiserating over lots of things, I cannot do anything about. Doing a task in the best, most efficient way I know how, like cleaning the toilet or scouring the bathtub and/or bathroom sink actually makes me feel fulfilled like I've accomplished something important for the day.

No one knew better than me what was good for my body, mind, and Spirit. Besides, if it were not for Big Pharma, most of the psychiatrists would be out of a job, so they do not really delve into the scientific information released and then suppressed for years now warning us of the dangers of most of these medications. Some of them warn us of suicidal ideations as a possible side effect. Hold on now. The medication is prescribed for depression, but actually Causes suicidal fantasies or possible death. For Christ's sake! Do you think consumers are stupid? Or deaf when we hear these commercials on TV!? It is my personal belief that most of these medications are perpetrated upon the public in order to keep them sick and to keep the large corporations and pharmaceutical companies like Merck and Bristol Meyers-Squibb in business. And to prevent people from taking responsibility for their own mental and physical health through healthy food choices, lifestyle, exercise, positive thoughts and feelings, and prevention.

My friend, Jeanette, advised me, "Meryl, don't you want to get out of there? Just do exactly as they tell you and you will be released." So, I played their game by being the good, compliant patient. Many of the patients I met while I was hospitalized twice at Princeton House and twice at The Carrier Clinic in Belle Mead had been there several times or at least twice. Obviously, something is not working.

ABRAHAM HICKS
WORKSHOP 9/2004

Beloved Ones,

Life just keeps getting better and happier for me since treating myself to the September interactive workshop with and Jerry and Esther Hicks at the Holiday inn in Philadelphia last Wednesday. Esther channels the non-physical collective consciousness of the non-physical teacher who refers to itself as "Abraham". I have been listening to their teachings on audiotape since the late nineties when a friend from the Universal Brotherhood Movement gave me their introductory tape. I consciously try to incorporate their basic teachings into everything I think, say, and do, from moment to precious moment. The longer I live the more I realize that the only thing that matters in my life is that I feel good. So, whenever I focus on some petty thing that does not bring me joy, I try to witness and just notice the thought that causes me discomfort and change it to one that is more soothing and pleasing since the limiting, negative thought does not allow my natural Well Being. It is so much simpler to allow Source Energy and connect with it when we focus upon the love, peace, joy, and beauty within and all around us.

The day passed quickly with so many folks asking questions, and I wanted to be called upon so I could express my love and gratitude to Abraham, Jerry, and Esther, for all they've given to me and thousands of others around the world since 1986, but scores of people had their hands raised around me with questions. The workshop was scheduled to end in thirty minutes, and I truly wanted to express myself, so I went out for a bathroom break where I could practice my MAT. pranayamas while visualizing myself being called upon. Sure enough, as soon as I walked back in, and I was chosen to be the next person to sit in the "hot seat" to ask my questions.

I immediately shared my love, joy, and humble gratitude with Esther, Jerry, and Abraham as well as a brief experience of my life with bi-polar illness along with my theories on kundalini awakening s well as my personal beliefs about psychiatric causing people with mental illness medications to become numb and unconscious of their deepest feelings and emotions.

Abraham agreed with me about all I shared and said" We want to tell you that as you sit there exuding so much love and gratitude that you are one of the most joyful people, we have ever seen in any of our workshops. Whatever caused you to want to take your life saying 'no more of this, I want that' is gone. You have left it behind you."

They told me not to be ashamed about attempting suicide because "we all do everything to ourselves;

and "all death is suicide whether one dies from a heart attack, stroke, diabetes, or a car accident. We all subconsciously bring everything upon ourselves, and there is no shame in whatever experience the soul chooses to have. We each have a non-physical counterpart on the "Other Side", they said which they called our "Inner Being". They also confirmed that I'd been seeing extra-terrestrial ships in the last few years. I've been seeing them en route to Maine on the way up to visit my boyfriend around the Cocksackie area while driving along the New York State Thruway. Esther said that I was of such a high vibration that I could perceive them in the same way that Esther is able to tune into the Consciousness of Abraham and share it with others. She said" Not everyone with whom you share will believe and will not be able to perceive the same way you do. There is never a crow out on the leading edge of thought, so don't expect everyone to join you."

Whenever I see a ship, I get a thrill of exhilaration that runs through my body.

After I left the workshop, I knew there was a free day at the Grounds for Sculpture in Hamilton, and I'd never been there before, so I decided to go from Philadelphia to Hamilton to partake of this beautiful place by my merry self. There were so many lovely statues and natural sculptures formed with the grass and grounds themselves as well as a towering statue of Marilyn Monroe from that movie in which her skirt gets blown up by the wind. There was another called "The Bread Line" which was so poignant and detailed showing lots of poor men with sad, pleading faces lined up to receive free food during the depression. It deeply moved me. I was still on the grounds during the remaining daylight hours enjoying myself very much and writing in my journal while sitting upon a bench, but once it began to get dark, I felt disoriented and was a bit lost, so I prayed and asked some people still left outside to help me find my way out of the park. I found my way and was so glad to get int a warm heated car.

It had been a beautiful, fulfilling, and joyous day, and I felt so grateful to return home safely to Sky who was in her room studying. God is great, filled with power and love, and so Am I. I am so thankful to be alive, and especially that He saved me in each hour of darkness to bring me to the happy, peaceful place I live in in this holy moment.

THE BIG BETRAYAL AND ARREST (2005)

In the spring of 2005, Lyle became very angry at me when we left family court, since the family court judge ruled in my favor, and I'd won an extra twenty-five dollars per week in child support. It went up from twenty-five bucks to a whopping fifty dollars per week. After court was over, we met in the elevator, where he threatened me, "You are going to be so sorry for this. You just wait and see."

I had not gotten a raise in child support in three years, so he was only paying $45 per week which barely covered her food, let alone clothes, or any other extras. The court sent me a letter saying it was time for a three-year review of both our incomes to see if Sky and I qualified for extra child support, so I simply said yes, I would agree to the review.

We both met in court with all of our wages and tax forms from the previous three years, and it was simply a numbers game. Lyle's income had increased whereas mine was just the same or had decreased; in fact, it was low enough that I was still receiving over $200 in food stamps, so the judge ruled in Sky's and my favor that she should be receiving $70 per week as opposed to the original 45. I was happy for Sky and me since I would not be worrying about how I would have to pay for "little things" like tissues, napkins, paper towels, deodorant, and an occasional lunch or dinner out for the two of us at the local Chinese restaurant or Panera Bread on Nassau Street which had very reasonable prices and lots of nutritious salads and sandwiches.

In October of 2005 I placed an advertisement for massage clients in US1 newspaper, a free local paper distributed to the banks and many local businesses in the area like Panera Bread restaurant. At the time I was offering Esalen massage for some of my clients. Esalen was big in California at the Esalen Institute in the nineteen seventies. It is a sensuous Swedish massage consisting of long, deliberate effleurage stroking performed on the recipient totally nude. The client is nude and the massage practitioner is partially or completely naked too. It is a not sexual in nature, but a beautiful, intimate way of connecting with another person's body, mind, and Spirit.

The following week I got a call on my advertisement in US1 from a man I did not know for a sensuous massage. The man was complaining from the beginning that he was having problems with his girlfriend from the very first session. I gave him an integrative Swedish massage topless because it was very hot and I happened to like the sensuous feel of it. The hour massage was over, and this client made another appointment for the next week. I am a very trusting soul, and it is rare I suspect anyone would deliberately do something to hurt me, not even my second ex-husband.

Lyle had taken it upon himself to call the local police pretending he was a neighbor saying he was concerned because he'd seen a lot of male traffic going to and from my apartment. He said he suspected my home was a house of prostitution. This was odd because I only had a part-time business as a massage therapist, so if I had five clients per week, it was a lot. I did have several male friends, and one special boyfriend from Maine who had just broken up with me that spring. However, five men visiting my home in a week did NOT constitute a lot of traffic, from anyone's point of view. None of my neighbors ever complained to me about anything. In fact, I had excellent, friendly relationships with most of my neighbors. Two of my women friends, Laurie and Julie, were neighbors who became massage clients. This one new male massage client came a few times for a massage and kept pestering me asking me if I massaged the genital area. He kept complaining about his relationship with his girlfriend so I told him" It's not something I usually do, but I am a licensed minister and I would be happy to pray for you and your relationship."

I placed my hands upon his back and neck and prayed aloud affirmatively that he and his gal would work things out in a harmonious way and gave him another one-hour integrative, sensuous massage. I asked how he liked the treatment, and he said, "You are excellent. This is one of the best massages I have ever gotten, but I'd still like to come back and get one of your naked massages and hope you will make me feel better." What would you charge for this?"

Again, I told him "It's not something I normally do, and I usually charge $150 for a 90-minute Esalen massage for my time. The man left, and said he'd call back to make another appointment. All along he was lying to me trying to entrap me and to set me up so that he could find some reason to arrest me. What a fool I was that I did not see this coming, but I had been doing massage for over thirty years and never had any problems before with any of my clients, so this was not anything I expected or was looking for.

Sure, some would ask me for prostate massage or on the phone asked if I gave a full body massage. Some creeps would say "Do you massage everything?" And I'd say "I massage everything but the genitals to keep away those undesirable clients.

Well, this particular man kept persisting and giving me the sob story about his girlfriend and him breaking up. The guy literally made me feel sorry for him by the third session. When he asked me that third time I said "I'll have to think about it and get back to you." He called me again, and I gave him a price for a sensuous Esalen massage in the nude. I do not remember, but possibly something incriminating may have been said during the course of that last phone conversation. He made another appointment for the following Monday at 11:30 AM.

My doorbell rang. I walked to the door looking pretty with my hair pinned up in a fancy hair-do wearing a short-sleeved blouse and white pants. To my surprise, instead of the male client, a policewoman was outside my door asking if I was Meryl. I did not know the policewoman and I said, "Yes, is there anything wrong? She barged her way into my apartment saying she was there with a search warrant to search the premises and that I was under arrest for prostitution. Wow, did that come as a shock. I then saw the client who kept pestering me for three weeks to give him a sexual massage behind her, with another male Princeton policeman. I could not believe my eyes. I had been betrayed and entrapped by this terrible man who had the gall to come into my peaceful home with the lady police officer and another investigator trying to find anything they could to incriminate me – for anything. Drugs. Whatever. These nasty police were judgmental, barged in and ransacked every room and every drawer in my immaculate, peaceful home looking for evidence they could use to convict me. They asked if

I took any medications or drugs or if I used insulin for diabetes. I said "No, I am very healthy, and I do not use any type of drugs".

My hands were then handcuffed behind my back which was very uncomfortable since I am a disabled person who cannot use my left hand, and I walk with a limp, so there was no way I could run away anyway. This was completely unnecessary. I do not use any illegal drugs at all, smoke, or drink because I happen to be a health fanatic and holistic health practitioner.

These blessed A-holes had me sit on my couch while they demeaned and taunted me with criticisms. The woman police officer sat beside me and one by one, removed all the hairpins from my hair while my home was ransacked by the two men including the bastard who had deliberately and illegally entrapped me. I was told she was removing all my bobby pins so that I could not harm myself or any others in the police station. Excuse me. These policemen who carry guns, are telling me that they are afraid of an unarmed petite, disabled woman who walks with a limp and uses a cane while walking outdoors!? What would I do with the bobby pins? Stick it in their groins? Wow, I would have liked to have kicked these prejudiced, judgmental hypocrites in the balls. One of the male investigators commented to me," I don't know how you can live with yourself."

I felt like crying but stopped myself and replied in an indignant tone, "I live just fine and happily, sir, and I have nothing to feel guilty about. I sleep very well at night. So does my daughter, but I was so glad she was busy at school while all this was happening. It would have been horrible for her to see her mom in handcuffs with these terrible men ransacking every drawer in my house trying to find something with which to incriminate me which, of course they did not.

It took about 90 minutes for the men to go through every drawer in my kitchen, living and bedrooms. They even opened up my hope chest and went through all the photo albums and papers lying on top. Not one drawer was left untouched, nor were any of them returned to its proper, orderly state. All the contents of the drawers were dumped out and after being ruffled through, were left on top of the dressers, desks, and night table from which they found nothing. In those ninety minutes I sat quietly on the couch with my hands cuffed behind my back in a daze and in shock wondering what the heck had happened and why. After wrecking my clean, orderly home they found absolutely nothing and left with $35.00 cash they took from my wallet, a bank statement which showed I had under $100 in my checking account and nothing in savings, a workshop flier on massage, a little black notepad I'd gotten in church, and my personal phone book. I was told that a trial date would be set and after the judge's ruling, I would eventually get my money, phone book, and other belongings returned to me. Then, like a criminal, I was escorted to the Princeton police station in handcuffs and forced to sit in the back of the squad car. It was one of the most humiliating experiences of my life.

The whole experience was traumatic, frightening, and embarrassing. So, humiliating. Some of my neighbors saw me being led to the police car. No one I knew well, fortunately. An extremely denigrating experience for a woman who was an ordained minister of Universal Brotherhood, a holistic health care practitioner, a mother of three children, and a gentle person who had never been arrested for anything in her entire life. I've never been in trouble before other than the usual parking or speeding tickets. But I always went to court or paid those online. This experience was completely foreign and different.

I'm the type of person who gives money back to the bank teller or cashier at Shop Rite if they give me too much change. That is how honest I am. I am an openhearted, loving, friendly woman who does kind things for people every day of my life. This experience was deliberately meant to denigrate and disparage me, especially when one of the officers criticized me and asked "How could I sleep with myself at night?" I felt like asking these men the exact same question.

Worse than that, when I got to the station, they asked me to remove my shirt after they fingerprinted me as if I was a common criminal who had hurt someone or stolen something. I asked why they were photographing me half naked. I was told that they needed to photograph all my tattoos for identification. I had tattoos on my left arm, right shoulder, one on my left thigh, and one on my chest, but this was way over the line. When I asked why they were doing this they said they needed these photographs for identification in case I ever got away and they needed proof of who I was. Excuse me. What kind of nonsense was this? I should have sued their asses for entrapment and defamation of character as well as unnecessary force. I was not capable physically of running away if I wanted to. And where would I go? Only back home to await my daughter's arrival home from school. The unfair treatment of an innocent, physically handicapped woman by these fools was not just ridiculous and unjust, but it was damaging to my child as well as to my career as a massage therapist. I'd been doing therapeutic massage since I was twenty-one, for over forty years, and in all that time nothing bad had ever happened to me, so this was crazy.

I had the opportunity to go to court if I wished, but they also did something terrible to my daughter, Sky, and I did not want to make things any worse for her than what they already had done.

When the cops could not find any evidence or loads of money to incriminate me as a Madame running a house of prostitution or even as a prostitute they went to my daughter's school, pulled her out of class, and interrogated her.

"Sky, do you know where your mom hides all her money?" Poor Sky. She was surprised and embarrassed by this attention not knowing what the heck was going on either. All she could say was "My mom doesn't have a lot of money. I don't know what you are talking about."

Luckily, after all the hubbub, the *Sergeant* was kind enough to drive me and my mom whom I called during the search for support, back to my place. The *Sergeant* said I was very cooperative, and he remembered me from 1999 from the time I'd been burned when he searched my home and found a kitchen knife in my drawer, which, at the time, I had been considering using in a suicide attempt in the midst of a horribly acute depression, but he did not know that. He just found it strange I kept a large kitchen knife in my night table drawer. He was very kind, and came to my mom's house in Franklin Park once I was released from the psychiatric part of St. Barnabas Hospital after I'd burned myself just to check on my well-being.

I so appreciated the sergeant's kindness which made me feel a bit more at ease in the midst of a terrifying and shocking experience. So, I was released shortly after they photographed, fingerprinted, and "processed" me. My mom met me at the Princeton police station after I called to let her know what had happened. Then, the kind *Sergeant* thanked me for my cooperation, wished me luck, and drove me back to my apartment where I felt happy to be home, but nervous and angry. I had a ton of papers and a heck of a mess to sort through, throw out garbage, and put what was left back into the drawers from which they'd been taken.

I felt some anxiety every time the doorbell rang after that for a few weeks. They also said I was not allowed to do massage therapy again until after the trial was over, so with all that had happened, I was not allowed to support myself in the way I was accustomed. After all, I'd been a massage therapist since I was twenty-one years old, and a certified, licensed one in Florida since I was 26 after graduating from the Sarasota School of Natural Healing Arts.

In retrospect, I wish I had been stronger and more courageous to have stood up to them by having my day in court. Several of my clients including Martin Kruskal told me they would have stood up for me and testified on my behalf. But I was terrified of the unknown and being naive about the whole court system, did not know exactly what was the best course of action for me to take. What they did to me was really an illegal entrapment since I had not done anything wrong and the officers never found anything in my apartment to prove my guilt. I was never a prostitute and certainly not a madame with women working under me.

Wouldn't it have been nice if I'd been having all the fun, they accused me of having as well as the big bucks that go along with being a Madame or high-class call girl? I could have bought myself a fancy car and a house for Sky and me to live in, and not just a small, subsidized apartment. What I was accused of just was not happening. To be totally truthful I had two very special friends who were clients of mine for at least eight years with whom I shared a special friendship which included both emotional and physical intimacy, but this was between me and them. No one was aware of my two special clients except for my mom. And I did not charge either of them for any intimacy we shared. I charged only for my time doing therapeutic Swedish massage, and any sensuous or sexual enjoyment that transpired was consensual and came from the friendship we shared over time. I was careful to see these two clients only once monthly in a private setting when Sky was at school or with her dad for the week-end. It was only our business alone, and besides, I never got paid for the sensual or sexual sharing. The love I shared with this man and one woman was a gift from my heart. I got paid for therapeutic massage and healing alone at one dollar per minute. That was my expertise and my job for over thirty years. In that time, I'd never had any kind of trouble, and it was all out of Lyle's lies and calls to the police that started all the problems in 2005. We found out he was the culprit who called the police posing as one of my neighbors saying he suspected a drug or prostitution ring going on in my apartment.

He did all this out of spite because he was ordered by the court to pay more child support, and I suppose he believed I was making a lot more cash than I was admitting or reporting, and hiding it. No such luck. With my disability I was rarely strong enough to take more than two clients per week anyway. I got money in SSI disability and Social Security that mostly covered my rent and other bills. Massage has always been a part-time gig for me.

We found out Sky's dad had been the culprit two years after the debacle when he was beating his new girlfriend, Julie, in their home in Indiana. Julie would call me every few weeks to tell me he was abusing her with her teen-age son living there in her peaceful home, and asked me what she should do about it. In one instance she called the police when he was chopping his head with a knife, and he was brought to jail. While Lyle was away Julie went through his safe and other effects. She was the one who found these letters in his safe trying to hurt me and Sky. He had also been calling and writing letters to DYFS saying that I was an incompetent, unfit mother who kept a dirty house with too many cats, and had sex with men in the apartment.

My boyfriend, Knowle, lived all the way in Maine and we'd just separated the spring before when he'd met a woman in his hometown that he liked just as well, so I had no man to protect or defend me during this crazy time. It was a frightening experience I would not wish on my worst enemy, and I would have dreamed each night before the whole thing came to be heard in the state court in Trenton. In the dream I saw myself in front of the judge and a whole lot of spectators where I would just look at everyone, especially the judge and say, "I swear I am not guilty. I did nothing to hurt anyone." I had never been to court except traffic court for speeding, and even that was a scary experience for me at times, so this incident truly frightened me. I really built it up in my mind as something. terrifying. In fact, I was so frightened and worried about the experience that I postponed my court date twice. Once due to snow and once because I said I was ill. My mom offered to come with me even though we had to be there early by 8:30 AM; in fact, she even drove me to the courthouse which I really appreciated, since I am not much of an early riser and am usually late for almost everything. Mom says "You'll be late to your own funeral". Anyway, she stuck by me through it all, as well as my son, Gabriel, and my best friend and fellow massage therapist, the Pan Man. And I got through it.

While waiting for my court date I held my head high as I did my daily tasks, errands, and went to art classes and shopping in Princeton. I was a board worker during elections for many years at Community Park School, and I still worked the November election. I had my hair done up and I wore my best red suit that day. I have an uncanny memory, and somehow, I would remember just about every face as well as the names of each person who would register in my line to vote. Everyone in Princeton knew me as the beautiful board worker with the big smile who always called them by name and inquired about their children, their jobs, and always had a happy disposition. I did not let the unfortunate incident disturb my equanimity while I was out working or playing in public.

Some people knew of my troubles because they read about the arrest in the Trenton Times, the Trentonian, and two of the local papers, but most people said nothing, or if they did say something, it was encouraging. People would say, "And this too shall pass". Or "Even bad publicity sometimes turns out to be good for business in the end."

I decided to take the pre-trial intervention as opposed to going to trial because the prosecuting attorney said it was like admitting I was "not guilty", and I'd just have to be on probation for only a year, but then it would all be over providing I did not get arrested again during the years' time I was on probation...

My friends and family told me to lay low for a while, and I was warned by the police not to work doing any more massages until I went to court, and the whole thing got cleared up, so I was without my livelihood for quite a few months. Even if I was permitted to work, the whole thing was so high profile in the Trenton Times, I was on national television, and I was a local sensation which scared off all my regular clients except for one or two women who came to me for a few years, and knew this whole farce was a bunch of nonsense. One of my regular male clients with whom I was and still am very close stopped by my home and left an envelope inside my door with $200 cash in it for me which was very kind of him, but he never actually called me or knocked on the door, so I found that kind of weird. It was very challenging for me to keep my head held high during the time I was "front page news". Not famous for a good reason as I had hoped one day I would be as an important, published author, singer, and inspirational public speaker, but as a notorious, unethical woman who was disparaging the entire massage profession reducing it to a sexual massage parlor type activity as opposed to the several thousand-year-old therapeutic healing techniques it truly is. I felt so sad and disappointed that this was my fate. But what could I do about it at that point? I was just doing all I could to survive and make some sense out of what was happening to me.

A close friend even told me they were making fun of me on the radio. I'm glad I never heard those two guys mocking me. They were making fun of me because I made a comment that I occasionally did prostate massage for a few men who had prescriptions from their doctors, but since I was inexperienced in doing this, I was not even sure how to do it because I wasn't sure how to find the male prostate gland. I was told by one of my clients that massaging his prostate every other week was helping to reduce the inflammation he had. I did not ever see this client after the arrest, and the next time I spoke to him by phone he shared that he ended up getting prostate cancer and nearly died. What people were gossiping about in regard to me would not have bothered me very much except that it was hurting my children to hear bad things said about their mom, and no one had any idea of the capable, loving, caring, honest person I am. I have very high ethics and I am an excellent massage therapist and facilitator of healing energy despite the fact that I have two disabilities – hemiplegia from the brain injury as well as a stroke, and manic depression.

Having manic depression causes me to not have very healthy boundaries. Sometimes I can be naive and I trust everyone way too much, as in the case of this investigator posing as a client and both my ex-husbands who have lied and done things to hurt me on more than one occasion. Other times I let people walk all over me like I do often with my ex-husbands and children occasionally, but I am slowly learning it is OK to say "No" when I feel tired, to have healthy boundaries, and also to walk away if someone is criticizing or disrespecting me.

Anyway, I felt terribly embarrassed for Sky, who was being teased and taunted at school, and for my mom who was also harassed outside my apartment when she came to visit me by the reporters from ABC news. A reporter from ABC news called me to ask if I wanted to go on the news to explain my side of the story. I agreed to do this, since I'd not really had time to speak rationally, from a place of discernment and dispassion. I was surprised and in slight shock when the incident first happened, and was feeling as if I had to defend my life and reputation.

The local news reporters and editors in US1 and the Times never asked me specifically for an interview, but were taking information they found on my website and in prior news stories, and other facts out of context just to make me look bad, foolish, and guilty.

I was particularly crushed by the way, Richard Rein, the Editor of US1, put a very negative spin on me and my business when I had advertised in the classifieds of his paper for many years, taking out small three-line ads that were just about all I could afford. Everyone just assumed I was running a prostitution business without doing real investigative work, so no one took the time to interview me or any of my friends or long-time clients. I had friends and clients write positive letters on my behalf that I was expecting to show the judge, but I was never given the opportunity to show the judge any of the letters since I took the pre-trial intervention. It was actually stupid on my part because it was a plea bargain. I was told by the prosecutor that taking the PTI. meant I was not guilty, and that after a year of just going to probation once per week and paying a small fine (which turned out to be $120) that the charges would be dropped just so long as I had no more arrests.

Even my pastor and minister from church did not support me in this endeavor when I really needed her. Fortunately for me, my dear friend and one of the senior ministers of the Religious Science Church (now called "Center for Spiritual Living – Princeton), Rev. Ian Taylor, not only stood by me, but also gave a sermon that seemed to have my plight as the theme, one Sunday when our regular pastor was not there. Ian spoke of unconditional love, of Unity, and how easy it is for people to criticize, to judge others without having walked a mile in their shoes, and to misunderstand things that are going on, especially how easy it can be to judge or misunderstand the motives or actions of another human being who is another individualized expression of the One Life that is God Consciousness.

Rev. Ian quoted the scripture that says "judge not lest ye be judged" and that we were ALL innocent, pure expressions of the One Source. Though he did not mention my name specifically, I intuitively understood he was talking about this because my case was so high profile, and most likely, other members and congregants knew about the arrest due to the negative media attention, scrutiny, and bad publicity I had been receiving.

I had been a longstanding member of the church and the choir for at least twelve years.

Rev. Ian always treated me with respect, honor, and kindness and addressed me as a fellow minister,

Reverend Meryl, whenever he greeted me. It was because of the kindness and respect from Rev. Ian and the prayer practitioners at the Unity Church and Religious Science International who prayed for me in the middle of the night when I could not sleep, that I was able to get through this challenging period in my life. So many people were talking about me, spreading lies about me, calling me on the phone at times to say horrible things, or strange men called occasionally to ask me if they could come over to spend the night. I was almost afraid to pick up my phone or answer the door sometimes because I felt so paranoid.

The cops even sent decoy clients to my door who would just show up without calling to make an appointment, to try to trick me into getting into trouble after I was told by the prosecutor's office that I was not legally allowed to work until the case went to court and was resolved. I always sent these strangers away immediately, even though I had no other jobs to pay my bills. My mom stood by me and went to the court in Trenton with me a few months later. I was so scared that I canceled the initially scheduled arraignment, calling to say I was ill. I was not physically ill, but mentally exhausted and physically tired from insomnia. I was worried and irrationally scared and anxious as heck about going to court for a felony. I'd never been charged with anything except for speeding and a few minor traffic violations in my entire adult life.

I was so troubled about the case and all the people telling lies and saying unkind things about me that I could not sleep through the night for two months, and I needed to go on Wellbutrin, an anti-depressant, and Ambien, a sleep medication. But I did have loving friends, family members, and clients write letters of good character to the judge for me and counsel me on the phone. It was those people, the true friends, who made it possible to hold my head high and get through this difficult time, and I actually made time to do my art, which is one of my passions – making collages and painting angel and cat sculptures at an art studio in the Princeton Shopping Center.

I could not believe my own pastor refused to back me up and write a kind letter of support for me, so I stayed away from my church for months after that. All I knew was that the one time I really needed the support of my pastor and church, the hardest time in my life, she was not there for me. Though I love and respect my pastor, that one action put a big strain on our relationship, and it took me a long time to forgive, but I have let go of that sad, horrible time in my life and reconciled with my pastor.

After three long months, I finally got to the state court in Trenton, where I was asked by the prosecuting attorney if I wanted to do a "plea" since I had no prior arrests or charges. Rather than waste the court's time I could plead not guilty and take Pre-Trial Intervention (PTI). I'd never heard of it, but basically, I was not required to go to court, but was just required to be on probation for a year and to report monthly to a probation officer. I was entered in a type of program for first time offenders in which I was not allowed to get into any more trouble. After a set time, the "criminal" record was supposed to be expunged automatically, I was told. Even though I was not guilty I'd already had enough of the sensationalism surrounding the case with press following me whenever I had a court date. Besides that, I felt that my sixteen-year-old daughter, Sky, and the rest of my family members should not have to be bothered by people talking about it anymore either. I was so naive about the laws and had no money for a very good attorney anyway. I just wanted everything to quiet down and to be able to move on with my normally happy, peaceful life. It was a good opportunity for me to trust God and surrender everything to Him in prayer. I had to let go of the fear and put all my faith and trust in my angels, my guru, and Lord Jesus, the Christ.

In retrospect, I wish I'd have done more research and actually gone to court to clear my good name. Several clients including the famous mathematician, Martin Kruskal, who'd been coming to me for massages for years, told me they would take the stand as witnesses on my behalf. I should have sued the hypocrites for illegal entrapment and defamation of character. I suppose they are just too frightened or not smart enough to go after real criminals who force women and children into sex slavery plus the men that control the poor prostitutes from the time, they are young and vulnerable when some are homeless and living on the streets.

But again, I just wanted to get the whole darn thing behind me with very little media attention and embarrassment to my family, friends, and neighbors, so I opted for the "quiet route".

My son, Gabriel, was very upset about the whole thing and wrote letters for me to the judge and my probation officer saying it was ridiculous that I was forced to attend this program and that I was unable to work.

Once the year had passed, I was sent a letter saying the case had been dismissed and I could go collect the things that had been taken during the raid on my apartment. Somehow, they had misplaced my phone book, which really irked me because I had phone numbers and addresses of all my relatives, neighbors, and many friends I'd met on cruises and other vacations as well as people I cared about that I'd never be able to contact again unless they happened to call me. It was nice to get back my small purse with the $35.00 back. Thirty-five dollars was still a decent amount of money to me back then. Thank God I was not carrying more money in my wallet that day. I would have been up a creek if I'd had $150 or more dollars on me to put in my checking account later that day to pay a few bills.

The cops often seize people's belongings and money illegally when they stop and search cars under false pretenses quite often these days if they find marijuana or something else in the car that makes a person look suspicious. Who knows if my purse might have been stolen or seized because it had been presumed, I'd earned money illegally through prostitution or drugs? Large amounts of money are seized, and large amounts of marijuana and property is often stolen when a police officer stops a motorist and searches their glove compartment and/or trunk. This money and the narcotics are never given back, of course, even when a person is found not guilty.

I heard once on NPR a man was carrying ten thousand dollars to purchase a pre-owned vehicle several states away, and the officer said he did not believe his story, so he put the man in jail overnight, seized his car, and took the money. Though the man was found innocent of some trumped up charges he was never able to get his money back. This is outright thievery and deception. It happens frequently, and regular law-abiding citizens do not have any say in the matter when it comes to getting back their property and money. Our laws and our country have become hypocritical and oligarchic. We are living in tyrannical times. And when former President Trump was in office things appeared to be worse than ever for immigrants, refugees, Mexicans, and people of color.

It has been years since the arrest and all the adversity I experienced during 2005 including the loss of my beau, Knowle, and the passing of my beloved grandmother, Lucy Vere, on September 11th, a month before the betrayal and arrest. It has been over eight years now, but in 2014 when I applied for a volunteer Grandpal position reading to school children through the Princeton Senior Resource Center where I do dance aerobics and take poetry classes I was interviewed and asked to get fingerprinted, though I'd already been a Grandpal several years prior at Johnson Park School reading to two second grade boys who are both now nineteen- and twenty-year-old men. When I was fingerprinted, it came up that I'd been arrested for a felony.

As far as I knew the case had been dropped, and this was supposed to be noted in the documents at the State Court. Thank God I found out that there had been a little slip up, and the clerk had forgotten to dismiss my case on the books. I went down to the proper court with my friend, Dan, a former attorney in CA and Washington DC, and asked what was going on. The clerk and another man there were very apologetic for this oversight, and made the proper notation. Unbelievable. I could not even get a job as a volunteer again reading to children even though I brought a note from the court saying this case was dismissed long ago.

Supposedly, according to Susan, the director of the Senior Center, their attorney said I could be a danger to the children, and they would be liable if something happened. That really burned me up. The reading is done in a public place with people in the library, and often for more than one student in a group setting. This is how strongly people are prejudiced when it comes to people who have been arrested even if they are not convicted. God forbid one is arrested, found guilty, goes to prison, and does his or her time in jail. They are judged, scorned, and scarred for life for as small a crime as possessing an ounce of marijuana. Look at poor Ruben "Hurricane" Carter who spent so many unnecessary, wasted years in jail due to the lies and deliberate framing of detectives and prosecuting attorneys on his case. And he is just one example. Our prison system sucks with so many innocent people being put into prison for petty crimes or crimes they did not commit because their skin is the wrong color.

I have a girlfriend from WV who was put into prison illegally for mail fraud as a psychologist, and she's written several wonderful books about the subject and become an advocate for others in prison.

In order for me to have the arrest completely expunged I have to pay an attorney several hundred dollars to fill out lots of forms, and it will come completely off the record. I will have to do this if I want to get a job outside my home working as a teacher or doing anything with children, but as of this writing I do not have that much money to pay an attorney to have the case completely expunged from all the records. I am not worried, though, because we all have our own karma, and each action has a consequence. All the people involved in this betrayal and entrapment will one day have to experience a karmic consequence for their actions. I have forgiven them, but I will never forget what deliberate harm they caused me and my family. Especially Lyle who started the whole business. "God bless them and forgive them for they know not what they do." I mean "did".

Meeting Angel Joan, Jeanette, Michael and Dan

One of my best friends in this incarnation was named Jeanette LeDoux.

It has been years since she made her ascension during a struggle with cancer, but I was reminded of her in 2018 when I was told to go to Edison Physical Rehabilitation for therapy, acupuncture, massage, and chiropractic by my good friend, Zara Rose. Coincidentally, the chiropractor there introduced herself as Diana LeDoux. I told her I knew that last name because of my good friend, Jeanette. She was surprised for a second and then shared "She was my sister."

It was so good we connected because neither of us felt totally "complete" about Jeanette's death, and we would be able to share our thoughts, feelings, and remembrances.

Jeanette LeDoux and I met at Angel Joan Fericy's Church of Divine Light in Somerset, New Jersey. Jeanette was beautiful, blond, intelligent, and had a caring, sweet personality. We had a lot in common since both of us were into holistic healing and offered therapeutic massage, reiki, and similar healing modalities. We both loved metaphysics, studying Science of Mind teachings, going down to the ocean and sitting on the beach any time of year. We also liked eating healthy, vegetarian types of food, and we even liked two of the same men. It was Jeanette who told me about Rev. Karen's Religious Science Church of Princeton (now called "Center for Spiritual Living – Princeton"), which I would check out just prior to Angel Joan packing up whatever she had not given away to make the move to California where her second beloved, Brucie, resided, after her husband, Richie, died of cancer. I was amazed that Joanie could sell just about everything, or give it all away in order to make a new start in another state with a former friend with whom she reconnected after her husband passed away.

There was a handsome musician named Doug who performed at Rev. Karen's church who was one of Jeanette's massage clients. He had colon cancer and a colostomy bag to boot. He was getting chemotherapy treatments weekly, but he still managed to work at a full-time job, attend Science of Mind classes, and attend church on Sundays, where he often performed original compositions singing and playing guitar, and sang in our choir.

I became close to Doug when Jeanette and I were still good friends. I considered her one of my best friends since she was one of only two or three, I felt I could trust with my vulnerability and weakness when I'd spiral into depressive, anxious periods. Sometimes I'd feel very frightened and anxious during times of chronic depression, and Jeanette was such a good person that she would offer to give me a free bodywork session and sometimes let me sleep over night at the house she rented in Milltown. Other times when I was not feeling as frightened, she'd offer to drive us down to Belmar Beach where we donned our bathing suits, or, if it was late winter and too cool, we'd just spread out a huge blanket, lay down in our pants and sweatshirts taking in the sun and smelling the delicious scent of the ocean breeze allowing the wind and sun to caress our faces. We might take light snacks with us or go to one of the restaurants afterward to relax and enjoy ourselves.

Unfortunately, I did not know that Jeanette also had a bit of a thing for Doug, but made the choice not to get involved since she was his healer, and thought it unprofessional.

Unlike me, Jeanette had good boundaries, discernment, and discrimination. Doug had been living with a woman for five years who broke up with him. I cannot remember how it happened, but we began dating. I suppose it was easy since we both went to the same church, had a love of music, sang in choir together, he was attractive, I was pretty, and he lived on Mt. Lucas Rd. in Princeton which was about two miles from where I was living. At the time I had no idea Jeanette liked him too, but was being cautious due to his delicate health.

One time after we'd been dating for a month or two, I stopped at my mom's house en route to another destination to introduce him to my mother. She liked him very much, but later that night on the phone mom said "honey, I get the feeling he's not going to live much longer." I did not think much about it at the time even though mom is psychic, because I like to see the world through rose-colored glasses and to live in the present moment.

Doug lived long enough to take me to the Beacon Theater for Valentine's Day of 2003 to see Al Jarreau. He felt very relieved because he was able to sit through the entire two-hour performance without having to go to the bathroom to empty out his colostomy bag. His oncologist declared him free of cancer of the colon. Doug and I became intimate pretty quickly, and I enjoyed the subtleties of his lovemaking, especially since he was a great kisser. Maybe I was a bit possessive, I'm not sure, but after a few weeks of our making love Doug decided he wanted space and we should break up. I was pretty upset, and little did I realize that my worst fear had come upon me. Doug and Jeanette had been getting together to play tennis. After a few weeks he asked her to go up to New England with him for the week-end, and I was bummed out. I don't think I've ever experienced so much jealousy in my life. Jeanette had no disabilities and was athletic, as I used to be. Plus, she was my good friend. I remember calling her up to find out how or where Doug was not knowing that they were already going together. It was hell.

I felt so shitty and jealous that night I knew they were coming back from New England that I could not stop obsessing about it; and I drove past Doug's rented house at least three times to see if his car was parked in the driveway yet.

I finally realized what a ridiculous frame of mind I was in, and decided to see a movie all by myself that night. Sky was away visiting her dad, none of my other friends were available at that time, so I went to see "Pollack" about the painter, Jason Pollack, at the Montgomery Cinema all by myself which distracted me enough to be able to take my mind off the whole stupid thing in order to get some sleep that night.

The next day I found out that a famous woman guru and meditation teacher from India was coming to a center in Hopewell, and I knew it would be valuable for me to get this saint's darshan. I'd read a book about all the current women saints from India, and they are miraculous. This guru was one of the women saints I'd read about. Just like Baba Muktananda and Gurumayi transforming the energy wherever they go and spreading God's grace through their words, their touch, will, or intention, all the women saints had this power to be "transmitting stations" of God's unconditional love and grace.

The Sunday morning, I arrived at the Hopewell Center, that same week-end I knew Doug and Jeanette were together I was about ten minutes late for Satsang. When I got there, I saw about forty devotees including my friend, Allan, sitting on the floor chanting, but Ananda Mayi Ma was nowhere in sight. I found out in a short time that she was feeling temporarily ill and was resting in her cabin. I was a bit disappointed that I could not receive her darshan, but I still stayed chanting with the other devotees for about forty minutes. When I finally decided to leave would you believe I had the great fortune of seeing her coming out of her cabin at that exact instant she'd be leaving, and with that one glance and my entire mood changed from one of agitation and hopelessness about my relationships with both Doug and Jeanette, to one of acceptance and peace? When I returned home, I picked up my pen and wrote a poem to Doug called "Moving on to our Greater Good" which expressed all my thoughts and feelings, bought one red rose and left both the poem and the rose in front of his locked door inside the room he rented. Once I did that somehow, I felt complete and had some closure in the relationship. I stopped talking to Jeanette for several months after that. But the weird thing is I surrendered the whole thing to God and wrote Jeanette a letter of apology while at the Universal Brotherhood Minister's Conference in Atlanta at the end of the summer. I would see her again at my grandmother's funeral in the end of September 2005. She rode in the limousine with me and some of my relatives. I was in shock at the time, so I do not remember if it was my mom or my brother sitting on the other side of me.

Subsequently, Doug found out the woman he'd lived with for five years was engaged to her massage client when I told him after church service one day. He broke up with Jeanette, started dating another woman he met at Angel Joan's church and took her to the Christmas Eve ceremony, but once he'd found out about his former beloved being engaged to marry another man it must have broken his heart, because his cancer metastasized from his healed colon into his lungs. I'd realized he was nowhere to be found anymore because he went into hospice, and he was dead a few months later at the tender age of 47.

The really weird thing is that Jeanette ended up also getting colon cancer. They say that by the Law of Attraction what we focus on expands. Now she had been focusing on healing Doug's cancer for about a year. None of us can heal anyone else. We can merely be a facilitator of the healing energy. I stayed pretty close to Jeanette while she had the colon cancer. I even introduced her to the man who would later become her lover and spiritual partner, Tom Campanelli. I was selling Young Living essential oils at the time and had one of those home parties. They were like Tupperware parties, but much more educational focusing on the healing properties of plants and flowers by distilling the essences. Tom and I had been lovers for a very brief period, but when he met Jeanette, he went ga-ga over her and decided she was his Indian princess from a former incarnation and the love of his life. He would be the one to love and care for her up until the end of her life. Tom even flew her down to a holistic healing clinic in Mexico in a last-ditch effort to save her, but by that time it was too late. Though her colon cancer was declared healed and her colostomy surgery reversed after several months, like Doug, her cancer would return, only the second time it metastasized in her liver. She had tried both allopathic and holistic means, but nothing stopped the progression of the disease. It was a shame because she'd finally found the love of her life, and they were planning to move down to Florida together. They'd already found a place.

Poor Tom was left with a broken heart, and with Jeanette's corpse, which he had to ship from

Mexico back to New Jersey. Her sister and her mother were shocked to find out she was dead. They knew she had cancer, but had no idea she was so close to death. At 62 years old Jeanette was still thin but curvy, radiant, and beautiful. She never told me her age, but I saw it on her driver's license one day, and I was quite surprised because she was so young looking and astonishingly beautiful. I thought she may have been in her late forties or early fifties.

The neatest thing is that shortly after Jeanette's death I had a vivid lucid dream about Doug. When I awoke, I felt his presence still with me? I was dating an author named Mason Loika at the time, things were not going so well after a few months, and I decided to buy myself a pink topaz ring on sale at J. C. Penney for 60 % off one afternoon. When I woke up from the dream I thought "I really miss Doug. Why don't I just go down to visit him and surprise him at his rented room on Mt. Lucas Road? Then it occurred to me that he had been dead for a year or more. In the dream, Doug and I were conversing, He told me he still loved me, and the dream felt so real.

A miracle happened shortly after that with a psychic named "Spiritman Joseph" who had done some channeling at Pebble Hill Church in Doylestown at our monthly New Hope Metaphysical Society meetings. I felt guided to see him privately at his house. His fee of $100 was steep for me, but I was very impressed with his short readings at the meeting, and he was recommended highly by a colleague, Susan Doyle, the owner of a holistic center in Pennsylvania, who'd gone to see and hear him privately for a reading. He told me not to say too much to him, and that he was going into a trance state and would tell me what he saw.

He saw a whole bunch of departed loved ones who wanted to come through in order to give me messages of love, healing, and encouragement. He even told me he saw I'd be buying a new car and that it would be blue. He was correct. I bought a royal blue Chevy Cobalt shortly after that reading.

But the thing that impressed me most was that both Doug and Jeanette came through to talk to me and send their love and good will. Joseph told me specific things they both wanted to let me know. When I told him I'd had a lucid dream about Doug a few nights prior, he said "That was a visitation. He wanted to connect with you to say he loved you and would marry you if you wanted. That is why he impressed you to buy that pink topaz ring you bought for yourself at J. C. Penney as a kind of eternal friendship and engagement ring. He loves you very much and is sorry for the way he treated you at the end. He also said that when he got very sick before he died and was too embarrassed to be with any of his friends and just wanted a quiet space to make his peace before he passed on.

Spiritman Joseph said "I see a beautiful woman in white in a bridal gown here with many of your relatives and friends. Wow. There are so many who want to speak. The bridal gown means that she has attained a very high state of divinity. She says she was your close friend, and because of your loving relationship she will channel the messages from all the other departed ones there who want to talk to you. She is the only one with the ability to do so."

After that Jeanette sent messages of love from my Grammy and Pop Pop who happened to be relaxed and happy on the "Other Side" with cats in their laps. One of them was kissing the cat, and the other was just petting its head.

There was also a message from my friend, Jackie, from the nude beach. She'd just died from a toxic overdose of alcohol several months prior to this reading. She appeared on a beach with a drink in her hand, so I would know it was her. I wrote a memorial poem for her called "Love Never Dies" which was read by our friend, Archbishop Herb, at her funeral.

The coolest thing was knowing that my friend and former beau, Doug, had actually decided to visit me on Earth in his celestial form to tell me he still loved and cared for me. Or was I in heaven while I was dreaming, I'm not sure. The dream felt so real. I could swear when I awoke, I could get out of my bed, don my clothes, and go visit him at his former house a few blocks away from me until finally it occurred to me, that he'd died a year or two before that dream.

So, we definitely know from near death experiences, channeling, Jesus' words, astral travel, and psychics that life is truly eternal. Death is an illusion, and "we will all eventually be singing around the same subtle campfire" in heaven as my former friend and teacher, D. R. Butler, wrote in one of the lessons of his course "Living in the Truth of the Present Moment."

Another of my dearest friends I still have in my life today after many years of being acquaintance friends at a special church for students of metaphysical science, is named Dan. We met at my friend and pastor, Rev. Angel Joan Ferricy's, Church of Divine Light, in Somerset, in the mid nineteen eighties. Dan dated another woman in the congregation which was fine with me because I was not too attracted to him. For whatever reason, after Dan broke up with that woman and Rev. Joan was moved to close down her church and move to San Diego, California, after her husband, Rich, died, Dan started calling me around November of 2008. Dan wanted me to visit him at his large home in South Brunswick to walk the grounds and hang out with him. We had never talked privately or dated prior to that.

Oddly, the day he finally asked me to visit him was just one day before he was moving down south to Maryland where he'd taken a job as a health worker and aide at a live in rehabilitation center. His house looked as if it was struck by a cyclone because everything was displaced with luggage everywhere, scores of vitamin bottles on his dining room table, clothes on the floor, and nearly everything in disarray. The only place to sit with him amongst this messy confusion was next to him on his couch. We started making out, and there was a bit of a spark between us. He showed me around his property and told me stories of his mom and his wealthy, industrious Italian family who had lived there in South Brunswick township for a generation before. I found him interesting, but the mess and the geographical distance between us turned me off completely. Our date ended, I drove back home, and never gave him a second thought.

In the meantime, I attended a UFO conference in April of 2010 at the Days Inn given in Bordentown, NJ, where I met another man named Michael, who was one of the presenters. He called himself the "Mystery Man" and did not have his name on the program, only "The Mystery Man". He spoke about topics I had an interest in like friendly, unconditionally loving extra-terrestrial beings who came from the dog star, Sirius B, and how they wanted to help the human race, and where humans came from originally, among other things. I found myself immediately attracted to this "Mystery Man" and after his talk was over, I approached him to say how much I liked it and to ask questions. When the conference was over on Sunday everyone was invited to dine together at a local diner, and I managed to sit close to this "Mystery Man", whom I found attractive physically, intellectually, and spiritually. He was tall, lanky, blue eyed, intelligent, intense, and handsome.

I saw him again at the monthly UFO meeting in Hamilton. Following the meetings most of the group would go out to the Golden Dawn Diner where interesting topics of discussion that began at the library meeting continued and folks relaxed while eating a bit of dessert, soup, or some small appetizer since it was already around 10:00 PM, and most all of us had already had our suppers. Michael and I sat across from one another, not by chance, getting to know one another better; and when we left the diner to go to our cars he hugged me while saying farewell in the doorway; then he closely ran his strong fingers up and down my spine giving me a really tingly, delicious massage up and down my back which really perked my interest in him. He had some type of "magic" in his hands that really attracted me to him physically, not to mention I was drawn to him intellectually, and spiritually, too.

I was already seeing a very nice, handsome man named John, originally from Kenya, whom I'd met at the Suzanne Paterson Senior Center, when he was playing ping pong and I was finishing my aerobics class. John and I had been dating just a few months, but I was unhappy because he lived in the Princeton home of the elderly man whom he was caring for; and with no home of his own he just brought me over there in secret while he was working. When I told Michael I was already seeing another man he said" That's OK. I work a lot, so I really don't have too much time for dating, but I'd really like to see you." However, I gave him my business card, he called, and by Mother's Day we made plans for a first date.

Michael did not seem to have much money because our date consisted of seeing our friend, Karin's, daughter, Abigail, sing at her spring concert at her grammar school in Lambertville. It was OK, though, because I love children and especially watching them sing or act in the same way I enjoy watching my own children perform in school plays and musicals. Since I loved both Karin and Abbey too, this was a unique and fun "play date" for me.

Afterward, we all met at the local McDonald's and had some small bites to eat while making good conversation. Michael is not a very large eater, and though he is a tall man, he is on the thin side, but with very strong runner's legs from being a track star in high school. I never felt satisfied when he would take me out to dinner to a Chinese place and share a vegetarian dish or some soup together. I realized he was not a big spender because he did not work regularly, but only part-time, so he had to be prudent. We were opposites. If I had money, I lavished it on myself and my children not even being aware of what I'd spent. I suppose I was accustomed to having more than I needed while married to David, so my habits did not change a lot after we divorced. Michael was much more careful and even saved all his receipts which he marked in a composition book in order to keep track of what he spent weekly.

After the date we shared with Karin and Abbey he drove me home to Griggs Farm and politely kissed me warmly after our date saying he enjoyed my company and he'd like to call me to set up another time we could get together. I eagerly accepted another invitation even though I realized he was not a big spender.

I suppose it was by our third date that I asked him if he wanted to lay down in bed with me to rest after we went out dinner and dancing, so since we were both already attracted to one another you can imagine what that led to. I can always tell what type of lover a man will be by the intimacy of his kisses and the subtle foreplay like kissing me on my neck or nibbling on my ears. Michael was a good lover; we connected in a really sweet way which led to gentleness and closeness the more we met. But other than to hold me and talk to me for ten to twenty minutes he was not much of an "after lover" which disappointed me. He always had work afterward or some errand to run for his landlady who would prove to get in the way of our evolving intimate relationship. He never seemed to be a free man making his own choices in his own time frame; he appeared to be caught on the "work wheel", a treadmill that keeps most men from being creative and truly enjoying the little, precious moments of their lives, like most men in our society. He did not pay rent, but bartered for a bedroom in his landlady's house by working four to five hours per day at whatever needed to be done. He was a handyman, a cleaner, painter, genius who could repair or make anything look clean, bright, and shiny. He even figured out how to do electrical work, plumbing, pool repairs, and helped his landlady teach swimming classes to very young children.

Besides our mutual interest in UFOs, the paranormal and metaphysics, we both shared a love of dancing and listening to music. When his landlady had regular parties at holidays our friends, Doug and Nancy, would play guitar and sing not just original compositions, but also fun rock songs like "Teach your Children" by Crosby, Stills, Nash, and Young, a song which was very easy to find harmonies that blended together. So, we'd all have a grand time singing song after song, harmonizing with one another while dancing to the music. I'm kind of perky with a lot of charisma, so I'd bring a lot of joy and energy to these parties when I did go. I was not normally invited by the hostess; I'd just show up being Michael's girlfriend, and I'd bring some appetizer like hummus, a dessert, or a bottle of wine since most of the folks at those parties enjoyed drinking alcohol.

The bad thing about Michael was that he did not have a place of his own either. He bartered for a small bedroom in the very nice home of this older woman he'd met through the UFO community. He had a small bedroom in her home and was able to use the kitchen, living and dining areas. We would spend nights in each other's' arms. I have many fond memories of the times we spent there, especially sleeping outside in her cottage near the pool.

Six months went by, and there was another UFO conference where a lecturer named Denis Denocla was flown in from France to share his experiences of some extra-terrestrial beings called Ummos. I missed Denis' 10 AM talk, but had the good fortune of getting to know him afterward when Karin, Michael Pat, Denis, and I went to a local Italian restaurant where a wonderful band was playing, and we all got to dance to golden oldies and familiar rock hits again. I enjoyed talking with Denis because I took high school and college French. It was one of my favorite subjects, and I'd rarely get to practice using the language unless I met a French Canadian up at the ashram or went to Cannes in the French Riviera while cruising the Mediterranean.

Eventually, I sent Michael a letter and asked him to come to live with me. I was beginning to become too attached and got possessive. After a date we made seeing the "Capitol Steps" one Saturday night he read the letter back to me expressing all the things he found untrue which upset him; and he broke up with me that night. He said" I'm not that available for a relationship, and besides, I am not as into having sex as much as you. But we can still be friends."

As in all my break-ups I went into a mild state of shock and could not hold back the tears. But Michael assured me we could still be friends and see one another occasionally in the future. Michael and I still continue to see each other as friends.

While Michael and I were dating and coming to know one another better emotionally, spiritually, intellectually, and intimately my friend, Dan, from Rev. Fericy's church kept calling me from Maryland which seemed very strange to me since we'd only had that one encounter the day before he moved from his home in South Brunswick to take a good job in the business office of a rehab center that helped recovering alcoholics and some men with mental illness. I was surprised to hear his voice because we had very little relationship while he was here in New Jersey except as acquaintances. I told him I was in a relationship with Michael, but he said it did not matter. "I just need you to pick me up at the train station when I come to New Jersey to visit my sister and aunt, and I'll pay you. Plus, we could have a good time if you let me take you out to a nice place in Princeton for dinner."

I finally gave in, and allowed Dan to pay me for chauffeuring services and for the benefit of my good company at a few dinners in town. Then he'd go back to Capitol Heights, MD and I'd just hear from him occasionally on the phone.

Somehow, Dan and I continued to date occasionally, though he was one of the most interesting men I met, a former attorney in California who loved dabbling in the stock market, he lacked confidence in dealing with women which turned me off. He did like to dance, have a good time with pretty women, and to spend money on me which did attract me. He cared so much about me that when he realized I was still sad and grieving over Michael after our break-up, when I told him there was a new Abraham-Hicks cruise facilitated by Jerry and Esther Hicks to the Panama Canal, Costa Rica, and Belize called the "Living in the Vortex" cruise and that I'd love to go with him, but I could not afford it on my own, Dan was so kind and generous he came up that week-end to deposit $1,000 into my bank account so that I could cover the deposit, the port taxes, the fee for the interactive workshop with Abraham, Jerry, and Esther, and have money left over for some of the outside excursions while in port like parasailing and other adventures.

There would be great fun, delicious food, interesting new friends of like minds out on the leading edge of thought, singing, entertainment, various excursions, and my most favorite of all, dancing at night into the wee hours of the morning. Now if that did not shift my focus and take my mind off sad thoughts about losing Michael, nothing ever would. I asked Dan if he would accompany me, but he said he could not come since they needed him at his job. I had the feeling, though, that even if he could get the vacation time he still would have bowed out because he'd have to take the risk of getting closer to me, like sharing a bed for ten nights, and he just lacked a lot of confidence as a lover. He told me the last time he had a very good relationship he was living with a wonderful woman in California, but broke it off because he had too much anxiety about studying for his exam to pass the bar and become a full-fledged legal attorney in California. He would regret this decision later in life, and look for Barbra, but she was hurt, angry, and when the investigator finally found her she told him in no uncertain terms to "get lost." None of his relationships after that were too fulfilling, so he came to be a loner with what one might call "social anxiety".

Michael and Dan both became part of my extended family in a sense. If there were celebrations for my mom for her birthday, Sky's birthday, Thanksgiving, Christmas, my other daughter, Kyrie's birthday or some of her singing gigs, both Michael and Dan would be invited. They are both dear friends of mine to this day.

I forgot to mention that Dan also invited me to a sex club shortly after Michael broke up with me. It was New Year's Eve, and two of my close friends from church, Ron and Audrey Franks, both passed away within a week of one another, and I was surprised and saddened by their deaths. Michael agreed to accompany me to Ron's memorial service given by our pastor, Rev. Karen Kushner, at a funeral home in Hamilton.

So, even though it was New Year's Eve I was not exactly in any mood to celebrate after losing Michael in mid-November right before Thanksgiving, though he did accompany me to our church service and carried in the 15-pound turkey I'd roasted in my oven beforehand for our annual Thanksgiving dinner after our "Gratitude Sunday" service. So, Dan, wanting to make me feel better and have something to look forward to, invited me to this sex club he'd been telling me about for months called "The Private Affair" saying that quality people went there, the food was good, they had music, dancing, and even a jacuzzi where people could go in naked and relax.

The sex part did not really interest me at the time, but the other things sounded like things I enjoyed, so I agreed to drive down to Capitol Heights to pick him up. I'd invited my friend, Karin, who also invited her boyfriend, John, who would meet us down there. Karin and I would drive down together. Her former boyfriend drove down by himself after work, and we met at the hotel where Dan rented a room for us for two nights.

Dan did not own a car and did not like to drive except for work, so I would be the one to chauffeur us to "the Private Affair". First, I found a boutique there that sold sexy nighties, negligee's, bras, and thongs, so Dan told me I could purchase anything I wanted. I got something pretty and sexy which I think I put on underneath the long black dress I was wearing.

I enjoyed the buffet, danced a bit with Dan and Karin. Afterwards Dan and I would get into the hot tub together because we were waiting for a photographer in the next room to take a photograph of us, and he had others waiting. While in the jacuzzi I met a nice, handsome guy, but I was really in no mood to make a close acquaintance of anyone because my mind was on Michael almost the entire night, not to mention my friends who had just died. Having sex or giving a blow job to someone I did not know very well was the last thing I cared to do. I was just kind of curious and watched others doing their thing.

My good friend, Karin, hit the jackpot that night. She met a couple soon after walking into the club who found her attractive and invited her back to one of the quiet rooms to be alone with them. She told me had a very pleasant threesome and even got their names and phone numbers to keep in touch.

I spent most of the night on the dance floor and ended up dancing with a very handsome, sexy man who said he and his wife had an open marriage, but he always had to get the OK from her if he wanted to bring another woman into their relationship. I thought that was interesting and wondered how they made it work without one of them getting jealous, angry, or possessive. I suppose their decision to be honest with each other and respectful as much as possible because each was #1 in the relationship. The others were apparently just meant to make the relationship more spicy and less routine.

Anyway, I was happy when the night was over and it was officially New Year's Day. Dan and I spent the last night in our hotel room, and upon awakening and showering he took me to Denny's for breakfast. My car had a flat tire, and upon calling AAA we discovered my spare which was a little doughnut, was not in good shape either, so I ended up having to call AAA a second time and was towed, along with my car, while

I sat in the front with the driver, all the way back to Griggs Farm in New Jersey. Luckily, I had the plus policy which allowed for up to five calls per year and many more miles as part of the tow. I immediately had all of my tires checked and repaired upon arriving home. My friend, John, told me about a guy in Toms River who sold used tires that were nearly new, so I bought five tires from him when I got down there.

Dan and I carried on a long-distance friendship with no sex for the rest of that year, and then he paid for me to go on the Abraham-Hicks cruise. He liked me so much he even wired money to my cruise account almost every day which was great because it meant I had extra money to get my hair done, go to the spa to get massages, and have the fancy diner for an extra $35 on the "special dinner" night. I was also able to buy some professional photos that had been taken of me by the cruise photographer on two of the formal nights and one when I walked into the ship upon arriving that first day. By the way, I'd asked Michael to drive me to the airport and to sleep over the night prior on my couch, but he refused. I was supposed to be at the airport by 8:30 AM for a 10:00 AM flight in Newark. He was an hour late arriving to pick me up. I gave him so much slack even though he was late, I missed my flight, and was forced to wait another five hours in the airport for the next flight to Tampa. I did not make a big deal about it. Luckily, I'd brought my journal and I'd still make it to the cruise ship on time, thank God. The cruise was so much fun, especially because I'd met several of the same friends I'd made on the last Abraham-Hicks cruise I took to Alaska on the USS Oosterdam. David Byrne was the man from London I'd come to know on the cruise to Alaska with whom I'd have a great time dancing, chatting for an hour in The Crow's Nest Lounge with our other Abie Friends until it was really late and time to retire. Then we'd usually run into one another again in the morning and sit together enjoying a late brunch. We'd make fun of my friend, Michael, being a little light in the loafers because I thought he was a bit effeminate.

Anyway, Michael's friendship turned out to be true blue and would end up lasting through the years even though we were not sexual for a long time. We did exchange massages and gifts at Christmas and he usually gave me something nice for my birthday. The first year we were together he gave me a beautiful light purple fairy shirt, a matching necklace and earrings with an abalone shell setting in both earrings, and in the necklace. He knew what I liked, and even though he did not have much money he always seemed to splurge on me at Christmas and on my birthday, so I suppose he must have still had genuine feelings and cared for me.

A year later Dan had a minor car accident in DC. where he was hit from behind while driving one of his clients to work. It left him nervous about driving, and he went to my chiropractor to try to sue this woman and collect a decent amount of money for his pain and suffering. After that accident he would not be the same and refused to drive ever again. His refusal to drive the clients from the Rehab center to work caused him to lose his job. He was distraught and asked me if he could come live with me for a while in New Jersey. I did not think it was a good idea because he would not fit into the income guidelines, and I didn't think there was enough space for the two of us anyway. I did, however, agree to pick him up with my new beau, Gary Torres, and Michael. Michael and I drove down in my car, and Gary drove alone in his Subaru Forester which had a pretty large station wagon area to store most of Dan's belongings.

I had room for his clothes and small boxes in my trunk. Dan offered to pay for the tolls, gas, dinners for all of us, and our time and trouble. He said he'd take us all out for a buffet dinner at one of his favorite dining places when we arrived. So, it was going to be an adventure. Dan had a cat, Dusty, whom he really loved, and was probably the only living thing that was a true female friend. He said he was going to give Dusty away to someone down in DC which I found sad because I knew how much he liked his cat. Dan was cheap and said he could not afford to keep the cat, so Gary said he would keep it in his home, and it was decided last minute we'd package Dusty in her little ca carrier and drive her the four hours on Route 95 back to new Jersey. Dan initially stayed with me for two or three weeks, but because he was such a cheapskate we fought like cats and dogs, especially when it came to Dan having to pay Michael for a handyman job, he did for him and his sister who lived on the property they both owned in Dayton. There was a place called "The Grange" which was originally begun for farmers as a place to socialize, and his sister was the secretary. The Grange needed a lot of work done inside and outside the property from painting to repairs, and it was decided Michael could do most of the work, but he was not licensed and insured, so he was being paid barely a living wage per hour, and this pissed me off because I knew Dan and his sister both had a lot of money. I knew that because Dan had to fill out an application to live with me in Griggs Farm, and I could not believe he had so much money in his checking account and owned stock, a home and property. He definitely did not fit the income guidelines in order to live with me in Griggs Farm, a subsidized housing apartment complex. I was only paying $286 per month when I first moved in 1995, and a mere $450.00 per month when I moved out more than twenty years later. I was living with a room-mate at the time, and we both split the rent, so technically I was only paying $267.50 per month for rent when I moved out and into Merwick Stanworth Apartments, a brand-new subsidized housing community closer to town.

Dan and I were like brother and sister who loved each other, but who just did not get along if we were too close to one another for extended periods of time, so we decided to move Dan into Gary's house where he rented half of Gary's office upstairs with Dusty, the cat living in his room with him, though Gary had to buy and pay for all the cat food and cat litter. Dan was so cheap and immature he even expected Gary to do the shopping for and pay for paper towels, napkins, toilet paper, and tissues with his own money. Dan might offer Gary ten or fifteen dollars for all the things he bought afterward, but he just seemed so immature and dependent for a man in his late sixties.

Dan, Gary, and Michael all have a great sense of humor, so we joke all the time. Gary, Michael, and I always make fun of Dan, and w even made up a dictionary of "Danisms". My favorite one was "redandant_-a tendency to make the same mistake over and again without ever learning to change one's behavior. Dandruff-a scalp condition, etc. Well, you get the picture.

Michael's relationship with his landlady began to deteriorate because she was not respecting him and often took advantage of his good nature by giving him way too much work without pay. He really wanted to leave her and get his own space, so eventually after I'd introduced Michael to Gary, I'd invite Gary to talk to Michael. Michael, now has a small room in Gary's neighborhood. He takes care of the grounds at Gary's house, maintains the appliances if anything breaks down, and is a property manager of sorts. In return, Gary allows him to store tools and supplies in his basement. There was a lot of work to be done before he could even begin to paint or refinish the basement. There was leaky sewage and the basement floor was covered with a few inches of cat litter cemented into the floor itself, so Michael had hours of work in front of him. He also was expected to do all the landscaping and repairs of anything that went wrong. He even fixed leaks in the plumbing. If appliances broke down like refrigerators or air conditioners Michael was expected to repair or replace them.

Technically, he had no rent to pay, but to me it seemed as if Michael was paying more in hours and repairs than if he was paying an actual rent. The only difference was that Gary was not demeaning or demanding, and was much easier going than Michael's former landlady, nor did he expect Michael to be the host at all of his parties. Gary rarely had guests or dinner parties until I arrived on the scene.

Famous Mathematician Martin Kruskal & "Lauragami"

Martin Kruskal was one of my massage clients. He was a very modest man, and it was only after his death that I discovered how famous he was as a mathematician. I later found out very much about him. He was born in New York City in 1925. His mother, Lillian Rose Vorhaus Kruskal Oppenheimer, founded the Origami Center of America in New York City, which later became OrigamiUSA. He studied at the University of Chicago and completed his PhD. at New York University. He worked at Princeton University, as a research scientist at the Plasma Physics Laboratory, then as a professor of astronomy, founding the Program in Applied and Computational Mathematics. He retired from Princeton University in 1989 to join the mathematics department of Rutgers University. Among his accomplishments was an elegant description of the spacetime structure of simple black holes. He received the National Medal of Science in 1993. Martin loved games, puzzles, and word play. He invented a "magic trick" that perplexed professional magicians because it was not a sleight of hand but a mathematical phenomenon.

Martin was married to Laura Kruskal, whom I met just before his death in 2006. "Lauragami" was well known as a lecturer and writer about origami and originator of many new models. Martin and Laura traveled extensively to scientific meetings and to visit Martin's many scientific collaborators. Laura taught origami workshops in schools and institutions for the elderly and people with disabilities.

The Kruskals were good friends with John Forbes Nash Jr. and his wife, Alicia. John was the mathematician who made fundamental contributions to game theory, differential geometry, and the study of partial differential equations. His theories are widely used in economics. The film "A Beautiful Mind" and a biography by Sylvia Nasar are based upon John's struggles with mental illness beginning in 1959 and his recovery in the mid-1980s.

My friendship with Laura Kruskal had grown after meeting her at the Senior Resource Center during one of her origami workshops. Her husband, Martin, had told me so much about her during his massage sessions or afterward, but it was not until Martin died that I finally met her during one of her classes in which I participated. After that I gave her a beautiful, long purple scarf for Christmas which I left for her at the Senior Center. Susan, the head of the Senior Center, shared with me that Laura was thrilled to receive the scarf as a gift, especially since purple was her favorite color. After that she invited me to her house one afternoon for some lunch and she also insisted on sitting me down to teach me how to make a little pink origami folder to keep a few of my checks in. I was about to decline the offer, saying I was too busy, but Laura insisted. Origami was her gift and her passion. One rarely got away without learning how to fold something special and practical around Laura.

While I was there, I noticed all of the news clippings with Martin's picture or some of the two of them together. I was very surprised to see the one newspaper article that showed Martin at the White house with Al Gore and President Bill Clinton where he was given the highest award in Science one year, something he never even mentioned to me in the five years I knew him.

I did know he worked at the university and was a worldwide lecturer and Math scholar because Art Dupre'e, an adjunct college math professor I dated for a short while used to attend his math lectures and told me how brilliant they were.

Laura was a cheerful, sweet, and talented woman who brought joy, fun, and wisdom wherever she went. She spoke several languages, and would use them if she wanted to communicate with someone of a different culture. She knew I could speak a little in French, so sometimes we would just speak some conversational French just for the fun of speaking in a different language.

Her home was filled with magazine cut-outs on the walls and on her outside door.

In 2015, the first "Heartscapes" poetry reading and concert took place at the Kruskal's home.

Laura passed away quietly in her sleep on February 6th, 2019, and though I knew she would not be here too much longer at 95, I just did not expect her to leave me so soon since she was still in relatively good health. She was such a strong, vital woman who never let anything stop her even with a lot of physical challenges like blindness in one eye, deafness in one ear, and pain from pins in her hips in a less than successful operation. She didn't drive, but people loved her and her teaching so much they would come from far distances to pick her up so that they could have her positive Spirit and special skills as an origami instructor for their students.

ABRAHAM-HICKS AND FIRST TRIP TO ALASKA (2010)

After reading her *Ask and it is Given*, I came to know, Esther Hicks, who channels the non-physical entity Abraham said that when Abraham first entered her body, she felt not just ecstasy, but almost as if her toe was plugged in to a light socket all the time. But eventually Esther became more comfortable with the high frequency of Abraham and eventually relaxed so much that there was not so much of a contrast between her and Abraham.

I asked her a question about my suicide attempts in a question-and-answer session in a workshop with Abraham in 2004 in Philadelphia. Abraham said I was one of the most joyous entities they had met and that I should have no shame about my suicide attempts because all death is suicide. He/they said "We all do everything to ourselves. Whether we died from a heart attack, diabetes, lung cancer, stroke, or whatever, we chose to do whatever was needed to our bodies in order to move into the next realm, so there was no shame in my wanting a change in my reality.

In July of 2010 I had the great fortune of taking a Holland America cruise with Jerry, Esther Hicks, and 450 other Abraham "Law of Attraction" metaphysical students to Juneau, and several ports in pristine Alaska. I had seen the photos in their photo album from their very first cruise to Alaska at the Holiday Inn in Philadelphia when I took my first interactive workshop with them. When I first perused the photos, I had the divine desire to go, but it seemed a bit expensive for this single mom living on SSI disability with only a small income from part-time massage clients, so it actually took seven years before the manifestation of my desire.

I decided to treat myself for my fifty-fourth birthday which was July 15th of that summer. The cruise ship was leaving on July fifth and returning on the twelveth. I could not imagine a more wonderful way to spend the week.

I had to preregister early with a certain amount for the deposit. The cash was not in my budget at the time, so I opted to put it on one of my new Capital One credit cards. My abundance consciousness was not very expansive at the time, so I did not sign up for any extra side trips. Besides, I was traveling alone and did not know anyone that was traveling in the Abraham group.

There were so many new things I needed to handle and had no man in my life at the time to help me. I'm not very good at using the computer, but I e-mailed all the info like signing of documents online over to my local Triangle computer store in Montgomery where my friend, David, understood how to do these things easily and did so for a small fee. All that remained to be done was book the flight out to Seattle, Washington. I booked it early enough so as to receive a good discount on the round-trip airfare. I had a tendency to be late for appointments, so I decided to make sure I'd be on time by arriving a day early in Seattle with plenty of time to take a bus or taxi to the port in Vancouver in order to rendezvous on time with the SS Oosterdam. That meant I needed to pre-arrange an overnight stay at an inexpensive hotel or motel nearby. I did some online research to compare rates, found a great Best Western and made a reservation. I'd stayed at their chain before. The rates were reasonable, the rooms were clean and neat, had comfortable beds, a desk and chair where I could do some writing, there was a large bathtub, and they gave you a light buffet breakfast in the early AM with your choice of scrambled or hard-boiled eggs, waffles, danishes, turkey sausage, bacon, coffee, milk, OJ, and herb teas. I had never been to Seattle and knew there was a lot to see and explore, but as a woman traveling alone, I had no desire to do anything but rest in my room, write in my journal, and figure out how I was getting to the port on time the next morning. The next time I go I'm traveling with a friend or mate and I'll opt to explore the city.

Anyway, my flight was terrific. The Best Western van picked me up at the perfect time at the airport with my two bags of luggage plus one carry-on I held on my arm along with my shoulder pocketbook.

Alaska was beautiful and pristine. I saw some eagles flying and the tails of whales from the ship. Every night after dinner I danced in the nightclub with the new friends I met. I dressed to the nines for dinner since I loved to get fancy occasionally, and I'd brought at least two or three gowns, a fancy cocktail dress, and a sequined top I wore as a professional singer that I paired with black silk pants. I even brought two fancy purses to match my dressy outfits for the captain's night and one other formal night when they take professional photos at our table and by ourselves. My photos came out gorgeous, and I also took a lot of personal shots with my digital camera. I made very good friends with one man from London named David Byrne and another man who looked like Santa Claus named Scott.

I treated myself to a massage, a manicure, and getting my hair done in the beauty salon as opposed to going on a lot of side trips. Oh, I did schedule a trip parasailing on a little island called Half Moon Cay prior to going on the ship because I had been parasailing once before on Daytona Beach with my boyfriend, Knowle, and I just loved that free feeling of flying twelve-hundred 1200 feet above the ocean. I was harnessed in with this lovely blond gal from the Ukraine, Alison, who was part of the Abraham group, and we had a blast. We shared the joy of our fun experience later that night after dinner.

After dancing five or six of us from the Abraham group would meet in the Crow's Nest Lounge to have a beer and chat. It was all the way at the top of the ship, and there was a great view. This was one of the best cruises I'd been on, and it was my eighth cruise. My first to Alaska and second with Holland America. The food was scrumptious, displayed beautifully, and plentiful. The cool thing about lunch and dinner was that if I could not decide between two appetizers or two different yummy desserts, they would bring both of them out, and I'd share them with one of my other Abie friends. I think I gained seven pounds on the cruise, but I lost most of it within a few weeks once back at home. I probably would have gained about twelve or more if I had not been dancing half the day and night for there was always a band playing somewhere. The house band called me "the dancer" and I talked with the members when they were on breaks making friends with a few of them.

Even though I was traveling alone as a person with a disability who uses a cane everything went smoothly for me everywhere I went. People were always kind and helpful, opened doors to be considerate, let me go before them in line, and when we had to move our baggage on a long line people in front or back would move it for me since they saw me struggling just using one arm. I felt so very blessed and well taken care of. It was probably my connection to my angels, guides, Jesus, and Abraham, and the fact that I was in a very positive mindset that all went so smoothly for me. I felt sad when the seven days were over and I knew I would not be seeing most of these people ever again, even the waiters and other members of the staff I'd come to like a lot. I did take phone numbers and addresses of a few of the Abraham students I'd come to adore like David, the fellow from London with whom I brunched or danced with nearly every day or night.

Michael picked me up from the airport in Newark. He could tell how joyous and uplifted I was from having such a delightful experience. My joy and happy memories would stay with me for a few months. Michael and I were enjoying some nice times together until we had a misunderstanding in November, and he would break up with me. I was very physically attracted to him which made me attached, so I felt heartbroken at the time. Michael did say he would still be my friend which softened the blow a little bit.

Trip with Pat, Michael and Karin

After Michael and I broke up in November of 2010 I was pretty down, but I did not stay there for too long because I was asked by Karin if I wanted to go down to Florida on vacation with her to visit her friends, Chuck and Gracie. I had affirmative prayer work for the success of the vacation done by a Religious Science practitioner at church.

Thank God, because neither Karin nor I had the needed funds, stamina, nor were in the best health to take the trip all the way down to southern Florida by car all by ourselves. At that point Karin asked her dad, Pat, if he wanted to accompany us on the trip, and thank goodness for the two of us, he did, and he decided we would drive his new car down there, and the three of us would share the driving. Unbeknownst to any of us at the time Karin was suffering from colon cancer. Every time we would stop to go to the bathroom Karin would stay an awfully long time, and eventually we'd find out that she was having very difficult, painful bowel movements. Karin did not go to the doctor to get it checked out because she thought she just had hemorrhoids – it was not until after we returned from this trip that Karin told her mom about her bloody stools, and her mom strongly encouraged her to go to the ER. to finally get this checked out. By the time she did she was in the second or third stage of colon cancer.

Prior to this we did have a pretty fun vacation. And her dad, Pat, was there to joke with us, serve as an escort, pay for Karin's meals when we stopped at Cracker Barrels on the way down to Florida and back, and he paid for half the amount of our stays at hotels or motels until we finally arrived in Florida, and we were able to spend nights with friends. We played music and sang together on the way down, Pat took us to the butterfly museum at one of the universities which was really cool, but when we got to Chuck and Gracie's place there was no one there. Thank goodness Karin knew where Gracie worked, so we were finally able to get her key to get inside the house after the long journey to Florida. It was Chuck's mom's birthday, and I was surprised to find he took his girlfriend rather than his wife to the birthday dinner out at a very nice restaurant. Gracie was from the Philippines and liked to work every day, but Chuck preferred she was home with him, so after a while there was an understanding between her and Chuck that when she was working or doing what she liked he would go be with his other lady friend. In fact, Gracie even agreed to let Chuck have his girlfriend move in at one point. That was my first exposure to a couple having a true polyamorous relationship which eventually was what seemed to work best in my life with all the different types of relationships I had simultaneously with various men.

While in Florida as Chuck and Gracie's guests or staying in the various hotels, Pat and I shared the same bed. Karin said she knew, and it was something she'd gotten accustomed to from the time she was young. We did not make a big thing about it and did not continue the relationship after coming home because Pat had his girlfriends at home, and I had my "home guys", but we always cared about one another as special friends. In a way Pat is like an uncle or father figure to me.

After visiting Chuck and Gracie's mom and Aunt we took off for Pat's friend, OJ.'s beautiful home in? where we had the good fortune to stay for several nights enjoying the beauty of OJ.'s back yard which had a creek with lots of aquatic life teeming in it. I picked up lots of shells while kneeling down by the creek where I saw lots of water birds, insects, snails, and mollusks. OJ. and Pat, being older and wiser, know how to just sit, relax, and "be" in the beauty of nature without having to do much of anything except chat, drink a beer or something cool, listen to good jazz, and enjoy some good home cooked food.

On that same car trip, we stopped in Leesburg in central, Florida, at an RV park to see my old boyfriend, Rick Huston, a former painter, carpenter, and window washer at Princeton University. The three of us slept over a few nights to visit while we availed ourselves of the two swimming pools, the jacuzzi, and the jazzercize classes. We also went to see a variety show given by the residents the first night we arrived. The singers were terrific, and there was a music quiz at the beginning where several notes of various songs were played, and the first person in the audience to guess which song was being played as well as the artist who sang the song, won a small prize. I managed to guess three out of the ten songs, but I told Pat one of them, so he could call it out in order to win the prize. I did not want to be a hog and a show-off.

One night we all sat outside under the stars while Rick built a beautiful fire. We felt the presence of Rick's dad in Spirit whom Karin tuned into with her psychic abilities. He gave Rick some special advice and personalized messages just for him.

It was during that trip that we realized something was wrong with Karin physically due to the protracted periods of time she was spending in the bathroom when we'd stop for gas. Karin had already contracted cancer by that time and was having pain during her slow, difficult bowel movements. She assumed she had hemorrhoids, so she was lax in going to the doctor to get checked out. Once we all found out she was in stage two or possibly three, cancer of the colon Michael, Pat, and I talked about taking her on a trip over her birthday the next year to give her something good to look forward to in order to make her feel happy and forget about her health challenges. It was my idea for all of us to take a cruise, especially because I wanted to have an excuse to vacation with Michael since I'd been holding a torch for him since we'd formally broken up. We remained good friends still seeing one another on our birthdays and giving each other gifts at holidays, but I was still missing the sex and romance we once shared.

I'd earlier found out about the discount cruises one could take through vacations to go.com if you paid for a trip in full within ninety days of its sailing. I always loved cruising – especially southern Florida or the Caribbean during cold winters in New Jersey. We were to fly in to Tampa where we boarded our ship; and our first port was Key West, former home to Ernest Hemingway, where we explored all sorts of treasures.

Karin and I shared a cabin together, and so did Michael and Pat. We had a few special dress-up for the captain's dinner, and special photo nights, and I'd brought several very dressy gowns for each occasion. Michael took one photo with me, and since Michael dd not want to go to the special dinner that cost an extra $30 apart from all the free food we ate at every meal one night Pat was my escort, and he took a lovely professional photo with me which I still have framed and sitting on my bedroom dresser.

Karin's birthday was on a Wednesday, March 6th. I remember she wore a long red and black dress, looked very pretty and was her usual vivacious self. The waiter brought out a nice cake for her after we finished eating dinner, and we all sang happy birthday. Little did we know she would only have two more birthdays on earth to celebrate after that special one where we all danced in the lounge, sang, and drank delicious pina coladas with fresh pineapple and strawberry daiquiris. We met lots of handsome guys, and they hung around Karin and me for the next few days of the trip. Michael met a nice blond lady too, and I got a little jealous even though they just shared some innocent conversation. She was rich enough that she had a cabin with not just a window, but which opened onto a balcony.

One day we went to Belize, and we took some nice photos, but it was rather poor and not as beautiful as I had expected it to be.

My favorite stop was in Roatan, Honduras where Michael and I were signed up for a snorkeling expedition in the lovely, clear turquoise waters of little French Key. We took a short ferry ride to get there, were given masks and flippers which we donned, and once in the Caribbean felt like we were in the warm waters of the Earth Mother's womb. The water was so clear we could see lots of colorful fish swimming right next to our moving arms and legs. The water was warm just the way I like it, and Michael held onto me to make sure I kept up with the group after we jumped from the small boat into the ocean. It was one of the happiest moments of the trip for me because I was swimming and sharing something physical in beautiful Mother nature with a man I loved very much.

The cruise was only a week long, and over the next few days, was jam packed with delicious meals, sightseeing, dancing, drinking, and chatting with new friends we made in the lounges The week passed by very quickly. Before we knew it we were back on the airplane to go home again.

ABRAHAM-HICKS TRIP: PANAMA CANAL AND COSTA RICA (2011)

On the Alaska cruise, I had made scores of wonderful new friends, two in particular whom I'd be lucky enough to see again the following year on the Hicks' "Living in the Vortex" cruise to the Panama Canal, Key West, and Curacao. I met a lot of new friends and danced and sang with the band on that cruise ship. Everyone loved me and complimented me as they always do, on my dancing and enthusiasm.

I met the same band again! The leader of the band and the bass player remarked to me immediately upon meeting me again, "You're that dancer we saw on the cruise to Alaska, aren't you?" They somehow recognized me right away as soon as I started dancing on the deck as we were leaving the port of Palm Springs... So, there you go. I may never be one of the famous dancers on Dancing with the Stars, but I can still enjoy dancing in this somewhat limited body just as I am and thoroughly enjoy myself as well as transform all the people around me wherever I go. I get a kick out of raising the energy and vibration by dancing, singing, walking just as I am, being kind, being witty and funny.

My cruise with Jerry and Esther turned out to be one of the most joyous vacation adventures I'd ever take, and it was Dan's loving care for me depositing a few hundred dollars per day into my cruise account so that I had no financial worries that helped to make it so carefree and fun. I could get my hair and nails done as often as I wanted, go to the spa to get a massage, buy my own pina colada drinks, jewelry, trinkets, or souvenirs at the various islands we visited, etc. Dan made sure I was treated like the Queen I am. Unlike now when according to Michael "Dan is tighter than an anal sphincter" Michael jokes a lot with him. We all poke fun at each other. Back when he thought he was "my guy" and I was "his gal" he was so kind and magnanimous probably hoping a permanent girlfriend/boyfriend relationship would come out of it, but everything would fall flat the first time he slept over my house one night. We were not compatible at all sexually, plus Dan was way too nervous and anxious for me. He tried to please me by going to a dakhini named Astarte in Philadelphia to learn how to massage one's partner and to learn tantric sex, but either there is chemistry or there's not, I find, with most men and women. Sometimes I may relate on two levels—an intellectual and spiritual, or like my flame mate, Ernie, on a physical, spiritual, and intellectual level, but it is rare when you find someone so similar like a "twin flame" that you are physically, spiritually, physically, and emotionally compatible. I know when I am doing my sadhana (Sanskrit for spiritual practices) of prayer, contemplation, chanting, or meditating in nature I experience the inner love within my own being; when this happens I am in touch with the love and joy of Christ within my own heart, then whomever is before me is my beloved, my "magic mirror", or my own divine reflection which I can see in the leaves blowing on the trees, in the red-orange sunset, in the red-tailed hawk soaring above my head, in the softness of the baby's cheek against mine, or the soft pink rose flower petals smelling delicious brushing up against my cheek, and in the love of my playful kitty rubbing up against my leg in this precious present moment. God is everywhere, all loving, all knowing, in everyone, everything, delighting in its own sport, this delicious Play of Consciousness.

In the spring of 2009, I saw on the Abraham website that there would be another cruise in 2010, but this time it would be to the Panama Canal, Costa Rica, Curacao, and Costa Maya, Mexico. This trip would be even more up my alley because I loved the Caribbean, swimming and snorkeling in warm turquoise ocean water, and sunbathing in my bikini on hot sands in the Caribbean. As usual, my money situation was not great, but I did have at least enough for the deposit on one of my credit cards. I also had a good friend I knew for many years from Angel Joan Fericy's, Church of Divine Light, in Somerset, New Jersey. His name was Dan, and we started dating even while Michael and I were in love. Dan had moved from South Brunswick, NJ to Capitol Heights, MD; and we shared a long-distance friendship from the time he moved from Jersey to MD by phone. Dan also asked me to pick him up from the train station when he would come in occasionally to visit his home and family in Jersey. Though he had a sister who lived next door to him he said he preferred someone else drive him since they did not get along well. But I think it was just an excuse to see me. He made the offer more attractive by saying he'd pay me. Dan had money, and he was unafraid to spend it on me. We went to a few nice restaurants in the afternoon or evening when he came to Jersey even while Michael & I were dating. Michael did not have a lot of money because he was self-employed as a carpenter, painter, landscaper, and whatever odd jobs he could get, so he was very careful with his budget. Michael was also tall and lanky without a very big appetite, so when we'd go out to Chinese restaurants we would split entrees, soups, and such. I'd always end up feeling hungry after Michael and I ate together unless he came to my house for date, and I would cook salmon and vegetables or spaghetti and turkey meatballs for him. So it was nice having someone treat me like Queen in the money department even though I was not physically attracted to Dan. I liked him intellectually, and he was interesting with a good sense of humor. He also was interested in polyamory which I'd been exploring myself for some time.

When Michael and I broke up I was very sad, grieving, and Dan tried very hard to make me feel soothed and better with phone calls, sending me money from Maryland, and he came to visit a few times on the week-ends. We had even scheduled two trips to be together—one where I'd drive down to MD, go out to dinner and check out a nearby sex club. I had never been to one before, but Dan said they had great food, a jacuzzi, dancing, and a lot of nice, classy people, so I said "OK, let's give it a try."

We had a fun time at the Indian restaurant, ate well, and Dan even bought me a pair of cotton Indian pants.

The sex club was fun for dancing, dining, and socializing, but the last thing I wanted to do was have sex with a stranger after losing my boyfriend. I did not even want to have sex with Dan. In fact, I kept calling Michael from the club or after we left to keep in touch since my heart was still with him.

Dan bought me a sexy lingerie outfit in their special store which I put on later that night and I got into the hot tub with him. Except that I may have kissed Dan I was not interested in any type of sexual exploration with strangers. I watched in amusement and curiosity while some of the other folks were enjoying themselves in the club. There was one black man to whom I was attracted, but I told him I'd just lost my boyfriend; he was sorry, but we danced anyway cause the music was good. and then I found out he was married. I danced a dance with the guy, but when I learned he was married I also realized his wife had to approve of any partners he'd choose since they most likely had a threesome, so that was not where I was at. Oh well. I liked the dancing, the jacuzzi, and the buffet was great, but I could do those things anywhere in New Jersey. I did let Dan convince me one more time to go to "A Private Affair" on New Year's Eve because they were having a special celebration with really fine food, but this time I drove down with one of my best girlfriends from the UFO crowd, Karin. Her boyfriend would also drive down after work to meet us there, so I figured it might be a nice distraction from not being with Michael on a special holiday like New Year's Eve.

Right before New Year's Eve two special friends of mine from the church, a husband and wife from Hamilton, Ron and Audrey Franks, who ran a metaphysical center from their home, both died within a week of each other. Audrey was very sick in a hospital practically near death, but Ron had a fluke accident while in his bedroom doing some carpentry work. He was found dead by his son-in-law, Scott, and all of us who knew how special he was from church and his metaphysical meetings were shocked and devastated. He was strong and healthy, but he was the one to die even before his wife, Audrey, who finally succumbed to her illness within a few days after he had passed away. The only thing we could think to explain it was that Ron loved Audrey so much he wanted to go prepare the way for her in heaven. I don't think the two of them wanted to live without the other.

Our pastor, Rev. Karen Kushner, was asked to perform the memorial service and their son, Scott Allen, would sing some songs he composed for the eulogy. I asked Michael to accompany me since I was sad and feeling vulnerable at the time.

The next day I was scheduled to drive down to Maryland to pick up Dan from the place where he lived and worked in Capitol Heights to go to an inexpensive hotel near the sex club where we would dress and get ready to participate in the New Year's Eve celebration at "A Private Affair". A big mistake. I'm not sure why I was not honoring my feelings of sadness and vulnerability. Dan so desperately wanted to help me feel good I guess I wanted to please him, and I had no one else who'd asked me to spend the New Year with them. Looking back, I guess I was afraid to be alone, but I could have just had a quiet night with my single mother or my daughter, Sky. It was sort of fun driving down to Maryland with my friend, Karin, though. We talked a lot about private things and became pretty close that week-end. Like me, Karin had an experience of sexual molestation by a family member in her youth. In fact, she was even younger than me when it happened, but she said she forgave him and realized while doing the Landmark Forum that she was responsible for all the circumstances she had created in her life, so she did not blame this person in her family for what happened.

Karin ended up having a great time spending a sensuous and sexy evening with three different couples who were attracted to her beauty, charm, and charisma. I was happy for her. I, however, was in no mood to do anything but dance and enjoy the delicious food that was provided at the buffet. I also wore a sexy pink fishnet outfit underneath my long black, not too dressy maxi dress. I would wear my dress initially, but take it off later on in the night when I got hot dancing and wanted to look sexier.

Dan wanted me to check out some of the rooms. I actually did get involved with some guy who was attractive for a little while after I got out of the jacuzzi. For some stupid reason I kissed him, and I think we even got more intimate with oral sex. I don't even remember. All I can recall is I felt terrible afterward. Dan kept saying how beautiful it was, and I felt horrible, like I'd betrayed my own heart. I finally admitted to Dan I'd made a poor decision telling him I'd spend New Year's Eve at a sex club right after my two good friends had just died, and all I wanted to do was just cry or have Michael hold me in his arms even though he was no longer available to me emotionally or physically.

One more good thing did come out of spending more time with Dan. He was beginning to like me more and more; and he asked me if I'd like to spend a week-end with him at the little hotel in Stockton, New Jersey called The Stockton Inn where we could get to know each other better and really enjoy ourselves. We had a pleasant time even though Dan tried to cancel the week-end at least three times before we'd actually go. He was afraid I'd reject him, so he wanted to forget the whole thing and not even take the chance.

We had a wonderful dinner at the inn with Karin and her daughter, Abby, for which Dan paid. The room was really classy with a fireplace, a king-sized bed with a really beautiful comforter and matching pillow shams. And we felt very comfortable with one another. No pressure for either of us, so we massaged each other, and that was a nice way to relax and be intimate without too much pressure. That week-end there was a Renaissance Fair in New Hope with different characters dressed up in Renaissance outfits. A poet made up a poem for me on the spot. Dan bought me some earrings, an outfit, and a harness for my new dog. He was very loving, kind, and generous. I was beginning to like him more even though I still was not really attracted to him physically. When I told Dan about the Abraham cruise to Panama Canal & Costa Rica, he said he thought it would be great fun for me. He knew I did not have the money for it. He said "You know I can't go because of my job." I replied,

"That does not have to stop me from going." Could you help me pay for the cruise?" Well, the sweetheart, he came up with a thousand dollars cash the a few week-ends later to put in my bank account so I could send in all the money required. I was thrilled to be going on another cruise with Jerry and Esther Hicks as well as participating in the group questions and channeled answers from the being Jerry and Esther called their spiritual guide, "Abraham" which they called themselves to signify "Teacher". Abraham said it was a group consciousness of like minds and had nothing to do with the Abraham mentioned in the Bible.

GARY (2011)

In the meantime, I met another man at my church, a quiet one at the Center for Spiritual Living in Princeton, one whom I had no physical attraction for whatsoever. He seemed kind, interesting, spiritual, and interested in seeing me as a friend who would take me out for lunch or drive me to Piscataway to a clinic where they did cosmetic testing for large corporations. I would often pick up a few bucks in between massage clients for testing different face creams, deodorants, facial peels, and the like. Clinical Research Labs also had regular cosmetic "Patch" studies where we would get twenty or thirty lipsticks or foundations of various colors taped across our backs to see if there would be an allergic reaction. These studies generally paid anything from $40 for a two-day sunscreen test up to $250 or $300 for a longer study with more visits to the testing site. After a while I stopped going to Piscataway because, with the money I shelled out for gas, I could not have been making more than 10-$12 per hour.

Except for my experience as a masseuse, go-go dancer, professional singer, and yoga instructor I did not have a lot on my resume'. Not for regular companies anyway. That was why I usually was self-employed most of my life making my own hours and setting my own wages, even if they were modest.

My new friend, Gary's, demeanor, was quiet and he did not say much unless it was important or funny. I found out later he had a type of learning disability called "Central Auditory Processing Disorder" which made him super sensitive to the sounds around him as well as any conversations going on while he was trying to focus on speaking or listening to just one person. He loved pets like myself. He had two cats like me, and at that time we met I had a puppy dog named Puja with whom he would enjoy playing in my living room if I was late coming home from somewhere for a date with him. There were several times I'd just "space out" when we had a date and call him from the road from my newly acquired flip cell phone, apologizing for forgetting about our date and running late, but he was always understanding, patient, and never upset with me about forgetting. Nothing much seemed to bother him. We'd been going out to lunch and then dinner for over three months and he still had not kissed me. I tried to kiss him after a date, but he'd usually give me a friendly kiss or a peck on the cheek. Little did I realize I was dealing with the only sixty-year-old available male virgin on the planet.

One night while I was doing dishes in the kitchen after we'd had dinner and he took me in his arms from behind and gave me a passionate kiss smack on the lips. Now that was more like it. This guy actually had some potential as a boyfriend and help mate.

One time I was working on the computer, but I never knew much about it and would get help learning to do e-mails, Facebook, and writing articles and papers from either my daughter, Sky, or my son, Gabriel. One Sunday I had a lot of questions about how to edit something I was writing, so I asked Gary if he could help me after church was over. He was so kind. He got into my computer and spent a few hours straight focusing on whatever it was, and it was finished very quickly-Voila. He was so nice he asked for nothing in return. He was just glad to be of service. I began to realize what a kind, gentle soul was in my presence. He seemed to be willing and able to give me whatever it was I wanted and needed.

One time I read in the newspaper my favorite musical theater actor and performer, Ben Vereen, of "Jesus Christ Superstar" and "Pippin" fame, would be coming to PA to the Bristol Riverside Theater to do a one man show, and I really wanted to see him, but I did not have any cash nor enough credit left on even one of my five credit cards. I told Gary about him coming, and voila! He was like an angel, my wish fulfilling tree. He seemed to want to satisfy all my desires. I particularly recall that date because it was a romantic, rainy day, and Ben Vereen's show was so amazing and inspirational. He began to recount his life in theater from the time he performed in "the King and I" as a child right through each and every one of his performances as an adult. He also shared amazing stories from his personal life like the time he was walking along the highway, had a stroke, and was hit by a car at night by a man who did not see him in the dark. It happened to be his friend famous pianist and musical producer, David Foster. He was told that he would never walk again. Anyway, he recounted his miraculous recovery from the stroke to go on to walk again and finally, after much rehabilitation, he went on to perform again too. He said his miraculous recovery was due to all the prayers and the love of his fans, friends, and little ol' ladies who loved him that was the reason for him standing back up where he is today. "I'm not sure what to call it. You can call it God, Allah, Jesus, the angels, love, or "the Force". But whatever your religion is, this loving force is the same in everyone and responds to the loving prayers of all of us." I truly believe this, and I am so grateful to this day to that Force of love and all those kind people and friends who prayed over me and for me for months until I came to a full recovery."

What a great man. What a beautiful story and show he put on for us at the Riverside Theater in Bristol, PA, the day I started to fall in love with this quiet man, Gary, who would eventually come to live with me and be my partner and full-time help mate.

Later that afternoon Gary took me through the rain back to his car where he drove me to the Red Lobster on Route 1 in Lawrenceville where we had a delicious dinner and quiet, romantic conversation. Though I was not that physically attracted to him since my heart was still with Michael, I still wanted to sleep next to him in his bed that night just as a loving thank-you for all his kindness and love for me.

Having a disability, it was difficult to keep track of my check card purchases and to record my debits when I used the automated teller machine or paid with my visa or debit card at the Shop Rite in Montgomery or McCaffrey's in Princeton; with people waiting on line behind me I always felt pressured to finish up my transaction, so I'd wait until I got back home to enter the purchase into my checkbook. Unfortunately, I'd get so busy and had so much on my plate that much of the time I would forget or I was just too busy to care. I never balanced one checking account statement because I was too busy, and it was too much trouble for me. I was very lucky to have a friend in the manager of the bank at First Union, which is now Wells Fargo. He was very compassionate because of my circumstances as a disabled single mom, and was kind enough to credit $560 of the bank fees back into my account. Thank God. Most of my checks were small and bounced by a matter of a few dollars or even fifty cents, but one or two $31 overdraft fees would cause my entire checking account to get out of whack.

Some of the checks I wrote were $8 and $10 donations to various charities. I felt extremely generous, but I could have used better judgment and discrimination in making a budget, paying my bills first, tithing 10 % to my church., or wherever I felt spiritually fed. I rarely had extra money to put in my savings account for my daughter's clothing and college needs. I never was practical or realistic about money as a single mom. God heard my prayers and eventually sent me a new attitude of abundance, and my Gary, a very grounded partner I met while at the Center for Spiritual Living. He has been my partner and special friend to help me in so many areas of my life. He was an environmental engineer with the state of New Jersey, but he was retired when I met him. He had a decent pension when I met him, and though he owns a home in Hamilton with a mortgage and much credit card debt, he was willing to allow me to move my old boyfriends into his office as well as a guy friend who was about to lose his living space. He even allowed a girlfriend of ours, Lorelei, to take over his very own bedroom briefly. She did not have much money to give him, but the point is that Gary is so kind and magnanimous he will not allow people to be homeless for any reason, whether it be due to a chronic illness like our disabled veteran friend, Wes, who originally chipped in $400 per month until he lost his job, then got COPD. Gary was and is so kind and generous to me treating me like his own child when I am so moody or deeply depressed that I become paralyzed with fear and cannot cook for myself, do laundry, or any of the normal tasks of life like shopping, for instance. Except when I am in a very dark depression, and then he just snuggles me at night and in the morning, and listens to me express my fears and dark thoughts until I feel safe and comforted in his arms. He is devoted as a husband would be to me, and I am blessed that he adores me the way he would a beloved wife. I was his first and only girlfriend, so he was inexperienced in romance when we first met whereas I'd had two husbands and slept with more men than Madonna and the Magdalene put together! We are both unconventional, and I've no desire to lose my benefits from the State, so I am not going to formally marry him. But he stays with me at my apartment in Princeton many nights.

Gary has his own challenges. He is nearly blind without his very strong glasses, and, even with the best and most expensive lens material available, his glasses distort his peripheral vision at close range, making housecleaning and repair work very difficult. He also suffers from central auditory processing disorder, a nervous system (brain) disorder which, in his case, makes verbal communication nearly impossible when there is a level of background noise that "normal" people wouldn't even notice. He is working on his own book about this and related disorders.

Gary behaves like a husband, and is the most kind and caring man I know. His two disabilities do not stop him from volunteering at church to set up and break down chairs and tables, run the Eckhart Tolle meet-up group, run the Princeton Singles, and be at my side 24/7 when he is not in service to the Center for Spiritual Living, the two Meet-up groups he runs, or running off to his house to drop off cat food for his cat. That is how much he loves me and is devoted to me. I am truly blessed. I'd probably be a basket case without him. Or in mental hospitals on a regular basis. I am so blessed to have my special mate in my sweet life.

After all, my income was still modest enough for me to qualify for over $150 worth of food stamps and SSI disability. In retrospect, it is easy to see that my bills and my daughter should have come first before any frivolous spending. Thank God my consciousness about money is finally starting to balance out more into the arena of abundance. The thrill I used to get from "living on the edge" financially is gone. It caused me too much anxiety, and sometimes the worry I felt about not being able to pay my bills would gradually cause me to go into such a state of anxiety and fear that I would get depressed thinking thoughts of lack. I felt overwhelmed at those times with ideas and outmoded belief systems that did not serve me when wanting to create a spiritually economic, abundant, and healthy, balanced lifestyle. It was not true that I would not be able to support myself and my daughter. We were always cared for even as a single mom, but my faith and practical application of the abundance principles I already knew. At those times I was dealing with first chakra issues, the lower ones dealing with actual survival of my physical being. Sometimes I'd get myself into such a state of anxiety over lack of money that I would become too stressed out at night to sleep. Or if I did fall asleep fine, I'd wake up between 3 and 5 AM worrying about how I was going to pay all my bills after having overindulged. If Michael, whom I still saw as a friend, suggested I save all my receipts, enter them into a ledger, and make a budget and stick to it I'd think, "Why? Way too much trouble and who wants to have all those little papers lying around anyway? Way too much trouble and clutter on my desk. Or in my already very messy file cabinet."

My partner, Gary, who is completely devoted to me, is not very physically active and rarely goes swimming with me. He prefers napping and cuddling with his lady and reading a good, metaphysical book over dancing or singing, but he will escort me to clubs and other places that have karaoke, live bands, and dancing. He enjoys watching me, sharing my good company, and will lovingly pick up the tab for our dinner, appetizers or a drink though neither of us drink much alcohol. Perhaps a little sangria or glass of wine occasionally. Like coffee, alcohol usually upsets my stomach and interferes with my digestion. Coffee will make me feel too revved up or even make me sick, so I stay away from it unless it is made from mushrooms by a company called Alphay. Their mushroom coffee and tea are actually healthy for you and always makes me have a good bowel movement in the morning upon arising.

My higher Self would assure me that God supplies me with everything I need and more when I think positive thoughts and feel happy doing whatever it is I am doing. I know you are thinking this is crazy, airy fairy type thinking. When I have more respect for money and for myself, I tend to use more moderation with spending money with discrimination, and in situations requiring me to have healthy boundaries. The Truth is that Substance is infinite. It is a matter of cultivating a "watchful consciousness focusing on all the abundant good within and all around me—my three children who treat me all the time to meals out or cook Thanksgiving or Christmas dinners at their homes with so much love, the grains of sand on the beaches everywhere underneath my feet, and the millions of blades of grass underneath my naked feet, as well as all my multitude of friends everywhere I go, millions of stars in the night sky, all the delicious food that I eat at every meal. And giving myself a decent night's sleep of at least six to eight hours.

Gary, stays in my apartment much of the time, mostly because I have a disability and need extra help, and I love going to bed snuggling with the same loyal, devoted man every night and waking up to his warm, fleshy body each morning; but he owns and maintains a home a half hour away by car in which two of his tenants are men I dated for several months whom are still close friends even though both relationships broke up. I love them both as special friends, and I talk to Dan just about every day several times per day. We are angel buds who do prayer work together. We've known each other for over twenty years since we both attended the Church of Divine Light in Somerset until Angel Joan Fericy left to live in San Diego. If I ever get anxious or depressed Dan will petition Mother Mary for me to give me extra special attention and love until I move through whatever is bothering me. We tease each other all the time just the way a brother and sister would do. We love each other and support one another spiritually, mentally, and emotionally.

I have a very small apartment which gives neither Gary nor me a lot of space, so my visiting my dear friend, The Pan Man, at his home to exchange sensuous massages and dance every few weeks works for me. I told my special friend, P. M., that sometimes I feel guilty because Gary does not date any other women, though he has other women friends from meet-up groups he leads, but according to "the Pan" it is very common in polyamory for one person to want to be monogamous while their mate or partner is more experimental and likes to enjoy more than one relationship because they are multi-faceted or multi-dimensional. Gary tells me "Being with you is like having seven girlfriends in one, anyway!"

I had a friend who is also a writer and teacher I'd met while attending the "Remember the Magic" IWWG workshops held every summer up at Skidmore College in Saratoga Springs, New York until a few years ago. She was married for some years, and then she met a lovely woman one summer up at Skidmore with whom she fell in love. She shared with me that she told her husband that she'd fallen in love with another woman and wanted a divorce because she and her lesbian lover both wanted to live together. He did not want to lose his wife, so he suggested my author friend move with her new love into a trailer on his property, so he could still maintain a friendship and relationship with healthy boundaries, so he could still share some time with his wife and close friend of many years.

So, my point is there are all types of relationships and unique friendships. Gary just shared an autobiographical song with me I'd never heard before recorded by both Jefferson Airplane, and "Crosby, Stills, Nash, and Young called "Triad". It was written during a time when both bands were sharing living quarters in California. The song is written to express Grace Slick's solution to the seeming problem that she was loved and in love with both David Crosby and her original lover, Paul Kantner, from the Jefferson Airplane. She proposes the only happy solution to their dilemma is "Why can't we go on as three?" It is a new world with new attitudes, and with the divorce rate higher than ever perhaps this open, inclusive relationship is the solution to some of the limitations and other challenges experienced by couples in a conventional monogamous marriage.

For the last ten years, Michael, Dan and Gary have been focal points in my life. Dan as my prayer partner and brother that I can kid, tease, and make fun of. We laugh a lot and enjoy kitties and the same types of old music like Nat King Cole, big band, and the like. Dan and I talk every morning and night like brother and sister over the phone. Dan was also so kind to me after Michael and I broke up. My heart was breaking and Dan thought it was his job to personally care for me and make me feel better by inviting me to go to a sex club with him in Maryland on New Year's Eve. It was my first experience at one of those, and probably my last. I drove down with my good friend and sister in Spirit, Karin. Other than dance a lot, dress in some sexy costumes Dan bought for me there in the boutique, eat from the delicious buffet, and go into the whirlpool naked with Dan, not much happened. Not only was I still healing from my break-up with Michael, but a dear friend of mine named Ron from the Center for Spiritual Living, died suddenly from an unexpected fall while his wife, Audrey, was in the hospital dying after having had an aneurysm or stroke. Michael had accompanied me to Ron's funeral the day before Karin and I drove down to MD to go to the sex club where she would meet her former husband, and I would pick up Dan from his residence to accompany me to "An Intimate Affair" for a night of food, sensuous fun, and dancing to bring in the new year, January 1rst, of 2011. So, I was dealing with both the grief of losing my boyfriend and lover, Michael, and two of my dearest friends who ran the Hamilton Metaphysical Society out of their home. Ron and Audrey were very special folks who loved and respected each other and all who came around them. They also had a lovely daughter, Robin, a son-in-law, Scott, who sang like an angel, who created theater stories and musical compositions for his father-in-law's memorial service which our pastor, Rev. Karen Kushner, officiated. Ron knew I was an ordained minister without a church, and Ron would acknowledge this by asking me to say a certain prayer or perform a blessing of some kind during his spontaneous, original, and unique service.

THE EPIC CRUISE (2012)

In 2012, on my most recent Caribbean cruise to Jamaica, Mexico, and the Grand Cayman Islands with my beau, Gary, people were constantly approaching me after seeing me dance to thank me for sharing my love of music and movement. One woman said," Hi, I am a nurse and I want to tell you what an inspiration you are. I've had patients like you that have had strokes, but they do not get out much. Some don't even get out of their beds or off their couches. You are such a strong, independent, and charismatic person who just doesn't let anything stop you. You make me feel happier about my own life. I will tell my patients about you the next time they tell me they cannot do something."

MOUNTAIN QUEST (2013)

I attended a Whole Life Expo in Edison once with my friend, Dan. While there, my good friend, the Pan Man, came over to me with a really interesting photograph he'd purchased from a woman named Alex Bennett. It seemed to be made of many points of light, and within the points, one could make out what looked like wizards or beings from the other side of the veil. I felt guided to go to the same booth to look at the photographs, and to meet the photographer. I purchased one of the smaller photos, which was all I could afford at the time, and struck up a conversation with the woman at the booth. Alex said she lived on a huge farm in West Virginia where she found she had a unique gift of manifesting beings from "the Other Side", not the earth plane, hidden in the morning mist, whether they were departed loved ones, angels, or whatever.

The Mountain Quest Institute is a 450-acre research and retreat facility near Marlinton, in the Allegheny Mountains of West Virginia, and is owned and operated by Alex and her husband, David Bennett. At the Whole Life Expo, Alex gave me a brochure of Mountain Quest that I kept for a few years. Then, after researching the institute, and the beautiful bed and breakfast inn located on its property, I decided it would make an ideal adventure and place for my beau, Gary, and me to go for several days on vacation. In preparation for our 2013 trip, I called Alex, who told me more about the inn's beauty and the uniqueness of each room. The inn contained rooms with different themes like the "Nautical Room", the "Fantasy Room", the "Asian Room", to put guests into their imagined fantasy places. I'd read that the grounds invited a person or a couple to deeply relax in nature, to feel comfortable just "being", as opposed to doing and thinking a lot. We were soon on our way.

Once Gary and I managed to get through all the tortuous turns, and several hours navigating the mountains, we were more than ready to just spend time rocking on the porch with a cup of hot coffee or tea in hand, like an old, retired couple with nothing to do, while watching the kitties or dogs move playfully about. The cats were friendly and allowed us to pet them. Gary and I both love cats and have some of our own, so we enjoyed making friends with each cat and calling them by name. When we leisurely finished our morning chai, we walked across the property to the fenced-in area containing pasturing horses and llamas to greet them too. I have always adored horses, so I loved petting their heads, giving them a bit of feed Alex had given me, feeling their soft muzzles and breath on my hand.

We had breakfast in the old farmhouse with other guests who happened to be there. Since I am sociable, and love to talk to folks, I enjoyed meeting some new people during our three-day visit. One guy had ridden his motorcycle all the way from Tennessee for the third time, because he liked Mountain Quest so much. Alex, the proprietor, also sat with us a little while, to find out more about us, and to share some things about herself. We were able to order a continental or hearty breakfast of two or three eggs made in an omelet or whatever style we preferred, with toast, and delicious turkey bacon or sausage. We also had long-cooking, steel-cut oatmeal, and more tea, coffee, and juice. Alex's son was a chef, and lived on the property. We enjoyed his meals very much.

I got to know Alex a bit during our stay and found out she'd been a professional opera singer, who had traveled the world and was in the navy, where she met David. I had the honor of hearing Alex sing a little even though she had completely given up performing. She told me, "Now I make up songs for my animals."

Alex and I talked a lot about the power of sound to heal, especially with a technique she learned at the Monroe institute. Called "Hemisynch", the method requires a person to put on stereo head phones, and to listen to special nature sounds and music with a binaural beat, produced by intentionally delaying the recording of one of the stereo channels very slightly. Listening to this program automatically induces brain-wave patterns which produce a state of deep relaxation and meditation, and can lead to accelerated learning.

When Gary and I first arrived, Alex gave us an MP3 player with a set of headphones, and invited us to choose one of the special audiotapes, which we could listen to at our leisure in bed, or while relaxing in a lounge chair. We both did this, and the tape I'd chosen, called "In the Garden", worked perfectly.

While we were there, Alex showed us more of her photographs. Alex's mother showed up in the mist in one. When she was in the navy, Alex had spent an entire day with Mother Theresa, whose spirit is in another one of the photographs.

Alex had a beautiful new photograph which was larger than most of the others, about 20 by 17 inches. It contained the "spirits" of her favorite horse as well as her favorite dog who'd passed away around the same time. She also pointed out as well as "the Angel of Compassion". The angel is a lovely pink and very smokey and curvaceous. It was $180, which was expensive for me, especially since the cost of the room was $149 per night plus tax, and I did not want to burden Gary with this extra money. When Alex learned that I was a professional, certified massage therapist, she agreed to barter, half of the cost of the framed photograph for a holistic therapeutic massage.

I had a most amazing experience during and after administering the healing massage. We were talking about my voice and how to project sound, so Alex sang a few notes of one of her arias, while lying there on her back. I could not believe the power of the sound emanating from her throat and diaphragm. She was a high coloratura soprano, with such a beautiful, clear tone it went right through me as I worked on her shoulders and neck.

When I finished the 75-minute massage, I went by myself into the jacuzzi for about fifteen minutes until I was completely relaxed and rejuvenated. I donned my clothes and walked outside to get back to our room, to retire for the evening. As soon as I came outdoors, I saw a white scintillating light everywhere I looked. I was ecstatic! I'd just been thinking about my friend, Karin, who had cancer, and my ex-boyfriend, Doug, who'd also died a few years before from cancer. But now it seemed that so much of the past was an initiation rite, through which I had grown, so that I could now see a new, brighter, deathless universe. My loved ones were all here with me!

Then, I wondered if what I was seeing was real, and if anyone else could see what I was seeing. In my excitement, I ran to my room to get Gary. Unfortunately, Gary was already half-asleep and, in his pajamas, and did not seem to share my enthusiasm for seeing the scintillating white lights. I opened the door to go back outside, but by that time, I was not as attuned to my surroundings, I suppose, because I was no longer seeing the stars in the same way I had when I first came out of the jacuzzi. I had the feeling that it was being with Alex, her singing for those few moments, and being surrounded by both of our guides and angels during the healing session, that had somehow attuned me to this exquisite state of perception. I've been to Arizona and New Mexico, and saw the night sky twinkling with thousands more stars than I've ever seen in New Jersey, but I had never seen anything like I did that night. I felt extremely blessed and filled with exquisite joy.

The next day after breakfast, Gary and I went into the town of Marlinton for lunch, and to explore. It was a beautiful, warm, sunny day, so we went to a small park where I wrote poetry and made entries in my journal. Then we went to town where I checked out a consignment shop and bought some West Virginia T-shirts as souvenirs, and I got post cards to mail to my mom and kids. I also bought one to mail to myself, which is something I always do when I go on a trip, as a thank-you to myself and memento of my trip.

The heat made me work up an appetite. We asked some of the natives about a lunch spot, and drove just a few miles to one of the local spots someone recommended. It had a large wooden outdoor patio overlooking a stream and waterfall where birds and ducks flocked, so we took some cool photographs while waiting for our lunch to come.

I love birds and feel very connected to certain ones like the great blue heron, hawk, robin red breast, and hummingbirds which look like mystical beings of pure joy to me. I feel the same connection with butterflies.

I was reminded of the time in Tuscon, Arizona, with my girlfriend, Zara Rose, when we were eating lunch at an outdoor cafe and a beautiful butterfly lit on my right shoulder and stayed for quite a while.

Then, it was time to return to the steep, winding roads, on the way back to Princeton.

Gary and I would visit Mountain Quest again, then visit the nearby radio telescopes, part of the Search for Extraterrestrial Intelligence (SETI) project. What a perfect setting!

MERWICK-STANWORTH

In 2013, new housing became available a few blocks from the Princeton University Campus and downtown restaurants. The Princeton Housing Authority conducted a lottery to decide which applicants for affordable housing would be the first to occupy the few affordable housing units mixed in with university housing. Sky had moved out of Griggs Farm, and I would not be allowed to keep my two-bedroom apartment. I'd gotten a new housemate by putting an advertisement in Craig's List seemed nice and perfect at first, but the day she moved in, she came very late and gave me "bad vibes" about the whole thing, and in time, it turned out she would be the most challenging live-in room-mate I'd ever have to deal with on a regular basis. I also soon found out that this would be considered as subletting the apartment, which would violate my lease. In a way I could call her the "room-mate from hell" if I want to look at the experience from a negative, subjective way, and even though I asked her to move out many times that year, she refused, so it was up to me to find another place to live.

Gary Mom and me

At first, she did not like the fact that my beau, Gary, slept over fairly often. However, it was my apartment first, and being a woman with not just one, but two disabilities, counted on Gary for many things, both physically and emotionally. She began keeping track of the nights he slept over and began writing letters to the landlord complaining that my boyfriend was living in the house, even though he would leave to go home to his own house most days and nights to sleep over after going to physical therapy on Tuesdays and Thursdays. This woman had even called the police on me and made a formal complaint to them for accidentally opening her mail.

The fact was that not only did I live there for twenty years before I ever invited her to move in so she could help me pay the rent and half the utilities and TV, but I paid all the bills myself hoping she would pay her share which never happened. In fact, I was forced to cut off our cable television so that she would have to separate the service and pay for hers on her own. She did not pay for half of our exorbitant electric bill either. Her excuse was that we had made an agreement for her to pay only $268 for everything, including her half share of the rent, which was never the case. She said she could not afford to pay half the utilities, and that it should not be her responsibility since Gary was living thee, according to her viewpoint, so she should only be responsible for one third of the electricity, cable and internet bills. She only paid $268.00 for half the rent, but she had not found a full-time job yet, and somehow convinced me to allow her to pay less than her fair share until she could get a regular job and could afford to pay half the utilities and cable bill.

Every day Doris would call to complain to the landlord that my boyfriend, Gary, was living in the two-bedroom apartment so many times that we began getting letters to cease and desist doing something against the bi-laws since Gary was not allowed to live in the apartment. Technically, he owned his home in Hamilton, and spent about half his time there, so I'd call the landlord and explain that to her, but Doris really hated him or was jealous that I had a boyfriend when she did not and one night, she threatened to call the police if Gary slept over again even though we kept my bedroom door closed and were extremely quiet, even when we were out in my living room watching television or using the computer to pay bills or looking at our e-mails.

Ironically, Gary was so nice to this new room-mate he helped her set up her computer with which she had trouble, and was so kind he assisted her with other things she was having trouble figuring out like paying bills with her smart phone.

The night she threatened to call the police we both felt frightened, even though we were not sure if we had done anything wrong or illegal. It was just that she was a very strong woman and could be negative and really nasty, if you know what I mean. While around her I felt as if I was walking on eggshells, always having a pit of anxiety in my stomach around her even though I tried to get along always saying "Good morning. I hope you have a happy and blessed day when she got a cleaning job, so and was very polite and trying to be nice to her, except one time when I awoke her from a nap because I was upset, she used some of my shelf space to put more of her kitchen things out in the cabinets when I was not home and without asking my permission.

I was not accustomed to giving up too much personal space because I'd been living there since 1995 moving there when Sky was only five years old, so I'd already been there for seventeen years, and Sky left when she was about twenty years old around 2010 because we were not getting along., and I asked her to find her own apartment since she had been working for years at various jobs from cashier jobs at McCaffrey's and Shop Rite supermarkets to working part-time with the young folks at Eden services for the autistic community, and I knew Sky could afford it.

Anyway, I gave Doris some shelf space in the kitchen and moved two shelves worth of stuff in the bathroom so she could put her cosmetics, toothpaste, and stuff as well as half the bottom closet where the bathroom cleaners were stored. She had a huge walk-in closet in her bedroom where she could store stuff as well, and a small space in the downstairs storage unit. I thought I'd been pretty fair, so I suddenly felt put upon and angry that she waited until I was out of our home before deciding to move some of my pots and pans so that she could put her own stuff on "my" shelf space, which, I realize, as I'm writing this now, was such a petty, egotistical thing to do. What a petty melodrama I created for myself. I recall knocking on her bedroom door and in a loud voice, saying Doris, could you come here please, while she was taking a nap in the evening, and confronting her in an angry tone about moving some of my things without asking so that she could put some of her stuff in the cabinet. She had been sleeping, so she was dazed and disoriented. I remember feeling so bad that I'd woken her up over something so petty, and actually yelling at her getting her very upset. I felt horrible afterward and humbly apologized an hour or so later.

Grownup Gabriel and me

The night she threatened to call the police on us if Gary spent the night again, we decided to go sleep over at Gary's home in Hamilton, which we did a few nights per week anyway when I attended Gary's Princeton Singles' coffee and conversation meet-up group from 6-8PM at a restaurant in East

Windsor as well as his Eckhart Tolle meet-up group on Thursday nights in one of the libraries near his house like Lawrenceville or Hamilton.

We slept in the next morning on a Saturday until 11 AM or so because we were so upset about the way my roomie had treated us, and we were not very confrontational folks. We were almost afraid to go back to my apartment We were both easy going, gentle, peaceful, harmonious type people and rarely fought with anyone. When we got back to my place in the early afternoon I found a note from Doris on my kitchen table saying that my new all white cat, Cookie, whom I had adopted from SAVE animal shelter in Princeton about four months prior, had escaped while Doris was bringing in some groceries late at night. Then she stated in the letter, that she tried to get it to come back into the house at two or three AM, but the cat never came home. I was very upset, and suspicious of what she told me, because, she had wanted to adopt a certain breed of dog when she moved in, but I told her she could not because we were only allowed to have two pets in my apartment, according to the bi-laws of the Association, and I already owned two cats, Ellie, of 12 yrs. Whom I'd also adopted from SAVE when I was a volunteer there. And Cookie, the newest one I'd adopted, who was skittish and probably about six years old, according to the animal shelter. She was a very beautiful cat, one of the most beautiful domestic short haired cats I'd ever seen with her all-white silky fur which I loved to brush while I petted her, and she was very loving and cuddly. She was the "Queen" of the house already, and had already formed a close bond with Gary and me. I was devastated when I read the note, but when I asked Doris e about it, she just acted like it was nothing, dismissing it as if it were the cat's fault, and mine for leaving the house to sleep over Gary's.

Mom and me

I have no doubt she deliberately put the cat out somewhere, and the poor thing got so frightened that she ran away. She needed to get rid of the cat in order that she be able to adopt the new puppy dog, she'd been wanting for months. She'd been showing me photos of him since the day she moved in, and I kept telling her he was cute, but that the landlord would not allow us to have another pet living in the apartment, so she made sure one of my cats simply got lost or ran away. I called SAVE to see if she had found her way back there since it was only a mile away, and we posted photos of her on the mailboxes in Griggs Farm, but no one ever found her or even called us with information that she'd been spotted anywhere in the neighborhood. We were sad, but there was nothing we could do about it, especially when Doris asked the landlord if she could get this new puppy. When we complained about it, the landlord said we had a month to find "Cookie", and if she had not returned by then, my roomie could go pick up her new puppy.

We had some new challenges when the puppy came into the apartment, and Doris wanted to put up a very large playpen for him in the middle of the living room. The dog was a cutie pie, so as much as we'd resisted his arrival, we ended up falling in love with the little guy. Luckily, she moved the playpen out of the common area because it was way too big and left no walking space to get around it to the computer or on the couch. Ironically, we liked the little puppy way more than his "foster mom", and we ended up playing with him a lot when he was allowed out of his crate and also took him on more walks than his mom.

Luckily, the complaint was dismissed by a judge and referred to a professional mediator.

I was on vacation with Gary when the lottery was held, and discovered upon my return that I had "won", and I would be moving as soon as construction on my new block was completed.

HEARTSCAPES 2015

My children have much better voices than me, and my daughter, Kyrie, has a lovely mezzo soprano voice, composes her own music and lyrics, and has already recorded a professional CD. for a talent scout and one of her original songs on disc. "That Certain Something," a song she wrote years ago, is a song she used to audition for the pop music and vocal program up at Berkeley College of Music in Boston. The lyrics are profound and much more mature than her tender age. She was seventeen when she wrote that song, and her voice and vocal style has improved by leaps and bounds since the time she recorded the song. She has several songs on video that you can watch on YouTube or if you click on her website. We also perform together at house concerts, churches, and places like "The Heart of Art" in Hamilton.

Kyrie honored me by singing several songs at my very first house concert entitled "Heartscapes" at the home of my friend, Mrs. Laura Kruskal, also known as the Origami Mommy, and her artistic home. the Princeton Origami Center. In honor of the passing of Natalie Cole, Kyrie graced us all with a rendition of "Unforgettable" that would have made both Natalie and her father, the renowned, Nat "King Cole, proud. It was unforgettable like the title. Kyrie's voice was so beautiful and her rendition so heartfelt and authentic I got chills from head to toe. At that concert, I also sang a few jazz standards and did performance poetry from my first published anthology of poetry entitled "Heartscapes", published in November, 2015, by Author House.

KARIN

Karin/s health had continued to deteriorate.

I recommended Karin see Dr. Van Beveren, a naturopathic doctor and biochemist friend of mine who specializes in nutrition, so she did. She did not work that long with him because of financial challenges, but he did help her for several weeks getting her on a plant based vegan diet which did seem to make her feel better for a little while. According to Van, though, Karin was in at least the third, if not, fourth stage cancer by the time he finally got to see her and studied her blood chemistry under a very high-powered microscope. Karin was very positive, though, and had affirmations and pictures up everywhere in her bathroom of her in perfect health. I think she was in denial, but I think she wanted to protect Abbey and her dad from the fact there was a good possibility she was dying. Her boyfriend, Mo, had already lost his wife to cancer, and this would be another tragic loss for him if Karin died.

Mo was by her side throughout everything. The doctors at Robert Wood Johnson Hospital in Hamilton did not give her much hope, so Mo and her dad had her transferred to one of the Cancer Treatment Centers of America at Philadelphia, PA where she seemed to be doing better with some chemotherapy, and was released three times from the hospital.

Karin told me she felt a baby growing in her stomach, and she wanted to get married to Mo and have a little boy baby with him. But Mo told me he believed the growth she was feeling was not a baby, but the cancerous tumor growing larger, and he feared she was not going to be around much longer. You could see having to deal with his loved one's health challenges were taking a toll on him; plus, he worked full-time at a very physical job, so one night while he was watching sports on TV. at Karin's house, and I was there taking care of dishes for her in the kitchen I offered to give Mo a massage in the bedroom. I offered it to him out of the purest love in my heart out of compassion for both him and Karin. I sometimes massaged Karin, too, either at my home or in her room after she was ill-just her back, or her back, neck, and shoulders. Mo came to my house for a massage after that first time to pay for a full body massage, and we began a relationship that was more than friendship that was not one of my better decisions.

I always seemed to be the type to think I should care for others' needs more than my own—like I started out in my own family by caring for the emotional needs of my mother and then submitting to the improper physical and sexual advances of my dad. I am still learning discernment and how and when to have healthy boundaries in my various relationships.

The third time Karin got out of the hospital there were complications, and she needed to go back in in June. After some tests and other things, the doctors said she was fine, and she could go back home for good the next day. Karin declared "This is the Last time I am going home. I won't go back in the hospital again ever."

As fate would have it, the day she was to be returning home for the final time, the Holy Spirit had higher plans for her. Though her beau, Mo, was sitting in a chair near her bedside and the nurses were at their station twenty feet away, Karin apparently awoke during the night to go to the bathroom and when she got up to get out of bed, fell down and landed atop her colostomy bag. She then bled out; and by the time the nurses found her she had expired; and it was too late to revive her.

Mo called Annie, our mutual friend and chiropractor the sad news. Then Annie called me, but she got Gary on the phone instead. When Gary told me she was "gone" I did not understand what he meant, and I could not believe that my precious, best friend was taken from us at such a young age. She was like the little sister I never had; and I was devastated by the news. I immediately prayed and went into action designing a T-shirt for her parents and friends with her picture on both sides, her name, and her dates of birth and death. One of the photos was of Karin on our trip when she was in Belize looking very beautiful. I distributed the T-shirts at her funeral. I sold some to friends for my cost and three of them I gave out to her father, her mom, and her daughter, Abby.

A day or two after she passed away, I also made a large pot of homemade spaghetti sauce for Mo and her dad which I placed in large glass jars so they would not have to worry about cooking for a few days. They could just add the sauce to a pot of their favorite pastas. The next day Karin kept sending messages to me, my daughter, Kyrie, and her friends, by sending butterflies, birds, and other totem animals. Kyrie met a woman whose name was Karen while I was talking to her about Karin's ascension. I know for certain that Karin's beautiful soul is alive, well, and living in some happier, higher, more expansive subtle dimension.

My journal entry follows:

Dear Journal,

It is July 16th at 5:50 AM, and I've been up chanting, writing and meditating since 4 AM. Yesterday was my 59th birthday celebration which we held at Amalfi's Restaurant in Lawrenceville. Except for Gabriel who could not come because he was detained at his best friend, Matty Collura's, barbecue, all of my beloved friends and family came to celebrate with me—save one glaring omission—my best friend, and spiritual sister, Karin, who made her untimely passing into Great Spirit's Divine Abode at forty years young on Friday morning, July 11th, before 8 AM, I am told. (Our mutual friend, Annie Monetti, called me after Karin's beau, Mo, called her.) It was a shock to us all.

Apparently, Karin woke up in her hospital bed in the middle of the night or early morning to go to the bathroom. Mo guessed that she got up and must have slipped and fallen on her colostomy bag. While the nurses were busy at their stations and Mo, slept soundly on the chair in her hospital room, our beloved Karin bled out to the death of her physical form.

It was so unexpected, and I am just beginning to feel the pain of losing my sweet friend and spiritual little sister. I have no real biological sisters. My step-sisters, Kathy, Debbie, and Suzie, though always sweet to me when I see them, have had very little contact with me over the past twenty-five years. I see them occasionally at one of my brothers, Pete's, functions, like a wedding or birthday party. First, I saw them at Pete's house in Bridgewater when Daddy was still alive. Dad and Joan chose to ostracize both me and Sky until Sky was ten years old. Who knows why for sure?

It could have been because I divorced my first husband who was financially secure whom they liked, in order to marry a young, black man I met in a mental hospital. Or could it have been because of my personal history with mental illness? Who wants to hang out with a woman who deliberately shot herself in the head when she had such a great life? Or possibly they did not want to face me when I told the truth about my dad molesting me as a teenager? That is a good possibility. Even though I do not talk about it know I did write about it in an article and while I was an in-patient at the Carrier Clinic in May of 1988, sent copies of the article to half the people in my family including my dad, brother, and step-mother, my paternal grandfather, as well as my dad's brother, my Uncle Henry.

I recently saw Kathy and her husband, Mike, my sister, Suzanne, in Cape May, at Pete's second wife, Kathy's, 54th birthday party. They were all very sweet to me, but it is never mentioned by any of them how or why none of them call me or invite me and Sky to Christmas, Thanksgiving, or any of their other parties during the year. Not even a phone call or card for my birthday. I send my sister, Debbie, a birthday card on March 8th or occasionally give a call, but basically, we are glad to see each other occasionally and briefly at funerals and Pete's parties, but then go back home to lead completely separate, unique lives, them with their successful husbands in a conventional, monogamous marriage, and me as a single mother with Sky who has had lots of men in and out of her life.

The bottom line is that all we have is NOW. We do not get to choose our family members. Except before we get here, I am told by Holy Spirit, from a more expansive perspective in order to learn certain life lessons. From my experience, we attract and gravitate to those precious people in our lives we consider our best, most special friends and part of our spiritual family. Karin was and is part of mine.

Sure, we had our fights and disagreements every now and then where I did not want to talk to her for a month or so. But that was OK. All close families fight at times. Then we let go of it and make up. But for the most part, we played.

We called each other a lot to shoot the breeze, shared secrets and dreams with one another, massaged each other sometimes, cooked and cleaned up together at holiday parties, and were there (here) for each other when it counted. When one or the other was sick or troubled, we could call each other and feel better just knowing there was someone who cared enough to listen and talk about anything.

"Karin, I miss you honey. I don't know how Abby will ever get over losing you at such a young age. How will I ever be able to comfort her? Or teach her the way you did about the ways of the world and the ways of God's chosen ones. I was not a very good mom to my own daughters either dealing with depression or mania so often. So many darn mood swings.

I feel as if I held Abigail in my arms right now, I'd start crying and never stop. I'm afraid to see her. As yet, she has not called me back. What do you want me to do?

I suppose I can just love her and be with all the feelings. I do love her as if she were my own. She is the youngest Crystal child in my life except for Sadie from Earthgate whom I do not get to see too often.

Abbey and I have so much fun whenever we are together. I'm still teaching her a little bit on the piano, and she is still practicing at home, it seems. She teaches me the songs by all the new groups and we sing and dance to them. We also love to do art work together. Especially painting and using markers.

Abbey must be devastated right now. How can I help soothe her pain and make her know for certain that you are still here watching over her and guiding her from the celestial realms? You are such a light in this world. We had so much in common. Even our love for Mo, Abbey, your dad, Michael, and all our mutual friends we shared through the UFO and paranormal family you and your dad had attracted throughout a quarter of a century. You were the one who was supposed to take over the reins of power and leadership once your dad retired.

"What the hell happened? Why did you leave us so early? You had just been declared all better, whole and healed from cancer at forty years old. Somehow the Philadelphia Cancer Treatment Center must have ravaged your body with the chemo and everything they used to cure you. Even the last six months of your life you were looking so radiant and beautiful. Healthy and much thinner. Pretty. You did not look like a sick woman. You were out and about. What the heck happened? Why did you leave us, honey? I miss you, Karin. You said you'd come to my birthday party and dance with me, remember?" I wanted you there last night to dance and sing with me. You never got the chance to see my new apartment. I wanted you to help me decorate, to have seances, and metaphysical meetings with your dad, Amy and John Giallucco. I wanted you to come to my housewarming party. I even wanted you and Lorelei to form a hot new all-female band with me and to take a road trip to Nashville, Memphis, and Austin, Texas, after my memoir is published. We both could have sung our hearts out for cash money and danced our pretty, sexy fannies off creating a huge new sensation. What happened to realizing all your dreams on this earth? And manifesting our dreams together? As friends? What about your dream of becoming pregnant again with a son? And getting married to Eric, Mo, or whomever you wished? Like me, you had so many men who were attracted to your beauty, your sensuality, your energy, and outgoing personality. You will be missed by so many besides your daughters. Annie, your Landmark friends, your mom and dad, Mo, Michael, all the folks who know you from the UFO and paranormal meetings.

Why did you leave us? Well, maybe you did not expect to leave when you did either—consciously. I know it must have been rough living with that silly bag attached to you. And a body that was all cut up in pieces. But now you are Whole again. Free to roam in the heavens on your chariot pulled by four white steeds, and you are free to be whomever and whatever you want to be.

I miss you and still need your love and our special eternal friendship, Sister of Light, who continues to shine Bright for all to see."

Even though your beau, Mo, was sitting in your hospital room, and the nurses were not too far all outside your door at their posts doing whatever nurses do, you had bled out completely without anyone finding you until it was too late. Your holy Spirit had already left and your physical body had already expired by the time your boyfriend, Mo, found you on the floor of your room next to our bed.

Annie, who already intuited Karin was not going to last more than a year. Michael, my other boyfriend, knew it in his heart as well, and told her dad not to expect his beautiful youngest daughter to live much longer either. I did not receive the phone call. Gary picked it up and gave me the sad news. I must have been overly optimistic or in denial myself because when Gary sat me on the bed and said in a serious tone "honey, Karin's gone." I asked him "Where?" When I figured it out that she had died I could not stop crying. I felt bad especially for her dad, Pat, her daughter, Abigail, and Mo. She had a lovely mom too, but I had never met her except once at one of the hospitals, so I did not know her too well.

My way of dealing with death is usually the same. I write a poem, create an art project, go into the woods or a park to journal and/or I make homemade food for some of the grieving relatives and friends. This time I decided to make my Grammy's homemade spaghetti sauce with magical herbs to make us all feel better-fresh garlic, onion, sage, rosemary, sea salt, and a bit of chili powder. I made a huge pot of sauce, saved some for Gary and me, and put the rest in jars or Tupperware containers for

Pat, Mo, Abby, Annie, and Michael. I'm not sure if it was really magical, but I believed it was from the heart because I chanted with great love and appreciation for Karin while preparing it, and it gave me something productive and kind to do as opposed to focusing on the fact that I'd lost one of my best friends.

I'm a Grandma!

I am a mature mother and grandmother in her sexy sixties.

Anyway, I am loving being a grandmother of a precious, charming, light brown mulatto boy. In June of 2015 I was blessed with this charming, handsome grand-baby, William, after my youngest daughter, Sky, gave birth at the beautiful new Princeton Hospital with nurse midwives on June 16th, 2015. William is the Light of all our precious lives, and I never believed I would be so happy at 60 years old still celebrating SEX and intimacy. And being an older, more settled polyamorous grandmother of a little, charming boy who just loves watching "Daniel Tiger's Neighborhood", "Paw Patrol", and "Dinosaur Train" now at three years old.

Sky is studying to become a nurse, and sometimes leaves William with me and Gary while she studies or goes to class. William does not watch much live TV in our house because we only have Verizon Basic FIOS (including a landline for my business). We do have a DVD player, an Amazon TV Firestick, and subscriptions to Netflix and Hulu, so we can watch many things. William loves to watch "Daniel Tiger's Neighborhood" and "Dinosaur Train".

We also paint together with acrylics and water-colors and listen to our Amazon Echo.

William also loves to water my flower garden and tiny vegetable patch with tomatoes, basil and dill which he helped to plant.

I think children and grandchildren keep us young. My only grandson makes me feel happier sometimes than my orgasm when we play ball together successfully catching up to sixty special throws in a row without dropping the rainbow-colored ball I purchased from the local Shop Rite for just 99 cents – a bargain. We play Frisbee, but William has yet to master throwing it to me. He is better at throwing a football, and with my disability I am not great at running back far enough to catch it, even when we are in the kiddy pool, I keep dropping the darn thing in only six inches of water. Must be "performance anxiety". I love to paint wish him, however making masterpieces better than any Chagall, Mirot, Rembrandt, or Peter Max

ANXIETY

Journal: Tuesday, October 14, 2015

I did not sleep well last night. I woke up around 4 AM, read about Edgar Cayce for a while, in Jesse Stearn's "The Sleeping Prophet" (the same one I read when I was fifteen years old when Daddy told me how good it was). Then I listened to some relaxing meditative audiotapes, but though I still feel very tired I have yet to fall back to sleep.

I massaged Allan, the painter, yesterday at 10 AM and felt uncomfortable through almost the entire massage. He kept saying "I'd be so happy if you surprised me and got naked so we could be sexual, and I could make you feel really good." I clearly did not want that. I kept telling him I was in a relationship now and had no desire to be with anyone but my boyfriend. He finally let it go, but the whole experience left a bad taste in my mouth. I started to feel ashamed about my former promiscuous behavior and I felt so disrespected that I am feeling somewhat depressed again.

Don came over last night and expected to have intercourse with me too like we usually do, but I felt very sad and resistant to it. I'm really different now. I respect myself much more and want to honor where I am at in my feelings. I just cannot behave in the same ways I did before. I find I'm feeling tempted to fall back into that trap of allowing men, particularly some of my clients, to manipulate me into doing something I've already resolved not to do to help make more money to pay the bills, but also because I feel guilty because we were intimate at one time, some part of me feels like I owe them something. I don't like that. I don't owe anyone shit, only my true Self. I must love, respect, and feel confident enough to be true to myself and say "No" when I am asked to do something I do not want to do including things my mother or Sky want when I am feeling way too tired or I have other plans like going swimming and relaxing in the jacuzzi at my health club, or to the senior center to do dance aerobics.

It makes me feel like a prostitute if I allow myself to be manipulated into doing something I do not want because I do not have healthy boundaries. I am definitely not. I am a priestess of love, a goddess, and a dakhini who deserves love, honor, and respect, and devotion.

I told Don I was exhausted after having therapy at 2 PM and then lunch with mom and asked him to work on me. He did, and I felt better because he is really intuitive and good at shiatsu. Then I worked on him for 40 minutes and told him I was too tired to continue. It meant less money, but I did not care. I just don't want to get back into those old bad habits of not honoring my own needs before another's. or disrespecting myself. And then I'd go into a depression afterwards.

There have been so many men I have shared sensual or sexual massages with that I can barely remember half their names or even what exactly happened. Now that I have Gary in my life I do not need or want that anymore!

Saturday afternoon Gary and I saw a great movie called "Kill the Messenger" about Gary Webb, the journalist who exposed the CIA in the Nicaraguan CONTRA scandal. The CIA was selling drugs to help fund the war the rebels were waging against their totalitarian government.

Later that night Gary and I went to see the Beatles cover band, Blue Meanies. I love them. But they are just not as good without Jeff, the former bass player, and their piano player who was playing with another band that night, we were told. The original bass player, Jeff, added so much vocally to the group. I really miss him.

Our friend, Elayne, from the Eckhart Tolle group was there with her husband when we arrived at Amalfi's Restaurant. She said she lives just down the road from there.

We joined her and her husband once we saw her; she danced several dances with me as well as another woman who came up to dance with us. Even her husband who usually does not dance as a rule, came up to dance with both of us. I love Elayne so much, what a sweetheart. It was so much fun, but after Elayne left I tired of the band, so Gary and I left early at 11:15 PM. We only arrived at 9:30 PM, but we needed a short nap and decided to eat a small meal before we left for Amalfi's.

Sunday morning was the 5K race for Matty Collura. I chose not to walk the entire distance this time since I arrived late, I had to park far away, and most of the runners and walkers were nearly done with the race. I wasn't registered anyway, so I could not get a T-shirt, so I watched Matty cross the finish line with his walker after I walked a bit in the park. His family and friends are always so proud of him. I had some water jugs in my trunk so I brought them to the open spigot that gives freely of spring water, filled them, and then met Kyrie, Gabriel, Marianne, and Matty and his mom near the place where the band was playing, and all the racers and walkers are having free burgers and hot dogs. They have veggie burgers too for folks like me.

There were lots of people there. It was so gratifying to see the kindness of all the folks who came out to support Matty and his family. What would we have done if Gabriel had injured his brain or spinal cord in a sports accident like Matty? His entire life would be completely different in the blink of an eye. Matty had to be put into a coma for three months until all the broken bones in his body healed after his spinal cord injury following his fall on the mountain while he was snowboarding. Like Christopher Reeve one day you are doing everything independently and a powerful, strong man whose career is going strong and about to get even better, and then, a fall from his horse, and suddenly he is dependent on a machine just to breathe.

Matty had just graduated from NYU just like Gabriel all ready for his career or graduate school; and then comes an accident in sorts with a traumatic injury and suddenly he is dependent upon nurses, doctors, rehab, physical and occupational therapists, and his parents for everything for at least a year or more.

The good news is that so many people love Matty, especially my son, Gabriel, his best friend, and they all stuck beside him to love, support, and encourage him through most likely the most challenging time of his life, and now in January of 2019 Matty is very independent, and has lived in a group home for people with traumatic brain injuries for three years, is a terrific writer and poet with his own blog, gets around easily with the help of a walker or a cane outdoors, and his speech has improved tremendously. He did a great job giving the toast at Gabriel's first wedding several years ago.

Pneumonia (2016)

I rarely seem to create illness or disease in my life, but I was surprised to find I had double pneumonia at the end of February of 2016 and was shocked to find myself waking up in a hospital bed with tubes coming in and out of me. My family was told my oxygen level was only 10 %, and there was a 60 % chance I could die. I had believed while at home I just had a chronic case of influenza which made me cough and sleep a lot, according to my beau, Gary, who usually stays with me. I rarely go to doctors or hospitals except for preventive maintenance. If I get a virus or occasional flu, I normally handle it myself by taking megadoses of vitamin C, ten or more drops of full-strength oregano oil, echinacea tea or fifteen drops of echinacea from Herbalists & Alchemists, my friend, David Winston's, company, which strengthens the immune system. For a stuffed nose or sinusitis, I take neosynephrine; or usually I'll rub my nostrils and chest with Vicks VapoRub, massage myself with tiger balm, eucalyptus or peppermint aromatherapy oil, rest in bed, and drink all kinds of herbal teas I prepare for myself.

I had been ill for about ten days with a chest cold which seemed like it was starting to turn into bronchitis and a virus, so I opted to go see Dr. Nair, my primary care physician, to get checked out and be on the safe side. She had told me to go to the hospital emergency room, but, for some reason, I failed to recognize the need for speed, and I wanted to complete the remaining two days of a study I was involved in.

My son, Gabriel, had to make the decision to have me intubated, or it was possible, according to Dr. Bejaj, the surgeon in charge of me and Princeton Hospital, that I might have expired. In fact, my son was told that if I'd come a day or two later, I might not be here right now. They were shocked that I was talking up a storm when brought into the emergency room upon a stretcher. Usually, the only times I have ever gotten sick was when I was over-stressed and my immune system was compromised due to poor diet, lack of exercise, or lack of sleep. One of my husbands had herpes when we met, but I never contracted the disease even though we never used condoms. Through his own research he learned to manage the disease very well through good nutrition, vitamins, exercise, and positive thinking.

When I chose to give birth to my second child at home the midwives suggested I get a blood test to make sure I did not have the herpes virus which could be passed on to my baby and is potentially fatal at birth. They had already lost one baby to the herpes virus, and did not want to risk the possibility of that happening again, so I was tested. My blood showed no signs of this virus or any other. I was very healthy and thriving. And still continue to choose that consciousness of abundant health.

So, to find out that I was put into the hospital without my knowledge was a traumatic shock. It was my home health aide, Anya, who made the decision to call the nurse when she and Gary could not lift me up out of the bathtub together. Anyway, she decided to contact the nurse who works with

Mercy Home Care, the agency I use out of Trenton to hire me the perfect home health aides. Anya was Russian, a terrific woman who was talented in every way, and had become a terrific friend and help-mate in the year she'd been coming to clean my home, wake me up in the morning, help me with dressing, bathing, and cooking my breakfast and help prepare a sandwich for lunch as well. She also aided me with dyeing my brown hair blond, styling it every two days, bought me birthday and Christmas gifts. She was amazing in every possible way. I loved her deeply as a friend even more than an employee. Though she was one of the best, most competent home health aides I have ever had, and was kind enough to even bring her dog, Goo Goo, around to spend time with me and Gary, because she knew I loved dogs.

Thank God Anya had the horse sense and wherewithal to call the nurse and EMTs or I might not be writing this now.

I got very depressed while in the hospital, especially because upon arising from the induced coma I found I was unable to eat, drink, or speak since I'd been intubated without my knowledge or consent. All I could do was lie there and sleep or watch television which became very boring after a while. Gary was a sweetheart and visited me twice per day, once in the early morning after feeding the cats, doing food shopping, paying both of our bills. Luckily, Gabriel was transferring enough money into my checking account every day so that Gary had enough funds to pay all the necessary bills from rent to phone and cable to my car payment and all my credit card bills. Gabriel and Gary were both menches.

Gary would let me have lunch, rest, and come back again in the evening before or after he had supper. Since I could not speak, I'd try to use sign or body language, or if I really needed to ask him something I'd write it on a piece of paper. Mostly he would sit quietly or tell me who called to ask about me and what was going on at home. A lot of people were concerned, and many people asked about me in e-mails or online on Facebook after Kyrie and Gary let a lot of my friends know what had happened to me and the asked for prayers and after I got out of ICU, told some of my closer friends or folks from church that it was OK for them to come visit me. I was very stiff staying in bed and could not even bear weight, let alone walk. I do remember my first meeting with the physical therapist at Princeton hospital which later became Penn Medicine. I forget his name now, but not his face because he was very handsome and charming. He was like me, always singing and in good cheer; he told me he had "musical turrets". Turrets syndrome makes people have uncontrollable movements of the face or uncontrollable outbursts of sounds coming from their mouths. My PT guy said whenever he heard certain words it would remind him of a song title, and he would just spontaneously begin to burst into that song. I liked him and I found this quality refreshing. We were both very much alike. If he had not told me he was engaged. I would have flirted with him and probably asked him if he'd take me out after I got out of the hospital.

Once my lungs were cleared of fluid Dr. Bejaj came into my room and said it was time for me to have the tubes removed from my nose and throat. Thank God. It was a relatively quick, easy process, and did not really hurt much at all. I was starving, but I was still denied food for another day or so because they said my throat was probably sore and needed to heal. The whole time, I was intubated I was dying for a drink of water. One night I was terribly thirsty, I told the nurses as much, and I think I remember them bringing me a few ice chips to suck on. Not being able to drink a cup of water really sucked! I swore to myself if I ever got out of there, I'd never again take for granted being able to drink full glasses of water several times per day. With or without meals. The twenty-four hours I had to wait before being given clear liquids for my meals seemed like an eternity, and even longer before I could eat solid foods like eggs for breakfast, a turkey or tuna sandwich at lunch, or just a piece f chicken with vegetables seemed like the most glorious feast a woman could ever hope to eat. The food turned out to be particularly delicious in that hospital, especially for "hospital food" which one never expects to be the best. The menu was varied and I could even have some Indian or Chinese food at some meals for dinner. I loved Asian food.

I was so appreciative of a few of the nurses that were so kind to me. One I remember in particular was named Katie, and when I was moved out of intensive care to the normal ward, I remember thinking how much I would miss her excellent company and great care. There was another nurse named Lorna who would ask me questions every day trying to keep my mind sharp. My daughters and I called her "Lorna Doone" like the cookie. After I returned home from Merwick Rehab Center and felt much better after returning home for a month I made it a point to go back to the hospital and ICU where I visited some of the nurses on the floor and filled out a form of appreciation, as well as a form on which I could vote for the best nurse on the ward. I think I mentioned both of my favorite nurses and expressed why I loved them so much. I was hoping at least one would receive the "Best nurse of the month award". I was getting my strength back, and one Saturday I received several visitors at once – my friend, Zara Rose, Gary, my mom, and my good friend, the black bus driver I'd met in Merwick Stanworth, the deacon Milton, who had his whole Mormon congregation praying for me. I had no make-up on, my hair was unwashed and a mess, and I was sure I looked like a wreck, but later Milton told me my eyes were clear and a beautiful hazel shining in the sunlight, and my face looked very good. I still find it hard to believe I looked OK with no make-up on or lipstick, but both Gary and Milton swore I looked just fine. Gary was not big on make-up anyway.

When it was time for me to leave the hospital, I had to choose which rehabilitation center I wanted to be moved to. Since Merwick Rehab was right next door I figured that was the easiest decision since I would not have to go in an ambulance. Somehow, I was just transported on a stretcher with blankets over me right across the street, but I don't remember exactly how I got there. I was put in my own room with a wardrobe closet, a table with a telephone on it, and a television like the hospital. Gary and my mom had brought some sweat pants, comfortable cotton shirts, some undies, pajamas, and other things for me to wear. A few of the tops matched the sweat pants, but I was not planning to win any awards for fashion while I was there. I was glad, however, that Gary brought me a hairbrush and my own toothbrush. I was finally able to get up on my feet after a couple of weeks PT. a few times per day, but though the rehab therapists had ordered me a cane they were not allowing me to use it except during physical therapy in the gym under their supervision. This was such a bummer because I wanted to get out of my bed and be able to walk out of my room and down the hall or at least to the bathroom, but I was not permitted. I had to use a damn wheelchair, and it was never easy for me to maneuver a wheelchair with only one arm. I had to wait for assistance to be transferred from out of my bed into the chair and pushed into the bathroom, shower, or to the elevator t go downstairs for physical therapy. I began to get very depressed while at Merwick Rehab and I felt like a prisoner who might never be let out. I was bored to pieces and became addicted to watching crime dramas like my favorite show, Criminal Minds, Law and Order, and CSI. The only relief I had from watching television were the two times I was brought down for physical therapy where I would ride a stationary bicycle and walk holding onto parallel bars on either side of me at first until I could bear my own weight, and after some time passed, I was able to walk up several wooden stair steps. I also practiced catching a ball of some kind and did some kind of an exercise with hoops or rings. Sometimes Gary would visit in the middle of my PT. session, and he was shown the window where he could watch me exercise, and I remember feeling happy and proud that I was progressing somewhat while Gary was watching me. My son came a few times to visit at both the hospital and the rehab center. Once he brought my published poetry book, "Heartscapes", showed it to the nurses and therapists, and read me some of my own poems telling me how proud he was of me for being a great writer. One Saturday at the rehab center he came in with his guitar and sang and played for me. It made me so happy to hear him play, and I sang along with him on a few Simon and Garfunkel and James Taylor favorites. Afterward, I'd ask him to take me somewhere in my wheelchair since I was so bored just sitting or lying in my room all the time. He'd wheel me down the hall, down the elevator, and all over the rehab center. Even outside for a breath of fresh air. Gabriel had no idea how much this meant to me, especially since I felt so depressed not being able to walk and not being able to shower on a regular basis and wash and blow-dry my own hair.

When I found out there was a beauty salon in the hospital, I quickly made an appointment to get my hair trimmed, blown dry, and styled.

In the middle of my styling a call came in from a nurse saying I had to go to the X-Ray room so that they could X-Ray my chest and take a picture of my lungs to make sure the pneumonia was all gone. I refused to go. I was in the middle of relaxing for the first time I'd been at the rehab center getting my hair done so that I could feel better, but they were wanting to spoil my fun and treat me like a sick patient when I was already discharged from the hospital when they discovered my lungs were all clear, so why do an unnecessary test now? I was livid, and refused to budge from that salon until after my hair was completely dried and coiffed. I could be stubborn that way. I've never been a good patient and rarely listened to my doctors if I felt I knew better what I needed to feel better.

Toward the end of my stay, I began to feel more uncomfortable because I was still wearing adult diapers at night., and when I called some of the night nurses to change me more than once they'd have a bad attitude, complained, and made me wait. Incontinence was not something that I could help, especially at night, so I felt totally demeaned if one of the nurses would make fun of me or complained about having to do what was supposed to be their job.

Easter was coming up, and I'd already been out of commission nearly six weeks between the hospital and the rehab center though it felt more like a year to this normally physically active woman who's a social butterfly. I wanted to go out of the hospital to celebrate Easter with my family. I put in an official request to my doctor, and permission was granted for me to leave the hospital for the afternoon to go out to dinner with my family at Ruby Tuesday's restaurant right across the street on Route 1 South. It was one of my favorite places to go. Gary and Gabriel picked me up in my wheelchair since the hospital staff was still being weird and overly cautious about me using my cane on my own, even though I felt completely comfortable using it by myself. My balance was fine, and I was steady. The wheelchair was always a pain in the ass for me to get into and to maneuver with one arm and hand.

We had a lovely dinner which sped by ever so fast, but I remember feeling a little uncomfortable and depressed because all my children and Gary were so animated talking about all the things they were doing and all the projects going on in each of their lives. I had to go to the lady's room and excused myself. Kyrie accompanied me for support. I was washing my hands next to a lady with whom I struck up a conversation. I told her that I was on a pass from the Rehab Center and that I'd just gotten over having double pneumonia. I'm not sure why, but somehow my problems seemed to make this lovely lady appreciate her own life more, and she told me her own problems did not seem so challenging to her anymore. "God bless you, girlfriend. You inspire me to go home and appreciate what good things I have in my life much more than I did before I met you."

"Really?" Thanks, that makes me feel so much better, too. Thank you so much for sharing that, I said as I left the bathroom to go back to our Easter dinner party. Funny, but when I finished dinner, I had no desire to go back to the rehab center. I'd not been to my own apartment in nearly two months, and I missed my two kitties, Ellie and Huckleberry, terribly. So, I convinced Gary to take me back to the apartment for a quick visit. We lie down to nap for an hour with the cats, and they seemed so happy to have me home in my bed near them. They purred away while we pet them. Ellie seemed a bit distant and angry at first, but after a while she began purring and relaxing next to me, too, like Huckleberry. Then it was time to get back before it was too late and we were locked out of the Rehab Center. We got back there by 6:30 PM, I think it was, but having a taste of being home made me yearn for getting back to my old life of activity, friends, dance aerobics, poetry classes, and Dance improv at the Princeton Center for yoga and Health.

I had one particular male nurse, a handsome black man with whom I became friends, and he always brought me a smile and some cheer. It's amazing how someone's kindness and positive attitude could make all the difference in how a sick person felt while in the hospital, and would spur me onto want to get better, just for their sake. This one nurse seemed to be attracted to me even in my unkempt, weak state and told me he'd like to keep in touch with me after I left, but I was so upset at how the other night nurses were treating me I complained to my son who called my doctor to say he was unhappy with how his mom was being treated and threatened to sue the hospital or something. I said I wanted to be discharged sooner than later. And, within a matter of a few days' plans were being made for doctors and social workers to visit me in order to have me discharged formally and moved back home with my cane since I could walk, but plans were made for a physical therapist to come to my apartment a few times per week to give me exercises and watch me do them. I felt a little nervous about going home, having to work and pay all my own bills again by myself, but it was better than the alternative. I celebrated the morning I was waiting for all the paperwork to be completed so that I could walk out of that rehab center which had become a prison to me at that point because they were not allowing me to grow. I had been numbed by too much television, bored from sitting upon my "asspirations", and was ready to get stronger and to get back into the swing of my happy life and family again. Gary was still living with me, and I appreciated his good company and help more than ever. Especially because while I was still recovering in Princeton hospital Anya came to visit me one afternoon with a fresh ripe avocado, she'd cut up for me into bite sized pieces before telling me she would not be coming back to my home anymore as my home health aide. Anya said she was taking a course in anatomy and physiology at Mercer County College and was not really wanting to be a home health aide much longer. I cried bitter tears of disappointment for several minutes when she gave me the sad news that afternoon. She felt bad, but did not know how to console me. She just said "don't cry. Meryl. The agency will get you another person to replace me soon enough. Actually, it took them almost a month to replace her. I was not ready to lose Anya as a friend or as an aide, especially at such a vulnerable time when I really needed her. But people grow and need to move on themselves, so what could I do but just accept the fact and learn to be in harmony with it? My next aide was from the Dominican Republic who spoke Spanish and English, and it turned out she had a beautician's license just like Anya, and would be able to cut, dye, and style my hair just as well as Anya, and we became very close until one day she decided to quit without any notice because she found a better agency to work for that paid her higher wages. But, in the meantime, she was very helpful to me, a great cook and a terrific housekeeper who cleaned my house as well as if it were her own. Cesy also did all my laundry, helped me take care of the cats, and eventually took one of my kittens, a tiny little one we got from Patty

B's house we named Dora, the adorable explorer who fit in the palm of our hands when we got her, but Cesy must have thought we had too many cats and decided to give it to her daughter. We did not really want to part with the sweet kitten, but technically our lease only permitted us to have two pets, and we already had three other cats though one was a larger, older kitten we'd also adopted from Patty B's brood in her backyard. We called that one Moondancer. Eventually, Cesy found a home for that one too. She had a powerful, dominant personality, and Gary and I were both very laid back, so we just went along with her ideas to give the kittens away to homes where there were no other pets.

TRAPPED

Journal: Saturday, April 9, 2016

Beloved Self,

At this moment which is ever changing I am living in a prison of my own making; though I've been here before I think/feel like am powerless over this negative frame of mind and death of spirit. I have tried to numb the pain of living in this weak and challenged body by watching television for hours on end and taking naps, but that in and of itself is like living in hell because I am out of relationship with my family and friends and avoiding life. I have to face whatever is really bothering me before I burst or before I try to harm myself again.

The worst thing about depression is that I feel so guilty because I am wishing again that I was dead when I have so much to live for. My beau, Gary, treats me like a Queen, and my children have to be the most loving, caring, happy people on earth. I have to tell the truth I am somewhat jealous of them because they all are healthy living in Whole bodies with good jobs and full lives. I had a full life until I got struck down in late February with pneumonia and influenza. I know my family would be devastated if I had died. Even as adults the love me a lot and need me on this earth."

The difference is that now I know more what to expect, know that others will support me, and regain hope quickly.

HAPPY

Journal: Wednesday, April 5, 2017

"Life is great. I am so happy. I love and adore myself, my children, and my grandson, William Samuel. Gary Bear is such a gift too. I spent a very happy, relaxed day with Gary having lunch at the Cracker Barrel in Hamilton Square and then watching and petting the pedigree pups at the Puppy Palace in Robbinsville, the place where I purchased my precious Malti-poo, Puja, for which Dan paid most of the $600 fee. I enjoyed him so much until I got into that bad depression one summer and was forced to give him to "Small Dog Rescue" where he ended up choosing a new owner with a yard and two other dogs that very same week-end he was brought to the outdoor place in Pennington where he was immediately rescued and adopted by a better mom than me. The new owner ended up sending me photos of him playing in the snow with his new buddies later that winter.

Anyway, it was fun spending the day with Gary not really having an agenda except a 10AM massage that I gave Lorrie Rette, my friend and neighbor. She did not have the cash to pay me, but I told her we could barter for a haircut later on down the road when I need one.

Tonight, Sky came over at 6 PM with William; and he stayed overnight. I agreed to babysit for a few hours in the evening beforehand so that Sky could study at the library for her anatomy and physiology exam. I had a great time playing with the little leprechaun, as usual. It was a lovely, warm sunny day the next morning. We both met and made a new friend at the swings named Malakai, and his mom, June. William had so much fun playing with Malakai that he did not want to leave the park. They both had so much fun playing with the little matchbox trucks and sliding down the sliding pond that neither of them wanted to go home to eat supper.

But I was tired, a bit hungry, and the wind started to blow making the day colder. William had a small tantrum when I tried to force him to come back home with me. He kicked his sneakers off onto the muddy ground getting his clean white socks all covered in dirt and wood chips. I wiped them off and asked June to help me put his sneakers back on and tie them which she did kindly. When she realized, William was refusing to go back home with me because he still wanted to play with her son she told William that Malakai needed to go back home to eat dinner, so finally he reluctantly began following me back around the sidewalk away from the playground toward the bike rack and eventually all the way back in to my apartment, but first he got distracted by an older brother and sister riding their skateboards near my place. William is such a friendly child and a social butterfly just like me and his mom. At 22 months old he is already such a charming little boy. I love playing with him. I've never been happier in my life even when I've been in love with a man. It does feel completely different from anything I have ever experienced before. Just to see him smile and light up whenever I walk in the room and he is sitting on the couch gives me such a feeling of joy and fulfillment. I feel so very blessed to be his grandmother.

And Gary is such a devoted partner as well as a terrific grandpa. I have more than enough love, joy, peace, creativity, and companionship to keep me satisfied and content for the rest of my life. I am so grateful to God and my angels for sustaining me and helping me through all the trials and tribulations that brought me to this special, satisfying time of my precious life.

UNCONVENTIONAL

I love being unconventional. I have already given birth at home naturally and in the Family born room of Helene Fuld Hospital in Trenton to three glorious Beings of Light (my precious children, Gabriel, Kyrie, and Sky), so I have no desire or need to be married. I live with one wonderful man with whom I have had a sweet and beautiful relationship. Gary has been an angel to me sent by God to help me through my crazy, sometimes inexplicable, irrational mood swings. The causes are complex, and I have been on several different medications from lithium (for about a week while hospitalized at Carrier Clinic) to departed, a mood stabilizer also used for seizures, I've been using on and off since 1991 when it was prescribed for me by Dr. Moss when I had my second psychiatric hospitalization at the Carrier Clinic because my husband, David, believed I was manic. I suppose I must have been a bit too high energy and euphoric because no matter how many hot baths and L-tryptophan I took to relax and calm me down, I just did not feel tired at 11:00 PM after dancing and chanting in ecstasy inside my own home with my little baby, Kyrie, who had just turned one year old, I would finally fall asleep around 1 AM, but I still would wake up several hours later euphoric, energized, and ready to start my happy day again.

I consulted with my primary care physician and nurse practitioners about my continued problem with insomnia; and they prescribed Seroquel and trazadone for sleep and depression, and a few other medications since my first chronic suicidal depression in 1981 after the sudden breakup of the intimate relationship I shared with my massage teacher in Florida. The medications have helped to some extent, but there are also undesirable side effects like constipation, dry mouth, weight gain, and some of the boxes say: may cause occasional suicidal thoughts, so I do not always feel like taking some of these medicines. In my experience I have found that regular exercise several times per week, dancing in the house and out at yoga centers with friends a few times per month, daily meditation, contemplation, and/or chanting practices, morning affirmative prayers, excellent nutrition, and occasionally a bit of organic beef, turkey, chicken, or fish help me ground the fast-moving kundalini energy when I become so joyous that I cannot get to sleep sometimes until 3 AM. Instead of feeling agitated or frightened as I used to be a lot in the beginning, now I am learning not to let it upset me so much anymore. I just watch my breath and say my guru's mantra, OM NAMAH Shivaya, the Universal Mantra which means I honor Shiva, the Hindu God representing the masculine, unmanifest aspect of God Consciousness. It also helps if I take some deep full yogic breaths or read before bed.

Back to today, I had a wonderful breakfast cooked for me by my home health aide, Yolanda, scrambled eggs with sauteed onion, garlic, and a bit of melted cheddar cheese, plus some plantains which Yolanda brought from home to make special for me since she is from the Dominican Republic and speaks mostly Spanish. I suppose plantains are a common food for people of her culture. They are delicious and not as sweet as bananas. I am just realizing how blessed I am to have such a loving friend and helper in my life so that I am free to write, exercise, or do other activities I enjoy.

After eating breakfast, I took a leisurely bath while Yolanda cleaned up the dishes, made an egg salad sandwich, and a delicious vegetable soup with dandelion greens, onions, organic carrots, celery, potatoes, and garlic which I suggested and supervised. She also threw in a load of laundry, swept and mopped the floors while I was singing to songs, I had asked Alexa to play on my Amazon Echo which can stream just about any song one asks for that is on the internet.

I always take my phone into the bathroom with me so I can call my three children just to connect and tell them how much I love them wishing them a great day. After all, love is the only thing that matters besides awareness of that Divine Lover within us which folks can call by many names which resonate for them. For example, God, Love, Infinite Intelligence, the Holy Spirit, the Force, Allah, Jesus, the Divine Friend, the Guru, Jehovah, Buddha, the Divine Mother, Awareness, the Truth, etc. All are names for the same thing, in my experience. No religion is right, wrong or more valid than another. We are all ONE Universal Consciousness that has become individualized, unique expressions of That One "I AM Consciousness" that is So beautiful. God dwells within you as you. Its nature is Sat-Chit-Ananda, according to the gurus and Master Teachers. Sat is Sanskrit for Truth or Being. Chit is Sanskrit for Chiti — the Divine Conscious Energy that has created and is inherent within all forms of matter including animals, plants, minerals, earth, fire, water, air, and ether. Planets, stars, extra-terrestrial beings, etc., and Ananda is the Sanskrit name for Divine Bliss, the kind of joy that is not dependent upon anyone or anything.

After I got out of my relaxing bath where I just took my time languishing, relaxing, merging with the lavender scented Epsom salted bath with a few bubbles, and talking to my son and my other dear friend and lover, Michael, on the phone, while my live-in-love, my beau, Gary, of six years, typed e-mails and checked out his Facebook posts from friends on his laptop computer.

What I've been trying to say for the last few pages in a circuitous manner is that I am an unconventional woman who enjoys polyamory at this time because marriage has never really worked for me except to have a stable, loving home to give birth to my children. Now that they are grown, I don't have to answer to anybody but myself and God who loves me unconditionally and wants me to be myself to follow my own joyous path-- free, happy, and to following my own bliss and inner guidance. I doubt Source has a lot of time to pay much attention to my genitals or anyone else's, though it seems our society makes such a big deal about sex and with whom we are sleeping.

I am probably the "Black Sheep" of the family, but, in a way, as the oldest of seven children including my two biological brothers, three step-sisters and one step brother, I have had to pave my own way through some trials as a teenager who experienced an unconventional relationship with my dad that included sensual and some sexual intimacy which molded me into the unique woman I am today. My mom loved and hated me which influenced me as well to put up defenses and armor of a certain type. Since I had my boundaries violated from the time, I was about four years old I was never taught what were healthy boundaries. When I began studying metaphysics and Eastern philosophy, I learned that we were all ONE, United, brothers and sisters, and divinely connected, so I figured "why the heck do I need to have any boundaries at all?"

It was not until the early nineties that I happened to be visiting my good friend, Bob Burgess, a psychologist by trade, whom I knew for many years from the ashram up in South Fallsburg, NY, that I found a book and audiotape on having healthy boundaries. I cannot remember the name of the audiotape and book by John Bradshaw, but my intuition told me to pick it up while Bob was out doing guruseva (divine work or free service to God and the guru) and to study it. Wow, did that book open my eyes and change my perspective. For the first time in my life, I realized it was fine and good for me to say "NO." It was proper and healthy for me NOT to say "yes" to everyone's requests of me, and that I did not have to be anyone's doormat.

Up until then I had been giving my body and my loving energy away to almost any man that wanted me or with whom I flirted because there was a physical, intellectual or spiritual attraction. I let my mom and certain other people, even my daughter, Sky, walk all over me, because I wanted their love and approval. And I did not know how to say "No" without feeling guilty. With men I felt ashamed and guilty if we became lovers if I did not have a commitment with them, or they were not my primary relationship. I also attracted a lot of married men in order to heal the weird triangle relationship between my dad, my biological mom, and my stepmother, a very close friend of my mom and dads with whom my dad fell in love after Joan's husband died suddenly from a heart attack in his forties.

Anyway, today after getting out of my hot bath and getting dressed into warm layers of clothing since it was a mere 34 degrees out, I put on some bracelets, a beautiful beaded necklace my friend, John, made for me personally, large enough that I can put over my head since I cannot use my left hand, and it is difficult trying to clasp anything with one good right hand. So, John added enough extra beads on a long string for me to put this necklace over my head. It is very beautiful and functional with many different colored beads. I wear it almost every day along with my rudraksha beads, a neck mala that I got in the ashram in India.

Having bracelets with a stretchy elastic string helps me to be independent and wear bracelets easily when I am guided to wear certain types of semi-precious beads and stones like hematite, turquoise, malachite, jade, onyx, tiger's eye, rose quartz, and amethyst due to their individual frequency and vibration. For example, rose quartz, a clear pink colored crystal, has one of the highest vibrations of stones and attracts unconditional love for Self, romance, and acceptance of WHO we are in the present moment. I also like to wear hematite a lot because of its beautiful silvery black color, grounding properties, as well as protection if one is feeling attacked by negative thoughts or entities from outside forces or other people. As an empath I am often affected by other peoples' thoughts and vibrations because I am a highly sensitive person who has a lot of compassion in my heart for the suffering of others, especially my mom who has had depression and anxiety on and off since I can remember as a child of twelve or thirteen. And in my first ten years I knew something was wrong when she would scream at me a lot for practically no reason. I forgive her and my dad for any mistakes they made as I was growing up, but I believe it might have a lot to do with my having confusion growing up which eventually evolved into a mental illness in my twenties. I'm not blaming anybody; I'm just sharing my personal experience growing up with two parents who were not completely healthy emotionally and spiritually because they were both abused themselves.

I'm guessing that most of us come from dysfunctional families, but as part of the evolutionary process to become ALL-That-Is, Aware, humane human beings we owe it to ourselves to contemplate our divine natures and reasons for being Alive. Let's give ourselves a break by realizing we are all doing the best we can, including us, so let's be gentle and forgiving of ourselves. We will never get it wrong.

We have eternity to grow, to love, to change, to learn from past mistakes and subconscious errors. Let us forgive ourselves and all others while we focus on our divine natures and spiritual purpose for being on this planet at this holy moment, a great time of Transition, the Birth of a New Life, a Unity of All Beings, a Renaissance like we've never experienced in a few thousand years as we are on the verge of this New Age, a Yuga (as it is called in the Sanskrit language) where Mother Earth is ascending to a higher level merging with the Grand Central Sun. Becoming a Star in her own right. There truly are no mistakes or accidents. What a relief and breath of fresh air to be able to forgive ourselves and everyone in our lives, learn what the lesson is from each and every relationship, every circumstance and experience for this Divine Mystery can be a new adventure into LOVE and communication with every person, animal, rock, the winged ones, and even the space brothers on other planets that you will eventually come to know and call friends just like you do your brothers and sisters on Mother Earth Herself.

TRIAD

In May 2017, my sex life was more fun and exciting than it had ever been. A few months earlier, I resumed my relationship with my ex-boyfriend, Michael, who lives in Gary's neighborhood. Michael takes care of the grounds at Gary's house, maintains the appliances if anything breaks down, and is a property manager of sorts. We had dated for six months in 2012. After he broke up with me because I was rather possessive, I was very upset, but he said he still wanted to remain good friends. Michael still visited me a few times per week and on holidays, and on my birthday, he still visited after work and gave me a special gift.

Even after I began dating my present beau and live-in partner, there was a void in my sex life since Gary was a virgin at 60 years old when we met. Gary also is not very physical, is legally peripherally blind and does not dance or swim like me, but he is gentle, kind, intelligent, and unconditionally loves and cares about me.

I invited Michael to take me to my daughter, Kyrie's, wedding, and my son, Gabriel's, first wedding in Brooklyn because I loved him still and he was and is a terrific dancer. After Gary and I became closer Michael began dating and subsequently moved in with another woman. I was disappointed especially when he brought her as a guest to one of my parties. She was surprised to find so many photos of Michael and I around my apartment which she asked me about, so I told her we had been boyfriend and girlfriend for seven months and still remained close. He was and is also a family friend. I was disappointed in Michael and left him in the company of his new girlfriend completely removing myself from the picture soon after. But within a year she became very insecure, possessive, and was critical of him, so they broke up too. Michael then moved into Gary's neighborhood.

Since Michael and I remained friends and we were both trained, certified massage therapists we somehow began exchanging massages in the evenings when Gary would leave to go to the Princeton Singles meeting on Monday nights and to lead the Eckhart Tolle meet-up group on Thursday evenings for two hours. The only therapeutic, relaxing massages were just that at first but relaxing conversations progressed into romantic dancing, flirting, and massaging one another on the bed when he was tired after a long day's work. There was such an incredible attraction between us since he has his Venus in Cancer and so do I as well as four other planets including my Sun in Cancer, so we had and still have a very romantic, sensuous connection while dancing which progressed into making love on the massage table and eventually in my bed. At first, I was confused about having two men to love because I believed it might hurt Gary, my live-in beau and daily companion. But I finally got up the courage to tell him especially if Michael came late and we spent most of our time talking, dining, or sitting outside in the lovely spring and summer weather, so I'd ask Gary if he could come home later so Michael and

I could spend some quality time relaxing. After a few times, Gary realized what was happening and once remarked in a light-hearted, comic way when he called to see if it was OK to come back home to snuggle and sleep "Is the orgy over yet?" Gary and I are honest and are together so often that we both truly need some space and time apart in order not to argue or be mean spirited or grouchy with one another. If either of us gets too hungry, tired, or Gary gets overheated or headachey in the summer we tend to argue over petty things that normally do not bother us.

Gary usually leaves the apartment on one weekend each month to visit best friend, Glen, whom he met at Lehigh University many moons ago, and to spend quality time with Glen's family. He sometimes sleeps at their house overnight on Saturdays. So, one week-end I asked him if he minded if I invited Michael to take care of me Saturday night into Sunday morning so I felt safe. Gary agreed in a very generous, expansive way. He remarked "Well, honey, you usually always do what you want to do anyway." That was true, for the most part except in the thick of winter when I got the blues and was in deep despair. I chose to be celibate and completely monogamous whenever I felt depressed mostly because I felt numb and asexual. Being only with Gary alone at those times and/or my immediate family made me feel safe. I knew he would care for me if I was sick in the hospital and through all my winter doldrums and many mood swings. He was a real trouper since I was no picnic. I would not wish this polyamorous, bi-sexual bipolar bear on any man who was not a bit crazy himself – especially if he has no idea what he is getting into.

Michael and Gary make up the "perfect man" in this triad relationship we share. Gary loves animals like me, has a very big, open heart, is focused, very spiritual and intellectual. Plus, he will do anything I ask except go swimming or dance with me. He will be my divine escort, be a fantastic, caring father to my youngest daughter, Sky, when she needs fatherly love or advice, and he is an amazing grandfather considering he's not had much experience around babies or little children. He cooks for me when I am hungry, makes me tea or mushroom coffee in the mornings, helps me dress and get out of the bathtub when my home health aide is off at night or on the week-ends, and he is one of two best friends with whom I can confide in about anything. He is a great counselor, spiritual teacher, and the perfect mother and father I never had.

Michael is more yang and I love that about him. We love to dance, romance, swim together or walk around the grounds of my apartment holding hands. And he is the best tantric lover I have ever had. He makes me relax and melt into his strong arms every time we are alone together. And that is very important to me. I am realizing at 63 that sharing sex and love are very important to me. I feel so happy now being able to have regular orgasms – even with myself.

It took years for me to learn that sex with a man was actually supposed to be pleasurable. Not something to be avoided or rushed. Nor faked just to get it all over with. I just believed something was very wrong with me and that I was frigid. How wrong I was!

However, to this day I still love and appreciate variety. I do not think there is any perfect man "out there" for me nor a knight in shining armor like they would have us believe in fairy tales. In fact, that was a real toad of a tale teaching young women to look outside of themselves to find something that can only be found within our own hearts and minds-the love, Light, and beauty of the radiant inner self which always radiates love and Light from within. For me, practicing tantric sex and sharing romance with a few very special partners with whom I have close friendships, is a way to connect with That Higher Self, the Goddess within me. And I write sacred, erotic, ecstatic poetry about my lovers and experiences connecting to this beautiful, loving, special part of myself.

I also have two other regular friends and lovers I have known for many years before ever meeting Michael or Gary.

One is my friend, Pan, who is also a certified, licensed massage therapist with his own successful practice like me as well as a tantra student, Master, and practitioner like myself. We have shared relaxing, intimate massages, naked, sensuous dancing since the late nineties. He was my best friend for so many years, but we were both married when we met and did not meet again until the nineties after we both divorced our spouses. For whatever reason, my angel buddy and I never became boyfriend and girlfriend, just best friends and clandestine lovers. We both agreed that in our "old age" that if neither of us were married or had a permanent live-in partner that we would move in together. But then I found Gary, and Pan met a lovely woman in a tantra class who he started dating, and recently they purchased a beautiful three-bedroom home together in a lovely town nearby. I met her and I saw their home one afternoon when the new girlfriend was out with one of her guy friends from her original hometown. I am so happy my buddy does not have to be alone in his twilight years. We still get together to exchange massages once in a blue moon, but things have changed for both of us since I respect the relationship, he has with his girlfriend now. Plus, she suffers from anxiety and depression, so I would never want to make her feel insecure or threatened by me. She would not understand our polyamorous relationship although my best friend and angel buddy told her exactly who he was when they first met and what were his interests – tantric sex, massage, weaving peace on the planet, dancing, making money without hurting anyone or damaging the planet in any way, and teaching his philosophy at beginner tantra classes and workshops, and polyamory.

Pan spent thousands of dollars learning about tantra, the subtleties of love making, and how to please a woman in the highest and best ways. Pan also understands stuck emotions and subconscious core beliefs that tend to "run us" if we do not take time to heal old wounds and negative subconscious beliefs from studying tantra, massage, and many other natural bodymind modalities. One cannot heal subconscious thoughts and wounds unless one actually focuses on the physical body which contains layers of fascia where the emotions get suppressed from traumatic experiences and stored being repressed for incarnations. It is only through accessing the soma of the bodymind that we can bring the wounds of the inner child to Light so we can heal our Spirits and connect to our Souls and higher guidance.

My second close relationship and lover is a man I met while doing massage at my apartment in Griggs Farm. Though he was married his wife had a popular incurable neurological disease which prevented them from connecting physically or sexually on a regular basis. Mr. Chase was very handsome, fit, and had similar political beliefs and interests as me. He was also a vegan who ate some fish, and I was a vegetarian who ate some fish, eggs, and occasionally fowl. Though I hardly ever ate the turkey at Thanksgiving. We were very attracted to one another and began kissing and holding one another from the first time we met. Eventually we would become close friends and lovers. After months of this special connection, I began charging him a lot more than my other clients since he was the only male client with whom I shared sexual intimacy. And I prayed over him. He always told me "You are magic because whenever you pray for me about my job, I always get a better job or a better paying position within the company. Though Mr. Chase was brilliant he was in his sixties, so he was not appreciated or compensated for his great accumulated experience and expertise. The bosses always seemed to take him for granted. He could not wait to retire from the corporate world, but due to his son needing to complete his college and graduate studies at an expensive, elite school combined with his wife's serious, debilitating illness sometimes getting worse as opposed to better, Mr. Chase wanted to play it on the safe side to make sure his family was always cared for, and that his wife had good health insurance. He was and is a really good guy even though he has shared this clandestine friendship and sexual relationship for over twelve years. I love my client and friend and always pray for him and his family's highest and best good. The only reason his wife does not know about me is because sharing this information would hurt her and make her feel very insecure. However, I believe that Mr. Chase is enough of a caretaker himself that he deserves a little extra nurturing and good sex in his life. I also love when he massages me, gives me foot rubs, talks to me about his interesting job as a consultant to a large banking firm, and he also does things I like that make me feel more energetic and happier when I am exhausted after a long day of massaging, going to PT, or going to different doctors for my hemiplegia, recently diagnosed arthritis in my knees and lumbar spine, and osteoporosis which I was shocked to find out I had just like my mother, Arleen because I eat very healthy, take supplements, swim, ride the exercise bike at the gym or rehab center I frequent in Edison a few times per week on a regular basis, dance aerobics a few times per week. walk regularly, and swim at least once per week.

As far as I'm concerned, this wonderful time is a crossroads, a time in a young woman's life where she learns she is a REAL woman who can have pleasurable intercourse, kiss, pet, neck, have regular orgasms, and make babies with a suitable, prospective partner or husband. Without us making eggs, having a bloody lining form in the uterine wall where eggs are deposited and kept safe just waiting patiently for a sperm to swim through the sacred cave, pierce the wall, unite with the egg, how would the human race continue? So, once the union takes place between man and woman, and a little tiny sperm happens to find its way into an egg in the vagina when a woman is most fertile, we would finally have cells splitting and re-creating themselves to make a human baby. Voila – Creation Begins!

I believe it is a magical process designed by God, Source, Infinite Intelligence (however one wants to define that Creatrix or Creator of Life. In my reality this Infinite Ultimate Creator of all things, created sex to have the human and animal species perpetuated upon this planet. It is a sacred, pleasurable process depending upon your attitude and what or how you have been taught and prepared for the unique and very pleasurable, holy experience—the union of a man and woman in love is one of the greatest things we have going on the planet. Life would get pretty dull and boring without it. Besides, there would be no people or new friends with whom to play and share life's gifts, blessings, and travesties.

Unfortunately, so many people are fucked up not knowing the difference between SEX and LOVE. The boundaries have been blurred. In my case there were no healthy boundaries since they were violated the first time my dad patted me on my growing buttocks calling me "Crisco" which progressed into him fondling my breasts from underneath my pink "Baby Doll" pajamas when my busy cooking mom told me to fetch my dad out of their bed for a Saturday or Sunday brunch at 10 AM.

Sometimes, it still gets a little complicated. If you don't believe me, go ask half the married men in Mercer County and all the way up to Maine! Not really. Well, maybe ten per cent. I am exaggerating just to shock you a little. I guess I like to ruffle your "conventional feathers", so to speak, just to see if you are awake and paying attention.

Nah, it really wasn't ten – maybe five per cent... Not even that. Now that I take the time to actually recall and count them. There were only four with whom I have had very special friendships. In fact, I still do have wonderful relationships with two of these men I have been privileged to know for at least ten years, but I won't name any names to protect the innocent. I mean the guilty. Whatever. I don't really relate to the concepts of sin or believe guilt is a worthwhile practice. I don't know what to say. We just could not help ourselves. I am cursed with a certain something God gave me that makes me, according to my dear friend, Fairy Elaine Silver's, husband, James, a "Man Magnet.". Believe me, it's not something I consciously asked for. I like it, but it can be quite a distraction from my purpose in this life. I mean it's taken me at least twenty years or more for me just to finish this memoir.

It's a curse— I literally attract guys like moths to a flame even when I'm not trying. Women too, for that matter. But though I am attractive and sweet, boys, you don't want to mess with me. Take it from me. Being with me long term can be dangerous to your health, not to mention your wallets. Ask my beau, Gary. Being with me is no picnic. Basically, we just never know which personality is going to rear its ugly or pretty head. With my sun sign and four other planets in Cancer I am probably one of the most sensitive, sensual, emotional, and moody women I have ever known. And I have known a few.

DOWN

Journal: August 2, 2018

Dear journal,

I don't know why, but I'm feeling so sad. I have so much abundant love, sex, friends, money, success, and joy in my life; so, I'm not sure why I am feeling this way except that it is raining today when I wanted to swim in the outdoor pool at Community Park, and I miss William so much. it's been three weeks already since Sky and I had that huge fight the night she came over early and Michael and I were supposed to share time alone together until 9:30 PM when Gary Bear and I would be babysitting and watching William overnight so that Sky could work at Allies overnight. It was so petty, but I was upset that Sky just decided to bring William over early at 6:00 PM when the agreement was for us to babysit at 9 or 9:30 PM since I already had made plans, which I'd made clear to her when she asked if we could babysit again. Gary and I had already babysat for the little guy nine hours a day or two before when her work meeting went overtime.

Anyway, Sky has now been using the fact that I lost my temper and blew my stack as a way to keep me from seeing William which is so unfair, but what can I do but wait? I already apologized for blowing my stack twice (and it was not even my fault), but she continues to block both mine and Gary's phone numbers.

This Sunday is the Butterfly Festival in Pennington at the Watershed which we took William with us to enjoy two or three years in a row, so I'm a little bummed out that she will not allow Gary and I to have William on our own without Gabriel as a supervisor; I have no idea why. Gabriel is going to Daphne's home in New York city now that she just got back to the states on Tuesday night. So, we have no chance of seeing William unless she has a change of heart. Oh well. God bless her. I know my mean-spiritedness hurt her that night as well as the fact that she felt as if she and William were being pushed aside so I could be a "horndog" with Michael. That's what she called me anyway. Polyamory is confusing for adults; I can only imagine it is so much more confusing to an emotionally immature child within a woman's beautiful motherly body. Sky has had so many more wounds to endure than either Kyrie or Gabriel.

Anyway, I have stuff to do like work on the memoir, take a nap, read Jaime Lowe's book "Mental: Lithium, Love, and Losing My Mind". She's done great research on bipolar illness, hysteria, and how psychiatrists in the past used to masturbate their patients to orgasm because that was what they believed to be the most helpful course of action. Can you imagine that? The stupid bastards!

Love & Light Beings,
Meryl

GETTING OLD IS A JOY

Memoir: September 2018

Who would have thought it would be just as fun to grow "OLD" like my grandparents and have the means, desire, and ability to be able to care for and love someone as much as myself? Or at 25, and 32 when my whole world fell apart after break-ups with my massage teacher at the Sarasota School of Natural healing Arts, then AGAIN seven years later during the Harmonic Convergence & I tried to off myself with that crazy 22 caliber Beretta handgun! My God, have I had some type of Loony Life and Times I never ever expected! Anyway, my point is that NOW in this present Holy moment hearing the lovely sound of the birds singing, knowing all three of my children – all born naturally at home with midwives and my two younger brothers in attendance – and my #1 grandson, Prince William, are happy, safe, healthy, successful, and living nearby I feel so incredibly blessed – like I AM the luckiest woman in the entire state of Equanimity (New Jersey) – planet (Earth), the WHOLE Universe, Cosmos, with my little contented kitty, Ellie, a 22 yr. old "Shapeshifter" in human years. In kitty years, is she 154? Do any of us realize what a glorious, blessed Life we are leading right NOW at this beautiful, precious, SACRED moment in TIME?! How blessed we are to be ALIVE?! How fortunate we are I AM to have God/Goddess Love Living in OUR VERY OWN PRECIOUS Hearts, MINDS, & SOULS – as well as the Infinite blessings in the various roles we play as moms, dads, lovers, friends, brothers, sisters, aunts, uncles, workers of infinite kinds, husbands, wives, and stewards of this Magnificent Mother Earth, Goddess Gaia, who provides for our every need AND loves us unconditionally like my grandparents did and still DO from the celestial realms, and how Lord Jesus, the angels, Archangels Michael, Gabriel, Auriel, Uriel, Ariel, personal guardian angels, gatekeepers, Hashem, Abraham, Jehovah, gentle Mother Mary, the Great White Brotherhood, Intergalactic Federation, and the entire family of man and woman. Infinite Intelligence, The Entire Company of angels, animals, plants, , fairies, guides, guardians, Gurus, and Teachers here to serve US and each other! I think that makes all of us pretty darn SPECIAL no matter how CRAZY things might be looking from our human perspective, Life is purrfect and unfolding exactly as it should be. Are we' blessed!? Despite the temporal nature of things, Life, in the Immortal Wise Words of Tony the Tiger, who went backwards in time and birthed Daniel Tiger of "Daniel Tiger's Neighborhood" – Life is GREAT – "Griffin"! We love, honor, and respect you all for BEING HERE NOW on this happy & blessed Monday! This little lady has a few dollars in her pocket which is all we ever need, my flowers in Sabrina's garden grow, food overflowing from my cabinets, refrigerator, fresh air to breathe, clean, potable water, all the clothes I will ever need, and more opulence than I ever expected.

NOW it is time for little Meryl, the Goddess, to GIVE Back to Father/Mother God for everything She has given me. I feel so blessed to be of service to my Guru, God, Shiva, Parvati, the "Holy Spirit, "the Force", the Creatrix, whatever the heck you want to call this Loving God Source from which we came and in which we always, eternally live, Move, and have our Being. Scroll down if you want to see my/our little guru and one of the many reasons I am SO happy to be ALIVE, WELL, and nearly 63 years young... Heck, even if I were 100 years young. It beats the alternative of pushing up daisies! At least that's what I am told. Earth is THE PLACE to be if you want a GREAT ADVENTURE. MOTHER Earth IS the VACATION PLANET, according to my good friend"Penelope", WHO lives on the "Other Side" of the veil and used to be channeled by my good friend, Virginia Ohara, who actually channeled her at the United Nations. Virginia Ohara called herself a "LARGE" rather than a MEDIUM for at the time she was Rubenesque, like me. We would like to say THANK YOU, precious beings who have volunteered for this experiment.

love & Light to all
I AM
Merylee Niranjani

WONDERFUL

Journal: December 20,2018

Today was a glorious day, and there is no time like the present to be grateful for Life and living in the Truth of the Present moment. They (doctors and psychiatrists) have diagnosed me as as a manic depressive, or a bipolar bear as I like to think of it in my own lighthearted fashion. Because what good is being here if we can't laugh at ourselves? I am just a happy go lucky gal, a yogini who is just learning to enjoy the Wild Ride, this adventure that has been my journey through ups and downs, grief, ecstasy, ins and outs, but due to my guru's and God's grace I AM slowly realizing that I AM the Divine Self, Master of my own ship, creatrix of this precious Life that is mine, part of the Divine Feminine Energy and Consciousness that has created this entire Universe. I am the entire cosmos which makes me cosmic. And I am also Shiva, the unmanifest masculine energy that is all part of each one of us as well.

Getting back to today I received an amazing therapeutic massage from Pan, my precious friend and lover of nearly 22 years; we've known one another since the summer of 1984.

Back to my massage with Pan it took quite a long time for him to relax me because I realized how much I'd been in my head focusing on the past or thinking about the future, so I stopped talking, thinking, and started to breathe deeply inhaling and then releasing the breath easily with a bit of sound and intention letting go of stress with each exhalation. After ten minutes or so I finally began to feel the pleasure in all the different parts of my body, and did it (I) feel good. I really understood from an experiential perspective how blessed I am to be a spiritual being inhabiting a physical body that can feel, taste, smell, hear, and see.

Pan had very relaxing New Age music playing softly in the background that had special sounds like Tibetan bowls, Atlantean quartz crystal bowls, and solfeggio frequencies that incrementally began to completely de-stress and relax my entire body; so, I was able to completely surrender to the quiet and go into a state of deep meditation and sublime peace. Eventually I felt authentic pleasure in each and every part of my body as he kneaded muscles, I forgot I had; he wrung out just about all the tension as if he were squeezing foul water out of a dirty wash rag. He twisted and deeply pressed acupuncture spots with intention with his strong thumbs and the rest of his fingers. At times he softly caressed my face and kissed my lips since that was really relaxing and such a beautiful way to honor a Goddess while expressing gentle closeness.

I never like when a man goes too far too fast like touching my breasts or vagina before I am ready.

He had not had sex in nearly six months, so he was a bit too ready and excited for my taste. I asked him to slow down and focus on connecting with my Spirit. That was when I really began to trust him and started to relax. Since Pan has a live-in girlfriend now and I found out recently he had one or two other sexual partners since tantra and the polyamorous lifestyle has also resonated with him for many years I was wondering if I was special to him. When Pan finally looked deep into my eyes saying "I love you so much Meryl. You really are one of my dearest, most precious of women friends. You have been and always will be the Sunflower in my fairy bouquet." I really need you here on this planet.

After not seeing one another since 1984 we met again at Ryder College at a Five Rhythms dance workshop given by the founder of Five Rhythms, Gabrielle Roth, a dancer, singer, and actress I met in New York City when I was twenty-one years young. I had the privilege of dancing with Gabrielle herself the first time I attended her Five Rhythms workshop. What an ecstatic experience it was for me. I realized then, as I do now, that dancing was my joy, my sacred path, and my gift to my friends, my family, and the world. Even with a disability I still absolutely love to dance. I feel as if my body is a conduit for joy, love, and enthusiasm for Goddess when I am dancing. It brings me more joy than almost anything, save making love to myself through masturbation or someone I truly love and connect with physically, emotionally, and spiritually like Pan, or Michael.

But then love making is a dance in itself. A tantric meditation and exercise in listening, in sensing, in feeling your partner close to you, and sensing his deep need for connection with the Goddess, with both the yang, masculine energy playing with the Divine feminine, that gentle, softer, receiving aspect of Himself. Of Herself.

It is the actual merging of these two sacred energies of masculine and feminine that has created all things on this planet. I love the beautiful way the 15th century realized Master and poet, Jnaneshwar, says in his poem, "Amritanubhava" "The lover out of boundless love has become the beloved. Both are made of the same substance and share the same food.

Out of love for each other they merge and part for the joy of being two. They sit together on the same ground in the same garment of Light.

From endless time they have lived this way in union and in bliss. Without the Goddess He is not, and because of him She exists. It is God alone in every form – the make and the female, Shiva and Shakti."

CALM

Memoir: May, 2019

In this current moment I am very healthy, happy, and have wonderful hobbies like writing poetry, singing. dancing. painting and making collages. I love traveling locally on sunny spring, autumn, and summer days. Driving to lovely places like New Hope and the Poconos in Pennsylvania is relaxing and fun.

Sometimes I still pretend I'm Judy Garland, Barbra Streisand, Debbie Reynolds, Doris Day, or Ginger Rogers gliding along in the arms of Fred Astaire. I often picture myself as Debbie Reynolds being swept off her feet by Gene Kelly in Singing in the Rain'. Whatever I am doing during my day I am having a grand old time, and I don't care who knows it. I like attending dancing saptahs at the Princeton Center for Yoga and Health. I especially loved Suzin Green with her melodic vibrato voice chanting and harmonium playing; I also used to dance at all the major saptahs during the summer up at Gurumayi's Siddha Yoga ashram in South Fallsburg in the Catskills.

I go on cruises to the Caribbean, Bermuda, Alaska, Costa Rica, Mexico, and other exciting places at least once every few years When it gets cold in NJ I like to fly south to Florida, usually for 10 days in February or March. I am definitely a snowbird and plan to retire in Florida within a few years.

Just 35 years ago I was having light contractions at a surprise birthday party for my mother, twelve and a half hours went by in a flash, and then, my magnificent Son of Light, Gabriel, was born on my bed and brought forth into this magnificent world as a tiny baby boy. Thirty-one years have gone by in a flash. He is now a happy, self-made man, and we have an incredible relationship.

However, when I was so depressed that I was contemplating killing myself time moved so slowly that I felt as if I was waiting for Death. I thought that I would never be well, and I did not want to saddle my husband, my son, and our baby daughter with the stigma of having a wife and mother who would have to live in a mental institution for the rest of her days! That was why I shot myself in the head. I did not want to be a burden to them. But this was false thinking. A lie I told myself when I was afraid to face all the feelings and thoughts that were coming up to be healed in the moment. It's shame I listened to these lies, but then it also turned out to be a blessing, in the end. This long winding path to Self-Realization has brought me to the perfect, happy Life I am living today. Or is that Life living me?

Just remember the media often focuses on negative stories or sensational happenings. So, I do not especially recommend watching corporate news. Is any of this really beneficial for people to see. Why do we have to bombard ourselves daily with so many negative images? Why can't we have a news station which is only focused on reporting ALL GOOD News and positive things that are taking place all over the planet???

Life force pulses through my body abundantly provided I get enough rest, eat well, and think happy thoughts. My chi is high and my sexual appetite for a 64-year-old is better than when I was in my twenties. I am truly loving and enjoying sex and all bodily sensations in a way that I have not since I was a young teenager. My menstruation stopped about a year after my ex-boyfriend, Knowle and I started making love, and I am happier and hornier than ever! Oh well, so much for that one. Knowle left me for a younger woman who lived in his home state, they moved in together, and they have now been happily married for some years according to our mutual friend, Dave. Oh well. All is fair in love and war. I was sad and angry about the betrayal and unexpected, sudden ending of that relationship for months, but it has not even been on my thought radar for many years.

Sky is now a grown woman with a child of her own. In the midst of my depressions, I never would believe I'd get through the fear and pain and be as happy as I am today and have been on and off for the last ten years. Life is and has been such a gift.

GROUNDHOG DAY
AGAIN (2020)

Right now, as of February 2, which is the celebration of "Groundhog Day"[9] and "Candlemas, or exactly mid-winter; and we just had a beautiful eight-inch blizzard since Sunday afternoon straight through until today. It stopped for a while in Princeton, but according to weather prognostications, we are supposed to get about another inch or so tonight while we are asleep. Governor Phil Murphy, Jersey's Democratic governor, declared a "state of emergency" on Monday, and asked people to stay home indoors and off the roads unless you were doctors, hospital workers, or emergency workers like firemen, EMTs, nurses, supermarket clerks, and pharmacists. He said "Stay home unless it is absolutely necessary for you to go to work—which is what all the governors and mayors of cities like New York and Philadelphia, have been warning us to do all along with the so-called "threat" of getting the corona virus.

The so-called "pandemic" which, according to Dr. Gary Null, the nutritionist, author, and listener sponsored radio announcer, on WBAI every day at noon for people who listen to him on the east coast, have declared the virus which truly has helped to exterminate millions of people, was created basically, by accident, in a lab by Dr. Anthony Faloci, and then sold to China. According to Dr. Null and other scientists as well as medical experts, declare it was Falci himself who went against President Obama's orders to stop the research that was going on which was "against nature; but Fauci was either naive about the possible negative results that might occur, and continued to defy the president's orders and the law he made, or he just did not care.

In fact, it was Fauci himself who continued to fund the dirty little lab in Wuhan, China, where there was the first outbreak of co-vid 19. I heard on WBAI that Bill Gates had a lot to do with this pandemic, too, predicting it on a TED. talk years ago, before it ever happened. Having mass vaccinations of folks around the world would make gobs of money for his foundation, not to mention all the pharmaceutical industries. Bill Gates was involved in this "hoax" perpetrated upon the American public along with many doctors and pharmaceutical companies.

Many scientists and doctors the world over are coming forth now on the radio and some in the newspaper or other media, to declare the whole thing has been blown way out of proportion in order

---

9   In the comedy movie "Groundhog Day", Bill Murray plays Phil, a man who is obligated to repeat the same day until he learns to treat everyone with unselfish love. In the Center for Spiritual Living, Princeton, we joke that this day is a high holy day, because of the movie's message.

to create fear and anxiety in order to control the population and take away our constitutional rights in a democracy which is now slowly eroding. Doctors and scientists from the US. Belgium, Germany, Sweden, Denmark, Australia, and all around the world who say this thing was created to create fear and anxiety as well as to control people the world over; and to have everyone manipulated into thinking they need vaccinations which have not even been given enough time to see what the long-term effects of it will be. Like SARS, HIV. and the pertussis part of the DPT vaccine, which, according to Dr. Null, contains formaldehyde and mercury, and very well, according to both parents and doctors, may very well be responsible for creating autism and Downs syndrome in little babies.

At first, getting the virus was no worse than getting any flu or virus; and if a person was healthy with a good immune system, would not be at risk. There were and are tons of preventive measures other than getting a vaccination that would stop any person from getting the corona virus, like taking megadoses of vitamin C, zinc, and eating herbs and teas like echinacea and oregano, which stimulate the immune system, especially if these folks ate a purely vegan or vegetarian diet, avoided sugars, wheat gluten and white flour. Not to mention that they live a healthy, happy lifestyle which includes exercising regularly, connecting with their higher Selves through meditation, yoga, chanting, writing in their journals, making art, painting, gardening, working with animals, children, or divine contemplation; or whatever makes them feel happy and connected to Source or his or her own higher power.

If a person were to think happy, positive thoughts and KNOW without a doubt that they, as creator gods, connected to Source Energy, not only deserve and create their perfect health as well as the circumstances of their entire lives through their thoughts, both conscious and subconscious, and emotions.

We each have choice to create everything we are wanting, from precious moment to precious moment, according to New Age thinkers as well as Conscious Beings, ancestors, gurus, and Masters on the "Other Side" like Abraham, Edgar Cayce, and Archangels Michael, Gabriel, Gabriel, and Raphael, the Archangel of Healing and Transformation. "Every day, every second, there is choice. If it were not so we would not be individuals." is a card I chose from the "Wisdom Card" deck by Dr. Ernest Holmes, whose teachings inspired the Science of Mind religious philosophy which, besides being a "New Thought" church, is now called the "Centers for Spiritual Living" so as not to be confused with "Scientology and Scientologists like the gorgeous and successful actor, Tom Cruise, who has been so successful using and applying the tenets of author and philosopher, L. Ron Hubbard.

A DAY OF REST

Journal: November, 2020

I am so grateful on this Sunday evening before Thanksgiving 2020 that I am finally taking the time to sit down and write at my computer. Due to some crazy negative thoughts, I was having three months ago with people all around me in a state of fear and anxiety about the novel "virus everyone is talking about, thoughts of the violence towards innocent black and brown children, adults, and animals, one dark, hopeless thought led to another, and I spiraled into a dark hole which made me feel unworthy, not valuable as a handicapped person. Not valuable as a woman. Super needy. And not even having a desire to get out of bed in the morning even if it was a sunny day. It was three months ago that the negative thoughts of sadness, hopelessness, and uncertainty began, a day after Labor Day, I was sad the summer was ending, and I would not be able to swim in the outdoor pool with my precious new friends anymore. I was a real basket case after a few weeks of thinking this way and feeling bad about it, and I felt so weak, embarrassed, and ashamed to be a minister who really ought to know better. I was "shoulding" all over myself. You know what I mean. I should be happy. I should be exercising. I should be out on the streets demonstrating and singing from cars with my friends. I should get others to vote. I should stop feeling sorry for myself and help others. Be of service. But I did not even feel able to prepare a meal for myself. And I had no appetite anyway.

After all, God has helped me get through worse times than the "novel corona virus. How about slowing down a bit and taking the time to write a great romantic novel with my beau, work a bit each day on my memoir, take long, slow walks in nature? There were endless possibilities. I was feeling guilty and ashamed knowing I had so many blessings like my mate, my family, and so many precious friends, two sweet kitties, and multitudinous blessings like mother Nature, the Sun, moon, stars, dancing, sex, massage friends and one or two clients. Poetry, reading good books. Learning new things. Helping my daughter by watching my precious, adorable, fun-loving grandson. I finally got myself into such a hole with the negative thinking that I got out of touch with my heart, my sweet, gentle soul, and passion for life in general. Oh, my goodness, I was in hell punishing this poor little angel fairy child with one negative, punitive thought after another. I was even too ashamed to tell my psychiatrist, Dr. Madaya, a lovely Indian woman I respect, even though I only met her face to face at AAMH (All Access Mental Health) two times, though we definitely have different ideas about the use of medications.

How dare I not feel my usual happy, peaceful Self who is eager to rise in the morning and see what great good the Divine Mystery has in store for me?! You are a bad girl. You need to get back to writing your book and tell the truth to friends and family about how shitty I was feeling. It was completely inexplicable. I'd feel too tired to go out shopping for food because I'd have to" mask up" out of respect and love for others who believe this is something that will prevent the spread of illness, but I already KNOW in my heart I create my own reality. When it's time for me to die I will not fear anything. I know it will be my time to translate into my subtler form where I will merge with God Consciousness again.

Besides, I know heaven is not ready for me yet. I have too many happy, wonderful dreams and goals I still want to accomplish, and I want to live to see my grandchild, William, grow up, get married, and have children of his own. Not to mention that my handsome, talented, and prosperous son, Gabriel Peter Olson-, is having a wedding of his own to a lovely lady named Daphne Tin, from Hong Kong sometime in the near future. They were supposed to wed in Hawaii on April 11th this past spring, and he'd already purchased the plane tix for Gary and me to go to the wedding and reception in Honolulu, as well as many of Daphne's family, whose parents and aunts and uncles were well into their seventies and eighties, I suppose.

Anyway, often times man and woman make plans, but sometimes God/Goddess laughs. We don't understand, and we get disappointed. But there is always a higher spiritual purpose to everything that happens. In the English words of Great Britain's other most famous rock group after the Beatles, Mick Jagger, Keith Richards, and the Rolling Stones "You can't always get what you want, you can't always get what you want, but if ya' try sometimes, you just might find you might get what you need."

So, the wedding in Hawaii as well as the reception had to be postponed until a more perfect time. Daphne and Gabriel Bear were married by a justice of the peace and have two lovely homes together, an apartment in Manhattan and still keep their house in Manalapan, New Jersey, which, I am so happy, for my sake, because I love, adore, and depend upon my son's grounded focus and industrious nature to create prosperity in the family which he then shares with me and his wife and other family members just like his dad did before him with his magnanimous nature. The reservations at the various hotels were promised to still be honored at the perfect time.

Besides, patience is an angelic quality, a true virtue in these crazy, fluctuating times of change and "all good things come to those who wait. "Seek ye first the kingdom of God, and all things shall be added unto thee." As you believe, so ye will receive. Gary and I made reservations at a hotel for a few extra days at the hotel where Gary and I were going to relax for just a few more nights at an inexpensive hotel the less expensive hotel closer to the airport since, originally, it seemed it was going to be such a whirlwind of a trip. the mind thinks of as being separate I try to never get too high anymore so I do not need to have an equal, opposing experience of depression, fear, or anxiety. Divine Light and Love bring up anything unlike itself to be purified and transmuted into a higher frequency which benefits the All Good.

"The only thing we have to fear is fear itself." Franklin Delano Roosevelt, which, is reminiscent of a Science of Mind teaching that affirms that" the only thing that ever needs to be healed is the Belief that something needs to be healed. Holy Spirit does not see me as handicapped in any way, shape, or form. It is just a limited thought in the ever-changing subconscious Mind. I KNOW in my heart that I am Perfect, Whole, and complete filled with unconditional Love, a radiant Being of Light in this holy moment, as are all of you. There is only One Infinite Life, one Divine Reality expressing in, as, and through each precious human being on this beautiful planet of ours, even at this time of seeming adversity, disharmony, political strife, unrest, violence, war, poverty, hunger, and on and on and on. No one ever dies. We are all eternal Beings. There is no endedness to life, despite what it seems.

Even though my grandmother, Lucy, died on September 11th, 2005, at 87, and I still miss her, I have such sweet memories of her unconditional love and, at times, can feel her subtle, loving presence as well as her husband, my "Pop Pop Vere, who passed away at 76 years young. But I know he is still with me. So much love there. And my Grandpa Olson, Henry Otto, and precious Grandma Anna, whose middle name I received from my parents in order to honor her memory.

My best friend, Jenna LeDoux, ascended into heaven after a bout with colon cancer which was healed and finally metastasized into her liver, and she ascended into the celestial realms before I ever had the chance to tell her how much I loved her, and how grateful I was to her for every kind thing she did for me—like taking me down to the beach if and when I got depressed, invited me to her beautiful home to give me free massages when I was frightened I'd not have enough money to pay my monthly bills. Poppycock. God has always provided for me through some special person or persons each day of my precious life.

I thought "Why did my best friend and sister, Karin, pass away at the tender age of forty years young from cancer, leaving behind her beautiful, young daughter, Abigail, father, Pat, mother, boyfriend, Mo, her brother, and many friends to grieve her passing, yet I am still here? It does not seem fair. And my friend, John Giallucco, who was married to my dear friend, Amy Ascordia, ascended less than two years ago Why am I so lucky, or perhaps unlucky, to be here at this auspicious time of change, of growth, seeming adversity with so many perceived obstacles to harmony and World Peace. I suppose to get stronger. I suppose it is a lesson in both faith, patience, coming together as One Big Family to care for one another and do our little part to serve and help all others of all races, religions, creeds, sexes… The One Great Spirit tells me "With God all things are possible." Listen to the angels' clarion call to Wake Up and care about yourself and to love and respect each other. We truly are our brothers' keeper.

If I start to doubt my own ability to live and make enough money just to pay all my bills and get by without much work like many others during this time of the Co-vid pandemic Archangel Gabriel and Lord Jesus whisper in my ear. "Have faith, dear child, and trust in Me.".

"Consider the lilies of the field. The Lord said "They do not toil or spin yet your heavenly father feeds and clothes them." And you, Meryl, as a human being, are worth so much more to him. The Lord will never desert or forsake his flock.

So now I can relax choosing now to surrender cares and worry about tomorrow to the One who always loves and cares for me –through other Earth angels on earth like my precious beau, Gary, my darling son, Gabriel, my daughters, Kyrie London, and Sky as well as all the friends, chiropractors, doctors and counselors I have on my team. Not to mention my home health aide, Sheira, and so many others who came before her to care for my basic physical needs, cook for me, do my laundry, and clean my simple home. I am grateful for all that I have today and all the better that is coming. I asked Archangel Metatron for help with my goals and dreams, Archangel Raphael, Mary Magdelene, and Mother Mary for healing of all the Divine Feminine sides of my self—to accept the handicap—or not. To love the way, I look in this moment and to do certain yogic exercises, swim, and specific physical therapy to help me improve incrementally each precious, holy day. I am told I will be guided.

In the words of Dr. Hook, Bing Crosby, and the Andrew Sisters "You gotta acc-entuate the positive, eliminate the negative, latch on to the affirmative, and don't mess with Mr. "in-between," Well, unless it happens to be in between my beautiful yoni, if you know what I mean, Jelly Bean!

As Lord Jesus said in his sermon on the Mount "Turn the other cheek." If someone slaps you on one side of your face, don't offer him the other cheek to be slapped. I think it means to turn your petty, thoughts and body away from the darkness and toward the Light if ever those silly, crazy thoughts ever plague you again, honey chile.". As a Light Worker for the Great White Brother and Sisterhood I am consciously choosing to dwell only in the Light from now on. And if an occasional crazy thought pops into my head again, I'll just witness it and be vigilant to replace it with what I am wanting. Anything to help soothe the savage beast. Gary tells me to invite the demons in for a cup of tea. Or I call one of the Science of Mind practitioners or the Unity hotline to affirm t God's divine Law through what we call "prayer treatment". There is no pleading or yearning. Just a simple statement of fact like "I am healed." I am already a successful, published author. So be it. Thank you, lord God that it is already so.

Besides me. All you folks with bi-polar and other mental illnesses are in great company. Comic geniuses like Robin Williams. Artists and painters like Vincent Van Gogh. Composers like Rachmaninoff and Beethoven also experienced powerful dark nights of the soul and mood swings. Vivien Leigh. Patty Duke Astin. Great actresses, singers and dancers like Catherine Zeta-Jones, Psychologist Dr. Kay Redfield Jamison.

Who wants to be normal anyway? Without writing, taking risks and sending out my stuff to publishers, how will my work ever get known? How will I ever become successful enough to get off public assistance and food stamps? How will I travel the world sharing my courageous story unless I actually write a little bit each day and enjoy the process? Isn't that what my angels have been trying to tell me each night in my dreams when I sleep? They say "You are talented. What you have to say is valuable. We believe in you, girlfriend. So, get to it! Finish the blessed book. We leave you with great love for a job well done. Congratulations, sweetheart. Nighty night, Abraham, Ascordia, beloved World.

LIFE IS CHANGE

Journal: November, 2020

Hey, how do you know it's time to make changes and get a life?"

"When you've watched so many episodes of "Law and Order". Criminal Minds", "the Closer", and it's spin-off "Major Crimes" that you know everything before it's about to happen!" Pretty sad stuff. Boring. As for me, I hate television now. I'm just so bored with most of the old shows I used to watch, including "Medium", "the Ghost Whisperer", and "Gracie and Frankie" with Jane Fonda and Lily Tomlin. I want to tell a new vision. As for me, I am enjoying making the movie of my own life more than ever. I love myself and am in touch again. Committed to my spiritual purpose to help and serve others in whatever small way I can. My time is much too valuable to procrastinate success and creativity one more blessed minute.1declare I will never waste time watching another re-run-on TV again. Time is just too precious. I declare. I am in service to God and my Guru, by whose grace and love I am alive and well. This is why I came to this precious planet in the first place.

I originally came from very far away from the dog star, Sirius B, where we never get too serious – seriously. At this moment in time, I love my simple, happy, uncomplicated life of dancing, singing, swimming, gardening, in the spring, summer, and harvesting the fruits of my labor in autumn. Painting "messterpieces" with William and enjoying the quiet, uncomplicated, divine companionship of my Gary Bear.

I adore chanting, making love, taking long, hot, Epsom salted bubble baths, getting manicures and pedicures to relax at Kim's Nail Spa in Princeton. I just got one this morning after exercising at Princeton Fitness and Wellness for a few miles on the stationary bike. I like sitting quietly in contemplation and meditating on my mom's former beautiful blue sofa with Gary in the early mornings by sunrise or before, Ecstatic dancing with Michael, Pan, and my beloved daughter, Kyrie OneLove at her Celebrating All People events that honor, respect, and celebrate people of all nations, colors, creeds, etc.

Gosh, I got so nervous while public speaking at the church this morning on Gratitude Sunday. I completely forgot to mention both my daughters, Kyrie, and Sky. Nor did I mention my son, Gabriel. Or did I? I'm pooped. Nighty night.

I try to going to physical therapy at least once per week in Edison where I am learning to speak Korean, get relaxing massages, acupuncture, hot packs on my back, and enjoy having the experience of deep relaxation.

But my favorite thing is being a good grandparent whenever William is free and his mom needs me and Gary to babysit. soccer classes. He is an excellent athlete and shines when he is trying out new things like jumping jacks, push-ups, karate chops, kicks, and flies up into the air and ends up in a full side split in front of me on my wooden apartment floor or on the green grass in warmer weather like the Nicholas Brothers of old. William has either a green or yellow belt which I think is terrific for five years of age. Or whatever belt or the next one up. I forget. He is growing up so fast. I recall the day he was born. Auspicious June 16th, 2015. What a happy and blessed day for all of us who actually went to the hospital in Princeton to be part of that sacred experience. Sky had a great midwife like I did. We missed his actual birth because Kyrie called us a bit too late to tell us it was happening.

The funny thing is I woke up in the middle of the night KNOWING something special was happening. I said to my honey, Gary Bear, who was sleeping beside me "Babe, something special is happening right now. God told me so. I think that Sky is about to give birth. And that's when we called and her message went to "voicemail". Then we heard from Kyrie who said Sky had just had a baby boy. She already knew from a sonogram that she was carrying a boy; and she had already chosen a name. I laughed when she told me the baby daddy, Charles, wanted to call him "Megavan". I said" What, is he nuts? The kids will make fun of him, and go around calling him "Meg". Like a boy named Sue, the song by Johnny Cash, one of my favorite country artists. Anyway, she chose to name him William. Sometimes she calls him William and other times she calls him 'Samuel'. Whatever it is she calls him, he knows he is deeply loved; he knows his limits; and I think she is the best single mother I've ever encountered, in my experience.

ARTISTS

Journal: August 31, 2021

Famous artists like Vincent Van Gogh were also deeply sensitive and haunted by suicidal thoughts and mental illness most of his life, musicians like Jim Morrison, Janis Joplin, Ray Charles, James Taylor, Karen Carpenter, and Brook Shields have all "come out", sharing their personal struggles with mental illness. Brook's story of her battle with postpartum depression was particularly compelling, surprising, and inspirational because she had temporary thoughts of driving over a cliff or killing herself and her baby in a car accident.

Even Naomi Judd, mother of Wynona, and half of the singing duo, the Judd's wrote a book about her life called "The River of Time". In it, she shares her struggles she experienced after the duo broke up; she ended up going through a period of turmoil that consisted of time spent in psychiatric hospitals after she and her husband could no longer face the chronic melancholia without help from a professional. In it, she shares she missed singing very much on stage performing with her daughter, and she missed not just the performing part, but traveling with her daughter, too. Naomi shares that the medications the doctors and psychiatrists all gave her did not help Naomi feel one iota better.

I suppose from what she shared so openly and honestly, she was not even in touch with her own trauma, sadness, and need to grieve for the losses of so many things at once. In my estimation, as someone who has had post-traumatic stress many times in my life, I was thinking how much she'd accomplished in life besides giving birth to two amazing daughters, nurturing them, singing everywhere with one of them, being there for actress Ashley's and Wynona's fame and success. Not to mention that Naomi became very ill and almost died, but through prayer, faith, and hard work, aligning with Jesus Christ and God's plan for her life, she got through it and became an overcomer triumphant in every respect/ a major health crisis, needed to grieve, I think, but, as a usually strong woman who has accomplished so much in her life, was probably ashamed of feeling weak and vulnerable could not face her sadness and the trauma of no longer being able to share her many talents as a singer, mother, performer, world traveler, etc. She had truly accomplished so much as the mom of not one, but two beautiful, talented, globally famous daughters; Ashley, the actress, was close to her mom at the time of her trials and tribulations with mental illness and tried to help, but Naomi, being the proud loving, kind mother she was, did not want Wynona to know anything about all the negative thoughts and feelings she was struggling with after they split. having a successful career as a performer-not to mention that she and her daughter "Wy, were no longer close. Wynona even met a man she would eventually marry without sharing this wonderful news with her mom, nor did she invite her precious mother to her wedding, probably the biggest event in her life next to giving birth to a baby. She shares that she did not want to bother Wynona with her troubles. I can see how deeply hurt and lonely she must have felt after they split because they had been so close.

That is an example of how lonely we get and how people with mental illness feel isolated even while we are in the company of other people, especially strangers, that the soul needs to withdraw for a while we tend to ignore our pain and true feelings of sadness or subconscious fear and anger; so sometime we, well, especially I, need to zone out in front of the "boob tube" so I can avoid feeling, my feelings of unworthiness or anxiety. I'd go into a temporary cocoon as well so that I could feel safe and take stock of where I've been. Naomi shares how she became addicted to watching endless reruns of "Law and Order". I was so happy she shared this because I did the exact same thing by sleeping a lot or, watching endless television since I do not take any drugs or self-medicate with wine or alcohol since I am very disciplined when it comes to the foods, drinks, and other things I put into my body. way by withdrawing from my family and friends by becoming addicted to fantasy". I went through the same thing two years back when I had one of my seasonal affective disorder things kick in when we changed the clocks back and it became darker earlier in the day around 5 or 6 PM. Or depression came like a thief in the night sometimes after a break-up with a boyfriend, stealing all my natural, inherent joy and peace of mind. Not to mention my desire to work, to dance, to make love, to want to watch the news, or to be able to leave the house to interact with folks in "the World". In winter when I did not want to get out of bed to face another day, I'd live just to watch old episodes of Mattock with Andy Griffith if I had very few massage clients that day, sometimes none at all; and I'd think to myself"

Why am I still here on this blessed planet if I can't make a profound positive difference for Mother Earth and Her children when so many of my friends plus my dad are no longer here to play with me?"

A little television for entertainment is fine if you are sick and tired of being lied to by the patriarchy and you are feeling rundown, I need of soothing, relaxing oneself with television and a cup of delicious tea, mushroom coffee, espresso, a beer, good clean fresh H2O. It helps the mind relax and be quiet for an hour or so, but then I'd get antsy if I lay in bed reading, trying to nap, or watch endless re-runs of Law and Order or Criminal minds. Then I'd drive myself to the nearest gym in Princeton

Well, from my experience, sitting on my asspirations watching TV all day long never got me one inch closer to realizing my dreams of becoming an inspirational singer, speaker, dancer, ad author.

as where we are going, not to mention that we need to grieve for that part of us we've left behind. still felt sick because her depression was resistant to all the medications she tried. with non-resistance.

Despite childhood abuse, sexual molestation, divorce, depression, shooting myself in the head, overdosing on pills and alcohol, poverty, single motherhood, and setting myself on fire, with God's grace and watchful loving eye I was able to survive all these trials in order to become an overcomer with great strength.\ Phew. Let's take a breath right there. Before you think I am some kind of nut case, let me tell you a little insane and I've had my share of troubles, like anyone, but with God's grace and a bit of Self effort I've come through each trial and tribulation with flying colors. I am also a loving daughter, mom, grandma, a legally ordained minister of Universal Brotherhood, and devotee of a great saint, Swami Muktananda, writing during a time of great change and upheaval on the planet. It is now the last day of August, 2021, and I've been living and writing this memoir since 1991 while a student at Mercer County College in West Windsor, New Jersey.

Boy, am I glad I got that past self-hatred and doubt out of my system once and for all! God is great and All Good—omnipresent. There is not a spot where He/She is not. — Divine Consciousness is omnipresent, and omniscient. Inside you, inside me, above you, below you, to the left and right of you, in all animals, nature, our precious pets, both living and deceased and wildlife everywhere; There is truly no spot where infinitely intelligent Conscious Awareness is not! And you yourself have become a unique expression of That precious divinity. Your body is only temporary and just a spacesuit you will only don for a finite period of time until it is your time in this incarnation to ascend with your beautiful Spirit to go back home and merge with infinite Love and Light!

At sixty-six years young I have barely begun to manifest half of my personal dreams as well as my visions for a more peaceful, happier humanity in harmony with Mother Earth and all her precious creatures. According to some American economic standard I still live below poverty level if you compare me to others who have way more material riches, but I personally feel like the richest woman in the world because of my guru's grace giving me the wisdom and discernment I've gleaned from so many varied personal experiences, including the ups and downs of being a "bi-polar bear".

And the infinite, eternal unfailing love of our Father, Jesus, the Christ Consciousness Who is still with us always. I recently had a direct, personal experience of His Presence. Today. While listening to my Alexa machine I asked for a particular song, but rather than playing the one I already knew and asked for the machine decided on her own to play "Miracles" from a children's Christian musical by a woman whose name I'd never heard before. Children were singing the words from the Bible that began with a Bible quote and played itself over several times until the knot in my heart just burst, and I sat on the couch crying as I felt waves of bliss and peace run through my entire body just the same way I did when I met my guru, Swami Muktananda, for the first time. Now I am trying to memorize the words and sing along with them because they are all so pure and true. I rarely read the Bible, but I do know many of these sayings from the New Testament because I was raised Catholic, and mom and two brothers are all "Born again Christians".

The childrens' voices are perfect for singing the truth of Christ's teachings about love, forgiveness, freedom, and true salvation. I've sensed Christ's presence around me before, but because so many Christians have tried to force their beliefs down my throat, I have almost always resisted reading the Bible, but I think I'll look at it with new eyes the next time I look at John or Matthew. I particularly love the sermon on the Mount and commands like "Seek and ye shall find". Also, knock and the door shall be opened (just for you) You can succeed too no matter how young, old, poor, disabled, or sick. If you feel truly happy inside no matter how much money you have, what job you do on a daily basis, or how many material possessions you have, you have already found the kingdom of Good within. Enlightenment is ordinary and need not take you to the ends of the earth, to a small solitary cave in the Himalayas where you have to meditate for hours on end, stand in a yogic position on one foot for hours, or sleep on a bed of nails. All those notions are ridiculous. Poppycock.

If you are truly happy with yourself and your accomplishments right now, grateful for all you have, even the adversity and challenging dark circumstances, how you have come very far in your search for the Truth and Light that is always inside your own heart and soul. It does not matter what others think. If you don't need anyone's approval but your own, you have become your own hero or heroine. God/Goddess, the angels, archangels, and saints are all so very proud of you. You are truly a noble being worthy of so much honor, gratitude, and appreciation. Each of us is already worthy as a holy Son or Daughter of the One God.; we each came here for a particular reason only we ourselves can know for certain and with a unique spiritual purpose. We are all lights like the facets of a sparkling, brilliant diamond! Never forget that That is Who you truly are a Being worthy of Love and adoration. you are an incarnation of God/Goddess, and you were not created to suffer. "Suffer" the little children to come unto me." actually meant "Allow" them to come hither. Many people misinterpret what the real meaning of suffering is. It only has the meaning we give it. It is not necessary once we have finally learned the beautiful lesson of forgiveness it has tried to teach us. Only you and you alone can add your talents and unique piece to the puzzle and beautiful tapestry of Love, Light, and infinite variety of expressions that has become our struggle here upon Planet Earth at this holy moment in time. The angels and archangels sent a clarion call for help at the time of 9/11 and now, with the challenges of the virus whose name I shall not mention here because I don't want to give it more power than it already has been given. I will give you a clue, though. There is a liquid ale in a green bottle that has the same name. Co-vid 19, -21 and all its seeming deadly variants, have absolutely no power over you or me because God only provides good and greater good for his precious children. It's all in what you have been taught and truly believe, whether it's been by your parents, your teachers, your doctors, seemingly knowing scientists like Dr. Fauci, or your politicians. What if it was all lies? That's something to really think about—a truly great thing to contemplate next time someone wants to complain about everything going on in the world as well as all his or her personal problems. Ever notice how misery loves company?

My mom is a real trouper, but she has a tendency to focus on the latest ill in her body. Even when she is completely healthy, she seems to find something to complain about, whether it's her neck, back, stubbed pinky or big toe. Then I ask her if the toes have healed. She says "Of course. They feel much better, but I broke my arm and wrist last Wednesday while in the bathroom, and I don't even know how I did it! If it; s not the aches and pains it's the diarrhea, the shape and color of her feces, or whatever. Give me a break. Stop right there., mom. Please tell me some good things that have been going on in your life and two or three things you are grateful for. I cannot take any more of this old story.

My friend, Dan, once said of my mom's front door to the house she lived in for twenty-two years "On the front door should be posted a warning sign that says "All who enter here, abandon hope." I know this might sound disrespectful, but I love my mom very much and just wish she could just try to Lighten up, find a better attitude and finally learn the value of positive thinking, appreciation and gratitude for all the abundant blessings she has in life. We all have these negative conscious or unconscious thoughts sometimes. It seems to be a part of the human condition unless we become aware that our negative thoughts, beliefs, and feelings are actually creating our "inner state" which manifests into our moment-to-moment, or daily reality. I, myself, know that I manifest my own reality with my own thoughts, words, and deeds. That's why I like to listen to a lot of different kinds of good music daily to inspire me, read Bible verses, pick Goddess, fairy, or angel cards as a way to tune into Holy Spirit. And I LOVE to Dance, or loudly chant and sing out sadness, temporary fear, self-doubt the negative or temporary doubts and fears away and out of my system, or to go for a pleasant walk-in nature. Like William Shakespeare once said "one touch of nature makes the whole World kin." That's why I love to watch for deer; they are gentle, innocent, and bring me deeper into whatever next adventure will be for me as a gift sent from the Divine Mystery, Jesus Christ, "the Force", the guru, or whatever you want to call this blessed thing we call "Life". We are each a blessing to the world and each other. And we all are so very blessed. I am so grateful and blessed that my precious Mom is still alive at 85 after all the trials and tribulations she has come through with a person who has experienced mental illness firsthand—chronic depressions leading to despair, loneliness, and suicidal ideations. She also attempted suicide as well as me-twice, but God, Lord Jesus, and I helped to save her from self-destruction. It was not her time yet, thank Goddess.

At 85 my "Ma" is still beautiful, intelligent, a great dresser, attractive on the inside and out, a caring and deserving person, whether she believes it or not. She is sensitive, psychic, a great organizer, and sometimes very open and friendly, sexy even. She used to tell dirty jokes when I was a kid and hostess a lot of parties for the Princeton Singles or her own family (me, David, the kids, my brother, Pete, Kathy, his second wife, and love of his life (who I'm sad to say, recently died from stomach cancer at 51, rose again, and her memorial service was coincidentally scheduled for Easter Sunday, the same day Jesus, the Christ, rose, so even though we are sad and grieving right now, there truly is no death for all who believe in love and everlasting life. It does not matter if you are atheist, agnostic, Christian, Jew, Muslim, Protestant, a Jehovah's Witness, gay or straight, God loves all His children equally. We are all the same One beautiful Being of love and Light, precious in His sight. because life is eternal,

Kathy no longer suffers from pain of the body and her beautiful, courageous Spirit and soul is now in heaven with her Lord) and their two children, Luke, and Caroline Grace, used to come to Grandma's lovely, immaculate condominium in Franklin Park, off of Route 27, but that was before she kept falling and forgetting to eat breakfast or lunch regularly, so now she is living in Cape May Courthouse in a beautiful, expensive assisted living residence called Brookdale where she has regular meals with other older friends, daily activities she can do besides rest in her room with her cat, Jade, and get daily medications or assistance with laundry, cleaning, or whatever she may need now that she no longer owns her own home, which amazingly sold within a day or two of being put on the market; so I told her that her Lord, Jesus, obviously had a hand in that because he cared very much about her loneliness, depression, and anxiety about living alone without a man , a room-mate, or daily caretaker, like I am fortunate to have here at my apartment because I chose to manifest that, knowing I am especially vulnerable, having two disabilities, hemiplegia and manic depression that pops up every few months without my even knowing why even if I am on mood stabilizing medication. God wanted only thoughts and feelings of Well Being and appreciation that all her bills and things are handled by my brother and the pleasant, competent staff at the residence. She always fussed so much with dinner, decorations, and a beautiful dining table set with sterling silver and cloth napkins at Thanksgiving and Christmas about ten or fifteen years ago. I was so grateful and proud of her. I wanted and still want her to know that I deeply love and appreciate he desire to survive, despite all her trials, and my deep appreciation for taking me in at terrible times of dark despair that was medication and therapy resistant; so, I am so grateful l my welcomed me into her home cooking lunch or dinners for me, and inviting me to sleep over many times I did not want to be alone. She was so kind and helpful, and I owe her a tremendous debt. She is a wise old elder even though she still complains about having to sell her house and not enjoying living where she is.

At some point she lost her job at Buckingham Place in Princeton where she worked part-time after I was fired, and her life seemed to go downhill after that. How can a "born again" Christian Not be born again anew each morning? It seems silly that we would not remember the unconditional love and complete acceptance our Lord has for us—especially after communing with Him/Her in our sweet dreams when we fall asleep and go to the astral plane until we wake up in the morning at sunrise or whenever.

Each day is an opportunity to begin anew. Start fresh. We can turn to turn to Him or ask the whole company of angels, a minister, priest, pastor, or Science of Mind practitioner to pray affirmatively for whatever need or desire we are wanting to manifest. The licensed Science of mind practitioner or minister will pray and Know the Truth for you, even if you temporarily forget. It is perfectly OK and encouraged by God and Mother Earth, our family and friends to have the courage to call a friend, or ask a family member for help if and when we feel weak, confused, unsure of ourselves and ask our Lord in heaven which path to take to make you closer to Him in order to manifest whatever goals you are hoping to manifest; or if it is just to feel normal instead of being afraid, lonely, and anxious at the time. How to take the next step forward, if we feel as if we do not want to get up and out of bed in the morning. I recently had that same experience. I felt that same weakness I've felt in the past when a lover left me, or a good friend moved away or died where I did not want to rise out of bed for three whole months after I lost my personal home health aide who was beautiful, bright, and cheerful. Carlissa was not only young and beautiful, but she felt like a daughter to me. She was like a ray of sunshine that brought light into every corner of my sometimes dark, messy, disorganized small apartment which I humbly call "The New Friendship Ranch". She would draw a relaxing hot bubble bath for me that contained lavender or eucalyptus scented Epsom salts to soothe my weary body and mind.

She cooked breakfast, usually fresh long cooking oatmeal scrambled eggs, or a fresh omelet with kale or a small green pepper packed with flavor, enzymes for digestion, and vitamin C, picked fresh from our vegetable and herb garden that morning.

She usually sauteed a bit of fresh onion or garlic with the eggs and added spices like sea salt, fresh pepper, turmeric, dill, sage, rosemary, or whatever to make it taste extra special... She made my herb or Lipton teas with honey and almond milk and brought them to me on my coffee table while I relaxed on the living room couch watching a comedy like Steven Colbert or a recent rerun of Saturday night Live; or after I got into the bath while she was lovingly cleaning the dishes in the sink or making my beautiful bed with spread, freshly changed flannel or cotton satin sheets every week, and she sponge mopped my kitchen and bathroom floors with a Swifter Jet mop. Get the picture. She was a very sweet, kind, industrious worker. It was a hard job and the agency did not pay much by the hour. No wonder she quit. She was also a full-time student, and I suppose she needed to go back to school full-time at Ryder College once the new semester began in August. She'd been away before that on vacation I the Dominican Republic; so, I'd gotten very attached to her, and so very disappointed when she came back and left me and the agency suddenly.

However, God is great, and already knew my needs before I even asked because I live in the land of plenty where everything is so abundant as the grains of sand upon the beach, the leaves on the trees which are beautiful now in autumn in jersey and Pennsylvania—a lovely combination of reds, yellows, golds, and now a little brown as they are beginning to fall on the ground. if we believe we deserve to have it all. We can truly be, do, and have what we want if we believe, trust, have faith, patience, listen to our inner guidance, and persevere. God always provides and mother Earth loves us dearly and has provided everything we need to be happy. We just need to think a better thought, and know there are some things we can control and others over which we have no control like the Laws of gravity or Attraction which is our friend and just means "Like thoughts and deeds attract like thoughts and things.

Carlissa organized my refrigerator which often contained fresh vegetables or fruits that had spoiled due to there only being the two of us, and many times we'd both be too pooped to pop or cook, so we just heated up microwaveable meals for both lunch and supper which Gary purchased early in the morning from Shop Rite or McCartney's to beat the oppressive heat, she mopped the bathroom and kitchen floors, shopped for us, did laundry, folded it and put it away. She even helped me plant new vegetables and flowers in the spring when she came. What a Godsend. I still consider her my precious friend and helper, like most of my former home health aides, Anya, Wilma, Yolanda, Cesserina, Sheira and my favorite Spanish aide, Carlissa was a beautiful, young 21 years old who came in with a sweet smile on her birthday as a brand new, home health aide with great energy, enthusiasm to do a good job for her very first client. She made me breakfast so I could relax and read, write, do e-mails or watch TV. She helped me plant new flowers in my garden or herbs; bending down and kneeling using a shovel and trowel to get deep enough into the earth so the roots of the perennial which are all tasks I used to enjoy doing all by myself without the help of a personal assistant or a man until my knees got painful, my legs were weak and my joints became sore. So now I ask for help because, as a person with two handicaps, I think I deserve it! Elderly folks and young children need our help, too. Wouldn't it be so great if we did not make such a stink about getting older and all respected and honored our elderly parents and friends. They have much wisdom gleaned from years of direct experience.

Carlissa helped me file a tax return and told me when and how to figure out how to get my stimulus check. She was so sweet, kind, and helpful. There was nothing she would not do for me in the three or four hours per day she spent helping me No wonder she chose to leave the agency after coming. That was part of the reason I went into despair and a temporary depression again. Plus Gary had to do all the things she used to do for me, especially on Tuesday or Thursday mornings it became difficult because he was supposed to go to his own home in Hamilton to take care of his own business like paying bills, checking up on his tenants or getting their rents, organizing his books and things in his "Pile" in the attic, etc.

Though it sometimes seems that we will never get better, especially when in the midst of crises and chaos, God never gives us more than we can handle, because with God, all things are possible if we just have the faith of a tiny mustard seed, quiet the mind, and listen to that "still, small voice within. He helps us handle all that we've been given and more, if we have faith. My path through a debilitating mental illness has made me a stronger, wiser, more compassionate person. After coming through so many ups and downs, I totally trust and have implicit faith in the Infinite One that is called God/Source, the Inner Being, Buddha, Christ, the Force, whatever it is you personally wish to call that omniscient Energy that created the Cosmos.

Navigating the ups and downs of mental illness as well as using various coping methods to deal with grief, loss, abandonment and egotistical melodramas in relationships has made my inner strength Herculean. And I do not even worry about the petty problems in life anymore. Life has become more playful and I feel light and joyful about most everything from one moment to the next precious moment. Life is a game to be enjoyed and played to the fullest, and I have immersed myself in the game. It has become a leelah (Sanskrit for "play") or Shiva's Cosmic Dance. Even the popular virus whose name I shall not mention since I know it has no power over me if I have strong faith and belief in a higher power that wishes to bring only goodness to His/Her precious children. There have been flus, bugs, and viruses since the beginning of time, and each one has run its course with or without vaccines.

After much education, information, and procrastination I made an informed choice to get conventional and doubly vaccinated myself with the Pfizer vaccine manufactured specifically for the dreaded "corona virus" with who knows which crap?! I personally believe the pandemic is just here as a clarion call to wake us up to the fact that we are all ONE' and we are our brothers' and sisters' keepers. Let's do unto others as we would have others do unto us! Be kind, for our sakes, please. A little bit of random acts of kindness goes a long way each and every day to make us aware that we are not alone here. I always feel better if I open the door at JC Penney for a mom with a stroller, a child, a person with a disability, someone in a wheelchair or an elderly person with a cane... They are not only grateful to me, but we smile at each other, and both feel better as we continue on along our daily journeys.

I believe there is a big paradigm shift taking place as Mother Earth is ascending, and anything unlike love is coming up for healing. There are lots of things that need to shift in order for everyone of all races, creeds, and colors, to be in harmony with one another, to let go of fear, greed, hatred, and judgments of all kinds, including judgment of ourselves.

I recently came out of a depression, and I realized after three months of sitting on the couch watching reruns of old Netflix series I'd never seen like "The Good Witch", "Virgin River", "The Queen's Gambit", and finally Shonda Rhimes' "How to Get Away With Murder" which was so compelling and fascinating that my beau and I got pulled into the fantasies of each character, just like a drug. We had become zombies like the walking dead, only we were the "sitting lazy kind; the only time we'd get off the couch to move was to feed ourselves with quickie microwaveable meals, to use the john, feed our two Manx kitties, or go to bed, and by that time we were stiff, achy, and could barely move. Life is never stagnant; without movement and a desire to grow spiritually, emotionally, mentally, intellectually, and to be part of the local community as well as global community, what's the point of having a body anyway? My beau and I never had sex, or when we were in bed together, we were too pooped or hyped up from the adrenaline of watching sex, drugs, and rock and roll on the TV screen was mesmerizing (actually there was very little music, but somehow the passion of both heterosexuals, bi-sexual, and homosexual sex and passion pulled us in like a drug. We even found the violence very interesting, too since we are rarely ever violent with each other, our children, grandchild, or our many friends, or ever filled anger, with rage or passion. It takes way too much energy and work. Gary is passive, I'm passive aggressive, and though I'm a very sensuous woman I'm still avoiding having sex with him after nearly nine years of being together. "Oh, no, Mr. Bill. Sex, what the fuck? So I either become a compete monk, not even having the desire to masturbate with my "Power tool", my Panabrator vibrator, or I'll occasionally fulfill my needs outside the relationship with one or two side guys who were formerly "ex-boyfriends. That seemed to be safer and more exciting. It was also clandestine for the guys, but not for me. I always told my beau about it, and he said it was just fine with him, but deep down I think he must have been hurt or felt unloved and unappreciated since he is the man who takes care of all my material, spiritual, emotional, and financial problems, all my emotional needs to be cuddled, cared for, and if I was sick or in the hospital, he'd be the one to show up every day and take care of all the bills at my home as well as his. Gary is definitely a 'keeper". He is an intellectual, philosopher, historian, and knows all the old songs I never heard Growing up as a long haired hippie in the sixties who went to college twice, got two degrees, and continues to grow as a liscensed Science of Mind practitioner who recently completed all the years of study necessary to get his degree from Centers for Spiritual Living in order to be a professional paid affirmative prayer practitioner, he works hard at growing as a man, a spiritual person, and a caring human in service to humanity and Mother Earth n the way of conservation and deeply caring for the environment. I am so very proud of him. I love his wit and the way he stimulates my mind and makes me laugh in bed as well as constantly throughout the day. It's hard to keep up with him intellectually and it's like living with Robin Williams or Rodney Dangerfield, Peter Sellers. George Burns, and Don Rickles all combined. I've got to be on my toes when we are together, or I'll miss the meaning of his many jokes.

He is very industrious, committed and loyal to me, has the biggest, kindest, most expansive open heart, and knows how to lead without being pedantic or egotistical; he's very quiet, a great listener, and just sees where the Eckhart Tolle group's members want to go next in their personal lives allowing each one a say in order to share exactly the experiences they are going through in relation to the book they are studying at the time. After mastering Tolle's two bestsellers, "A New Earth" and "The Power of Now" Twice, they studied the teachings of Byron Katie, and now they are reading books by Michael Singer, a man who wrote *The Surrender Experiment*, as well as *The Untethered Soul*. I am now reading a book he read already and is on another with the group called *Your Spiritual Power* Both books are by Michael Singer and I love the one entitled "The Surrender Experiment" after Gary suggested reading this because he told me this Zen student and philosophy teacher knew both Ram Dass and Swami Muktananda, my precious guru and teacher.

I read slowly and sometimes it takes me months to get through an entire book of less than three hundred pages because I have to read the same passages over and again to imbibe exactly what their meaning is. I don't mind though. I've loved to read since I was a kid — especially non-fiction, romance novels, and murder mysteries like those of Agatha Christie with her famous characters, Hercule Poirot and Mrs Marple.

Gary is slightly unconventional, whereas I am usually very unconventional; I used to go to the nude beach and walk around topless in nature on a regular basis back in my forties and fifties. I am more conservative now, but at one time I wanted to live in or start my own "clothing optional", polyamorous, free love community, but as I age and I love being a grandmother more each day, those older needs are shifting and changing each day. I love writing, and I still have a dream to finish this long book someday soon — perhaps this year. I've been living and writing this "masterpiece" of a life since 1992 when I was first a student at Mercer County Community College after coming out of a mental hospital in Piscataway where I spent three months after divorcing my first husband whom I still loved, and leaving my two children with him. Even though we had joint custody of our two little ones, deep down I still missed the old comfortable, joyful life we shared together as parents and daily companions on a spiritual yogic path that began in the autumn of 1982 when he asked me to move in with him after a whirlwind romance of just three weeks of dating, no sex, just a proper courtship, though he had been pursuing me for nearly eighteen months when he first met me at the Freehold Meditation Center, but I thought he was a skinny, intellectual geek, so I went out with the other two available males there, Steve, and Art. Both very nice guys, but not the perfect ons for me. I was looking for a good father for my children and someone who could provide well for me and the children. So, when he asked me one day while we were walking and singing together n route to the East Brunswick Mall just a few miles from where we lived in the comfortable home built by his millionaire strict Orthodox Jewish father, Eli, I said

"No. Definitely not. Are you crazy"? I barely know you. If I were ever to do anything like that, you'd have to marry me. I had already had my heart broken too many times before without a long courtship which led to a legal and spiritual commitment for life. Until death do us part. All that, and marriage just turned out to be no more permanent or exciting than a long, smelly fart! No, truly. I jest. David was a great provider, terrific dad, relatively good husband when he was not controlling, or psychologically abusive. We both had too many issues from traumatic childhoods to be able to relate sexually or intimately at all. We only "hooked up", if you know what I mean, jelly bean, about once per month, on the full moon, whether we liked it or not. Most of the time we did everything to avoid enjoying ourselves in bed; so, when we finally did, the sex was quick and terribly unsatisfying for me. I know he got his rocks off, but I take a long time to just relax; I need lots of romance, deep kissing, and stimulation of my thighs, breasts, and other erotic erogenous zones just to be able to relax and get wet. As a mom I always had so much on my mind, and we had a "Family Bed" when Gabriel was born at home. And he never left it. It was not conducive to having much good, if any, sex. I don't think I ever thought about my own sensual or sexual needs until I was in the wedding band, "Smooth Sailin" with Tony Paritzi when I was twenty-nine years old in 1984 six months after Gabriel was born, and I could finally shine onstage in clubs singing and dancing for small to medium sized audiences in small, intimate clubs down the Jersey shore like "The Chanel Club where I first met Tony. He was tall, dark, handsome, Italian, and plays a mean piano. With a smooth, sexy voice that sounded just like Neil Diamond. He was also married to a beautiful blond, French woman with whom he had a daughter and son. They shared a lovely colorful home of lavender, pink, purples, and greens on the porch in beautiful, spirit filled Ocean Grove a few blocks from the beach that was filled inside with angels, a piano, opera on the "C. D.s, and coincidentally, these two were not having sex anymore either. What a set-up for excitement, adventure, a clandestine affair, and two failed marriages within a few years of knowing one another.

I loved performing in this band which paid excellent money for mostly part-time week-end work, though I spent most of my wages on beautiful costumes, long dangling rhinestone and black earrings and other bangles that shone on stage almost as much as me., Once we played for a political function. And another time for my husband's former boss, John Krahnert, at Equitable Insurance Company Sometimes we performed at fairs on the beach or other corporate functions. I was having the time of my life! It was so much fun and it gave me time to shine away from the house where I was always

being a great "supermom, part-time career woman as a massage therapist and healer at the Awareness Health Service" run by herbalist, lecturer, and renowned teacher, David Winston, founder of the 'Herbalist and Alchemist tinctures. He and his mom started that small company in his mom, Marilyn's, living room until it went viral and now his tinctures are in many of the local health food stores including "The Whole Earth Center" here in Princeton. After several months of working for David, he taught me about Native American sweat lodges, smudging, the sacredness of the Native American connection to Mother Earth, her plants, wild creatures, as well as a few other more things Biblical in nature, if you understand my meaning. Gosh, what a wild, untamed wife and mother was I! Retreat 4/2021

In April, 2021, I went on a spiritual retreat in Texas with the nutritionist, author, and host of a daily radio show on WBAI, Dr. Gary Null. I put the cost of the $2,500 retreat as well as the air fare – not to mention the wonderful therapeutic 90-minute massage I received there – on three different credit cards, two of which had high percentage rates.

I had problems sleeping just before I left on the trip and a gnawing feeling in my gut like I was a bit frightened to go by myself without my boyfriend or another person helping me with my luggage and other things my home health aides at home would normally help me with, such as daily bathing, dressing, cooking.

I did not realize it would be OK for me to take my medication because I mistakenly thought I was going to be part of a special "study group" where lab work was done and other things. Besides, I'd already decided to go off the meds after reading a book about them that made me realize most of them were emotionally and chemically addictive, and many of them had negative side effects.

I had wanted to go on one of Dr. Null's retreats for years, So, I had the warning signs, I had already paid for the trip. So, I ignored the warnings, and went on the retreat in this beautiful, pristine villa surrounded by beautiful flora and fauna with animals like guinea hens and colorful, proud peacocks walking freely around the property helping one to relax in the lovely surroundings and being able to commune with some of these beautiful animals Dr. Null had rescued like a pony and a kitty too. He said he'd rescued lots of animals which was something that truly attracted me to him. I love animals myself; and if I had the money, I'd do the same thing. He is quite a philanthropic humanitarian. He always shares that he does not charge for any of his services; he gives away most of his gifts for free because that is what his mother told him to do.

I loved listening to all of Dr. Null's stories and lectures. However, being with Dr. Null was like being around the guru. After a while, all the shift finally comes up and hits the fan, if you know what I mean. This was a vegan retreat. I had every desire to be vegan, or at least vegetarian, like we were when my first husband, David, and I were up at the ashram,

I really loved Dr. Null; his beautiful home which he was so kind to share with us during the retreat, was like an ashram to me, and he was like the guru. I started to revere him and put him above myself because he was so successful, so rich in money, in homes, and in all his accomplishments. He had written many books that were successful and making a great difference in peoples' lives, He was curing supposedly "incurable illnesses by helping to influence or change peoples' diets and lifestyles. As a man in his early sixties, he was incredibly young looking and "fit", still running marathons in New York City; and I began to compare myself to him. As a person with a disability, I still get around pretty well and I can dance in ecstasy on any dance floor even with some arthritis in my knees and other joints right now. But that's probably because I hang out at the wrong joints every now and then. Actually, that is a lie. Wherever I go, whether it be a bar, nightclub, or restaurant I bring my loving kindness, deep interest in other people, and fun-loving nature.

The retreat facilitator, Barbara, and LuAnne, a psychologist, nurse, and former nurse at a regular allopathic hospital, went to every length to see that I was comfortable – including moving me from the hotel far from the retreat center where I was on the second floor and had to climb a lot of stairs while holding onto my cane and an outside railing. I shared my room with a lovely black lady named Melissa, who was very competent, intelligent, sweet, and caring, and who advocated for me. No one seemed to think I should be on the second floor in that particular hotel.

Luckily, there was a Best Western much closer to the retreat center in a different town that had a room available on the second floor, but the guru is great. Gurumayi and Baba knew I needed two things—an elevator to help me get up there easily with my luggage, and, lo and behold, scrambled eggs! Finally, the extra protein my body was craving for some grounding. Even though I felt a little guilty about going against Dr. Null's protocol, I knew this was what my body needed to ground me and get better sleep.

I had been in the habit of eating some eggs or some fish for protein nearly every day, so the sudden change to a completely vegan diet at the retreat did not work for my particular constitution. I stopped sleeping at night: I had way too much energy. By that time, my mood stabilizer and the quietiapine I took to have a full night's sleep, were completely out of my system. I'd already stopped seeing or talking to my psychologist at home and my psychiatrist, Dr. M at Al Access Mental Health in Princeton told me if I was unwilling to take medication any longer, she was no longer needed, so she had dropped me too; so, I felt as if I'd lost all my support systems. And my largest support system, my beau, Gary, was back taking care of our home and cats in New Jersey besides keeping up with his own home, bills, and friends' needs in Hamilton.

I told Barbara and LuAnne about my plight, and that I felt very anxious from not sleeping well three nights in a row. From experience, I know that that means I am out of balance in some way and starting to go down the rabbit hole of fear and doubt. I apologized to the two women because it was such a wonderful, peaceful place to be; and they had been so helpful.

I left the retreat early and flew home, depressed and three thousand dollars poorer...

At home, I was already drinking two completely vegan juices daily that either my home health aide or Gary would prepare for me on the week-ends. One was all carrots, apples, berries, and whatever other fruits that we had fresh in the frig. My morning drink was made of a ripe banana, an apple, spinach or kale and parsley from our own garden, a teaspoon of maple syrup, if needed, and a teaspoon of flax seed. So, I was already juicing and eating pretty well for my particular constitution; and when I'd go to Princeton Fitness and Wellness to swim or exercise in the therapy pool and ride the stationary bike, I'd usually stop at Chris' Cafe to get a protein and berry drink and/or a sandwich made with avocado which Gary says means "no vocado" Avocado is one of my favorite foods; and is actually a fruit which I just discovered. It is almost all fat, but the delicious, healthy kind of fat that lowers cholesterol.

So, what I am saying is I was already treating my body/mind with a lot of love, nutritious foods, regular exercise, dance, walking in nature several days per week just by waking the grounds of my own home or occasionally in the park, but almost daily to the mailbox several blocks away with Gary and our black and white, long haired Manx Zen kitty, Lovey Bear following behind us just like a dog would follow his Master. My upstairs neighbor, calls him "Bunny Cat" because he looks like a bunny when he runs to chase squirrels around our property.

But I had failed in my attempt to improve myself and had wasted money! You know the nature of the crazy, judgmental, subconscious or even conscious ego-mind, whatever you do is just not good enough as another. Gosh, the mind goes on and on about not being good enough. And then there's the "shoulda, woulda, coulda syndrome. Or the "if onlys" and/or the "what ifs". "If only I hadn't shot myself. If only I was not disabled and hemiplegic. If only I wasn't so old. How can I begin to realize ALL my dreams now while I'm already in my sixties? The adversary, or demonic ego mind has so many ways to trick us into not doing what we love to do by making us think we are not good enough or we don't deserve. And the comparisons! Some other person has written way more books than me while I've only written and published one anthology of poetry. Come on. You know Linda Ronstadt and Barbra Streisand has made way more money, starred in Broadway musicals and movies, got grammys, or has made many albums and has touched more lives while I have barely gotten started." Talk about self-sabotage.

DEPRESSION

This is what I feel like during times of depression, from my journal end of May 2021.

Ever since I've returned from the Gary Null vegan retreat in the end of April I have been spiraling from a place of anxiety and fear into a deeper place of depression, anxiety, and apathy in which I really don't feel like myself and don't care to get up when I wake up in the morning which is so not like me.

When I'm indoors I just don't want to do much of anything. I have no interest to look at my e-mails, check my Facebook posts, or even call anyone because I am so embarrassed and I feel ashamed when I get into these dark states of mind. I wish I could just love and accept myself when I'm like this, but I am completely judgmental, and I rarely see a way out when I get like this even though I know it is a temporary funk, especially because I've been here before.

If I go for a walk outside it feels like I am afraid of everything. I don't want to go to shopping or to the gym even though I know it will make me feel somewhat better.

It's difficult for me to dress, especially to put my bathing suit on; and I've not had a home health aide in months since Carlissa left, and I only had Cesy for a very short time to replace her. Gary has to do just about everything from all the food shopping, cooking, laundry, pay all my bills, and sometimes even drive me to PT. if I've not slept most of the night.

I've not had a psychiatrist or psychologist from AAMH (All Access Mental Health) since the end of March because I stopped taking the quietiapine (seroquel) and also went off the Depakote in March; so, Dr. Mudiah discharged me.

When I came back from Texas where I did not sleep much for four days straight while I was out there on a completely vegan diet of liquids and vegetables, grains, and stews; and I got so very anxious about that I decided to start back on both the medications I'd been taking for manic depression. I had a lot of both the Depakote and seroquel left over which I had not thrown out, just in case; and then before those ran out, my primary care physician, Dr. Nair, agreed to write prescriptions for me to hold me over until I could get back into the system.

Unfortunately, it takes a few months because they have to go through a whole in-take process again which is a pain in the butt, especially when one is anxious or having suicidal thoughts. I know I would not have acted upon them; but just the same it is pretty scary to observe the crap going on in your mind and feeling as if I have no control over the irrational, negative thoughts. The medications do not seem to work at all when I am this down except that they do manage to get me to sleep. Unfortunately, I never stay asleep for more than several hours before I have to pee; and then I don't always get back to sleep for a while.

I've not been to church since March, and this is unfortunate because I know it would help me because I would be better able to combat these lies from the negative entities surrounding me and replace the icky thoughts with ones of Truth.

Fortunately, the angels and animal totems are still with me because every now and then my malaise and boredom are interrupted by a moment of joy and peace when nature presents me with the gift like a glimpse of a baby rabbit running in front of me as I walk down the street to go to the mailbox or a brilliant red male cardinal on a holly branch on the side of my apartment while swinging quietly on the swing bench. I also saw a lovely female which has a lovely red crest and is like a light brown or gray in color. Maybe that's his mate.

I was also blessed to see a little tan fawn coming out of a thicket at Mountain Lakes Reserve where Kyrie and I danced and drummed with Ange Chianese a few times and some of our friends from Dance Improv Live. Gary drove me there so we could go for a walk. Nature really does help with improving these horrible states of mind. So does walking.

I remember being very euphoric in February after going off the medications slowly, so I suppose this is just the opposite polarity.

Gary and I have been sitting a lot on the couch just watching lots of different series on Netflix like "Virgin River" and "The Queen's Gambit" which I really enjoyed, and "Viola Davis in "How to Get Away with Murder" which we stopped watching in midstream because I realized we were both so addicted to it, and watched for many hours per day instead of being in "real relationship." Television is an addiction just like a drug, I realized. Other than the fact that I could temporarily relax and lose myself in a fantasy world where I did not have to think much about my problems, it really was not very therapeutic. I certainly had no motivation to write or work on my memoir or anything else, but like everything else, I know this, too, shall pass. If I could only stop feeling so ashamed for being weak and imperfect, in my eyes. The funny thing is I know that God, my angels, and guides, are not judging me at all. It's all just me. Stop it, Meryl. You don't deserve to be punished like this.

CARING FOR THE EARTH

Due to my love of and for animals and the ecology of the planet. I know veganism, or at least vegetarianism, is a healthier way to live, especially at this moment in time, with all the terrible climate changes like flooding, tsunamis, uncontrollable fires in California, droughts, babies and children dying from starvation in many parts of the world including some parts of one of the richest countries in the world, the US A. I am so sad about how we, as a human species, can be so inhumane to one another, to our precious Mother Earth, her children, and her creatures with terrible hydrofracturing of Mother Earth which leads to who knows what horrible consequences. Anyway, I'm getting off track here.

HOPE

Journal: Saturday, November 6, 2021

My beau, Gary, treats me to delicious, nutritious food, fulfilling relationships, a fulfilling career, great sex, orgasms, and all the wonderful blessings this life has to offer! When I personally allow myself to slow down to receive these things, I feel great!

I know anything is possible with a dream, a bit of faith, determination, patience, and God's help. Because with God, all things are possible. "Ask and ye shall receive." Just like it says in the Bible, though I don't read it much these days, preferring my own wise counsel of the school of hard knocks, direct life experiences that come from lots of failures and direct experiences. Like Natasha Beddingfield says "I am unwritten. Sometimes my tries are outside the lines." We've been conditioned to not make mistakes I also like gentle hatha yoga, stretching, dance aerobics, swimming in the local community pools outdoors or indoors when it gets too cold outside, living and planting flowers and herbs like basil, and dill. in my garden of green Love Light while singing beautiful songs to my plants. Sometimes I'll sing Joe Cocker's "You are so Beautiful to me", sometimes new and spontaneous words and feelings come to me, and they sing back to me in deep appreciation, but in quieter tones. I love communing with nature and noticing the natural beauty within and all around me. Sometime I am in awe of it. Like the magnificent orange and pink sunsets I can see when in Sarasota, Florida off Siesta Key Beach when you just know in your heart there has to be a god because who could paint such a magnificent tapestry of colors with the azure blue sky above with big, fluffy white cumulus clouds fading into the blue green clean ocean with the radiant Grand Central Sun, reflecting that radiant reddish orange all the colors of the rainbow love that we are with a gift of a big orange beach ball sitting setting magnificently right onto that coolish clean blue green water like a young maiden lover sits upon her man gazing deeply into his big brown beautiful eyes of love, as if for the very first time.

It's a new, holy present moment, and we are alive together. Precious. Presence. New. Sacred. Light. As a feather. Free floating through the water, ether, air, and noticing how the sweet flames of love flicker in the firelight. Right now, All of us. One Big Bliss-ball of a Being. Centered in the heart. Caring deeply about each and every one of us—equally. No one is better or worse. Each one is unique as a crystal. As a snowflake. Are we not blessed to be here now at this sacred time in Mother Gaia's Herstory?! It makes you just want to dive right into it now as you are reading it while it still feels warm and yummy on your skin and in your mind, doesn't it? The liquid love water, I mean. Not me.

Speaking of love and special experiences. I remember one my friend's, a student, fellow dancer and model who had a great body and who could dance very well with me at the Patio in Sarasota. Anyway, after lying on the beach one afternoon we got into the warm ocean together. We'd never made love, had sex, or even held hands because I was interested in my teacher, Sid, and my old beau back home, John Jay from Toms River, but just as good friends and fellow Light Workers we share heart energies in the womb of the Mother Ocean's sweet embrace. Heart to heart. The water would move us toward the shore as the tide came in, but he, being a bit taller than me, making sure I would not go too far in or too far down; we just matched up all our sweet chakras, and let the ocean bathe us in her Liquid Love. It was heavenly ad so pure. I could have let him hold me in his strong arms like that forever. It was timeless, safe, and I still got to keep my precious virginity. For one more day, at least. Even though I'm a mother of three grown kids and grandmother to one charming six-year-old mulatto grandson, I am still a virgin to this day. Virgin comic that is. I still would love to try to be the next Mrs. Maizel. What a great, funny life of adventure that courageous lady leads.

There's nothing like making love or just holding your lover in the ocean, by the way – dancing to one another's rhythmic rhyming heartbeats until the curtain of darkness suddenly closes upon the beauty of the sunny day and you are finally ready to leave the ocean or rivers' gorgeous Godly divine embrace like the happy prancing dancing, loving fairy dolphin mermaid you are, girlfriend. All you mermen, too. Then you deserve a romantic dinner of yummy Thai, Indian, Italian, French, or Japanese sushi, whatever floats your boat. The choices of where, when, and how you eat are infinite! That's how sex, romance, and lovemaking is. But you got to know you both deserve it, and just make time for it. Take a few moments to just look deep into one another' eyes after listening to your favorite romantic music like Al Jarreau, Barry White, Earth, Wind, and Fire, Freddy Jackson, or Luther Vandross. Unless you are more into Sinatra, Ella Fitzgerald, or Stevie Wonder. Like life, love and food is an infinite smorgasbord of fun, filled with travel to beaches, romantic places, or you can just do a "Staycation" at home. Dim all the lights. Pour the wine. Start the music. Time to get ready for cuddling, relaxation, and love.

But first you must be still. Silence all cell phones, televisions, doorbells, children, and breathe together' be willing to go into the silence. Dance together wherever you are. Do the vertical mambo if you are too exhausted to stand up.

Right here in Princetonius where I have a lovely westerly view if I walk a few blocks to the west before the sun sets. I love to watch the sun set slowly while meditating, quietly chanting OM or om Namah Shivayah to myself before Gary and I finally hold hands on the couch for a while before making out.

By the way, this has yet to happen. We spent the last two months watching other actors in the divine drama have sex and act out their passion on a television stage just for our benefit during co-vid so we have only just begun to explore the subtler aspects of lovemaking since we both have physical disabilities. I am hemiplegic and he has auditory processing disorder, and is legally peripherally blind, so I make him take off his thick lenses and feel his way around my voluptuous map. He is a stubborn male, and never has to ask for directions.

He also happens to be very funny, witty, and tired in bed, and once one of us starts joking or thinking of different songs to play we laugh like crazy for hours at a time, but that's a good thing. but ==And we are committed to getting our bodies into better shape since we have a strong desire (at least I do) to be more flexible and stronger, especially on the left side of my body which has been way weaker ever since shooting myself I head on June 1,1987.

I love chanting, singing, dancing, and showing off my assets while Gary is much quieter and humbler, but we balance each other out. Whenever I get too excited or enthusiastic about music, a show, a performer, God, or chanting kirtan, Gary says "Honey, where are those tranquilizer darts I ordered?"

I like private discussions with my own counsel of twelve, usually during my dream state. And sometimes I think my beloved and I meet over there because even when he is home in Hamilton two nights per week and I am here in Princeton he still has a tough time sleeping, I still think if I "Seek with a pure heart that I shall find solutions to every seeming problem – especially when I ask Lord Jesus Christ Consciousness directly for His precious, divine guidance from moment to moment. He tells me "Knock and the door shall be opened unto you, my precious Daughter of Light and Fun. You are Loved, he says. You are my beloved child, tender, sweet, and mild. I will never abandon or forsake you in your time of need from now or until the end of time which is not. We will be lovers for eternity, my precious one.".

REFLECTIONS

Depression and having a physical handicap have taught me humility, to slow down and "smell the roses", and to have much more compassion and empathy for others and myself. It has also taught me that it is all right to be human and to ask for love and support from others when I need it. I don't always have to be the Herculean caretaker of others and the one who is usually in control. As I allow myself to receive from others, I am creating a blessing for them as well as myself.

I've also met lots of new friends I never would have chosen to meet as a result of this adventure through mental illness and because I have a physical handicap. Prior to this I was afraid to approach or relate to someone who was blind or confined to a wheelchair. I would have feelings of sympathy, but I'd see people with handicaps as somehow less than or different from myself.

Now I see the beauty and strength of others with mental illness, or physical or mental disorders. Their special gifts would have remained foreign to me had I not chosen to experience life from this unique perspective. Through this I've come to realize that people with "different" abilities are easy to talk to and no different from anyone else. We all share the same divinity, human feelings and needs.

At Griggs Farm I was very inspired by a friend and neighbor who was blind. I used to think that if I'd become blind from the gunshot to my head I wouldn't even want to get up in the morning. But the truth is that most people with disabilities learn to adjust after a while and lead regular lives like most everyone. It's a bit more challenging having a disability, and we have a unique contribution to make to others who are seemingly perfect. We are all perfect just as we are, disabled or not. And we all face challenges in life no matter how perfect we seem to be. All souls experience adversity of some type or other. The author, Charlotte Bronte, had the wisdom to say, "if we had no winter, the spring would not be so pleasant. If we did not sometimes taste of adversity, prosperity would not be so welcome."

I know sometimes it seems impossible to still all of our negative thoughts and judgments. Difficult at first, but very possible. Not you, you say? You think you are unworthy or unlovable. No, my dear ones. No matter what you've done or how guilty you feel, God loves you exactly the way you are. are. Without you God would not experience Him/Her/Itself perfectly! So, I'd say that makes you very important. You are Spirit incarnate in a beautiful physical form out here on the leading edge of thought! My non-physical friend and teacher, Abraham says,

"The basis of our life is freedom. The purpose of our life is joy. We are only here for a short time just to experience a few moments of joy, so lighten up and relax a bit because as eternal beings we will never get it all done." It is the journey that truly matters, not the destination. Your destination back to the One God is already assured. It's part of your divine blueprint. No matter how hard you try you cannot separate yourself from Source, the God within and all about you.

It's been years since I planned and executed the shooting, and I still am unable to use my left arm and hand after putting a bullet in my precious head. The entire nightmare seems surreal now it was so long ago and so unlike my nature it is hard to believe this experience ever really happened. But I still walk with a limp and can no longer jog or run, but I've made the best of the situation over the years, and now accept how lucky I am just to be alive, and try on a regular basis to put my attention on the present moment and all the things I CAN DO.

I use my right arm and hand for practically everything, including driving and swimming, massaging myself, friends, and clients. And I have a perfectly good Spirit, great heart, and healthy body for making love. Sometimes I use my mouth to assist in dressing myself if I have no one to help me.

To open jars I put them between my thighs to stabilize them, and in order to cut vegetables or fruits I use a cutting board I got in rehab at JFK hospital with a nail stuck through the board which I use to impale and stabilize the onions or other veggies so that I can chop them with my right hand.

I have my beau, Gary, other friends and assistants who help me with dressing sometimes and putting on my jewelry if I have a show or a wedding to attend. Otherwise, I am fine dressing myself with a little extra time and effort.

The bottom line about getting my arm and hand working the way it once did is that I am not really attached to the results. I feel so happy just as I am that I do not really care one way or the other if I get back the use of my left arm and hand. There is little I cannot do now that I did before as a WHOLE woman, and possibly I am a bit less intimidating having a physical disability. I happen to be an extremely powerful person who is very intense with a LOT of energy and enthusiasm. When people see me walking with a limp and not as strong as some others, they do not expect much from me or feel threatened by me. But then they hear me sing or dance at a concert or club, and they are amazed by the way I move and how joy exudes from each pore in my body.

I always laugh at myself – especially when my children make fun of me. Sometimes I laugh so hard from the way they make fun of something I said or the way I walk funny or dance crazy that my laughter becomes a guffaw and I just cannot stop. Gary makes me laugh so hard that, at this age, I have to remember to wear a mini pad because I end up peeing in my pants. There is nothing I need to change, no special exercises I must do, to be my Beautiful Self.

Nothing you must change or do to be "Your Best, most beautiful, glorious Self filled with energy, love, wisdom, enthusiasm, wonder, and awe at the Divine Mystery of Life as we know it, here and now."Just recognize and love yourself just as you are in this precious, holy moment. You are God and Goddess, expressed in form, and you are Glorious in every way, my friends! You are so unique and beautiful that even God himself cannot remake you if you were to destroy yourself, which you cannot truly do, anyway. You have always existed, and you will exist for eternity, so just relax and enjoy the ride even when it gets bumpy.

I enjoy hiking up small mountains and through pretty, winding trails at the Sourland Mountain Reserve and Pettoranello Gardens in Princeton with my beau, Gary. I also love walking near and around the lake at Mercer County Park. And writing poetry there about birds, foxes, and deer, and the Great Blue Heron who come to visit me at Pettoranello Gardens in Princeton.

Each one of us has our own special totem animals that give us guidance from the wild. My own personal totems are deer, turkey vulture, cat, Great Blue Heron, wolf, and turtle. I am very attuned to the deer. They are my main totem animal, and give me messages all the time about my next adventure, or help me find my way when I am lost on the road. Hawks do that as well. Sometimes red fox comes into my life to remind me of the importance of camouflage and secrecy.

Once, several years ago, I was extremely tired of driving late at night and got temporarily lost on my way home from my bass player, George's, house, so I was guided to get off the highway and stop for a rest in this park. There I saw an amazing BUCK with eight points on his antlers who brought me clarity, energy, and helped me to get grounded. Moments later I felt quiet and centered enough to turn around on route 78 and proceed on my journey in the RIGHT direction. It was deer bringing me strength, peace, and who helped me to ground all the energy running through me at that time when I was feeling somewhat manic. I am a petite woman, and at times it has been challenging for me to stay grounded and centered when I feel the fast-moving Kundalini energy moving quickly soaring up my spine. At those times lying on the ground quietly feeling Mother Earth beneath me helps to calm the energy and relax my mind if I start to feel a bit frightened by all the energy coming through my body.

One of my many home health aides, Anya, and I had the great fortune of seeing a beautiful male red fox outside my bedroom window when she was styling my hair a few four years ago. It was coming as a gift from the wild to bring peace, harmony, leadership, and to remind me not to be arrogant or dominant, but appreciative that Anya did so much for me even though she does not always stay as long as I'd like. We had just had a small disagreement, and I was thinking I should call the agency she worked for to complain she did not give me enough hours, but after seeing fox, I realized I was being petty, and rather than focusing on what she or anyone did NOT give me, fox reminded me to be more be appreciative of all the kind things she DID do for me very efficiently in a short amount of time. She not only did most of the housework, did most of the laundry, and cooked breakfast for me and my beau, Gary, but she helped me made soups, stews, and turkey meat loafs by cutting up vegetables that would take me longer due to my disability. Anya also did nearly all my laundry, made my bed and changed my sheets every week. And she graced us with her joyous greeting in the morning and sometimes brought her dog, Goo-goo, with her to visit; he sat with us on the couch and allowed us to pet him for as long as we wanted. That way I did not feel dog-deprived since I love dogs a lot, but I have such an active lifestyle that I either gave away my last few dogs due to depression or financial hardship, and sadly lost my favorite Maltese puppy, Murphy, right after his third birthday, to Addison's disease. So I really appreciate when other people share their dogs with me or let me pet their pups. I especially love when they lick my face and kiss me on the mouth. I felt so blessed to have Anya and Goo-Goo as my special friends whom I saw on a regular basis. Anya had to leave my service while I was in Merwick Rehab following my hospitalization for pneumonia, but I still miss her.

Now what the hell do all these ridiculous labels mean, and do they actually serve any practical purpose to help the millions of people afflicted by mental illness? Well, maybe a few. If you believe you are sick, and it helps you to think taking a pill or multitude of pills is going to help, more power to you. I was on Depakote, a mood stabilizer, on and off, for twenty-three years, and sometimes Wellbutrin, an anti-depressant, and I believe they are helpful for some of the time, but it is just a temporary "fix". I still got depressed while taking the medications if the circumstances of my life are challenging emotionally or economically. When I was not allowing God's energy to flow through me, or if I allowed my vibration to dip so low that I became fearful of just making ends meet financially.

You know what I mean. The rent and the car payment are due at the beginning of the month. The price of of groceries and Medications is exorbitant. Sometimes it can all just be overwhelming if one is living at or below the poverty level which I have been for most of my life as a single mom except for the five and a half years I was married to my first husband, David, who was very industrious and had a knack for making lots of money.

Luckily, for all our sakes, even though we are divorced, he has been kind and generous to me, our children, and my youngest daughter, who is not even his child. David was so kind and magnanimous he helped my son pay off half the new Chevy Cobalt I'd purchased in a hypomanic phase in 2006 for $18,000, eighteen years after we'd divorced. It was my son's idea because I was truly struggling with the $313.00 monthly payments on it, due to a bankruptcy I filed in the year 2000, and poor credit at the time. Gabriel asked me to find out what was the balance on my loan after I'd been paying for about seventeen months while living below poverty level, getting food stamps, and governmental assistance with utilities. A small bit of SSI and part-time income from massage was barely enough to cover rent, groceries, and clothes for me and my daughter. Let alone a new car payment.

Then there are utilities, phone, cell phone if you have one, cable TV, and then on top of all that, the price of gasoline is exorbitant. Sometimes, even if a poor person or single mom receives food stamps, that person may have no extra money for little things like toothpaste, napkins, toilet tissue, paper towels, and diapers. No wonder I got depressed. Just writing about it know I am thinking "Just shoot me now and put me out of my misery". Nah. I've already been there, done that. Besides, if I was gone, who would clean up mistakes left by the rest of the unenlightened human race?! Each one of us needs to take responsibility NOW for some small facet of the many sad problems and circumstances technology has created. Like the devastation of our environment for hundreds of years. We must ALL love our Mother Earth, Goddess Gaia, and become stewards of our precious planet now before it is too late. Before there is No planet upon which to live and thrive. We could just blow ourselves up right out of existence if we ever had a Third World War. And some of what our government does and condones today is leading to that. So, let's have peace, guys, by acting in a peaceful, loving, kind, compassionate manner and being the peace we seek. Hatred and violence only begets more of same. Love begets love. If our Lord Jesus, had an inkling (and he does, I am sure) of all the violence, torture, and murder that has been committed in His holy name he would be turning over in his tomb! Seriously, folks, can't we all just get along? Whatever happened to "Do unto others as you would have them do unto you? And "Love thy neighbor as thyself". As far as I'm concerned, I AM my brothers' and my sisters' keeper, and I try to be kind and compassionate to as many people I can the world over, if not in person, at least in my prayers, chants, intentions, and donations to organizations that help those who are temporarily less fortunate and cannot help themselves.

Kindness goes a long way. In little things in our daily lives, and in BIG THINGS like people engaged in warfare or large disputes over territory.

If I could go from years of imbalance, mood swings, relationship addiction, co-dependence, lethargy, exhaustion, and boredom with my comfortable life to one in which I appreciate every precious moment as a gift from God, know that you can too. I still have occasional challenges in relationships and managing money, but I am always learning and growing, so I'm never anxious or fearful anymore no matter what is going on in my outer world. I realize I am a deliberate creator of all the people, circumstances, and activities in my sweet life. I constantly create my reality anew, and I know my outer world is a projection of my own inner consciousness and thoughts. When I attract an experience or person, I don't like I know there is still something for me to learn about myself; there is a subconscious belief or attitude I must change. God is truly All there is, and if I'm seeing something other than God, I'm observing or projecting a quality onto someone or something that I don't like about myself. Underneath all outer appearances and illusions there is only Consciousness expressing itself uniquely through each individual according to his or her own understanding.

If someone is angry with me, I try not to react immediately, or to take offense. Usually that person is overtired or unhappy with themselves, and just calling out for love, so I just send them a mental blessing instead of a "Fuck you" in return because I know that underneath they are just calling out for love. Even crazy New Jersey drivers who often seem to be in a hurry to go nowhere are just stressed out, tired, or impatient because of the fast-paced life we live here in the northeast. I simply send love and a mental blessing. I always let people cut in front of me on Route 206 or Route 1, or they would never get out of their parking lot after work during rush hour. I am courteous, polite, and kind, so I usually create the same kind of people even in traffic tie- ups that treat me with kindness, compassion, and generosity.

This is not to say that I never have moments of despair. But I know that I will recover, and I do recover more quickly.

SPIRIT

We are eternally loved and we are That Love itself. God, the only Life there is, dwells within us as us. This Infinite Intelligence thinks through our mind. Creates with it. And experiences the wonders of Life through our precious bodies, the temple of our very own soul. If we could quiet our minds right now in this instant, go inside; observe the perfection of the breath going in and out, we could open our hearts to That Supreme Love. We will feel it and know without a doubt that what I say is true. Ask wholeheartedly and the Truth shall be revealed to you. And it will set you free from the prison and duality that the limited, false thinking has created.

You and I are precious Daughters and Sons of God, and One with That Source itself. We are here to remember who we truly are. The only creative Power there is works through us to create whatever good we desire to see in this human form. Source never judges whatever it is we want to create in this illusory world of opposites. We are here to experience it all. For how would we come to appreciate the dawn until we have experienced the darkness of night? How could we even know the difference?

In order to experience Light and Truth we needed to imagine darkness. How could we really know and feel the fullest capacity of pleasure in human form until we have known pain? The beautiful former folksinger and head of the Siddha Yoga music department, Shambhavi Christian, says it so beautifully in her song, "Just love". "God is just. There is no high or low. The laughter and the weeping both create a rainbow. So just love. ". We are here to experience it all and make new choices in each moment based upon what we have learned and what is our innermost Truth and desire for our brethren, our planet, and ourselves in each new and holy moment.

There is no devil and you are not a sinner. You are pure, you are taintless, you are Consciousness, you are made from Love and this is your very nature. The only "devil" that exists is within your very own mind. That is judgment and FEAR. You make it real by giving these thoughts power.

I have experienced the power of fear directly and it will expand and manifest as whatever you believe if you don't put a reign on it. I've even "thought" myself into mental hospitals by dwelling for long periods in the place of fear and negativity. But it will have no power over you if you honor it and replace it with positive thoughts – ones of gratitude and love, hope, and faith. Because of the Law of Attraction, what we think about and dwell upon attracts more of the same types of thoughts. They then expand and manifest as our reality eventually in the physical world. Like attracts like. Happy, uplifting thoughts of love and appreciation attract more joy whereas negative thoughts bring us more of the same negative circumstances, so it behooves us to think about what we are wanting rather than what we are lacking. Keep your eyes on the prize until you have achieved and attained the object of your desires, my children.

Faith is the element, the "chemical", which, when mixed with prayer, gives one communication with Infinite Intelligence. It is the only agency by which the cosmic force can be harnessed and used by peoples of all faiths and traditions, in all cultures and walks of Life. According to Napoleon Hill, author of "Think and Grow Rich", "it is the eternal elixir which gives life, power, and action to the impulse of thought." Faith is the starting point of all accumulation of riches, whether they are physical, material, emotional, or spiritual. Faith is the basis of all miracles and mysteries, which cannot be analyzed or proven by the laws of science. Have faith in yourself, dear Ones, and faith in the Infinite.

Thoughts mixed with emotions constitute a magnetic force, which attract similar related thoughts. According to Hill, " A thought magnetized with deep emotion may be likened to a seed which, when planted in fertile soil, germinates, grows, and multiplies itself over and over again until that which was originally one small seed becomes countless millions of the same brand of seeds."

In that way the Law of Attraction will give you more of the same. For example, let's pretend that one night you can't get to sleep because something is disturbing you like poor finances, a bad relationship, poor health, etc., and that you wake up the next morning, "on the wrong side of the bed" feeling grouchy. You may rise with a negative thought in your mind like, " Oh, it's cloudy and rainy. It's going to be a terrible day." And through your expectation that is exactly what you create in your experience.

First, you stub your toe on the way to the bathroom. Your mind says, "I knew this was going to be a lousy day."

The next thing you know you burn the toast in the toaster, which the "evil housemate" set on the dark position. And you hate blackened toast! While you are running to save the burning toast, you turn your back on the poached eggs in the overflowing pan of water. The water boils all over the electric stove you just cleaned the night before. This has been my previous experience. Sound familiar?

Again, your mind says, "Oh, I just knew this was going to be a bad day. It's always something. I just can't win. I am so stupid – so incompetent. Poor me. I' m such a victim of circumstance." But, in reality, you created every last detail of your unfortunate morning with your original negative thought when you arose. The Law of Mind and Attraction is neutral. The Universe just said, "Yes" to your original idea about it being a bad day. And with every new negative thought you re-created the same scenario.

Let's look at a different scenario now.

You go to bed around 10:30 PM and get a full eight hours of deep sleep, waking up feeling rested and refreshed at 7:00 AM. You take your time to stretch slowly like a cat as you put on your fuzzy cat slippers and get out of bed. You rise with the sun thinking, "Wow, the sun is shining. It looks like it's going to be a beautiful day. I can't wait to shower, dress, eat breakfast, and wait for the adventure to unfold. I wonder what wonderful, pleasing friends I will meet and make today. What exciting adventures and circumstances will Life bring to me today? God, Nature is abundant and so am I. Money comes to me with ease and grace. I have the 'Midas touch'. Everything I touch turns to gold. My heart is golden, and I am kind. I am generous and giving of my time, talents, and energy.

God is unconditionally loving, omniscient, peaceful, beautiful, orderly, and creative. And so am I.

"I am forever light, beautiful, and youthful. Instead of aging, I am actually 'youth-ing'. I look and feel more beautiful, healthy, vibrant, sexy, and radiant than I did years ago! And I mean that sincerely. I am a divine expression of God in human form. It is through my own body and Mind that the Infinite experiences itself. I am the most important person in my Whole universe. No one deserves love or abundance more than I do. I deserve the best in life. I create positive, joyous experiences. God and I love myself unconditionally.

"I am healthy. I am wealthy. I am wise. I am balanced. I am clear. I am thriving. I am so grateful to be alive in a human form at this auspicious time in our history. I am so pleased and utterly thrilled with all the contrast in the Universe. It's like a humongous Divine Kitchen with thousands of ingredients to choose from to make my 'uniquely divine Soup of Life' experience. If there are some ingredients, I find I don't like I just put them back on the shelf once I've tried them out. No need to control or to judge them. I don't even have to give them a second thought. Manic depression. Schmanic depression. It's behind me now. It's in the past. And I'm enjoying the present too much to give the past another thought."

However, if you become too attached to a particular form, this kind of thinking can turn into....

The Fantasy

"....I think I'll move on to becoming a millionairess, marrying my handsome, sweet, talented and creative lover, buying a dream home on an island like Hawaii, Bermuda, or wherever Goddess sends us. Finishing my books, my two compact discs of original music and poetry, and enjoy watching my children grow and thrive for the rest of their happy lives. Then my beloved and I can spend more time alone together holding hands while we walk along the shore, watch movies and videos together, and just enjoy the simple pleasures of life like taking walks together, candlelit dinners, cuddling, great music, great sex, and each other's good company. God, it's all so good. We could even live in a community where there are no restrictions. One that is clothing optional where we are free to have as many wives, husbands' friends, and lovers we are wanting. It could be great fun, don't you think, my dearest One? All the love, sex, fun, vacations, money, music, and fame we've ever envisioned in our imaginations is a potential possibility for each one of us who is truly desirous of this free way of life. When we take responsibility for our own happiness we'll have little need for guns, jails, policeman, elected officials, lawyers, doctors, or the like. It's called the art of self-governance. And self-healing. Self-pleasuring. Yummy. Sounds good to me." Want to come joins me in this divine Play, my dear ones? There is no room to be free and happy just because you ARE!

After the Ecstasy

In his book *After the Ecstasy, the Laundry*, Jack Kornfield warns of another kind of excessive attachment, following supposed spiritual leaders or organizations which have lost their direction. A true leader will not demand that you accept his or her dogma, but will allow you to become your true self.

I had made my Holy Communion and confirmation as a Catholic in accordance with my mother's wishes, but I was totally dissatisfied with what I believed were false teachings of the Catholic Church in which I was raised. I found their teachings narrow minded, arrogant, limited and a negative, powerless approach to spirituality. The ancient patriarchal teachings regarding sin, punishment, and death in a fiery hell sounded like bullshit to me from the time I was a little child. I now know that some people get a lot of value and have mystical experiences in Catholicism, but it was never for me. My grammy was Catholic, and loved going to mass, so I honored her choice and recognized it as a Path that works for some people. I personally just find it oppressive, and believe it dishonors the Goddess and represses the natural sexual beings we are.

There is so much sexual dysfunction in the Vatican and priesthood that many former altar boys and other grown male and some female adults have now come forth to make allegations of sexual abuse and molestation. It is about time the church is becoming aware of this very prevalent and long overlooked problem. The very men who were supposed to be trusted and looked up to by the youth were taken advantage of and betrayed. The perpetrators merely get a slap on the wrist, but the victims must live with the memories and shame of what happened to them for the rest of their lives. It is a traumatic shock, and the devastation takes a long time to heal. The sexual force is a divine, natural, and powerful force. When it is suppressed or repressed, it often comes out in violent or inappropriate ways.

The same kinds of problems – abuse of power – are found in many religions.

Masters

Thank you, my dearest Lord. My precious Baba, Gurumayi, Archangel Michael, Jesus, Buddha, Mother Mary, Sinanda, St. Germaine, Lady Kwan Yin, Melchezedek, Abraham, Penelope, Ascordia, Astoriel, Gabriel, Gabriel, Amy and John Giallucco, Tony Kenton, Virginia O'Hara, Ernie Kara, Georgia, Jessica, Pan Les Fina and the priestesses, Rev. Jeanette LeDoux, Leigh Shaw, Rev. Carola Van Dusen, Rev. Gregory Possman, Z bird, Rick and Jeni Prigmore, Rev. Tom Campanelli, Rev. Amelia LeBer and you, beloved Meryl, for creating the sweet Life and friends you've always dreamed of having. You are a Master, priestess, and Goddess of Love. I/We honor you, dearest One. "You've come a long way, Baby"

I knew with certainty that God or some higher Power loved me unconditionally and Jesus never once said I needed a mediator to whom I must confess my sins. As far as I was concerned, I didn't have any sins. I was so frightened of going to confession the first time when I was seven years old. I felt compelled to make up sins to sound good in order to get my mom's and the priest's approval. I didn't have the courage, as a child, to share my belief that I was already pure, and God and Jesus loved me exactly the way I was. That didn't mean I didn't make mistakes many times. I wasn't perfect. Sometimes I'd disobey my mother and I fought with my younger brother, Pete. I did more frequently than I wanted to admit, but I always felt sorry afterward, resolving not to do it again, and asked my family directly for forgiveness.

I was led to the practical teachings of Ernest Holmes, who contributed to the founding of New Thought religions along with the Fillmores of the Unity Churches. Holmes established Religious Science[10] in the nineteen thirties. This was a teaching with which I'd become familiar in my early twenties. I received the Science of Mind magazine for a few years at the same time I discovered the Psychic Science Temple of Metaphysics in Paterson led by Reverend Bill Daut when, I was a mere twenty years old and chose to become a Spiritualist and Psychic Scientist.

Sixteen years after meeting my Master, I moved to Princeton, and returned to the teachings of

---

10 Religious Science is not to be confused with Christian Science. Holmes studied Christian teachings, as well as other world religions. While much of his writing uses terminology from Christian writings, he also drew from Eastern texts.

Religious Science and the text *Science of Mind*.[11] It became a practical way to integrate what I'd learned in Psychic Science, Siddha Yoga and meditation. It helped me to approach God and spirituality by connecting with spiritual Law and Divine Mind by using the power of mind to do "spiritual mind treatment" in order to manifest the life, love, and the circumstances I truly want. Daily positive affirmations by a trained or licensed practitioner

"As a man thinketh, so is he." Jesus had completely mastered the power of his mind and that was how he was able to perform all the healing miracles, including resurrecting Lazarus from the dead. His faith was more than that of a tiny mustard seed. It was steady and unswerving. After years of study and purification in the East, Jesus knew it was His Father who did the works through him, at all times, because he and God had become One in Spirit. However, Jesus said that we would do all the works that He did, and more. He knew that it was the nature of God and Love to expand. So even as He was continually growing greater and gave himself freedom and more responsibility to care for all God's people from the celestial realms, he knew that we were also destined to live eternally and become "Christ Conscious" as he did. Jesus was just as human as you and me, and went through tremendous struggle, hardship, purification, contrast, and learning just like we are going through right now. He is no greater or lesser than any one of us! If you ask and listen to your heart you can communicate with his great loving consciousness in this very moment without ever having to open up your Bible again. The human race has distorted most of his pure teachings through the many translations and individual perceptions in the various gospels. There are so many varied interpretations of what his life and passion were all about. I am most strongly attracted to the Gnostic gospels and the information in the Dead Sea Scrolls. I personally believe Jesus lived a much happier and more normal life as a great teacher, husband, and father than most of us have been made aware of.

I suggest you read some of the writings about Jesus that come from Princeton scholar, Elaine Pagels, if you want to get a more varied and truthful perspective on who Jesus was and what his teachings were all about. It was out of his personal trials, tribulations, and triumphs that he was able to purify the lower ego personality to become the Ascended Master he became. He could be on this earth right now writing through this very channel. He could even be you or your next-door neighbor. I can almost hear him saying, "Come unto me, little children. I am here in the golden silence of your own hearts, not in some remote foreign land or heaven. I am right here within you now expressed through your very own heart and mind. Just call upon me directly if you need to ask a question. I am always listening. I will respond with great love, joy, and enthusiasm. I honor you. There is no need for you to open an antiquated book that truly does not express the power of this very moment. We have a divine connection right here right now through the words she is speaking. You have the same capacity to listen to your own individual guidance and channel the Truth that is right for you. I honor you all as the Master Avatars you have become since my transition into the higher planes of Consciousness. My teachings are expressed everywhere. Not just in the holy Bible." His teachings and wisdom can be found in books like *The Course in Miracles*, *The Celestine Prophecy*, and *The Tenth Insight*. You will glean some of my teachings by reading Allen Cohen's book, *The Dragon Doesn't Live Here Anymore*, *The Peace That You Seek*, *Rising in Love*, *Are You as Happy as Your Dog*, and *I Had it All the Time*. Recent books like Jack Canfield's *Chicken Soup for the Soul*, Neal Donald Walsh's *Conversations with God*, and

---

11 *Science of Mind* by Ernest Holmes is a large volume, and some find it hard to understand. I am presently enjoying *This Thing Called You*, a much shorter and simpler treatment of the same principles, also by Holmes.

many others you have been attracting through the desire of your soul to know itself, are valuable and reflect much Truth.

At the heart of every major spiritual tradition is one Truth. You might use different words, and you may call yourself a Muslim, a Hindu, a Buddhist, or even an atheist. You will be attracted to the perfect books and teachings that will resonate with you, my dear Ones. All of the books are saying the same things in different ways and they are all valid. The only thing that matters is that you experience a loving connection to your Source as you read them. You are out here on the leading edge of thought, my dear ones, creating so many new and wonderful ideas and inventions that have never been before. Even God herself is impressed with your progress and creativity! So keep up the good work. But don't work too hard, my children, because you will never ever get it all done. This Universe is infinite, eternal, and ever changing. So just sit back, relax, and play to your hearts' content. It is not your destination, but your joyous journey that matters. There is never any need to hurry. What is the big rush? Where are you going? There is nothing to do but what you like. There is nowhere to be but here now, present in this beautiful, peaceful moment filled with love and joy. It is inside of you, my dearest ones. Become like the animals, plants, the fairies, gnomes, divas, and nature spirits. We are all having a great time. Don't you think it's time to slow down and not take yourself so seriously? There is plenty of time to grow and achieve all that you are wanting. See if you can be content as you stand in your present moment as another fresh desire is springing up within you to be more, do more, and have more. It is all-divine. It is all-perfect. You are all divine. Aum. Poornamidam Poornamidam. Poornah. Poorna Mudachyate. Poornasyaa. Poornamadayah. Poornavevavashishate. Om Shanti. Shanti. Shanti. Sadgurunath Maharaj ki J'ai! Om. That is perfect. This is perfect. From the perfect springs the perfect. If the perfect is taken from the perfect, the perfect remains. Om. Peace. Peace. Peace. Hail to your true guru. Your inner Self! As Rick Prigmore of the Universal Brotherhood says so succinctly, G-U-R-U. Gee, You Are you, are you not? You could not be anything but your sweet divine Self, my beloved Ones. I am in you, and you are in Me. It is truly a spectacular, wondrous adventure, this life of ours, is it not?

Bliss is God's inherent nature. My guru, Swami Muktananda, said" That is why we are always searching for happiness. It is OUR TRUE NATURE, but it is not out there. It is WITHIN our own hearts and it is called our "Inner Being".

Since the three-dimensional world is an illusion, and the mind's attempt to understand many dimensions, nothing matters and everything matters. We give every thing and person whatever meaning it has for us. If God cares for all the trees, feeds the birds on the wing even in the winter, how much more do you think He cares for you, one of his own children? Source adores you. God is impersonal and yet the most personal, intimate relationship an embodied physical entity can have. It is a precious, growing, expanding relationship. There is nothing more important in our lives than the relationship we have with this One, our special Divine Friend. How much longer will we wait until we open our hearts to Him or Her?

How much longer will we roam from door to door, job to job, this one to that one, from conquest to challenge, project to project, trying to compete and/or keep up with the Jones' and the Rockefellers? How long will we go from door to door, my beloved ones, just picking up dust? When will we go inside and open up to the love of your very own Self? It is not outside of us, my dearest ones. It is ever moving, flowing like a river rushing to its ultimate destination, the Ocean of God's Love. It is filling me up like a large cup, a Holy Grail until I am filled up with so much love that I am crying tears of sublime ecstasy. I drink deep in grateful humility.

We are such blessed divine children of God. Joy, love, sublime inner peace, and abundance are our divine inheritance. Jesus says so through the prophets in the Bible and the entire Earth is our divine playground. Let us love, protect, and respect her. All its inhabitants are our playmates. Life is our divine gift.

The Indian saints tell us this in the Vedas, the Upanishads, and Shaivite scriptures, and we KNOW from within our hearts that freedom, love, and joy is our destiny. The reason why we are always seeking joy outside of ourselves is because ecstasy is our very nature. The unbounded, unfettered bliss of God is our True Unchanging Nature. It is much more lasting than temporary glimpses of joy found in sense pleasures, material objects, fantasies, and the like. Though I must admit that in my experience giving birth and having tantric sex and regular orgasms makes me feel more connected to God and Self than any church service or ritual has ever done. I did enjoy, however, the special rituals we did in the ashram, like the arati, which was taken from ancient practices in order to honor of the Self and the Mother Goddess. My heart still bursts open with love, and I am still moved to tears, when I chant the Shiva Arati and the Guru Gita.

Because of the nature of duality, and laws that create the perfect harmony in the universe, we are always subject to the play of opposites in the third dimension. So with feelings of love, there also exist the potential for feelings of hatred. With hot there is cold, with happy there is sad. And so on. So we must learn to go beyond these polarities, by practicing contentment in all these fleeting circumstances. The Self remains unaffected by all these changes and temporary states. So dear ones, we can always go within to discover our true natures. Or just go sit quietly in nature and observe its beauty. Meditate upon the beautiful, colorful fractals in nature. Gardening is one of the most therapeutic and enjoyable things I do. Once my seeds have blossomed in the spring into beautiful yellow daffodils, lavender and white hyacinths, variegated pink and white petunias, yellow and purple pansies, and tall golden yellow sunflowers reaching for the sky, by summertime I sit quietly contemplating the beauty of my efforts and vision. I did so little to grow them. Just an idea of a variety of beautiful colors in my mind nurtured with some water, sunshine, and weeding produced a magnificent creation of beauty for the entire neighborhood to enjoy. I did so little. Goddess and grace did the rest. Life is so easy and simple when we just allow ourselves some time to just "Be". A few moments of meditation or contemplation before bedtime, or when I wake up in the morning, makes all the difference in how my day unfolds.

It is because of the divine Self that we are able to experience the sweetness in food, drink, sex, and to feel love in relationships within ourselves, for our families, animals, and for other people.

No matter how depressed you feel in this moment, know that it is temporary and "this too shall pass." Start by accepting yourself exactly as you are. Appreciate that you are a survivor. Give thanks and praise that you are alive and will make it through this experience too. Adore yourself, rather than criticize. Be gentle with yourselves, my dear ones. You have so many gifts. And you are a gift to God and yourself!

Try not to put yourself under pressure to be a certain way, or to achieve too many goals. Don't "should" on yourself, as the New Age teachers might say. For several years, I didn't write much of this book, and I really beat myself up about it. I felt guilty, ashamed, and sad that I was procrastinating on a project that I believed was my spiritual mission.

Finally, my higher guidance said not to put so much pressure on myself and that it didn't really matter whether I wrote the book or not. That I was perfect just the way I was. And I could simply write because I wanted to, and because it made me happy to do so. Boy, did that free me up. I stopped punishing myself for what I didn't accomplish and began praising myself for whatever I felt guided to do on a particular day or days. Then when the book began to flow, I was able to sit down with all the little pieces of patchwork quilt I'd already written, and they started to all fit together just like a jigsaw puzzle. Now I am very excited about my project taking form, which spurs me on to writing more. Sometimes I will write now for six or seven hours straight, without even checking the time, until the wee hours of the morning. I am very focused. My creativity is flowing, and I am so grateful the Divine is using me as an instrument for its expression of Truth and beauty.

So don't "should" on yourself about anything. It's just another form of self-criticism and punishment for being other than Who and What you are. You are perfect just as you are. You are doing the best you can do each moment. No need to change or do a thing. God loves us unconditionally exactly as we are. Make a New Year's resolution or a daily prayer to love yourself unconditionally and to always be gentle with yourself as if you were a little child, because you are God's beloved child. You are so precious, dear ones.

Baba Muktananda said, "The Self is already attained." All we need do is to quiet our minds in order to experience That pure peaceful state of Being, of pure Consciousness. There is nowhere to go and nothing to do. I sometimes wonder why I am always in such a hurry here in the East scurrying around like a chicken with its head cut off, when I could be down in Florida, where I feel relaxed, or out west where the lifestyle is so much more relaxed and easy. My family members including my precious children and grandson all live in New Jersey, so I guess that is why I stay.

I suppose that is why I need to take regular time each day for a long, hot bubble bath for a few moments of quiet meditation, and affirmative prayer. Chanting the Guru Gita in the morning or sometime during the day in my car while en route to Edison Rehabilitation where I go for PT. Massage, and acupuncture, always makes me feel grounded and connected to the Source of my Being. Writing in my journal, and sitting out in my garden, watching the happy neighbors go by with their children and dogs, is seemingly such a simple life and these little things bring me so much pleasure and contentment. Giving, receiving massages, and making love are my favorite ways to become quiet and go within to that sublime state of peace, joy, and equanimity. I also love to swim, dance, sing, get facials, pedicures, manicures, get my hair washed and styled, and to garden as I mentioned before. And of course, now that I am a grandmother, spending time playing with the Light of my life, William, is one of my most favorite activities. Entertaining friends, making collages and painting, going out to dinner, watching movies with my boyfriend, and going to local concerts, and Broadway shows is great fun too. I love variety and my precious life is filled with it.

Think about what brings you joy and do that. When I am feeling a bit depressed, I know that moving the energy by taking a walk outside or dancing in my living room will make me feel much better than if I just sit on the couch spacing out and watching television. Though sometimes that is very relaxing too. Sometimes I am so driven to succeed that I overdo, and I have no energy left. Then I just plop in front of the "boob tube" where I don't have to think or work at all for an hour or two. I can just relax, be entertained, and use my imagination to live in another reality for a short while, or I watch comedians or romantic comedies. Sometimes I think it might be better if I just took a nap or listened to quiet, gentle music at those times, But I must admit that I do learn a lot from watching television and movies, too. I particularly like watching shows about nature and particularly animals.

The Shadow

My chronic, suicidal depressions and fears are at the nadir of existence whereas Love and Ecstasy are the zenith. Fear, anxiety, greed, rage, and jealousy are called our "SHADOW" or Dark side. It has been written about a lot recently in books like Debbie Ford's "The Dark Side of the Light Chasers", but it is a complex topic and deeply misunderstood. The Christians would see this part of one's self as evil or as actions of a mythical "devil".

The Buddhists or Hindus might call it the ego. I just call it part of Life, a contrasting experience. We can choose to experience all these "not feeling good" states for as long as we wish for this is a Universe of free will and co-creation. When I got bored of feeling depressed, anxious, poor, poverty stricken, negative, weak, and a hopeless victim I finally was sick and tired of thinking and feeling that way; so, I made a conscious decision to Choose with my own free will, and intended to CHANGE my thinking, which, with God's and my guru's grace, CHANGED my life circumstances. But, even before circumstances changed, I felt a sense of serenity and inner peace just as things were, when I surrendered my negativity and my ways that were not working to Spirit, in prayer or meditation. Sure, complete transformation and Realization of all of your wildest dreams is not going to happen overnight, but through knowing what our preferences and desires are NOT, and what is NOT working in our lives at any given time, we then have the opportunity to see things differently, feel worthy, and KNOW without a doubt what it is we ARE WANTING. We can then choose a NEW THOUGHT, make a new plan, be grateful for WHAT IS, and ALLOW wisdom, discernment, and new good to come from these seemingly negative experiences. As Louise hay would say to whatever we are thinking or experiencing, "It's just a thought, and a thought can be changed."

For me, having had manic depression half my life has not been easy, but at the end of the day, I can say I am a richer person because of it. I have more depth, more character, more courage and strength, and more compassion for other humans and animals on the planet who are suffering. I deeply care about my life, and about every person I meet. I unconditionally love and accept The Whole of humanity, Mother Earth Herself, and I take more responsibility for myself and the whole world when I am in the flow, connected to my Lord, and to my Gurus' infinite, precious eternal LOVE. Being in the depressed state, feeling weak, and needing help taught me to rely on God and my higher Power, and to actually ask for help and prayer no matter how difficult it was for me to be authentic and vulnerable. I was always ashamed, as a minister and holistic healer, that I could still sometimes fall into a place fear, anxiety, and sadness instead of the joyous, ecstatic state normal to me. How egotistical of me to think that I am so special, that I have no right to be human and make mistakes. I learned humility the hard way sometimes having to get down on my knees to pray and surrender my Life to the One. However, I gained much wisdom gleaned through all my manic-depressive experiences.

Now that I have seen and deeply experienced this SHADOW side of myself on many occasions, I can truly say it's not necessarily a "bad" thing. That is just a judgment my mind has made about this darker part of our Consciousness. Of course, it is a lot easier to accept and embrace our shadow once we have come to the other side of a challenging situation or come through a depression successfully.

In fact, without this contrasting experience, how would I have been able to feel the depth of All That Is, and experience the variety of infinite colors of our multi-dimensional SELF? I would not be able to recognize or feel my Light as deeply and joyously as I do now. This seeming negative or SHADOW side is something to be felt, experienced, embraced, and integrated, not despised. Though the SHADOW is seen as BAD by the Christians and other patriarchal religions, labeled "SIN" and attributed to a terrible, mythological evil deity called "the DEVIL", this part of ourselves and human Consciousness is not something to be shunned, scorned, or run from. We are all in the process of becoming complete beings as we integrate the "SHADOW" Remember, the SHADOW KNOWS".

In the Course in Miracles it states, "What we resist persists." Please, folks, take it from a person who has been there, not just once, but several times, the longer we run from our feelings by numbing ourselves with sleep medications, television, drugs, or alcohol, the longer we are going to stay in our depressed, fearful, or angry state of mind. There is always a way through the bad situation and darkness once we relax and let go of wanting to run from it. The path to God is not necessarily an easy one. It can be as sharp as a Razor's Edge or hotter than a fire. Our emotions are to be felt and moved through. Emotions can be seen as ENERGY in MOTION. The more we try to stop or damn up this energy the more disconnected and confused we feel. When the emotions get trapped, we become stuck, contracted, and misaligned from our true Selves. From our misalignment and confused thinking we sometimes create illness and dis-eases of all kinds – like cancer, diabetes, high blood pressure, and all sorts of other things to let us know we need to stop, slow down, and pay attention. Symptoms like these make us stop whatever we are doing in order to re-evaluate our lives and lifestyles. Are we really doing the things in life that bring us everlasting joy and fulfillment, or are we just in a comfortable place doing the same things over and again without any sense of wonder, newness, or growth? Many times, during the excitement and energy of spring I'd be involved in so many activities that, even though many were joyful, I often felt as if I was a hamster in a cage spinning around on a wheel.

Are we truly happy in our nine to five, five day a week working world, or would we be happier as an artist, a musician, a dancer, or a painter? I don't care what our parents said about being practical. I'd rather be doing what I love like holistic healing, massage, reflexology, and writing, and am passionate about the few artistic things I do that make just a little bit of money. I'd much prefer to do a variety of part-time things I enjoy as opposed to being engaged in a nine to five job I just tolerate to eek out a living. I love being self-employed. Though I have worked for others at various times in my life, I am too independent, and I enjoy variety and creativity so much, that I do not think I could ever work for a company or a store again. I really love my freedom, and I really love being creative and happy. I love doing a variety of things during my work day and at night. If I was stuck in a nine to five full time job I would just wither and die – unless it is something I really love like dancing, singing, or working with children and utilizing all my special talents.

EMOTION AND EXPRESSION

Emotions are part of our inner guidance system, letting us know how close we are to our Source, our Center, our inner Being. Though God is always within and all around us, sometimes it is easy to forget WHO WE ARE. When we consciously choose to change our thinking and reconnect to our Inner Being through prayer, meditation, holotropic breath work, rebirthing, massage therapy, being in nature, or another type of healing modality we can relax for a moment and remember to live and enjoy the PRESENT Moment. In this PRESENT we can KNOW with all our hearts that no matter what temporary things are going on in our lives or the World, we are OK. All is truly well. God is in charge and life is unfolding as it should. As my mom's mechanical Santa says at Christmas. God IS "Large and in charge." Totally EXPANSIVE, Omniscient, Omnipresent, Abundant, and Eternal.

Our consciousness is so much more expansive than we can possibly imagine, and so much is happening on so many levels of which we are not aware. In retrospect, just about everything seems to make sense, like the unraveling of a tapestry. Love is the greatest POWER in the Universe. This LOVE also has the power to bring up anything unlike itself. When I began my spiritual path, I had no idea that I'd have to suffer through many of the challenges I've had in life, like manic depression, abuse in my marriages, divorce, losing my children, censure by the community, and ostracism by my father and stepmother for telling the truth about the incest I experienced as a teen. I've sustained many other losses, but each experience has made me a stronger, more loving, humane, and compassionate person. Every experience that has come to me has taught me something about life and myself.

Life is so fleeting. We cannot hold onto anything for too long, for it may be gone in an instant. That's why we must appreciate this precious, holy moment. My dad used to say "The only thing we can be certain of is CHANGE." It's kind of scary, but if we just relax and flow with the tides, we are happier in that rhythm. I like to think of myself as a mermaid at times. Often, I like to be in the ocean, or under the ocean, swimming with the tides. Sometimes I prefer to be on land, but I find I have to be flexible and adaptable. If a hurricane is coming, I might want to dive deep under the water, find a cave, and stay there until it is safe to come out to the ocean to surface again.

If we repress our emotions, we can become ill. Repressed grief and anger are stored in the intestines. Courage and joy are also stored there. We must be willing to, and allow, all the emotions. The more sadness or grief we are able to express and allow the more joy and laughter there is to feel.

Fear is stored in the area of the solar plexus. Have you ever felt like you've been smacked in the tummy or were unable to breathe when you were really frightened? We have a tendency to hold our breaths when we become afraid. That's why it is so important to take a deep breath and exhale fully with a sigh whenever we are feeling anxious or afraid.

Love is stored in the area of the heart. So is the rejection of love. I'm sure we could prevent many heart attacks and strokes if we allowed ourselves to feel more love and forgiveness for others and ourselves.

We tend to store rage and anger in the liver. If we were to flush out the liver and large intestine with a colonic, herbal cleanse, or some kind of emotional release work, we would most likely rid the body of cancer, cirrhosis, grief, despair, candida, and a host of other diseases. Much disease begins in the mind, the liver, and the colon as a result of a poor diet of refined, unnatural or genetically engineered foods, chemical toxins, lack of exercise, lack of sunshine, lack of clean, pure water, and negative thinking. There is a part of the being that is not at ease with itself. You have watched too many television commercials about illness. There is no need for you to create illness of any kind for yourself, unless that is what you are wanting for some reason.

When we become ill, we slow down. Everything stops for a while, doesn't it? We put all our activities on hold, so that we can rest and address the problem at hand. When there is pain, depression, or illness, it is a sign from our inner being that we need to pay attention to something it is trying to tell us. If we take a lot of drugs to stop the pain, or make us go unconscious, we are merely choosing to shut out the signals the body, mind, and Inner Being is giving. It's time to be still and listen to our inner guidance, for it wants to communicate something important to us. Maybe we hate the job we've been slaving at for forty years. Maybe we have no intimacy in our relationships. Maybe we are longing for sexual connection with our mate, or a deeper connection with God within. Maybe we are overworked, stressed out, or just not doing the things in life we enjoy. Sometimes our body needs a rest, and it wants us to spend a whole day in bed relaxing, watching funny movies, mysteries, or old musicals.

ABUNDANCE

According to one of my spiritual teachers, Abraham, a nonphysical collective consciousness channeled by Esther Hicks, there is an abundance of all things, and that includes whatever we desire. So, we can choose to focus on what it is we have and desire, and to be grateful for all of it, or we can think about, talk and complain about what we lack, and attract more of the same deficiency.

Complaining, and thinking we never have enough money, creates the inevitable circumstances of not having "enough" money, no matter how much or how little we have. Former billionaires have been known to commit suicide, when they got down to their last few millions! Complaining and telling all our friends about our problems with money, with relationships, or whatever makes us feel bad, will just make us feel worse, and create more of the same problems over and again, through the Universal Law of Attraction. What we think and talk about today will become our circumstances of tomorrow.

Just like gravity, the law of Attraction is a Universal law we cannot escape. Jerry and Esther Hicks, say in their book about the Law of Attraction, that it is our friend. Like karma. You are either driving a good karma or a bad karma. Now would you rather drive a loaded Porsche, or BMW like my son, or a used slightly banged up lemon? My point is, that it is up to you. We choose our own reality. We are the drivers, the authors of our lives and most of our experiences. Of course, there are some karmic experiences we bring in from past lives, but even these can be changed by how we view the circumstances. The same person can either view an event as a curse or – using a positive mindset and attitude – as a learning experience, an opportunity, or a blessing. Even an illness or other "bad" experience, like a divorce, can be seen as positive,

In my experience, I have discovered that, when I "seek first the Kingdom of God", all good things, including material wealth, have already been, and continue to be, given to me. It's in my connection to the Great Spirit that has me relax into God's quiet embrace, and feel His – and my loving guardian angels' – divine Presence. I realize each day that I am so deeply loved by my Creator, by my personal guides and guardian angels that I am always provided for even if I am temporarily sick and, in a hospital, like the time I got double pneumonia in February of 2016 and was taken by emergency ambulance to Princeton Medical Center and intubated without my conscious consent or knowledge. Even then always had enough food, water, air, clothing, and shelter, and all the abundance I needed to pay all my bills and fulfill every one of my needs. Holy Spirit is always giving me brilliant ideas for books, services, art, poetry, and other things that inspire the soul and bring beauty and peace to our minds and living space. When I feel connected to Spirit and Source through meditation, chanting, prayer, yoga, contemplation, or by being relaxed in nature my perception is clear. I have the clarity of the Divine Mind. I feel so different after meditating for just twenty minutes in the morning or evening than when I am in a stubborn funk experiencing anxiety, focusing on lack, and feeling victimized or very needy. When I feel my Divine Connection to Source, I am at peace and in a place of humility and gratitude for all that I have and all that I AM. I am in a place of pure love and appreciation for ALL-That-Is and in a pure place of receptivity allowing myself to circulate the good that comes to me and through me.

While doing my daily spiritual practices and being kind to myself and others my heart is completely open and I feel generous and expansive. In this place of experiencing Divine Connection, I am grateful for everything I have, no matter how little materially, and have positive expectations about receiving more of my Universal Good. This good is available to all people and beings. It is our divine inheritance as divine Daughters and Sons of the One God and also expressions of That One Great Life! "There is a divine power for Good in the universe and we can all use it," according to the creator of "Science of Mind", author and teacher, Dr. Ernest Holmes.

We are so blessed, and we are each a blessing to one another. Every thought and action we think, speak, and take affects the Whole, so it behooves us to focus upon the good, joyous, and TRUE. When we speak it is best if we leave one another feeling good, happy, encouraged and inspired as opposed to indulging in petty gossip, complaints about our jobs, bosses, other people, or the ever-changing weather.

My higher Self would assure me that God supplies me with everything I need and more when I think positive thoughts and feel happy doing whatever it is I am doing. I know you are thinking this is crazy, airy fairy type thinking. But it is the Truth.

There has been a spiritual reason for me to go through all that I have and still survived to be a happy, healthy person so grateful to be alive. I was meant to be here now at this moment to enjoy my family, especially my children, and to help others going through the same challenges with mental illness and suicidal ideations like me.

There is a way out of every dark night of the soul. But it takes faith in the Creator of your being, courage, determination, faith, and prayer. Along with that, positive thinking, unconditional love, and self-acceptance. Dear ones, don't despair. Once you've reached the light on the other side of this tunnel you will experience the most exquisite love, joy, clarity, wisdom, sublime peace, and understanding. The recognition of your own divine Self as a unique expression of God!

WHO ARE WE?

You are a conscious, intelligent divine being connected to the Source of All-That-Is. Think about that for a moment. God dwells within you as YOU exactly as you are in this very moment. You don't have to do or change a thing. Just be exactly Who you are. Simply quiet your mind and listen to the language of your heart and Soul. You are a beautiful, unique expression of God. No one in the world is just like you. Your presence on this earth is needed. If you were to destroy yourself even Consciousness Itself would have trouble remaking you. As Eckhart Tolle' says, "You are here to enable the divine purpose of the universe to unfold."

God, the creator, would have no experience of itself without you, without all of us. Never believe you are anything but infinite Potential. Infinite Intelligence is operating through your very own mind right now as you are reading and interpreting these words. How will you use this gift? Will you use it constructively or try to hurt, control, and destroy? The choice is yours and yours alone to make.

Will you use this "force", your innate intelligence, for good or for "evil"? Will you benefit yourself and humankind or watch the destruction of the earth and its inhabitants with violent thoughts of fear, terror, greed, and weapons?

The older I get the more I realize that nothing in this temporal world is certain except change. The more I want to hold onto a person, a particular way of thinking, a circumstance, resentment, or anything for that matter, the more unhappiness I create for myself. Whenever I try to control another person, like my daughter or a man with whom I'm involved, I feel miserable. The only person I have control over and the power to change is myself. Living happily in our world is not about domination. We are here to learn of the power within ourselves to be, do, and attract anything good we desire through the power of our own minds – not to have power over someone or something. Freedom is our nature. It is also the nature of God, of Love, to expand. And with expansion oft comes dissolution and destruction of limited beliefs, outmoded ways of being, and even our very bodies. How could the butterfly emerge from her chrysalis without casting off its old caterpillar body? How can we usher in the New Age of enlightenment in which we all experience our loving connection to God and one another, as brothers and sisters of Light if we do not let go of our outmoded, destructive ways of being and thinking? The only "axis of evil" is in our own minds. There is truly no "evil" in any human soul. We are all pure and made of light and divine love energy. We must look within ourselves before we blame and criticize others for the violence we see in this world. We must wash the mirror of our own hearts. Did Jesus not say, " Love thy neighbor as thyself"? This was the greatest commandment for me next to Love the lord thy God with all your heart and soul and mind". What about "Thou shalt not kill"? Did all the men involved in warfare not understand? How can "compassionate conservatives" believe that the death penalty is a good thing, but taking away a woman's right to choose is not? Abortion is bad, but is killing a healthy living adult human being that made a mistake a good thing? I don't understand the reasoning behind this.

God, Jesus, and the Divine Mother teach us to forgive everyone and to have mercy. How can a leader call himself a Christian when he is killing innocent people every day in unethical wars? I am not standing in judgment of him. I am just trying to understand his true motives. I suppose, like us all, he is learning and doing the best he can, according to the dictates of his own conscience and his own unique, but limited understanding.

Whoever says he loves God, and hates his brother, is a liar... "(1 John 4:20) [12]

Consciousness is always moving. Ebbing and flowing like the tides of the ocean. Expanding and contracting like a laboring mother in the midst of childbirth. And so are we. But the universe is dynamic and never moves backward; it is always spiraling upward toward greater levels of love, awareness, harmony, and creativity. Love, Bliss, and consciousness is its very nature, so we can just relax and allow it. Quiet the mind and in the silence, you will know without a doubt that essentially you are the image and likeness of God. The divine Friend is closer than your very breath.

Sometimes, when I think I've fallen to the depths, and lost ground on my spiritual path, I see – in retrospect – that the seemingly negative experiences have made me stronger and wiser. The times I've spent in the dark, in the caverns of unknowing have actually catapulted me to some greater understanding of myself, and have given me more clarity. It is through the delicious contrast in the universe that we learn what our preferences are. I am learning that all problems eventually resolve themselves with God's help. Once I give birth to a question, Source hears it and answers it immediately. All I must do is remove my attention from the problem, and then I am able to allow the solution and answer to flow. It is really a very simple thing to do. God answers all prayers immediately. We must learn to receive the gifts that are given, and be open to receiving, or we can block the immediate demonstration of the greatest love that we can ever know, the unconditional, expansive love of our very own Selves! No romantic love or anything of the earth can compare with this great love. It is formless, free, and cannot be truly described in words. It must be felt within the sacred quiet of the heart in prayer or meditation.

By experiencing what I don't want, I am free to make a new choice and to create the happy Life I desire. My Light, my Being, has never changed, and remains totally unaffected by my thoughts, feelings, or experiences. This Light We Are, and have always been. The Light we shall remain. I have no guilt or shame about any of the choices I've made in past. Even going into the dark and trying to commit suicide has taught me a lot about myself and the preciousness of each moment of my life and yours too. Feeling tremendous despair caused me to yearn for the experience of joy and connection with Source on a constant basis. I feel more joy on a daily basis than almost any person I know. My heart just bubbles up with love, enthusiasm, and fun all the time. I take delight in my own ecstasy and see it revealed everywhere I go-in the beauty of a pink, orange, and blue sunset, in the morning sunrise, in the colorful flowers and majestic trees, in a baby's eyes, and in all the children and older people that come into my sphere of reality.

---

12 Regarding the Ten Commandments, please read about the Good Samaritan (Luke 10:25-37)

ANGELS, MEDIUMSHIP AND AUTOMATIC WRITING

Channeling is a simple process, which almost anyone who meditates can do. All I do is listen to quiet music or chant to clear the thoughts from my mind. At first, I just observe my breath going in and out and sometimes I count the breaths. If I notice myself thinking I simply become a witness. I don't judge myself and I don't continue thinking random thoughts. I just become an outside observer of my mind and return to focusing on my breath. When I am in a very calm, relaxed state I ask my guides or Higher Self a question. In this case I just asked something general. In my mind I telepathically asked my guru, angels, and non-physical guides, "Do you have any information for the people who attend church at the Church of Divine Light in Somerset?" After a few moments this is what my fingers began to write: This is called "automatic writing" in the metaphysical circles.

I had only heard about angels when I was little. I knew they were mentioned a few times in the Bible, but in Catholicism we were not really reading the Bible when I was seven years old in catechism nor when I made my confirmation.

THE truest HEAVEN is HERE NOW ON EARTH Right WHERE I AM/You ARE in this precious, holy moment! With God's Grace we will all make it through every challenge together – with a little or a lot of help from our friends and family. And angels. They really do exist, you know.

There are actually TEN PHYLA or types of angels—completely pure, innocent beings created before humans – from plain old, everyday angels to personal guardian angels to Seraphim who love to sing and praise like me, and others like Archangels who PROTECT the planet and its beings in BIG WAYS, like Archangels Michael, Raphael, and Gabriel. And believe it or not, they use me as one of their ambassadors here on Earth. Hey, I bet you thought I was going to say that I was an angel myself. Hell, honey, I'm no angel. In the immortal words of Ms. Mae West, "When I'm good I'm VERY GOOD, but when I'm BAD I'm BETTER!" If you don't believe me, go ask half the married men in Mercer County and all the way up to Maine! Not really. Well, maybe five per cent. I am exaggerating just to shock you a little. I guess I like to ruffle your "conventional feathers", so to speak, just to see if you are awake and paying attention.

LABELING

In retrospect, I have come to the conclusion that there is absolutely nothing wrong with me. Nor is there anything wrong with people who feel a tremendous sense of love or connection to Jesus or some deity, when doctors believe they are manic or psychologically sick, and should be medicated to stop these powerful feelings and thoughts. These are merely signs that a person's kundalini has been awakened and is rising through the chakras. The kundalini is the coiled inner meditative energy that is represented in the West by the caduceus.

Feeling love and connection is not negative or bad. It is a good thing. More doctors should feel as open-hearted as their psychiatric patients, in my opinion. A person should not be hospitalized because they feel a deep, overpowering connection to the Lord Jesus, or with a deity with whom they personally resonate. There is so much more going on than what meets the eye. When a devotee's kundalini is awakened by a sadguru, or some other means, lifetimes of karmic experiences come up to be healed and integrated. I wish I had understood more about kundalini when my husband and doctors wanted to medicate me during manic phases. I am a petite and formerly thin woman who had a challenging time holding that much energy in my small body. Rather than trying to stop the energy, what I needed to learn was how to ground it, and eventually feel more comfortable with it. I did learn about eating more root vegetables like carrots, potatoes, beets, parsnips, etc., and to just lie on the grass and relax into Mother Earth's embrace. Meditating and doing hatha yoga is helpful, as well as listening to songs, playing drums and chanting OM, concentrating on the color red (which corresponds to the root chakra) and taking a lot of Epsom salts baths to soothe and relax my muscles.

Anyway, back to being "crazy". Don't you know all the great geniuses and brilliant artists of our time were a bit touched in the head? Thank Goddess. Who wants to be ordinary anyway? Both my parents were conventional, ordinary humans, who worked very hard from 5:00 AM until night time when they could finally relax watching TV after a good supper, and what did it get them? Dad is dead, and mom is 83 going on 100 from the way she complains about her health.

Now, what the hell do all these ridiculous labels mean, and do they actually serve any practical purpose to help the millions of people afflicted by mental illness? Well, maybe a few. If you believe you are sick, and it helps you to think taking a pill or multitude of pills is going to help, more power to you. I was on Depakote, a mood stabilizer, on and off, for twenty-three years, and still take it sometimes. I was also prescribed Wellbutrin, an anti-depressant, and I believe they were helpful for some of the time, but it was just a temporary "fix". I still got depressed while taking the medications if the circumstances of my life were challenging emotionally, economically, or way too stressful. When I was not allowing

God's energy to flow through me, or if I allowed my vibration to dip so low that I became fearful of just making ends meet financially I still got depressed even while taking the medications.

Each person is a unique individual with a unique past, a childhood that is directly responsible for her biology, and has a special, unique personal history. A person should not be treated as if they are crazy or labeled and pigeon-holed into some generalized stereotype and categorized into an impersonal blanket of mental illness using the same types of drug treatment for Psychosis, schizophrenia, bipolar, or depression. As individuals we should not be compartmentalized or disparaged. The body, mind, and Spirit are connected, and most of the practitioners in the medical community today do not recognize this fact. The doctors are not God with the ultimate answers to all our physical, mental, and emotional problems. They should honor their patients as uniquely individual human beings. As divine beings all the biological systems are interconnected. Our thoughts influence our emotions, and how we feel influences what goes on within the body. And vice-versa. How the body feels affects the thoughts in our mind. And thoughts in our minds create the health or dis-ease of the body. Everything is connected. We are holograms.

The people with mental illness or physical dis-ease are first and foremost spiritual beings having a human experience. They may be temporarily ill at ease, but one must focus on wellness and have an intention to thrive in order to get better. Focusing on symptoms and masking or removing them does not cure anything. In fact, the symptoms are a sign from Divine intelligence that the body or thoughts in the mind is out of kilter; and there is something awry. If we have a fever in the body, we should allow it to do its job to destroy all the germs and toxins in the body instead of taking aspirin to bring the temperature down unless ones' temperature got to a deadly level, of course. If it were not necessary to purify the body and get back into balance Infinite Intelligence would not have caused our temperature to rise in the first place.

Let's listen to our innate intelligence and signals the body mind is giving us because they are being given to us, as a sign there is a problem to be addressed. It is much to our advantage to work with the divine urges and intuitions as opposed to masking or suppressing them. Many of the allopathic doctors in the United States today are going about the problem of illness in reverse. Problems eventually always resolve themselves when the attention is taken off of the problem and turned toward solutions. Focus on wellness, and you will allow the natural well-being that is your abundant birthright. In order to get to the subconscious roots of these mental, emotional and physical problems we must address the cause, not the symptoms. Without deep self-contemplation and analysis, bodywork, and an individualized approach to mental wellness that respects the divinity and dignity of each patient's spiritual, psychological, and emotional well-being, these doctors are not addressing the core roots of the problem. Besides, it is not in the physician's best interest to cure the patient because he or she would then lose business. Instead of paying for "health insurance", might it not make more sense to keep a general practitioner on retainer as long as you stay healthy, and to have free, universal coverage for true emergencies?

When each person takes responsibility for his or her own health through correct positive thinking, healthy eating, regular exercise, and by focusing on thoughts, feelings, and actions that make us feel good there is no room for illness; there then would no longer be a need for doctors. Well, except in cases where we have accidents and get our bones broken, get seriously burned, or something of that nature. This, of course, is just my personal opinion, and you can accept it or reject it if it does not resonate with your way of thinking and being.

I am a true chameleon who wears a coat of many colors with God's energy just pouring through every pore of my body. After all, I am a multifaceted, multidimensional being, but the psychiatrists at Princeton House would probably term me "manic depressive with possible multiple personality disorder". Hey guys let's throw in a little bit of borderline personality just for fun. Not really. I just made that one up. I don't even know what it means.

What about those of us who are "OUT PATIENTS? Thousands of us listening to that dangerous box we call a "Boob Tube" for it mesmerizes one to the point where a human brain does not have to be original, creative, or actually think for itself. Lots of thought control going on here if you are sitting in front of that box being bombarded by hundreds of commercials and a hypnotic frequency for hours per day. No wonder most humans are unoriginal, mediocre, complacent creatures who just allow themselves to be massively manipulated to think things like killing human beings in other countries and torturing animals is actually a beneficial thing for the race. Even if the majority of individuals disagree with these horrible, unethical practices, it seems like none of us has the courage to stand up for what is right by going against the politicians in power. Especially the killing of other humans because they are of a different skin color or religion which has happened frequently over the last few years. It's so hard to believe our police are actually given legal license to seize, brutalize, and murder innocent young teens just because they are of a different, darker race. Whether they be brown, black, Muslim, Christian, homosexual, autistic, mentally retarded, or anything that makes them different from the usually preferred and accepted male WASP who has been in charge and put in positions of power for thousands of years now on this planet.

PRACTICE

We can choose to focus on what it is we have and want and be grateful for all of it, or we can think about, talk and complain about what it is we don't have and attract more of the same. More of what we are not wanting. That is called creation by default.

Anytime I catch myself complaining or gossiping to a friend about someone or something I don't like in my life I notice what I'm doing and stop it. I know that if I continue in that fashion, I just make myself feel worse and create more of the same problems through the Law of Attraction that will manifest as unwanted circumstances later on that day, the next week, or five months down the road. It is only when I am feeling connected to my Source and feeling happy, grateful, and appreciative that I am in the place of creating more of the joy and abundance I am wanting to manifest.

Things that work for me when I am down, spiritual practices I like to use on a daily basis are chanting holy mantras in Sanskrit, singing kirtans with others, relaxing in NATURE, or just lying in my bed or on the couch petting my cat.

Cats are completely relaxed and always living in the moment. They are Zen Masters in their own special, quiet way. The easier it is for us to quiet the chatter in our subconscious and conscious minds, the easier it is to Remember and re-experience the quiet contentment of our deepest SELF, out TRUE NATURES, and truly KNOW WITHOUT a DOUBT, that ALL is WELL. No matter what negativity the corporate media likes to bring into our living rooms, there is much more joy and good things happening to many people on a daily basis. WELL BEING REIGNS. God's LOVE and the protection of our angels is more powerful than any dark forces or temporary dis-ease like co-vid 19 or unwanted circumstance.

Practices do not have to be "serious", only sincere.

I love fresh flowers, planting in my garden, and admiring the lovely flowers and bushes after I have finished planting. I like to use aromatherapy as well as Bach Flower essences if I am really depressed or out of sorts. Recently I used OAK to slow myself down when I'd get addicted to cleaning and organizing everything in my home to the point of perfectionism. It was exhausting, and taking ten drops of Oak remedy in the early mornings before or after breakfast helped me to relax and give myself badly needed rest.

The peace that the Bible speaks of as the "peace that passeth all understanding." is inside us and has nothing to do with outer circumstances. Sometimes I experience this peace while I am making love or during meditation, or after I have given myself a really prolonged orgasm with my vibrator. Oh my God. I have just mentioned one of the unmentionables. How can she be spiritual if she is talking about SEX and ORGASM?

Well, let's face it. We would not be here without it. Goddess Herself made it So pleasurable to have sex in order to perpetuate the species. All of them. They all do it. We all do it! Just like Cole Porter's song says, "Birds do it, bees do it, even educated fleas do it. Let's DO it. Let's fall in love."

Thank Goddess for "it". It makes living on the earth plane so much sweeter – especially amidst the hustle and bustle of everyday 9 to 5 existence. Time. A man-made construct. Does it truly exist?

I love to watch romantic comedies and musicals when I am ill or tired because they make me relax, smile, and laugh. The brain produces endorphins from gut laughter that will really make you high. You'll never need to take drugs again if you find what makes you happy and causes you to have a good belly laugh. Ellen DeGeneres, David Letterman, and Conan O'Brien crack me up. Everyone from the former casts of Saturday Night Live like Jim Carey, Bill Murray, Dan Akroyd, John Belushi, Chevy Chase, Jane Curtin, Gilda Radner, Steve Martin, Billy Crystal, Robin Williams, Eddie Murphy, and all the more recent members of the cast and guest hosts are so silly and creative. Watching them perform their crazy skits and antics makes me forget my problems and laugh hysterically. Laughter is the best medicine for me. I can't help but guffaw when I watch the antics of the Blues Brothers while they are on their "Mission from God". Well, we are all on our own personal mission from God, as God, are we not? When I am ill at ease or sad, I need nurturing and rest, so I go over to moms and get served with some of her delicious homemade chicken vegetable or turkey soup, get some warm hugs, and have some friendly "girl talk". I also make sure I get lots of hugs from friends, cuddles, and sensuous massage.

RITUAL

Though Catholics celebrated Jesus Christ's birth, death, and resurrection during a mass with two rituals symbolizing the Last Supper of Jesus in which he told his twelve apostles to drink of his blood and eating of his flesh, the Bible was only read a few times throughout the service, and these were select passages read to us by the priest ritual of drinking the blood of Christ with the priest drinking wine from a chalice and the parishioners were able to metaphorically "eat" of the body of Christ by taking a blessed wafer, a very thin paper-like substance which melted into our mouths.

Every spiritual path has rituals and symbols which, taken at face value, make no sense to practitioners of other paths. Based on the ritual just noted, some people historically even believed that Christians were cannibals! Instead, everything in the preceding paragraph has a purely symbolic meaning. So many "arguments" between adherents to different world religions have resulted from misunderstandings of symbols – sometimes by the very practitioners of the religions from which the symbols originate. It is easy to understand, for example, why many Muslims accuse Christians of *shirk*, the belief that there is another besides God.

ENCOURAGEMENT

Take heart, my dear ones. There is more awareness than ever before about mental illness. There is medication. There are natural God given herbs and essential oils like frankincense, sandalwood, myrrh, peppermint, rose, and lavender to calm your mind and uplift your spirits. There are trained counselors and natural health care practitioners. There is a tremendous amount of support from mental health groups and institutions. There is genuine love and concern for you from your family, friends, and the Divine Mother. There is much compassion. And most important, there is Source energy, God – the Truth of who you really are. This creative force is within you and is the solution to all of these temporary feelings and problems. When you go within and reconnect with Source all the illusory problems and sadness will disappear.

Whatever you do, don't put yourself through what I did by feeling ashamed, guilty, and worthless because you've had negative, suicidal, or disparaging thoughts about yourself. First of all, you are not alone. It is not you or your rational mind talking. It is a symptom of the illness and our thoughts, both conscious and subconscious beliefs that determine our experience of reality. We are not our thoughts or emotions. They are temporary, and will tend to go up and down. But the essence of you, your soul and Spirit does not change and will never die.

Blessed brothers and sisters, you are not alone. You are in excellent company. In fact, you are in the company of geniuses! Brilliant artists like Vincent Van Gogh, composers Rachmaninoff and Peter Ilyitch Tchaikovsky, poet Sylvia Plath, author Virginia Wolf, actresses Vivien Leigh, Patty Duke Astin, and Catherine Zeta-Jones,, comedienne Joan Rivers, newscasters and talk show hosts, Mike Wallace and Jane Pauley are some who have also been afflicted. Most of them have managed to come to a place of balance. Those who did not like Vincent Van Gogh, Sylvia Plath, and Vivien Leigh were glorious beings of Light who lived during a time when they did not have all the awareness, understanding, and medications like they have today and had more challenges to surmount. All of the aforementioned were unique expressions of divine intelligence who have made great contributions to society with their brilliant ideas, books of poetry, music, memoir, drama and art that reflect their genius, talent, and creativity.

The psychologist and author, Dr. Kay Redfield Jamison has made unique contributions to the research and treatment of bipolar disorder having experienced the illness firsthand. Her book, <u>An Unquiet Mind</u>, inspired me greatly. I am listening to it again on audiotape, and she has a wealth of wisdom to contribute to bipolar patients, their families, counselors, and doctors. Gary and I had the honor and pleasure to meet her in person when she gave a lecture at Labyrinth Books in Princeton a few years ago.

There are millions like us, just in America alone. And that counts for only those of us who have had the strength and courage to seek help from a psychiatrist or medical doctor and were therefore counted and diagnosed. There are still many more confused and depressed souls who suffer alone in silence. Don't let yourself be one of them! Please pray for guidance and go to a minister, priest, therapist, or doctor for help. Don't be afraid to tell your friends, family, and people closest to you because your illness is also going to affect them too.

Have no fear, my dear brothers and sisters of the Light. There is definitely hope for all of us who have experienced this kind of imbalance. In fact, there is always hope for everyone, no matter what kind of disease we might have, or how dire the circumstances in which we find ourselves. Within every problem lies a solution. When you have a problem, a desire exudes forth from you. God hears this desire and answers it immediately. Once you remove your attention from the problem, you then allow the solution. Giving birth to the question and then surrendering the problem to Source energy allows the answer to come, and all problems resolve themselves. I know from experience that when we feel deeply depressed it feels like we'll be that way forever, but please KNOW without a doubt that it is only temporary and that it too shall pass. We all must walk by faith, not by sight. Most of what we see in the world is illusion anyway, seen through a veil of forgetfulness and limited understanding, but this veil is becoming thinner and thinner, as our awareness of Who we truly are are grows.

When we allow ourselves to become still, quiet the mind, and just become a witness to the constant stream of thoughts eventually we come to realize we are not our bodies, thoughts, or emotions. We are the pure Consciousness beyond the thoughts that is aware that we are thinking. This Consciousness is One with everyone and everything. We constantly create our reality anew with our thoughts and attitudes, so it behooves us to master the mind. Control or witness our thoughts. We can change them from negativity and disillusionment to hope, faith and acceptance. The more positive our thoughts, the more positive thoughts, feelings, and circumstances we will attract. Go within the heart to find that source of unconditional love, equanimity, peace, joy, and success. Then we will thrive, and allow the natural state of Well-Being and bliss that is our divine nature, to pour through our physical vehicle from That Realm of Eternal, Omniscient Source from whence We came. There is nothing more important in life than that we feel good. Nothing! Feeling joy and contentment is our natural state of being if we just allow it. We are all here for one purpose. That is to experience and express the pure joy that is our nature! The basis of our lives is freedom, and we are free to be, do, or have absolutely anything and everything we want as co-creators with the One Magnificent Reality!

Source loves and adores you unconditionally. It is very proud of all that you are doing to contribute to the expansion of All-That-Is. So do not worry, my dear ones. All is well. In fact, well-being Reigns no matter what it looks like from our limited human perspective. All is working together for Good according to the Universal Laws of Attraction and Deliberate Creation. We are magnetically attracting every person, circumstance, and experience through the power of our focus.

No matter how sick a person seems in body or mind that person is still able to achieve perfect health. But the attention must be taken off what appears, and put upon that which is preferred – that which they desire. A new idea is the beginning of all deliberate creation. In this moment we project through thought and word what we choose to experience in our future. There is nothing more powerful than this moment. You summon Source energy each time you have a divine urge. All creative powers are at work bringing to us the object of our desires. Keep focusing on your dreams and visions, dear children. Imagine what you seek, and expect it until it appears.

"Right Thought"

There is a potential gift in every illness or adversity-a chance to learn and experience something new about you. People with disease are just temporarily ill at ease or out of harmony with some aspect of themselves. They are like magnets attracting unto them that which they are not wanting re-creating the same disease over and over again through their own thoughts by dwelling on what they are not wanting.

Those without money are dwelling upon lack. Those in poor health are dwelling on illness rather than accepting and allowing the perfect health and vitality that is the reality of Who they truly are. Most disease is psychological or unconscious in nature. When we discover the roots of the dis-ease we can prevent illness or heal it from the inside out. It is usually very simple. Just take the path of least resistance and focus on wellness.

Listen to your heart and pray for guidance. We all have a guidance system within because we are all connected to the Source of All-That-Is. Our higher Self or Inner being is our best friend and is always giving us guidance in the form of emotion. If we are feeling negative emotions like frustration, anger, rage, resentment, despair, or depression, it s a sign from our God Self that we are thinking a negative thought that does not match up with Who we truly are. There are only two emotions. One feels good, and the other feels bad. Go with the good feeling thoughts that bring about the positive emotions like gratitude, peace, contentment, appreciation, hope, enthusiastic expectation, and joy. As we are grateful for Who we are, and for what we have in the present moment, we allow our natural Well-being to flow and thrive. We feel light, and get into vibrational alignment with the abundance, love, and joy we desire.

MIND

Only you have the power to master your own mind, but sometimes it helps to have the support of others who have gone through a similar experience. Having the support of a competent, compassionate psychiatrist, a wise therapist, or one who has already mastered the mind through the power of God's grace and his own self effort like a true saint or guru was the way to balance and great physical and mental health for me. This is the great fortune of having an enlightened Master who always experiences Him/Herself as the Truth, one with the Infinite, eternal, Omniscient I Am Presence that creates, sustains, and eventually dissolves the Universe back into Its own being. This was my great blessing when I found a true guru, Swami Muktananda Paramahansa, an enlightened God Realized Master.

I'd like to pose the idea that everyone, even so-called" normal" healthy people have negative, judgmental thoughts at times about themselves or others. There is nobody in this world who has not, at one time or another, listened to the false, negative tapes in the mind. All human beings have had occasional dark times in which we thought, "I am not good enough." "I can't make it through this experience". Or, " I am lazy, my mother told me so". "I am fat and ugly". "No one will ever love me." "I will never be a success". "I am stupid". "I am sick".

We have thousands of such false beliefs our own egos, our parents, ancestors, and the mass consciousness have perpetrated upon us. But once we become aware of these annoying, judgmental inner critics we can thank them for teaching us what we are not wanting. It is never wise or practical to compare ourselves or our achievements with another human being because usually it will only make us feel unworthy or "less than". I know how I have felt whenever I think about other famous, successful, prolific writers, novelists, and poets like Danielle Steele, Steven King, Toni Morrison, or Maya Angelou. I would feel defeated before I even began to pick up a pen. In fact, I used their success as a way to bash myself over the head for being a failure and never attempted to try writing a novel or a play. Even if I had written something I liked and believed might be good I was afraid to send it out to a publisher, editor, or literary agent for fear of rejection.

I survived at least ten suicide attempts until I was finally diagnosed with manic depression and eventually led to the perfect combination of psychiatrists, counselors, medication, social workers, nutritionists, books, and audiotapes on the subject. Please have hope, faith, and the belief in yourself and your "Higher power" that you can too! Though I already had met my spiritual Master at 26 years of age, there was still much pain and anger from childhood and past life memories in my subconscious mind that needed to be healed. Since much of it was repressed, I needed to feel the emotions, process, and release them. Having a living Master, a loving family, supportive friends, psychiatrists, counselors, and teachers helped me to get through a living hell with this illness so that I could eventually come out on the other side feeling stronger and happier. It is much easier for me to embrace what one may call my shadow side now, to acknowledge and feel my emotions without judging or getting embroiled in them. If I feel sad or angry it is easy for me to express those emotions, and then I contemplate what was the thought that caused me to feel angry or sad in the first place and change it to one that soothes me and makes me feel joyful instead.

I believe with all my heart that each one of us can make it through all painful experiences, no matter how challenging. I believe in you and the power of God's love. I believe in the power of your own love that has guided you through each trial and tribulation you've been through throughout all time! We are all in the process of healing wounds and false beliefs that have been in the collective human consciousness for eons. Most people believe we are all separate from each other, and separate from God, but this is NOT true! Each one of us has a mission – our part to contribute to the healing of humanity. We are embarking on a great spiritual journey of ascension that will transform each of us into the gods and Masters we are destined to be.

Each one of us is a teacher and a healer and has as much to contribute to the growth and development of many others including the psychiatrists, nurses, and social workers in the mental health field. If they had all the answers, why is it that most of their patients continue to fall ill and become hospitalized over and again the way that my mother and I were? I was hospitalized at least seven times. My mom was hospitalized about four or five times and made two serious suicide attempts in which I became her rescuer and support person. Many of the patients I've befriended at these institutions like the Carrier Clinic in Belle Mead, Marlboro State Hospital, Helene Fuld in Trenton, and in Princeton House had been repeatedly hospitalized again and again during the course of many years. The doctors and nurses would like you to believe and will tell you that it was because these patients went off of their meds that they became unstable and needed a medication adjustment, but I propose that this was not usually the case. Often there are underlying triggers from birth, childhood or past life traumas that caused us to go into post-traumatic stress and a major depressive episode. Some can be caused by natural circumstances like a dear friend or mate dying or becoming ill, getting fired from a job, or whatever challenge a person must face in life.

Sometimes a person may have a strong negative reaction as their kundalini becomes awakened, and the negative samskaras or impressions located along the sushumna nadi, the central channel along the spine, get purified. This is called the sushumna nadi by gurus and yogic adepts like my teacher, Swami Muktananda. When all of the chakras, or wheel-like energy centers are open and cleared a jiva or individualized soul will eventually become a jivan mukti or Self-Realized Being where he or she experiences himself as One with God and feels sublime peace, joy, and ecstasy in each and every moment. This is the major goal of all incarnations – to reunite with the Divine. All of this is here for us to experience a few moments of joy, peace, and love. And then we return to that Ocean of Love from whence we came.

In my mind, being honest with oneself and others is the best policy. How many married couples stay together arguing and feeling miserable and unappreciated just for the sake of the children? Since children learn what they live and model their parents' behavior, I do not think this is something we want to pass on as healthy behavior. When I was married to my second abusive husband, at one point I felt as if I was trapped and would never be able to get out of the relationship. Thank God this proved not to be true or I would have stayed stuck and felt abused and miserable for more years than we actually stayed together. We were separated soon after getting married, but we did have a baby together, so it was at least six years of confusion, comings and goings before a divorce settlement was finally reached. But, even as a single mother with financial and emotional challenges I felt so much happier. And I learned to become stronger through yoga, meditation, prayer, going to college, counseling, and just being on my own.

DOCTORS

It may seem that I have problems with the entire medical profession. This is simply not so. I will address alternative medicine below, but I have also had a few "regular" allopathic doctors who have helped me tremendously. And I have learned to take advice from them, or to suffer when I didn't.

According to the author and publisher, Louise Hay, who wrote "You Can Heal your life", abundant health is our natural state of well being and it is only one good thought away.

I am so very grateful, however, to the surgeons, nurses, burn technicians, and medical doctors who repaired my body following my two serious suicide attempts after I shot myself in the head in 1987 and in 1999 when I set my pajama tee-shirt on fire. The surgeons, nurses, burn technicians, doctors, and social worker at St. Barnabas Hospital in Livingston made me feel welcome, hopeful, and best of all they made me laugh and smile in the early mornings when they washed my burns with oil. I am indebted to them for their knowledge, kindness, compassion, and expertise[13].

Sometimes, too, my body tells me I need a break, but I rarely if ever, get genuinely sick, and if I do, I do not usually need a doctor. However, I have a wonderful, competent, caring, young Indian woman, Dr. Nair, as a primary care physician who is someone I trust to help with preventive maintenance or being there for me if I get a bit too careless about physical tests like cat scans, mammograms, and/or a colonoscopy. Once I did not listen to her right away when she wanted me to go to a specialist to take a picture of my lungs. I did not realize it was so important since I just believed I had a simple case of the flu, so I waited to get the sonogram or whatever, and it turned out I had double pneumonia. I thought I'd just had influenza which I picked up from kissing one of my old boyfriends who had been ill and was taking an antibiotic. That'll teach me to fool around! Anyway, that was a close call, but my doctors and angels saved me from death for the umpteenth time. If it wasn't for my son, Gabriel, who'd just returned from a vacation in Belize, trusting the guidance of Dr. Bhajaj, the head of the ICU at Pen Medicine in Princeton, who told him I needed to be intubated because I was only operating on eight per cent oxygen in both my lungs; so my son was asked to sign an agreement in order for me to have this procedure done in order to save my life since my boyfriend, Gary, was not related to me and therefore unable to be a legal signer in order for me to get intubated and have my lungs cleared of mucus or whatever it was that saved my life.

---

13 I would return to St. Barnabas in 2016 to visit Gabriel's friend, Matty, who was healing from a spinal cord injury.

There have also been some excellent psychiatrists, psychologists, chiropractors, and counselors over the years who have helped me tremendously like Dr. Betsy Wilson, Dr. Moss, Shashi. Dr. Swapna Nair, Dr. Vince Kiechlin, and Dr. Khouri.

I have had so many wonderful doctors, both holistic and allopathic, on my "team". I'd just like to mention a few more. I met a Muslim doctor and physical therapist at a rally for Palestinians one year at Hinds Plaza in Princeton; he gave me his card and said he thought he could help strengthen my weaker, hemiplegic side. He was such a kind and wise man who would prostrate on the floor in the middle of a work day with several other doctors at his office to pray toward Mecca to Allah for the health and well-being of all his patients while I was there on the medical table; I thought that was such a beautiful gesture for everyone to slow down in the middle of a day to think of God and the welfare of their patients.

I also love my current physical therapist, Dr. Dae Kim who runs Edison Rehabilitation and Acupuncture. He is a great physical therapist and intuitively brilliant acupuncturist. And everyone on his staff. In particular, I love my chiropractor, Dr. Park, whose hands are like magic. He always massages my cervical and tense shoulders before adjusting me which makes my axis go into place so much easier. Jay Hun, my favorite massage therapist, also gives me a very intuitive twenty-minute massage on my back before I even get to Dr. Park for my chiropractic adjustment. Most people think chiropractic care and massage therapy are just for bad backs and aligning the spine, but both actually work on all the systems of the body; and each vertebra has an emotional component and organ that it helps stimulate or heal.

Dr. Eric Evans is a wonderful chiropractor, too, with a practice in hamilton, and he is an expert in nutrition and certified in "functional medicine".

HEALING

I have been dealing with manic depression and serious mood swings for half my adult life, and believe me, it's not been an easy road. For me or the friends and family of a manic-depressive person. I would not be here now if it were not for my "Support Team" --my mom, children, my ex-husband, David and his wife, Laurie. If it were not for the unconditional love, support, an encouragement of my best friends, Zara Rose Zagerman, and Pan, my chiropractic neurologist, Dr. Vince. My other dear friend and chiropractor, Dr. Annie Monetti, the kindness of my many home health aides at Mercy home Care like Anya and Cesy as well as the aides I met through the agency, Carefinders like Masiel and Sheira Garcia, I would not be here now writing this so that you could read my memoir and possibly be helped by it also. It takes a lot of loving people to care for a person like me with a mental illness and a physical disability.

Rev. Karen Kushner, my close friends and prayer practitioners at the Center for Spiritual Living - Princeton helped me get through so many challenging times by just listening to my problems with respect and concern while simultaneously Knowing and affirming the Truth for me-- that all is truly well, and I am perfectly healthy, Whole, and complete, in their affirmative prayer treatments. The church was formerly known as the Religious Science Church, but changed its name to avoid confusion with Christian Science or Scientology.

And all the doctors, nurses, psychologists, and counselors who treated me since 1988, when I was finally diagnosed one year after shooting myself in my precious head. My chiropractic neurologist, Dr. Vince, has been a Godsend, and my favorite female chiropractor, Dr. Annie Monetti, literally changed my life within three months of bi-weekly adjustments and conversations that were so deep and helpful I felt like I was having a conversation with God at each appointment. Dr. Annie is a "Wonder Woman. Not only does she have a successful practice as a healer and chiropractor, but she has five children, a husband who works in Washington DC, and three dogs for whom to care besides her many patients. My life is so much better and happier because of these two wise and caring beings. I have two other wonderful chiropractors who have become my friends—Dr. Park at Edison Rehabilitation and Dr. Evans in Hamilton, New Jersey.

Dr. Van Beveren helped me immensely to understand I had an imbalance in my minerals and helped me with better nutrition. A few good psychiatrists like Betsy Wilson at the Community Mental Health Center in Piscataway, and Dr. Moss whom I met while at Carrier Clinic in 1991 who recognized my mood swings for what they were—a biochemical imbalance, and suggested trying Depakote, a drug they use for preventing seizures to help stabilize my moods so I could lead a healthy. normal, happy life. She said I would not have the highs anymore, but neither would the lows be so extreme and devastating. She was right even though I never lost my enthusiasm for life.

I also love the doctor, scientist on anti-aging, daily radio personality on WBAI and clinical nutritionist, Dr. Gary Null, who does not believe in mental illness as a disease in and of itself, but who believes most illnesses, whether they be mental, physical, emotional, or spiritual, can be reversed easily through proper nutrition with a vegan diet, daily supplements, exercise for at least one half hour daily, and stress reduction by using meditation, hatha yoga, walking in nature, connecting to God or ones spiritual nature on a regular basis, and by being kind and helping others as a way of life. Dr. Null himself never charges for his services as a nutrition and holistic health counselor. Gary has all sorts of interesting speakers on his show at noon every day on WBAI, public, listener sponsored, radio, which is very progressive and opens one's mind to all sorts of new viewpoints and perspectives from teachers' doctors, and politicians who have had direct experience with the dangers of using drugs and medications through Big Pharma as well as the dangers of getting required and forced vaccinations, especially when one is an infant. There are many other differing viewpoints and perspectives on his show that I will not go into here, but I highly recommend listening to his show or opening up the WBAI archives to get a completely different and unconventional perspective from the rest of the masses who are controlled by the media owned by big corporations and such. Dr. Null has science and multiple studies to back up each and every claim he makes. He has personally reversed dozens of supposedly incurable diseases of all kinds-from autism to full blown AIDS. to every type of cancer, diabetes, multiple sclerosis, and Alzheimer's. In my estimation, after watching one of his many documentaries on veganism and how animals are tortured and murdered by factory farmers for man's greed and unethical appetite, I was moved to tears and felt as if I should make the trip into Manhattan to see him about my manic-depressive illness without using medications I no longer believe in, especially since Dr. Null says he has never charged a patient a single penny. They just need money for the foods on his protocol as well as the money to purchase vitamin supplements. Gary does not make a dime off any of the formulas he creates in the laboratory specifically for us, as a gift to us in service to humanity and for the preservation and respect of animal's welfare and the benefit of the planet Herself.

SPIRITUALITY

My brother, Pete, is a chiropractor who has been there with me as a happy, committed, and devoted Christian family man who knows personally through direct experience, of Jesus Christ's deep, personal love for each one of us as well as His personal sacrifice on the cross as well as His power to heal absolutely anything if we have faith and believe in Him as our own personal Savior. That was never my path for many years because I despised Catholicism and its false teachings of sin and shame, so I was was not drawn to Christianity at first, being more attracted to Buddhism, Hinduism, and the teachings that came out of the East. Then, I found my first true teacher and guru, in the Indian saint, Swami Muktananda, and then his successor, Gurumayi Chidvilasananda, and his brilliant student, the teacher, writer, and meditation Master, Donnie Ram Butler, who wrote the Siddha Yoga Correspondence Course back in the seventies which eventually morphed into the e-course "Living in the Truth of the present Moment", which I am still reading and studying NOW in this holy moment. Though Ram, who humbly referred to himself as just a typist for his personal guides and former Master teacher, ascended into heaven (passed away) in September of last year, in 2019, the course is still continuing due to the industry, diligence, and kindness of his beloved wife and partner, Kunti Kay Butler, who lives in a lovely home in Forest City, PA, but due to the power of computers and the internet, is still easily able to e-mail the course to thousands of Siddha Yoga students and devotees of God and the guru throughout the world.

Now I personally draw upon the teachings of all these many saints, guides, guardians, angels, and infinitely interesting paths that are many but always lead an aspirant seeking enlightenment back to the One Source of All Beings from whence we came. God Him/Herself, in, as, and through all beings and people everywhere.

BODY

Image

It's sad that when I share with most people like some of the members of my church that I am a nudist and naturist who enjoys suntanning at Gunnison Beach, a nude beach in Sandy Hook, NJ, in my birthday suit that they automatically think I am a nymphomaniac, whore, or even worse, a prostitute to be shunned and scorned from the church community. It is terribly tragic that violence is something completely tolerated by our society, but when it comes to something as natural as breastfeeding your baby in public the way I did my newborns, or nude sunbathing, most conventional people are in an uproar about it.

First of all, in case you did not notice, we were born naked. And God deemed the body beautiful. Our bodies, the temples that house our souls, should be treated with love, kindness, and reverence. To me, that means eating fresh fruits and vegetables, nuts, seeds, and grains, and limiting foods, drinks, alcohol, chemicals, and substances that do not contribute to its Life force. I am very careful about what I put in and on my precious temple. The few times I experimented with drugs or other mind-altering substances when I was much younger, I was sorry.

I dry brush my skin vigorously in the morning before my bath to rid myself of dead skin cells and stimulate circulation. After a hot Epsom salt bath, I dry myself and then apply Edgar Cayce's Aura Glo or olive oil on my skin while massaging my muscles and joints at least every other day.

The fact that some people find a naked body offensive completely puzzles me. I suppose they are not too comfortable in their own skin or do not love their own bodies very much. The only reason we are wearing clothes is to protect us against the elements, folks. Oh yes, and as the years progressed, people liked clothes for "adornment" and then it became the "fashion" to wear things like loin cloths, kimonos, togas, skirts, kilts, pants, halter tops, etc. But when we first started out, we were naked and so beautiful and pure just as we were. We invented clothes like buffalo, wolf, and deer skins for protection against the cold and other elements. Then years later the patriarchy got the idea that our genitals were bad and dirty and must be hidden. Also, women's' breasts and especially her nipples. What nonsense.

I am a sun worshiper and would be very happy to live in my own clothing optional community in Hawaii, Bali, a Caribbean Island, or some tropical island paradise. But for now, I enjoy living adorned in fashionable clothes, halter and bikini tops in the spring and summer Princeton

HEALTH

As a proponent of natural healthcare, I rarely take antibiotics for anything unless I've exhausted every other alternative, because the antibiotics compromise our own natural immune system. They destroy the natural, healthy flora located in our guts. God gave us a perfect machine in the form of our bodies with a terrific guidance system that automatically heals and balances itself just so long as we don't poison or neglect it. In fact, the human body is designed to last for over a hundred years if we maintain it with proper nutrition, daily exercise, and positive thinking. My grandmother, Lucy, lived to be almost ninety-eight years old and was thriving up until the last two years when she got COPD. and ended up in bed a lot. Three of her Italian brothers lived to be happy and healthy up until their mid-nineties.

My paternal grandfather, Henry Olson, lived to be a vibrant, active ninety-two years young. In fact, he still had his license and was driving his car up until he was about ninety. My uncle told him to stop driving when he kept having little fender benders the last few years he was driving in Sarasota and Venice, FL on the highways.

Nutrition is key to maintaining a healthy mind and emotional balance. I discuss this topic below.

DANGERS OF PRESCRIPTION DRUGS

Rather than just assuming that the "cure" for everything is a drug, we should consider alternatives.

I had a session with a man from Sedona, Arizona, named Christopher Fromkin whom I'd met at a meeting of the New Hope Metaphysical Society. He did some special psychotherapy called Byron Katie's "The Work". I met him at Pebble Hill Church when he was a featured speaker at the New Hope Metaphysical Society in Doylestown, Pennsylvania. I felt an incredible connection with him after hearing him speak and watching him do Byron Katie's work on another volunteer in the room that night. I hesitated to raise my hand because I did not believe I had any issues to work on at the time. Still, I was very impressed with what I saw and felt guided to do a personal journey with him. His relaxed and available Presence reminded me of another teacher I'd worked with named Paul Lowe. I experienced Paul as a unique, free, unconventional, open-hearted and wise teacher. I'd taken a workshop with him in New York City at the suggestion of my dear friend and lover, Ernie. I also saw some of Paul's audiotapes and read a book he wrote with his wife, Ava, whose given name was Grace. I used to watch Paul teach classes on video with Grace sitting quietly holding the energy by his side. She was just beautiful, peaceful, and quietly powerful.

The work Chris did with me at the home of a friend in Pennsylvania was spontaneous, creative, and profound. I got in touch with some deep seated, subconscious sadness and powerlessness I felt when being molested by my dad as well as some rage, hatred, and anger towards my mom when she was verbally, physically, and psychologically abusing me at the ages of four, five, and fourteen. I had reservations about making the appointment because I was living on the edge financially and needed more money with which to pay my bills, but the Universe told me that I deserved the best work possible as an angelic healer. I knew that if I put out the $100 check out for the session that I would be rewarded in some great way. Right after my session two new clients called to make appointments for an Esalen massage for which I charge $100 per ninety-minute session. I had a truly transformative, healing session. Not only was it unique, profound, and transformational, but I made a good friend.

After we were done Chris asked me if I had any desire to get off the medication I was taking for bipolar illness. I said, "Yes, of course. Eventually someday I had hoped that I would no longer be dependent on taking a tranquilizer to keep me in balance. He shared an audiotape with me of a Young Living conference in which the actor, Clint Walker, and a psychiatrist, Dr. Ann Blake Tracy, were the featured speakers. Wow, the information I heard on that tape changed my life and attitude forever about taking serotonergic anti-depressants. Dr. Tracy had been researching the effects of drugs like Prozac, Paxil, Effexor, Seroquel, Wellbutrin, Luvox, Zyprexa, Risperdal, and others with which I was not familiar. The results of these studies were astounding.

Apparently, after having removed any suicidal patients from the clinical trials, the incidence of suicide in these trial subjects increased from zero to 65 % in a testing sample of nine hundred patients on drugs like Prozac, Effexor, Zoloft, Paxil, Luvox, Lexapro, Serafim, Remeron, and Lubamil. What these results indicated were that people taking these prescription drugs had a 65% greater chance of being more likely to attempt suicide while taking the anti-depressants than if they had not taken any medication at all! The risk of suicide jumped 3 per cent to 68 % for people taking anti-psychotic drugs like Zyprexa, Seroquel, and Risperdal.

The world has been told that when you are depressed that you have a problem with your serotonin level being too low. According to the research over the last sixty years what is actually low in depression is your ability to metabolize serotonin. When one cannot metabolize serotonin, the level goes down. The way the anti-depressants work is by impairing your ability to metabolize serotonin, which was the problem in the first place! It is the inability of the body to metabolize serotonin due to poor eating and living habits, which causes a biochemical imbalance, and is the actual cause of depression. Through her research since the nineteen seventies Dr. Tracy found that people with anxiety had serotonin levels that were eight times higher in patients who suffered from high anxiety. When one cannot metabolize serotonin, the levels build higher and higher from the use of these drugs.

Many disorders like psychosis, schizophrenia, depression, mood disorders, autism, anorexia, mental retardation, organic brain disease, violent crime, insomnia, and suicide result. Taking these drugs has resulted in very violent suicide attempts, violent nightmares, exhibitionism, hostility and argumentative behavior, arson, substance abuse, chemical dependency, schizophrenia, Alzheimer's, road rage, and impulsive murder. This list is what patients have reported as the typical side effects from taking these prescription drugs which inhibit a person's ability to metabolize serotonin.

Dr. Tracy believes that these drugs are responsible for many of the impulsive mass murders like those at Columbine and Mattawa, Washington. There a seventeen-year-old student named Corey Badascar who was a religious Mormon boy, an Eagle Scout and very active in his church, tried to murder his fellow classmates while first on Paxil and later Effexor. After a year on Paxil the doctor switched him to Effexor which is the same drug that Andrea Yates was on when she drowned her four children. Corey was only on Effexor for three weeks when he had a bad reaction. He told his father he did not feel well, went to bed, and when he woke up, he was in jail. He woke up from a violent nightmare, got dressed, got his father's gun, and then held twenty-three students in his classroom at gunpoint. Fortunately, the teacher was able to persuade Corey to give her the gun before he was able to hurt anyone. He apparently had the same kind of violent reaction to the medications that the two boys did at Columbine High School.

Mark Taylor was the first student shot in the Columbine High School Massacre. He is now the director in the state of Colorado for the National Coalition for Drug Awareness. Mark will tell you that the reason he is alive today is to tell the world that the reason the students at Columbine were murdered was because of the use of these drugs. Mark was shot seventeen times in the chest, and prayed for an hour and a half that God would spare his life as fifty kids ran over his limp body. Mark was so near death that his body was thrown underneath all the other dead bodies in a police car and actually brought into the coroner's office of the hospital where the attending physician was very surprised when Mark began talking to him.

Corey, the school shooter and Mark, the injured victim of a deranged shooter on antidepressant drugs, have joined forces this past year and gained the attention of the United States Senate. They gathered together many parents of the suicide victims to testify at Senate and FDA hearings.

According to Dr. Tracy, another man named Doug Williams who put his faith in doctors and psychiatry was on Zoloft and Celexa when he shot and killed five co-workers when he then turned the gun upon himself.

Michael McDermott, the man who perpetrated the Edgewater technology shootings was also a victim on Prozac for depression when he killed seven coworkers. Mathew Beck shot five of his coworkers before killing himself.

Many more tragic murder suicides are believed to be the result of the use of these dangerous drugs. When will the medical community realize that these drugs are not a panacea for the cure of mental illness? In some cases, these drugs are the actual cause of the physical and emotional problems that are so prevalent in our society today.

Having been in the mental health system myself for over twenty-five years I can say from experience that drugs and psychotherapy were not responsible for the major part of my healing, and in some instances the medicines were the cause of a few depressive episodes. It was because of my desire to be well and whole and because of my love for Self and my faith in God that I was able to persist and overcome all the obstacles I've encountered along the spiritual path. The causes of my mental illness were deeply rooted in my subconscious mind, which began as negative self-talk caused, by early birth trauma, childhood physical and psychological abuse, and negative past life memories. It has only been due to my own personal yearning and search for mental, physical, emotional, and spiritual well-being that I am as happy and healthy as I am today. It was due to the contrasting experiences I had while suffering in the dark that gave me the strong desire to be in constant divine communion with the Source of my being, my very own divine bliss filled Essence. It has been quite an exciting and arduous adventure, which has contributed to great growth, strength, and a desire for wholeness. My exciting journey is still unfolding and joyously expanding each day I'm alive.

The company who started marketing the antidepressant drugs they are pushing today put out Prozac first and was the same one that manufactured LSD and PCP, telling people that these chemicals would be a cure for alcoholism, mental illness, and an aid in psychoanalysis. There is a sixty-eight per cent greater rate of suicide using the anti-psychotics that are serotonergic like Zyprexa, geodome, Risperdal, and Seroquel. While I was a patient at Princeton House, my psychiatrist put me on Seroquel for ten days. Not only did I feel lethargic and drugged like a zombie, but I also felt so depressed that I needed to be released into my mother's care feeling more hopeless and suicidal than when I'd entered the hospital two weeks before.

My good friend, Fiona Miller, who lived in Griggs Farm up until her death by suicide several years ago, was only eighteen when she took her own life while at Earth House in Princeton. Her mother, Ruth, another massage therapist, and I, became good friends following her death. Ruth said Fiona was given Paxil while at Earth House. The doctors diagnosed her with bipolar disorder, but apparently the drug did not do its job. Just a few weeks after being on the drug Fiona disappeared. The nurses, aids, and other people at Earth House searched for Fiona for three months and could not find her.

Ruth became quite concerned and posted a sign at the Whole Earth Center in Princeton where Fiona worked as a cashier urging her daughter to call pleading with her to come home. Ruth must have been beside herself with worry; she must have thought Fiona had run away from the hospital. Unfortunately for Ruth, her brother, Andrew, and everyone that knew and loved her, this was not the case. Her boyfriend, John, had visited her the night before and Fiona told him she'd done something for which she was ashamed. Apparently, she had made a poor choice while on the drugs and the shame she felt made her feel guilty enough to hurt herself and end her temporary misery.

After three long months of searching and worry on her family's part, Fiona's lifeless body was finally found hanging from a tree outside somewhere on the grounds at Earth House. She had hung herself in a tragic moment of despair and hopelessness. How was this tragedy allowed to take place? Ruth totally trusted the hospital, psychiatrists, doctors, nurses, aids, and medications when she put Fiona into Earth House. She put her into the hospital expecting that she would be kept safe and that her condition would improve, not deteriorate to the point of insanity. Is it possible that being on Paxil caused Fiona to take her own life? My young friend and neighbor, Fiona, was a beautiful, creative, gentle soul who brought sweetness and joy to her family, friends, neighbors, and many in her community. It is a tragic shame what happened to her as a consequence of taking these potentially dangerous and fatal drugs. Her life was so precious, and I will never forget how she touched mine. I do not want her sweet life or her death to be in vain. How many more lives will it take before the psychiatrists, pharmacists, and nurses realize that these drugs are not a panacea for all society's mental and emotional problems?

I recently read a book written by a psychologist and medical doctor called "Your Drug May be your Problem".

I also detest Big Pharma and how they start getting people hooked on dangerous medications at a young age—like Ritalin for hyperactive children, for example. Kids are naturally energetic and creative. It is not necessary to calm them down or to tame the natural, inherent energy that is their divine birthright, by forcing them to take a medication that stunts their creativity and probably has negative side effects that will cause them to have to take other medications to counteract the negative side effects. It's a vicious endless cycle that only keeps the pharmaceutical industry in business long term and truly cures absolutely nothing.

Once people start on these medications with their negative side effects it becomes a daily habit and very challenging to stop. I believe sometimes they have been useful for me on a temporary basis, but I've also used other means of quieting the powerful Kundalini energy like chanting OM Namah Sivaya and meditation. I've also preferred at times to use flower medicine like the Bach flower essences and young living aromatherapy. The doctors and psychiatrists convince us we will need these medications for life, but I do not believe this in my heart anymore. There are Christian Scientists I know personally with bi-polar disorder, broken bones, and misaligned shoulders who have used just the Scientific teachings in the Bible to miraculously heal both mental illness, fractured bones, and a girl's shoulder that went out of place while she was playing basketball. Not quackery. Not miracles, but deep relaxation, trust, and faith in the alchemy created instantaneously through the power of Belief in God. The belief that God is in man and everywhere present at all times in all places.

One of my best friends, Diana Dawley, has also experienced the ineptness of the psychiatric profession. Diana had been on and off different drugs for years, but she never found one that got to the core of her depression or supposed manic states in which she felt completely One with Jesus Christ, her divine lover and precious best friend. She had a sister who was also a victim of suicide while a patient in Marlboro State Psychiatric Hospital. I'm not sure how it happened, but her sister was able to hang herself by the neck with a pair of her own blue jeans. Was it her illness that caused her to become suicidal, or was it the medications she was on? To the consternation and upset of her family, we still do not know. My loving friend, Diana, went to Costa Rica to care for her ailing elderly father and expected to return to Princeton as a millionairess. Her father died after a few years, and Diana was lonely and alone. She was supposed to inherit her dad's finca, but a claim was put on it by the former common law wife who'd lived with her dad for years before she arrived. Diana's moods went up and down for the five years we kept in touch, but eventually she stopped calling and writing to me. One year I mailed her a special birthday card, gift, and Christmas present altogether because her birthday was right before Christmas. I did not receive a card that year nor did I get a call or card thanking me for my gifts. A year later my gifts were sent back by the post office to my surprise and consternation.

To this day I do not know the fate of my precious friend, Diana. I do have the feeling in my gut that she is finally with her Lord and Savior, Jesus Christ.

At one point she told me she'd lost her job as a home health aide, her cable TV had been turned off for nonpayment, and she had fallen and was put into the hospital where they discovered she was dehydrated and malnourished. I wanted her to return to Jersey and told her she could move in with me somewhere, but she said she did not have the money for a plane ticket. To this day I have not heard from her brother in Texas and am unaware for certain what was the ultimate fate of my beautiful friend.

I also became good friends with a lovely dark-haired woman named Pat at the Community Mental Health Center in Piscataway when I was hospitalized there for three months in the autumn of 1988 following my divorce from David and sudden remarriage to Lyle. Pat was very sweet and friendly and she shared that she'd already been a patient at the hospital for three months the first day I arrived as a voluntary patient. Pat appeared to be improving after a few months and her doctor released her into her husband's care. Pat had a beautiful eighteen-year-old daughter who'd come to visit her with her dad. They were both thrilled when mom was ready to come home. Unfortunately, the weekend after she was released the staff and patients received some sad and shocking news. Pat had hung herself downstairs in the cellar while her family was out of the house. Her poor daughter found her mom's lifeless body and was devastated, of course.

I remember it well because I was supposed to go home with Lyle on a weekend pass, but all the patients were kept in the hospital due to the tragedy. There was a meeting with a social worker and one of the nurses for us to talk about the tragedy so that we could share our feelings and concerns. Not only was I disappointed that I would not be able to go home for the week-end to sleep in my own bed with my husband and pet my cats, but I was so sad and angry that Pat had hurt herself. She was loved dearly by her family, friends and many of the nurses and patients who'd gotten to know her at the hospital were terribly saddened by the loss of such a beautiful, vital, special human being.

Unfortunately, for reasons of which we are unsure, the medical doctors who participated in Dr. Tracy's clinical studies ten years ago somehow neglected to call her back when they had gotten in all the test results. The study had been sitting there for years, but the doctors deliberately neglected to share these astonishing findings.

I wonder if this little slip had anything to do with the connection between the FDA, the physicians, and the multi-billion-dollar pharmacological industry. Many of the doctors who do this research get exorbitant grants, and these negative findings would not boost sales of the companies who authorize the research. Depending upon who pays the bill often influences the outcomes of the various medical research. However, in this case there was no mistake.

In September of that same year there was an investigation and trial in Washington DC. in which the parents of suicide victims of children nineteen years of age and under testified before the Food and Drug Administration and the Senate in order to have the dangers of these drugs made known. Despite their obvious negative findings, the FDA opted not to take most of these dangerous drugs off the market, though they did ban the use of Paxil in anyone under the age of nineteen. They merely told the manufacturers of some of these dangerous drugs to put stricter warning labels on the bottles. It seems that our children's lives are not as precious as the almighty dollar or as powerful as the multi-billion-dollar pharmaceutical industry, medical, and psychiatric profession.

In June of 2004 England, Ireland, Wales, and Scotland banned Paxil for anyone under the age of eighteen. Nine clinical studies that were kept hidden mysteriously appeared after twelve years, and it was proven that Paxil produces suicide, self-mutilation, violence, psychosis, and medical damage at a rate of two and half times to 3.2 times greater than a placebo. Paxil's manufacturers are now facing possible criminal charges for withholding that information from the public. Even the US. Food and Drug Administration finally moved on this information and acted on it this past autumn by banning Paxil in the use of anyone eighteen years old and under. With the help of Senator Chuck Schumer, a concerned Senate subcommittee listened to the testimonies of Coalition for Drug Awareness director, Lisa Van Sickle, and other concerned, grieving parents. Lisa's daughter was severely harmed by the use of these drugs, and other parents lost their children by means of suicide from the use of these dangerous antidepressant drugs.

The physicians and pharmacists are making millions of dollars off of our sickness and uninformed choices. Many of these drugs are contributing to the diseases and illnesses you and I are now experiencing! The side effects from the medication you are taking to prolong your health may just be the actual cause of your untimely demise!

What do you think of that? Don't you think it is about time that you began doing your own research into a more holistic approach and taking responsibility for your own health as opposed to relying on doctors who want to make a profit off of your illness? Your body is their product, and they are trying to sell you on the idea that you need them in order to be healthy. Just look at the hundreds of commercials promoting fear, illness, depression, heartburn, allergies, indigestion, restless leg syndrome, social anxiety disorder, and hundreds of other nonsensical maladies. Give me a break. Take your attention off the television and the crap they are trying to sell you before you are brainwashed into believing it's all true.

Recently, while listening to the nutritionist, author, and famous radio personality, Dr. Gary Null, he talked about a new documentary he was working on about reversing so-called "incurable diseases". He mentioned he had a panel of "expert allopathic doctors and psychiatrists, whom he asked if there was actual clinical, scientific proof that mental disorders like depression and bi-polar illness were caused by biochemical imbalances in the brain. He said not one on the panel of ten physicians had any scientific proof that mental illness was caused by a biochemical imbalance in the brain. Not one. This documentary will be coming out shortly. It is now the summer of 2020, and with all the crazy beliefs about the corona virus being "in the air" and its seeming causes, I am excited to see Gary Null's newest scientific documentary. I am especially excited because Gary Null is one of the only holistic doctors, I know who has taken ten HIV patients with full blown AIDS and completely reversed the disease by changing the person's diet to a vegan one without sugar, wheat gluten, and dangerous additives and put them on a regular protocol of daily aerobic exercise, fresh juicing, and added nutritional supplements. Dr. Null offers his services for free and even donates his time on the air and complete salary as a gift to WBAI, so it is obvious he does not have a personal agenda or motive to lie to the public. I heard several patients and clients on his show share the amazing results they received from following his suggestions and protocols on reversing aging.

In my opinion, gleaned from experience, the drugs and medications used for "so called" mental illness only bring temporary relief anyway; they numb us to feeling the emotions which are our guidance system, and from what I could see while institutionalized, turned most people who are temporarily hospitalized into walking zombies, who can be easily controlled and manipulated. Many "illnesses" are only believed to be real because we have been conditioned by BIG PHARMA, all the pharmaceutical companies and corporations who benefit from our taking hundreds of expensive medications for decades now and commercials and advertisements everywhere, from magazines to Billboards, that we actually NEED these chemical pills. We have been literally bombarded by these messages for over a quarter century. Decades of false programming and mind control has completely ruined our RACE Consciousness of Natural Well Being and Abundant Health into one of terminal illnesses caused by flus, viruses, and other "bugs" we can easily catch. We do NOT need most of this crap with all its horrible side effects. Not to mention the exorbitant cost of the medicines. Nor do we need rampant vaccinations which have been shown by studies and parents to cause autism, other illnesses, and sometimes even lead to death! I heard the woman doctor and virologist who was the head of the AIDS program sharing why she resigned from being in charge of distributing the vaccine used to control HIV and AIDS. The vaccine called, AZT scientists had invented to cure HIV/AIDS, according to her, actually killed a quarter of a million people. The homosexual partners who saw their loved one die from using the vaccine made a lifesaving decision not to use AZT after seeing how it affected their partners. The facts are there according to many doctors, but they have been silenced by the BIG corporations that make these vaccines. Even people who were given the vaccination for smallpox eventually died. Their immunity to smallpox decreased every year after they were given the smallpox vaccination.

Thousands of African children were killed who were given the vaccine for polio. And now, in the age of "the novel corona virus, we are expected to believe some miracle cure is being concocted for everyone in a lab somewhere to save humanity; and this will be a forced global vaccination that will be mandated by governments.

First of all, I have a perfect immune system. I was tested for co-vid 19, as was my eighty-four-year-old mother, twice, with positive results. I mean the test came back that I was and am perfect, whole, and complete in every way! I think and treat myself in only positive ways as far as food choices, exercise, and give myself time to meditate and receive massages which lower all my stress levels.

Tell me now, what sane person would take a medication advertised often on commercial television for depression which has the possible side effects Of Depression AND suicidal thoughts or actions? That is what it says on the side effect label for Quetiapine, or Seroquel, the antidepressant I was prescribed. First of all, it caused constipation which never made me feel very good. "Excuse me, ma'am, just in case this medicine has a few unhealthy side effects that might kill you, or practically kill you, I am warning you about it in advance, so go take it anyway just in case you might feel a little relief after a few doses. It may cause damage to your liver, your heart and your kidneys. And if that's not enough reason to influence a healthy person to NOT take this pill, they warn you a person taking this medicine on a regular basis might possibly become so chronically depressed and crazy that he'll have suicidal thoughts and/or want to kill himself! Isn't that WHY we are taking the medication in the first darn place, you idiots?! What the hell are they thinking? We are NUTS?! You'd *have* to be a desperate, insane NUT CASE to take these medications with all these potentially fatal side effects after hearing all that! But that's BIG PHARMA for you. They have been making millions, no billions of dollars off us "consumers" for so long that it has now become status quo. It has just become the norm over the last seventy years to take a chemically manufactured pill as opposed to eating healthy foods, connecting with Mother Earth by actually growing a garden of your own, or planning a larger one with friends in a community setting where you could be growing your own food and herbs. And taking one half hour per day in meditation to just relax and feel our own natural well-being. We are not encouraged to. tune into our own divine inner guidance, listen to our intuition, or try using the medicine from plants like echinacea, sage, astragalus, or oregano to stimulate our own immune system in order to prevent getting a virus, flu, or whatever illness we are all creating in order to slow us down so we can re-evaluate our lives and heartfelt desires and dreams at any given moment. At least that's my take on why I feel sick sometimes.

I tried adding Wellbutrin to my usual dosage of Depakote because I was not able to sleep at night. I was feeling frightened and depressed again for the first time in years. I was rather concerned because I started to go into a downward spiral again and felt suicidal for the first time since November of 1999, even though I had not changed my medication in years. I was feeling depressed, frightened of losing my mind, tired, and was having trouble sleeping at night. I'd also lost my appetite and was barely cooking for myself again. I lost my therapist, Chloe, over at Princeton House several months before, and I was sad because I really enjoyed our conversations. I reapplied to the Advancement for the Association of Mental Health because I'd been a client there from 1997 to January of 2000. I asked my new psychiatrist, Dr. Serostelsky, to put me on the anti-depressant, Wellbutrin, for a while along with the Depakote, but it did not make me feel much better, and after three weeks I started to feel somewhat anxious and manic. I still would wake up several times during the night to urinate, and then could not get back to sleep. I was worried about finances and started to feel anxious and fearful about my life again. My doctor lowered my dosage of the antidepressant, and I started to feel better. After going off Wellbutrin I remained on Depakote and began to stabilize again. Since our circumstances, unique biochemistry, and emotions are ever changing it is important to be open to new medicines or holistic remedies when it comes to making ourselves feel better.

We are literally bombarded by these messages of disease, aging, and illness as the "norm" in our society. Decades of false programming and mind control has completely ruined our RACE Consciousness of Natural Well Being and Abundant Health. We do NOT need most of this crap with all its damaging side effects. Though there are many people like Dr. Kay Redfield Jamison and Patty Duke Austin who swear by lithium and give it the credit for being their wonder drug which controlled their manias, but it has also damaged kidneys of friends I know when taken on a long-term basis. I have a close friend who lost one of her kidneys from taking lithium for so long. Now it looks like she needs a new kidney to replace the second damaged kidney, so what is the cost? Not to mention the exorbitant cost of the medicines monthly. Nor do we need rampant vaccinations which cause autism, other illnesses, and sometimes lead to death! The facts are there according to many doctors, but they have been silenced by the BIG corporations that make these vaccines.

BENEFICIAL HERBS AND SUPPLEMENTS

God gave us plants, the original healers, who were designed by God to nourish our bodies and keep them healthy for hundreds of years! That's right. God designed our bodies to be so intelligent and efficient that if we care for them properly, we can actually live like some enlightened beings, like Thoth from Egypt, to live for hundreds of years!

I, personally, have used two things for years to stimulate my immune system if I felt a cold or flu coming on; or if i already had a virus and that's herbalist and Alchemists echinacea; or echinacea capsules; i also take oregano in capsule form or use several drops of oregano oil. It tastes vile; but it will kill any bug in a day or two. These are two plants God gave us to keep us healthy and thriving.

Now that I'm no longer using medications like Seroquel or Depakote to cure depression and/or to help get me to sleep due to their negative side effects like apathy and suicidal thoughts, but I am using several capsules of magnesium threonine a few hours before bed, and I get to sleep right away. Valerian, lavender, melatonin, and 5HTP all work, too. I love Sleepy time tea because it is relaxing, like a cup of hot milk, to drink right before bed, and has no negative side effects.

Since stopping my anti depression medication and mood stabilizer several months ago I've been using the Bach flower essences frequently and my boyfriend uses applied kinesiology (muscle testing) to figure out exactly how many drops of which essences I need. My favorites are Vervain which I use when I feel too enthusiastic or a bit over-the-top with energy and the essence, mustard, if I feel a bit sad or depressed. It restores inherent, natural joy.

As a single mom I'd often feel hopeless in the dark of winter, and then I used Elm; and Willow was great for forgiveness which helped brighten my outlook in just a few days. There are scores of Bach flower essences and even flower decks you can study to understand the positive and subtle uses of flowers. Look up Dr. Bach and you will be intuitively guided to the perfect one for you.

NUTRITION

Proper nutrition is necessary for mental, emotional, as well as physical, health.

I give my body lots of fresh spring water, mineral water, nutritious, healthy foods close to nature, over ten different types of nutritional supplements daily including vitamin C, a B complex, Vitamin D, multivitamin and mineral, calcium, magnesium, glucosamine chondroitin for my joints, and MSM. Nutrition and eating healthy, LIVING foods are key to maintaining a healthy mind and emotional balance.

At times of depression, I was so exhausted that I could not or Would Not cook for myself. Sometimes I'd go for days without eating any fresh fruits or vegetables. It became so bad that I actually created an "eating disorder". Sometimes I'd be so depressed and felt so bad about myself after getting fired from a job or not getting enough work that I would eat practically nothing in the morning. I'd get out of bed after 11 AM, eat the tiniest bit of cereal or possibly an egg if I was starving, and then I'd wait until 3 in the afternoon when I was so hungry, I could barely get off the couch where I was watching reruns of Mattock, CSI, or other mindless shows on television for hours just so I did not have to feel or face my pain and depression. I felt so embarrassed that I did not really want to live anymore. I'd hide from everyone except my mother and my children. I could not face the world in my weakened, unworthy state, so I would drive to the local Burger King where I'd order a junior Whopper with extra pickles and tomatoes. I'd ravenously devour the burger in minutes so happy to be able to eat the delicious tomatoes and extra fresh pickles. There were times I was so depressed I could not even taste food at all. The usual enjoyment I had while eating vanished, and things no longer tasted good to me. My sense of taste may not be as acute as others because after shooting myself in the brain I lost my sense of smell. The only things I can smell are things that are really pungent like eucalyptus or peppermint. But, during a chronic depression I could barely taste the deliciousness of food. Eating so poorly worsened my depression, and my usual good health would become compromised. Unlike my mom, dad, and brother, Pete, who lost his appendix at a young age, I was healthy enough to keep my appendix until I was in my mid-fifties, but after a few of these depressive episodes and crises where I refused to eat raw fruits or vegetables, or whole foods for long periods of time I eventually irritated my colon enough that sluggishness and constipation became chronic; and that inflammation turned into acute appendicitis after several bouts with chronic depression and poor eating habits. I remember taking a hot bath and suddenly feeling the most intense pain I'd ever felt physically, much worse than the labor contractions associated with childbirth. I also believe a lot of the grief I felt that was unexpressed during different periods of my life lodged itself in my large intestine.

When I was so chronically depressed, I literally lost my appetite for food just like I 'd lost my appetite for life. I ate little bits of food just so that I would not wither away and die. Some people who are lonely or depressed eat lots of food to fill that emptiness, but I had the opposite problem. I just had no energy or desire to eat anymore. It's a slow, painful way to die. Look at people like Karen Carpenter, Princess Diana, and others who secretly had an eating disorder which was so acute they became anorexic. Then there are bulimic women who eat as much as they want and then deliberately vomit so as not to gain any weight. This is a dangerous illness because it can hurt one's esophagus and cause inflammation of the stomach and small intestine too.

At times, when I was chronically depressed and could not feed myself, I'd drive to my mom's house a lot because I knew she would cook for both of us. She was a good cook, and I'd ravenously eat whatever she put on my plate. Even if it was meatloaf or a hot dog and sauerkraut which I normally did not like to eat because it was more meat containing nitrites and nitrates, preservatives to give it the pinkish red color. I also spent the night over her place on week-ends when Sky was with her dad knowing I'd have some loving company at night and in the morning when I woke up, some snugly pajamas to wear, a quiet hour or two when I did not have to think, and a nice breakfast in the morning. It was my mom who got me through the really rough, dark depressions many times until my precious beau, Gary, came into my life.

When I was not eating anything or choosing a quick whopper from the take-out window of Burger King on the run, I didn't feel like I loved myself enough to take the time to prepare a fresh salad, a soup, or chicken and vegetables in the crock pot, and by not making extra effort to cook or prepare a decent meal I was choosing a slow death over a joyous, energetic LIFE. My poor daughter, Sky, has shared with me how often she was hungry after school and sometimes went to her friend's house to ask for food. I did not remember this happening, and I felt just terrible when she told me this happened during some years of her childhood when I was chronically depressed.

Starving yourself or over eating is the worst thing we can do during a depressive episode. It is partially the lack of B Vitamins and other precious nutrients that are factors in causing the depression in the first place. There is no life force in potato chips. None in fast foods like Whoppers and Big Macs. Very little in canned foods, and microwaveable meals. It was only when I saw Dr. Van Beveren, a nutritionist and biochemist in my area in desperation during a very bad fearful time of acute anxiety and depression when I was not sleeping again, who recommended certain supplements as well as a vegan diet that I started to change my way of eating to a healthier one. I had been vegetarian at different points in my life, first when I was a yoga student and also when I was married to my first husband and pregnant with Gabriel. Even though I was vegetarian I was very careful to eat complete proteins like beans or tofu with steamed veggies and whole grain rice or quinoa together at a meal. I loved almond butter on a rice cake. I also took a lot of supplements because David was wealthy from my perspective, and money was never a concern when I was married to him. When I became a single mom thing changed because I was poor enough to qualify for the food stamp program and to receive SSI disability.

Dr. Van Beveren, my friend and a renowned biochemist and naturopathic doctor in Skillman, had been monitoring my blood using a high-powered microscope and advised me on nutritional issues on and off for years... I was on a strict wheat and acid free vegetarian diet for four months eating mostly raw fruits and vegetables and some whole grains, soy and rice-milk shakes, but no bread. He also recommended several supplements.

I knew I did not have the money I needed to purchase all the supplements Dr. Van had recommended, so I started small by shopping for lots of fresh organic vegetables and fruits that were in season at Wild Oats and the Whole Earth Center, the two health food stores in Princeton at the time. It was more expensive than Shop Rite, but the quality of the produce was better-organic and locally grown, and just making this small shift in my eating made me feel stronger and better about myself. I felt as if I was now CHOOSING LIFE and not giving myself the option of a slow suicide by not eating properly.

Over the spring and summer, I was very strict about my diet until I started to feel healthier and more energetic. I started to shop mostly at the health food stores in Princeton for organic produce and juices. I started to add ground flax seed meal to my morning shakes, soups, and salads in order to get the omega three oils I needed. I also decided to go for colonics, an excellent way to detoxify one's large intestine using a machine called a toxigen where water is put into the colon through a tube inserted in the anus. Since most disease begins in the large intestine or gut this was a very healthy thing for me to do at least once or twice per season.

When I went on vacation for two weeks to Cape Cod and Salem, Mass I drank and ate mostly healthy things as opposed to going off my diet just because I was on vacation. Though I did take advantage of the New England's delicious clam chowder and lobster with my good friend, Bob Burgess, a precious friend I've known from Siddha Meditation since 1981. Due to my intention to feel better and changes in my diet I began to feel much more energetic and the lethargy, depression, and arthritis that was plaguing me for some time just disappeared after a few weeks. I still enjoy eating mostly vegetarian except for occasional meals of tuna fish or turkey sandwiches for lunch because I find a little bit of fish or foul grounds me if I begin to feel too euphoric or ungrounded in the spring or summer.

I make lunch my largest meal of the day when I am at home and add assorted steamed veggies, and occasionally modest portions of chicken or wild salmon with brown rice or gourmet pasta as a side dish. For dinner I eat lighter and enjoy fresh salads made of spinach, arugula, romaine, or Boston lettuce with local organic produce in season like carrots, sprouts, yellow squash, zucchinis, red cabbage, or chickpeas along with lunch or dinner.

I vary my breakfasts between organic brown eggs from free roaming chickens, oatmeal, pancakes made from gluten free grains with fresh blueberries, French toast, gluten free waffles, or a fruit shake made with bananas, fresh pineapple, strawberries, rice dream, almond or coconut-milks. During the several months I was eating raw vegetables, fruits, and whole grains like oatmeal, brown rice, quinoa, and couscous I also consciously cleansed my liver and colon. I got a few colonics from my friend, Ursula Szypryt, a registered nurse.

For more guidance concerning excellent nutrition consult these books I've read by Dr. Gary Null: *Nutrition and the Mind, The Healthy Vegetarian,* and *Women's Health Solutions.* I listen to Gary Null every day at noon on WBAI and he always has excellent up-to-date advice on the best supplements and healthy vegan or vegetarian foods to consume. He is a brilliant man with a doctorate in nutrition, is a registered dietician, and quite a philanthropist who is not just an advocate for animals, but rescues animals and cares for them on his own personal property at his own expense. He has reversed or cured many non-curable illnesses like A.I.D.S., cancer, and Alzheimers using mostly diet and lifestyle changes. He inspires me every day with his courage to tell it like it is as well as his kindness.

EXERCISE

Light exercise like regular walking, folk dancing, swimming, and bicycle riding is so important for we need to circulate oxygen and get aerobic daily in order to have a healthy heart and lungs. It also creates natural serotonin, the neurotransmitter derived from L- tryptophan that is involved in sleep, lack of depression, memory, and other neurological processes.

Movement is good for the soul. All the women in my dance aerobics class at the Senior Center who are over eighty years old all tell me they have to keep on moving every day, and that is the key to longevity and happiness.

I found when I did not move or dance for hours or days, I would stay stuck in a depression for at least two or three months. Why waste that much of our lives? Even medications did not really help. Sure. Some of them helped to drug me and get me to stay asleep for most of the night. But the medicines did not help me to want to get up in the morning. It was prayer by others as well as myself that got me back into my body and out of my head. And movement. Dance and movement got the energy moving so I could shake off whatever was bothering me deep down. Sometimes I wondered if my negative thinking had somehow attracted ghosts, devilish spirits, or some type of negative entities.

ALTERNATIVES

Sometimes I'd go in my car when I was all by myself and scream my heart out. That gave me some relief from all the negative thoughts asking for my attention. Or I might take a soothing drive in my car while listening to the radio and singing as loudly as I could without disturbing people who were in listening range... Singing has always helped me to feel better. Using my voice from any part of my register started to bring me out of my head and back into my body. Chanting Sanskrit mantras in a group of people or especially alone with the chanting tapes in my car always made me feel better no matter how anxious, fearful, or depressed I was feeling at the time. Chanting with others, especially devotees of Muktananda and Gurumayi Chidvilasananda, at certain times during the day like 5:30AM or the Guru Gita, a bit earlier, let's say 4:15 AM for the Shiva Arati, if one is inclined, and disciplined enough to arise at 4 AM so you could be showered and ready to sing, do hatha yoga, meditate, chant, or whatever your personal unique sadhana is inviting you to do at this holy moment in time. Now that you have some structure in your life, really think about and envision in each moment what it is you absolutely LOVE to do with ALL your HEART & SOUL! Each moment in time is so precious. Let's not fritter it away with anything that is not for our highest and best good. Well, that is what you have to DECIDE NOW. Take stock of where you have come from, where you want to go, and make a plan, Stan, for getting there.

The trick is enjoying the journey, and NOT rushing around like chickens with their blessed heads chopped off. Running to and fro, like most human beings, to arrive at your destination. Take our time, dear hearts. There does not have to be the same dull routine each day. FIRE and PASSION go together. You can invoke it with the Violet Flame of Saint Germaine when you light your sacred candles in the early mornings.

What is a colonic, you say? Well, my friend, Dr. UFO, Pat, thinks it is a higher education enema. Really now. That's what he said on our vacation to FL last year. I kid you not.

I was trained and certified at the Sarasota School of Natural Healing Arts by my nutrition teacher, Marilyn, to be a colon hydro therapist, and it is an extremely beneficial habit to get into in the spring or autumn when it is a good time to detoxify your liver and your colon. Actually, almost anytime is a good time for fasting and detoxing the large intestine because of all the refined foods we eat, processed meats, and "fast foods". I did a twelve-day juice fast when I was studying to be a massage therapist when I was a mere youth of 25. Along with daily enemas and four colonics during that time, I was able to get rid of about ten pounds of "crap" I did not need along with mucous and stuck fecal matter that had been slowing me down for at least a decade. When I finished fasting and detoxifying, I felt like a million dollars. I was filled with energy, enthusiasm, and ready to truly appreciate fresh food in smaller amounts and every single precious bite I ate when I was finished fasting after the twelve-day period I imposed upon myself. Besides being filled with new energy, I was twelve pounds lighter, and my mood was very light. I enjoyed the fast so much I would have continued for another week, but it was interfering with my social lunch and dinner calendar. And wow, did I appreciate the taste and juiciness of that first Red Delicious apple the day I broke my fast!

Except for a healing "crisis" which I experienced on the third day when I was vomiting and had diarrhea, the "cleanse" was very easy and did not tire me out. I drank herb teas, fresh carrot apple, beet, ginger, parsley, and celery concoctions I made fresh daily in my juicer. And lots of spring water to wash the walls of my colon. There is nothing like drinking lots of fresh spring water daily to improve cellular growth and keep all the systems of the body moving better. After all, we like our mother, are made up of mostly water. I think we are eighty %, aren't we?

Truly now, a colonic is a high Irrigation enema, NOT education, Pat, you silly goose, and I get them regularly so I can stay "regular". I do not like to get all backed up. That way I can eat all the Lindt chocolates, tapioca pudding, and Junior's cherry cheesecake I want! I can live like the eternal bird of youth I am. I am getting younger every minute. Instead of aging I Am "youth-ing".

Just like Ike, Mike, and Dick Van Dyke! I'm serious. Have you seen Dick lately? He's over eighty and looking Great! Still dancing up a storm, and probably doing the horizontal mambo with his new, young wife on a regular basis. Dancing, singing, having regular sex, being active, and involved in your passions, that is what keep people living into their nineties and beyond. Like my Grammy, Lucy Vere, who lived to be almost 98 and was still active, happy, and going strong at Buckingham Place, the assisted living residence in Princeton, where I worked as a concierge for under a year, and saw my grandmother bless every person who lived or worked there.

AROMOTHERAPY

Ursula Szypryt also got me into using the young living oils again. Ursula came back from a young living conference in Hawaii with so much enthusiasm I knew that I wanted back that same kind of abundant passion for life and the energy I once had. I started using a blend called Transformation as well as lavender and joy for peace, calming, balance, and energy. I substituted the Depakote with lavender oil at night and a supplement called 5HTP in order to help me sleep through the night when I was having insomnia in the spring from anxiety or mania.

The Joy blend has rose oil in it, which is the highest of all the plant frequencies. Rose is the smell that permeates the air whenever angels like Padre Pio, Mother Mary, or Mother Theresa are around. After I shot myself, my husband used to bring me a dozen red or pink fresh roses each day and put them by my hospital bed while I was in Robert Wood Johnson Hospital in New Brunswick, but no matter how hard I sniffed I could not smell the sweet fragrance I was once able to do with such ease. It was such a sweet, loving gesture on his part, and I enjoyed looking at them very much. It did seem odd to me that I could not smell them at all. For some reason, my sense of smell became compromised after the head injury. It has been improving, though, with the use of the essential oils and the work Dr. Vince has been doing with me for two years. The first time Dr. Kiechlin worked on me in the spring I reported to him that I was able to smell freshly mowed grass for the first time since shooting myself in the head. This past summer I was able to smell the scent of body odor from perspiration while working on a massage client. I know this sounds weird, but to be able to smell this was not unpleasant and gave me great joy after not having been able to smell this type of musky scent in years. I used to burn pots and pans like crazy because I could not even perceive the smell of something burning until I started to use the aromatherapy with young living essential oils.

The transformation blend contains lemon, Idaho balsam fir, Dr. Young designed this blend in order to replace negative beliefs with revitalizing new thought patterns; once the thoughts are changed, a transformation in behavior is possible. I was guided to use it in order to help reverse the depression I went through last spring even though I was still on the medication after my boyfriend in Massachusetts left me for a woman, he'd met in his home state.

CHIROPRACTORS, PHYSICAL THERAPY AND MASSAGE

Recently, I've been getting treatments from a chiropractor, Dr. Vince Kiechlin, who is also studying to be a neurologist and is therefore knowledgeable about the brain. He is now a board-certified chiropractic neurologist, and we have become close friends who share knowledge about holistic health, and he is an amazing doctor since becoming a neurologist. Though there is a hole in the right side of my brain from the gunshot Vince discovered that it was the left hemisphere of my brain that was very weak. He has been giving me exercises and working through my eyes and applied kinesiology to strengthen the left side, which he calls "the happy brain". The left side of the brain is also responsible for the proper functioning of the immune system. We are working together with chiropractic, applied kinesiology, and aromatherapy using the young living essential oils in order to strengthen my immune and nervous systems in order to lessen or go off the medication I've been on and off for over twenty years.

One chiropractor would see me just about any time if I had a headache or I was starting to feel out of balance. He knew exactly what neuromuscular points to press and adjusted my cervical and pelvis so that I was back in perfect postural alignment, and my body healed itself after that. I usually go to a chiropractor at least once or twice per week for preventive maintenance, get a physical with a medical physician once every few years just to check in, and I find that I'm usually always healthy and thriving. If I get too overworked or not enough sleep my immune system gets compromised, and I am more prone to a cold or flu.

I go to a chiropractor regularly (once a week or every two weeks, for preventative maintenance and the dentist twice per year for a check-up and to get my teeth cleaned as a part of good oral hygiene. I also floss my teeth twice per day with a flossing sword made for one hand. I eat according to my intuition and in moderation. My health is perfect and my body is thriving, for the most part. I am filled with abundant energy, vitality, and enthusiasm in the spring, summer, and fall. In winters I feel more tired and need more sleep.

And after twenty-eight years of non-use and little or no therapy on my left hand or arm I worked with an Indian physical therapist named Dr. Ahmed Shafiq at Olympic Rehab in Hamilton, NJ whose expertise is rehabilitating people who have head strokes and brain injuries. I began to see improvement in both my left leg, left shoulder, and arm muscles. My left pectoralis major is moving better and getting stronger than ever before. It's not big progress, but it is a great start, and the flexibility in all the other muscles used for abduction, adduction, wrist flexion and extension are getting more loosened up each time I saw Dr. Shafiq. Some other doctors and therapists gave me a poor prognosis for complete rehabilitation of my left side saying that whatever I got back in a year would be about as much progress as I would make. They were wrong. I have progressed incrementally ever since I shot myself. Sure, there were periods where not much was happening, and other times when I felt depressed and could not even move off my bed or the couch where I'd space out for hours watching old movies and mysteries on TV, but as of today, I drive, I dance, and do just about anything I choose to do.

Most of my physical therapists in the past few years would always just focus on relieving stress, pain, and arthritis in my right arm, shoulder muscles, and knee due to over exertion. They completely ignored the left arm and hand believing it was useless to do anything. I believe in the POWER of God and Dr. Shafiq's belief in himself, Allah, and me. He even does his daily prayers during my sessions in the afternoons with other Muslim doctors right on the floor in his office sometimes. I heard him and the other doctors praying once while I was resting after an intense therapy session.

One day, I had the privilege of sitting in a chair in the reception room while waiting for one of the beds to be free, and I watched them pranam (Sanskrit for to bow) to Allah right on the white blanket and carpet in front of me. It was so beautiful and touching to watch these doctors of all ages incorporate God and prayer into their daily work day. It was so beautiful and inspiring. I heard them pray for all their patients and for the relief of arthritis and other ailments. A few weeks back Dr. Shafiq told me he was praying for me and all the other patients. How wonderful to meet a doctor who combines his knowledge of science with a belief in Allah, his Almighty Source, the One God who is the power behind all healing and everything that has life in this Universe. I feel so grateful and honored to be able to work with such a holy man as this, one who has reverence and love for God and all beings.

I have more recently worked with some other excellent healers, including Dr. Kim, a South Korean physical therapist who has his own rehabilitation center in Edison, New jersey, where I receive" free" acupuncture, massage, physical therapy, hydrocollator packs, electric stim, and use two or three of the machines there for pain management or to make my legs stronger, especially my left one. When I say all those services are free, I just mean they are covered by Medicare, and I usually do not have to pay one dollar because Dr. Kim is so kind and generous he takes whatever Medicare offers him.

MEDITATION

There are many forms of meditation, and many variations of each form. The important thing is to find a form that works for you and, most importantly, that you will do consistently. When asked what was the best form of meditation, Lama Surya Das replied, "the one you actually do."

Siddha Meditation

Siddha Meditation has been an important part of my sadhana (spiritual practice) since 1981 when I met Swami Muktananda and his translator, Malti, who would eventually become initiated as Gurumayi Chidvilasananda and take over as the head of the Siddha Yoga lineage when Baba Muktananda died on October 2nd, 1982. My particular love and a way to still my mind and open my heart is to chant the divine name. And it does not take very long. One will find if they just chant alone for twenty minutes or in a group for a bit longer their mind will begin to slow and quiet down. There is a ninety-minute chant in Siddha Yoga called the Guru Gita which is probably my most favorite chant and discipline in the early mornings since, at the ashrams, it is usually chanted after morning chai, from 5:30 until 7:00 AM. Then we would quietly meditate for at least twenty minutes after that before going to do guruseva (work) or service to the guru in something we usually enjoy and for which we have a special talent.

Sit quietly and meditate.

Watch your breath. Witness the thoughts as if they were some interesting friends. Just do not get caught up in them. Baba Muktananda often said "Oh, my MIND, please be my FRIEND." We are so easily distracted, it seems, doesn't it, my precious child? We love the fresh flowers that add a variety of colors, scents, and beauty to your living environment; and if you wish you may wear the same clean white or other colored meditation clothes every single day during meditation time for at least twenty minutes to start and work up to one hour in the morning eventually. You will notice a great difference in how your day unfolds. We can choose to use the same white woolen or cotton asana upon which to do your meditations that contains all that same charged shakti particles if you use it every day and evening before going to sleep. You know you can purchase one at a Siddha ashram, center, or even at the Princeton Center for Yoga & Health in town. It truly IS the FIRST DAY of the rest of your precious LIFE!!! A few minutes of regular meditation will not only give you energy, but it will calm and center you for a long day of many activities. Meditation, massage, and chanting have always grounded, centered and relaxed me. My inherent joy was already present.

A very simple meditation could be to just enjoy and appreciate the beauty of one special flower that attracts you. Being in nature and appreciating the beauty of it is so calming and soothing.

If you are indoors, light a candle and burn some delicious smelling incense. After you wave the incense in front of a picture of your guru or special teachers you can just sit quietly in a chair with your back erect or if you are very tired, just lie in your bed with your hands, palms opened to the ceiling while you watch your breath and deeply breathe with your diaphragm with your hands resting upon it with fingers slightly separated, so you can notice how deeply you are inhaling and exhaling easily but for a certain count you choose like six, eight, or ten seconds. This will help you to learn to focus your mind on one thing—observing your breath and counting the rising and falling of it by watching it raise and counting the number of six, eight or ten count inhalations and exhalations. If your mind gets distracted by thoughts, just go back to the number where you remember leaving off.

There are also guided meditations on "Headspace" and other places on the internet that will lead you through the meditation, and I find them very helpful, especially if I've not taken the time to meditate in a while. That is why it is best to decide to keep up a regular, disciplined practice at a certain time each day. Early morning is best, but if you cannot find time before work, do ten minutes of deliberate, slow breathing on your lunch break at work and then, before you retire at night while upright in bed. "Headspace" offers meditations in the evenings too as well as ten minutes of soothing sleep sounds, there are also audiotapes and CDs with nature sounds on them and ones by? Where you learn to put your awareness in every single part of your body until it is completely still even if it was hurting or tight before you started.

I happen to love my guru's mantra "Om Namah Shivaya" the best of all before the meditations. They have a fast version of the singing chant used preferably during the day to give you energy, but my favorite is the slow version because it really slows me down and quiets my mind, especially if I feel so high and busy that I cannot get very grounded, and my mind just wants to chatter away. There is a lovely, slow version of this chant by Craig Pruce and "The Singers of the Art of Living" I play a lot on my Alexa Amazon Echo.

I love to get grounded by placing my bare feet upon the earth, but the weather is not always conducive to this practice. Though I heard or read somewhere that there are people who go barefoot all the time, even in the cold of a frigid winter! For me, it is easiest to meditate and pray while in a hot bath tub in the morning or evening prior to going to bed. Sometimes I do some gentle, basic hatha yoga stretches to help my body feel better which then leads to better meditations

Once we relax and breathe in the present moment and present experiences, we can then accept ourselves and our circumstances and just be grateful for it all in the present moment. In this glorious PRESENT we can breathe deeply and feel safe knowing that we are OK. Our Well Being reigns. Most of us have everything we need to be happy and healthy right now. Somehow, we get fed, clothed, and taken care of each day in every way, even when we are sick or so over tired that we need an entire day in bed to rest and recuperate. We are deeply loved by God, our Creator. The angels and archangels. And we are His children-- each of us is a divine expression of THE DIVINE, and we can eventually, with practice, feel content with whatever is happening in the present moment.

From this place of acceptance, we can feel that state of humility and be grateful and accepting of ourselves and for our magnificent, intelligent bodies, minds, and our circumstances just as they are. From this place of deep relaxation, we are also able to have hopeful, positive expectations for better in the future. The more we relax and appreciate each thing or person in our lives, the more things we will notice to appreciate. We will create more and more wanted things and experiences for us to appreciate and for which to be grateful. Eventually we will find that it will become easy to be grateful for every experience the Great Mystery brings our way. Even the so called "bad" experiences. Everything is an opportunity to choose, to learn, and to grow in awareness. To be in service to Great Spirit and Man.

Our true nature, the nature of the eternal SELF, the unchanging, eternal ESSENCE of all of us is Ananda – Joy. Chiti or Consciousness is WHAT all human beings ARE. Love and sublime peace are our true divine nature, and it is because of the SELF that we are naturally Joyous, Bliss filled beings. It seems that we humans in search of our true nature are constantly seeking joy outside of ourselves.

When we don't get the car, the money, or the boyfriend or girlfriend we want in the time frame we want we become frustrated, and then we feel overwhelmed. And the emotions spiral down from there into anxiety, fear, and depression. That's when it is time to let go and let God/Goddess. There is so little that we can actually control. In times of doubt and fear we must go inside our minds and hearts to pray, and ask the higher Power, God, Source, Allah, Jesus, Gaia, Aphrodite, Moses, Abraham, whomever it is you call God, for help. You can resonate with whatever works for you.

MANY PATHS

Every person and relationship are unique, so we must all follow our own hearts. Ultimately, there is only one beloved, and That is the One that exists in us as us inside our very own hearts. I don't believe that I have ever found what I was searching for as far as fulfillment "Out there". It has always been, and still is, inside me. Whomever is before me is a reflection of the One Beloved that exists as God within me.

There is not just One path to God. There is just One God, but there are many paths, and you have to be true to your own heart.

I followed a Guru, Swami Muktananda, a realized saint for half of my life, and I still ask for his guidance to this day, but at times just sitting quietly listening to the wisdom of a flower, hugging a large tree in times of despair, or listening to the wisdom of a totem animal like deer or wolf, may give me the insight I need in the present moment. Sometimes I ask a rock or a crystal for knowledge and wisdom.

Whatever you believe in, whatever you put your faith in, is what works best for each one of us. There is no ONE DEITY who is the best for all. *Or, rather, each person relates to the ONE in her or his own unique way.* We are all students and teachers for one another. Sometimes I will have good advice or guidance for another, or at times of weakness, another person or this same person, may comfort and guide me through a challenging period I happen to be going through. It is so helpful when one is clear headed and may have had a similar illness or circumstance that challenged them, and they are able to give guidance that has been gleaned from his or her own personal experience.

That is why I am writing this book. I hope my life's ups and downs will be able to help at least one, if not many, others going through similar experiences in the hope that others will not have to go through the pain and suffering of depression. Or the mistakes one makes during periods of mania. Depression is unnecessary, but it can be a teacher. It can and will make you humble. Make you stronger and more compassionate. More patient. At least that is what I have found in my experience.

If you let your attitude become so negative and fearful for extended periods of time it is most likely you will slip into a depressed state without even realizing you are spiraling quickly downward. Because of the Universal Law of Attraction, our attention to the negative aspects of any subject will just attract more of the same types of thoughts. These negative thoughts just bring more negative people and experiences into our lives to match our inner attitudes and beliefs. Like complainers. Like naysayers. Beware of the company you keep. They say "misery loves company", and if you are happy and tend to visit a complainer, they can easily bring you down vibration ally. I'm not saying we should hang out with only happy people, but when we are hanging round people who are constantly complaining about their health, the weather, the government, the economy, or whatever, it is really easy to come down to their level of misery if we are not careful. That has happened to me a few times with my own mom.

I have seen movies of the poorest people in Africa, but their attitudes are so happy and these people tend to be grateful for whatever they have. Why can't we Americans live our lives in this state of grace and joy?

As above, so below. And as within your consciousness and belief system, so you will manifest experiences and circumstances to match your vibrational level. If you are focusing on lack and hardship believing in a bad economy, that life is a struggle, life is tough, and one must work very hard to manifest wealth, you will probably be working two jobs for low pay, and always just get by or never have enough money. Everything depends upon our attitudes.

Releasing negativity allows us to open to new possibilities. We can create new experiences, new jobs, new ways to serve, new ways to receive our good and new ways to have fun.

Many times, I have wanted to go on vacations, but at that time in my winter I had no extra money to do so. Yet, each time, Great Spirit heard my prayer and divine desire, and provided the perfect vacation for free through some other avenue.

For example, in 2002 I wanted to go to Florida in the winter, but my massage practice was slow, and I did not have the extra resources. I was going to book a four-day free cruise over the phone in the Bahamas, but the extra money I needed for the port taxes and fees was not available at that time, so I just forgot about my wish to leave New Jersey to vacation in a warmer climate and went about my business. A week later I received a phone call from my dear friend, Rev. Greg, a friend and fellow minister I'd met two years before in Hershey, PA at the annual Universal Brotherhood Ministers' conference. We did not know each other too well because he lived out west, and I was in Jersey. But he knew me well enough to know I was another healer, fellow minister, poet, and nudist like himself. He called to share great news. He'd just won a three-day trip in a raffle to the Grand Lido Braco, a naturist resort, in Jamaica. The woman he usually traveled with was unavailable, so he called me and invited me to come meet him in Jamaica for a week. He paid for my plane fare and four more days at a Comfort Suites Hotel in Ocho Rios with no strings attached. What a wonderful vacation we both had, and what a wonderful gift from Greg and Great Spirit. The water in Jamaica is turquoise and warm, and the flora and fauna so colorful. I particularly enjoyed the colorful costumes of yellow, black, green, and orange the dancers wore one night when they performed in the moonlight not far from the water as well as their carefree joy and enthusiasm while dancing and singing. There are huge banyan trees that keep growing tall and wide. The leaves are beautiful, and when the vines die they lay down on the ground where artists make their mark in the bark creating people's faces and other interesting things in the dead bark. A new branch springs up out of the old, and the tree grows huge – tall, wide, and magnificent. So many pretty things to see in Jamaica.

Another example of the grace of God and gifts of the Spirit was in the summer of the following year when I wanted to fly to Atlanta for the next annual Universal Brotherhood Ministers Conference, and as usual, due to my refusal to make a budget for myself in the spring and summer, my funds were tight. I waited until the last minute to book my flight because I was saving money for the plane fare. I went to a AAA travel agent to book my flight after I had the necessary funds, but for some crazy reason the computer kept jamming and crashing that Saturday afternoon. I was supposed to visit my best friend, Jeanette, later that afternoon, so I just lost my patience with the process. I realized after ten minutes of these challenges with the reservation that I was not meant to book my flight that afternoon because Great Spirit had something better in mind for me. I only had five more days until I left for the conference, so I was wondering if I was supposed to drive down like I had once before with my friends, Carola and Ursula, and split the cost of the gas and tolls. But Great Spirit had a better, easier way of traveling in mind for me. At a much better price.

The next day was Sunday, and I went to the Religious Science Church (now called "Center for Spiritual Living – Princeton), as usual. There, after service, my best friend, Jeanette LeDoux, introduced me to a new friend, Barbara, she'd just met a few weeks before. Barb Bentzin was a lovely, intelligent gal who also happened to be a junior pilot for Continental Airlines. I was happy to meet Barbara, and said, "Hey it's great to meet you. I think you are the person Spirit wanted me to meet because I have five days in which to book a plane flight to Atlanta. Where should I go at this late date to get the best deal, the internet? Travelocity, perhaps?"

Barb replied, "No. I happen to have several buddies passes I've not used yet, and they must be used before the end of this year. Would you like two of them?"

I had never heard of a "buddy pass" and did not understand what they were, but of course I said "Sure. Thanks a lot. "Barb explained what they were and how to use them.

Basically, I was going to be on standby, and if all the seats were not sold on the plane, I would have the opportunity to fly as a guest of Continental in an economy seat for free. That is exactly what I did on the way down though I had to sit way in the back of the plane, but the flight back was even less crowded, so I got a great window seat in the middle of the plane. That was back in the days when we actually got free meals and did not have to pay for luggage either. What an incredible gift from Barb and from Great Spirit! I had never met Barb Bentzin until that day, but something prompted her to give me those buddy passes, and I felt so grateful and blessed that she liked me that much upon first meeting me to extend such kindness.

After church Barb, Jeanette, and I decided to travel together to the Balloon Festival at the Readington Airport not far from Flemington, NJ and enjoyed ourselves immensely. What a lovely gal and great friend was she. Barb ended up meeting a guy in Belize in her travels, married him, and moved out of state, so I have not connected with her in a long time, but I so enjoyed our friendship for the year or two she was here in Princeton.

The world is as we see it. From a place of chronic suicidal depression, I saw and misperceived everything in my life as bad, sad, angry, dark, hopeless, and negative. Changing your thinking Will change your life. All our experiences come from a conscious or subconscious thought, and "a thought Can be changed" according to Sondra Ray. I know this from personal experience. If it were not through my own conscious intention, I would ask holy Spirit to help me because I knew at times, that I felt weak, not confident, felt unworthy, and did not believe in myself or my own power, so I gave it all to Him. He always knew what was for my highest and best good. Even when it came to lovers, beaux, or permanent boyfriends. The choices he made for me were so much better than the ones I chose for myself.

HUMANITY

If we, as loving human beings, just stopped for a moment and allowed ourselves to feel all the pain and suffering we have inflicted on animals, other human beings, and ourselves through our own greed, selfishness, neglect, ignorance, and indifference we would just break down and cry. Our hearts would break. But it would also lead us to feelings of compassion and forgiveness, and to a path of action to make changes for the better. We must call upon the decency and compassion of caring people like ourselves to unite in a vision of positive action to stop the killing, destruction, and insanity in our world by first starting with loving and honoring ourselves by loving and caring for our individual selves first, our families, friends, and serving our communities in whatever small and humble ways we can. There is a phrase "Bloom where you are planted" which I really like. I always try to offer a smile to each person I meet whenever I am outdoors and a little pat on the head to the dogs being walked in our neighborhood or on the main street in Princeton.

Each one of our individual efforts of loving-kindness makes a huge difference. We are like one Light, a huge force for peace and oneness that has started within each one of our own hearts and continues on as a Great Big Wave of Divine love. We are all longing for God and God's infinite Good... We are all yearning to be one with That sublime Truth, with that One Beloved who has manifested in form as everyone and everything we can see, taste, touch, and experience in this physical and non-physical world. There is a greater part of us that exists in the non-physical celestial realms simultaneously that is broader, omniscient and in constant communication with us, my dearest ones, through the divine gifts of emotions.

There are only two emotions. We call them all sorts of things, but there are only two. One feels bad, and the other feels good. Go for the good feeling thought. Go for what you are wanting. There is no greater being outside of you that stands in judgment of anything you do. God Herself is extremely pleased with everything you are doing, so we need not be so hard on ourselves, brothers and sisters. The lover, out of boundless love has become the Beloved, and That beloved is You!!! There is nothing outside of yourselves that is more beautiful, worthier, more deserving of every good thing Life has to offer. So go for it, dear friends. Go for the gold. You are the most glorious expressions of divinity and Light God has to offer. Embrace and accept your unique expressions and desires. Your preferences are divine urges. So go create anything your big golden heart desires. God/Goddess will be here on Earth watching, applauding your every step until it is time for you to merge again into All that We have become.

Let us become peaceful within and become aware of our own violent feelings, thoughts, and actions so that we may heal our own hearts of pain, rage, and vengefulness. Even though I try not to get angry, sometimes I am aware of myself being passive aggressive with my partner, my mother, or one of my close friends that pushes my buttons, if you know what I mean. Sometimes I still project the lies about myself in my subconscious onto others, but for the most part once I realize something I can work on by surrendering it to Divine love and forgiving myself so that I can change for the better.

We have forgotten that the "Japs", the "Commies", the North Koreans, and the Muslim terrorists that your fathers and forefathers have been encouraged to kill in the name of peace in defense your country, also had mothers, wives, fathers, sisters, and brothers who were devastated by their deaths just like we were when our sons were sent back in body bags.

Where is the rationality in killing and terrorizing other human beings? They are our brothers and sisters, my dear ones. They are a reflection of our own inner consciousness. Where is the peace of mind in knowing that you, your husband, son, or country destroyed a whole village of schools, hospitals, temples, and homes? Some men are brainwashed into raping women and terrorizing frightened elders leaving little children without parents or grandparents all for the sake of peace? How can a country prepare for and prevent war simultaneously? This is an impossibility. It goes against Universal Law and everything you have been taught about God and loving thy neighbor as thyself. We are our brother's keeper. Not just one brother, but All of our Brothers and Sisters. All this senseless fighting has been done in our Lord's name, in the name of God and country – in the name of honor. I see no sense in it. Violence only begets more violence, pain, destruction, and resentment.

The poor men who come back from these terrible wars where they acted so courageously out of duty to fight for our country were convinced it was an honorable thing to do. Despite their fears and inner conflicts, they traveled far from their homes and families to protect or rescue innocent peoples, but ultimately, they have to live with the devastating consequences of their actions for the rest of their lives. It is not an easy thing to destroy another human being. It is a spiritual assault to force a man to kill another. I don't care if you can't see their faces when you drop a bomb upon their homes, families, and towns. We brainwash our young boys in order to kill, in order to stop respecting and honoring the preciousness of human life. We are all brainwashed by men and women in government and positions of power to believe that we can stop violence, terrorism, and war through our own means of terror. The only way to truly overcome evil is with love, understanding, compassion, communication, and patience. We must be peaceful and truly care for our fellow human beings in all countries, not just our own. Let us behave in a civilized, peaceful manner ourselves. Let us commit to look at and address core problems of hunger, poverty, and crime. In this way we can help transform what is truly the underlying cause of violence and terror. Let us become the peace that we seek. "My peace I leave with you. My peace I give unto you" is what Jesus said in the Bible. And this peace had nothing to do with killing, judgment, or the like. Jesus was the embodiment of unconditional love and forgiveness. We are made in his image and likeness.

Now, after the events of 9/11 we are supposedly engaged in yet one honorable war after another, the wars in Iraq, Afghanistan, and Iran, and so on. I am not an advocate of terrorism or one who believes in not taking action to make things right, to make our world situation better. But there is a better way to resolve our conflicts with others than by behaving in a terroristic manner ourselves. Great leaders like Mahatma Gandhi and Dr. Martin Luther King both knew he way of peace takes a lot longer and requires much patience, effort, and courage, but it is truly the only way. We must address the underlying problems and issues that foster a climate in which war is likely to erupt. Let's not damage ourselves spiritually or hurt more of our innocent brothers and sisters through more acts of violence. Even killing something as small as an ant has a consequence. Let us all practice the

Indian philosophy of ahimsa, non-violence. Gentleness, service, and random acts of kindness each and every day will have far reaching effects toward creating a world of Universal brotherhood. Become as gentle and peaceful as the deer. Learn from all the animals. Did you ever stop to think that maybe the animals here were really beautiful beings that each had something special to teach us in the way that they live their lives? They are totally present in each moment, enjoying each and every moment. They come in love and complete service to humankind. Don't you think it's time we stopped treating them so poorly and loved and honored them the way they do us? Would you ever be able to destroy your own pets for food? That would be the last option, I would think. It is possible to live completely off the plants or just the oxygen in the air if that is what you are wanting. If you do hunt and kill in order to feed yourselves, then do it with love, do it with respect, and honor the animals, my children. Do not torture and maim them. Live in harmony with them and become truly grateful for all the gifts they give you, even the gift of their precious bodies! Think about how loving and evolved that is. They love you so much that they allow themselves to be hurt and neglected, tortured, tested upon, all in the name of love, for the advancement and upliftment of humanity. Some of the same animals have chosen to return to your lifetime after lifetime – and in between, too!

Terrorism and war tend to incite retaliation and so perpetuate more violence. It becomes a viscous cycle. When we wage war against our brothers and sisters, we are waging war against ourselves. If we truly embrace our Judeo-Christian teachings, we will remember that Jesus said to "love thy neighbor as thyself" and "as we do unto others, we do unto ourselves". In Proverbs in the Christian Bible it also states, "As a man thinketh, so is he."

We are not victims. We each create our reality moment to moment, attracting people and circumstances to ourselves with our thoughts, words, and deeds, so it behooves each of us to think loving, peaceful, positive thoughts. When we come together in Truth as part of a group, we have unlimited power to change the world. Jesus said that all we needed were "two or more gathered in His name and there He would be in our midst. The Truth is that we are One collective consciousness of the One Magnificent Creator—the I Am of All-That-Is, and we all share the same loving heart. It is a fearless, unconditionally loving heart. It is a heart that understands the power and necessity of forgiveness, mercy, and compassion.

Instead of using violence to solve our problems let us change our thinking. It is possible to create agreements, concepts, and feelings that foster World Peace. It is also possible to live in harmony with each other, to respect and care for all peoples, our animal friends, and our environment. Let us not ignore the commandment "Thou shalt not kill." Let's remember the preciousness of all life. Let us respect and honor the ancient teachings of our Native American ancestors to love, preserve, honor, and revere all life, and to protect the mother's precious resources. If you don't there will be nothing left to share and use. Then Mother will become displeased with you and move along without you. She can only take so much violence amongst her beloved children. Her heart is aching for you to love one another as She loves you.

People in every country are the same no matter what their race, religion, sex, or culture. A Palestinian mother who loses her child is no less devastated than an Israeli, Iraqi, Afghani, or American one. Or a father, sister, or brother. We all have the same needs for survival, and we all feel pain, anger, joy, love, and fear. Now is the time for everyone everywhere to realize our unity and to learn the value of forgiveness, compassion, gentleness, mercy, and kindness before it is too late. Through communication let us build bridges of understanding, tolerance, and peace let us have empathy for one another and judge no one but ourselves. We must each walk in our brother's shoes and in beauty noticing the beauty within and all around us. You are beautiful beings of Light, love, Truth, and goodness. Each and every one of you. There are no exceptions. Even the terrorists are doing the best they can according to their own cultural upbringing and limited understanding. All things will balance out in the end and justice will prevail. It is All God's divine Leela, the Play of Consciousness being acted out on the huge dramatic stage of life. You are the divine actors and actresses, you are the Authors of the divine play, and you are its audience. You can make it a sad, dramatic play or a light-hearted happy one. It is totally up to you. God has given us all the ingredients for a happy, healthy life free of war, conflict, bondage, and disease. Out here in the celestial realms there is only sublime peace, joy, bliss, harmony, and greater states of ecstasy and divine communion. There can be nothing else beyond a certain level of understanding. We choose only thoughts and realities that foster harmony, joy and communion with one another. We are here to serve you and all humanity. There are many of us here in many realities beyond those of the third dimension. You are all ascending too, and all is well no matter how it looks from your limited perspective. Everything that you do is done in the name of love. Every action you take is for your own joy and upliftment, is it not? Ultimately, that is why any of us does anything. Underlying each and every thought, word, or deed we want to feel good. We want to be happy. We want to experience our true natures. We want to experience true freedom and become intentional co-creators with the Divine. Freedom is our natures, and we are here to create beauty, music, or whatever we choose and to experience greater levels of peace and bliss.

Since we are all made in the image and likeness of our Creator and each share That Divine spark of Consciousness and Light that is a part of the One Great Spirit, let us make it our top priority in life to know that Reality within ourselves. Since we were all born from unconditional Love out of a desire of God, All-That-Is, to know it, we are free to experience all the amazing contrast within the vast universe and make preferences about what it is we are wanting. When I experience this love within myself it is so easy to love all others—even my so-called "enemies". I love the rapist, the murderer, the jailer, the children, the politicians, the oppressors and the oppressed equally.

I see every person everywhere as my precious Brother and Sister, as a reflection of my very own Self. So why would I not do everything in my power and capacity in this lifetime to help as many as I possibly can? We are just passing through this life briefly, so we may as well make as big a difference as we can. Or why should I be here in the first place? All is well, and everything takes care of itself in time. Well Being reigns. It's been that way for thousands of years, and it will continue to be so because God and the angels are at the helm. The Earth herself has even survived Two World Wars, hydro-fracturing of her precious body, and other sad things, but the Earth and her children will survive and thrive. This is our experience from the higher perspectives of the star peoples. directing our steps from within as well as from the celestial realms. There is never any reason to worry about anything. Deep down, most of us know everything is all right and will be fine in the end, even in the midst of a crisis or challenge. But if we worry or feel very frightened about our finances or not getting that perfect job or mate, that is exactly the circumstance we will create in the near future. For what we fear and worry about we will attract. It's so simple. There is an abundance of all things and that includes a lack of what we are wanting.

We are eternally loved and we are That Love itself. God dwells within us as us. This Infinite Intelligence thinks through our mind. Creates with it. And experiences the wonders of Life through our precious bodies, the temples of our very own souls. If we could quiet our minds right now in this instant, go inside; observe the perfection of the breath going in and out, the constant beat of our hearts we could open our hearts to That Supreme Love. We will feel it and know without a doubt that what I say is true. Ask wholeheartedly and the Truth shall be revealed to you. And it will set you free from the prison and duality that the limited, false thinking has created.

You and I are precious Daughters and Sons of God and One with That Source itself. We are here to remember who we truly are and have the power to create whatever it is we would like to while in this human form. Source never judges whatever it is we want to create in this illusory world of opposites. We are here to experience it all. For how would we come to appreciate the dawn until we have experienced the darkness of night? How could we even know the difference?

In order to experience Light and Truth we needed to become consciously aware that there was also darkness. How could we really know and feel the fullest capacity of pleasure in human form until we have known pain? The beautiful former folksinger and head of the Siddha Yoga music department, Shambhavi Christian, says it so beautifully in her song, "Just love". "God is just. There is no high or low. The laughter and the weeping both create a rainbow. So just love." We are here to experience it all and make new choices in each moment based upon what we have learned and what is our innermost Truth and desire for our brethren, our planet, and ourselves in each new and holy moment.

We are not meant to lead lives of mediocrity or to just "survive". Nor are we here just for "getting and spending". Acquiring hordes of personal possessions is meaningless to me now. Besides, they require lots of care, space, and effort to maintain. When I lived with my wealthy first husband we owned a home, two cars, two televisions, and way too many toys, clothes, and other items that I spent most of my day cleaning, organizing, or shuffling our belongings from one place to another. It seemed like such a waste of precious time.

I've found through experience that having some basic possessions makes life simple, more orderly, and less stressful. When I had more possessions than I truly needed I found they began "owning" me. I will admit, though, that I do truly appreciate having a reliable nearly new pre-owned vehicle, some basic comfortable furnishings, a computer, electric piano, a modest collection of music and books, and a CD and audio-cassette player because I love music, singing, dancing, reading, and writing.

Wow, that's something that we all take for granted, isn't it? There are people in this country who can still not read or write. As well as many other war-torn countries where poor children are just trying to survive and keep themselves strong until all the chaos around them has subsided. When will we all learn to live together as brothers and sisters respecting the unity, dignity, and divinity of all human life? Each and every individual is so precious. My guru says that it takes a very long time to obtain a human birth. So, we should contemplate this and waste not a moment because time is precious, and we could each be gone in the blink of an eye. We never know when the hour of our death might come.

So, let's live each moment as if it were our last-- loving, appreciating, feeling thankful and enjoying our precious lives, Mother Earth, all her inhabitants, and ourselves. According to one of my non-physical teachers and friends, "Penelope" Earth is truly the vacation planet, and each day could be a vacation or a struggle to just survive. It is our choice. It all depends on what we want and what we are all collectively wanting as a human race. We can become humane, unconditionally loving and forgiving just like the Christ or we can remain miserable and without divine intent and spiritual purpose. It is totally up to us, my dear ones. We are free to choose. We can be, do, and have everything and anything we want as we give our attention to whatever it is that we desire. We were born with a magnificent emotional guidance system that lets us know in each and every moment what exactly is our vibrational content. We are all vibrating at a particular magnetic frequency. We are all made up of only energy. The Law of Attraction, which magnetically matches us up, with the focus of our desires and thoughts is then matching this up. As it is our desire to feel good, we learn to practice good feeling thoughts. There is nothing more important in this world than that we feel good. Then only good things will come to you. It is as easy to create a castle as it is to manifest a button or a parking space in busy downtown New York!

Kindness brings a smile to people who are struggling with low self-esteem, poverty, depression, or whatever problem. A helping hand goes a long way. As does a smile to a stranger.

Not long ago, a kind man working in my mom's neighborhood saw me tentatively climbing up an icy snow bank over a curb and ran a hundred feet warning me to stay where I was put until he got there to give me his hand to stabilize me and help me safely get over the snowy hump. He also prevented me from getting unwanted mud on my sneakers which would have upset my "Winner of the Immaculate Housekeeping Award" mom very much if I had tracked that mud and loose dirt onto her clean-living room floor which she just vacuumed and swept with her Swifter jet mop.

So, kindness does go a long way. In little things in our daily lives, and in BIG THINGS like people engaged in warfare or large disputes over territory.

VOLUNTEERING

I, personally, used to volunteer as a yoga teacher and singer in the Siddha Yoga prison program back in the nineteen eighties. I felt so humbled after sharing my story of god's grace and overcoming suicide and manic depression when these very large, muscular men at Manhattan Correctional Facility who would approach me after my talk and yoga class. I shared an original song I wrote about God's grace entitled "By Your Grace" that moved some of these men to tears. They were filled with gratitude, love, appreciation for my courage, and inspiration when they would come to thank me for sharing my challenges and inspirational story with them. I could only think how fortunate and blessed was I to be able to serve these precious men, who, for the most part, were just like you and me, but they happened to run into a bit of bad luck. They were incarcerated behind bars as opposed to being incarcerated inside a home or in a negative, complaining state of mind where we become obsessed listening to that constant "inner critic" that so many of us do.

SOCIAL JUSTICE

Not so long ago, an entire global awareness of anti-racism was ignited when the poor innocent black man, George Floyd, after allegedly passing a counterfeit twenty-dollar bill in Minneapolis, Minnesota, was deliberately executed by a Minneapolis police officer who had a history of violence when it came to arresting black and brown men. Poor Mr. Floyd was murdered by the arresting police officer, Derek Shavan, while being forced to the ground with a knee pushed onto his chest for nearly nine minutes. The poor man was murdered right in front of three other officers while the entire incident was caught on videotape. The police officer, Derek Shavan, was arrested and charged with second degree murder after mass peaceful protests in the United States and around the world. People the world over saw the blatant disregard police officer Shavan had for this unfortunate black man's life. Was it truly necessary to restrain Mr. Floyd in this cruel and brutal way with his knee on Mr. Floyd's neck for over eight minutes while Mr. Floyd said over and again "I can't breathe", called for his mama, and pleaded for his life? Of course not. Violence that leads to Murdering another precious human being should have only been employed as a last resort. Didn't this police officer have a taser or a night stick? These same police officer had been known to have been abusive to brown and black men in the past and was cited for police brutality. If it were not for body cameras and videos on smart cell phones this might have been just another brutal police killing to be swept under the rug and not acknowledged. Most likely this would have been the case since this type of police brutality has been going on for many years and unfortunately, even when the police have been arrested, as in the murders of Medgar Evers, the brutal killing of an innocent young fourteen-year-old, Emmett Till, seventeen-year-old Trevon Martin killed by a gunshot, twelve-year-old Tamir Rice.

Michael Brown, an eighteen-year-old, innocent unarmed Negro boy and a recent graduate from Normandy High School in Missouri was only two days away from beginning college, was shot six times, twice in the head, by Officer Darren Wilson, in Fergueson, Missouri, but the officer was found not guilty in this horrible crime. He had no real legal reason to hurt or kill this innocent young black man who was not just innocent and a very good student about to begin his life as a good college student with the potential to be a great, law abiding citizen and family man who contributes to the betterment of his community, but like all these other innocent black and brown men I've mentioned, is killed by policemen with a history of violence way before his time, so he had no opportunity to live and create the beautiful life he was meant to create. Eric Garner, an unemployed father of six, was murdered by a police officer who tried to arrest him for selling loose cigarettes on the street to make money to buy food for his large family, died when he was put into an illegal choke hold. This officer was not arrested or charged with any crime either.

Come on people. Are we back in the age where lynching's of black and brown men was not just legal and tolerated, but encouraged by the plantation owners and Confederates of the South who used lynching's as a way to control their slave population to keep them from running away to the north to escape a life of prison on plantations where they were owned by white men and kept chained in a life of hard labor and continuous servitude. If we do not protest these killings en masse right now as free men and women, whether white, black, brown, Christian, Jewish, Muslim, or agnostic, standing up for blacks, browns, American Indians, Japanese and Chinese, young Palestinians and Israelis alike, young men and women of every color and creed everywhere, this will continue for decades more to come.

How many billions of dollars does our US government spend on military defense weapons to keep us safe? How many millions and billions could be better spent investing in peaceful means of defense and social programs that uplift the poor, homeless, hungry, and disenfranchised.? I mean using just a quarter of that military money to feed our hungry, house our homeless, give people with mental illness a job to make them feel better about themselves, and create programs for teens and children that will help keep them safe, nourish their naturally creative abilities in art, music, gymnastics, poetry, home economics, cooking, etc.

Money could be used at the state and local levels to rebuild infrastructure and to fund community programs like a community garden, fund the senior centers and soup kitchens. The government would have more money for education of our prisoners who, for the most part, don't get a good education, and most likely, when they are let back into society, due to stigma and economic hardships, will most likely commit crimes again just to survive. There is no real rehabilitation going on, and the people who are teaching prisoners at New Jersey State Prison in Trenton and other prisons are volunteers who give of their time on a weekly basis. I know of one such program in Princeton where Princeton University students are involved that I learned about while attending the One Table Cafe at the Nassau Presbyterian Church in Princeton one Friday evening a few years ago in which university students go out in their "free" time to teach prisoners, and it transforms their lives. Both the prisoners AND the student volunteers.

Most of us are living like dullards in a state of dull, uncreative minds being comfortably numbed by television, music CDs, news programs, fast food, and a typical nine to five existences. Are any of us truly happy? How many of us come up with an original idea or have the courage to deviate from the societal norm of going to 23 years of schooling, getting married, having 2.5 children, and a boring 9 to 5 existence just making ends meet? I know there are a few of us who live in a state of childlike wonder, new thoughts, and gratitude or a place of God Centeredness from moment to moment, but, for the most part, that is a rare human being. Mostly, we are already pre-programmed to live like automatons in a state of reactivity, just content to be living a comfortable existence where we do not grow much or have the courage to make too many waves even if we know there are unethical things going on around us like the torturing of animals, enslavement and abuse of young women, and the killing of young, innocent black men. How many of us are strong enough to stand up for what is right like Dr. Martin Luther King, Jr., Rosa Parks, or Gandhi? To stand up for climate control and loving, respecting, and deeply caring for our Mother Earth and Her environment, the one in which we live, move, and have our Being?

How many of us will stand up against horrible things like hydrofracking and greedy, unethical companies like Monsanto who are making genetically modified soybeans and corn without proper labeling or regulation? Or standing up to boycott Phillip Morris who was still trying to peddle its

Marlboro death sticks even after knowing the dangers and diseases caused by smoking like lung cancer, *emphysema*, and COPD.? How many of us are courageous enough to go to jail for a just cause? It takes someone really unafraid and special like Daniel Ellsberg or Julien Assange who had the courage to be a whistle blower for Wikki Leaks.

Reform America's prison system that is so unfair and unjust. There is no rehabilitation in our prison system. Mostly torture of the poor, destitute, and especially our black and brown men. It's like the white man saw a way to legally reinstate slavery fifty years ago and get all the free labor they wanted again by placing so many of our poor black and Latino males in prison who committed very petty crimes or who were completely innocent but happened to be in the wrong place at the wrong time.

Where is the mercy, compassion, and rehabilitation we've been trying to implement for years? Nobody truly cares about the rights of our prisoners, and many are incarcerated for crimes they did not commit. Then there are rich men like OJ Simpson who've committed horribly heinous crimes, but because of their wealth, power, and charm, are able to lie and fool people. The rich and powerful hire high-powered lawyers who get them off the hook It makes me so sad and angry people like this literally get away with murder. Nicole Simpson and Ron Goldman, I love you and your lives are not forgotten. I read your best friend, Nicole's book, and I do believe O J had such a terrible hold over you, and he was terribly abusive too. It is a shame you did not leave him before this terrible tragedy occurred. I am also a victim of spousal abuse by both my husbands.

We still have such a long way to go for civil rights equality with young and old black men getting shot right and left by police officers just for standing in the street late at night wearing a hooded sweatshirt or even in broad daylight.

These murders are happening on a weekly and sometimes daily basis for the last ten years or so. Police brutality and condoned murder is worse than slavery because at least, for the most part, the black slaves were kept alive for the white man's profit and to tend the fields, pick the cotton, be butlers, clean the house, cook, raise the white woman's children.

My heart goes out to the poor black women slaves who were forced to undergo such humiliation and degradation of their precious bodies in order to just stay alive and keep the Master happy without the Mistress finding out. If the poor black slave were to get pregnant, she usually was forced to give up her baby, and it was raised as part of the white man's brood. How sad, powerless, and humiliated these poor women must have felt! If I have any say over this travesty or my own body and POWERFUL MIND, I will not allow this to be tolerated anymore.

I also have a six-month-old brown grandson, William, and I will NOT tolerate this type of environment of prejudice and injustice against a black, brown, or Latino man or woman. Not to mention the poor Native American red men and women whose land we stole and raped. The indigenous peoples knew the value of our "Mother" Gaia.

The difference between the extremely rich and extremely poor is at the root of many evils. There were and are many times I saw homeless men or women on the streets of New York while walking somewhere with Gary and once in Tucson with my friend, Zara Rose, that I would give my last few dollars to these unfortunate folks while stopping to talk to them about what was going on and how I might brighten their world. It always bothered me when I saw poor homeless people lying down on the ground in the subway station or outside in the rain, and people in New York would just walk by or step over them pretending they did not even exist. It was obvious they were in trouble. How could so many people just turn the heads and not notice the plight of so many people in such a sad state? Gary and I were in Manhattan once to be in the audience of the TV Show "Who Wants to be A Millionaire". While walking back to the train station we saw a woman with a child sitting on the ground. It was obvious she needed money, and I had already given away the last of my single dollar bills to several other homeless men I saw sitting or lying on the ground. I could not, however, turn away from a woman with a child. I said to Gary, "Honey, do you have any money left? We need to help this poor woman and her family." Gary only had a couple of bucks, but I insisted we stop and talk to the unfortunate woman and bless her and ourselves with just a little bit of cash that might lift her spirits knowing someone cared even if we were mere strangers.

We are all just like the tree Sky and I planted at Griggs Farm. Starting out as small seeds, a sperm and egg unite to form cells which multiply over and over until they become a large, completely Conscious, innately intelligent human being. What a miraculous process Life is. Depending on which thoughts we choose to use to nurture this body and mind will be what determines what type of trees we will become, but we will all grow larger and expand to fill up the space we have inhabited just like my tree. Always growing in awareness, from good to greater good, all-in divine order and timing. This "Consciousness" of ours is always evolving, becoming better and better, out here on the Leading Edge of Thought creating time saving machines like refrigerators, dishwashers, washing machines, dryers, machines for better communication like the telephone, telegraph, and finally computers, airplanes, space ships and other intelligent machines. Infinite ideas have gone into building boats, ships, huts, buildings, and gigantic architecture. However, let us not forget where we came from. Without Goddess Gaia, our precious Mother Earth, none of this would be possible, so along with human innovation and the growth of civilization we should remember to respect Nature for it is She who sustains us. She gives us life, nurtures and sustains us, but if we take her for granted, we could become extinct in the blink of an eyelid. She just may decide humans were an interesting experiment if we don't wake up and begin to love, honor, and respect the Goddess and all her inhabitants. We must live in this beautiful world in harmony with Her, her animals, elements, and each other, or not at all.

War and greed must become a thing of the past as it is not serving anyone except for those elite who are in power at this time, but they will fall eventually. Any tyrant who has reigned over others may enjoy his power for a brief period, but unless a ruler has the best interests and welfare of his subjects in mind, he or she is no leader at all. And his empire will fall like the Greeks, the Romans, Hitler, Genghis Khan, British apartheid, black slavery, and all the others.

I want to speak about the poor veterans coming home after many months or years on the front lines who feel alone, abandoned, unappreciated, tormented, and traumatized. I know many of them feel abandoned, undervalued, and unappreciated. Confused about the horrors they experienced while fighting for our country many attempts suicide every day. Some are successful at killing themselves. This is such a travesty, people. Please do not hurt yourself, my precious ones. It was NOT your fault! You are loved, honored, and your heart was and still is in the right place. You young boys were and are brainwashed to think killing is necessary and actually give your whole lives, sometimes losing body parts in service to a country who is just manipulating you to practice violence and murder when it is, for the most part, NEVER justified. Nonviolent communication and PEACE is the only way to resolve differences. Our country must address the underlying causes of most conflicts like poverty, hunger, lack of resources and education.

How many hundreds of trillions of dollars have our politicians created in debt due to mismanagement of US funds, natural resources, etc. All I know is, when President Bill Clinton left office there was a large surplus in the treasury which Bush and Cheney squandered away on the WAR MACHINE, going to war against Iraq for their billion-dollar oil. Now with all the monies being spent on weapons like. Atomic bombs, guns, warships, ammunition, war planes, etc. it appears as if we are on the road to SELF DESTRUCTION, and we, the people, are the only ones who have the power to STOP this travesty. WAKE UP PEOPLE from your deep slumber. NO GOD OUT THERE is going to rescue us if we are not WILLING and ABLE to STAND UP FOR OURSELVES!

ME TOO

The "Me Too" movement was given that name in 2017, but it existed long before that.

My first experience with sex contained feelings of toxic shame and guilt by that first interaction with my dad. I kept recreating the same circumstances over and over until I could learn radical forgiveness of my father and myself. I am now a free woman listening to my own inner guidance using my head and heart to make new, better choices in sex partners and life-mates. I am now choosing only men that are for my highest and best good, those men who see how special I am and truly love, honor, respect, and appreciate me.

As of 2022, we were living in "Loony Times". I am discovering that I am not the only woman who has been sexually abused, harassed, and disparaged. More and more famous women are having the courage to speak out in television, movies, and the workplace. The "Me Too" movement has been growing ever since. First, the "allegations" of sexual abuse began several years ago with many women comings out against the actor Bill Cosby, though only one woman took him to court. The others did not want to go to court. Cosby's wife said the allegations were absurd. Mr. Cosby denied them, as just about all sexual abusers do, like former presidents. Trump, and Clinton. Why can't people, especially the members of the powerful male patriarchy, just be responsible, own up to their actions, and be honest? The truth always comes out eventually anyway.

In 2017, film mogul, Harvey Weinstein, accused by actress, Ashley Judd, daughter of famous country singing star, Naomi Judd, and quite a few others of rape, sexual harassment, and creating an entire racket of intimidation and fear in which others were complicit in keeping these clandestine rapes and inappropriate advances toward many of the actresses in Hollywood.

Then, after that was announced in the newspaper, suddenly there was a "rash" of accusations against newsmen like Charley Rose, who was accused of walking around naked in front of his staff, making inappropriate jests, and fondling some of his fellow newswomen in inappropriate ways. Charley Rose not only apologized for any appropriate sexual misconduct, but was subsequently fired from CBS News.

More recently, I looked on in horror and surprise as one of my favorite anchors, a man I would never ever suspect of inappropriate sexual behavior, a very "nice" family man, Matt Lauer, was fired from his anchor position at NBC after one woman made claims against him of sexual harassment. After that, several other women spoke up as well.

Well, what can we expect in a climate that looks the other way when women are bullied by the police, raped in prisons and mental hospitals, and senior women who should be respected just for their age and wisdom, are treated with disdain in nursing homes and hospitals, as if they do not matter and have nothing to contribute to society anymore? Not to mention that young girls are still being mutilated by having their clitorises removed in some countries in Africa. Some Muslim women still have so few civil rights in some countries that it is even illegal for them to drive cars or show their faces. They have to completely cover up their bodies with a black break, and if they show their faces in public, apart from their husbands, they are considered immoral, and many of them are having acid thrown into their beautiful faces by their husbands to make them unattractive on purpose. In fact, I saw a show on public television where a surgeon was donating his time on a weekly basis to surgically remove the scars to fix these poor women's brutalized faces so that they would be able to live a normal life out in public. Eleanor Roosevelt asked for her own home, Val Kill, in upstate New York knowing that her husband had a mistress living in the White house with her husband! Rose Kennedy ignored her husband's behavior.

Poor Princess Diana knew practically from the start that Prince Charles had Camilla Bowles as his mistress almost from the start of their marriage. She had to deal with depression, anxiety, anorexia nervosa from having to keep silent about that and so many things that were "allowed" while being part of a "Royal Family".

Poor Anita Hill was practically laughed at while trying to tell the truth about justice Clarence Thomas in front of the Senate Judiciary Committee During the times he was being considered as as Supreme Court Justice Senator Joe Biden asked her questions almost as if she were on trial. Anita Hill reluctantly shared these insults to her as a woman in the workplace with the Ethics Committee only because she was sent a subpoena to appear. She said she had shared these things with someone she worked with at the ERC in confidence, and never even tried to accuse Clarence Thomas in public of any inappropriate sexual harassment in her work environment because she was too embarrassed about it. She said Clarence Thomas had treated her like "one of the boys" from the time she worked at the ERC, telling dirty jokes, bringing in pornography, referring to a male porn star's penis as "Long Don, and other things that made her feel uncomfortable and disrespected."

Well, it looks like it's high time all women came out of the closet to share our stories and tell our personal truths so that this BAD BOY Behavior can be stopped right now. This disrespect and denigration of women has been going on behind closed doors for way too long now! No more abuse. No more indignities! No more rape or disrespect. Not only toward women in general but toward our precious mother Earth, the Goddess herself who has been raped, violated, disrespected, used, and abused for a very long time—especially now with hydrofracturing and still taking oil from the ground that usually ends up in her clean oceans killing tons of fishes, otters, turtles, birds, ducks, and generally destroying the natural habitat and environment. How long will it take before we love, honor, and appreciate the One who loves us unconditionally and who provides us everything from food, clothing, delicious clean, flowing water, shelter, sunny days, moonlit nights, animal playmates, to beauty, bread, and roses? I am so grateful to our mother for sustaining me. My personal family as well as the entire human family. I am trying to recycle, use less plastic, pick up litter and waste I see when I go walking in nature, around my development, on the beach, etc.

Sex and touch should be wonderful, pleasurable experiences for most men and women, but people like me who have been molested, not educated about sex or how to have healthy boundaries with men, healthy sensuality has been a continuous life long process for me to learn and experience, I am sad to say. I was forty years old before I truly began to enjoy sexual intimacy with a man.

It should be obvious that children do not experience sex in the same way as adults. Suppressing a child's exploration of its physical form or, at the other extreme, forcing an adult viewpoint or activity on a child, can do serious harm and long-term damage to the child. My boundaries had been violated by both my father and my mother. Mom insisted that I suppress my sexuality, while Dad encouraged me to express it, but in the context of a father/daughter relationship.

At five years old I had a healthy curiosity about my body and especially my breasts and vagina. One of my girlfriends with whom I played outdoors took me inside her cool garage one hot summer day when her mom was not home and we played being "BIG" Girls. She played the guy's part, and of course I was the girl. She touched me "down there" (as my good Catholic mom would refer to my vagina which she told me was my "Cooley".) Anyway, Christie pulled down my pants and began fondling my private places between my legs gently opening up my labia, getting me wet, and eventually fondling my clitoris until I had an orgasm – at five, can you imagine? She literally taught me how to masturbate, and I was excited and really grateful. I started to experiment on my own after that without my mom ever knowing because I knew somehow, she would not approve. Sometimes I'd rub my little "button" up and down against our clothesline pole which was totally enclosed by a wooden fence, so I had lots of privacy where I felt free and comfortable to be my natural, sensuous, curious little Self figuring what ways to make myself feel the best and eventually climax.

I'd touch myself privately later on in the bathroom or at night after I got tucked into bed for the night in my bedroom. Just once my mom found out I had been playing with my genitals. It was a winter afternoon. I had just masturbated on my bed with the door closed during the day, and I got so hot that I needed help taking off a very heavy knit sweater which went over my head. My tiny fingers still had the delicious musty scent of "cum" on them, so when mom helped me to pull the sweater off, she was able to smell my pussy juices on my fingers. Mommy said

"Meryl, you don't touch yourself "DOWN THERE, do you?"

"NO, of course NOT, Mom. Never." I didn't feel bad about lying about this because I figured if God had made touching my pussy feel so good, why would he not want me to enjoy it.

"I sure hope you were not touching your private parts because it is a sin" she admonished.

Sin or not, it felt pretty fantastic to me, so I was not about to give up giving myself this new pleasure which I so enjoyed. At five I was pretty precocious. I was already kissing boys in kindergarten.

Eventually, my suppressed sexuality would reassert itself. I even became a very successful go-go dancer in New Jersey for five years in order to express my suppressed sexuality. Once a man got close enough to become intimate with me when there was a commitment, I would subconsciously shut down the feelings in my genitals which gave me a good excuse to look outside the relationship and move onto the next man. When I would begin to feel dead "down there" I just believed I was frigid, thought there was something seriously wrong with me, and I would never be able to marry or have children of my own.

As a Cancerian with five planets in Cancer, this was disconcerting, because, having a loving family was as important to me as breathing, so I sunk into a very deep suicidal depression a few times in my mid-twenties after serious break-ups with men I believed were "the ONE" for me. I was interested in my career as an entertainer when I was younger, but not at the expense of having a family and the "man of my dreams".

At the other extreme was my early relationship with Dad. He was my knight in shining armor –

my protector, defender, playmate with me and my two brothers at home and at our resort home in the Poconos, where we went on vacation. He was my first lover, of sorts.

He was the first man to touch my breasts when I was thirteen, pat me on my buttocks when I was 12 calling me "Crisco" because I was meaty in my hind end. And the first man to give me an orgasm. He was the first man to make me feel pleasure in my nearly hairless pussy. He was also the first person other than myself, who knew how to make me orgasm just with his skillful touch, from behind while he was tucking me into my bed at night. He read me a story first, tickled my back underneath my pajamas, and it progressed down into my yoni from there.

I cannot lie. It felt absolutely relaxing and exciting at the same time. I did not know it was coming the first few times it happened, so it may have been the element of surprise that got me so wet and excited. I was fourteen years old, and things with him and my mom were not going so swell according to her, I would find out later at 16 when my dad left mom to court and eventually marry my mom's best friend, Joan. I had surmised as much because I found centerfolds of Playboy playmates in the Playboy magazine's left in the upstairs bathroom for me and my brother, Pete, to find plus the older issues which he kept stored away from me and my brothers in the bottom of his light brown oak night table drawer next to his bed.

I loved the beautiful playmates, and often fantasized I would have big beautiful breasts like all those perfect, older young women when I grew up to be eighteen or nineteen. That seemed like the ideal dream. To be loved, honored, and cherished for my beauty and sensuality by these handsome men like Hugh Hefner and my Daddy, Pete, who loved his little girls like me, Raquel Welch, Sophia Lauren, and the actress, Ursula Andress, who was in James Bond 007 with gorgeous Sean Connery, and Barbie Benton, Mr. Hefner's main squeeze who was all of nineteen years old.

Anyway, I occasionally saw Miss Benton on TV on Rowan & Martin's "Laugh-In" for a few years when my parents would let me watch with them in our recreation room downstairs on a Friday or Saturday night, I forget which. This show came on past my bedtime, so I had to get permission from them to stay up to watch this really cool show with one-liner jokes, funny, risqué' parodies that starred women and men who would eventually become famous actresses, actors, or comedians like the skinny, goofy, wide eyed, giggly blond bombshell, Goldie Hawn, who danced as a go-go dancer in the cages along with Judy Carnes. Goldie was a better dancer and wore crazy tattoos all over her body like PEACE, POWER, and sayings like Body Paint, EAT ME blazoned upon her tush, and other provocative sayings I was just learning were nasty because of what I saw and heard from TV, magazines, talks with my girlfriends, and books. I was curious about how to make babies, and just wanted to know if they came out of your belly button, and how does one actually "Do It".

Once I read a question in Ingenue magazine from a reader, a letter to the editor, saying "how will I know if I'm still a virgin if I don't have a hymen.

I knew what a hymen was because my mom and I had "the talk" about menstruation when I was ten so I would be prepared if I started bleeding early like Aunt Erna, my grammy's older sister, did, at ten years old. Mommy told me she got her "Period" at ten years old and barely knew what was happening to her. When my mom got hers at 12 or 13 my grandmother was frantic and not very helpful in this minor crisis. She just shoved her off with an "Oh my God" and a sigh, saying "You poor thing". So, it begins. "Go talk to your sister, Marlyse." Gram did not want to have anything to do with sex, sex education, or the "dirtier, more shameful things of life we women have to bear and endure. Except it was all worth it because we were the lucky ones to give birth to beautiful babies like me, Pete, and Scott.

Can you imagine? Something so wonderful, magical, and natural being disparaged, denigrated, and experienced as terrible, dirty, and shameful?

Can you imagine how embarrassed I felt when Daddy, who was born under the astrological sign of Scorpio, which meant he was oversexed, after reading his Playboy magazines, would reach for me, his precious charge, a thirteen-year-old virgin with no knowledge or experience of sex, or even knew how to make babies, or how to even kiss a boy or a man? I could not even look my dad in the eye or confront him directly about it because I felt so embarrassed and ashamed. I could not even share what was happening with my mother, friends, or siblings since this was so taboo. Plus, he warned me not to say anything or my mom might divorce him and he would have to move out which I did NOT want to happen since he protected me from my mom's spankings, yelling, and psychological abuse.

I had been kissing boys since I was in kindergarten. My first was a handsome little brown-haired boy named Frank Cachera. I fooled him by telling him I had a secret to share with him alone. He bent down so I could whisper in his ear; and after the whisper I kissed him on the cheek. I was such a naughty little girl then who turned into a very naughty young woman and crone thirty years later after being married twice, giving birth to three children by three different men. And I chose to marry two of them. They were both Pisces and either caring, loving, or psychologically and sometimes physically abusive. Freud would say I married my mother not once, but twice! What the heck was I thinking? I suppose it was all subconscious so that I could heal these wounds from childhood that had been stored there for decades. At least that's what seems rational and logical to my adult mind now.

I still love sex more than ever – especially because I have no more eggs since my Fallopian tubes were tied in 1991 after I was admitted to the Carrier Clinic for bipolar depression when it was discovered by doctors that I had an ectopic pregnancy, which meant that the fetus was developing in my fallopian tube and not my uterus; so, I no longer had to or have to worry about getting impregnated. I've had my three beautiful children, now adults.

As a woman who has experienced a unique relationship with my dad – one of both physical and emotional intimacy, from the time I was thirteen years old, it has really been challenging to have healthy relationships with men who care about me and to embrace my natural sensuality and sexuality without having shame and trust issues. I was never someone who understand it was OK for me to even HAVE healthy boundaries. I mean I believed in my heart and mind that the incest was my fault, and that I should be ashamed for having attracted my father. I felt guilty and ashamed that I did not confront him right away, look him directly in the face and tell him to "STOP – you are making me feel very uncomfortable."

It was not until 1990, with my second marriage failing, that I experienced that breakthrough.

ECONOMICS

The rent and the car payment are due at the beginning of the month. The price of of groceries and Medications is exorbitant. Sometimes it can all just be overwhelming if one is living at or below the poverty level which I have been for most of my life as a single mom except for the five and a half years I was married to my first husband, David, who was very industrious and had a knack for making lots of money.

Then there are utilities, phone, cell phone if you have one, cable TV, and then on top of all that, the price of gasoline is exorbitant, though at this moment it seems to have gone down a LOT. Hurray! Sometimes, even if a poor person or single mom receives food stamps, which, at this writing, were just cut by the Republican conservatives in Congress by billions of dollars so they could fund their military spending, a mom may have no extra money for little things like toothpaste, napkins, toilet tissue, paper towels, and diapers. No wonder I got depressed. Just writing about it now, I am thinking "Just shoot me now and put me out of my misery". Nah. I've already been there, done that. Besides, if I was gone, who would take care of my children as well as clean up mistakes left by the rest of the unenlightened human race?!

Getting back to economics, I'm very easy about all of money and abundance now because it is not my top priority, and it has always been easy for me to acquire when I do what I love doing. My children are all grown and doing well financially. In fact, they are all doing better than me financially, and often help me out, and this truly makes me happy. In depressed states I was a little jealous of their prosperity, but not anymore because I know my gifts of writing, healing, singing, dancing, and teaching are unique, and will bless and serve others. Basically, that is truly all I really want to do is serve God, and my gurus in my own sweet, humble way and provide a few needed services for humanity.

Money is useless unless we use it as an instrument for good. If we allow God to work through us in order to use His unlimited abundance for the good of ourselves and in service to humankind, we will feel happy and fulfilled. Why should I eat like a Queen every day if I know my little neighbor is starving in Trenton, Philadelphia, New York, or even around the world in Syria or Africa? I care deeply about myself, my family, my friends, my immediate community, and my World community, so I donate and tithe regularly to my church, the Center for Spiritual Living, and organizations that feed the world's poor like Heifer international, Feed the Children, World Vision, and others I am guided to be helping. My mom regularly donates to all the charities that help animals like the Wild horses, elephants, rescue dog and cat shelters like SAVE now in Skillman. When they were close by in Princeton, I used to go there on a regular basis to volunteer my services by petting and holding the cats as well as taking out one of the smaller dogs, brushing it, and showing it a lot of affection after I walked it.

ECOLOGY

You and I are a part of Mother Nature. We have the gift to be able to go outside and meditate on the wonders of the stars, the sun, sky, and moon. I have friends in prisons that are not free to do that. Anyway, let us give thanks for the "little things" – like the fact that we can breathe and walk. The infinite intelligence that is operating in the Universe is the same intelligence that dwells within <u>our</u> very being! It is the same one that keeps the stars and planets in place in all our solar systems and galaxies. It is the same one that animates our bodies, makes our hearts beat, and performs all the infinitely complex functions like digestion, assimilation, and elimination without us ever having to think about it.

Each one of us needs to take responsibility NOW for some small facet of the many sad problems and circumstances technology has created. Like the devastation of our environment for hundreds of years. We must ALL love our Mother Earth, Goddess Gaia, and become stewards of our precious planet now before it is too late. Before there is No planet upon which to live and thrive. We could just blow ourselves up right out of existence if we ever had a Third World War. And some of what our government does and condones today is leading to that. So, let's have peace, guys, by acting in a peaceful, loving, kind, compassionate manner and being the peace, we seek. Hatred and violence only beget more of same. Love begets love. If our Lord Jesus, had an inkling (and he does, I am sure) of all the violence, torture, and murder that has been committed in His holy name he would be turning over in his tomb! It's almost Easter and he is laughing at me even as I write this now, but seriously, folks, can't we all just get along? Whatever happened to "Do unto others as you would have them do unto you? And "Love thy neighbor as thyself". As far as I'm concerned, I AM my brothers' and my sisters' keeper, and I try to be kind and compassionate to as many people I can the world over if not in person, at least in my prayers, chants, intentions, and donations to organizations that help those who are temporarily less fortunate and cannot help themselves.

We can challenge Big PHARMA, corporations like Walmart who do not care for their workers, and those who support the military industrial complex. We must love and care for Mother Earth NOW, deal with pollution and climate problems before it is too late and there is no Planet left for us to enjoy. With so much war, selfishness, and greed taking place upon our planet mother Earth is about to explode. She loves us so much She allows us free will in order to learn and grow, but unless we stop terribly damaging practices like hydro-fracturing we will create more toxic waste, deplete ground water and dry up natural streams in some parts of the country. Hydrofracking injects waste water underground which causes earthquakes. Big Oil and Gas plants do not have to disclose what toxic chemicals they are using due in part to intensive lobbying by the former Vice President, Dick

Cheney, who did extensive lobbying for exemptions from critical statutes in all the major environmental laws including the Safe Water Drinking Act as well as the Clean Water and Clean Air Acts. Among those toxic chemicals being used, many cause cancer, neurological problems, and birth defects. Do you remember the movie "Erin Brockovitch? If it were not for her steadfast determination to help all the poor farmers and residents of the area who were getting cancer and dying from the toxins that ended up in the local water supply from the large gas company at the time these people who knew what they were doing was dangerous to human health, would have gotten away with murder. Many women and children were being poisoned daily by the toxic waste that had leaked into their drinking water from this damaging process of hydro-fracturing Mother Earth. Sure, many of the families who were affected were given thousands or even one million dollars. But how can one put a price on a human life-or on one mother's or child's suffering? Nothing can bring back a child or any human being who has suffered needlessly.

What about the Earth Mother? Do you think she has no feelings Herself? She is a sentient being who loves her children and all the beings who live upon her precious body. Do you think she does not suffer when we go to war with one another and torture innocent people and animals? Do you think that destruction such as was created by the atomic bombing of Hiroshima and Nagasaki had no effect upon her? It's time to WAKE UP, precious beings of Light and take responsibility for all the damage and destruction we have created over the eons. If it were not for the Archangels, the love and intervention of many Ascended Masters, and Space Brothers, Man would have experienced a global catastrophe more than once already. The devastation that took place on 9/11 was another clarion call for man and his crazy technocratic society to WAKE UP NOW. Let us love one another as brothers and sisters before it is too late. Let us not make Money and greed more important than loving God and one another. We are each our brother's keeper. Let's do unto others as we would have them done unto us, as Christ Jesus said in the Bible. Let us exist in love with and appreciation for all the beautiful plants, trees, animals, insects, and other species which share residence with us upon Goddess Gaia. We must become aware of the needs of others, not just ourselves, and become stewards of our precious planet, Do NOT rape Her resources, do NOT do terrible things to our blessed mother like hydro-fracturing and drilling through her body for oil... Do you think that our mother goddess cannot Feel this horrible insult inside herself? She became a planet so that she could feel the joy of all her precious children walking upon her body. She has chakras just like we do. She has infinite love, compassion, and more powers than we can possibly imagine. Do you believe, for one second, that she could not destroy us before we, as fools, explode another atom bomb upon her body hurting, maiming, and murdering millions of innocents as has been done twice before? This will NEVER be allowed to happen again. The Truth has been and will continue to be revealed. We are One and we are all connected. Whatever we do to our neighbor we are doing to and for OURSELVES. WE must learn to be kind, love one another, our precious neighbor at home and across the globe as our own self, and SHINE our LIGHT of UNITY as ONE LOVING Consciousness in HARMONY with all beings as ONE FAMILY and then we will experience the DAWN of a NEW AGE of sublime PEACE, BEAUTY, creativity, Unity, joy, contentment, and Divine LOVE. There are many Masters and people who have gone before who are guiding and assisting us. It is time to STOP, go within, and ask for personal and planetary guidance from those who are watching and waiting to be of help. We are all on the verge of a PLANETARY AWAKENING, a GRAND Polar SHIFT in Conscious AWAREness where we all care for one another as if we are caring for a newborn child. We can tap into this Infinite Intelligence at any time by just asking and being still. The answer and solutions to all our questions will be provided.

I like bartering for services and have never felt the desire to be rich like some folks. I am starting to have a desire for more wealth as my prosperity consciousness grows, but mostly because I like to give a lot as gifts and to charity. I also love to travel. Allowing, receiving, and manifesting more prosperity has been a gradual process. But there is no need for hoarding or greed. God and Mother Nature provide everything that we need for us without us having to make much effort. Life can be so simple if we want to make it that way. Simply allow the flow of abundance that is our divine birthright. All of us have unique gifts and talents that we trade for dollars. There is no need for any of us to struggle. In fact, when we do the things that bring us joy we are much more in a vibrational countenance to attract and allow the very abundance that we believe we will get from working hard and struggling. We will achieve nothing from struggle and hard work but discontent and resentment. It is much better to make money doing the things we love to do. Even if we did not make millions doing what we loved doing at least we would be happy. And what is more important than that? In my mind, the fact that I am mostly happy or content doing whatever job I am doing makes me a success.

I believe it is a very good thing to recycle. We must learn to conserve and take care of the mother's resources and care of the environment while we still can. That's why I hope to purchase a "hybrid" electric car that also uses gasoline for my next new vehicle.

Community and Support

I first fell into a suicidal depression it was the winter of 1981 after finishing massage studies at the Sarasota School of Natural Healing Arts. My lover had betrayed me and my best friend had moved away. The situation is described in the previous chapters "Massage School and Life in Sarasota" and "The First Breakdown", and I will not repeat it here. Suffice it to say that I attempted suicide several times and was institutionalized and began a regime of medication that has continued off and on ever since.

If you ever feel this bad, please don't stay by yourself and allow things to get out of hand the way I did running from the pain and negative emotions. Emotions are not negative. If they are not felt and the energy is not moved along the hurt, anger, rage, and resentment will get trapped and stored in your body, particularly your organs like your liver, gall bladder, and intestines. If you find yourself in a situation like this, my dear ones, please don't hide away by yourself feeling toxic shame, unworthiness, and confusion. You are loved and supported by God, your angels, and God's angels on earth, the other human beings who have become our dearest friends, family, doctors, prayer partners, and counselors. We are all connected, and at one time or another, have all suffered. We are all united as One BIG Cosmic Family. We are so connected that what one person does affects another because we are all related. If you feel alone and trapped in a crazy state of mind, please go seek some help. Please do not be ashamed. You are intelligent and courageous to look for a counselor, go to a doctor, a spiritual teacher, pastor, or a psychologist. Whatever you think will work for you personally, someone you trust and whom you can be vulnerable enough with to cry and express your deepest feelings.

Please do not hesitate to call someone. Or visit your mom, your dad, your spouse, your best friend, your priest, minister, doctor, counselor, or call the suicide hotline for help—please, my beloveds. The phone number at NAMI, the National Alliance for Mental Illness in Mercer County is 609-799-8994. Please call someone to talk about how you are feeling before you make a terrible mistake that cannot be undone. Take it from me. Trying to run away from pain and suffering by attempting suicide is just not worth it. Whatever caused the pain in the first place does not go away until you just DEAL with it. You will be sorry later if you do anything foolish to hurt yourself.

I have heard so many sad stories on the news lately about teens committing suicide due to bullying. This is something that's got to stop. If you are a teenager who is bullied at school or on the internet, please do not let anyone else influence you to think you are unloved or unwanted. You are completely worthy of LOVE and friendship. Adored by God, the angels, and I'm sure you have at least one or two good, kind, close friends who DO appreciate you. Do not listen to anyone who does NOT appreciate the beautiful person you are inside. It is ONLY the inside that counts. You may be of a different race or religion, be attracted to the same sex, or confused about your sexuality, but you are beautiful just as you are in this holy moment. Like Mary Poppins you are practically perfect in every way. With all our human failings and faults, God loves us unconditionally and accepts us completely just as we are, so do not listen to the judgments of a hypocritical religion, church dogma, or any other person's opinion of you unless it is kind and helpful. The kids that do that to other kids are not worthy of your friendship anyway. It's so sad what kids do to other students out of jealousy or because they are being abused or neglected at home by their OWN parents and need to abuse someone, they know to make them feel temporarily better about themselves. NEVER EVER let anyone tell you are BAD or not worthy of love. You are beautiful to God/Goddess no matter how you look, feel, or think.

You are DIVINE in nature. God most High dwells within you AS YOU right now, and in time you will KNOW this for certain in your heart of hearts. Never let anyone put you down, blame you, or humiliate you, my precious ones.

If you are feeling hopeless, filled with despair thinking you'd be better off dead, precious ones, PLEASE tell someone who can help. Suicide is NEVER the answer. Find someone who truly cares and an organization like the National Alliance of Mental illness who can lead you to a good support group. There is also survivors of suicide support groups. Whatever problem or circumstance you are in, guys and gals, is just temporary, though I know when we are suicidally or chronically depressed it is difficult, no nearly impossible, to think rationally. We feel so hopeless, lethargic, exhausted, and helpless that we do not believe there is any hope out of our current circumstance or challenging situation. But DON'T BELIEVE IT! That's just the "Adversary" talking. If you can just pray, meditate, or quiet the incessant thoughts in the mind with some dancing, meditation, or some type of movement you might be able to hear your guardian angels and the archangels who are always guiding, guarding, and protecting you.

These dark moods feel seemingly endless and time literally drags on for so long that minutes seem like hours. We feel as if we cannot breathe or take a deep breath. Believe me, I know exactly how you are feeling. I have been there on many an occasion, but each time the love of God and the grace of my guru prevailed with just a few prayers to All-That-is and my angels and guides, and though I did not believe it at the time, somehow, some way my Lord's grace, like a precious mother or grandmother Who cradles her infant and tenderly puts her face to its cheek, Mother Goddess, Gaia, Mother Mary, and the Divine Feminine will cradle you in this time of need holding you in the Light of Her love so that you can feel safe, nurtured, and soothed until you can think a more positive thought about yourself. And have a bit of hope and faith.

There is nothing more powerful than God's Love, than this Force or Being we call God. Great Spirit. Father Sky. Lord Jesus. Allah. Shiva. Krishna. Buddha. Bahah Ulah. The Guru. It is known by many names, but it is only One Divine Being expressed as infinite beings and forms. Love is truly All there is, and you are a divine expression of That Love itself. You yourself are a divine expression of this Great ONE and without you, my beloved friend, God Himself would not have a conscious experience of its own DIVINITY. Let that sink in for a few moments. This AWARENESS lives inside us all the time, and we can choose to listen to our higher guidance, or we can say "I can't. I won't, complain about everything under the sun, live in fear, and be a victim. Why waste another minute in this hellish state of mind?

Reclaim your personal power, my friends, and surrender to the DIVINE WILL of the ONE Great God, the Great Central Sun, the power of Source that created all the planets, maintains, recreates and destroys cells, planets, and entire Universes. Yet, nothing is ever destroyed because this energy is invincible, eternal, never was born, and will never die. So, vow to reclaim your power, embrace your loving, creative natures, and above all, be gentle with yourselves, my beloveds, if you are feeling down and out.

You are not the first person and won't be the last to feel overwhelmed, hopeless, and in a state of fear and anxiety. It's all part of the process of being "human". We are all learning, by contrast, what are our personal desires and preferences. No matter how crappy or unworthy you are feeling in this moment you still deserve love. We must love ourselves first before we can love anyone else. Give your Self that kind, tender loving care and respect that you offer to others. You deserve it, sweetie. Love, nurture, and honor what you are going through and please, do not get down on yourselves, precious ones, like I did, if you are feeling temporarily weak or unworthy. When you become humble and surrender your problem, mistake, circumstance, and eventually entire Life to the ONE GOD you will actually discover He resides within You just as you are in this precious, holy moment. Things will come to you as if by magic, and life will then become a game to be played, and all your human friends and animals here will become your playmates. Each being before you will become a holy reflection of your beautiful, powerful, pristine, Glorious, beautifully sweet Self. It may take a little time, but just start small by loving one or two things about yourself. Feel grateful for your breath. Feel grateful that you can use your legs and go take a walk. Get up off the couch, turn off the TV, leave the cell phone behind, and take a walk down the street, around your yard, and notice the beauty of the trees and flowers.

If it's winter you may not want to go outdoors, but at least get off the couch or out of the bed, put on some music, and move your body. It will make a difference in how you feel. Movement and your favorite music will change your brain chemistry and strengthen your vagus nerve.

Living Life is about movement and growth. Staying young and having a positive attitude about aging and growing older takes a bit of change in your thinking and perspective because most people in America do not honor people that are elderly like the Asians do and the Native American Indians do as part of their cultures. The "elders" are seen as wise beings and accorded respect just because of their life experience, wisdom and the knowledge they've acquired. Unfortunately, the consciousness in the United States is mostly that getting older is a sad, terrible thing that makes one ill and unable to do the things he or she was once able to do with their bodies and minds is, unfortunately, a human "race belief" that we must look at and see it for the lie it is. One of the things I keep being reminded of each day, especially if I'm feeling achy or have some type of pain in my joints, is that I have control and choice over whether or not I [pay attention to my body and honor it as the powerful vehicle of infinite Intelligence and temple of the soul that it is. Even as I write these words now Holy Spirit reminds me that I feel so much better if I make a point to get up and stretch or move around a bit by dancing or stretching in the midst of writing this material on paper for more than a few hours. or walking outside after an hour of sitting at the computer. Any more than that and I begin to feel stiff and get a little tired.

Sometimes I get into a flow and I might write for five or six hours straight without being aware of the time, but my physical body is usually sorry afterward, so now I try to set a timer or just check the clock, so I make myself stretch, do neck and shoulder rolls. Actually, I'm going outside right now to do some cat and cobra poses on the grass. The sun is lower in the sky, and it is a lovely, warm evening.

Perhaps the hardest thing is to ignore negative remarks, bullying and abuse, but it is possible.

When I was about fourteen, I sat on the bus with my girlfriend, Susan, whose family owned a farm, and she did not have a lot of really nice, cool clothes like some of the other kids and the teenagers who were older than us in the upper grades that rode the bus with us. She wore the same two outfits all week long. I remember two older teens making fun of Susan all the time even before I got to know her well, but it did not stop me from sitting next to her on the bus and talking to her as if they were not there. We would have nice conversation, and I'd tell her they were idiots and to just ignore these two girls.

I found out many years later Susan, who was just an average student when I knew her, really excelled later in life and got a terrific job at Bell Laboratories in Holmdel where we lived and married a nice man too. So, luckily, this verbal abuse did not affect my friend enough to stop her from living a happy life and making a success of herself.

Please children, and adults: think before you say something that could hurt someone else's delicate feelings. It could be you-or your child, or your mother who is being deeply affected by your words. So, unless your words are kind, true, and necessary, do not speak them. I have learned that the hard way many times in my life.

I have opened my BIG MOUTH too many times to share something that inadvertently or unintentionally hurt another person, or reacted angrily to something a family member said to me calling them a horrible name and saying things I did not mean, wishing I could take my words back later. So be very careful about the words you choose.

Speak your Truth. Be HONEST. Be KIND. Honor and establish healthy boundaries. But respect others' boundaries as well. Always pretend as if these words are being spoken right back to you or someone you love very much like your own mom, your favorite sibling, or your child because every person is a divine expression of the ONE BELOVED LIFE, God, in all these holy human and animal forms. Even our so-called enemies. Everyone is our teacher.

Be careful how you speak to your pets too. They have souls and love us unconditionally. It's not so much WHAT you say, but the tone you use when you speak to them, They are very sensitive and know when we are sad, depressed, out of sorts, ill at ease, or need some extra TLC., so please try not to snap at them either. No one deserves more of your love, kindness, and tender, sweet words of appreciation than our pets. Cats, Dogs. Birds. Hamsters, ferrets, turtles, fish, snakes, chameleons, frogs, or whatever. I do not care what type of pet you like to keep in your home. They all deserve loving kindness and sweet words from you, their owners.

Even plants respond to our tones and love. I sing and chant to my plants and flowers daily and tell them how beautiful they are. In my mind I tell them I appreciate their divine beauty and presence in my precious life. I sing and chant OM NAMAH SHIVAYA for them while I am watering or pruning them. I love and hug trees on a regular basis.

CHANTING

I love chanting, especially the Guru Gita, the song of the guru. It explains the guru disciple relation in 188 Sanskrit verses with English translations in the book "The Nectar of Chanting which I have kept in my library for over thirty years because it is such a sacred text and, when chanted regularly or even occasionally, brings multitudinous blessings. It can be a wish fulfilling tree for attaining material wealth and the best thing of all, spiritual knowledge. It cannot be explained. It must be felt by direct experience because it brings focus and takes much discipline to sit still for ninety minutes until one gets to the Arati Karoon at the end which puts me personally into a state of sublime peace, contentment, joy, and deep bliss as the mind finally becomes quiet and one remembers how very lucky they are to have found a true guru and meditation teacher like Swami Muktananda, his predecessor, Bhagwan Nityananda,(whom I never actually met, but I felt his power through the large pictures of him hung in the ashram in South Fallsburg, New York and hearing the stories Baba would tell about him Gurumayi Chidvilasananda, who has been the current head of the Siddha lineage for over thirty three auspicious years. was so fortunate to meet Baba once just before he took mahasamadhi (the final liberation, death, ascension when the soul leaves the physical body to merge with God Consciousness Awareness eternally. I met his best student, a lovely woman named Malti, his translator, who'd been studying with Baba from the time she was a young girl, but through divine grace, discipline, fortitude, and obedience to her guru's teachings, became the Guru herself at the perfect divine time years later.

In my understanding yoga is a Sanskrit word which comes from the root word, yug, which means yoke, or to put it simply, to unify the individual soul with the greater Cosmic Soul by purifying the lower, base chakras by doing hatha yoga (physical asanas and exercises, pranayama (special breathing practices that awaken the kundalini energy,) jgana yoga, the yoga of knowledge and wisdom through contemplation. This energy begins at the base of the spine, referred to as the muladhara, or root chakra and continues upward from the coccyx bone from the lower spine and continues all the way up to the sahasra where One always Knows that he has never left God. He/She is one with the Realization that He/She is God at all times, in, as, and through All things living and non-living, through each direct experience, under all circumstances of adversity. Or, as my precious guru, Baba Muktananda, would say "God dwells within you as YOU. The individualized soul is not different from the Conscious Self. One then Knows all things necessary to live a very happy life now in the precious present moment. As the mind grows quiet through the spiritual practices of meditation, contemplation, chanting, and tantra, we eventually experience contentment, and Bliss Divine under all circumstances. Cares melt away as the individual merges with the One Beloved WHO has become His or Her own precious Self in physical form.

Baba would say" The reason we can experience the joy while tasting food, through sexual expression, creative pursuits, also with our children, spouses, and while being in nature is because of the jiva' (individualized Soul connection to God, whose very nature is Sat, Chit, Ananda. Truth. Consciousness, and Bliss Divine. Awareness of Being, and divine Ecstasy. There are many paths to this experience of divine love, Truth, and joy. I am mentioning just a few that I have experienced which worked for me personally.

I personally have seen the "Blue Pearl" in meditation, which, Baba says, is very auspicious after chanting for a long period of time at home in my meditation room with my former husband, Girish. However, it is not necessary to have any goals in mind while sitting quietly for meditation for ten or twenty minutes in the morning and possibly before you go to bed. Baba suggests we get a clean white woolen asana, a pretty shawl for warmth if we need it, with the wool asana placed upon a high-backed chair or couch if you have trouble crossing your legs in a lotus posture. a comfortable chair in a clean place, light a candle, watch the breath go in and out. Become aware of your breath and once the mind gets quiet after letting go of the thoughts and coming back to the breath just watch what happens. Witness of your breath going in and out or count them if you choose until the mind become still and thoughts stop wandering. to sit upon each day because it will hold the Shakti, and since I've not meditated in quite a while myself due to some crazy fears, I had during the time of the crazy virus whose name I shall not mention because I do not believe it has any power over me at this time or ever will in the future. I even got tested for it at my mom's urgent care at the suggestion of my newest chiropractor, Dr. Evans. So, I did. And guess what they told me when they called to tell me the results of the test. I was Positive! Positively healthy, Whole, and complete—just as I KNEW in my heart it would be since I was born perfect, Whole, and complete in every way.

I Am the Master of my personal starships, the captain of my soul, and I am creating my own personal reality in each holy moment with each thought I think, feeling I feel, and each holy action I take. I forgive myself and others all past transgressions, and my love and joy, sublime peace, and Wisdom contribute to the Collective Whole of Humanity. As are you.

If I get stuck or become contracted by focusing on something I don't want, I try to catch myself, notice it, and make a conscious decision, a Choice to think something that makes me feel better. Focus on my gratitude for all the love, prosperity, and blessings in my life now knowing God's great good is boundless and being thankful with positive expectation of more to come.

HUMOR

One of the greatest assets for any person is a sense of humor. Stay tuned for my next book "A Funny Thing Happened on My Way to Becoming Queen"

Not the End

Life is not what it appears to be sometimes. The saint often appears to be the sinner and vice versa. Maybe we are all just players on the Big Stage of Life acting out God's own personal drama. He acts through and as each one of us in these magnificent human bodies! We are all out here on the leading edge of thought adding unto everything that ever was and ever will be. What do you think of that idea, my dear Brothers and Sisters? Does that sound crazy to you? Does that sound like the ideas of a madwoman? Or yet are these the inspired words of a teacher, visionary, a philosopher, and a prophet? I could be any, none, or all of those things. It does not matter to me what you think of me. I am personally happy, content, and feel fulfilled each and every day of my precious life; and I feel my joy expanding each and every day. So truly nothing really matters to me, yet Everything matters to me. I am detached from all of the outer stuff. I'm just witnessing the divine play of love unfold. I love myself, my family, and friends with my whole heart, and it is because of this love that I was determined to be persistent through all the lows and highs of this illness. Love is what kept me moving forward and continuing this story until I reached its glorious end. And that is where you have finally arrived—at the conclusion of my story. Thanks very much for reading about me.

AFTERWORD: FINDING HELP

Organizations

My good friend, Janet Berkowitz and her husband, Phil, now deceased, established a very special phone line people can call with anonymity and not fear being put into a psychiatric institution against their will due to having suicidal thoughts and fears on a regular basis. She lives in New Jersey and runs the organization "Creative Communication Builders.

National Organizations

https://www.samhsa.gov/find-help/national-helpline
SAMHSA's National Helpline
a free, confidential, 24/7, 365-day-a-year treatment referral and information service (in English and Spanish) for individuals and families facing mental and/or substance use disorders.

National Alliance on Mental Illness
https://nami.org/Home

Mental Health America
https://mhanational.org/